The Future of Large Dams

Dealing with Social, Environmental, Institutional and Political Costs

This book is dedicated to the tens of millions of river basin residents who have been unfairly impoverished by large dams

The Future of Large Dams

Dealing with Social, Environmental, Institutional and Political Costs

by Thayer Scudder

London • Sterling, VA

First published by Earthscan in the UK and USA in hardback in 2005 and in
paperback in 2006

ISBN-10: 1-84407-155-3 (hardback)
         1-84407-338-6 (paperback)
ISBN-13: 978-1-84407-155-5 (hardback)
         978-1-84407-338-2 (paperback)

Typesetting by MapSet Ltd, Gateshead, UK
Printed and bound in the UK by Cromwell Press
Cover design by Yvonne Booth

For a full list of publications please contact:

Earthscan
8–12 Camden High Street
London, NW1 0JH, UK
Tel: +44 (0)20 7387 8558
Fax: +44 (0)20 7387 8998
Email: earthinfo@earthscan.co.uk
Web: www.earthscan.co.uk

22883 Quicksilver Drive, Sterling, VA 20166-2012, USA

Earthscan is an imprint of James and James (Science Publishers) Ltd and publishes in
association with the International Institute for Environment and Development

A catalogue record for this book is available from the British Library

Library of Congress Cataloging-in-Publication Data

Scudder, Thayer.
The future of large dams : dealing with social, environmental, institutional and
political costs / Thayer Scudder.
      p. cm.
   Includes bibliographical references and index.
   ISBN-13: 978-1-84407-338-2 (pbk.)
   ISBN-10: 1-84407-338-6 (pbk.)
    1. Dams. 2. Dams–Social aspects. 3. Dams–Environmental aspects. I. Title.
TC540.S435 2005
333.91–dc22

                                                                    2006002665

Printed on elemental chlorine-free paper

Contents

List of Figures, Tables and Boxes

FIGURES

TABLES

BOXES

List of Acronyms and Abbreviations

ADB	Asian Development Bank
AIEQ	Association of Quebec's Electricity Industry
AMP	Accelerated Mahaweli Project
ANEEJ	African Network for Environmental and Economic Justice
ARCH	Action Research in Community Health and Development
ARD	Associates in Rural Development
ARPAC	Arquivo do Património Cultural
AVB	Authority for the Development of the Bandama River Valley
BBC	British Broadcasting Corporation
BOOT	build, own, operate and transfer
BP	best practice
CAMPFIRE	Communal Areas Management Programme for Indigenous Resources
CAO	Compliance Adviser/Ombudsman
CAPCO	Central African Power Corporation
CFE	Federal Electricity Commission of Mexico
CFRI	Central African Fisheries Research Institute
CGE	computable general equilibrium
CGIAR	Consultative Group on International Agricultural Research
CIDA	Canadian International Development Agency
CIEL	Center for International Environmental Law
CSE	Centre for Science and the Environment
CSS	Centre for Social Studies, Surat
CTC	Ceylon Tobacco Corporation
CYJV	CIPM Yangtze Joint Venture
DBSA	Development Bank of Southern Africa
DDP	Dams and Development Project
DFID	Department for International Development
DRIFT	downstream response to imposed flow transformations
DWAF	Department of Water Affairs and Forestry
EAP	Environmental Action Plan
EAUDRL	Egyptian Authority for the Utilization and Development of Reclaimed Land
ECA	Export Credit Agencies
ECGD	Export Credit and Guarantee Department
ED	Environmental Defence
EGAT	Electricity Generating Authority of Thailand

ENDESA	Empresa Nacional de Electricidad SA
ESSG	Environment and Social Services Group
FAO	Food and Agriculture Organization of the United Nations
FCFA	Franc of the African Financial Community
FMG	Five Member Group
GAP	Southeastern Anatolia Project
GEM	Environmental Monitoring Group
GOB	Government of Botswana
GOG	Government of Gujarat
GOZ	Government of Zambia
GTRDP	Gwembe Tonga Rehabilitation and Development Project
HIV/AIDS	human immunodeficiency virus/acquired immunodeficiency syndrome
IAG	International Advisory Group
ICID	International Commission on Irrigation and Drainage
ICJ	International Court of Justice
ICOLD	International Commission on Large Dams
IDA	Institute for Development Anthropology
IFAD	International Fund for Agricultural Development
IFC	International Finance Corporation
IFR	instream flow requirement
IHA	International Hydropower Association
IRN	International Rivers Network
ISP	Income Security Programme
IUCN	International Union for the Conservation of Nature and Natural Resources
IWGIA	International Working Group for Indigenous Affairs
IWMI	International Water Management Institute
JBDC	James Bay Development Corporation
JBNQA	James Bay and Northern Quebec Agreement
JPTC	Joint Permanent Technical Commission
JVP	Janatha Vimukthi Peramuna of Sri Lanka
KLCC	Kariba Lake Coordinating Committee
LHDA	Lesotho Highlands Development Authority
LHWC	Lesotho Highlands Water Commission
LHWP	Lesotho Highlands Water Project
LTTE	The Liberation Tigers of Tamil Eelam
M&E	monitoring and evaluation
MAB	National Movement of Dam-Affected People
MARD	Mahaweli Agriculture Research and Development
MASL	Mahaweli Authority of Sri Lanka
MDB	Mahaweli Development Board
MEA	Mahaweli Economic Agency
MIGA	Multilateral Investment Guarantee Agency
MP	Member of Parliament
MP	Madhya Pradesh

MW	megawatt
NBA	Narmada Bachao Andolan
NBR	Nottaway–Broadback–Rupert
NDD	Narmada Development Department of MP
NEDECO	Netherlands Engineering Consultants
NGO	non-governmental organization
NNT-NBCA	Nakai Nam Theun National Biodiversity Conservation Area
NORAD	Norwegian Agency for Development Cooperation
NRC	National Research Council of the US
NRG	Northern Rhodesian Government
NT2	Nam Theun 2
NTEC	Nam Theun Electricity Consortium
NTSEP	Nam Theun Social and Environmental Project
OD	operational directive
OECD	Organization of Economic Development and Co-operation
OED	Operations Evaluation Department
OKACOM	Okavango River Basin Commission
O&M	operations and maintenance
OMS	operational manual statement
OMVS	Senegal River Basin Authority
OP	operational policy
PA	Provincial Administration of NRG
PDR	People's Democratic Republic
POE	panel of experts
PMU	Planning and Monitoring Unit of the MASL
R&R	resettlement and rehabilitation
RAP	Resettlement Action Plan
SAM	social accounting matrix
SAPP	Southern African Power Pool
SCOPE	Scientific Committee on Problems of the Environment
SIDA	Swedish International Development Agency
SMEC	Snowy Mountains Engineering Corporation
SOIWDP	Southern Okavango Integrated Water Development Project
SRC	Social Research Center of the American University in Cairo
SSP	Sardar Sarovar Project
TCTA	Trans-Caledon Tunnel Authority
TERRA	Towards Ecological Recovery and Regional Alliance
TISS	Tata Institute for Social Science
TVA	Tennessee Valley Authority
UDI	Rhodesia's Unilateral Declaration of Independence
UK	United Kingdom
UN	United Nations
UNDP	United Nations Development Programme
UNEP	United Nations Environmental Programme
UNESCO	United Nations Education and Science Organization
UNP	United National Party (of Sri Lanka)

US	The United States
USAID	United States Agency for International Development
UXO	unexploded ordnance
WB	World Bank
WCD	World Commission on Dams
WCS	Wildlife Conservation Society
WFP	World Food Programme
WHO	World Health Organization
WTO	World Trade Organization
WWC	World Water Council
ZESCO	Zambia Electricity Supply Corporation
ZRA	Zambezi River Authority

Foreword

On 16 November 2000 in London the World Commission on Dams (WCD) released its Final Report *Dams and Development: A New Framework for Decision-Making*. The launch drew as much global interest in the landmark publication as in the unprecedented process by which it was born. With its mandate fulfilled, the WCD decommissioned itself that same day, whereupon its legacy might slide quietly into oblivion, its example might fade and its Report might collect dust on a shelf.

And pigs might fly. For its work and words refuse to die. Even today, four years later the imaginative fires of both our product and our process continue to blaze on brightly at new forums and in different languages, fuelling discussions from riverbank village to corporate boardroom, living on through the United Nations, generating more light than heat.

Opinions vary as to why it still thrives. Perhaps its past was a prologue. For our outcome was no spontaneous combustion; it was painstakingly kindled in an intense global context. Nor could we afford to let our delicate flame flicker out or flare up out of control; too much was at stake in terms of lives, funds and ecosystems. Yet the crucial factor, I think, was how ignition of the initial spark required the friction of 12 volatile elements – one of whom wrote this book.

Facing the rest of the world in public, the Commission collectively remained 'quick to listen, slow to speak'. Facing each other in private was another matter, of course, but few commissioners individually embodied this motto better than Ted Scudder. He was as laconic as he was attentive. So in the pause before Ted articulated his point, his question or his argument, the reaction among many of us was double-edged: anticipation and anxiety.

Anticipation: because his life experiences shaped a mind so deeply and widely versed in the nuances of dam politics that his words would raise the level of debate, whether our topic was the political pressure to store water or the definition of 'prior, informed consent'. Anxiety: because one never knew whether those reasoned words would bolster our own position, or debunk it. Now, opening this book, one feels that double edge again, but all the more keenly as his voice is in print.

To prepare myself for what Ted might write, I tried to recall where he was coming from, and for whom he was inclined to speak. As it happens, neither is clear-cut. And that's his secret. He's unpredictable.

In one of our last conversations, Julius Nyerere, then Premier of Tanzania, urged me, 'Always remember and speak up for the South'. His advice guided my spirit throughout the Commission, both personally and professionally, as I strove to balance perspectives across the North–South divide. Like many people from the South, my life followed a familiar pattern, leaving my home, family and native lands for higher education, work opportunities, and exile in the developed world. Some stay there. I was fortunate enough to be able to return home and test what I had learned abroad in my beloved country, representing South Africa's first democratic government.

So what are we to make of this American – from a country often considered one of the most provincial and inward looking in the world – who did the exact opposite? Ted left home, family, comfort and excellent education and career in the US to immerse himself not only in developing nations, but also among the lives of the poorest of the poor and dispossessed in those nations. Some may consider such a life to be a moral crusade, evangelism or missionary work. But Ted's research was never motivated by anything more than an insatiable drive for answers to questions most would rather not ask. Through his investigations, he created a field of study, a discipline of his own, where none existed. He documented – disinterestedly but not dispassionately – the voices of the voiceless, the lives of the nameless.

His immersion and travels make it impossible to pin down Ted's identity, his sense of place, let alone his politics. You see at once that he is more comfortable crossing a Southeast Asian paddy than sitting in a Washington office building, more at ease among the Tamil or Sesotho or Tonga than among classmates at his Harvard reunions. So should he have been counted among the commissioners from the North, or lumped in with those of us from the South? Neither, perhaps. Or both. Or in between.

If he appears healthy and agile, perhaps that is because his diet consists largely of ink and paper. One day at the end of an exhausting three day meeting, Ted announced out the blue that, to get a fuller sense of the big picture, he planned to read every one of the knowledge base reports over the next two months. This included, I should mention, 17 thematic reviews, nine case studies and hundreds of contributing papers. Several thousand pages, stacked to eye level from the floor.

His remark sank in. There was the usual silence that followed whenever Ted spoke up. He wasn't boasting, or challenging. But we knew he wasn't bluffing either, and no one else attempted either to match his reading page for page or rescue our dear colleague from his self-imposed high-fibre document feast. He was fuelled by hunger, driven by the need to test his own experience against that of others. He wanted to know not just what we can say and how to say it, but why it must be said.

Many observers attempted to tuck every individual WCD commissioner into a neat, definitive pocket of being either 'pro' or 'anti' large dams. They rarely met with success, and never with Ted. He remained among the wildest of 12 wild cards in the Commission's deck, and he had a distinct advantage. Most of us had some vaguely defined constituencies that we primarily spoke for and to: environment, engineers, government, shareholders, people's movements etc. Ted, the professional scholar, was beholden only to the University, to intellectual honesty, to Truth.

Truth is, of course, the most notoriously fickle and demanding constituent. It may change its mind without warning. That is why I was so curious as to whether Ted's individual research and analysis in the coming pages might contradict, supplant or make obsolete what we collectively had crafted four years earlier.

But there is no comparing the two. *Dams and Development* emerged from the fullest possible range of dam perspectives. Our relentless inclusiveness was our greatest strength: it led to endorsement by all 12 commissioners, acceptance of our rights and risks framework and seven strategic priorities by advocates and critics alike, and gave the Report a *gravitas* for deep and widespread penetration. A thousand thoughts melded into one 'Truth'.

That said, the act of a dozen authors writing with one hand can also become a weakness. For, by definition, this process curbs the untamed edge, style and passion of the individual mind. As each of us worked on the Commission to reach unanimous agreement based on the first comprehensive global and independent review of dams to date, we became aware of the small individual compromises such unanimity demands. A word cut here, a qualifier added there, an active voice edited and modified there.

To this day, no one on any side of the debate has found fault with the accuracy of the WCD's Global Review, nor with the clarity articulated in the Way Forward (although some found its facts too painful, its recommendations too sharp). Nevertheless, what the Report lacks, by its mandate, is the ferocity of perspective that a solitary voice can bring. Looking at the past and at the future, we deliberately had to omit the deeply *personal* Truth. Happily, Ted did not. And that is what he provides here.

In *The Future of Large Dams* Ted has stepped out of his role as one of the WCD chorus to provide a solo performance that none could control, or predict. In the process his voice has not only retained his pitch-perfect intonation, he has gone on to create a poignant melody, set against the WCD's background harmony, a song that carries us forward and outward into the field, without missing a beat.

Kader Asmal is Member of Parliament, South Africa;
Professor, University of the Western Cape, South Africa;
Minister of Education, 1999–2004;
Minister of Water Affairs and Forestry, 1994–1999;
Chair, World Commission on Dams, 1997–2000.

Acknowledgements

I doubt that I would have written this book if I had not been involved, as a commissioner, in the work of the World Commission on Dams (WCD) between 1998 and 2000. Serving on the Commission was a wonderful experience during which I profited from discussions with fellow commissioners and from our travels. I am especially indebted to the Commission's Chair, Kader Asmal, who also agreed to write the foreword to this volume. My years on the Commission coincided with my last two years as a Caltech faculty member in which time my only obligation was to be a full-time researcher. As a result, I was able to devote most of my time to reading about dams, including the large number of documents and submissions prepared for the Commission.

Four years in the writing, this book reflects nearly 50 years of research and thinking about large dams. I especially wish to thank the thousands of resettlers and downstream people who have patiently answered my questions over the years. It was in the autumn of 1956 that I joined Elizabeth Colson in initiating our long-term study of 57,000 people soon to be resettled owing to the construction of the Kariba Dam on the Middle Zambezi. That study, which continues at this time, has had a major influence on my thinking. I am especially grateful to Elizabeth Colson, who invited me to join her in 1956, and who was one of four readers of the initial draft of this book. I also wish to thank three colleagues who joined us in the 1990s to continue the study as a second generation of scholars. They are Lisa Cliggett, Samuel Clark and Rhonda Gillett-Netting. Just as Elizabeth Colson initiated me as an academic field worker, so too did Gilbert F. White play the major role in guiding me to work with United Nations and other agencies to apply the policy implications of what I had learned.

I also owe a major debt to the other three readers who were: social anthropologist, David Brokensha; mathematician and social scientist, John Gay; and engineer and fellow WCD commissioner, Jan Veltrop. My debt to John Gay is especially great since he not only emphasized the need for the statistical analysis presented in Chapter 3, but also provided essential help in crafting the 50 dam survey presented in that chapter. He also read and commented on each chapter as did the other readers. So did Robert Goodland, who I subsequently learned was Earthscan's principal reader, and who gave me invaluable advice on how to cut what was originally a 600+ page manuscript down to its present size. Special thanks also go to David McDowell and James Morgan who reviewed the manuscript at my request. Thanks also go to other readers who read and commented on specific chapters. They are

Randolph Barker, Michael Cernea, Ron Coley, Robert K. Davis, Theodore Downing, Patrick Dugan, Jean Ensminger, Hussein Fahim, Geoffrey Howard, Lakshmi Jain, Jacques Leslie, Ronald Manley and Peter Rogers.

Over the years I have also profited from conversations and/or joint work in the field with Nanda Abeywickrema, Michael Acreman, William M. Adams, Gordon Appleby, Dan Aronson, Ramesh Bhatia, Jeremy Bird, Asit Biswas, Malcolm Blackie, Donald Blackmore, Geoffrey Bond, Harrison Brown, Joji Cariño, Rita E. Cestti, Chris de Wet, Gamini Dissanayake, Michael Dow, John Eriksson, Carlos Escudero, Robert Fernea, Henry Fosbrooke, José Goldemberg, Ginny and Leo Goodfellow, J. Green, Thuso Green, Lawrence Haas, Jonathan Habarad, Judy Henderson, Robert Hitchcock, Michael Horowitz, Charles Howe, Alois Hungwe, Jeffrey W. Jacobs, Jonathan Jenness, Barbara Rose Johnston, E. A. K. Kalitsi, Sanjeev Khagram, Charles LaMuniere, Véronique Lassailly-Jacob, Stephen Lawry, John Ledger, Goran Lindahl, Sarah Jane Littlefield, Wynand Maartins, Chris Magadza, L. K. Mahapatra, David Martz, Andrew Macoun, Patrick McCully, Mike Mentis, Robert Mertz, Reatile Mochebelele, Elizabeth Monosowski, Deborah Moore, Marshall Murphree, Isaac Muzila, Enoch Nane, Roger Noll, Donal O'Leary, Engelbertus Oud, William Partridge, Anil Patel, Medha Patkar, William Payne, Jean-Yves Pirot, Norman Reynolds, John Roome, Muneera Salem-Murdock, Thea and Tom Savory, Monica Scatasta, M. Sekwale, Henry Shatford, Bennett Siamwiza, Pete Smith, Achim Steiner, Lee Talbot, A. R. D. Taylor, Martin ter Woort, Ralph Townley, Stephen Turner, Kapila P. Vimaladharma, Rangit Wanigaratne, Tim Whitmore, James Workman, Edmund Wright and Abdel Hamid El Zein. At Caltech I would like to thank engineering colleagues James Morgan and Norman Brooks for helping me better understand issues that lay outside my expertise. Special thanks go to Victoria Mason without whose editorial help this book would still be a work in process.

I was especially pleased that Earthscan, as publisher of the Final Report of the World Commission on Dams, agreed to also publish this volume. Special thanks go to Rob West, Ruth Mayo, Camille Adamson and David Smallbones.

My wife, Mary E. D. Scudder, has been supportive throughout, joining me in the field as colleague and best friend when her career allowed.

1

The Large Dams Dispute and the Future of Large Dams

INTRODUCTION

I analyse large dams in this book as a flawed yet still necessary development option. That was also the conclusion of the World Commission on Dams (WCD) on which I was one of 12 commissioners. For that reason this study is, in a number of respects, a follow-on volume to the Commission's Final Report. On the one hand, it endorses the analysis and conclusions in the Final Report and uses the Commission's seven strategic priorities[1] to examine how the decision-making process for water resource and energy development should be structured and, should a large dam be selected as the preferred development option, on how planning, implementation, operations and maintenance, and handing over of assets should proceed.

On the other hand, it extends and updates the Commission's Final Report. Extension is needed since the Commission had neither the time nor the authority to explore some issues in detail, examples being multiplier effects associated with dam construction, impacts on deltas, institutional issues, resolution of conflicts among stakeholders and, especially, how to deal at the international level with project authorities and national governments that violate human rights and other international declarations and covenants relevant to the planning and implementation of large dams. Updating is important because five years have passed since the Commission's Final Report was produced – five years during which the report has influenced not just the dams debate, but also the planning process for specific dams. Yet the debate continues about the future role of dams and the utility of the WCD report.

Large dams are flawed for many reasons. Benefits are overstated and costs understated. Especially serious are the adverse environmental impacts on the world's river basins, impacts that tend to be irreversible where dams are built on mainstreams and large tributaries. Implementation continues to impoverish the majority of those who must be resettled from reservoir basins and project works, and to adversely affect millions of people who live below dams and whose living standards are dependent on natural flood regimes.

The scale of large dams, and the uncertainties and risks associated with manipulation of such important life support systems as river basins, raise important questions as to whether governments and project authorities have the institutional capacity to deal with the complexity associated with such large infrastructure projects. Then there is what is apt to be a long planning and implementation process during which changes in priorities and policies, and the not infrequent occurrence of unexpected events, need be addressed but often are not. There are also the problems of corruption associated with the large financial requirements of such projects, as well as the lack of political will to follow state-of-the-art procedures, especially those associated with environmental and social issues. Finally there are legitimate questions as to the continued appropriateness of the development paradigm that large dams epitomize.

Yet, in spite of such flaws, large dams remain a necessary development option to deal with the needs of a human population that is expanding beyond the carrying capacity of the world's life support systems. That is the tragedy. A development strategy that over the longer term is degrading critical natural resources remains necessary, at least over the short term, to supply water resources in those late-industrializing countries where the large majority of future dams will be built as a means of addressing the poverty and rising expectations of billions of poor people. Large dams will be needed to store and transfer water to rapidly expanding urban populations; to provide electricity to those populations and to the industries that must employ them if poverty is to be alleviated; to increase irrigation in countries such as India where small reservoirs dry up during periods of drought; and, in countries such as Laos and Nepal with few other natural resources, to provide foreign exchange for development purposes by exporting hydropower.

The number of new large dams, however, should be reduced by weeding out those for which better alternatives exist and by better management of existing dams. One WCD approach was to emphasize an improved options assessment process that actively involved all concerned stakeholders. That is important, but the WCD approach should also be complemented by an international adjudication and compliance process, perhaps modelled on the World Trade Organization (which has the capacity to impose sanctions), when the disadvantages of large dams are such that they should not be built or, if built, could be redesigned to expand benefits and reduce costs.

Large dams are the focus of this book. The International Commission on Large Dams (ICOLD) defines large dams as those rising 15m or more from their foundation or, if between 5 and 15m in height, as having a storage capacity of over 3,000,000m^3. Over the past 50 years, their number has increased from 5700 in 1950 to approximately 50,000 today. Although large dams are present in over 140 countries, nearly 80 per cent are in five countries – China, the US, India, Spain and Japan. Before 1949, China had less than 100 large dams; today it has approximately 22,000, or nearly half of the global total. The US has over 6000 large dams, India over 4000 and Spain and Japan over 1000 (WCD, 2000, p9). Looking to the future, construction emphasis has shifted to late-industrializing countries, with Brazil, China, India, Turkey and countries in Africa expected to be the dominant dam builders.

While the WCD's terms of reference were to address all large dams as a category, my emphasis is more on those of 60m or more in height. They comprise 78 per cent of the 50 dams surveyed in Chapter 3, whereas dams 60m and higher comprise only 11 per cent of those in ICOLD's 1998 register of 22,748 large dams. Forty-four per cent of those in Chapter 3 are at least 100m high as opposed to less than 3 per cent of those on ICOLD's list. It is these larger dams, and especially those on mainstreams and larger tributaries whose future is at risk because of unacceptable environmental and social costs that have dominated the large dams dispute. They are the ones that heads of state support and for which international firms compete for feasibility, design and construction contracts.

The future of large dams is dealt with in two ways. One way, the more general, is to chart the way forward by relating WCD's strategic priorities to key issues that must be addressed. The emphasis is on environmental, social, institutional and political issues, WCD having dealt in detail with economic and financial issues, including cost overruns. The other way is to focus in greater detail on what analysts have emphasized as large dams' most unsatisfactory features. These are environmental impacts on river basins and social impacts on riverine communities.[2] Large dams continue to impoverish tens of millions of poor people as well as to degrade the river basin ecosystems on which they are dependent. Those impacts need to be documented and explained, for such a situation is unacceptable; indeed outrageous. It is also unnecessary and counterproductive to impoverish affected people since there are known opportunities for helping them become project beneficiaries (for more details see Chapter 4).[3] Dealing with adverse environmental impacts, on the other hand, is more difficult since some, such as those found in deltas, are irreversible.

A focus on resettlement in a number of chapters provides an important mechanism for assessing when dams are an acceptable water resource and energy development option and when they are not; for assessing how the decision-making process should be structured; and, should a dam be selected as the preferred option, for working out a planning, implementation and asset handing over process that enables the majority of resettlers to become project beneficiaries. Used in this way, resettlement becomes an optic for examining the entire large-dam-building process. The sustainability of that process, for example, requires attention to be paid to environmental impacts within each river basin, as well as to impacts on tens of millions of people in downstream communities. It also requires a detailed examination of the institutional structures that are required for an acceptable development process to proceed.

ORGANIZATION

Two-thirds of this book deals with issues and one-third with case histories. The case histories are important because they detail the complexities, the difficulties and the unexpected events that so often keep large dams from realizing their expected benefits. The remainder of Chapter 1 deals first with the large dams dispute, including what I refer to as the WCD process and, after the Commission's 'termination' in November 2000, the origin and initial years of the United Nations Environment Programme (UNEP) Dams Development Project (DDP). Next, I outline my own career to illustrate how and where I obtained the information on which this comparative analysis is based, and to make explicit my current position as it relates to large dams as a development option. The chapter ends with a brief consideration of categories of affected people and a longer section introducing resettlement as a major issue. Chapter 2 deals in detail with our current understanding of the dynamics of the resettlement process by integrating into a single theory the previous analytical frameworks of a number of scholars.

Chapter 3 shows that impoverishment is a well-documented fact. It includes the results of the first statistical analysis of resettlement outcomes in connection with large dams and ten short case studies. According to a recent survey, violation of human rights is another major risk of all types of development-induced displacement.[4] But, 'The resettlement issues surrounding dam projects are inherently more difficult than those of nondam projects' (Picciotto et al, 2001, p2), since both the homes and livelihoods of large numbers of people are affected.

Chapter 4 analyses the types of opportunities that must be implemented if a majority of future resettlers and other project-affected people are to improve their living standards. In addition to incorporating affected communities as project owners and such project-specific opportunities as irrigation and reservoir fisheries, opportunities include the multiplier effects that can characterize well-planned and well-implemented water resource development projects, but which are usually ignored by those planning and implementing large dams.

Chapters 5 and 6 include case studies of five projects in which I have been involved as adviser, consultant and/or researcher from the 1950s to the present. These are Zambia–Zimbabwe's Kariba Project, Sri Lanka's Accelerated Mahaweli Project, India's Sardar Sarovar Project, Botswana's Southern Okavango Integrated Water Development Project and Canada's Grande Baleine (Great Whale) Project. Four of the five cases were the largest single project within the country or countries in which they were constructed or were being planned, while the fifth, Hydro-Quebec's Grande Baleine Project may well have been the largest being planned in Canada prior to its cancellation. These projects illustrate a number of important points that are dealt with in detail in the text. These points include the inability or unwillingness of countries to follow their own policies and guidelines, Sri Lanka's Accelerated Mahaweli Project and India's Sardar Sarovar Project being examples. They also illustrate the important adverse effect that unexpected events can have on outcomes, and the impoverishing effect of the resettlement that resulted.

Chapter 7 deals with the impact of large dams on downstream communities and habitat, and on catchment management. The importance of environmental flows for mitigating adverse impacts on people formerly dependent on a river's natural flood regime and on riverine wetlands and deltas is emphasized. In Chapter 8, the wide range of institutions are assessed that need to be involved in planning, implementation, management, monitoring and evaluation if favourable outcomes are to be realized. The final chapter sums up circumstances under which large dams warrant or do not warrant consideration as a legitimate development option. The way forward with existing dams and with dams as a future development option is illustrated by ways in which WCD's seven strategic priorities can be implemented.

THE LARGE DAMS DISPUTE

Introduction

Pushed as a development strategy by a powerful coalition of politicians and civil servants, multilateral and bilateral financial institutions, and parastatal agencies and private sector engineering firms, the construction of large dams has been justified on economic, social and political grounds. A pioneering example, subsequently emulated by India with its Damodar Development Authority and by other countries, was the Tennessee Valley Authority (TVA). Established in the 1930s as a major component of President Roosevelt's New Deal, TVA was intended to raise the living standards of residents in one of the US's least developed areas.

During their construction, the biggest dams tend to be the largest project in countries where they are being built. Drawing on cases where I have been involved, a 1950s example was Kariba, which was the first mainstream dam in Central Africa on the Zambezi. Examples from the 1960s are the Volta Dam in Ghana and the Aswan High Dam in Egypt. On filling, the Kariba, Volta and the High Dam reservoirs became the largest man-made lakes in the world, each having approximately four times the storage capacity behind the Hoover Dam in the US. A South Asian example from the 1970s is Sri Lanka's multi-billion dollar and multi-dam Accelerated Mahaweli Project, followed by India's Sardar Sarovar Project in the 1980s. China's Three Gorges Dam is the largest current example today.

In each of these cases, as in many others, no less a person than the president of the country pushed the project forward. President Nkrumah saw the Volta Dam not just as a pilot project for the industrialization of Ghana, but as a symbol of that industrialization, with a commemorative issue of postage stamps that showed him with the dam in the background (communication from David Brokensha). Egypt's President Nasser stated 'In antiquity we built pyramids for the dead. Now we build new pyramids for the living' (Fahim, 1981, p14 after Heikel, 1973, p62), while President Nehru eulogized large dams as 'the temples of modern India'.

Benefits can be major. They include hydropower generation that pays the bills, as well as irrigation, urban water supply, navigation, flood management, and recreation and tourism. Today generation of hydropower provides nearly 20 per cent of global electricity, with the figure closer to 100 per cent in

Norway and 80 per cent in Brazil. Although accurate statistics are not available, WCD estimated that approximately 15 per cent of world food production is based on large dam-supplied irrigation, while Los Angeles – the second largest city in the US – and much of Southern California; Gauteng, the industrial hub of South Africa; and Nairobi, Kenya's capital, are all dependent on dam-supplied water for residential, commercial and industrial use. Governments also claim strategic and political justification. During the apartheid years, the Nationalist Government built the Gariep Dam on the Orange River during its efforts to convince the world that South Africa was a modern industrial nation worthy of respect, while it has been argued that Argentina's advocacy for the Yacyretá Dam, built in partnership with Paraguay, was in good part a response to Brazil's construction of the Itaipu Dam, also built with Paraguay, further up the Parana River.

Initiation of the debate

Given such benefits and justifications, why has an increasingly adversarial dispute arisen over the construction of large dams? Although the history of the large dams debate has yet to be written, it is important to emphasize that by the mid-1960s researchers, myself included, and practitioners already had begun to criticize undesirable and unnecessary environmental and social impacts. They were also emphasizing the need for considering dams as only one of a number of possible options. At a 1965 symposium on man-made lakes at London's Royal Geographical Society, six papers dealt with environmental, public health and socio-economic 'Problems Arising from the Making of Man-made Lakes in the Tropics' (Lowe-McConnell, 1966, p51). In 1966, the Committee on Water of the US National Academy of Sciences – National Research Council, with Gilbert F. White in the chair, produced a report titled *Alternatives in Water Management* that noted 'the possibility that there may be many alternatives to water development for promoting regional growth' (NAS-NRC, 1966, p60).

In 1972, the International Council of Scientific Unions' Scientific Committee on Problems of the Environment (SCOPE) Report on *Man-Made Lakes as Modified Ecosystems* began with a section on 'Alternatives to Man-made Lakes'. Key statements noted: 'Unfortunately, with reservoirs as with other major modifications, only a few careful assessments have been made of the full range of impacts of their construction' and 'whatever the circumstances, reservoir construction never is warranted without prior examination of the other possibilities' (Scientific Committee on Problems of the Environment, 1972, pp11–12). That same year, Farvar and Milton edited the Natural History Press' influential *The Careless Technology: Ecology and International Development*, in which over 50 prominent scholars and practitioners wrote critical chapters including ten dealing with irrigation and water resource development.

Drawing on such sources, non-governmental organizations (NGOs) subsequently linked adverse environmental impacts with adverse health, socio-economic and human rights impacts in a telling critique of large dams not just in the tropics but worldwide. Leading the way were articles in *The Ecologist* followed by Goldsmith and Hildyard's edited two volumes on the *Social and Environmental Effects of Large Dams* (1984, 1986). Subsequent books, including Pearce's *The Dammed: Rivers, Dams, and the Coming World Water Crisis* (1992) and McCully's *Silenced Rivers: The Ecology and Politics of Large Dams* (1996, 2001), also questioned the extent to which justifying benefits forecast in feasibility studies were being realized.

The World Commission on Dams (WCD) and the WCD process

In April 1997, the International Union for the Conservation of Nature and Natural Resources (IUCN) and the World Bank invited 38 participants to a workshop in Gland, Switzerland, to discuss what had become an increasingly adversarial debate. Representing the range of interests involved, 35 delegates were able to attend the two-day workshop. In addition to IUCN and World Bank Group officials, participants included three from academic, government and non-profit research institutions; eight from major firms and consulting agencies involved in dam feasibility studies, construction and operation; and three from river basin authorities and government ministries.

Also present were the presidents of the International Commission on Irrigation and Drainage (ICID) and ICOLD. NGOs, including such strong dam critics as the Berne Declaration (Switzerland), International Rivers Network (US), Movimento dos Atingidos por Barragens (Brazil) and Narmada Bachao Andolan (India) sent six representatives. After lengthy discussions that included evaluating several background documents, including one by the author (Scudder, 1997a), the participants unanimously recommended the formation of an independent WCD. Terms of reference included reviewing the development effectiveness of large dams; assessing alternatives for water resources and energy development; and, where dams were the selected option, developing internationally acceptable criteria, guidelines and standards for the planning, implementation, operation and decommissioning of large dams.

The intentions of the April workshop participants were that the Commission would commence operations that November. Delays in selecting a balanced group of commissioners, whose number increased from 8 to 12 in the process,[5] and delays in weaning the Commission from IUCN and the World Bank as sponsors of the April workshop, sponsors who had continued to play a major role during the establishment process, delayed the Commission's start up until February 1998 (Scudder, 2001). During the next few months, a secretariat was established in Cape Town, South Africa, under a Secretary General with a full-time support staff that grew to 10 experts and 8 financial and administrative staff and who were assisted by 6 temporary programme staff, 7 temporary finance and administration staff, and 19 temporary research fellows selected from 16 countries.

The full Commission held its first meeting in May 1998. With most members meeting for the first time, emphasis at that meeting and thereafter was on creating a working group of people who knew and liked each other. That proved to be very important as it subsequently allowed commissioners to discuss, as friends, the most contentious issues and make what compromises were necessary. During the next two and a half years, the Commission completed what is likely to remain the most comprehensive review of large dams. A total of 1400 individuals from 59 countries attended four consultations in Sri Lanka, Brazil, Egypt and Vietnam at which the commissioners heard, and asked questions of, submissions that had been selected to cover various viewpoints.

Eight detailed case studies of specific dams in Brazil, Norway, Pakistan, South Africa, Thailand, Turkey, the US and Zambia–Zimbabwe were contracted out, as were country studies for China and India and a briefing paper on Russia and Newly Independent States. Seventeen thematic reviews were outsourced and supported by over 100 contributing papers. They dealt with social, environmental, economic and financial issues; electricity supply, irrigation and water supply options, and flood management; operation, monitoring and decommissioning; planning approaches; institutional frameworks; regulation and compliance; and participation, negotiation and conflict resolution. Experts also produced working papers on health and management of cultural resources, while the secretariat designed and distributed a detailed questionnaire, the results of which dealt with 123 dams and were analysed and presented as a cross-check survey.

Submissions to the four consultations and at other times totalled 947. All materials were incorporated into a WCD knowledge base, catalogued by subject and listed on the WCD website (www.dams.org). This provided a communication tool unavailable to previous commissions. Not only was e-mail traffic estimated at over 250,000 missives during the Commission's life span, but the website received top ranking from two global ranking firms.[6] Communication was also via nine issues of the Commission's official newsletter, summary reports following the four regional consultations, a July 1999 Interim Report and three meetings of a forum. The purpose of the forum was to serve as a check on the WCD process. The 68 members were drawn from within and without the April 1997 workshop to represent the full range of stakeholders in the dams debate.

Up until the time that the Final Report was written, WCD emphasized transparency, which was facilitated by the four consultations, the existence of the forum and the website. The Final Report was the responsibility of the commissioners, working in close cooperation with the secretariat to ensure commissioner familiarity with the WCD knowledge base. No drafts were circulated for comments. Although that procedure was subsequently criticized, WCD had already been in operation longer than intended. Given the intensity of the dams dispute, if drafts had been made available, their circulation would have had to be unrestricted. Coping with the expected volume of comments would have been very difficult if not impossible.

The Final Report was released on Thursday, 16 November 2000 at a ceremony in London. Up to 300 people were expected and perhaps 30 media representatives; in fact over 400 people attended including more than 90 journalists. That same day, thousands followed the proceedings through the WCD website and hundreds attempted to download the Final Report.[7] All 12 commissioners were present at the ceremony. Nelson Mandela, the former President of South Africa, was the main speaker. Other speakers, in addition to WCD Chair Kader Asmal, were the Crown Prince of the Netherlands, the President of the World Bank, and the Secretary General of IUCN. Mary Robinson, UN Human Rights Commissioner, who was unable to attend, also made comments.

Throughout the rest of November, various commissioners and members of the secretariat travelled the world and held meetings to present the results of the WCD process. On Friday, 17 November, Kader Asmal presented a copy at the United Nations (UN) to Secretary General Kofi Annan. Also present was Klaus Töpfer, Executive Director of the United Nations Environment Programme (UNEP), which subsequently was to sponsor a continuation of the WCD process. Meetings were held during the next few days in Germany, Pakistan, the Netherlands, the US, Sri Lanka, Senegal, South Africa, Russia, Brazil, Thailand, Japan and Norway.

WCD was 'decommissioned' as intended following the release of the Final Report on 16 November. A core staff of the secretariat stayed on until the end of March 2001 to further distribute, and facilitate discussion of, the Final Report. A CD-ROM was prepared that included the Final Report, report summaries in nine languages, and the WCD knowledge base including the over 500 submissions that were in electronic format. As for the website, it is still accessible, having been converted to serve as a WCD archives.

In February 2001 a third meeting of the forum was held in South Africa. It had been requested by the forum's 68 members and was to be run by the forum over a three-day period. Its purpose was to discuss the way forward with the WCD process as well as to provide members with an opportunity to react to the Final Report. A total of 50 of the 68 forum members attended along with 28 observers and several former commissioners. As the Commission's former Chair, Kader Asmal presented opening and closing remarks. By the end of the proceedings, a decision had been made to further institutionalize the process started by the Commission whereby a representative forum liaison group would work with other forum members and the core secretariat to reach agreement on three issues.

One concerned the formation of a dams and development forum drawn from previous forum members but including more members from national governments. A second was to link the forum liaison group with UNEP, which was 'ready and committed actively to contribute to the follow-up process.'[8] The third was to institutionalize the follow-up process in a small Dams and Development Unit by 1 August 2001. Its function over a two-year period would be to coordinate the meetings and activities necessary for 'facilitating the exchange of information among all stakeholders about initiatives and outcomes relating to dams and development in an impartial way' (*DAMS*, 2001).

The UNEP–Dams and Development Unit, now called the Dams and Development Project (DDP), came into existence in November 2001 to promote a 'dialogue on improving decision-making, planning and management of dams and their alternatives based on the World Commission on Dams (WCD) core values[9] and strategic priorities' (DDP website). Pledges of financial support were received from five European countries. The six-member forum liaison group was reconstituted as a 13-member steering committee to represent the forum's 13 stakeholder groups. It was confirmed by UNEP as one of its official advisory bodies from which guidance would be sought before UNEP took 'decisions on policy and substantive matters affecting the work programme of DDP' (*Confluence*, 2002a). Temporary staff members were drawn from the former WCD secretariat while new members were being recruited throughout 2002.

A new website (www.unep-dams.org) was formed and the first meeting of the dams and development forum met in Nairobi in July 2002. A total of 64 forum delegates, along with 22 observers, discussed the range of important issues that DDP should address. Concerns were expressed about the need to further engage governments, as well as other stakeholders, in DDP to complement the 11 forum members and 5 observers from government agencies. Subsequently the forum was increased to over 100 members, including 55 from the initial 68-member WCD forum. The next month, August 2002, DDP hosted a multi-stakeholder panel in Johannesburg at the World Summit on Sustainable Development and staffed an exhibition booth. The following March an afternoon session on 'Dams and Development: Promoting dialogue for improved decision-making' was held as part of the Dams and Sustainable Development theme at the Third World Water Forum in Kyoto, Japan. In July 2003 the new DDP secretariat was shifted to Nairobi with a second meeting of the forum in September 2003 that dealt with the options assessment process.

Impacts of the WCD Report and WCD and UNEP–DDP process

Impacts have been of two major types; both were pioneering. One was to set a precedent for dealing with major international issues and the other related to moving the dams debate forward. The World Resources Institute, Lokayan and the Lawyers' Environmental Action Team (with funding from the MacArthur Foundation) researched the Commission by attending WCD meetings and conducting wide-ranging interviews. A 136-page report, *A Watershed in Global Governance? An Independent Assessment of the World Commission on Dams*, was published during 2001. It contrasted WCD with previous commissions in regard to a number of features, concluding that they 'added up to a Commission structure and process that was path-breaking by historical standards' (Dubash et al, 2001, p119). The commissioners, for example, represented the range of viewpoints present in the dams debate rather than coming from a 'broad middle' and were mainly 'active practitioners in international networks, rather than the eminent persons of past commissions' (ibid). The Commission was also characterized by a commitment 'to incorporate good governance principles in its work' (ibid).

The Report concluded that the WCD, despite flaws, was 'essentially robust' (ibid), with the Final Report actively engaging the range of stakeholders. What its final contribution would be, however, would 'depend upon stakeholder willingness to continue dialogue on the Commission's findings and recommendations' and on 'champions in financial institutions, industry, government, and civil society working to implement the recommendations' (ibid). That, I believe, was a prescient conclusion, discussion of which requires consideration of negative reactions to the Final Report, UNEP–DDP's effectiveness in moving the WCD process forward, and ongoing obstacles that the WCD and the UNEP–DDP process faces.

China, with nearly half of the large dams in the world, and one of the major dam-building countries of the 20th century, was quick to reject the WCD Final Report, as was India. Other major dam-building countries such as Spain and Turkey were highly critical of the Final Report. Also critical were officials in ICOLD, the International Hydropower Association (IHA), and ICID who believed that far too little emphasis had been placed on the benefits associated with large dams and that following the WCD guidelines would greatly restrict the construction of future dams.[10]

UN agencies and several European governments, on the other hand, endorsed the report, emphasizing that from then on it would influence their policies as donors. In addition to UNEP's support, the World Health Organization (WHO) stated on 30 November 2000 that the 'Report of the World Commission on Dams is a landmark report for all development stakeholders. It pays attention to the environmental and social aspects of dams, including the health problems associated with their development. It provides a roadmap for a leap forward in development planning, through its rights-and-risks concept... If the report meets with broad support from all development stakeholders, then the scene is set for truly sustainable development in the 21st century.'

Especially supportive was the German Government, detailing its position at ICOLD's 69th Annual Meeting in September 2001. The previous January, the Minister for Economic Cooperation and Development had invited relevant German stakeholders to review the WCD Final Report. Considered remarkable was the 'way in which the main stakeholders on the German side, including industry and non-governmental organizations, agreed that the WCD recommendations have pointed the way forward... This encouraged us to adopt the WCD recommendations as binding standards for German development co-operation' (German Government, 2001, p36).

Wisely UNEP–DDP, having become operational during 2002, chose to concentrate on stakeholder agreement rather than differences and on being a facilitator for dialogue as opposed to being an implementer of the WCD Report (*Confluence*, 2002b, p5). That meant concentrating on the five core values and seven strategic principles that all stakeholders had found to be of value, and this is the approach that I have taken in this book. Reiterating the WCD viewpoint that procedures followed in different countries must be 'home grown', the Dams and Development Project opted to use the five values and seven principles as a discussion framework among stakeholders both within and without DDP; hence, for example, the emphasis on options assessment during the second forum meeting in September 2003. That approach has paid dividends in regard to bringing representatives into the forum from governments that initially had taken strong objection to the WCD Final Report. China joined the DDP forum late in 2002, with the Ministry of Water Affairs the lead government agency and China's State Environmental Protection Agency also involved. Turkey also decided to join the forum. The forum steering committee concluded: 'Over the past eighteen months, we have seen a remarkable change take place in how people view the WCD report' (ibid).

Positive change definitely has occurred; however, major obstacles remain to continued forward progress. That is because critics continue to ignore, marginalize and/or not advocate the WCD and UNEP–DDP process. Three examples follow relating to the World Bank, the World Water Council and the 2003 Camdessus Report on Financing Water for All. In July 2002, the 12 former commissioners wrote a joint letter to the President of the World Bank reminding him that the Bank had stated in its December 2001 Board-approved official response to the WCD Report that 'it shares the WCD core values and concurs with the need to promote the seven strategic priorities' and that the Bank's draft Water Resources Sector Strategy would be the Bank's primary mechanism for integrating the WCD report into its policies and practices. Yet that had not been done, even though the strategy paper's emphasis on large dams playing an important role in the Bank's future as 'high risk/high reward' projects provided an excellent opportunity to integrate the WCD approach. The Bank's reply came in August via the Vice-President for the Environmentally and Socially Sustainable Development Network, rather than from the President himself, and was not reassuring in regard to the Bank's willingness to play a lead role in pushing forward the type of new decision-making framework for water resource development that WCD had advocated.

The March 2003 Third World Water Forum in Kyoto, Japan, was sponsored by the World Water Council and the Global Water Partnership. The main theme dealing with dams during the Forum of 16–23 March was titled Dams and Sustainable Development. According to the preliminary programme, and at the request of the Japanese organizers, it was to be sponsored jointly by the World Water Council and UNEP–DDP with an open plenary session in the morning and a less formal discourse in the afternoon. In mid-February, less than five weeks before the commencement of the Forum, for which planning had begun in 2001, I received a telephone call asking me to be one of four speakers in the morning session with the President of the World Water Council (WWC) in the Chair. Because I was not directly involved in UNEP–DDP, I wondered why there was no DDP speaker involved. What I learned during the next week was that a small group of prominent officials or former officials in a number of WWC member organizations, including

ICOLD, IHA and ICID, not only wished to marginalize DDP's role but, as a minority, had succeeded in getting DDP removed from the Plenary Session.

Had I accepted the invitation to participate, I would have had an excellent opportunity to explain how best to deal with environmental, social and institutional issues, which I knew to be even more serious than presented in the WCD Final Report. But to accept would have been at the expense of DDP, for, as I stated in my e-mail of 18 February to the organizer declining to participate, 'It is clear to me that colleagues in UNEP–DDP are, and remain, very concerned that some members within the World Water Council are trying to marginalize the involvement of UNEP–DDP and of the World Commission on Dams in the Third World Water Forum's Dams and Sustainable Development dialogue.' Presumably my withdrawal had some effect, for the final group of four speakers in the morning session included two members of the DDP Steering Committee, while UNEP's Director General co-chaired the closing session with the WWC President, and DDP and WWC cooperated in preparing the theme statement.

The 2003 Camdessus Report was sponsored by the World Water Council and the Global Water Partnership and was presented at the Third World Water Forum. Chaired by the former Managing Director of the International Monetary Fund, its 20 members included the Presidents (or their delegates) of the African, Asian and Inter-American Development Banks and of the European Bank for Reconstruction and Development. Although correctly emphasizing the critical need for major increases in financial flows if the number of people without access to water and sanitation were to be halved by 2015, the report included additional dam storage, along with other types of infrastructure, without addressing the policies necessary for dealing with past inadequacies that presumably would be necessary for obtaining additional funding. In a letter of 10 April 2003 to the Chair of the Global Water Partnership, former WCD Chair Kader Asmal wrote that 'I am both astounded and disappointed that the World Panel's Report chooses to effectively ignore the framework proposed by the World Commission on Dams. Moreover, the only reference to the WCD Report – in footnote 13 – implies that the WCD did not recognize the need for water storage and hydropower development. This is clearly a misrepresentation and potentially damaging... I will regretfully have to reconsider my patronage to the Global Water Partnership.'

MY EXPERTISE AND CURRENT POSITION ON LARGE DAMS

Expertise

The analysis in this book is based on several hundred cases. Although distributed throughout the world, the large majority are in late-industrializing countries, where the large majority of future dams will be built and where tens of millions of people are still dependent on the natural flood regimes of innumerable rivers. Included are 20 large projects that I personally have studied, 10 of which are among the largest river basin development projects in the world. Until the spring of 1956, I doubt that I had ever thought about involuntarily displaced people or others affected by the construction of large dams and other river basin development projects. That was soon to change, however, because of a course I took that spring. It was on Southern and Central Africa and was taught by Professor Elizabeth Colson at Boston University – nothing similar was available at Harvard where I was enrolled as a graduate student in social anthropology. Still doing fieldwork in Central Africa today, Colson had initiated research in the mid-1940s among the Plateau Tonga who were one of Central Africa's largest ethnic groups. Subsequently she became the director of the Rhodes–Livingstone Institute, one of three British colonial social science research institutions in Africa.

In the mid-1950s, a decision was reached to build the first mainstream dam on the Zambezi in what was then the Central African Federation (now the independent states of Zambia, Zimbabwe and Malawi). Called Kariba, the main purpose of the dam was to provide hydroelectric power to the Northern Rhodesian copper belt. Aware that the dam would require a major resettlement component, Henry Fosbrooke, at that time director of the Institute, persuaded the copper industry to fund 'before and after' resettlement studies of those involved, the large majority of whom were Gwembe, or Valley Tonga. Because of her previous work among the Plateau Tonga, he asked Elizabeth Colson to undertake the study and she in turn asked me to join her. So, in October 1956 I ended up not in the mountains of East Africa, which had been my preference for doing the necessary fieldwork for my PhD dissertation, but at the bottom of what was one of the hottest, most disease-ridden and isolated rift valleys in Africa. What followed were 48 more years of research and consulting in river basins with special emphasis on impacts on river basin communities and habitats.

Our Kariba study, now in its 49th year and the most detailed long-term study of a population undergoing dam-induced resettlement,[11] began with pre-relocation 'benchmark' research. My initial involvement was primarily academic. While some of the British colonial civil servants responsible for planning and implementing the resettlement programme may also have had some interest in our work, Colson and I were not expected to think through, let alone help government officials apply, their policy implications. Throughout 1961–1962, I was involved in a similar pre-relocation 'benchmark' study of approximately 50,000 Egyptian Nubians soon to be resettled in connection with the Aswan High Dam project.

Colson and I returned to the Middle Zambezi Valley in late 1962 to carry out a one-year post-project study of the impacts of Kariba resettlement on the 57,000 people who had been relocated and on how they had responded to those impacts. A few years later, we decided to convert our 'before and after study' into a systematic long-term study of change and continuity in the people's lives.

By the 1960s I had become increasingly interested in the application of research to policy issues. Several consultancies were instrumental in this. One was a World Bank consultancy with three economists and an agronomist that produced over a three-year period the two-volume *Experiences with Agricultural Development in Tropical Africa* (de Wilde, 1967). A second was the opportunity provided by the Ford Foundation in 1965 and the Food and Agriculture Organization of the United Nations (FAO) in 1966 to design, with colleagues at the Nigerian Institute of Social and Economic Research, a pre-project research programme designed to improve resettlement and environmental outcomes for the Kainji Dam project on the Niger River. Further FAO consultancies in 1966 and 1967 dealt with fisheries development in connection with Zambia's Kafue and Kariba Dams, while three consultancies with the United Nations Development Programme (UNDP) in 1969, 1970 and 1973 involved resettlement planning for the Ivory Coast's Kossou Dam.

While our Kariba study has influenced my thinking about river basin development more than any other single project, the comparative analysis of others has helped me decide which impacts and trends have global applications irrespective of geographical, cultural and political differences and which are project specific. Seven activities have been especially important in the evolution of my thinking. Three involved broad comparative analyses. The first was a global review of large-scale irrigated and rain-fed government-sponsored new land-settlement schemes in the tropics and subtropics (Scudder, 1981b). It involved field and archival research over a several-year period and was financed by the US Agency for International Development (USAID) through the non-profit Institute of Development Anthropology that David Brokensha, Michael Horowitz and I had founded in 1976. The second review was a desk study that dealt with World Bank-financed government-sponsored land settlement (World Bank, 1985a). As in the first review, the second included both voluntary and involuntary resettlers. The third activity was a detailed overview of the African experience with river basin development that was financed by USAID under its cooperative agreement with Clark University and the Institute for Development Anthropology on Settlement and Resource Systems Analysis (Scudder, 1988).

The fourth activity involved a detailed ten-month evaluation in 1991–1992 for IUCN of the Government of Botswana's Southern Okavango Integrated Water Development Project (Scudder et al, 1993). The fifth involved repeated consultancy visits to a number of large river basin development projects, including Ghana's Volta Project at Akosombo (three visits: 1967–1989), Sudan's Jonglei Canal Project (three visits: 1976–1978) and Rahad Project (two visits: 1979–1981), Sri Lanka's Accelerated Mahaweli Project (nine visits between 1979 and 1999), India's Sardar Sarovar Project (four visits between 1983 and 1989), Mali's Manantali Project (six visits: 1985–1989) and China's Three Gorges Project (three visits: 1986–1987) as well as individual consultancies dealing with, among others, Hydro-Quebec's Grande Baleine Project, the Jordan Valley Irrigation Project and China's Longtan Project.

More recently, the sixth activity has involved membership on independent panels of experts dealing with environmental and social issues in connection with the Lesotho Highlands Water Project (16 visits: 1989–2000), Laos' NT2

Project (eight visits: 1979–2004) and Swaziland and South Africa's Maguga Project (two visits: 1998–2000). Serving as a commissioner on the World Commission on Dams from 1998–2000 was the seventh activity.

Current position on large dams

For much of my life I have been a supporter of large dams. As a child I spent days building my own dam on a small stream in the Berkshire Mountains of Connecticut. During the early years of my career, I believed large dams could facilitate, even catalyse, equitable river basin development. By the mid-1980s, however, I saw that this was not happening. On the contrary, inequitable development and environmental degradation were occurring. I now consider that in most cases, large dams, and especially those over 60m in height, are part of a flawed paradigm that causes an increasing disconnection between the necessary environmental health of river basins and the current needs of people and governments for the provision of water, energy and food.

The dilemma for planners over the short term is that dams may be the most desirable option when needs reach crisis or near-crisis proportions. Examples include the need for water in South Africa's urban industrial heartland or in Northern China, where rural and especially urban populations grow as aquifer and surface water is depleted. In such cases, which occur in many late-industrializing countries, large dams and/or inter-basin transfers remain a possible development option. For that reason, a major emphasis in this monograph is how to reduce costs and increase benefits in cases where a participatory options assessment process concludes that the construction of a large dam is the best way to deal with current needs in spite of irreversible longer-term costs. Such an options assessment process, however, should be informed about the many environmental, social, institutional and political costs and problems that are associated with dam construction, points that are also emphasized in this volume.

First, irreversible environmental impacts, especially in deltas and wetlands, should be expected. Second, unacceptable social costs continue to be imposed upon people who must be involuntarily resettled from future reservoir basins and upon the tens of millions living downstream from dams. Third, governments and project authorities are often unwilling to follow the guidelines of multilateral organizations and professional pro-dam institutions such as ICOLD. Acceptable policies and plans are not being implemented and compliance with agreed-upon guidelines does not occur. More specifically, the necessary political will, finance, institutional capacity, stakeholder participation and development opportunities for addressing environmental and social issues are lacking. Fourth, unexpected events, including changes in government, unfavourably alter outcomes because large dams are so complex and take so long to build. A fifth problem, with scale again being a factor, is corruption.

In the future, large dams should only be built after participatory decision-making demonstrates that better options are not available. But that alone is not sufficient if dam builders continue to ignore the WCD's five core values and seven strategic priorities – values and priorities that have received near universal approval. Even more basic is the importance of expanding the WCD approach to water and energy resources and to river basins everywhere. Moreover, the WCD report has yet to foster the type of discussions that could lead to the necessary new paradigm for the 21st century and beyond.

Adverse and irreversible environmental impacts continue to occur and improved policies have yet to yield improved outcomes for project-affected people. This conclusion applies to some of the largest dams recently completed or currently under construction, including Lesotho and South Africa's Highlands Water Project, India's Sardar Sarovar Project and China's Three Gorges Project. Unless dam builders can show that they are willing and capable of implementing WCD's core values and strategic priorities, they should not receive international finance or support. Of course, countries can, and will, continue building dams with their own capital, but that does not mean they should escape internal and external pressure. Major human rights issues can and should be raised.

The international community needs to be proactive, using a 'carrot and stick' approach, to minimize adverse environmental and socio-economic effects. The 'carrot' is to reward implementation of the WCD framework. The 'stick' must involve a willingness on the part of the international community to challenge national sovereignty where governments attempt to implement destructive projects. River basins are international heartlands. To meet the needs of future generations, their current degradation must be stopped. Examples of where both the 'carrot' and the 'stick' approaches are necessary include the Government of India's proposal to divert its northern rivers to Southern India, which could adversely affect the human rights of tens of millions of people in Bangladesh, and China's dam construction on the Upper Mekong River, which is proceeding without consideration of adverse impacts on tens of millions of people living in downstream countries of Southeast Asia. In such cases, moving forward will require the existence of appropriate international institutions and a willingness to impose sanctions where necessary.

My present position has evolved over the past 48 years as I have documented not just the unacceptable costs of large dams but also their failure to realize their potential, including the potential that water resource development projects have for achieving major multiplier effects. Although I was aware in the mid-1960s of underestimated environmental and social costs (Brokensha and Scudder, 1968), nonetheless, as a visionary, I tended to emphasize the development potential of large-scale river basin development projects. Referring to such African dams as Aswan High, Kariba and Volta, I wrote, 'In terms of regional development, these projects offer an exceptional opportunity for planning and implementing an integrated river and lake basin development program. Aside from power generation, flood control, and improved transport, such a project should include irrigation and fisheries, market and small industrial centers, conservation zones and national parks, residential areas, and tourist and recreational facilities' (Scudder, 1965, p6).

As for the resettlement of tens of thousands of people, I believed then that 'more highly productive environments can be created with new ground rules to maintain and increase resource potential. Through experimentation, new production and extension techniques can be developed which will better meet the people's rising expectations. They will also help to take the pressure off overcrowded urban centers to which impoverished rural residents are migrating'(ibid).

I continued to reiterate such views during the 1970s and 1980s but with increasing awareness of the possibility of failure. In 1979, my colleague Kapila P. Vimaladharma and I began a series of evaluations of the irrigation component of Sri Lanka's Accelerated Mahaweli Project. As planned during the 1970s, I initially found the Mahaweli Project very exciting, not just as the country's most ambitious attempt to foster a process of integrated river basin development involving over 500,000 settlers, multiple dams and inter-basin transfers, but as a means for addressing Sri Lanka's increasing ethnic strife.

The Accelerated Mahaweli Project has never realized the potential that Vimaladharma and I saw in the late 1970s and early 1980s. Indeed, it actually increased communal strife between the government and the Hindu minority (Scudder, 1995a). Elsewhere I continued to document disappointing results. In most cases, economic benefits tended to be overestimated and environmental and social costs underestimated. I offer many reasons in this monograph. Here I wish to emphasize the lack of political will on the part of governments and project authorities to realize the potential that I still believe is there. This is especially true in terms of creating the development opportunities needed by project-affected people, especially resettlers, host populations and downstream residents, if they are to improve their living standards.

It has taken me nearly 48 years to evolve this position. Readers will probably sense the anger I feel at the unacceptable and unnecessary costs that large dams have caused to tens of millions of people. Indeed, rereading sections in this monograph on the stress and trauma associated with resettlement infuriates me. I do not expect my position, or my anger, to change unless governments and project authorities begin to implement state-of-the-art guidelines.

CATEGORIES OF PROJECT-AFFECTED PEOPLE ANALYSED

The emphasis here is on people who live within, and are dependent upon, river basins within late-industrializing countries, in which the majority of future dams will be built. They are the major risk-takers when dams are built and they are the people who historically have been most adversely affected. Three categories are emphasized. Located above dams, the first category includes those who must be resettled from future reservoir basins, while the second category involves the host populations who receive them. Located below dams, the third category covers those whose lifestyles are adversely affected by dams, primarily because their economic systems are focused on naturally flowing rivers and recharged aquifers and include such components as flood recession agriculture, flood recession grazing, fishing and other activities that are dependent on the natural flood regimes of pre-project rivers. The number of people included in these three categories is in the hundreds of millions. According to WCD, the number of those resettled in connection with large dams exceeds 40 million and may be double that number (op cit, p104). Although data are lacking on the size of host populations as well as on the number of adversely affected people downstream, their combined number is much larger.

Of course not all households and communities in the above three categories have been adversely affected by past projects. Among resettlers, for example, a minority can always be expected to use resettlement as an opportunity to improve their living standards. The same is true of a minority of hosts. Moreover, the fact that a majority have benefited in a number of cases found throughout the world shows that the potential is there to increase significantly the proportion of beneficiaries. The same is true for downstream residents, especially where they are incorporated within well-planned and well-implemented irrigation and agro-industrial projects.

In the analysis that follows in this chapter and in the next three chapters, resettling communities will receive the most attention, simply because they are the group on which we have the most data; dam-induced community resettlement has been the topic of innumerable publications (Guggenheim, 1994) as opposed to the scant attention paid to host populations and downstream residents. My emphasis is on the development-induced resettlement of communities rather than on individuals and households that move as separate units because of natural disasters, famine and political strife. The extent to which responses may be similar as a result of such dissimilar causes is an important topic for analysis but is not dealt with in this book.

While the literature on resettlement sometimes distinguishes between resettlement and relocation, based primarily on the distance moved, I consider the two terms to be synonyms. That is because such a distinction confuses the basic issue: that the majority of those relocated respond in the same way regardless of whether a move is to a distant locale or to somewhere nearby, such as when a riverbank community is shifted to the edge of a future reservoir. Throughout my analysis, dam-induced resettlement, or other river basin development-induced community resettlement, is considered to be involuntary, since it remains to be shown that plans, no matter how good, can convince the majority to take the risks associated with being required to leave a familiar environment for an unfamiliar one. This involuntary element does not mean, of course, that subsequent to removal, a majority cannot come to like the new location or improve their living standards. Indeed, that is the goal to be reached.

Frequent mention will also be made of two other categories of project-affected people. One includes immigrants. The other includes people living in the catchments above dams. Immigrants tend to be better-educated people with more capital and more experience who come to seek the development opportunities that accompany dam construction. Some come as labourers and decide to stay on after construction is finished. Others seek specific opportunities such as reservoir fishing or incorporation within irrigation projects. In both cases they are apt to restrict opportunities available to less well educated and less experienced local people unless a special effort is made by project authorities and other agencies to provide training, technical assistance, credit and other facilities.

The activities of people living in catchments are relevant as to whether or not increasing sedimentation will threaten the functional lifetime of downstream dams. In rivers with a high silt load, such as the Yellow River and the Yangtze, deforestation in upper catchments is a major threat, as recently admitted by the Government of China. Current planning for the Nam Theun 2 (NT2) reservoir in Laos is supposed to include a major effort to stabilize the agrarian systems of approximately 6000 indigenous people living in the $3500km^2$ upper catchment area.

FOCUS ON RESETTLEMENT

Introduction

In assessing criticism of WCD's Final Report, I detect an unsupported and unsupportable sense of disbelief and denial that tens of millions of people have been resettled and that the situation is really as serious as the Commission presented it to be. Hence 'business as usual' remains acceptable, even though I believe that a continuation of that approach will intensify future conflict at the expense of water resource development and poverty alleviation.

Perhaps denial is understandable given the lack of easily accessible data on social impacts and the lack of familiarity of most planners and practitioners with resettlement issues, including the multidimensional stress involved. Even researchers such as myself risk underestimating the associated trauma until we are reminded again and again by those involved of the difficulties they must face. But ignorance only partially explains why such people's needs, rights and cultures, including their strong symbolic ties to their land and communities, continue to be ignored. Could a more important reason be because the large majority of resettlers as well as downstream inhabitants are poor, uneducated and relatively powerless rural residents who include a disproportionate number of indigenous people (as in the US and Canada) or people of lower caste or status (as in India)? That is a question that has been increasingly asked by a wide range of human rights and environmental NGOs as well as by the affected people themselves; it is a question that helps explain the increasingly adversarial nature of the large dams dispute.

It is important to repeat that the evidence, presented in Chapter 3, is overwhelming that the construction of large dams has impoverished the large majority of those resettled. Within the major dam-building countries, including the US, China and India, I am aware of none that can document that they have been able even to restore the incomes of the majority of resettlers. Take, for instance, the TVA, which became a model for other countries. According to Grant, 'studies show that families forced by TVA to move were worse off than they had been before the coming of TVA' and 'the tenant and poor land owner bore the brunt of readjustment' (1990, p75). That outcome was not intended. As TVA's sponsor, President Franklin Roosevelt intended the Authority to provide major social benefits to such people.

The introduction of World Bank resettlement guidelines in 1980 and the introduction of more recent guidelines from such professional societies as ICOLD and ICID, from the Organization for Economic Development and Co-operation (OECD) and from such countries as China and Sri Lanka, have brought increasing attention to environmental and social issues. Yet they are either inadequate, as in the case of the World Bank's guidelines (Chapter 8), or they are largely ignored, because the construction of contemporary large dams continues to impoverish the majority of those resettled as well as to adversely affect millions of downstream residents.

Numbers of dam-induced resettlers

A disquieting example of the extent to which people involuntarily displaced by dams have been ignored by project authorities and their governments is that no accurate figures exist of the numbers involved. That is the case even with World Bank-financed large dams where all phases of a project cycle from project identification to completion are supposed to be carefully researched and documented. In the mid-1990s, the Bank's Operations Evaluation Department reviewed 50 Bank-financed large dam projects (1996). In seven cases, no resettlement population estimates were available. In another case, the Bank assumed that no people had been removed when in fact a number of indigenous families had been displaced.

When figures are available, they are more likely to be underestimates than overestimates. Also in the mid-1990s, the World Bank's Environment Department reviewed 192 Bank-financed projects that involved development-induced involuntary resettlement during the 1986–1993 period. According to that review, 'the total number of people to be resettled is 47 per cent higher ... than the estimate made at the time of appraisal... Data supplied by many borrowers at preparation and appraisal have commonly understated the number of people affected. The real number became apparent only part way through the project' (World Bank, 1994a, p2/2). In this case, the underestimate at the time of appraisal was 625,000 people whose resettlement would not have been adequately budgeted for! While the Bank's review included all types of development-induced resettlement, 'dams and reservoirs are the most frequent cause of displacement, and account for 63 per cent of the people displaced' (ibid, p2/6). The first large dam financed in Africa by the World Bank, Kariba, illustrates the type of underestimate that is all too common. There, 57,000 people were eventually resettled as opposed to an initial estimate of 27,000. In the statistical analysis of 50 large dams discussed in Chapter 3, in the 20 cases where sufficient before and after figures were available, earlier estimates of numbers of resettlers on which planning and budgeting was based was approximately 50 per cent of the final tally.

The World Bank's 1994 Review was 'Bankwide' in that the Bank's regional and country offices were required to undertake resettlement reviews for submission to the Environment Department. As part of the review process, the Bank's resettlement team – at that time the largest and most experienced team in the world dealing with development-induced resettlement – 'has recently generated the first worldwide estimate of the magnitude of development-related population displacement. According to our analysis, each year about four million people are displaced by approximately 300 large dams (above 15m high) that on average enter construction phase annually... In addition six million people are displaced by the urban development and transportation programs that are started each year. Thus a total of about 10 million people every year, or at least 80–90 million people over the past decade, are displaced as a result of infrastructure programs for dam construction, urban, and transportation development, taken together' (Cernea, 1997a, p6).

If we take Cernea's lower figure of 80 million people, of whom approximately 40 per cent have been relocated because of dams, we get 32 million involuntarily relocated from 1987–1996 as a result of only 3000 of the world's 45,000 large dams at that time, or 10,666 per dam. Figures presented in the 1994 Bankwide Review increase that total to 56 million resettled as a result of 4000–5000 dams during the 1980–93 period. Based on estimates from the Bank's China and Mongolia Country Department, Cernea states in another Bank publication that 'more than ten million people were involuntarily resettled over a period of 40 years' because of dam construction in China (Cernea, 1997b, p4). Jing (1999) considers that figure conservative, believing that dam construction in China's Yangtze Valley alone is responsible for the resettlement of an estimated 10 million people, while Fernandes and Paranjpye estimate that 16–38 million people were resettled as a result of large dam construction in India (1997, p17). Even leaving aside such estimates from independent researchers, the estimates of the World Bank team suggest that WCD's statement that 'the overall global level of physical displacement could range from 40 to 80 million people' as a result of dam construction could well be a conservative one. Since the global experience is that such resettlement impoverishes the majority of those involved, such a number is an incredible indictment of the socio-economic impact of what are supposed to be broad-based development projects.

The stress and trauma associated with involuntary resettlement

Introduction

Oliver-Smith refers to development-induced involuntary resettlement as a 'totalizing' experience that is 'one of the most acute expressions of powerlessness because it constitutes a loss of control over one's physical space' (2002, p6). It is also impoverishing because 'it takes away economic, social and cultural resources all at the same time' and 'it takes away political power, most dramatically the power to make a decision about where and how to live' (Koenig, 2002, p10).

Educated, mobile professionals continue to be unaware of how stressful involuntary resettlement is for people with strong ties to their homes who have had little education and experience of the 'outside world'. Dam-induced resettlement is especially stressful, since entire communities are involved including the young and old and the healthy and sick. Agrarian populations, women and the elderly in particular (lack of research on the effects on children continues to be a major gap), with strong ties to the land are more seriously affected than those in urban communities that have been resettled, though in this case too stress is involved (Fried, 1963). Academics such as myself also run the risk of underemphasizing the trauma involved; yet such trauma also applies to our own spouses and children when we uproot them to further our careers by relocating to jobs elsewhere.

Weissman and Paykel are psychiatrists with an upper-income clientele in New Haven, Connecticut. They were surprised by the number of distressed spouses of Yale University professors who sought their help (Weissman and Paykel, 1972). Such patients had recently left familiar places to accompany relocating husbands. In the process they had left behind familiar habitats, friends and networks of aid-givers that provided security in meeting day-to-day demands. The same was true for their children, who were also 'involuntary resettlers' forced to leave their schoolmates and other peers. Other examples of the trauma of removal for more educated people relate to those elderly who, for one reason or another (such as safety after an earthquake in California), are required to move from a familiar institutional setting to an unfamiliar one. In these cases, death rates can be expected to exceed what they would have been if removal had not occurred.

Although the number of people involved was too small for statistical analysis, Mary E. D. Scudder and I also found resettlement stress during a study of airport expansion that significantly increased noise over one of the wealthiest communities in the US (Scudder and Scudder, 1981). Whereas husbands tended to leave home for work before increased noise from plane take-offs and landings became noticeable, their wives were primarily homemakers who remained in the area throughout the day. Yet even when they moved to quieter locales, the types of tensions they continued to suffer were similar, in our opinion, to those of people involuntarily removed from what had once been a known and preferred habitat.

The multidimensional stress of dam-induced resettlement

Introduction

I have found it useful to break stress into three synergistically related components. This concept of multidimensional stress categorizes the more generalized stress that is referred to in innumerable case studies of different types of involuntary resettlement (Hansen and Oliver-Smith, 1982). The various dimensions are physiological, psychological and socio-cultural.

Physiological stress
Physiological stress refers to the various health impacts associated with removal. Although careful pre-project demographic and socio-economic surveys are now expected by donors, equally important health impact assessments remain uncommon. For that reason, information on resettlement-induced increases in morbidity and mortality tend to be anecdotal or restricted to a few case studies. Nonetheless, especially in the tropics and subtropics, what data are available suggest that historically, the incidences of poor nutrition and disease, as well as higher death rates, have increased immediately after resettlement, or have occurred later where public health initiatives are lacking or impoverishment results.

Fahim reported what he believed were heightened Egyptian and Sudanese Nubian death rates following Aswan High Dam resettlement (1973, 1975), while Clark et al (1995) and Scudder (1975) reported a rise in death rates immediately following Kariba resettlement and from the 1980s to the present (Clark, 2001). Overcrowding in denser settlements and inadequate water and sanitation facilities get most of the blame. In the Egyptian Nubian case, 'Communicable diseases such as dysentery, measles, and a form of encephalitis quickly spread in the suddenly condensed population. These conditions, aggregated by the high summer temperatures typical of the region, caused a rapid rise in mortality, especially among the very young and the very old' (Fernea and Kennedy, 1966, p350).

In the Kariba case, inadequate food and water supplies were a serious problem immediately after removal, and remain a serious problem for tens of thousands of first, second and third generation resettlers today. During the first two years following resettlement, 56 children and women died from a 'mystery illness' during a period of food shortage in the Lusitu resettlement area (Gadd et al, 1962), while seemingly large numbers of children also died of dysentery. Among 1600 Gwembe Tonga resettled on the Northern Rhodesia Plateau, 41 children died within a three-month period. Across the reservoir in Southern Rhodesia, an outbreak of human sleeping sickness (trypanosomiasis) killed an unknown number of people (Scudder field notes). More recently, cholera – formerly rare in rural Africa – has become a serious problem in the two most densely occupied Zambian resettlement areas.

It is ironic and inexcusable that inadequate water supplies in inland resettlement areas of many past and current projects continue to be a public health problem for people who formerly lived besides free-flowing rivers and were forced to move because of the formation of large reservoirs. More than five years after their removal, less that 50 per cent of Basotho communities affected by the construction in the mid-1990s of the World Bank-financed Katse Dam had received the promised water supplies and sanitation, while four years after removal, Stage 1 resettlers from the Bank-financed Mohale Dam to the planned community of Makotoko continued to haul water from an adjacent host community.

Nutrition is also likely to deteriorate immediately after removal as a result of food shortages. According to the WCD, such shortages have been reported in Asia, including Vietnam, China, Malaysia, Thailand and India, as well as in

Africa (2000, p119). Several reasons may be involved. The quantity and quality of food supplies may be inadequate because resettlers often cultivate less land immediately before removal and have yet to clear, plant and harvest enough land to regain food self-sufficiency during the initial year or years after resettlement. Reduced access to such common property resources as wild food plants, fish and game also tends to occur. Where food relief is supplied by the project authorities, it may be limited to items insufficient for a balanced diet, as was the case with Katse resettlement during the early years of the Lesotho Highlands Water Project.

The creation of reservoirs and resettlement to a different habitat also bring people into contact with new diseases or result in a higher incidence of old ones. Documented case histories include occurrences of malaria, schistosomiasis, leishmaniasis, trypanosomiasis, encephalitis, haemorrhagic fevers, gastroenteritis, intestinal parasites and filariasis (Jobin, 1999; Lerer and Scudder, 1999). Changes in water quality caused by excessive build-up of toxic cyanobacteria may also have an adverse effect on health, as does methyl mercury when people, especially pregnant women, eat fish from the end of the food chain (WCD, 2000, p118). More recently, in Africa and Asia the influx of construction workers with HIV/AIDS has put local communities at risk. Such examples show the need for proper clinics and other health facilities to be made available at the time of removal and thereafter.

Psychological stress
Psychological stress has two aspects. Following Morton Fried's terminology from a study of urban redevelopment in the US (Fried, 1963), I labelled one aspect ' "the grieving for a lost home" syndrome. Here "home" refers to community in the widest sense, as well as to the surrounding landscape, especially where it is incorporated into origin myths, historical accounts, and religious symbolism' (Scudder and Colson, 1982, p270).

The second aspect involves anxiety over the future. Generally speaking, women are more adversely affected by this than men (Colson, 1971, 1999; Koenig, 1995; Mehta and Srinivasan, 2000; see also Weissman and Paykel, 1972). Almost invariably, relocation planning is done 'by men for men, with the result that men receive title to the land..., regardless of what the land tenure situation was prior to removal. At the same time, opportunities for women to earn money are rarely built into the project, and extension work among women is restricted largely to non-income-producing home economics topics... As a result the woman's position as a productive member and decision-making partner in the family is reduced, with concomitant loss in social and economic status' (Scudder and Colson, 1982, p285).

Reporting on her University of Cambridge PhD research in one of the 19 Gujarat villages affected by India's Sardar Sarovar Project, Hakim notes that problems associated with separation of villagers at different sites will be 'greatest for women, who often consider this as the worst consequence of resettlement... Women maintain a close relationship with their families, even after marriage' (Hakim, 1995, p156).

Both aspects of psychological stress characterized Gwembe Tonga women in the Kariba case. Mostly illiterate with travel largely restricted to visiting kin within the Middle Zambezi Valley or on the adjacent plateau, they were uncertain about what the future would bring. Of even more concern was leaving the burial sites of kin and fields that had been passed on from one generation to another. On arrival at resettlement sites, few women were able to lay claim to arable land. But women were not the only people stressed; also stressed were religious leaders whose status was tied to particular sites and sacred shrines that could not be moved. And unless they were still heads of households strong in labour resources, elderly men also faced an uncertain future, as did political leaders who had lost the trust of their constituents by failing to prevent the move or by collaborating with it.

Socio-cultural stress

Socio-cultural stress is precipitated by threats to a community's cultural identity. It is closely related to the unintentional simplification of a society's cultural inventory that tends to accompany removal. Especially difficult during the initial years following removal is temporary or permanent loss of livelihood-support patterns and comforting customs, institutions and symbols dealing, for example, with birth, puberty, marriage and death. Such loss can occur for a number of reasons.

Loss of livelihood-support practices occurs where economic activities, such as those involving crop production and livestock management, are not suited to the new habitat. Small entrepreneurs may find it difficult, if not impossible, to transfer their businesses and skills because of loss of clientele during resettlement or competition with better-capitalized and more experienced hosts. Development opportunities may not yet be available, or land and other resources not ready for use; only 10 per cent of arable land had been prepared for irrigation when over 40,000 Egyptian Nubians were relocated to the Kom Ombo resettlement area (Fernea et al, 1991, p192). Sixteen years later, Fahim found that only 60 per cent had received new land (1983). Having been relocated inland, women could no longer practise rituals associated with life beside the Nile. Other religious customs, as with rituals associated with Gwembe Tonga neighbourhoods, may also be lost because they are tied to specific sites, and hence cannot be transferred.

Because of the increased government presence associated with involuntary resettlement, other customs and practices may be at least temporarily reduced because they are associated with illegal but important income-generating activities such as the cultivation of marijuana and other narcotics, liquor production and smuggling. Still others customs are curtailed because of fear of ridicule by government officials or the host population. This can happen when people with distinctive rituals and other behaviour patterns are resettled among those who claim greater sophistication – examples being the movement of indigenous people in India, Laos or Sri Lanka to Hindu or Buddhist host areas.

Involuntary resettlement also often fosters insecurity by undermining local leadership at the very time that strong leadership is needed. Before and during removal, political and religious leaders tend to find themselves in a Catch-22 situation. If they agree to resettlement, they are likely to lose credibility simply because the majority do not want to move. For that reason they may turn against leaders seen as collaborating even if, through cooperation with project authorities, such leaders had been able to negotiate a wider range of benefits than would have otherwise been the case. This happened among the Gwembe Tonga where the people turned against the chairman of their local council who was the only Gwembe Tonga with some overseas education. In return for his support of the project authorities, he had been able to negotiate a number of favourable benefits for resettlers including eventual return to the edge of the reservoir as well as promises that no changes in agricultural techniques would be required and that all resettlement areas would be cleared of the tsetse fly, carriers of a disease fatal to cattle. Yet he never regained the credibility that he had enjoyed before removal. Leaders 'against' resettlement also tend to lose credibility when removal occurs in spite of their opposition. Exceptions are most likely to occur when followers perceive a leader's resistance as improving their livelihood conditions after resettlement occurs and where leaders remain within their own territories as was the case with the Allegany Senecas' resettlement in connection with the Kinzua Dam in the US (Bilharz, 1998).

Adversely affecting leaders, as well as all resettlers, are all too frequent and stressful conflicts with the host population. Leaders, for example, will find themselves at a disadvantage if hosts require them to defer to, or serve under, their own political and religious leaders or at least to delay the time when they can re-establish their own influence or authority. If hosts are not fully involved in, accepting of, and benefiting from resettlement decisions, they can make the life of resettlers miserable. This was the situation in 2001 for 22 Mohale Dam households that had agreed to shift from the mountains of Lesotho to a lowland area called Makhoakhoeng on the outskirts of the capital city of Maseru (LHDA POE, 2000b). Although the land on which they were resettled was legally acquired by project authorities from the Maseru Municipal Council, it was still land within the traditional territory of the Makhoakhoeng host population. Unfortunately for the resettlers, one of the hosts was a key minister in the Lesotho Government who had taken umbrage at his non-involvement in resettlement planning and land acquisition. As his feud with the project authorities escalated, he influenced the host population to reject the presence of the resettlers, not even allowing them to bury their dead in an adjacent cemetery. The stressful dispute continued until pressure from the World Bank forced the government to make a cabinet decision to allow the resettled community to remain at their new site.

Even where the host population, or at least their leaders, agree to incorporate the resettlers, eventual conflict is hard to avoid simply because more people are competing for the same limited land base and other natural resources (such as grazing) and the same job opportunities – resources and opportunities that otherwise would have been available to descendents of the host community. Such has been the case with many of the 6000 Gwembe Tonga resettled to the Lusitu area downstream from the Kariba Dam. There the local chief and headmen agreed to the resettlement on the understanding that local schools and medical facilities would be improved, as in fact they were. At the village level, initial relationships were friendly, with resettlers using their oxen to plough the fields of host 'friends' in return for the use of fertile land along the Lusitu River and in its delta. But 30 years later, with population and land scarcity increasing, many hosts – claiming that the fertile land had only been loaned – have demanded back most of those lands. The best approach is to attempt to reduce future conflict by fully involving the host population in all decision-making situations as well as involving them as part of a process of livelihood improvement.

Because of the tendency for resettlers to cling to the familiar as a coping response to uncertainty, most prefer to remain within a familiar habitat with people who share the same culture. In Laos' NT2 case, the project authority and the government hoped that the 6000 future resettlers would be willing to move to the lowlands where the potential for irrigation and the greater proximity to markets would provide better conditions for improving living standards. Except for a few families, however, all the villagers preferred to relocate not just within the future reservoir basin but also within their existing 'spirit' territories. As elsewhere, the important lesson here is for policy-makers to involve local people in the decision-making process from the start and to avoid trying to introduce from above radical changes in production techniques and social organization at the time of removal.

If changes in household and community livelihood systems are necessary for providing new development opportunities, resettlers should be familiarized with them as early as possible through pre-resettlement consultations, training, pilot projects and visits to appropriate projects elsewhere. In the Kariba case, training villagers to use gill nets in flooded Zambezi backwaters before removal prepared them to participate actively from the start in the future reservoir's artisanal fishery. In the NT2 case, settling three families on the developer's experimental farm in the reservoir basin not only enabled them to begin raising their living standards using new farming practices, but also provided a pilot project for training other villagers (NT2 POE, 2001).

The time dimension

Multidimensional stress is especially prevalent during the years that precede resettlement, during physical removal and during the years immediately after resettlement, although in the case of an unsatisfactory outcome, stress can continue for a much longer period. Prior to their removal, Colson and I found the Gwembe Tonga in denial in 1956 when the first rumours began circulating about possible resettlement in connection with Kariba.[12] We hypothesize that such denial is a coping response to minimize an otherwise stressful possibility. Once the certainty of future resettlement is realized and the time for removal draws near, people begin to cut back on life support activities, which causes further stress to the households involved. Labour migrants come home to help their kin with the move, hence foregoing income that would otherwise be forthcoming. Exhausted fields are not replaced with newly cleared ones; indeed, in anticipation of removal, smaller areas than normal may be planted.

Physical removal to a new habitat is especially stressful. Even after 45 years of research, I cannot grasp how, for example, 50,000 Sudanese Nubians – relocated in connection with Egypt's Aswan High Dam – perceived and coped with leaving their desert environment around and immediately south of Wadi Halfa for a resettlement area over 700km away. On relocation, their formerly isolated communities would be integrated into a single resettlement area with a previously unknown ethnic group. There they would find new diseases such as leishmaniasis and malaria and would be incorporated within a large-scale irrigation project, whereas in their former homes they had practised flood recession and small pump agriculture along the banks of the Nile. In their new environment, they would be subjected annually to several months of rainfall as opposed to the almost rainless climate of their former Saharan habitat.

In the case of the Gwembe Tonga, we have a better idea of the fears and reactions of people at the time of physical removal. That is especially the case with 6000 Lusitu resettlers. Based on their preferences, initially they had been allowed to move to a location on the tributaries which entered the Zambezi close to their homes. After they had begun clearing new fields and preparing new home sites, a decision was made by the project authorities to raise the height of the dam. Already hard-pressed to find sufficient land within the reservoir basin where the Gwembe Tonga preferred to remain, resettlement officials selected a relatively unpopulated area on both sides of the lower reaches of the Lusitu River, which joined the Zambezi below the dam site.

Unlike other areas selected for Kariba resettlement, the Lusitu area was occupied by a different ethnic group. Called the Goba, they spoke a different language and had distinctive cultural differences such as burying their dead in cemeteries identified by sacred groves rather than in individual graves near the house of the decreased. Furthermore, the number of cemeteries appeared excessive in comparison to a relatively small living population. While the logical explanation of this situation was past epidemics, such as influenza in 1928 or an epidemic of the Rhodesian variety of human sleeping sickness that periodically plagued the Zambezi Valley, the explanation preferred by the Gwembe Tonga was a particularly virulent form of witchcraft.

Fearing the Lusitu area, 6000 Gwembe Tonga refused to move. The danger of confrontation increased when the government sent in mobile police and villagers took up spears and fighting sticks to emphasize their resistance. Inexperienced, the mobile police fired when they felt threatened by what appears to have been a 'mock', symbolic charge on the part of the protesting villagers. Eight men were reported killed and many more were injured. Shocked and subdued, the 6000 resettlers were loaded onto lorries and trucked over 100km to the Lusitu.

The agony of that trip and its immediate aftermath is best told in Colson's *The Social Consequences of Resettlement*, which, after 30 years, is still in my opinion the best resettlement case study. During the evacuation, 'Vomiting women and children hung over the sides of the lorries. Drinking water and water for cleansing was gone long before they reached their destination. This was near nightfall. They emerged exhausted and sick to find themselves in what they regarded as a wilderness… They struggled to cook and eat. Then they lay listening to the trumpeting of the elephant… Next day they rose to the task of turning a strange land into a home' (Colson, 1971, p44). All this in spite of the efforts of a well-intentioned, though inexperienced, staff of government resettlement officials who wanted to do a good job and one of whom is reported to have had a nervous breakdown later in the resettlement process. Although less extreme, such staff 'burn-out' is a worldwide phenomenon.

The years immediately after removal

Multidimensional stress continues immediately after removal for a number of reasons, including the stress of adjusting to a new habitat, to the hosts as new neighbours and, more often than not, to an increased government presence. In all cases that I have observed, the living standards of the majority also drop following removal, thus adding to the stress load. Researchers at China's National Research Centre for Resettlement at Hohai University have reported the same phenomenon, noting falling production and living standards for the majority during what they refer to as the moving stage. Such declines are yet another reason why the only acceptable policy is to provide whatever development opportunities are necessary to help project-affected people become beneficiaries.

2

Theories of the Resettlement Process

INTRODUCTION

In the early 1960s David Brokensha, having used the Volta Dam Project at Akosombo for policy-oriented student training while teaching at the University of Ghana, stated in a *Human Organization* article the need for 'a sociology of resettlement' (Brokensha, 1963, p286). Since then the study of the resettlement process has become a field with many practitioners, as well as one with a substantial body of theory that focuses on two complementary theoretical frameworks or models.[1] Both deal with development-induced involuntary resettlement associated with dams as well as with other types of situation.

The first was my four-stage framework that theorized on how the majority of resettlers can be expected to behave during a successful resettlement process (Scudder, 1979, 1981a, 1981b, 1985, 1993a, 1997b; Scudder and Colson, 1982). Its application was restricted to development-induced involuntary community resettlement and to land settlement schemes involving volunteer households. Cernea's 'impoverishment risks and reconstruction model' followed in the 1990s (Cernea, 1991, 1995, 1996, 1997a, 1997b, 1999a; Cernea and McDowell, 2000). It dealt more broadly with the impoverishment risks that accompany involuntary resettlement, and with corrective reconstruction procedures.

This chapter has two purposes. The first is to combine the two approaches into a single theory. The second is to integrate into that theory the principal criticisms of both approaches by other resettlement scholars and practitioners. Criticisms include the underemphasis of several important factors, namely, the wider political economy and institutional context in which development-induced resettlement occurs (Wali, 1989; Ribeiro, 1994; Aronsson, 2002); the political dimensions of involuntary resettlement (Bilharz, 1998; Koenig, 2002); gender issues (Salem-Murdock, 1989; Koenig, 1995; Colson, 1999); and the cultural dimension, especially the symbolism dealing with space and time (Downing, 1996).

THE DYNAMICS OF THE RESETTLEMENT PROCESS
AND THE FOUR-STAGE FRAMEWORK

Introduction

I first developed the four-stage framework to deal exclusively with a *successful* process of involuntary resettlement in connection with dam construction, with success simply defined as development that is environmentally, economically, institutionally and culturally sustainable into the second generation. Representing an extreme example that throws human actions into relief, dam-induced resettlement provides the researcher with a quasi-laboratory setting in which 'before and after' studies can be completed and compared. In the early 1980s, I asked Elizabeth Colson to join me in applying the framework to other types of involuntary resettlement (Scudder and Colson, 1982). I also extended it to government-sponsored voluntary and spontaneous land settlement (Scudder, 1981a, 1981b, 1985; World Bank, 1985a). The theory that follows, however, is directed specifically at involuntary community resettlement associated with the construction of large dams.

Unlike Cernea's impoverishment risks and reconstruction model, the four-stage framework is behavioural. It focuses on those who must resettle and, specifically, on how a majority of resettlers can be expected to behave if sufficient opportunities are available for them to become project beneficiaries. It is also predictive. Drawing on case material, it explains why resettlers are the key resource for achieving a positive outcome. The statistical analysis of resettlement in the next chapter shows that government policies and the activities of project authorities have been the main factors constraining a successful resettlement process.

In the four-stage framework, the first stage deals with who is to be resettled and with the planning for their removal, rehabilitation and development. The second stage deals with the physical process of resettlement and the years immediately following removal. During this second phase, the behaviour of the majority tends to be risk averse and their living standards can be expected to drop. The third stage, in that small minority of cases where it occurs, confirms that a successful resettlement process is possible. It deals with the process of community and economic development, during which risk-taking occurs and the majority of resettlers are able to improve their living standards. Development continues or is maintained in the fourth stage when handing over and incorporation occurs. Two types of handing over occur: the resettlement project authority or authorities hand over institutional responsibility and assets to the resettlers, line government ministries and other agencies, and the first generation of resettlers hands over to the second generation. Incorporation involves the integration of the resettlement area or areas into the surrounding political economy in which ongoing success requires that the second generation be able to compete for their share of national resources. The entire process takes two generations.

The use of stages as a device to analyse the dynamics involved draws attention to the fact that projects involving involuntary resettlement have remarkably similar histories and that people and the complex systems in which they are embedded and interrelated (including government agencies) respond in predictable ways. Stages, however, are 'merely tools for coming to grips with a complicated and dynamic process. They amount to simplifying assumptions which attempt to break the settlement process into a series of critical time periods during each of which a range of basic issues need be addressed by settlers and settlement planners alike. Although the stages appear to have a certain universal validity, at least in broad outline, the details and the sequence vary with locally specific conditions' (Scudder, 1981b, p92).

Previous authors had found stages a useful device for analysing complex development projects 'as entities which change over time' (Chambers, 1969, p226). Because they also deal with the settlement of new lands, I have found Michael Nelson's and Robert Chambers' frameworks especially useful. Dealing with both spontaneous and government-sponsored land settlement in Latin America, Nelson (1973) used a three-stage framework in which a pioneer stage is followed in succession by consolidation and growth stages. Chambers also uses a three-stage framework based on African projects with special emphasis on the Mwea Irrigation Scheme in Kenya and Ghana's Volta Dam at Akosombo. His stage one deals with the pre-settlement period, stage two with project organization and the initial years of settlement/resettlement, and the third with devolution of authority and increasing specialization. Dealing with two dam-induced resettlement projects in West Africa, Butcher makes the important distinction between an initial resettlement stage followed by a development stage (1971, p6).

Like Chambers' and Nelson's frameworks, my four-stage framework deals with participants and project authorities. It is a general theory since it is based on the hypothesis that the majority of resettlers throughout the world respond in the same way to dam resettlement irrespective of differences in geography, culture and the organization of the project authority. Where it breaks new ground is by predicting how the majority of participants will respond to different phases in the resettlement process when well-planned opportunities are implemented. Because of its emphasis on the few long-term studies that have covered all four stages, it is most innovative in dealing with the last two.

The first stage

Stage 1 I have labelled the *Planning and Recruitment Stage*. Like Chambers' first stage, it deals with the lengthy pre-resettlement period. Because of the emphasis on success, special attention should be paid to the early involvement of affected people in the planning and decision-making process as discussed in the concluding chapter. On the basis of the evidence available, it is assumed that the concern of the majority increases as the time of their removal draws closer, although it is also assumed that increased involvement in the planning process will reduce, but not eliminate, the stress reflected by such concern.

Special attention must also be paid to development opportunities for enabling resettlers and hosts to contribute to the stream of project benefits as beneficiaries, rather than emphasizing compensation and income restoration as allowed in contemporary World Bank guidelines.

The second stage

Stage 2, *Adjustment and Coping*, begins with the initiation of physical removal, which can take a number of years if large numbers of resettlers are involved or if dam construction is delayed. For the majority, it can be expected to last at least a year after the completion of physical removal. In reviewing 32 cases of voluntary and involuntary resettlement in the late 1970s, I found only one where the length of Stage 2 was less than three years following removal (and that was two years) while 11 cases were between five and ten years and 15 cases were over ten years (Scudder, 1981b, p112). In over half of these cases, for many elderly people, Stage 2 would end only with their death.

Initially Colson and I labelled Stage 2 as a 'the transition stage' to draw attention to the transition from one habitat to another and to emphasize its temporary nature if the next stage is to arrive. On the other hand, the word 'transition' has the undesirable connotation of suggesting that people move from one steady state to another – from one equilibrium stance to another following a major perturbation. While equilibrium concepts are useful in explicating responses during Stage 2, 'they do not help us understand what is going on during the stage of ... development when people behave in terms of an open system' (Scudder and Colson, 1982, p276).

Stage 2 has two important identifying characteristics. One is that the living standards of the majority can be expected to drop following the completion of physical removal. The other is the tendency of the majority to behave conservatively – to be risk averse – for one or more years after arrival at their new sites. Living standards decline for a number of reasons. One, discussed in Chapter 1, is multidimensional stress. Another is the large number of adjustments that resettlers must make if they are to adapt to a new habitat; new neighbours; and, more often than not, to larger communities, new economic activities that planners consider more appropriate, and more government oversight. For many households, labour resources are inadequate or strained during the first few years, especially where everyone is expected to build new homes and clear new fields at the same time, as in the Kariba case.

Expenses may also rise following removal. Agrarian societies cultivating fertile riverine alluvia, for example, frequently are moved to less fertile lands that require such purchased inputs as chemical fertilizers if yields are to replicate pre-resettlement conditions. That is the case currently with the Lesotho Highlands Water Project with regard to resettlers from both the Katse and Mohale reservoir basins. Extra funds may also be required to purchase formerly available foods such as fish, game and gathered produce that are not available in more densely populated resettlement areas, as is the case with many Indian projects. There, as elsewhere, safely transporting livestock is fraught with difficulty. Owing to the non-availability of common property resources, on arrival a further problem is the lack of available grazing, with resettlers forced to sell livestock at reduced prices.

Stage 2 is also characterized as a period of coping with, and adjusting to, involuntary resettlement. In this adjustment period the majority tend to behave conservatively – to be risk averse. 'Risk-aversion appears to be a coping response to the stress and uncertainty associated with moving into a new habitat – where settler families need not only to come to grips with a new physical and biotic environment, but also with new neighbors, an increased government presence and frequently with a new host population... They favor continuity over change; and where change is necessary, they favor incremental change over transformation change' (Scudder, 1981a, p14). Colson and I 'suspect that this response is necessary in order to allow the majority to reconstitute their lives after a major insult to their physiological, psychological and socio-cultural well-being' (Scudder and Colson, 1982, p271 after Audy, 1971).

In clinging to the familiar, Stage 2 resettlers behave as if a socio-cultural system was a closed system. This is one of the more interesting hypotheses embedded in the four-stage framework. While long-term research in anthropology shows socio-cultural systems to be dynamic open-ended non-equilibrium systems (Foster et al, 1979; Kemper and Royce, 2002), during Stage 2 the majority in most cases behave as if their way of life was indeed constrained within a closed system.

Behind the 'clinging to the familiar' response is multidimensional stress; people attempt to cope by changing their behaviour and institutions as little as possible. While specific exceptions are many, the general approach is to try to recreate the security formerly provided by familiar structures, institutions and symbols. Examples include replicating former house types; transferring crops and productive techniques regardless of their relevance to the new habitat; and relocating in social units of resettlers' own choice, including extended kin groups, residential units within communities, and entire communities as well as networks of communities linked by marriage, ritual or other ties. Such a preference makes sense because it allows resettlers to adapt to new conditions with the support and assistance of familiar people. Indeed, the stress of resettlement, as in the Kariba case, may reunite brothers and other kin who, prior to removal, had split apart during the normal process of fission within kin groups as new families and lineages are formed, or because of previous conflicts.

Downing provides a number of examples from Mexico's Zimapan Dam resettlement of the extremes to which resettlers will go in trying to re-create previous cultural patterns. Three adjacent peasant communities were relocated from their riverine habitat to a newly constructed community on an adjacent, but arid, plateau. When permitted to name the main street, not only did they call it River Boulevard, but apparently they also tried to realign themselves along that street as had been the case along the river. Several months later they named the community Bella Vista del Rio, even though 'the river is nowhere to be seen' (Downing, 1996, p42). Another example from the same project of resettlers trying to reproduce a known past was a relocated Catholic community that increased what was formerly an annual visit of their patron saint to each household to weekly visits, with the saint 'moving from one relocated household to the next as the community struggled to reaffirm and re-establish its identity' (ibid, p39).

Where successfully transferred or reformed, social networks and religious practices tend to inhibit the type of social and cultural disorganization that can occur if policies place more emphasis on compensation than on opportunities for development and on tangible rather than intangible losses. Where cash compensation is given to the male head of household, for example, he may be tempted to use it for the purchase of consumer goods – a motorcycle as in the Pak Mun case in Thailand – rather than for the wider benefit of family members. Or he may use it to marry a younger wife at the risk of leaving his previous wife and children destitute. Where a 'land for land' compensation policy is followed without other development opportunities, kin groups can break apart when one family member – the oldest son, for example, in a family where the registered owner of the land has died – attempts to register compensatory land in his name alone. Stress among kin is also exacerbated when family members disagree as to where to relocate – a not uncommon problem in India where some family members may wish to migrate to urban areas and others to stay as close to their current rural home as possible.

The existence and duration of Stage 2 has important policy implications. In his analysis of agricultural land settlement, Goering wrote 'typically, evaluation of settlement projects three to five years after the start of implementation shows economic rates of return at least 50 per cent below those in project appraisal documents' (World Bank, 1978b, p16). I would suspect the same to be true with dam-induced involuntary resettlement. Given the 'closed system' approach of a majority of resettlers, it is unreasonable for policy-makers to expect rapid development during Stage 2. Another problem is the short duration of most donor-financed projects, which are rarely more than five years in length. Such projects may stop before Stages 3 and 4 occur, these being the crucial stages 'if living standards and productivity are to rise and if continuity and development are to continue' (Scudder 1981a, p13).

The third stage

Introduction

Stage 3, *Community Formation and Economic Development*, to me is the most interesting. At its commencement, people's behaviour changes from a risk-averse stance to a risk-taking stance that eventually characterizes the majority. At the same time wealth differentials increase, as does social stratification (Scudder and Colson, 1980). Because there are so few successful resettlement projects, and so few studies of them, further case studies and comparative analysis such as that in the next chapter are required to determine the extent to which such a transition can be generalized. Kariba's Gwembe Tonga case aside, most illustrating studies, such as those from Indonesia (both Sulewesi and Sumatra), Sri Lanka, Egypt, Kenya, the Sudan and Peru, involve irrigation projects rather than systems of rain-fed agriculture. And they include both voluntary settlers and involuntary resettlers.

The dramatic changes associated with Stage 3 are only possible under two sets of conditions. The first requires resettlers to change their behaviour radically. The second requires development opportunities (see Chapters 3 and 4) into which settler initiative can be channelled and appropriate infrastructure, such as feeder roads and service and marketing centres. Opportunities must be sustainable. Otherwise, constraints such as environmental degradation, political strife and inappropriate government policies can counter innovative behaviour and, at worst, cause the initial transition into Stage 3 to be followed by increasing impoverishment, as in the Gwembe Tonga case. Though not dam induced, involuntary community resettlement to Parigi in Sulawesi prior to World War II (Davis, 1976) provides an excellent example of the importance of infrastructure and access to markets. There, development really began 'to boom in the late 1970s in large part because of major government investments in road construction – both in connection with the improvement of the cross-island highway to the provincial capital of Palu and the construction of the west coast trans-Sulawesi highway' (Scudder, 1981b, p103).

Attitudinal changes among the majority of resettlers

Important questions relate to the circumstances under which the transition from risk-aversion to risk-taking occurs, how to identify and measure its commencement and trajectory, and how to facilitate its continuation. A prerequisite, I believe, is a situation where the resettlers must first come to feel 'at home' in their new physical and biotic environment and with the host population. Another is the regaining of household self-sufficiency in foodstuffs, which can be measured by calculating crop yields and household food consumption.

In cases that I have studied, a number of other indicators are suggestive that a shift toward risk-taking is underway. One is the realization on the part of the resettlers not just that they have survived, but that they have successfully been able to overcome the difficulties associated with removal. Like coming to feel 'at home', that realization is reflected in a range of symbolic behaviours such as decorating housing with traditional motifs, 'taming' the new habitat by naming or renaming physical features, plants and animals, and incorporating the resettlement area into dance and song, poetry and other narrative forms.

Community formation

Easier to document is the point at which family members begin to pay more attention to community formation activities than to their initial emphasis on reconstituting their own households. One of the earliest community-building activities is forming a burial society, followed by farmers' unions, water user associations, cooperatives, and rural and municipal councils.

Also indicative is a willingness to improve schools and clinics and to build housing for teachers and medical personnel on a self-help basis. Building and staffing religious structures is also a key indicator. Examples include Buddhist temples in Sri Lankan settlement projects such as the Accelerated Mahaweli Project; Hindu temples and churches in Indonesia's Parigi Project; Islamic sheiks' tombs at Kom Ombo in Egypt; and the renewal of ritualized community drumming in the Gwembe Tonga case. Participating in religious pilgrimages as well as travel to distant locations may also be involved. Re-emergence of old political leaders and the rise of new ones who are now able to advance resettler interests with project and government authorities, and with the host population, is another indicator.

Re-emergence of community religious activities may also foster what amounts to at least a temporary cultural renaissance whereby the resettlers emphasize their cultural 'ownership' of their new habitat. This occurred in Parigi with the elaboration of Hindu shrines at the household and community levels. It also occurred among Egyptian Nubians at the High Dam resettlement site at Kom Ombo. The same occurred in the Gwembe Tonga case at the beginning of Stage 3 in 1963. In addition to the reappearance of household hunting shrines, which had gone out of fashion before resettlement, the major indicator was a resumption of funeral drumming and ritual. Although I do not know what has happened at Parigi since the late 1970s, in the other two cases the 'renaissance' phenomena was temporary. Although ethnicity remains important, in the Nubian case 'loss of language, traditional customs and ceremonies, even the commercialization of dance and music' have occurred as the Nubians have become increasingly incorporated within the political economy of Egypt (Fernea et al, 1991, p198). In the Gwembe Tonga case, the people's distinctive culture has also suffered because of incorporation within a wider political economy and the social disorganization that has accompanied the economic downturn within Zambia since the mid-1970s.

Economic development

Appropriate development opportunities are essential not just for raising living standards but also for minimizing the dependency syndrome and 'complaints culture' that project authorities the world over tend to believe characterizes resettlers when, in effect, such a response is often a result of the non-availability of adequate development opportunities. On the other hand, some dependency and complaints are to be expected. After all, resettlers are being uprooted against their will and need assistance with compensation for assets lost and with development opportunities if living standards are to be raised.

When opportunities are available, it is interesting that resettlers around the world tend to follow the same development strategies. Once self-sufficiency is reached in the production of food staples, the trend is to diversify economic activities and investments. A gradual shift occurs into higher risk, higher value cash crops, while investments are made in livestock and children's education. Investment in children's education is an especially important indicator since it shows a willingness on the part of parents and other supporting relatives 'to forego returns from the labour of those children in agriculture in exchange for possible remittances and other support ten or more years later' (Scudder, 1981a, p14).

While still concentrating on their household plots and fields, family members in the more successful households next begin investing in a wider range of farming and non-farming activities. These may include renting out a room in an upgraded house to farm labourers or officials, or a wife opening a small house boutique or using an acquired sewing machine for manufacturing clothing for sale, while husbands practise other crafts. Plough animals and eventually a two- or four-wheel tractor and trailer may be acquired both for own use and rental. The next challenge is to open up a non-farming business in the nearest service centre or town, with the most successful resettlers eventually diversifying their economies into urban real estate and business, as I have observed in several African and Asian countries. Educated children and other dependents can also play an important role in the diversification of household production systems by running non-farming family enterprises or developing additional family-purchased farmlands, as happened in Kenya's Mwea project and Sri Lanka's Accelerated Mahaweli Project.

As living standards improve, resettlers worldwide also tend to improve their living arrangements and consumption in similar ways. Housing improvement is universal, as is adding more variety to the diet. Within upgraded houses similar furnishings are acquired: cooking utensils; improved lighting in the form of a Petromax lamp or electricity; table and chairs for family meals; a set consisting of a stuffed sofa and matching chairs; a glass fronted cabinet in which family valuables are displayed, including a tea or coffee set, children's toys and miscellaneous souvenirs; walls decorated with calendars, a wall clock and pictures of family members; a sewing machine; a radio/cassette player; and a TV – battery operated if no electricity is available.

Paradoxically, as John G. Kennedy originally pointed out to me (personal communication), the reduction of cultural inventory that contributes to multidimensional stress during Stage 2 may subsequently make innovative activities easier than if relocation had not occurred, simply because post-removal behaviour is less culturally constrained. This is especially the case where pre-project customs restricted land access and inheritance to a small elite, or where income-generating activities were disproportionately controlled through a class or caste structure. More often than not, resettlement within a new area allows land to be allocated to, or opened up by, a larger number of people. Resettlement also provides new opportunities to an initially small minority of innovators, some of whom may previously have been landless or impoverished, who are willing to take risks even at the beginning of Stage 2. Resettlement may also allow new and more dynamic political leaders to arise, as happened with the Allegany Seneca in the Kinzua Dam case in the US (Bilharz, 1998).

The fourth stage

Stage 4, *Handing Over and Incorporation*, involves the second generation of resettlers. It brings the resettlement process to a successful end as project areas and populations are integrated into the political economy of a region or nation. Three conditions must be met, the first of which may have occurred at an earlier date. This first condition is a handing over process whereby specialized project agencies hand over assets to settler institutions; to line ministries dealing with agriculture, education, public health and other routine government responsibilities; to the private sector; and to NGOs.

Handing over can be a difficult and complicated process. Hierarchical project organizations without a twilight clause may resist devolution of their authority or restrict it to certain assets. Where asset handover is attempted, it may proceed too rapidly, as can happen when ministries of public health have neither the personnel nor the budget to take over project medical facilities that had been established to cater to the dam-building labour force. The same applies to handing over roads. Organizational jealousies may also interfere to the extent that line ministries do not want to take over assets that they did not develop or were developed at their expense (as when project authorities lured away professional staff with high salaries). All these problems currently occur in connection with the Lesotho Highlands Development Authority.

The next two conditions relate directly to the second generation of resettlers. On the one hand, their living standards must continue to improve at least in line with improvements in neighbouring areas. On the other hand, community members must have the institutional and political strength to compete for their fair share of national resources.

While the community formation and economic development of Stage 3 had begun in the Gwembe Tonga case and institutional handing over had occurred in the mid-1960s, neither of Stage 4's further conditions occurred. In regard to living standard improvement, insufficient arable land was available for the second generation, and yields dropped because of degradation in much of the land already in use. Living standards began to drop in the mid-1970s for other reasons as well, including unfavourable rural–urban terms of trade and other adverse government policies that placed rural residents throughout Zambia at a competitive disadvantage. The war for Zimbabwe's independence also disproportionately impacted upon the Gwembe Tonga, who lived facing the international border.

This economic downturn was accompanied by detrimental socio-cultural changes such as increased domestic violence, intra-community crime and a very detrimental increase in witchcraft beliefs (Scudder, 1993a), as well as a broadening of those suspected as witches (Colson, 2000). Drought, HIV/AIDS and cholera worsened the situation still further in the 1990s. These are examples of the type of unexpected events, unrelated to the resettlement process, that can also have an effect on outcomes (Chapter 3).

Resettlement of Sudanese Nubians at Khashm el-Girba in connection with the Aswan High Dam is another example in which resettlers made the transition from Stage 2 to Stage 3 but then were unable to proceed through Stage 4. Research by Sørbø and others indicates that many Nubians had reached Stage 3 by the early 1970s when they began playing an important role in developing commercial activities in New Halfa township – 'both in regard to their own investment there and their stimulation of other investors ... through purchase of a wide range of production and consumption goods and services' (Scudder, 1981b, p101).

Community formation had also advanced when Nubian-only cooperatives were expanded into a broader federation that purchased wheat for its flour mill from both hosts and resettlers. Resettlers and hosts also worked together to form a Tenants' Union (Agouba, 1979). At the time of my 1979 visit, however, reduction in irrigation water and non-availability of functional project authority tractors were having an adverse effect on agricultural operations. With approximately 50 per cent of its tractors inoperable and with reduced efficiency for providing agricultural requisites, the project authority had become a major constraint to the resettlers and hosts proceeding to Stage 4. Not only was agriculture suffering but new business construction as well as old business expansion was being adversely affected with some businessmen moving their operations to the newly operational Rahad scheme (Scudder, op cit, p102).

Criticism of the four-stage framework

Criticism has tended to concentrate on two general themes. One centres on a concern that the framework operates at such a high level of generalization that it does not deal adequately with variation. Aside from making that point, critics note specific cases where resettler behaviour varies from that expected and predicted by the four-stage framework. The second theme queries the utility of stages. Both criticisms raise important points that warrant a reply.

De Wet succinctly sums up the first criticism with the comment that the four-stage model 'is formulated to explain the similarities, rather than the differences in people's reactions to involuntary relocation' (1993, p322). That, of course, is its purpose as a generalizing and simplifying theory and the source of its success if it explains events documented in a wide range of cases, as I believe it does. On the other hand, de Wet and other critics are correct to emphasize the wide range of behavioural variations associated with the resettlement process.

In Hansen and Oliver-Smith's 1982 volume on *Involuntary Migration and Resettlement* (in the final chapter of which Colson and I applied the four-stage framework to the editors' 13 case studies), Partridge, Brown and Nugent criticized my earlier comparative analysis of the resettlement process as being over-influenced by the Gwembe Tonga case (1982, pp260–262). With Kariba Dam resettlement, they pointed out, one was dealing with an isolated homogeneous population, whereas the population relocated in connection with the authors' Aleman Dam case in Mexico was heterogeneous and hierarchical, consisting of owners of cattle estates, mestizo family farms, single-crop plantations and Native American mixed farms.

Although the 25-year gap between Aleman Dam construction and the authors' study precluded a thorough testing of the four-stage model, it was clear that resettlement from the start opened up opportunities for a significant minority of entrepreneurial resettlers who, among the Native Americans, for example, formed novel alliances with new patrons who had power, including shopkeepers, government employees, resettlement officials and others. In the process a new 'group of elite families ... rise to dominant positions... As time passes the new leaders and their dependents govern access not only to local resources, but also to wider government, educational and commercial resources. Their offspring obtain relatively powerful positions in the world outside the community' (Partridge, Brown and Nugent, 1982, p261). So, during Stage 2 what was formerly a relatively closed, hierarchical system became for an unknown proportion of resettlers 'more open', while 'after transition the system again becomes closed and the hierarchical structure is preserved' (ibid).

Actually, in the Gwembe Tonga case a minority also was able to respond as risk-takers during the early years of Stage 2. In that case, they responded to the opportunities offered by the new Kariba reservoir fishery, from which initial profits allowed them to start (with ox traction) mixed farming of cash crops, open small businesses and educate their children, who were able to sustain their upward mobility during the years immediately following Zambian independence by filling the positions of departing British colonial civil servants (Scudder and Colson, 1980). To quote Bilharz, what is different between the Aleman and Kariba cases is not the simultaneous combination of 'cultural conservatism and innovation' (1998, p150), but rather who can respond and the way in which they respond to the available opportunities and the reduction of cultural inventory that characterize Stage 2. Presumably, the more opportunities that exist, the more people can respond innovatively.

Another example of variation relates to gender impacts and roles. Impacts on, and roles of, women can vary significantly from case to case without invalidating the general model. Although trauma can be generalized globally, in the Kinzua Dam case the status of women began to improve almost immediately after removal, between 1964 and 1966. Reasons were related to both resettlement and external factors. Summarizing data from Bilharz's PhD dissertation, Weist states 'that their position changed with the fight against the dam, and they were given the right to vote in 1964 and the right to hold office in 1966. In 1969 the first woman councillor was elected, and women continue to be politically and economically active' (Weist, 1994, p12).

As initially formulated in the late 1970s and early 1980s, the four-stage framework was too influenced by the Gwembe Tonga case. That dealt with only one ethnic group, whereas projects elsewhere, such as Mexico's Aleman Dam and India's Sardar Sarovar Project, can involve a range of societal types in which different behavioural responses can be expected. Furthermore, responses can be expected to vary according to the knowledge of resettlers and the resources available to them. Not only was Kariba the first mainstream dam on the Zambezi but it was also the first in Central Africa that involved community relocation. Largely illiterate as well as isolated within a rift valley, the Gwembe Tonga were the rural pioneers of development-induced involuntary resettlement. Not only did they have no knowledge of what to expect but there were no knowledgeable individuals or organizations apart from the government officials responsible for resettlement to provide them with assistance.[2] That kind of a situation no longer occurs because of the increasing anti-dam advocacy of local and international NGOs and the increasing emphasis on participation and transparency within existing guidelines.

Having national and other state-of-the-art plans, however, does not mean that they will be implemented, nor – as Partridge notes in his 1989 Colson Lecture – that project authorities will be supportive. Moreover, increased awareness, education and NGO and other assistance does not eliminate the stress of relocation. Bilharz's research is illuminating here. Although the Seneca received the assistance of prominent outsiders (including Arthur D. Morgan, a former TVA Commissioner) and fought a good fight through the court system, when they lost and resettlement followed, they did suffer stress. In particular, Bilharz provides important information on how Seneca children responded during Stage 2 and thereafter. Although families remained close and supportive during the resettlement process, 'that did not protect the children from great trauma. Seeing but not understanding what was happening increased their anxiety; parental attempts to protect them from stress served only to increase it' (Bilharz, 1998, p151). To summarize this section, although the complexity of human behaviour and conditions is such that exceptions should always be expected, I remain convinced that the majority must cope with, and come to terms with, the trauma and lowered living standards associated with Stage 2 before they can move on to Stage 3.

Moving on to the second criticism, Weist queries the emphasis on stages as a means for assessing the dynamics of the resettlement process. Stages, she notes, 'have a static quality' (Weist, 1994, p20) that does not do justice to the dynamic coping strategies involved. The point is a good one. Stages do tend to 'reify' the various processes that characterize them, implying that those processes cannot occur at other points in time. But of course they do. In the Allegany case, Bilharz and Weist see little difference between the first two stages since the Seneca began to actively fight the dam and to cope with the associated trauma from the time of the first rumours, which preceded construction by 30 years. In other cases, handing over and incorporation may occur before the economic development emphasized in Stage 3 gets underway or the two processes can occur simultaneously, hence fusing the two stages. Moreover, as in the Allegany case, emphasis on education may begin almost immediately following removal.

Goodland (2000) raises an analogous point when he suggests that improved resettlement planning and implementation will allow the large majority to become beneficiaries immediately following removal, hence eliminating Stage 2 behaviour. In his favour is the increasing knowledge that the majority of affected people will respond to opportunities; the increasing global emphasis on the importance of making them beneficiaries; and the increasing number of countries, including China, India, Nepal, Sri Lanka, Uganda and Vietnam, that have drafted (but in some cases not yet approved) national resettlement policies (Martin ter Woort, personal communication). Other factors are the increasing awareness of those threatened with future resettlement of the risks involved to their welfare and the increased capacity of local and international environmental, human rights and indigenous people NGOs to help them resist removal.

That said, it remains to be documented that improved resettlement planning and implementation can eliminate the drop in living standards, the multidimensional stress, and the initially conservative coping behaviour that characterize Stage 2, or that they can alter the involuntary nature of dam-induced resettlement so that a majority of resettlers welcome resettlement as a means for improving their livelihoods. Under conditions of extreme poverty, as in the case of Laos' NT2, the majority may be convinced that resettlement can improve their living standards, but they will still have to live for years with uncertainty as to whether that will be the case and with the risk that improvement will not occur. Throughout that period their lives can be expected to be stressful. As for their living standards, they did drop during Stage 1.

In responding to Weist, I can think of no way to emphasize core characteristics and key hypotheses associated with the resettlement process and resettler behaviour during that process other than by aggregating them into a series of stages. Notwithstanding a wide range of variation, in case after case Stage 2 is associated with multidimensional stress for the majority that is exacerbated by residential shifting, lower living standards, reduction in cultural inventory and conflict with host populations. In response, the majority of resettlers can be expected initially to cling to the familiar and to be risk averse. In contrast, the distinguishing features of Stage 3, if it occurs, include risk-taking, community formation and economic development.

CERNEA'S IMPOVERISHMENT RISKS AND RECONSTRUCTION MODEL

Introduction

The World Bank recruited Michael M. Cernea in the mid-1970s as their first full-time sociologist/anthropologist. To educate his colleagues as to the relevance of those disciplines to Bank activities, Cernea organized a series of seminars, at one of which I gave a 1976 paper on involuntary resettlement in connection with Bank-financed dam construction. As the first comparative analysis of the poverty-inducing impact of Bank projects on resettlers, that paper furthered Cernea's previous interest in the topic. His activities between then and the present have had a major impact on resettlement theory and on the way both international and national development institutions deal with the policy and planning implications of that theory.

There had been prior attempts to apply what was already known to the resettlement component of large dam projects. In Africa, the Ford Foundation-funded Nubian Project under the direction of Robert Fernea provided policy-relevant information in the mid-1960s to Egypt's Ministry of Social Affairs, which had responsibility for resettling approximately 50,000 Nubians in connection with the Aswan High Dam project. In Ghana, social scientists Amarteifio, Butcher and Chambers worked with resettlement issues within the Volta River Authority under economist E. A. K. Kalitsi, who subsequently became the Authority's Chief Executive.

Also in the mid-1960s, I completed a consultancy for FAO during which I worked with colleagues from the Nigerian Institute of Economic and Social Research to design a pre-construction socio-economic and natural resource management programme for Nigeria's Kainji Dam Project. Several pre-construction studies were subsequently completed. Anthropologist Jonathan Jenness did a one-year study of the riverine fishery and geographer Wolf Roder did the same for the existing system of small-scale irrigation and flood recession agriculture. Both were employed in FAO's comparative study of large dams and man-made reservoirs in Africa. After moving to FAO, in 1971 Butcher wrote the FAO's resettlement manual, which was largely based on experiences with the Volta Project and the Ivory Coast's Kossou Project, where I was also involved as a UNDP resettlement consultant between 1969 and 1973.

None of the above activities, including Butcher's manual, however, had an impact that extended beyond the projects and activities of which they were part. That distinguishes them from Cernea's activities. Over the years Cernea was the force behind the recruitment of additional social scientists, including Butcher and Scott Guggenheim, that in time became the largest group dealing with development-induced resettlement. With Butcher on board, Cernea wrote the first set of policy guidelines for development-induced resettlement. This was Operational Manual Statement 2.33 – Social Issues Associated with Involuntary Resettlement in Bank-Financed Projects (World Bank 1980). Revised by Cernea in 1986 (Operations Policy Note 10.08) and in 1990 (OD 4.30), these guidelines remained unique among multilateral and other donor organizations until OECD, under Cernea's influence, issued a similar set of guidelines in December 1991.

Between 1986 and the present, Cernea's influence also played a major role in the Bank's publication of a series of reports on development-induced resettlement dealing with urban redevelopment, industrial development and roads as well as dams. In addition to Cernea's own publications (1986, 1988, 1993, 1994, 1996, 1997a, 1997b, 1999a), these included *The Economics of Involuntary Resettlement: Questions and Challenges* (1999a), edited by Cernea, and *Risks and Reconstruction: Experiences of Resettlers and Refugees* (2000), edited by Cernea and McDowell.

Other volumes included Guggenheim's *Involuntary Resettlement: An Annotated Reference Bibliography for Development Research* (1994) and a series of single-country and more general case studies. Of particular importance were the *Resettlement and Development: The Bankwide Review of Projects Involving Involuntary Resettlement 1986–1993* (World Bank, 1994a), for which single-country and regional studies were prepared, and two sets of publications by the Bank's Operations Evaluation Department. These were *Early Experience with Involuntary Resettlement* (World Bank, 1993), consisting of an overview and four case histories, and *Recent Experiences with Involuntary Resettlement* (World Bank, 1998a) that included an overview and case studies from China, India, Indonesia, Thailand and Brazil.

Mining this World Bank data base, as well as studies by Chambers, Colson and myself, Fahim and others, Cernea formulated his impoverishment risks and reconstruction model during the 1990s (Cernea, 1990, 1996; Cernea and McDowell, 2000). This model advanced the state of the art in the sociology of resettlement in a number of ways. First, it approached systematically the impoverishment risks presented in case studies, dealing with the large majority of development-induced resettlement projects that are unsatisfactory by my definition, as well as with the experiences of refugee communities. Eight risks were identified: landlessness, joblessness, homelessness, marginalization (involving downward mobility), increased morbidity and mortality, food insecurity, loss of access to common property, and social disarticulation.

Second, Cernea's model incorporated in detail resettlement policies necessary to improve living standards. Third, and most original, the model emphasized the importance of extending risk analysis to affected communities. As stated in his introductory chapter to *The Economics of Involuntary Resettlement*, 'Conventional risk analysis selectively focuses only on the risks to capital investments, but not on the various kinds of "post-normal risks" (Rosa, 1998) that displacements impose upon affected people... Moreover, it is also common practice for governments to provide guarantees against various risks incurred by investors in infrastructure projects... Yet when the same private investments *create* risks to such primary stakeholders as the residents of the project area ... the state does not provide comparable protection against risks to these affected people... The current methodology of risk analysis at project level must be broadened to recognize risk distribution among all project actors and address equitably the direct risks to area people as well' (Cernea, ed, 1999, pp15–16). Incorporating Cernea's risk analysis for affected people, the final WCD report broadened the risk analysis concept to include the physical and biotic environment.

Testing the impoverishment risks and reconstruction model

In the late 1980s Barbara Harrell-Bond, as Director of Oxford University's Refugee Studies Centre, invited Elizabeth Colson to spend part of 1988 and 1989 at the Centre. Together the two initiated what has become an active programme in the Centre dealing with development-induced displacement and resettlement. In 1989 the Elizabeth Colson annual lecture was inaugurated with the World Bank's William Partridge lecturing on 'Involuntary Resettlement in Development Projects'. With Cernea playing an active role and with World Bank assistance, the Centre organized two conferences in the mid-1990s that effectively applied Cernea's framework to case material in various countries and settings, as did various authors writing at a later date.[3] Mahapatra, for example, used the risks and reconstruction model in his analysis of development-induced displacement in India (1999a). WCD also found the model useful in its assessment of the social performance of large dams (2000, Box 4.2) as did Robinson (2003) when writing the final report for the Brookings Institution–SAIS Project on Internal Displacement.

In the testing process various authors showed that eight risks should not be seen as a magic number. Mahapatra added educational risk (ibid, p15), which Robinson broadened to include other community services (2003, p13), while Downing considers violation of human rights to be a major risk. I would add loss of a society's resiliency, especially in cases where indigenous and tribal people lose access to natural resources (in particular arable land and common property resources) and to critical support components of their socio-cultural systems that are not replaced following incorporation within a wider political economy as a result of resettlement.

COMBINING AND BROADENING THE TWO ANALYTICAL FRAMEWORKS

Introduction

I believe that combining and broadening the two analytical frameworks can provide policy-makers with a powerful tool for planning and implementing a more successful process of development-induced involuntary community resettlement. Although looking at the resettlement process from very different angles, Cernea and I both believe that success is possible, but only if planners adequately involve affected people and provide significant development opportunities for resettlers and hosts alike. In Chapter 3, the two frameworks provide the mechanism for the first detailed statistical analysis of dam resettlement outcomes. In the paragraphs that follow, the substance of a unified and broadened theory is explained.

Combining the two frameworks

The two theories are complementary in that they offset each other's major weaknesses. The major weakness with the impoverishment risks and reconstruction model, and of the writing of scholars and practitioners who embrace it, is that it does not deal with the behaviour of resettlers as the key actors in the resettlement drama. This is especially the case with reconstruction, which obviously will not occur without the majority of resettlers emphasizing the community formation and economic development associated with Stage 3.

The major weakness of the four-stage model, on the other hand, is that it deals primarily with that minority of cases around the world in which a 'successful' outcome occurs. Of the 44 cases analysed in the next chapter, only 3 (7 per cent) involved living standard improvement and only another 5 (11 per cent) achieved an outcome that restored the living standards of the majority. In the other 36 cases, the resettlement outcome was to leave the majority worse off. Another weakness of the four-stage framework is that it does not deal in any detail with the 'backsliding' that occurs when an initial period of community formation and economic development associated with Stage 3 is not sustainable, as happened in the Gwembe Tonga and Sudanese Nubian cases. For such reasons, Mahapatra finds it of 'limited value in the Indian context' (1999b, p193) simply because there are so few, if any, cases there where dam-induced resettlement has raised, or even restored, the living standards of the majority.[4]

Cernea's impoverishment risks and reconstruction model complements the four-stage framework by providing an analytical framework for examining and explaining the much larger number of unsuccessful outcomes, while also providing a means for better understanding why an initially successful resettlement process was not sustainable. In the Kariba case, for example, five of Cernea's eight risks played a role in the 'backsliding' from Stage 3 that occurred in the mid-1970s. These risks were increasing landlessness, marginalization, increasing morbidity and mortality, food insecurity and social disarticulation. On the other hand, the four-stage framework complements Cernea's model by concentrating on the active behaviour of resettlers, which is so necessary if a successful outcome is to occur.

Broadening the two frameworks

Introduction
Combining the two frameworks should be further strengthened by addressing other issues that receive insufficient attention. One relates to unexpected events, which are analysed in the next chapter and which I found had a major impact on outcomes in nearly 60 per cent of 44 cases. Five other issues are dealt with in the paragraphs that follow. These are resettlement complexity; the wider political economy and institutional contexts in which resettlement occurs; the role of political leaders within populations undergoing displacement; gender issues; and such intangibles as human rights and concepts and symbols of cultural importance.

Complexity
Just as the planning, implementation and management of a large dam may be too complex a development option for dealing with water resource and energy development in a sustainable way, so too may the complexity of development-induced involuntary resettlement exceed the capacity of most project authorities to accomplish satisfactory outcomes. One particular aspect of complexity is an inconsistency between the goals of heads of state or other powerful politicians and central planners with those of low-income and often marginalized communities living in river basins that are to be dammed. The

former, as analysed by Scott, have a vision of the future involving mastery of nature that is 'unscientifically optimistic about the possibilities for the comprehensive planning of human settlement and production' (1998, p4), whereas, in reality, the lives of affected rural communities are interwoven with nature and especially with the annual regime of free-flowing rivers. Yet, for favourable outcomes to occur both categories of stakeholders must cooperate (Chapter 3).

As a result of such inconsistencies and other complexities, Colson doubts the possibility of a successful outcome writing, in exasperation, 'how many negative cases do you need to establish futility' in the margin of an early draft of this chapter. De Wet may be moving in the same direction after directing the Refugee Studies Centre's 1997–2001 project on Development-Induced Displacement and Resettlement. In a 2003 paper titled 'Does the Complexity Inherent in Involuntary Resettlement Put Successful Outcomes at Risk?', he argued that the type of inputs associated with Cernea's risks and reconstruction model, important though they are, are not sufficient. There are additional complexities that require 'us to find a way to build in open-endedness and flexibility into the more structured frameworks and procedures that are an inescapable part of policy formulation and its application, and to find ways of capitalizing and incorporating the creativity and entrepreneurial talents among resettlers'.

I agree. Resettlement may well involve too much complexity. In the first edition of *Putting People First*, Cernea wrote in an introduction to my chapter 'A Sociological Framework for the Analysis of New Land Settlements' that 'Agricultural development through new land settlement is socially the most complex of all development interventions, both to design and to implement' (Cernea, 1985, p119). Although he qualified that in the 1991 edition by calling agricultural land settlement 'one of the most difficult of all development interventions,' he added that '*involuntary* population resettlement has turned out to be a process even more complex and painful' (Cernea, 1991, p145). In 1993 I drafted a paper, eventually published in French (Scudder, 1995b), in which I concluded that 'Due to the complexity of resettlement, coupled with the paucity of successful cases a generation after people have been moved, I conclude that increasing pressure should be put on policy-makers and donors to minimize the numbers of people who must undergo removal'. Cernea would agree, minimizing numbers being the first option emphasized in the World Bank's resettlement guidelines.

On the other hand, Eriksen has shown that the higher proportion of successful outcomes associated with new land settlement projects colonized by volunteers rather than by involuntary resettlers is primarily caused by differences in project authority inputs. In the case of development-induced displacement, project authorities 'clearly treated the involuntary resettlement component as subordinate to construction processes and schedules ... and as an economic externality with poorly identified costs and no defined "benefits"' (Eriksen, 1999, p86). His conclusion is consistent with my earlier comparative research on land settlement projects involving voluntary and involuntary resettlement (Scudder, 1981b, 1985), while the statistical analysis in the next chapter supports Eriksen's views about the importance of inputs.

The two types of resettlement do differ in certain respects, of course. But those are neither consistently positive nor negative. In the involuntary case, for example, the shifting of entire communities makes social reconstruction an easier task than in a voluntary settlement scheme where an aggregate of separate households are mixed together in a new scheme. That provides an advantage, whereas the involuntary nature of the move is more likely to be a constraint.

To sum up, the complexity associated with development-induced involuntary resettlement is an important constraint to achieving a successful outcome. It should be considered a reason during options assessment for selecting an option that does not involve involuntary resettlement. But should involuntary resettlement be unavoidable, the case record shows that a successful outcome is possible provided the necessary inputs and opportunities are there. If they are, the majority of resettlers can be expected to respond to them in a fashion that will allow living standards to improve.

The wider political economy and institutional contexts

The wider political economy

Both Cernea and I know that the wider political economy has an important relationship to the resettlement process. Although I deal with external factors in Stage 4 in connection with the handing over process and incorporation of resettlers into a wider regional context, we do not emphasize enough the importance of the wider political economy or illustrate why and how that importance influences resettlement outcomes. A number of authors have shown the way, starting with Wali (1989) and including Ribeiro (1994). Wali's research is especially relevant to resettlement theory because it illustrates how resettlement outcomes are influenced by government policies at the national level and by immigrants responding to those policies. She examines Panama's first major dam (the Bayano Dam) in the wider context of Panama's development. In combination with the Pan-American Highway that crosses the middle of the Bayano reservoir, the dam project opened up a remote region of Panama settled mainly by two Native American groups.

The Bayano Dam was completed in 1976. The same year the government created the Bayano Development Corporation, which became the dominant economic and political force in the region. Although it absorbed those responsible for implementing the resettlement programme and was supposed to deal with the development of the reservoir basin where the larger of the two affected Native American peoples chose to resettle, it concentrated its activities on the downstream area below the dam. Within a year of its establishment, the Corporation was running short of compensation funds for resettlers and was unable to effectively implement promises made. By the time of Wali's return visit to the Bayano region, both Native American groups had become marginalized (Wali, 1989, p166) and had lost economic and social status to the colonists and other immigrants who had increased a population of about 5000 in 1980 to an estimated 20,000 eight years later. The resettlers' predicament was also adversely affected by the failure of the government to demarcate a new reservation for the larger of the two ethnic groups.

In his study of the binational (Argentina/Paraguay) Yacyretá Project, Ribeiro notes that specialists had identified a range of better non-dam options as well as better sites for a dam. Yacyretá went ahead because, in Ribeiro's analysis, of Argentina's desire to expand economically and politically into an 'outpost' area and in competition with Brazil over 'regional hegemony' involving the upper Parana River and Paraguay (Ribeiro, 1994, p73). Such political economy explanations have also been applied to the Aswan High Dam (Waterbury, 1979) and to Hydro-Quebec's James Bay Project and the Southern Okavango Integrated Water Development Project (Scudder, 1996, p74).

The institutional context

More than other writers on development-induced resettlement, Rew has emphasized that too little attention has been paid to organizational structures for managing resettlement as opposed to policies and guidelines that all too often are not followed (see also Rew et al, 2000). He has also pointed out that where the importance of management is emphasized, too little attention is paid to why a particular style of management was adequate or inadequate (Rew, 1996, p202). And while such issues as commitment, budgetary resources, legal frameworks and the nature of compensation are important, so too are such issues as legitimacy, staff direction in the field, and staff skills in dealing with conflict resolution and people's participation.

Based on his experience in Asia with different types of development-induced displacement, Rew concludes that managers, regardless of institutional structure, need to know what their responsibilities are in regard to project-affected people and what they can feasibly do to meet those responsibilities. Also necessary is the type of understanding of the lifestyles of local communities that I have found can only be acquired through adequate benchmark demographic, health and socio-economic surveys. A third conclusion relates to the need for a realistic understanding in policy and guidelines of the resettlement process, an understanding that must be related to what is occurring step by step at the field level.[5]

Management is crucial. Yet there is no best organizational structure that can be superimposed in the field in case after case within the same country, let alone between countries. Rather, management structures need to be related to national and local conditions. I found the same to be true when evaluating 34 World Bank-financed government-sponsored land settlement projects. In that study the two most critical issues were management and the nature of the farming system. No one type of management, however, was clearly superior throughout the project cycle. While centralized and well-funded parastatal organizations, for example, could be effective during the early stages of the settlement process, they were 'apt to resist handing over management responsibilities at a later stage' (World Bank, 1985a, p30). They also had problems dealing with other agencies, as was the case for the Mahaweli Authority of Sri Lanka (Chapter 5).

Resettler political leadership

How local leaders have responded to the threat of resettlement, and how their constituencies have responded to their leadership, has changed over time because of increasing knowledge and support by local and international NGOs. Because Cernea's framework does not deal sufficiently with resettler behaviour, the responses of local leaders to the resettlement process are not dealt with; in contrast, I initially placed too much emphasis on the negative impacts of removal on local leaders. Research by Bilharz and Weist provides an important corrective here by emphasizing how the threat of resettlement can also strengthen leadership institutions.

Referring to all three Native American populations involved in her North American case studies, Weist stated 'all had dynamic leaders who challenged the "development makers" and mobilized support from their members' (1994, p19). In the Seneca case, while older leaders were ill-equipped to take on the Federal Government, 'younger leaders who were better educated and more experienced in non-Indian ways were waiting in the wings to assume leadership. Their ascent to positions of power was hastened, not caused, by the dam fight' (Bilharz, 1998, pp53–54). Especially impressive is how Hydro-Quebec's James Bay Project became the means for integrating nine separate Cree Bands into a Grand Council which played the major role in stopping the Grande Baleine Project (Chapter 6) and subsequently negotiated a partnership agreement with Hydro-Quebec. In that case, university researchers and NGOs provided important assistance and can be expected to play an increasingly important role in the future in alerting river basin inhabitants to threats to their existence, in representing their interests in national and international councils, and in working with them to build up their institutional capacity to influence the water resource and energy development options assessment process and, should a dam be selected, the nature of the resettlement process.

Gender issues

Although Colson dealt with gender issues in detail in her 1971 *The Social Consequences of Resettlement*, their importance has been inadequately dealt with in published accounts of the four-stage model and the impoverishment risks and reconstruction model. Apart from a relatively small number of articles,[6] the same applies to the dams and the resettlement literature. Jobin's monumental *Dams and Disease* (1999), for example, pays scant attention to gender, except in regard to women's fertility. In trying to flesh out their submission on gender for WCD, Mehta and Srinivasan tried, without success, to obtain case material through e-mail consultation. These are not exceptional examples, with Colson (1999, p24) stating that multiple identities, including those associated with gender, 'tend to disappear' during development-induced resettlement.

The case material that is available indicates that women were and are particularly vulnerable and disadvantaged by involuntary resettlement. As a result, their general welfare as well as their status within the household suffers. They, and their children, are vulnerable to more physical abuse from husbands and other male relatives whose sense of self-worth has been undermined by displacement. As for women being psychologically, economically and socially disadvantaged, two major reasons are mentioned. One is that women are more tied to their homes and hence more stressed by physical removal. The other is that planners tend to ignore opportunities for restoring, let alone improving, their economic and decision-making roles. Looking to the future, women will continue to suffer until they are incorporated within the options assessment and decision-making processes to the extent that the necessary economic, social and political opportunities are also made available to them.

Parasuraman's chapter, 'The Consequences of Displacement for Women', illustrates how women are disadvantaged. Generalizing from case material from India, he concludes that no special provisions are made in what are called 'resettlement and rehabilitation policies' for women even though 'they are one of the more vulnerable groups for whom specific R&R provisions were lacking' (Parasuraman, 1999, p211). Women are vulnerable, he explains, because they are more dependent than men on common property resources, on kinship and other social ties, and on services and provisions that are essential for the welfare of their children and because they have less access to wage labour. Unless access to such resources are restored or replaced, impoverishment can be expected to occur not just to the women involved but also to their children.

There are exceptions, however, that emphasize the need for detailed pre-removal benchmark socio-economic surveys that are gender sensitive. Bilharz's initial hypothesis was that relocation in connection with the Kinzua Dam would have a more severe impact on women than on men. True, they did report 'slightly greater trauma' because they had to deal with 'the daily problems of removal'. On the other hand, they 'seemed more pleased with the improved housing, which definitely made household tasks easier'. But 'to a surprising extent the benefits that came to women were greater than those for men. This is most apparent in the expansion of political and economic roles for women' (Bilharz, 1998, pp130–131). In particular, this was caused by the increased size of the Seneca Nation of Indians' Government, which provided more jobs for women, while Community Action Programmes 'provided leadership and management experience'. Women also benefited more from the education programme, with continuing education providing college degrees for some. And the right to vote 'gave women their long-sought entry into the formal political structure' (ibid).

While Bilharz's research is a partial corrective to an overemphasis on Kariba data by those searching for impacts that can be generalized (Colson, 1999, p37),[7] far more attention needs to be paid to the differential impacts of involuntary resettlement not just on men and women, but on different categories of men and women, and on hosts as well as resettlers. This is because the reordering of gender relationships during the resettlement process 'emerges from previous assumptions about gender and the gendered experience of those involved' (ibid, p27).

Human rights and cultural intangibles

Emphasis on dam impacts on affected people as a human rights issue was detailed in Chapter 7 of the WCD Final Report on Enhancing Human Development: Rights, Risks and Negotiated Outcomes. Here, the 1945 UN Charter; 1947 UN Declaration of Human Rights; and subsequent covenants, including the 1986 Right to Development, were used as a global framework for achieving sustainable development and as a means for putting pressure on individual nations as signatories. An important contributing paper was Rajapopal's 'Human Rights and Development.' The more recent Brookings Institution–SAIS study on internal displacement extended a rights approach to all forms of development-induced displacement (Robinson, 2003).

Downing (1996) is correct in criticizing resettlement theory and practice as paying too much attention to economic rehabilitation to the neglect of the necessary cultural reconstruction. When crafting the four-stage model, for example, I emphasized economic development more than community formation as a corrective to the planning emphasis at that time, which paid close attention to housing but less to social services and very little to the economic opportunities necessary to restore and improve living standards. As for the World Bank's guidelines, they explicitly refuse to address non-material aspects of culture. Downing is also correct in noting that 'so-called "social costs" and "social impacts" are mentioned again and again without clearly explaining what is meant by "social" ' (1996, p34).

Impoverishment is indeed both social and cultural, with Downing arguing that 'involuntary displacement forces people to re-examine primary cultural questions which, under routine circumstances, need not be considered. Key among these is... Who are we? Where are we?' (ibid, pp33 and 36). These are questions that relate to a people's 'social geometry' and which relocation requires people to re-examine and where necessary, to reconstruct. This process not only involves uncertainty, which is stressful, but it takes time, which is yet another reason why I believe that the reduction in cultural inventory and overall decline in living standards associated with Stage 2 is a universal characteristic of development-induced involuntary community resettlement. Downing's emphasis on culture is also a reminder of the multidimensional nature of resettlement-induced stress.

SUMMARY

The evidence is overwhelming that the construction of large dams has impoverished the large majority of tens of millions of resettlers. That evidence applies to all the major dam-building countries, past and present, including Brazil, China, India, Turkey and the US, none of which have been able even to restore the incomes of the majority of those removed. Even in the small minority of cases where living standards have been restored, and the still smaller minority where they have been improved, the resettlement process has been stressful, with living standards dropping in the years immediately preceding, during and following physical removal.

Looking to the future, options assessment for water resource and energy development should be a transparent process in which all participants are aware of the social and environmental costs that are associated with most large dams. Since involuntary community resettlement should be avoided, such dams should be considered the least-desirable option and should be restricted to situations where essential needs cannot otherwise be met.

Where involuntary community resettlement is unavoidable, combining and broadening the four-stage model and the impoverishment risks and reconstruction model into a single theory can provide policy-makers with the means for improved resettlement planning and implementation. The two theories have complementary strengths. One focuses on the resettlers as the key resource if a successful outcome is to occur. It deals with how a majority of resettlers can be expected to respond during the different phases of a well-planned and well-implemented resettlement programme. The other theory identifies eight major impoverishment risks and specifies how to avoid them.

The combination of the two frameworks is further strengthened by incorporating a number of other issues. One relates to unexpected events. Five other issues that need to be incorporated are the complexity of resettlement; the wider political economy and institutional contexts in which resettlement occurs; the role of political leaders within populations undergoing displacement; gender issues; and such intangibles as human rights and concepts and symbols of cultural importance.

The range of risks that involuntary resettlement involves are such that successful outcomes cannot be guaranteed. For that reason alone, dam-induced involuntary resettlement should never be emphasized by planners as a benefit of dam construction. Because it is involuntary, it is not an opportunity for those involved. Water resource and energy development options that involve involuntary community resettlement should only be considered a last resort; where resettlement is unavoidable, major efforts must be made to minimize the numbers of people involved.

A Comparative Survey of Dam-induced Resettlement in 50 Cases, with the Statistical Assistance of John Gay[1]

INTRODUCTION

This chapter emphasizes two contrasting points. The first is to reinforce and quantify to the extent possible the WCD conclusions that the 40–80 million estimated global dam resettlers 'have rarely had their livelihoods restored' (WCD, 2000, p129), let alone improved. Improvement is the WCD's, ICOLD's, and my definition of a successful resettlement process. Furthermore, unacceptable resettlement continues today as shown by dams that have been completed during the past ten years. On the other hand, analysis of individual cases shows that there are indeed a range of available opportunities which have the potential for helping the majority of resettling households to become project beneficiaries. Such opportunities were sufficient in 3 of 44 cases analysed in this chapter to raise the living standards of the majority and to restore them in another 5 cases. Even cases with unsatisfactory outcomes included high potential opportunities that if combined with others could have improved outcomes. Examples were reservoir fishing and utilization of the drawdown area.

The evidence presented in this chapter and the next shows that those involved will respond to appropriate opportunities where available. It is the responsibility of governments and planners to make sure that such opportunities are available and that whatever programmes are necessary for extending them to resettlers are implemented. That will not be an easy task. In addition to lack of opportunities, major reasons why the record to date remains unsatisfactory and unacceptable include lack of planning and implementation capacity, lack of funds, and lack of political will on the part of governments and project authorities. Also important is lack of participation on the part of resettlers.

INTRODUCING THE 50 DAM SURVEY

Lack of information provided by project authorities and governments on dam-induced resettlement is the major reason why it has been so difficult to assess outcomes. That conclusion applies even to WCD and World Bank attempts to generalize about the nature of the resettlement process. While WCD initiated a cross-check survey of 150 dams to broaden its database, in only 68 (54 per cent) of the 123 replies received from project authorities was resettlement even mentioned, and in only 12 of those 68 cases (18 per cent) were valid resettlement data received.[2] As for World Bank surveys, they too were inadequate for purposes of analysis since they were restricted to a still smaller number of Bank-financed projects.

Initially I did not intend to undertake my own survey. Comments by two readers on early chapter drafts caused me to change my mind. My WCD colleague Jan Veltrop pointed out that while my individual case studies could document a failed resettlement process, my broader generalizations about resettlement outcomes were at best only 'informed opinions'. To correct that deficiency John Gay urged me to seek information on a large enough sample to allow statistical analysis. My search during 2002 turned up 50 cases for which there was sufficient data to code over 150 variables.

The survey was designed to achieve two purposes. One was to examine outcomes for the majority of those resettled. The other was to examine the utility of my four-stage framework and Cernea's impoverishment risks and reconstruction model for explaining why those outcomes occurred. As with WCD's survey, data inadequacies also illustrate the inattention that the large majority of project authorities have paid, and continue to pay, to resettlement issues.

Only households that were physically displaced by dam construction and reservoir formation were dealt with, since data were virtually non-existent for those displaced by such associated project works as roads, transmission lines and irrigation canals or those who lost their land and other natural resources to the reservoir and the dam site but not their homes.

Because of the small sample size, efforts at quantification were limited to use of frequencies, means, and correlational analysis. Significance was suggested only by a value of $P < 0.01$ or below, whereas values between $P < 0.05$ and $P < 0.01$ suggested a possibly significant relationship. The word 'suggest' is used intentionally because the small sample size increased the possibility of confounding factors influencing results when relationships between two variables appeared to be positive. For that reason, emphasis was placed on trends where a number of possibly related results pointed in the same direction. An example was where increased staff capacity, funding and political will within project authorities were all associated with improved outcomes.

DATA SOURCES AND BIASES

Data sources

Lack of data constrained the survey to 50 large dams. They are listed in Table 3.1 along with host country or countries, date of completion, numbers of resettlers, stage reached at the time of last data collection and outcome. Three sources of information were especially important. Publications and reports on the resettlement process by environmentalists, historians and social scientists covered the largest number of projects. They included 12 PhD dissertations. The second source was a series of reports in 1993, 1998 and 2001 by the World Bank's Operations Evaluation Department on the resettlement component of nine World Bank-financed projects. The third source was six WCD case studies of specific dams.

A much wider range of sources provided complementary data. These included the WCD database, other World Bank reports, NGO reports and the internet. In March 2002 I spent several days at the former Commission's Cape Town office going through what survey information was available for public disclosure. That included 34 of the 68 cases in which resettlement occurred but only 10 cases with useful data on resettlement outcomes. Although not covering the range of data that I needed, the most useful World Bank sources were *The Economics of Involuntary Resettlement* (Cernea, ed, 1999), the 1994 *Resettlement and Development*, and the various Operations Evaluation Department's case studies.

NGO reports and the internet were most useful in providing more recent information on specific projects. Especially valuable were NGO submissions to WCD consultations in Sri Lanka, Brazil, Egypt and Vietnam and the International Rivers Network's *World Rivers Review*. The usefulness of the internet for providing updated information surprised me. With only a few exceptions, a search for a specific dam accessed informative websites that were especially valuable in updating information on dams completed before 1980. Two topics were especially useful for providing information that was not otherwise available. One dealt with demand for, or provision of, reparations. The other dealt with the development of tourism around major reservoirs and the competition between resettlers and immigrants over opportunities associated with dam construction and reservoir formation.

Data biases and significance

Critics of the survey might point out that the 50 dam survey contained a disproportionate number of very large dams in comparison with ICOLD's 1998 report covering approximately half of the world's large dams. Since larger dams do tend to cause more resettlement, might size be related to outcome, and especially to a worse outcome? Among the 50 dams, however, we found no significant difference in outcome between dams causing the resettlement of over 25,000 people and those causing the relocation of much

Table 3.1 *The 50 dams*

Name of dam	Country/ countries	Date of completion	Number of reservoir resettlers	Stage (date) when last data collected	Outcome (2)
Kariba	Zambia(1)	1958	34,000	Stage 4 (2002)	Four
Aswan	Egypt (1)	1967	50,000	Stage 4 (1999)	One
Kainji	Nigeria	1968	44,000	Stage 4 (1991)	Two
Narayanpur	India	1982	30,600	Stage 4 (1997)	Four
Shuikou	China	1993	67,000	Stage 3 (1997)	Two
Yantan	China	1992	43,176	Stage 3 (1997)	Two
Kinzua	US	1964	550	Stage 4 (1997)	Three
Katse	Lesotho	1995	1470	Stage 2 (2002)	Four
La Grande	Canada	1995	One village	N/A	N/A
Grand Coulee	US	1939	2000	Stage 4 (1999)	Three
Nam Theun 2	Laos	Planned only	6000	N/A	N/A
Pak Mun	Thailand	1994	1205	Stage 2 (2002)	Four
Zimapan	Mexico	1993	2452	Stage 2 (1997)	Four
Nangbeto	Togo	1987	10,600	Stage 2 (1997)	Four
Itaparica	Brazil	1988	26,000	Stage 2 (1997)	Four
Garrison	US	1953	1625	Stage 4 (2001)	Three
Fort Randall	US	1952	95	Stage 4 (2002)	Four
Oahe	US	1962	2100	Stage 4 (1994)	Three
Kedung Ombo	Indonesia	1988	24,000	Stage 2 (1997)	Four
Khao Laem	Thailand	1985	11,694	Stage 2 (1999)	Four
Kpong	Ghana	1982	5697	Stage 2 (1992)	Four
Pantabangan	Philippines	1973	13,000	Stage 2 (1988)	Four
Bayano	Panama	1976	4123	Stage 2 (1994)	Four
Tucurui	Brazil	1984	23,924	Stage 2 (1999)	Four
Manantali	Mali	1988	9535	Stage 2 (1992)	Four
Mohale	Lesotho	2002	2000 est.	N/A	N/A
Pong	India	1974	150,000	Stage 2 (1994)	Four
Tarbela	Pakistan	1976	96,000	Stage 2 (1999)	Four
Morazan	Honduras	1985	3618	Stage 2 (1995)	Four
Hirakud	India	1958	>110,000	Stage 2 (1988)	Four
Ukai	India	1972	52,000	Stage 2 (1882)	Four
Arenal	Costa Rica	1980	2500	Stage 3 (1983)	One
Ramial	India	1988	5000	Stage 3 (1995)	Four
Yacyretá	Argentina/ Paraguay	Ongoing construction	>68,000	N/A	N/A
Nam Ngum	Laos	1972	3500	Stage 4 (2001)	Four
Cahora Bassa	Mozambique	1975	>42,000	Stage 4 (2002)	Four
Aleman	Mexico	1952	19,000	Stage 4 (1999)	Four
Ceyhan	Turkey	1984	5000	Stage 2 (2000)	Four
Kossou	Ivory Coast	1972	75,000	Stage 4 (1995)	Two
Chixoy	Guatemala	1985	1500	Stage 4 (2002)	Four
Pimburetewa	Sri Lanka	1971	120	Stage 4 (2001)	One
Victoria	Sri Lanka	1984	29,500	Stage 4 (2001)	Two
Alta	Norway	1987	None	N/A	N/A

Table 3.1 *continued*

Name of dam	Country/ countries	Date of completion	Number of reservoir resettlers	Stage (date) when last data collected	Outcome (2)
Sardar Sarovar	India	Ongoing construction	>200,000	N/A	N/A
Kiambere	Kenya	1988	7500	Stage 2 (1995)	Four
Saguling	Indonesia	1986	13,737	Stage 2 (1999)	Four
Cirata	Indonesia	1988	27,978	Stage 2 (1996)	Four
Norris	US	1936	14,249	Stage 4 (2001)	Three
Cerro de Oro	Mexico	1989	26,000	Stage 2 (1999)	Four
Akosombo	Ghana	1964	78,000	Stage 4 (2002)	Four

Notes:
1 Although Kariba involved both Zambia and Zimbabwe, only Zambian resettlement was analysed. In the Aswan High Dam case, analysis was restricted to Egyptian Nubians.
2 One = Improved living standards for the majority; Two = Restored living standards for the majority; Three = Restored or improved living standards for the majority but not project related; and Four = Living Standards for the majority worsened.
N/A = Not applicable or relevant.

smaller numbers. Indeed, perhaps the disproportionate number of very large dams such as the Aswan High Dam, Volta and Kainji in the 50 dam sample would be more likely to attract international attention, including funding and supervision from multilateral and bilateral donors, which could lead to improved outcomes. In that case the 50 dam survey would contain a larger proportion of favourable outcomes. We found, however, no significant difference in outcomes between dams supported, for example, by the World Bank and those not so supported.

DAM LOCATION AND DATE OF COMPLETION

Of the 50 dams, 19 were in Asia, 13 in Africa and the Middle East, 10 in Central and South America, 7 in North America and 1 in Europe. Coincidentally, this distribution roughly reflects the regions in which most future dams will be built. For the purpose of comparing outcomes over time, dates of completion were combined into three categories – before 1980, between 1980 and 1990, and since 1991. The earliest category pre-dates the World Bank's pioneering in 1980 the first global guidelines for development-induced resettlement. It includes 22 dams (44 per cent). A total of 19 dams (38 per cent) were completed during the 1980–1990 period, while 9 dams (18 per cent) were either completed after 1990 (five cases) or are yet to be completed (the remaining four cases).

CHARACTERISTICS OF RESETTLING COMMUNITIES

The total number of resettlers from the 50 projects is estimated at nearly 1.5 million, the majority of whom in 26 cases (54 per cent) are categorized by the various researchers as indigenous or tribal people, or as belonging to other ethnic minorities.[3] The situation varies from country to country, however. The disproportionate number of minorities applies to case studies in most countries, including Canada, India, Mexico and the US, but it does not apply to China. Nor would it apply to Korea and Japan if case studies from those relatively homogeneous countries had been included. Data analysis does not indicate that outcomes worsen as the percentage of minority people increases or that their homelands are intentionally sought for siting dams. Rather their predominance in the sample is due more to the location of acceptable dam sites in rugged terrain that has been colonized by minorities or into which they have been pushed over the years.

Although towns may be involved in each of the various geographical regions, as was the case for the Aswan High Dam (Egypt–Sudan), Kainji (Nigeria), Victoria (Sri Lanka) and Yacyretá (Argentina–Paraguay), the large majority of resettlers were poor rural farmers. The primary or secondary economic activities of the majority in 39 cases (78 per cent) involved agricultural production for both home consumption and external markets or agricultural production combined with migratory wage labour. These activities were only weakly linked to the national economy at the time of resettlement,

Even weak linkages are important since they show that the large majority had already been incorporated within a wider political economy, an incorporation that would be accelerated by the improved access and arrival of immigrants associated with dam construction and operation. Moreover, even in the 11 cases where both primary and secondary activities were oriented toward household consumption, communities were not shut off from the outside world due, for example, to the penetration of a great world religion in all but three of these cases. The socio-cultural systems of the large majority of resettlers were potentially dynamic, open-ended systems characterized by both continuity and change.

RESETTLEMENT OUTCOMES

Living standard improvement involved only 3 (7 per cent) of 44 cases.[4] Restoration, allowed by the World Bank's current policy, characterized another 5 cases (11 per cent).[5] As dealt with in detail in Chapter 8, I do not consider restoration to be a legitimate goal, because what evidence is available indicates that a restoration policy tends to leave the large majority worse off than before resettlement. I include restoration here as a 'positive' outcome, however, so as to allow a more detailed analysis of differing resettlement experiences.

In the remaining 36 cases (82 per cent), the impact of the project was to worsen the living standards of the majority. Furthermore, in several of the 8 cases where living standards have either improved or been restored,[6] questions remain as to whether living standards at the time of last data collection were as sustainable in the new communities as in pre-resettlement ones. Problems for the future relate to inadequate availability of arable land, resettlement on less fertile soils and greater dependence than had previously been the case on government policies or – as in the case of resettlement within an irrigation project with unreliable water delivery or drainage – on external agencies.

Special attention was paid to whether resettlement outcomes had improved during the three time periods between 1932 and the present. Although the results seem to suggest that outcomes during the 1980–1990 and 1991–2005 periods were actually worse than those before 1980, no significant evidence of changes in implementation outcomes over time was found. That conclusion might appear at odds with recent conclusions in World Bank studies.[7] In fact it is not. What the Bank is saying is that its requirement of a Resettlement Action Plan at the time of project appraisal, and Bank supervision of the implementation of that plan, has resulted in resettlers becoming less poor than they would otherwise have been. The Bank's evidence suggests that this is true, because, more often than not, housing and social services have improved. So have income levels and general living standards but not to the extent of either restoring or improving pre-project income levels and living standards, which is the Bank's policy goal.[8]

WHY FAILURE? WHY SUCCESS?

Introduction

The first section involves analysis of a range of variables on which quantitative data is available, such as the capacity of project authorities and resettler participation[9] in planning and implementation. The qualitative section that follows is based on an analysis of the eight most successful cases, as well as two other cases that illustrate important issues. Setting the stage for the next chapter, the qualitative section emphasizes the types of opportunities that can play a role in enabling a majority of resettlers to achieve relatively successful outcomes.

Quantitative analysis

Introduction
Analysis focuses first on the nature of the project authority. That is followed by analysis of project-affected people including resettlers, hosts and immigrants. The last two sections deal with unexpected events and impoverishment risks.

Project authorities
Institutional responsibility for resettlement
Four situations were analysed that dealt with institutional responsibility for planning and implementing resettlement. They were 'no specific unit', 'the

project authority working alone', 'the project authority cooperating with other institutions', and 'other government institutions'. Cross-tabulation results were significant ($P < 0.001$), with only project authorities working alone being associated with more positive than negative outcomes. Although the number of cases (three negative and five positive) is small, making a single agency responsible for all aspects of project planning, financing and implementation certainly simplifies what would otherwise be complicated and potentially non-cooperative inter-institutional relationships (see Chapter 8). Furthermore, where other agencies are given unasked-for resettlement responsibilities, case studies indicate inadequate commitment, funding and staffing capacity are to be expected.

Capacity

Capacity was defined in terms of staff expertise and numbers, with funding dealt with separately. No attempt was made to generalize a specific definition of expertise or ratio of staff numbers to numbers of resettlers because conditions vary from case to case. Rather, coding was based largely on comments made by case study authors. Examples are drawn from several World Bank-financed projects for purposes of illustration where the Bank made a major attempt to build project authority capacity to a level sufficient to implement Bank guidelines. Nonetheless, in large projects such as India's Sardar Sarovar and Argentina–Paraguay's Yacyretá, resettlement 'is adversely affected by failures to assign key staff', with Bank supervision in each case finding 'at one point or another ... staffing to be half or less than agreed levels' (World Bank 1994a, p6/11).

In Mexico's Bank-financed Zimapan Dam, the project authority (CFE, the Federal Electricity Commission) and the Bank 'tried to make Zimapan a model project for resettlement... The CFE met the new demands for the Zimapan project by creating a group of 84 professionals... The majority of them came directly from university and lacked work experience... It seems obvious that this group of young professionals had not been sufficiently prepared for the field. During informal talks, they claimed that they had not been trained in participatory methods, poverty analysis nor social situation analysis' (Aronsson, 2002, pp114–116). Such lack of expertise has occurred in case after case, while lack of staff numbers can be related to such other factors as initial undercounting of resettlers and inadequate finance.

A major lack of capacity was coded in 27 (66 per cent) of 41 cases where data were available and reservoir resettlement had been completed (Table 3.2). The outcome of the resettlement process at the time of last available data was adverse in every one of those cases (100 per cent). A minor lack of capacity was coded in ten cases (24 per cent), in seven of which a positive outcome occurred (70 per cent). Capacity was coded as adequate in four cases (10 per cent), in three of which (75 per cent) outcomes were positive. One of these positive outcomes was Costa Rica's Arenal Dam, where living standards of the majority had improved at the time of last data collection, and another was Nigeria's Kainji, where living standards have been restored (Roder, 1994;

Table 3.2 *Adequacy of planning capacity – Cross-tabulation P < 0.000*

Nature of Capacity	Adverse outcome	Positive outcome	Total
Major lack of capacity	27	0	27
	(100%)	(0%)	(100%)
Minor lack of capacity	3	7	10
	(30%)	(70%)	(100%)
Capacity adequate	1	3	4
	(25%)	(75%)	(100%)
Total	31	10	41
	(75.6%)	(24.4%)	(100%)

Ayeni et al, 1994). In the third case, the Kinzua Dam in the US, planning had not been a project responsibility and living standards had improved because of development opportunities that were not project related. Ghana's Kpong Dam was the fourth case and did not have a positive outcome. Although the government had learned valuable lessons while implementing a failed resettlement process at Akosombo, the outcome was adverse because funds and opportunities were insufficient to implement Kpong's much-improved plans. Table 3.3 deals with capacity in more detail for the 36 cases where information was coded on staff numbers and expertise.

Adequacy of funding
The authors of the World Bank's *Resettlement and Development* consider 'Timely availability of adequate funds is a severe constraint in a large number of projects; it may be the single most powerful explanatory operational

Table 3.3 *Numbers and expertise of staff – Cross-tabulation P < 0.000*

Staff numbers and expertise	Adverse outcome	Positive outcome	Total
Numbers and expertise inadequate	23	1	24
	(95.8%)	(4.2%)	(100.0%)
Numbers adequate but expertise lacking	3	3	6
	(50.0%)	(50.0%)	(100.0%)
Expertise adequate but numbers inadequate	1	0	1
	(100.0%)	(0.0%)	(100.0%)
Numbers and expertise adequate	1	4	5
	(20.0%)	(80.0%)	(100.0%)
Total	28	8	36
	(77.8%)	(22.2%)	(100.0%)

variable behind the failure to implement resettlement operations well' (World Bank 1994a, p6/11). Moreover, resettlement cost overruns in the Bank's active projects in the mid-1990s 'have generally exceeded overall project cost increases considerably' (ibid, p5/19). As with staffing, funding must be based on a careful analysis of the resettlement situation, which in turn requires detailed pre-project demographic, epidemiological and socio-economic surveys. While one 'rule of thumb' postulates that environmental and social costs should average approximately 10 per cent of total project costs, obviously that proportion will vary according to the number of resettlers, land availability, restoration opportunities and other factors. What is clear, however, is that properly planned and implemented resettlement is expensive. Estimated costs for Laos' Nam Theun 2 Project in 2002, for example, were US$21,075 per household and US$3819 per capita (NTEC Resettlement Action Plan, 2002, p9-1). If large numbers are involved, as with China's Three Gorges Project, properly implemented resettlement can become the largest single project cost.

In the 50 dam survey, funding was inadequate throughout the resettlement process in 25 (58 per cent) of the 43 cases coded (cross-tabulation $P < 0.001$). A positive outcome was achieved in only one of those 25 cases. That was in connection with the Ivory Coast's Kossou Dam where inadequate funding and a minor lack of capacity were offset by strong political backing for the resettlement process, a major attempt to implement opportunities for raising living standards, and integration of resettlement into an attempt at regional development. In two additional cases (5 per cent), in both of which outcomes were adverse, funding was adequate only for physical removal. In a further nine cases (21 per cent), initially inadequate funding was increased for resettlement and rehabilitation purposes. In five of those cases a positive outcome was achieved. In the other seven cases (16 per cent), four of which had adequate outcomes, funds were sufficient for implementing the resettlement process.

In addition to adequacy of funding, there is a possible correlation ($P < 0.04$) between the ratio of funds for resettlement purposes to total project costs, with a trend toward more successful outcomes where resettlement funds rise above 10 per cent. Looking to the future, the origin of funds is likely to become increasingly relevant where governments must rely on international funding. As NGOs, in particular, step up their monitoring of funds provided through international agencies, export–import banks and other national parastatals, and private banks, such agencies can be expected to pay more attention to 'best practice' guidelines[10] and their implementation.

Interestingly enough, in eight of the nine cases where funds did not involve major external donors, there was a significant association of an unsuccessful outcome with lack of political will ($P < 0.008$). Six of these eight cases involved the US, with the other two being Mexico's Aleman and Cerro de Oro Dams. The one case in which political will was present involved Canada's La Grande, for which resettlement involved only one downstream community.

Political will
I have defined political will as a commitment on the part of project authorities
and governments to implement a resettlement action plan that is intended to
restore or improve resettler living standards. Unfortunately, such commitment
has yet to characterize a majority of projects. Among a small number of
recurrent implementation problems that the World Bank emphasized in its
1994 *Bankwide Review* was '**Lack of government commitment to resettlement**'
(World Bank, 1994a, p6/11; bold print in the Bank text). I have had similar
experiences with Bank-financed projects. Although an extreme view, in one
case the chief engineer, who had also assumed responsibility for resettlement,
had become increasingly perplexed as to why I and the Bank were so concerned
about resettler welfare. What resettlers needed in his opinion was
'sterilization'. Comments by authors researching projects that have not
involved the World Bank have also emphasized lack of political will as an
implementation problem.

Political will was inadequate in 22 (54 per cent) of 41 cases coded (cross-
tabulation $P < 0.001$). Although the presence of political will may be a
necessary condition,[11] political will alone is insufficient. Although political
will was present at Kariba (Northern Rhodesian side only), along with
adequate finance, the resettlement process failed there due primarily to lack of
opportunities and unexpected events. A case can also be made that political
will was present on the part of the project authority at Thailand's Pak Mun
Dam. The resettlement process failed there, however, because of inadequate
feasibility studies, inadequate planning and too much reliance on cash
compensation as the major component in the resettlement action plan that was
implemented.[12] Political will was also present in connection with Mali's
Manantali Dam, but the resettlement process failed there because planners, on
the one hand, provided insufficient land for the majority of resettlers to
continue their existing system of shifting cultivation, and, on the other hand,
did not provide the irrigation necessary to intensify that system.

Opportunities
The definition of opportunities includes those that arise as a result of a specific
dam project. They also include project-funded training, credit and extension
for employment during the construction and operations phases as well as for
on- and off-farm employment outside of the project area. The range of possible
opportunities is dealt with in detail in the next chapter as well as later in this
chapter. Opportunities include incorporating resettling communities as project
'owners' and rain-fed and irrigation-based agriculture as well as farming and
non-farming multiplier effects associated with a well-planned and implemented
agricultural component. Also included are utilization of the reservoir
drawdown area, reservoir fisheries, aquaculture, tourism, catchment
management and establishment of natural reserves.

Opportunities also include a wide range of small-scale commercial
opportunities such as small general stores; recreation facilities such as tea,
coffee and liquor establishments; and carpentry, masonry and other services.

Although largely temporary, project-related employment can provide savings for funding other development opportunities, as has been the case with Sri Lanka's Mahaweli Project and is reported for Nepal's Kali Gandaki project. Employment outside a resettlement area is also possible and important but is more difficult to achieve. While project-implemented education, training, credit and extension can give resettlers a comparative advantage, job creation requires a favourable regional and national development environment as well as commitment by government, the private sector and other agencies to create new rural and urban industries.

Implemented opportunities were coded as 'inadequate', 'adequate' or 'eventually adequate but not project related' in relationship to outcome (cross-tabulation $P < 0.003$). Of 42 cases coded, implemented opportunities were inadequate in 37 cases (88 per cent). In two other cases (both in the US), eventual opportunities were not project related (5 per cent), so that adequate project-related opportunities were only implemented in three cases (7 per cent).[13] Furthermore, in none of these three cases was the full range of available opportunities utilized, adding support to my overall conclusion that the potential is there for implementing a favourable resettlement outcome in more cases than the record indicates.

Project-affected people
Numbers of resettlers
All guidelines dealing with development-induced involuntary resettlement, starting with the World Bank's 1980 guidelines, emphasize the importance of avoiding or minimizing resettlement to the extent possible. Options dealing with dams include changing the site, reducing dam height and building embankments to restrict reservoirs from flooding certain areas. Such options influenced design in only five (10 per cent) of the 50 cases. In the Pak Mun case the site was changed and a major reduction was made in height. Such a height reduction actually eliminated the need for resettlement in the case of Norway's Alta Dam, although the reservoir had an adverse effect on the economy of the indigenous population through reduction of grazing for their herds of reindeer. The height of the Philippines' Pantabangan Dam was reduced 3.5 metres to avoid flooding a town. In the remaining two cases, Nigeria's Kainji and China's Shuikou, reservoir towns were protected by dykes.

During options assessment for hydro-projects, the World Bank's environmental adviser also emphasized several other criteria for avoiding resettlement and for selecting 'good' hydro. They included the absence of vulnerable ethnic minorities and a high ratio of power to area flooded and numbers of resettlers (Goodland, 1996). Although I am not aware of these criteria influencing choices among the 50 dams surveyed, increasingly NGOs are using them, as well as other environmental and social criteria, in their critique of dams which are 'on the drawing board'. As with the Final Report of the World Commission on Dams, their advocacy has in turn influenced the donor options assessment process, as have the concerns of Goodland and others within donor agencies.[14]

One example of the lack of attention paid to resettlement by project authorities is the frequency with which the number of resettlers is underestimated and the magnitude of that underestimate. In the 50 dam survey, estimates of numbers of resettlers at different time periods such as project identification, project approval, implementation of physical removal and following removal were available for 20 cases. In nine of these 20 cases, data were available on numbers of resettlers at the time of project identification as well as during implementation (one case) or after the completion of physical removal (eight cases). The initial estimate in these nine cases (73,638 resettlers) was only 52 per cent of the later number (140,541). In 12 cases (one of which was among the previous nine) the number of resettlers estimated at the time of project approval (271,604) was only 55 per cent of the total counted (495,590) during implementation (two cases) or after the end of removal (ten cases). In only two of the 20 cases was the final total less than the earlier estimate, while the same was true in three other cases in the 50 dam survey that involved relatively small numbers of resettlers (120 to 5000 resettlers).

Major underestimates were also reported in the Final Report of the World Commission on Dams and in the World Bank's review of a wider range of development projects involving involuntary resettlement. The magnitude of such underestimates is one reason why the financing and staffing of resettlement are inadequate.

Resettler participation in project planning

We created an index of resettler participation by adding together the scores for their level of participation in site selection, in choosing the size of relocating units, in selecting social services and in choosing options for economic development. Each of these four variables is on an ascending scale from no participation to full participation. Thus the resulting index of participation ranges from the lowest value that means no participation in any aspect to the highest value which means full participation in all four aspects. We then calculated the mean value of the participation index when outcomes were adverse and when they were positive. The means were significantly different (Table 3.4), with a score of 7.0 for the adverse cases and 11.0 for the positive ones. This suggests that resettler participation had a significant influence on the outcome of the resettlement process.

Table 3.4 *Resettler participation in relationship to outcome P < 0.005)*

Outcome	Mean	N	SD
Adverse	7.0	23	3.4
Positive	11.0	9	3.1
Total	8.6	32	3.7

Note: SD, standard deviation

Resettler ability to compete with host populations and immigrants

One unexpected result of the 50 dam survey was that resettlers found competition with immigrants to be an even more frequent problem than their ability to compete and integrate with host populations. Inability to compete with immigrants was mentioned in 43 per cent of 47 cases. Inability to compete and integrate with hosts was reported in 32 per cent of 44 cases. The frequency of competition difficulties with both immigrants and hosts requires that planners pay more attention to the issues involved – issues that can be expected to require quite different approaches.

Immigrants tend to be better capitalized and more experienced individuals who arrive to exploit new project-related opportunities such as reservoir fisheries and sites overlooking the reservoir for tourist facilities and vacation homes. In India access to reservoir fisheries and/or marketing is often given by government or project authorities to outside concessionaires, while a fish-marketing monopoly has been given to a single concessionaire at Laos' Nam Ngum reservoir. In Africa, small-scale immigrant fishers tend to come from established fisheries, as was the case with Mali's Manantali reservoir, the Ivory Coast's Kossou reservoir and Ghana's Volta reservoir at Akosombo. As in the Kariba case, and as is currently planned for Laos' NT2 project, resettlers and hosts need to be given a competitive edge before the arrival of immigrant fishers. This is best provided by initially restricting access to reservoir basin residents such as resettlers and hosts, who are provided with training and ongoing extension, as well as with credit for purchasing gear.

The problem is more complex where elite immigrants seek out desirable sites along reservoir shorelines as has been the case with a number of dams in Thailand as well as with the Kariba Dam in both Zambia and Zimbabwe. In Thailand's Khao Laem Dam, the forests surrounding the reservoir are 'dotted' with the illegal 'resorts of well-known politicians, senior government officials, and businessmen' (*Bangkok Post*, 1999). On the Zambian side of Kariba, similar elites have bribed chiefs or convinced local councils to give or lease them what were previously limited-access, communal lands under customary law. Another type of problem characterizes the Zimbabwe shoreline, as well as Costa Rica's Arenal and various reservoirs in Thailand. That is where governments designate communal lands as national parks or forest reserves. Important as such parks and reserves are for catchment and biodiversity protection, these purposes should not be at the expense of the land rights of local people. Solutions, although seldom implemented, are to make use of indigenous knowledge and local participation in the management of such areas, which is planned for the upper catchment of Laos' NT2 Dam, and to allow local people to utilize designated resources, as is happening in extractive reserves in Brazil.

Dealing with host populations requires a planning approach that understands the extent to which resettlers can be expected to impact upon host arable lands, grazing, fuel and other common property resources; employment opportunities; and social services. The only way to offset resettler competition over such resources is to actively involve the host population in the planning and implementing of, and participation in, such new opportunities as project ownership and management, irrigation, reservoir fisheries, wildlife management and tourism, and new industries as well as improved social services. While such an approach increases initial financial costs, it also increases the number of future beneficiaries and reduces costs associated with future impoverishment and conflict.

Unexpected events

Ignored in most analyses, including those of the World Bank, major unexpected events had a significant impact on resettlement process outcomes ($P < 0.008$). Such events may be political, economic and/or environmental. They were coded as major in 26 of 44 cases. Although their relative importance as an outcome explanation is unknown, it is interesting that only two of these 26 cases had positive outcomes, while outcomes were positive in 44 per cent of the 18 cases where such events were coded as minor.

In the Mahaweli case, in addition to a flawed planning process (which failed to capitalize on the full range of available opportunities) and an overestimation of available water supplies, drought unexpectedly reduced yields in the first system that was settled. A worsening of civil strife also interfered with implementation of the settlement process and access to otherwise available finance, while a change in government led to a shift in national priorities that adversely affected what was still Sri Lanka's most important development initiative. In the Kariba case, unexpected environmental degradation combined with inadequate government policies at the national level were instrumental in causing living standards to deteriorate after an initial period of improvement.[15]

Impoverishment risks

Introduction

While Cernea's impoverishment risks were especially important in explaining failure, the frequency with which the most important occur is itself a condemnation of the nature of resettlement outcomes in connection with the 50 dam sample. Sufficient data for analysis was available for seven of Cernea's eight impoverishment risks, five of which we combined into a 'well-being' index, which had a significant relationship to outcome ($P < 0.000$, as shown in Table 3.5),[16] as did each of the five individual risks.[17]

Table 3.5 *Resettler well-being index in relationship to outcome ($P < 0.000$)*

Nature of outcome	Mean	N	SD
Adverse	6.6	31	2.4
Positive	10.9	9	2.2
Total	7.6	40	2.9

Landlessness

Landlessness was a problem in 86 per cent of 44 cases.[18] Bearing in mind that the large majority of resettlers were relatively poor farmers, the importance of claims to arable land that can be handed down from one generation to another is hard to overemphasize. Looking to the future, the importance of landlessness can be expected to rise as an increasing proportion of dams are constructed in the tropics and in China and Turkey, where rural residents constitute the large majority of the population. Yet these are the countries where land scarcity can be expected to be a problem as a result of population increase and environmental degradation.

Joblessness

Joblessness was a problem in 80 per cent of 41 cases.[19] Although project proponents often use job formation as a project justification, the record shows that comparatively few project-specific jobs are available to resettlers (and those available are mostly temporary) and that efforts to train resettlers for jobs elsewhere have been fraught with problems including non-availability and, as in China, the failure of industries for which resettlers are trained and to which they are assigned. Moreover, as illustrated by Thailand's Pak Mun Dam, jobs are no substitute for lost natural resources. Based on 1996 data, the World Bank concluded that Pak Mun resettlement was one of its most successful cases because living standards of many resettlers improved after they found employment in Bangkok and other urban areas. During the Asian economic crisis that followed, however, those who lost such jobs were less able to return to fishing and farming in their home villages because of the adverse effect of the project on the riverine fishery and, to a lesser extent, on agriculture. Even where jobs remain permanent, retirement benefits often prove inadequate. Nor are jobs a resource like arable land that can be passed on from one generation to another.

Notwithstanding serious problems with job provision for resettlers, increasing scarcity of arable land and of common property resources requires much more attention to be paid to job creation in the future. Dealt with in the next chapter is the important need to pay more attention to realizing the documented multiplier effects that have been associated with well-planned and implemented irrigation, and to the job-creating potential of multipurpose dams. More emphasis needs also to be paid to providing resettlers better access to temporary and permanent project-related jobs. The Kali Gandaki project, for example, was able to provide one job for each resettler household, and the income received was used, in at least some cases, to diversify the family's livelihood options (Cernea, personal communication). In the Lesotho Highlands case, local chiefs created registers for job seekers among resettlers who Mohale project contractors were contractually bound to hire first for unskilled and semi-skilled jobs.

Food insecurity
Related to landlessness and loss of common property resources, food insecurity
was a problem in 79 per cent of 42 cases; hence, the ability to restore food self-
sufficiency was significantly (though barely) associated with outcome ($P < 0.01$).

Marginalization
Cernea defines marginalization as occurring 'when families lose economic
power and spiral downwards; it sets in long before physical displacement,
when new investments in the condemned areas are prohibited' (1999a, p17).
But as Cernea also points out, 'it is often accompanied by social and
psychological marginalization, expressed in a drop in social status, oustees'
loss of confidence in society, and in themselves' (ibid). What is occurring is a
threat to the socio-cultural system in which resettlers' livelihoods are
embedded – a major cause of impoverishment that planners seldom
acknowledge and that is inadequately dealt with in such guidelines as the
World Bank's.[20] Yet marginalization had the highest association with an
adverse outcome of any of Cernea's impoverishment risks ($P < 0.000$).

Common property resources
Failure of planners to consider the importance of common property resources
was also a significant variable in helping to explain adverse outcomes. Given
the high proportion (relative to their number in the national population) of
relatively poor ethnic minorities undergoing resettlement, as well as of other
poor households, common property resources that provide access to arable
land (for example, along the drawdown area of soon-to-be-dammed rivers as
well as in inland areas), grazing, fuel, building materials and edible and
medicinal plants can play a major role in a people's livelihood, to the extent
that their loss can be expected to increase impoverishment. Yet few planners
make allowance for such losses. It is interesting that in the minority of cases
(23 per cent of the 35 coded) where those responsible for planning and
implementing resettlement had at least some awareness of the importance of
common property resources, five of the eight cases had positive outcomes.

Issues not dealt with by the 50 dam survey

The number of issues dealt with in the 50 dam survey was constrained by lack
of data. Two issues that could not be explored were the complexity of the
resettlement process and the lifestyles of resettling communities. As discussed in
the previous chapter, complexity does pose major problems that need be
overcome. As for the socio-cultural systems of resettlers, critics may suggest that
I am mistaken to have left them out as a major constraint, especially in the case
of indigenous communities and communities whose lifestyles vary significantly
from that of the political economy into which they are being moved.

I do not accept this viewpoint. Regardless of culture or environmental
setting, the best-documented case studies show that if opportunities are made
available, along with appropriate assistance to benefit from them, the majority

of resettlers will take advantage of them. This is a crucial conclusion that will be further documented in the next chapter. Although policies must be designed to minimize what project authorities have referred to as a 'culture of dependence' on project and government largess, what evidence is available indicates that the main cause of such dependency is the lack of available, achievable and affordable opportunities or their belated availability. To cite 'dependency' as a cause for a failed resettlement process is a 'blaming the victim' excuse that has little case history justification.

Qualitative analysis

Introduction

The preceding quantitative analysis was concerned with the first purpose of this chapter, that is, to support, in a more rigorous fashion, the World Commission on Dam's conclusion about the unsatisfactory and unacceptable nature of large dam resettlement outcomes. This section is concerned with the chapter's second purpose, which is to show that such unsatisfactory outcomes were also unnecessary since 'good practice' cases in the 50 dam survey show that it is possible for a majority of resettlers to become project beneficiaries whose improved living standards can contribute to a project's stream of benefits. The case study examples that follow also provide an introduction to the next chapter, which deals in more detail with the range of project-relevant opportunities that are available.

Ten cases are briefly described. The first three illustrate projects where improved living standards were coded The next three examples involve projects where living standards appear to have at least been restored. In the seventh (Kossou) and eighth cases (Yantan), available data suggest that living standards are trending toward restoration, although in both cases livelihoods of the majority may not be sustainable. Although the ninth case (Ramial) deals with a failed process of resettlement for the majority, resettlement of a minority within the project's command area may allow a significant number of households to raise their living standards. The tenth case (Pak Mun) shows how quickly a reputed 'success' story can turn into a failure. Emphasis in each case is on opportunities that have potential for application elsewhere as well as on future risks to the maintenance of improving living standards.

Aswan High Dam (Egypt)[21]

The construction of the High Dam in the 1960s required the relocation of over 100,000 Egyptian and Sudanese Nubians. The 50 dam survey dealt only with the 50,000 Egyptian Nubians. Their resettlement illustrates the importance of the project authority providing the necessary opportunities as well as being willing to allow resettlers to respond to them in their own culturally congruent way, even though the responses were different from what the planners had intended.

The initial opportunity that allowed a majority of resettlers to improve their living standards was the provision by the government of the resettlers' own major irrigation scheme in the command area location where the majority wished to resettle. Following a difficult Stage 2, which researchers believe involved higher death rates than during the years preceding resettlement and that lasted over five years because of delays in completing the necessary irrigation facilities, a majority of the resettlers used their irrigated holdings as a resource for diversifying their household economies. Combining diversification with the education of children and political activism allowed the resettling population to eventually become the leading force in the political economy in the encompassing province. Since those resettled were an ethnic minority, resettlement was also followed by a reinforcing of the people's ethnic identity. Because economic diversification has enabled the resettling population to become less involved with their irrigation holdings, the majority of which are cultivated by non-Nubian sharecroppers, the main risk to sustaining current living standards is the national political economy rather than the resettlement process.

A legitimate question that needs addressing is the extent to which the policies that contributed to the positive resettlement outcome of the High Dam are transferable to other countries. Did, for example, the Nubian experience with three previous impoverishing resettlements as a result of the building and subsequent raising of the first Aswan Dam play an important role in their subsequent ability to influence government policy for their benefit? The same applies to the government's desire to avoid the extent to which the Nubians had been disadvantaged by past development efforts. Important as these situational variables are in explaining the Nubian case (and other variables may also be significant, such as experiences gained by Nubians as labour migrants to Cairo and other major cities), the most significant development intervention was provision of a command area irrigation project for the large majority of resettlers. That intervention is transferable.

Pimburetewa (Sri Lanka)

Completed in 1971, Sri Lanka's Pimburetewa Dam required the physical removal of only 120 resettlers. As in the High Dam case, success was related to the resettlers' incorporation in a downstream irrigation scheme in which they were a minority among government-sponsored voluntary pioneer settlers. Their living standards benefited further from their incorporation in the 1980s within the Accelerated Mahaweli Project (Chapter 5), which allowed the double cropping of paddy with a more reliable water supply. Although still relatively poor, since even the double cropping of paddy on small holdings makes it difficult for the majority to move beyond subsistence, living standards remain higher than prior to resettlement. The main risks for the future are a renewal of the civil war between the government and the Tamil Tigers[22] and, if the economy does not allow diversification including non-farming employment, increasing subdivision for the benefit of future generations of what were already small holdings.

Arenal (Costa Rica)

Completed in 1980, Arenal is the first of the three projects involving actual or potential improvement without any irrigation. It is an interesting case for a number of reasons, including institutional capacity and political will on the part of the project authority and the principal donor, and good resettler participation. Unfortunately the only sources available to me are a report submitted by anthropologist William Partridge to the Inter-American Development Bank that deals with resettlement five years after removal and a subsequent Partridge article, also dealing with that time. The majority of resettlers found themselves in Stage 3 and considered themselves better off. Even Partridge, whom I consulted, is unaware of what has happened to the resettlers over the past 20 years.

The Arenal Dam was built in humid tropical ranching country. Construction required the resettlement of approximately 2500 people. A small minority was employed on two large ranches whose wealthy owners took cash compensation and left the reservoir basin without their employees. Before resettlement, the majority of resettlers lived in two communities, one of which was a service centre with a bank, a primary school and basic health facilities, and the other was on outlying ranches. No commercial crops were cultivated, although some households continued to practise subsistence farming of maize, which had dominated the economy before giving way to ranching.

The project authority, an electricity parastatal, established an Inter-Institutional Task Force that Partridge noted included anthropologists from the University of Costa Rica. Not only was resettlement coordinated with the construction timetable but apparently was completed several years before the dam. To replace the two existing communities, two new settlements were built and handed over to local government two years before the completion of dam construction. Thereafter the project authority remained actively involved for another three years. Planning was based on 'financial packages' for each household that sized house and farm plots according to such criteria as family size, labour resources and value of household assets. Fairness of distribution within each community, according to Partridge, was facilitated by the use of community leaders familiar with kin networks and household preferences.

Throughout the initial years of resettlement wide participation occurred. Community formation began almost immediately after removal. With assistance from the parastatal's resettlement unit, a church group was formed which organized its first mass with a visiting priest during the dam construction period. A similar group was organized for school construction and the provision of agricultural extension. Economic development began two to three years after removal. Those two to three years, according to resettlers interviewed by Partridge, were difficult, with households relying largely on subsistence agriculture. In 1980, however, credit became available for adding coffee as a cash crop. A coffee marketing cooperative was established that year and by 1981 most small farmers had planted coffee. Dairying was also emphasized rather than beef production, assisted by the introduction of a new fodder crop that tripled the carrying capacity when appropriately harvested.

Partridge noted future risks. The host population had been ignored and no soil surveys had been carried out. Nor had attention been paid to the environmental and socio-economic impact of the livelihood changes that had been implemented. While it is not possible to conclude whether improved living standards have been passed on to the second generation, recent information on the internet notes the formation of an Arenal Conservation Area that is said to prolong the project's life. In addition to being a stopping point on organized tours, the reservoir is also noted as an important place for windsurfing and fishing. No mention is made about the relationship of such activities to the resettled population.

Shuikou (China)

When completed in 1993, China's Shuikou Dam, financed by the World Bank, required the resettlement of 67,200 rural residents and 20,000 urban residents belonging to China's Han majority. The case study dealt only with the rural residents. Although China's development-induced resettlement in the earlier years of the current regime, and especially during the Cultural Revolution, increased poverty, during the 1990s China became the first country to legislate its own resettlement with development policy. A major effort was made at Shuikou to implement that policy and the World Bank's Guidelines.[23]

The rural population to be resettled lived in one of the most fertile areas of Fuzhou Province and marketed a range of agricultural products to surrounding cities. During construction, households were allowed to continue farming their river basin holdings until they were inundated. Because of a shortfall in replacement lands, resettlement policy and planning emphasized agriculture for older farming households and non-farming occupations (including cage aquaculture in the reservoir, and village and urban non-farming industries) for younger farmers. A 1997 survey completed four years after removal indicated that a majority had been able to restore their incomes and that they were expected to pass the income levels of a control group 'since the resettlers' occupational structure was forced to shift more rapidly to the fastest-growing components of the economy' (World Bank, 1998b, p11). Overall living standards had also improved including resettler-built housing, water supplies and social services.

Although the World Bank considers Shuikou one of its most successful cases, if not the most successful, four years after removal is too soon to reach such a verdict: there are just too many future uncertainties. One relates to an impoverishment risk related to landlessness. Because land availability per capita fell from 0.06 to 0.02ha, a significant number of resettlers were required to shift from agriculture to non-farming enterprises and services. This increases their dependence on China's ongoing economic development.[24] Not only has the amount of land that can be passed on from one generation to another decreased, but the impoverishment risk of food insecurity has also increased since the proportion of formerly consumption-sufficient households that must now purchase rice has increased. A survey of 524 households found that during 1994, grain purchases after resettlement increased '145 per cent. This shift reflects the loss of paddy land and the shift to a money economy' (op cit, Annex A, p30). In making such a shift, those involved and their second generation descendents 'will no longer qualify to share the village land or some other village-owned assets' (ibid).

Planners also miscalculated land availability for those who remained farmers. According to the original plan it was expected that land was sufficient for 52 per cent of the resettlers. By mid-1997 only 30 per cent of that 52 per cent estimate had been allocated land. Although the Bank report does not discuss land quality, the fields to be cultivated with market-dependent cash crops are described as hilly land. Presumably their fertility is considerably less than that of the farmers' now-inundated alluvial soils.

Kainji (Nigeria)

During Kainji's construction, most of the 44,000 resettlers relocated around the reservoir, while a small minority moved into improved housing in a new town constructed close to the dam site. I found the Kainji case one of the most difficult to evaluate; indeed, it is the one case where my rating perhaps should have been living standard improvement as opposed to restoration. Ayeni, Roder, and Ayanda consider resettlement to have been a success 'because it aimed at replacement of lost villages, and left the people undisturbed in their social, economic, and cultural life' (1994, p120). They also refer to an earlier survey of 513 households in which two-thirds of the respondents considered themselves better off three years after removal (Oyedipe, 1983). Roder also believes that living standards have improved for the majority 'as a result of many individuals pursuing their families interests and well being' (Roder, 1994, p162) in a reservoir basin with a very large and productive drawdown area. The area under smallholder irrigation has increased, as have the number of small pumps and the number of cattle. Moreover, Roder 'judges' that 'the volume of trade per capita has also increased' (ibid).

On the other hand, there is no evidence that health has improved; indeed the figures that Roder quotes of death rates of children five years of age and under suggest that death rates may well have increased (1994, p146 after Adekolu-John, 1980). The provision of other government services also has been unsatisfactory. Not only have government plans for large-scale agricultural development not been implemented, but 'The lake area urgently needs maintained farm to market roads, schools in which young people can learn, health centres which serve the community, and communications by telephone and post to support the lively trade in fish and food.' Roder expects local initiatives to continue but only 'if the government can maintain and improve the infrastructure needed for every day commerce, health and education' (ibid, p163).

Victoria (Sri Lanka)

Another case in which living standards of the majority may have been in the process of improving involves those resettled because of the construction of the Mahaweli Project's Victoria Dam (Rew and Driver, 1986; Scudder and

Wimaladharma, field notes; and Chapter 5). Conclusions in the Victoria case are difficult to make for several reasons. One is that the actual number of resettlers is unknown, with estimates varying from 28,000 to 35,000 (Rew and Driver, 1986, p7). Another is that the context in which the resettlers lived was as favourable as any among the 50 cases, with the possible exception of Shuikou. Unlike the isolated condition of most resettling communities, the Victoria resettlers lived within 25 to 50km of the important Sri Lankan city of Kandy, where the farming community could market their vegetables and other crops.

A third complexity was that resettlers had the option of relocating to one of two very different locations. At least 75 per cent opted to relocate to one of the Mahaweli Project's downstream command areas where they received a 1ha irrigated holding and a 0.25ha home lot. What evidence is available suggests that the majority, and especially the relatively high proportion of tenant farmers, have been able to at least restore their living standards provided they did not become too indebted or required to subdivide their holding among adult children. Options for the remainder who chose to stay within the reservoir basin or elsewhere above the dam included a residential site selected by approximately 76 per cent of households, a home lot and agricultural land selected by 21 per cent, and a business site selected by 3 per cent. This group has done less well. Problems outlined by Rew and Driver include dispersal of population over a wider area without attention paid to previous social and economic networking (hence bringing to bear Cernea's social disarticulation risk), insufficient attention paid to employment generation for those selecting residential sites, less fertile land for agricultural resettlers, poor siting of business plots, and potable water supply problems.

Kossou (Ivory Coast)

Resettlement of 75,000 people during the 1970s was coded as possibly non-sustainable restoration of the living standards of the majority. Uncertainty as to outcomes is caused by a number of factors. One relates to the project authority. Although adequate political will was present, opportunities were either inadequate or ignored. Land availability was inadequate,[25] but the agricultural potential of the drawdown area was ignored. Capacity was also limited. Budgetary constraints became a problem as the resettlement process proceeded. A second factor deals with the complexity of resettlement. Large numbers of resettlers were aggregated in 54 consolidated communities in two very different ecological zones, where some households were able to restore and improve their living standards, while others were impoverished. The fact that the detailed research of Lassailly-Jacob focused on only one of five affected districts[26] also makes it difficult to generalize outcomes for the majority of resettlers.

A special agency (the Authority for the Development of the Bandama River Valley or AVB) was established in 1969. It was responsible to the President of the Republic and was to plan and implement resettlement and the regional development of the central portion of the Bandama River Basin. It was closed down in 1980 with its responsibilities handed over to line ministries and other existing institutions. Although detailed resettlement planning did not get underway until after the commencement of dam construction, the process of physical removal was competently executed. Adequate political will played an important role due, in good part, to the fact that the majority of resettlers belonged to the largest ethnic group in the country to which the President also belonged. They had previously lived dispersed in over 300 small savannah villages and hamlets practising shifting cultivation of food crops and cash cropping of cotton and tree crops. During resettlement they were concentrated in 32 new communities in the forest zone downstream from the dam site and in 22 in the savannah zone.

Housing and social services improved in the new communities, but evidence for any improvement in economic status is mixed. In both zones, a major effort involved intensification of rain-fed agriculture.[27] It was most successful in the forest zone, where a forest reserve was declassified and each household provided with 1ha of arable land to be planted with coffee and cacao. Lassailly-Jacob considered outcomes there to be fairly successful (2002, personal communication) in regard to relatively secure land rights, income generation and relationships with surrounding people. On the other hand, recent reduced prices for the two tree crops and the probable subdivision of 1ha holdings among the second generation raise the question of longer-term sustainability.

The situation in the more densely populated savannah zone is more complex and less favourable. As in the forest zone, resettlement reduced the arable land resources of most households. The government also emphasized agricultural intensification, but only for a minority who volunteered to become tenants on a rain-fed block and semi-mechanization scheme based on the strip cultivation of four rotating crops over a five-year period. Yams were cultivated first followed by a combination of maize and cotton, and then rice. A green manure crop that was also intended to provide fodder for livestock was to be cultivated during the final two years of the rotation. Despite the crop mix being ingeniously designed to maintain soil fertility, the scheme had failed by the 1980s. Some of the departing tenants were able to renew their former lifestyle by reclaiming their pre-project lands because the reservoir only covered approximately two-thirds of its expected surface area.[28] Others who had lost their land to the reservoir moved into the new settlements.

The problem with the new savannah settlements was that the government had never given the AVB the authority to acquire arable land from the host population. As a result the majority of residents could only farm borrowed or leased land. Not only were most unable to do that, but even relatives found themselves in competition for what land was available. In the district where Lassailly-Jacob did her research, population densities had increased by 31 per cent following reservoir inundation and the construction of eight new communities for the 13,000 resettlers. Under these conditions, pressure on land resources increased for both hosts and resettlers, with the result that host–resettler relationships were poor from the start and deteriorated over time.

Host communities left out of the development process and expected to share limited land with the resettlers, resented the improved housing and social services that resettlers had received. They increasingly refused to allocate arable land to resettlers, including those to whom they were related. They also placed fetishes on land leased out during the early years of the resettlement process as a way to reclaim it by scaring off the cultivators (Lassailly-Jacob, 1994).

While the AVB's agricultural intensification programme for the savannah failed, a successful reservoir fisheries programme was implemented with technical assistance from FAO and financial support from UNDP. According to Lassailly-Jacob, not only were approximately 3000 fishers trained and outfitted, but a significant proportion were able to compete successfully with more experienced immigrant fishers from the Niger River Basin in Mali. That 'new activity became very attractive and financially rewarding for thousands [of] new skilled fishermen' (2002, personal communication). Including dependents, the new fishery presumably supported over 10,000 resettlers and hosts. Fishing also provided income to resettlers who were able to reclaim their former lands from the reservoir basin, but according to Lassailly-Jacob, the potential of flood recession agriculture was ignored by the government and by the resettlers and hosts living close to the reservoir.

To sum up, the first generation of resettlers in the forest zone at least restored their living standards and may have improved them, although the sustainability of that outcome for the second generation remains uncertain. In the savannah zone at least some fishers were able to improve their living standards, as were some farmers who were able to combine farming of their former land with fishing. On the other hand, the living standards of those who remained in the new towns had become increasingly dependent on non-project-related employment elsewhere in the Ivory Coast. Their living standards most probably have worsened because of the inability to acquire land from the host population and the uncertainty associated with finding jobs elsewhere.

Yantan (China)

Yantan is the first of two cases (the other being Pak Mun) where an outcome considered adequate by some may eventually be classified as a failed resettlement process. On the other hand, Yantan also illustrates a number of best-practice criteria. These include the world's first national dam-induced resettlement policy; use of revenue from electricity sales for the benefit of resettlers and the environment; and efforts to increase reservoir basin opportunities through cage aquaculture, cultivation of fruit trees on sloping lands above the reservoir, and reforestation. Also present was the political will on the part of planners to at least restore the income of all citizens, including ethnic minorities in the Yantan case.

But Yantan also points up the extent to which the insufficient availability of land for a population of poor rural farmers can jeopardize achieving policy goals – in this case to raise the living standards of the majority to the encompassing province's poverty threshold. Aware that land resources were insufficient to allow households to regain food self-sufficiency as farmers, the project authorities emphasized job creation, including job creation that required resettling people outside the reservoir basin. Such a strategy is risky for two reasons. On the one hand, job creation for resettlers has proved to be a problematic option throughout the world because of the non-availability of sufficient jobs. On the other hand, removal from a familiar habitat, as within a reservoir basin where resettlers have both skills and support networks, increases the risk of impoverishment for those who are resettled in contexts with which they are unfamiliar.

Yantan, a World Bank-financed project that spanned the second half of the 1980s and the early 1990s, required the resettlement of 43,176 people plus assistance for another 19,256 who lost land but not their homes to the project. In 1997, five years after removal, the Bank's Operations Evaluation Department funded a survey that concluded that resettler incomes in three dam-affected counties substantially exceeded 'pre-dam incomes: more than double in two of the counties. Thus, the project has succeeded in restoring the standard of living' (World Bank, 1998b, p22).[29]

This conclusion is overoptimistic for a number of reasons. As the Bank study points out, the non-availability of land suitable or available for agriculture within the reservoir basin or immediately downstream required resettlers to shift to 'radically different lifestyles' (ibid) including wage labour for approximately 15,000 affected people who were moved to distant government-owned farms, on two of which resettlers became labourers on sugar estates – hardly a very satisfying form of employment assuming that the majority became cane cutters.

Bank project documents and reports also tend to assume that restoration of income is the same as restoration of living standards. This is blatantly false where farmers must shift from agriculture to non-farming wage labour, because under these conditions income must be spent on food, fuel and other resources that the household previously had been able to grow or collect from common property resources.

Even if economic criteria are met, people may find themselves worse off in other respects, given the psychological and socio-cultural implications of leaving a familiar habitat, supportive kin and community-based networks for an unfamiliar environment where resettlers become a minority among an unfamiliar host population. In China and elsewhere, substantial numbers of people resettled under such conditions opt to return to overcrowded reservoir basins. That was the outcome for innumerable Danjiangkou resettlers from the 1960s onward and is being reported today for Three Gorges resettlers who have been moved to distant coastal and other provinces. As rates of unemployment rise in China as a result of the closing down of state-run enterprises, impoverishment risks for policies that attempt to find employment for resettlers who were formerly farmers can be expected to increase in the cases of Yantan and Three Gorges.

Ramial (India)

India, like the US, is a country with one of the worst records with dam-induced resettlement. As in the US, the capacity to do a better job is there – indeed India probably has more resettlement expertise in its research institutions and universities than any country in the world. Lakshman Mahapatra, a former vice-chancellor of Utkal University and head of Utkal's Department of Anthropology, exemplifies that expertise. He accepts my definition of success as encompassing the first and second generation of resettlers, but says that 'This has never happened in India' (Mahapatra, 1999a, p12). Referring to various types of development-induced resettlement, he further states that 'In India, we rarely come across studies of reconstruction of livelihoods after resettlement. Even rarer are reports on social reintegration as a part of such reconstruction' (ibid, p143).

A major problem is that the central government and many of the states do not have the necessary political will, a result of which is that national and state policies have been inadequate. A major example is the *Land Acquisition Act* of 1894 as well as its 1984 amendment that continues to impoverish resettlers by offering them market rather than replacement value for land. Land scarcity is also a major problem made worse by the *Forest Conservation Act* of 1980 that prohibits resettlement in government forests as well as by the unwillingness of project authorities to implement various *Land Ceiling Acts*. Furthermore, despite having a large number of NGOs willing to work with resettlers, project authorities continue to implement what Baxi refers to as 'development without participation' (1989). Indeed, as Mahapatra notes, 'there is no genuine consultation with the affected people even on such cultural issues as the desirability of a project or the selection of resettlement sites after displacement' (Mahapatra, 1999b, p197–198).

Outcomes vary from state to state, however. Orissa, in which the Ramial Medium Irrigation Project is located, has perhaps the best record as well as the best state policy. Studied over the years by Lakshman and Steela Mahapatra, Ramial does illustrate one example of 'best practice' that may have enabled some resettlers to restore and possibly improve their living standards. This was provision of irrigated lands[30] for four 'colonies' of resettlers in the project's command area as well as home plots large enough to include household gardens. Because land quality varied within the command area, and not all the 'colonists' received irrigated land, outcomes ranged from impoverishment to improvement. Furthermore, 'colonists' constituted only a minority of the resettled population. The majority apparently ended up worse off for a variety of reasons, including receipt of no land or other benefits for those that the government considered to be encroachers on state lands even where such lands constituted common property under customary tenure.

Another problem with Ramial was the lengthy period of project construction that so often has characterized dam construction and irrigation projects (WCD, 2000, p42). It lasted from the mid-1970s to the end of the 1980s. Also characteristic of involuntary community resettlement in India is delayed, inadequate or non-payment of compensation. More than ten years later, the need for adequate Ramial compensation was still being brought up in debates within India's parliament.[31]

The number of people resettled in Ramial's 22 affected villages, 6 of which were completely flooded and another 7 partially flooded, is unknown.[32] The Mahapatras' research concentrated on a minority of 383 households who were resettled in four colonies within the command area of the project. At this point it is important to emphasize that Ramial's inclusion as a possible success story is based only on outcomes relating to those 383 households. Piecing together what other information is available suggests that the project impoverished the majority of those required to resettle. Moreover, the Mahapatras' evidence suggests that even among the 383 households, income levels and perhaps living standards deteriorated because even irrigated land 'is not very productive' (1999a, p139).

By the mid-1990s 51 households (13 per cent) of the 383 had returned to their pre-project villages. Furthermore, 17 per cent of the 383 were allocated land unsuitable for agriculture (12 per cent of whom were among the 51 households who left the 'colonies' to return to their pre-project villages), while the arable land of a number of others could not be irrigated because it was above canal level. In comparison to the situation in their pre-project villages, access to common property resources, and especially to grazing, had worsened. Although the Mahapatras were impressed by efforts of the colonist households to reorganize themselves as communities, displacement had also involved 'a loss of joint family and village solidarity and social and religious networks' (ibid, p142), while relationships with the host population were considered unsatisfactory.

There was, however, some evidence that overall living standards had been improved for at least some households. The majority, including some formerly landless households, had received irrigable but not very productive land. The Mahapatras concluded that 'the landless families and the families who have got good, irrigated lands have got a better deal for life after resettlement' (ibid, p136). The new irrigation economy also provided more jobs for agricultural labourers and for service providers such as blacksmiths as well as additional non-farming employment in the colonies (and presumably within the command area). Among new businesses, the Mahapatras listed 11 shops, 3 rice hullers, and 23 petty businesses. Educational services had also improved with colonists supplementing project-provided primary schools with a secondary school. Although health services were also better, community health had not necessarily improved because of an increase in irrigation-associated diseases such as malaria. On the other hand, self-built housing for the majority had improved, while better communications, and especially better roads, were seen as a benefit. Overall, a very mixed result for the first generation and one that could be expected to worsen for the second generation as the relatively small irrigated holdings are subdivided.

Pak Mun (Thailand)

Located on the Mun River 5.5km from its confluence with the Mekong, the reservoir behind the Pak Mun Dam filled during the 1994 rainy season. Living standards of approximately 6000 households in 31 villages were adversely affected by the project. A total of 1700 underwent resettlement because of loss of residence, land or other natural resources (including fish), while dependence on a declining fishery adversely affected the living standards of the other 4300 households.

World Bank publications in 1998 and 2001, based on 1996 data, concluded that 'with few exceptions, resettlers have done well in terms of both increased incomes and quality of life' (2001, p59). This outcome, the Bank concluded, was caused by two major factors. One, a project-related factor, was the generous cash compensation that the project authority gave to the affected households. The other, not project related, was an assumed acceleration of a pre-project shift from agriculture to wage labour because of loss of land and other natural resources to the project. Based on data collected in 1999, the WCD-contracted Pak Mun case study concluded the exact opposite (Amornsakchai et al, 2000). Although the Asian economic downturn, an unexpected event that commenced in late 1996, was a contributing factor, it was the project that had made the majority of the population worse off.[33]

This difference in opinion illustrates serious weaknesses in the project authorities' feasibility studies and the World Bank's project appraisal, in the Bank's over-reliance on cash as the major form of compensation, and on the assumption that the continuing development of the Thai economy would enable those who lost the basis of their rural support to shift to non-project-related wage labour. The World Bank assessment also shows the risk of concluding the project to be a success too early in the resettlement process.

Feasibility and planning studies had several major deficiencies. One was inadequate resettler participation in planning. As a result resettlers rejected one of the project authority's two major plans for living standard restoration and improvement. Rejection was predictable because acceptance would have involved displacement from a familiar habitat to an irrigation project with core housing and improved civic infrastructure on another Mun tributary. Following the rejection of the irrigation option, the project authority made no attempt to design an alternative development intervention.

Another deficiency involved the faulty assumption by both the project authority and the Bank that a major fishery development programme in the reservoir would more than offset any drop in the productivity of the pre-project riverine fishery. That assumption underestimated the importance of fish migration into the Mun River Basin from the Mekong and the importance for breeding of rapids that would be destroyed at the dam site or inundated by the reservoir. These errors were compounded by the failure of both the project authority and the Bank to realize that the main source of food and income for the majority of the affected population came from fishing rather than from farming. According to the WCD Pak Mun case study, before the project 'villagers perceived themselves as fishermen who depended on fishing as their major source of income' (ibid, p55). Fish were a major food. They were also sold for cash and traded for rice. By 1999, the proportion of upstream households 'dependent on fisheries as a primary or supplementary source of livelihood and income' declined from 95.6 per cent to 66.7 per cent (ibid).

Although the World Bank's own guidelines warn against reliance on cash compensation as the main strategy for rehabilitating a displaced population, the Bank accepted the project's reliance on cash compensation. Predictably, few households used the liberal funds received to purchase arable land or other means for income restoration. Rather, 33 per cent went into savings, 24 per cent was spent on improved housing, and 19 per cent was shared with children and other kin. Household furnishings and other consumer goods, including motorcycles, were also purchased. Less than 6 per cent was used to purchase land, in spite of the loss of fisheries and other common property resources, riverbank gardens and rain-fed fields (World Bank, 2001, pp64–65).[34]

The assumption that wage labour in the cities, especially in Bangkok and to a lesser extent on agricultural estates, would provide a viable alternative and was happening anyway without any project influences, was misinformed for two reasons. First, having underestimated the importance of fishing in household economies, it overestimated the pre-project importance of the trend toward wage labour. Second, it assumed that national development in Thailand (as one of the major Asian Tigers) would continue to provide employment opportunities that would not only substitute for lost local resources and opportunities but improve upon them.

Ironically, the year following the 1996 survey contracted by the Bank, the Asian economic crisis began. Then, as the WCD-contracted case study states, affected villagers were no longer able to find 'nonfarm employment in urban areas'. Nor were they able to find employment by returning home since 'there has not been any investment in the area to generate employment' (Amornsakchai et al, 2000, pp59–60). Reduction in resettlers' resource base and the physical displacement of 1700 families also created social and cultural problems of a kind that project authorities as well as the World Bank continue to underemphasize in safety net guidelines and in practice. According to the case study 'the new social arrangements have disrupted former social relations and changed patterns of interaction among the villagers. Before the Mun river serve[d] as the stage for their social life. Villagers met, interacted, developed network[s] of exchange, and helped each other. The traditional communal ceremony usually organized on the river bank could not be held [due] to the submergence of the ceremonial site and, in part, due to the social disintegration of the communities' that intensified as protests and demonstrations that continue to this day 'created mistrust and deep social rifts' between villagers who opposed the project and those who supported it (ibid, pp98–99).

CONCLUSION

Analysis based on the 50 dam survey documents the unsatisfactory and unacceptable impact of large dams on those who must involuntarily resettle from future reservoir basins. The chapter also documents that such outcomes are unnecessary. They are unnecessary because positive outcomes have occurred and their analysis illustrates what is required to enable the majority of a resettling population to become beneficiaries and, in the process of becoming beneficiaries, to contribute to the stream of project benefits.

Living standards in the 50 dam survey were coded as improving in only three of 44 cases, while living standards were coded as restored in another five cases. Whereas the World Bank believes that policies and planning have improved over the years, their implementation has yet to be associated with positive outcomes in the large majority of cases. The complexity of the resettlement process is such that a number of key factors are necessary if a successful outcome is to be achieved. Among variables analysed in the 50 dam survey, a combination of project authority staff capacity, funding and political will, implementation of adequate opportunities, and resettler participation helped to explain every one of the more successful cases.

That does not mean, however, that all five variables are necessary or that their presence is sufficient to guarantee success. The resettlement process is full of impoverishment and other risks. Best results are achieved where a single project authority is responsible for both construction and resettlement planning and implementation. Adequate pre-project surveys are necessary since the global tendency to undercount the number of potential resettlers is associated with underfunding. More attention also needs to be paid to incorporating host populations within plans and to reducing conflicts between resettlers, hosts and immigrants. Also important is a favourable regional and national development context as well as the absence of unexpected events at the local, national and international levels.

4

How River Basin Communities Can Benefit From Resettlement

INTRODUCTION

This chapter deals in detail with what should be a win–win situation whereby resettled communities become project beneficiaries and contribute to, rather than detract from, a project's benefits. But is a win–win scenario realistic? Are lessons learned from the small number of successful cases widely applicable? Based on the evidence available, the answer is a provisional 'yes', but only provided such issues as institutional capacity, funds, political will, opportunities and participation are adequately dealt with. And even if they are adequately dealt with, unexpected events can interfere with the process. Furthermore, it should not be assumed that sufficient opportunities are present, especially in heavily populated areas where land and employment opportunities are scarce. All such issues should be explored during options assessment.

The first half of this chapter, after a discussion of resettler involvement, provides a detailed assessment of the type of opportunities that large dams can provide for resettlers. Especially important are project partnerships that include resettlers as managers, owners and/or shareholders; irrigation, with multiplier effects if possible; rain-fed agriculture; creation of rural and urban industries; and marketing and social services. Reservoir drawdown utilization, reservoir fisheries, access to common property resources, natural resource management and tourism, and job training are also important.

Next, a range of other important issues not dealt with in detail in the 50 dam survey are assessed. These include ways for avoiding or reducing involuntary resettlement, the financing of resettlement, selection of sites and resettling units (deciding who resettles with whom), and housing. The chapter ends with a discussion of the importance of combining cultural continuity with change.

INVOLVING RESETTLERS

Introduction

The definition of how affected people should be involved in river basin development has evolved over the years. In the 1950s, best practice was to involve them in the resettlement process by encouraging them to stipulate where, and with whom, they wished to resettle and discussing with them what compensation and development opportunities they could expect to receive. This was the approach in the 1950s with Kariba resettlement and in the 1960s with resettlement in connection with the Aswan High Dam. Today best practice is to seek the consent of resettlers, hosts and other affected people by exploring various managerial and partnership arrangements. The word 'exploring' is used intentionally since the most interesting arrangements are either still being discussed or have only recently been implemented. They include resettlers managing the use of at least some of the funds allocated for the resettlement process, sharing project revenue with affected people, and planning and implementing a project as a joint venture.

At the very least, involving resettlers requires not just their active participation in decision-making, but also the involvement of their expertise and their lifestyles. Participation should start during the options assessment process because that is when the environmental, social and equity implications of various options will be first considered. Should those options include a large dam, the views of potential resettlers should play a major role in the selection process.

If a large dam is selected, then it is especially important that resettlers be actively involved in planning where they will move, with whom they will be grouped and how they can become project beneficiaries. As for planners, and they should include resettler representatives along with project authority planners, it is especially important for them to be aware of the multidimensional stress that is associated with physical removal and the period immediately following resettlement. Although the majority of resettlers can be expected to behave conservatively at first, as described for Stage 2 of the resettlement process (Chapter 2), this does not mean that new opportunities cannot be made available to resettlers who are prepared to experiment with new occupations from the start and thus demonstrate their potential to others.

Participatory involvement

Within future reservoir basins, the increasing heterogeneity of communities that previously were more homogeneous creates problems for participation that continue to receive inadequate attention. The problem 'who is to participate' becomes even more complex if different cultures and societies are involved, as was the case with Mexico's Aleman Dam.

The best approach to such complexities is to bring potential resettlers into the decision-making process at the time when the initial assessment of water resource development options is underway. Bearing in mind that leaders who are identified to work with project authorities may lose their influence with their constituency if they are perceived as supporters of an involuntary move, every effort should be made to broaden community participation. Should the decision be made to build a dam, a feature of the necessary demographic and socio-economic surveys should be to identify ways in which wider community participation can be achieved.

NGOs can play a major role in helping communities understand the issues at hand and building participatory institutions that increase the ability of resettlers to represent their own interests. Communities should also be encouraged to employ their own consultants to help 'level the playing field' between them and the project authorities. When the Eisenhower administration reopened the issue of the Kinzua Dam in the US, the Allegany Senecas hired Arthur E. Morgan, one of the three original Tennessee Valley Authority commissioners, to represent their interests. Although his suggestions of alternatives to reduce the flooding of Seneca lands were rejected by the project authorities, Bilharz credits his activities with delaying construction long enough to allow the Seneca to organize better representation of their interests (1998, p51).

The financing of resettlement should include funds to enable communities to recruit the necessary expertise such as lawyers and engineers, NGOs, social scientists and health practitioners. In recent years Hydro-Quebec has been playing a pioneering role in providing money to the James Bay Cree for undertaking their own surveys and research dealing with project impacts – one example being the threat posed to Cree consumers by methyl mercury in fish at the end of the food chain. The James Bay Cree also provide an example of the participatory and decision-making clout that a previously unorganized indigenous people can develop (Chapter 6).

Lifestyle involvement

For resettlers to become active participants in decision-making, it is important for project authorities to obtain a better understanding of what resettlers know, what they do, and what they value. Such knowledge should be sought from resettler representatives and organizations during the options assessment process and, if a dam is to be built, through participatory pre-project socio-economic surveys. Especially important is an understanding of existing economic systems for making a living. Within each community and society these tend to be based on a range of strategies as a means for dealing with risks and uncertainty associated with both the natural environment and the wider political economy of which resettlers are part.

Knowledge of such local but diversified systems of production is important for a number of reasons. One is that the majority of resettlers can be expected, at least initially, to prefer the replication of these systems following their removal as one of a number of ways to 'cling to the familiar' while 'getting back on their feet' and coming to 'feel at home' in their new environment. This is the kind of behaviour predicted during Stage 2. Those responsible for implementing Kariba resettlement allowed the local council to influence, and even set policy, when they formulated a ten-point agenda that included such issues as not being forced to change agricultural techniques and allowing resettlers the future option of building homesteads along the edge of the reservoir and utilizing the drawdown area as they had previously utilized the banks of the rising and falling Zambezi. In China, although young people may prefer to switch from farming to employment in village industries, they and their elders nonetheless desire to retain sufficient land to meet their annual needs for grain staples (Scudder field notes).

Helping restore certain aspects of their previous economies, kin and social networks, and belief systems does not mean that new opportunities cannot be introduced. Indeed, they must be introduced if the majority are to become beneficiaries. What is needed is an appropriate balance between continuity and change so as to avoid Cernea's marginalization and social disarticulation risks. That balance can be expected to vary from one project to another and, within a particular project area, from one community and one society to another. It can also be expected to vary over time as the majority of resettlers become willing to take risks in the third stage of community formation and economic development. For such risk-taking to occur, the type of opportunities that are discussed in this chapter must be available.

INCOME GENERATION AND RAISING LIVING STANDARDS

Economic development and improving living standards following physical removal have been found to be the most difficult tasks to implement. Lack of success applies to World Bank-funded projects as well as to others. As stated by the World Bank's 1986–1993 review of its projects involving involuntary resettlement, 'although the data are weak, projects appear often not to have succeeded in re-establishing resettlers at a better or equal living standard and that unsatisfactory performance still persists on a wide scale' (1994a, px). Subsequent Bank reports have made the same point, with the Bank acknowledging in its 2001 *Involuntary Resettlement* that 'the record on restoring – let alone improving – incomes has been unsatisfactory' (2001, p9).

For success to occur emphasis must be placed on making resettlers project beneficiaries. This requires the careful planning and implementation of a wide range of opportunities, including land and water, farming and non-farming, and rural and urban development opportunities. Over-reliance on a single option, or even several options, is a mistake. Such over-reliance does not mirror the type of diversified production systems that pre-project resettlers had and which they will attempt to achieve as a means for raising their living standards. It is also risky since new opportunities, even important ones such as commercial irrigation and non-farming employment, depend on external factors such as pricing policies, availability of inputs and jobs, and finding and getting produce to markets over which resettlers, newly incorporated within a wider political economy, have little control.

For resettling farming households, the most important single requirement of a project authority is to make available arable land with legally valid property rights for such households whether previously they were legal owners, users of commons, leaseholders, sharecroppers or agricultural labourers. Unlike jobs, land can be passed on from one generation to another. This fact is often forgotten by planners and project authorities whose concept of time is more focused on the shorter construction timetable. Moreover, arable land is a life-sustaining resource upon which resettlers can fall back when other opportunities such as commercial and industrial ventures fail and jobs are lost.

Not all rural households, however, are farmers – another fact that is often ignored. Chuta and Liedholm, for example, note that 'one fifth or more of the rural labor force is primarily engaged in nonfarm activities' in the large majority of the 18 late-industrializing countries that they surveyed (1979, pp3–4). The proportion for India was 20 per cent, for Indonesia 24 per cent and for the Philippines 28 per cent. It would be higher in China because of the development of village industries. The World Bank's *Rural Enterprise and Nonfarm Employment* (1978a) presents a similar picture, noting that non-farming activities provide the primary source of earnings and employment to the labour force when rural towns are included, with over half of non-farming employment in Africa as well as Asia being in rural areas.

These publications by Chuta and Liedholm and the World Bank cover the 1970s. In regions where incomes have been rising since then, as in India's Punjab or in Eastern China since the initiation of the responsibility system, the proportion of non-farming employment can be expected to be higher. In the mid-1980s, for example, I found over 50 per cent of the village population in two Yangtze River Basin villages employed in rural industries. The desirability of such a trend is the reason why planners need to consider as wide a range of opportunities as possible, with special emphasis on those that can be expected to have significant multiplier effects and to integrate rural and urban enterprises (through agro-processing, for example) within the same area.

ECONOMIC DEVELOPMENT OPPORTUNITIES

Introduction

Drawing on specific examples, the range of opportunities that could be made available to resettling communities is discussed along with problems that must be overcome. Although the record shows that it is possible for resettlers to become project beneficiaries, this seldom happens. All projects discussed in this chapter have problems, the nature of which can be expected to increase with time as available land and other resources become scarcer, as host communities become more densely populated, and as communities of resettlers become more heterogeneous. For such reasons, future water resources and energy development decision-making must pay more attention to a wider range of options including those that do not force communities to resettle and, where resettlement is unavoidable, involve resettlers as co-project managers and shareholders.

Resettlers and other affected people as shareholders and co-project managers

Joint ventures with affected people as shareholders

Currently being pioneered in Canada between project authorities and Native Americans, joint ventures between affected people and project authorities are the way to go if a more equitable development process is to occur. Joint projects also provide an important approach for ensuring not just participation but also consent, hence eliminating expected conflicts over future dams. In the case of the Minashtuk Hydro Project in Canada, Hydro-Quebec and the Band Council of the Montagnais of Lac Saint-Jean formed a limited partnership, owning 49.9 per cent and 50.1 per cent of the shares, respectively. Operational since May 2000, the project involves a run-of-the-river facility with an installed capacity of 9.9 MW. It is owned by the Minashtuk Limited Partnership Company which sells all electricity generated to Hydro-Quebec for a 20-year period that is extendable for another 20 years. A total of 75 per cent of project funding came from a long-term bank loan, with Hydro-Ilnu (owned by the Band Council that represents a population of about 4600 Native Americans) 'mandated to conduct the feasibility studies, obtain all the governmental authorizations, have the project built under a turnkey contract and operate the facility' (Egré et al, 2002, p57). In addition to profit sharing, the joint venture 'allows the Montagnais to design a project according to their priorities and in the long-term reinvest the profits in a manner that supports the economic development of their community' (WCD, 2000, p257, footnote 11).

For the Montagnais/Hydro-Quebec approach to work, governments must be willing to acknowledge community rights to their land and water resources. While the situation in many African countries where the State owns the land poses a major constraint, the joint venture is an option that warrants increasing attention as a rights-based approach. This approach has also been recommended by the World Bank-required independent panel of environment and resettlement experts (the panel or POE) for the development of fisheries, reserves and tourism in the Lesotho Highlands Water Project.

Affected people as co-project managers

Co-project management involves giving resettlers responsibility for using at least some funds available for the resettlement process or giving them access to funds derived from project revenue. In the case of Brazil's Ita Dam, one community to which funds were allocated was able to build larger houses and a larger warehouse at a lower cost than was the case with project-managed building in another community (Bermann, 1999). Reynolds, as a result of his involvement in the Lesotho Highlands Water Project's *Organization and*

Manpower Study, recommended that the management of resettlement funds be handed over to the resettling communities, while the Lesotho Highlands Development Authority (LHDA) POE suggested that the Reynolds approach be piloted in the 'Muela reservoir basin. While both recommendations were considered too ambitious and risky, subsequently a policy was approved and implemented whereby compensation funds for loss of communal resources would be placed in community trusts for local management once an institutional structure, in the form of a cooperative, is set up (Maema and Reynolds, 1995).

Two cases in which project revenue is available for use by local communities involve national policies in Brazil and in China. In Brazil a portion of project revenue from Itaipu, Tucurui and other dams is shared with the municipalities whose land is inundated, while in China a portion of revenue from energy sales goes into a remaining problems fund to which resettlers can apply for credit.

Irrigation and associated multiplier effects

Introduction

Direct and indirect benefits of a well-planned and implemented irrigation scheme are one of the most important opportunities that can be provided by a large dam for raising the living standards of large numbers of rural resettlers, hosts and members of other local communities. The importance of that statement for resettler welfare requires elaboration. While not all large dams have an irrigation component, 'Half of the world's large dams were built exclusively or primarily for irrigation' (WCD, 2000, p13), including the majority of large dams in Africa and Asia. Although estimates vary according to the bias of the gatherer of statistics, estimates used by WCD state that '30–40% of irrigated land worldwide now relies on dams' (ibid, pxxix). Yet only rarely have project authorities emphasized the opportunity that resettlement with irrigation provides for raising living standards.

A total of 23 of the 46 dams dealt with in the 50 dam survey had a significant irrigation component. Yet in only three cases (13 per cent)[1] was a serious attempt made to integrate a majority of resettlers within the project's irrigated command area. All three were among the minority of cases in the 50 dam survey (18 per cent) for which living standards were either improved or restored.

Attempts, all inadequate, were made in six other cases (26 per cent) to provide resettlers with some irrigated land. In four of those cases,[2] a small minority of resettlers was resettled in the project's command area. While command area resettlement also occurred in Pakistan's Tarbela case, only one-third of resettlers were considered eligible to receive replacement land. Not only was land received after displacement occurred (Asianics Agro-Dev International, 2000, pxi), but half of the land to be allocated was in another province that subsequently refused to allocate 65 per cent of the land designated. Those who did receive land had difficulties integrating themselves into a more arid area (Sind Province) differing in social organization and culture. Conditions were even more difficult in the case of India's Pong Dam where the resettlement policy was to send resettlers receiving land to the problem-prone Rajasthan Canal Project in a dissimilar desert environment in another state. Hari Mohan Mathur sums up the situation by stating 'The plain fact is that the area selected to resettle the displacees ... was simply not liveable at that point in time' (1995, p11). Furthermore, over 15 years after inundation, 'only 5814 out of 16,000 eligible persons could actually get allotments of land for their resettlement in Rajastan ... even those few who got allotments have not lived in peace' (ibid, p14). As for the remaining 14 cases (61 per cent), receipt of irrigated land was not a resettlement policy option.

The sections that follow cover four main topics. The first reviews briefly the benefits and costs of irrigation to society, with emphasis on large dam-supplied irrigation schemes. The second deals with dam-supplied irrigation's potential as a resettlement opportunity that enables farmers to pursue globally consistent development strategies. The third emphasizes that enabling those strategies requires irrigation to provide both direct and indirect benefits, the indirect benefits being potentially the most important. The fourth and last section deals with the way forward if resettlers are to benefit from large dam-supplied irrigation.

The benefits and costs of irrigation

The future need for irrigation places society in a dilemma. On the one hand, irrigation's importance as a provider of food for an expanding world population is expected to grow during the present century. Already irrigation is used in the production of 40 per cent of the world's food supply (Postel, 1996, p15). According to Vermillion and Merrey at the International Water Management Institute, over the next 30 years 80 per cent of 'the additional required food supply will have to be produced on irrigated land' (1998, p166). On the other hand, society has yet to deal effectively with irrigation's adverse environmental impacts and with its consumption of 60–70 per cent of the world's increasingly scarce water resources.

The bias of governments toward large dams involves a built-in bias toward large-scale irrigation projects as opposed to other options. By 1998, large dams were supplying water to 30–40 per cent of the 271 million hectares estimated to be under irrigation (WCD, 2000, p137). The large majority of such irrigation is gravity flow with or without conjunctive pumping of groundwater, as used in Northwest India and in Pakistan. Where inland gradients allow, pumping from a reservoir provides a less frequent option. A current example is the Grand Coulee Dam on the Columbia River in which hydropower is used to pump reservoir water to serve a left bank irrigation area. A future example, now under construction, is Egypt's Toshka Project where current plans are to irrigate eventually over 200,000ha of land by pumping water from Lake Nubia.

There are major costs to society of this large dam-supplied irrigation bias in addition to increased resettlement and adverse environmental impacts.

Agricultural budgets have favoured large-scale irrigation not just at the expense of millions of farmers dependent on small-scale, community-oriented irrigation, but also at the expense of rain-fed agriculture. There have also been costs to large dam-supplied irrigation farmers themselves. One is a reduction in food grain prices of about 50 per cent since the 1960s. This is especially disadvantageous to small-scale farmers in countries where government policy – as with Sri Lanka's Mahaweli Project – stresses food self-sufficiency, because cropping of food grains such as rice and wheat can no longer be assumed to help farmers move beyond subsistence. Small farmers also are apt to lose out to larger farmers, as in India, in the competition for large dam-supplied irrigation.

Working out a balance between rain-fed and irrigated agriculture will not be easy. The same applies to the balance between small-scale and large-scale irrigation. Although their proportional importance will vary from nation to nation, both are needed and both are problem-prone. In arid and semi-arid lands and in monsoon climates such as in India where rainfall is concentrated in a few months, large dams remain an important option for providing storage since small-scale reservoirs such as tanks dry up in South Asia during drought years. Per unit of irrigable land served, small-scale reservoirs also inundate more land than would be the case with deeper reservoirs.[3] In addition small reservoirs have higher rates of evaporation and are more threatened by siltation, with community-supported maintenance requiring annual de-silting at a time when local communities are becoming more heterogeneous. As a result, there is a real risk of being unable to mobilize the labour necessary for tank and small-scale irrigation system maintenance.

Dam-supplied irrigation as a resettlement opportunity

Adequate implementation of a dam-supplied irrigation scheme can provide not only improved housing and social services but also sufficient income to allow farming families to diversify their household economy into a range of higher value farming and non-farming activities. There are major problems to be overcome, however, if first and second generation resettlers are to benefit. Major problems are threefold: environmental, institutional and technical, and distributional. Archaeologists and historians consider the degradation of irrigated lands caused by increasing salinity and water logging as a major cause for the decline of civilizations in arid lands in the Indus, Tigris and Euphrates Valleys as well as in the desert fringe of Peru and for the possible decline of classic Maya civilization in Central America. While installation of appropriate drains and the conjunctive use of groundwater with dam-supplied surface water have reduced salinity and water logging problems, they have not eliminated them. According to a former International Water Management Institute (IWMI) Director General, more land may be currently going out of cultivation as a result of land degradation than is being reclaimed (Seckler, 1996). And where dams are involved, siltation threatens their sustainability, with reservoir storage capacity on the average reduced by 0.5–1 per cent per annum.

Institutional and technical constraints have been more responsible for the failure of irrigation to meet expected targets than has been the case with other components of dam projects such as power generation. The WCD ascertained that the extent of the area planned for irrigation development, as opposed to the area actually irrigated, has fallen short of expectations. In addition to not meeting physical targets, 'Large irrigation dams have typically ... failed to recover their costs, and have been less profitable in economic terms than expected' (WCD, 2000, pp42–43). The causes are both institutional and technical. They include overcentralized system management linked to inadequate cooperation and water management relationships with, and among, farmers; inadequate infrastructure for water distribution; poor land preparation; inadequate financing for operation and maintenance as opposed to construction; inadequate soil surveys; overestimation of water supplies; poor drainage; overoptimistic assumptions relating to recommended farming systems; and major construction delays.

Major delays in completing irrigation infrastructure create special hardships for resettlers, with many Mahaweli settlers having to wait two or more years to receive their first irrigation water. In the case of some Sardar Sarovar resettlers, that delay now exceeds ten years. Distributional problems relate to inadequate water for those at the end of the irrigation system ('bottom enders') and the ability of larger farmers to manipulate the distribution of water to their own advantage.

The main victims of environmental, institutional and technical constraints are national consumers and irrigation farmers. Irrigated agriculture is hard work from which farming households expect reasonable returns. Where expectations are not met, farming families often reallocate labour to other activities with a presumed higher value, with on-farm crop production used to satisfy family food requirements. The Accelerated Mahaweli Project is an example of this, as are large-scale irrigation projects in the Sudan that draw their water from the Nile and the Atbara. As for distributional constraints, the tendency has been to benefit wealthier host farmers or immigrants rather than those undergoing resettlement.

If large dam irrigation is to realize its potential as a mechanism to improve resettler living standards, all three major constraints require much more attention. This includes not just a commitment to extend irrigation benefits to resettlers, but also to complete irrigation infrastructure on adequate soils with proper drainage; to provide water in the proper amounts at the proper time to bottom enders as well as top enders; and to integrate effectively farmer institutions into operation and management. These are necessary but not sufficient requirements. Without an appropriate pricing and marketing system involving appropriate terms of trade, the potential for the irrigation component to help resettlers become project beneficiaries and to achieve major multiplier effects will not be fulfilled.

Multiplier effects of dam-supplied irrigation[4]

Introduction

The dynamism of resettler investment strategies worldwide (Chapter 2) is why it is so important to assess the extent to which well-planned and implemented irrigation schemes can provide the type of multipliers that will allow farming families to diversity their household economies into higher value farming and non-farming activities.

Multipliers in this case apply to the indirect and induced benefits of an irrigation project that are defined as linkages between irrigation outputs and the rest of the economy. Indirect benefits refer to backward and forward production linkages such as the purchase of fertilizers and farming equipment. Induced changes would include changes in food prices and income expenditure patterns and their impact on the overall economy.

A long-held planning assumption has been that there is no need to assess the indirect and induced benefits of a given infusion of capital because they can be expected to be the same for different development initiatives. While that may be the case under conditions of full employment and normal price fluctuations, neither condition applies to late-industrializing countries in which the largest number of new dams will be built. Whether in China, India or Turkey or in countries throughout Africa, Latin America and the Middle East, unemployment and underemployment are serious problems. In addition, prices for major food grains have halved since the 1960s and 1970s. Furthermore, case studies show that different multiplier effects are associated with different development inputs. Water resource development projects have been associated with higher multipliers. I would expect the same to be the case with agricultural research, education (with special emphasis on that of women) and public health.

Multipliers are expressed as the ratio of total impacts of an irrigation project to its direct impacts. An early study involved Malaysia's medium-sized Muda irrigation project, where double cropping of rice during the 1967–1974 period produced a multiplier of 1.83 (Bell et al, 1982). Of the 83 cents of indirect and induced impacts generated per dollar spent on the project, 33 cents came from indirect production linkages and 50 cents came from induced impacts related mainly to the increased purchasing power of farming families. In addition to noting the Muda example, the World Bank's Task Force on Multiplier Effects prepared four case studies. Three dealt with large dams associated with large irrigation projects: Brazil's Sobradinho Dam, Egypt's Aswan High Dam, and India's Bhakra Dam. The fourth, also discussed below, dealt with two check dams in India's Bunga Village that together irrigated 250ha. Although all four studies produced significant multipliers, the indirect and induced effects were highest for the Sobradinho and Bhakra Dams.[5]

Multipliers are calculated through the use of multisectoral models that can be applied to countries, states within a country, regions or locales. The two principal models are input–output models based on input–output tables or social accounting matrices (SAMs) and computable general equilibrium (CGE) models. For the World Bank's 2003 study of dam-induced multipliers, the

Brazilian study relied mainly on a 1992 input–output model of the Northeast region complemented by analysis of a 1995 national level SAM disaggregated to the regional level. The Bhakra Dam study relied on an extended SAM-based input–output model for the state of Punjab, whereas a GCE model of the Egyptian economy was used for the Aswan High Dam.

In dealing with such case studies, three important caveats are necessary. The first is that all such studies suffer from data limitations that require various assumptions to be made. For this reason, what I find of interest is the comparison between the different cases and the possible reasons for the differences, rather than the specific ratio that is derived from what data is available. The second, discussed below under the check dam case, is that small-scale irrigation projects are also associated with significant multipliers for village farmers. The third is that the magnitude of the multipliers noted should not be construed as an argument favouring large dams as a development option. The purpose of the discussion is purely to illustrate that a dam-supplied irrigation project that is associated with multipliers can be, and should be, an important source of farming and non-farming employment and enterprise development for resettler households. Multipliers can also be negative. That is especially the case with environmental multipliers because mainstream dams can have adverse impacts on deltas that are irreversible.

Brazil's Sobradinho Dam

The Brazil study produced the largest multipliers, with values ranging from 2.1 to 2.28 'depending on the assumptions regarding hydropower generation and irrigation area contraction under the "without project" scenarios' (Scatasta, 2003, p46). Of greatest importance are 'income–expenditure induced effects'. The study focuses on the Médio sub-basin of the São Francisco River Basin that contains the Sobradinho Dam as well as the Itaparica Dam. Irrigation received special emphasis, with Sobradinho providing irrigation to 72,000ha.

In explaining her preliminary conclusions, Scatasta was especially impressed with irrigation's record 'which presented the same level of dynamism demonstrated by metropolitan regions' in Brazil's North East (ibid, p26). This, she concludes, is largely linked to 'the switch to higher-value crops, mainly for export, and their link with agro-processing business' (ibid). Starting in the 1980s, farmers switched to vegetables and fruits as major crops, with the total area planted with fruits and coconuts being nearly 100,000ha within the basin and growing, on average, at 9000ha annually. The irrigation area immediately below the dam is especially important 'accounting for 80% per cent of Brazil's grape exports and for 70% of mango exports, with its products headed primarily for Europe and the U.S.A.' (ibid, p30).

In terms of enterprise development, especially important was the planners' incorporation of irrigated areas within the same agro-industrial development districts (*pólos*), with inter-industry linkages larger 'when food processing is treated as a directly affected sector' (ibid, p46). As for employment generation, irrigation was by far the lowest cost generator of new jobs when compared with nine other activities, including the auto industry, construction, pulp and paper, and wood processing.[6] Few of Sobradinho's 70,000 rural and urban resettlers would have been major beneficiaries of this development, however, since Sobradinho was yet another case where no attempt was made to incorporate resettlers within an irrigation scheme and little or no compensation was received.

India's Bhakra Dam

The Bhakra Dam was completed in 1963 as a multipurpose project and as the first dam in the Bhakra System that links through inter-basin transfers all three of the Indus River tributaries allotted to India under the World Bank-mediated 1960 Indus Water Treaty with Pakistan. Once complete, the Bhakra system was able to irrigate 3.5 million hectares in three states, with canal seepage estimated to allow a doubling of the number of tube wells in use outside the canal-irrigated area. As part of the World Bank's Task Force on Multiplier Effects, Bhatia and Malik focused on the impact of the Bhakra Dam on the regional economy of the state of Punjab, which receives nearly half of the water from the Bhakra system.

Their analysis[7] drew on an input–output study (Bhalla et al, 1990) of the Punjab economy for a 12-month period in 1979–1980. Estimated multipliers ranged from 1.78 to 1.90 'depending on the assumptions regarding the impact of canals on groundwater availability' (Bhatia and Malik, 2003, p44). Estimated from the project's agricultural and energy sectors, they included 'the effects of inter-industry linkages as well as the consumption-induced effects' (ibid, p4). As expected, the project had 'its biggest impact on the output of agricultural commodities, especially the output of wheat, paddy, cotton, and oilseeds' (ibid). Since the major crops were low value food grains, presumably multipliers would have been even higher for higher value, locally processed crops. And, as the authors emphasize, they would have been much higher if they had included remittances from an agricultural labour force that came mainly from two poorer states and involved nearly 400,000 labourers during the lean season and double that number during the period of peak activity. The project also played a role in reducing the percentage of the Punjab's rural population living below the poverty line to 6.35 per cent as opposed to an all-India figure of 27.09 per cent (ibid, Table 5). In 2000–2001 Punjab contributed 39 per cent of the food grains acquired by the Government of India for use in its national 'Food for Work' programme.

In this case, the authors report that 30 per cent of resettler families requested resettlement in the Bhakra command area where they received 13,200 acres and were resettled in 30 villages (ibid, p55). The total number of resettler households was estimated at 7500 families, 5027 of which received cash compensation for self-resettlement.

The Bhakra multipliers are impressive. The project, however, is not without major environmental and social problems. According to a 1999 report from the International Water Management Institute, '[i]n the Bhakra Irrigation System, the practice of allocating and distributing canal water supplies ... leads to the current high productivity of water. The long-term sustainability of agricultural productivity seems threatened, however. In some areas, saline water tables are rising, and soils are becoming sodic, while in areas that have fresh groundwater, water tables are falling. There is an urgent need for the irrigation agency to thoroughly examine water management problems on the farm, regionally, and systemwide' (Sakthivadivel et al, 1999, pp20–21).

There is also a dam-induced flood management problem. As recently documented in connection with the Kariba and Cahora Bassa Dams on the Zambezi, sudden releases of large flows from dams can have devastating impacts on downstream communities and especially on those who, believing themselves protecting by a dam, have moved onto previously flooded alluvial soils. In the Bhakra case, McCully writes 'In 1978 nearly 65,000 people in the Punjab were made homeless by floods exacerbated by forced discharges from Bhakra Dam... Eleven years later a similar flood occurred' (McCully, 2001, p147). More difficult to assess, but required for a broader impact analysis of Indian and Pakistani dams in the Indus basin, would be the relative role of each dam in reducing the biological productivity of the Indus delta at the expense of hundreds of thousands of residents.

The very success of the irrigation component also may involve adverse socio-economic effects for small-scale farmers. Bhatia and Malik mention increased combine harvesting and the sinking of private boreholes and sale of water. This suggests that the number of pre-project farming units have decreased while, with the project, the area per household and percentage of wealthier farming families have increased at the expense of marginal and small farming households. Bhakra resettlement also remains problem-prone. Nearly 40 years after the dam's completion, at least 784 resettler families remain to be rehabilitated according to the government's own assessment (*The Tribune*, 2001).

The Indian case study of the Bunga check dams
The World Bank's Bunga case study is important because it shows that water resource development projects can have important multipliers regardless of scale. While large dam-produced multipliers benefit urban and rural residents alike when built for electricity generation and irrigation, the main multipliers associated with small dams go to the villagers who construct and maintain them. Sites for large dams are far fewer than sites for small ones. In most countries large dams also serve a smaller proportion of the low-income rural population. That is why far more attention should be paid to a better balance between large-scale dams and small-scale village projects, a balance that should favour the latter when poverty alleviation is the major goal.

The Bunga case study is located in the Shivalik Range of Haryana where 102 community-managed water harvesting structures were built in 60 villages during the 1976–1999 period. Facilitated by an Indian activist and the Ford Foundation, the check dams 'have contributed significantly to the increase in income to villagers and others around these villages' (Malik and Bhatia, 2003, p5). These are not the only benefits. Others include reduction of rainy season village flooding from upper catchment heavy runoff, reduction in erosion caused by catchment protection, and, at least in the Bunga case, a raised water table that allowed the introduction of tube wells. Although not mentioned, in this region where small rivers dry up after seasonal rainfall stops, such check dams might also restore perennial flows in some rivers for the benefit of downstream users. Such an outcome would depend, however, on how much water was utilized for irrigation in upper basins; Perry pointing out that a large number of upriver water harvesting schemes could also reduce seasonal and perennial flows downstream (2000 personal communication).

Bunga is a relatively small village of 178 families with a total population of about 1100. Malik and Bhatia's study of 'with' and 'without' check dam scenarios drew heavily on a detailed analysis of household economies during the 2001–2002 season by researchers from the University of California, Davis. Two check dams were built in the mid-1980s. Both would be classified by ICOLD as large, with one being 15m in height and the other 16m. Malik and Bhatia's multiplier value was 1.41.

Of importance among direct and indirect impacts were creation of a more complex production system at household and village level; significant increases in food crop yields; first cultivation of fodder crops for stall feeding, with buffalo numbers more than doubling; more apparent production–consumption interactions; regional interaction in regard to inputs and outputs (especially the sale of milk); and more employment for landless households.[8] Especially relevant in regard to poverty alleviation was the conclusion that marginal and small farmers increased their incomes by a greater percentage than medium and large farming households. Environmental benefits were several. Agreement to stall-feed large livestock allowed forest planting in the catchment and grazing control. Impoundment of monsoon rainfall raised groundwater levels to the extent that seven households purchased the first tube wells with sale of extra water benefiting a larger number of families.

Management functions were the responsibility of a village-level Hill Resources Management Society. Income received also allowed improvement of the local school with the result that literacy rates improved. A village tube well was installed for providing drinking water, while street maintenance and that of a pond for watering livestock were also financed, as was restoration of the village temple.

The major problem, and it is a problem elsewhere with similar projects, is siltation. Both dams are at risk, with siltation gradually reducing the extent of the area irrigated (which at best only served part of the population). This problem has in turn had an adverse effect on cooperative behaviour within the Hills Resources Management Society, lack of which once again has put the catchment at risk. Prior to the colonial era in India and in the drier zones of Sri Lanka, cascades of such check dams and tanks were desilted and maintained on an annual basis. Through neglect, increasing siltation apparently now exceeds village capacities. That, according to Bhatia (personal communication), is the problem now with the Bunga Dams. Given the seriousness of the problem both here and elsewhere, what is needed – in addition to research on the nature of the problem, how to cope with it technically and the finances required – is an approach involving local communities cooperating with outside government, NGOs and research agencies.

Other case studies
Other case studies of irrigation projects supplied by large dams deal mainly with more qualitative data on employment generation and enterprise development. Egypt's Kom Ombo Project served by the Aswan High Dam has provided employment opportunities for thousands of non-Nubian sharecroppers and labourers. The counterpart irrigation project (served by the specially built Atbara Dam) for High Dam Nubian resettlers living in the Sudan has contributed to the diversification of the local economy with 'a consequent favourable effect on the industrial development and employment of the Khashm el-Girba region' (Agouba, 1979, p42).

In 1978 the total population on the Khashm el-Girba scheme was estimated at 336,000 during the peak agricultural season, of which 216,000 were members of farming families living on approximately 19,300 tenancies, 50,000 were permanent or semi-permanent farm labourers, and 70,000 were seasonal labourers. Assuming half of farming family members to be children, the number of hired labour was at least equal to the number of adult settlers. The scheme was also served by a new town with an estimated population of 35,000 in which El-Tayeb's 1981 survey data indicated there were approximately 0.64 permanent non-farming jobs and 0.50 seasonal non-farming jobs for each agricultural tenancy. Throughout the scheme he estimated that there were approximately 1400 non-farming businesses.[9] Other case studies that indicate a significant increase in non-farming employment and enterprise development following irrigation development involve Indonesia's Metro project in Sumatra, Kenya's Mwea project and Peru's San Lorenzo project.

More quantitative in regard to employment generation was Wimaladharma's study of four irrigated settlement schemes in Sri Lanka (1982). In three cases non-farming employment was approximately 50 per cent of farming employment. The major exception was the Minneriya scheme that is generally considered to be the most successful settlement scheme in the country. There non-farming employment was 50 per cent greater than farming employment. The difference between the schemes Wimaladharma attributed to more reliable water supplies, better service and support facilities, larger agricultural and household allotments, and higher household incomes at Minneriya. There settlers pioneered during the 1970s the cultivation of higher value crops such as chillies, onions and tobacco and diversified their household economies into non-farming activities. Increased consumption of pumps, two wheel tractors and other farming equipment, household furnishings, children's toys, clothing and other goods and services in turn helped support what may well be the most dynamic rural town in the Sri Lankan dry zone.

The way forward

Introduction

The way forward will not be easy since incorporating resettlers within project-supplied irrigation must overcome a range of difficulties. Especially difficult are institutional hurdles and opposition from host populations and immigrants. Another major problem occurs where resettlers must not only learn new techniques to grow what may be new crops, but do so in an unfamiliar environment occupied by a different host population. For such reasons, priority should be given to rehabilitating inefficient irrigation schemes before new dam-supplied schemes are built.

Where dams are built another priority is to emphasize smaller dams, including the type of check dams discussed under the Bunga case study. Not only would smaller dams reduce the number of resettlers, but they could also be expected to have better returns. According to WCD, 'dams with heights less than 30 meters and reservoir areas of less than 10 km^2 tended to be closer to the predicted targets and demonstrated less variability for command area development, actual irrigated area and actual crop intensity' (WCD, 2000, p44). In the Commission's sub-sample of 52 irrigation projects, all of those 'below 90% of area and intensity targets were larger than 10 km^2 and higher than 30 meters' (ibid).

Dealing with institutional constraints

Dams whose primary purpose is irrigation tend to be planned and executed by irrigation ministries as in India or ministries of water resources as in China. Unless overseen by a higher authority such as the office of the prime minister or a policy-making interagency panel with political clout and funds, critical agricultural issues including soil surveys, cropping strategies and market potential tend to be underemphasized, not to mention the usual risks of overemphasis on the construction phase and underemphasis on project operation and maintenance and farmer involvement.

Dealing with host populations and immigrants

Another major constraint is a large host population in the irrigation command area. It is not accidental that all three of the successful irrigation projects in the 50 dam survey analysed in Chapter 3 were built in unsettled or sparsely settled areas of Egypt and Sri Lanka. As populations continue to increase, fewer such areas can be found. In more heavily populated areas, host opposition should be anticipated as a major constraint for incorporating resettlers. In Mexico, the intention of the Cerro de Oro project authority to utilize the command area immediately below the dam for resettlement was thwarted by large land owners in the host population. Politically influential immigrants, including corporations, large land owners, government officials and politicians can pose a problem for the host population as well. Examples include the eviction of hosts in Mauritania by dominant government elites following the completion of the upriver Manantali Dam, with a similar situation occurring in South Africa when Zulu elites moved into the Makatini irrigation project below the Pongolapoort Dam and in Somalia where elites sought command area land in the Juba River valley in anticipation of the Baardeera Dam being built.

To deal with such constraints, project authorities need to develop, and be ready to enforce, two sets of policies. The first is to give priority for irrigation waters to host populations and resettlers, as has occurred with many Sri Lankan irrigation schemes including the Accelerated Mahaweli Project. The second is to set a legal ceiling on the amount of irrigated land per household and to have the political will and ability to enforce it. Implementation of a well-planned irrigation scheme can be expected to double yields under a single-cropping system and quadruple them where double cropping is expected. Although India has land ceiling laws, the political will to enforce them does not exist. China, on the other hand, does have an enforceable policy for ensuring that hosts share irrigated lands with resettlers. Here it is important to keep in mind that irrigation agriculture is hard work, with the second generation of successful farmers often preferring non-farming occupations. While the Government of Gujarat claimed that there was insufficient land in the command area under the Sardar Sarovar Dam for resettlers from the two upstream states, in fact there was a significant number of large land owners who were willing to sell land with one purpose being to obtain funds for furthering the non-farming careers of their children.

Facilitating the shift of resettlers to areas under irrigation command
Worldwide, a majority of resettlers prefer to remain in a familiar habitat settled by familiar people. That is why so often they choose to resettle within the reservoir basin. Not only should they be allowed to do so, provided life support opportunities exist and will be made available, but project authorities should also assess the type of difficulties that can be expected should policies advocate, and resettlers accept, command area resettlement. Host opposition is to be expected, as is competition over common property resources, new health problems and a need for a strong agricultural extension programme.

The best way to deal with the host–resettler problem is to fully incorporate the host population into whatever development plans are implemented. Otherwise it is logical for the host population to resist encroachment on their land resources, social services and employment opportunities. The common property problem can be especially difficult if the resettlers have been dependent on large areas of common property for grazing and foraging. Such resources can be expected to be scarce in command areas, so ways to address such scarcity need to be incorporated within project planning. Especially in tropical countries, increased irrigation-associated risks of malaria and schistosomiasis must be anticipated and dealt with through appropriate medical services. The same applies to a wide range of water-borne and other diseases and parasites that can be expected when population densities are increased, as they usually are in command area communities. Especially important is provision of adequate supplies of potable water. To help resettlers adjust to new agricultural systems and techniques, extension must be targeted at both women and men. And all planning, starting with assessing resettlement location preferences, must be fully participatory.

Rain-fed agriculture

Wherever possible some irrigation should be made available to resettlers, including irrigation for both field crops and home lots. That does not mean, however, that rain-fed agriculture should be neglected, including the possibility of supplemental irrigation for rain-fed crops. As with irrigation, it is important not to overemphasize a single crop. Whether coping with poverty or trying to further develop an upward trending lifestyle, the global experience is that settlers favour diversified household production systems that include both farming and non-farming occupations. The benefits of such diversified production systems extend beyond risk-aversion and/or income generation because they also give both spouses as well as children and other dependents the opportunity to contribute in various ways to the household economy and to their own status within the household.

In Asia, Africa and Latin America, rain-fed tree crops have been able to improve resettler livelihoods. In Thailand, what are probably the two most successful resettler outcomes are associated with a farming system based on rubber that planners implemented in connection with the Bang Lang and Rajjaprabha Dams (Suwanmontri, 1996, 1999a, 1999b). The Rajjaprabha case is especially instructive for illustrating the potential of tree crops to raise living standards. At the time of commissioning in 1987, 385 families had been resettled. Pre-project incomes had been obtained in the mid-1980s from 165 of those households. Ten years later net incomes controlled for inflation had nearly quintupled because of rubber sales and were much higher than those of 112 households that were surveyed that same year in a neighbouring non-affected village. They were also equivalent to provincial incomes in spite of the higher incomes of urban households.

In addition to provision of a good cash crop, the Rajjaprabha case illustrates a number of other best practices. The project authority (the Electricity Generating Authority of Thailand or EGAT) was also responsible for planning and implementing resettlement through its Relocation and Resettlement Construction Division. Careful soil surveys were completed and the resettlement site was located within 4km of the dam site with electricity and water provided. A living allowance was provided while the rubber trees were maturing. Plans complemented rubber with other agricultural and non-farming opportunities. Farming opportunities included poultry farming and cultivation of fruit trees and vegetables, while an agricultural cooperative and credit facilities were provided. Non-farming opportunities included training programmes including 'training in reservoir fishery work' (Suwanmontri, 1999b, p13).

On the other hand, the resettlement process must have been particularly stressful for the resettlers. It was non-participatory, Suwanmontri relating that fact to communal strife involving communist groups that attacked project camps, although EGAT has been criticized for non-participatory resettlement elsewhere. Security issues and non-participatory resettlement may have been a reason why resettlers that had previously lived in 22 hamlets were aggregated into one site from which some households subsequently departed. Although EGAT was correct to hand over management responsibilities to line ministries, handing over within three years of project commissioning was too soon, with the result that roads and other infrastructure were inadequately maintained because of insufficient budgets. Halving of farm size is also likely to create a problem of sustainability for the second generation if land holdings of about 3.5ha are subdivided. At US$35,000 per household financial costs were high, presumably due in part to the security situation but also to provision of new land in addition to cash compensation for pre-project land holdings.

In the Ivory Coast's Kossou project, Laissailly-Jacob considers the most successful resettler outcomes to be associated with households cultivating coffee and cacao in the forest zone or those concentrating on fishing the reservoir behind the dam. In the 50 dam survey reported in Chapter 3, Arenal in Latin America – where the main component of the resettler's production system was coffee – was one of only three cases out to 44 where living standards had improved at the time of last data collection, although it was too early to know how sustainable they would be.

There are also cases in Asia and Latin America where tree crops have played the major role in raising the living standards of settlers on government- and private sector-sponsored land settlement schemes involving the recruitment of volunteer households. The three top performers of 34 World Bank-financed Government-sponsored settlement schemes were oil palm schemes in Malaysia and Papua New Guinea, while citrus played an important role in Peru's San Lorenzo scheme (World Bank, 1985a, p8). According to several writers, Brazil's Northern Parana scheme may well be Latin America's most successful example of regional development planning (Katzman, 1977, p53; see also Nelson, 1973, p121).

The Northern Parana case is especially interesting because of the attention paid to a range of critical variables. The project was initiated by a private development company that bought approximately 2.5 million acres in the mid-1920s in a sparsely populated frontier area. The first few years were spent completing the careful soil, hydrological and other surveys that are so crucial to the successful settlement of new lands. Plots were then sold to smallholders who received from the start secure land titles – another key requirement that all too often has been neglected in dam-induced involuntary resettlement.

With the proceeds from land sales, the company then built the necessary feeder roads as well as a railway along which they built market towns. The cropping system included coffee along with a variety of food crops. From a population of about 100,000 in 1940, the number of people increased to over a million by the mid-1960s. With 39,000 farm holdings and an urban population along the railroad that was estimated at 40–50 per cent of the total, 'it would appear that more than one non-farming job had been created for every farming job' (Scudder, 1981b, p169).

Tree crops are not without risks, however, and these should be offset by the cultivation of other crops as well as by non-farming opportunities. As Montri Suwanmontri points out (1996), net incomes drop below what they were preceding resettlement during the years before tree crops begin to produce. That was the case with both Bang Lang and Rajjaprabha. While such drops are a predictable characteristic of Stage 2 immediately following removal, they can be expected to be worse where there is no income from the main component of the farming system during the initial years of resettlement. There is also the risk of drops in producer prices where too much emphasis is placed on a single crop. That is currently the case in West Africa where an unknown proportion of smallholders are uprooting their coffee plants because of falling prices. And then there is always the problem of unexpected events such as the heavy frosts in the mid-1970s which affected 'close to 100% of the 915 million coffee trees in Parana' (Margolis, 1980, p 231).

Clearly tree crops and other rain-fed cash crops need be complemented by a range of other farming and non-farming opportunities. In Costa Rica's Arenal case, coffee was complemented by a range of household consumption crops. Smallholder dairy was also pushed by the authorities with carrying capacity increased by the introduction of a new fodder crop. Wherever possible, irrigation should be provided for resettler home lots as is the intention for the 6000 people to be resettled in connection with Laos' NT2 project. That will allow households to grow a range of crops included a small plot of paddy, fruit trees and vegetables, and fodder crops. A further strength of the planned production systems at the household and community levels for NT2 resettlers are drawdown farming and grazing, reservoir fisheries, wage labour and community-based social forestry.

Reservoir drawdown utilization synchronized with managed floods

Most large dams are built to regularize the annual regimes of natural rivers by reducing flows during the flood season and increasing them during times of decreased rainfall and inflow. Especially in climates with seasonal rainfall, demand for electricity, and water for irrigation and urban consumption, increase significantly as the dry season progresses. Where built for flood management, it is also important to draw down reservoirs before the commencement of the next rainy season. As a result of increased outflows after the end of higher rainfall periods or when reservoir inflows are less than outflows, reservoir levels drop. The zone between the annual high and low reservoir levels is called the drawdown zone. Although its extent varies from year to year, tens of thousands of hectares may be involved.

Dam operators can influence the commencement of reservoir drawdown and its extent by managing outflows. With access to data on inflows from upriver meteorological stations, they are also in a position to inform agricultural officials and farmers when drawdown can be expected to commence and to give a rough estimate of how many water free days can be expected at different levels. Such knowledge is important. On the one hand, it will enable extension personnel and farmers to select appropriate crops, including fodder crops, for cultivation. On the other hand, it will decrease the risk of crop loss when refilling commences. In some climatic zones, it may also be possible to combine drawdown management with the release of environmental flows for the benefit of downstream ecosystems and communities, the productivity of which had been dependent on a river's pre-dam natural regime (Chapter 7).

Benefits to be derived from utilization of the reservoir drawdown area have been one of the most overlooked opportunities by resettlement planners. Synchronized with managed floods from dams, reservoir drawdown could have benefited literally millions of resettlers and downstream residents who have been impoverished in the past by dam construction. And it could benefit millions in the future if built into the planning process and the design and operation of dams. Because of increasing awareness of the damage that dams have caused to so many downstream ecosystems, interest in environmental flows and managed floods, as well as in the decommissioning of dams, has increased in recent years. Such has not been the case, however, with drawdown utilization. As for linking reservoir drawdown and managed floods in an integrated development plan, I am aware of no examples.

Except where too steep or rocky, drawdown zones have value for agriculture and grazing by domestic stock and game at a time when both are under stress elsewhere unless irrigation is provided. That is especially true throughout much of Africa as well as in the semi-arid zones of South Asia where the drawdown area reaches its greatest extent toward the end of the dry season. The importance of such uses for resettlers and other local residents should not be underestimated. The Lake Kariba drawdown area, for example, has become the major producer of maize in the reservoir basin during recent drought years. It also supports one of the best livestock grazing areas in Zambia. Zoning is important to reduce conflicts between local users and between local users and government when planners wish to establish forest and biodiversity reserves or game ranches. Such zoning should be linked to the area immediately behind full storage level. Otherwise immigrants, in staking claims to sites for tourism, commercial fishing, game ranching and other business enterprises may deny access to adjacent stretches of drawdown which could more beneficially be used for cultivation and grazing.

The best examples of planning for drawdown utilization have been in Africa and Indonesia. In the late 1960s and during the 1970s, the UNDP-funded/FAO-implemented/host country man-made lakes research programme was interested in drawdown agriculture in connection with five major African dam projects. Only with the Aswan High Dam, however, has a national government become actively involved in an ongoing project, and there the emphasis is more on the high-cost pumping of irrigation water to scheme areas above the full storage level. On Ghana's Volta reservoir behind the dam at Akosombo, a successful pilot project involving soil surveys, cropping trials and local participation was implemented. Project funding ended in the early

1980s, however. Although the Volta River Authority's Chief Executive saw drawdown utilization as an economic development possibility (Quartey, 1988, p12), 'there was no adequate Ministry of Agriculture structure to continue assisting the project nor extend the results effectively to other resettlement and host villages along the lake shore region' (Perritt, 1988, p68). In Indonesia, planning for resettlement in connection with the Saguling and Cirata Dam projects combined drawdown cultivation with fish cage culture on the reservoir.

Why this opportunity continues to be overlooked by donors and project authorities alike is hard to understand. Leaving aside a lack of interest, which is hard to document but probably important, I suspect that institutional limitations and ignorance as well as concerns about water quality and water use are involved. Effective utilization of the drawdown area requires a range of expertise, as would its linkage to managed floods. So that farmers know when reservoir levels can be expected to drop and for how long, simple hydrological models based on recent meteorological data need to be developed and presented to farmers and extension workers at the right time. Soil surveys need be completed so that drawdown areas can be zoned for different uses such as crop agriculture, livestock management, natural resource management, wetland and other reserves, and recreation and tourism. To develop appropriate cropping systems, pilot projects are needed. So that producer prices are not adversely affected in quickly saturated local markets, improved transport and market access are necessary. What institution can be expected to play the lead role in such a programme, especially when ignorance as to its existence and benefits continues?

Concerns about water quality continue to dominate the thinking of project authorities, while those dominated by ministries of irrigation or energy are reluctant to allow water to be used for other purposes. In Swaziland the binational authority wanted to fence the entire perimeter of the reservoir formed in 2002 behind the Maguga Dam. In Indonesia cultivation of the drawdown area behind the Wonogiri Dam was prohibited 'since it is believed to carry a greater risk of farmers causing more silting, pollution and eutrophication of the reservoir' (Winarto, 1992, p460). While concerns about water quality and water use are legitimate, restrictions on use of the drawdown area by local residents is based more on a mindset imported from smaller reservoirs in Europe and the US than on project-specific surveys. Lake Kariba, for example, is nutrient poor so that the manure from grazing animals contributes to the productivity of the reservoir fishery and to a healthy grass cover that reduces the risk of siltation.

Since conditions can be expected to vary from reservoir to reservoir, whatever restrictions are placed on drawdown utilization should be based on accurate knowledge of local conditions as opposed to a misguided application of conventional wisdom. The same applies to resource hoarding by specific ministries or project authorities. In Southern Africa, for example, the existence of the Southern African Power Pool allows sub-optimization strategies where reservoirs such as Kariba could serve a number of functions rather than trying to maximize power generation or another single purpose at the expense of other development opportunities.

Because of project authorities' lack of interest in, or prohibition of, drawdown utilization, or their concentration on irrigating or otherwise developing areas above the full storage level, it has been left to resettler and host communities to pioneer drawdown use by adapting former systems of flood recession and flood rise land use to reservoirs. And this they have done in Africa, Asia, Latin America and the Middle East. In the Lake Kariba drawdown area, crop agriculture has been combined with livestock management. While the same is true with Nubian and Upper Egyptian communities along the shores of Lake Nubia, the reservoir has also become a major resource for transhumant pastoralists in the Eastern Desert, some of whom are settling down near the reservoir in the same fashion as pastoral people have settled the banks of the Nile during previous millennia.

The crops grown and other drawdown uses vary from project to project. In the Volta reservoir basin the maximum drawdown area during a 'normal' year has been estimated at over 100,000ha. Residual moisture can support cropping for 40–60 days, which can be extended by the use of small pumps drawing water from shallow wells within the drawdown area or the reservoir itself. As elsewhere, drawdown cultivation provides an important source of food and income by extending rain-fed cultivation into the dry season, with its importance increasing during periods of drought. Crops grown include important staples such as maize, rice, cassava and sweet potatoes as well as a wide range of vegetables. Once operational, the Ampaem pilot project developed under the auspices of the UNDP/FAO-supported Volta Lake Research and Development Project provided expertise to over 2000 small farmers who used supplemental irrigation to grow tomatoes as a cash crop. Following the termination of UN funding, an NGO (Catholic Relief Services) has provided support to a farmers' cooperative, including provision and maintenance of the necessary irrigation equipment (Perritt, op cit).

In Nigeria's Kainji Lake Basin, the Gungawa have adapted their pre-dam system of small-scale pump irrigation of onions to the reservoir margin (Roder, 1994). Resettlers have also pioneered a new system of land use in which they harvest a colonizing species of *Echinochloa* as fodder during the dry season and for sale to transhumant pastoralists. Secondary uses include providing thatching grass and fuel for smoking fish. As an indication of the importance of this resource for resettlers and pastoralists, Morton and Obot estimate that the total crop available is 'in excess of 110,000 t of utilizable standing crop'. Of this, 75 per cent is harvestable according to the authors' model (Morton and Obot, 1984, p694).

In Indonesia, as in Africa, resettlers have pioneered drawdown cultivation at least since the 1970s. The Wonogiri Dam is a case in point. Well suited for cultivation, the maximum drawdown zone there was 5000ha with less than a 2 per cent gradient. Yet according to Winarto not only was 'the drawdown environment excluded as a potential resource' (1992, p458), but its use was prohibited. Nonetheless local residents pioneered its use as they also did in connection with the Jatiluhur Dam in West Java (Tjitradjaja, 1997). Although government land in both cases, cultivators treat the drawdown zone as 'free land' in Winarto's words. Aware that use prohibitions are not backed up with legal regulations, they assume that the government is 'permissive of cultivation at their own risk' (op cit, p460).

Two crops a year can be grown, with local farmers experimenting with the interplanting and sole cultivation of different cash and food crops under varying soil and moisture conditions. As with flood recession agriculture along undammed rivers, a cropping sequence is used as reservoir waters recede. Buckets and small pumps are used to provide supplemental water where necessary. For the landless, cultivation of chillies and soybeans at Wonogiri provides an important source of income, while other crops provide food, fodder and fuel. Yields are high and 'benefits in terms of production, social equity and employment can be considerable' (ibid, p461). Winarto also notes that the farmers believe that the way in which they use the land does not have an adverse effect on water quality and siltation. The fertility of the land reduces the need for fertilizers while intercropping reduces insect damage and hence the need for pesticides. They also believe that the minimum tillage and plant cover associated with intercropping, and the bunds associated with rice cultivation, reduce soil erosion and hence siltation.

As a result of less favourable conditions at Jatiluhur, only 10 per cent of the 3600ha drawdown area is cultivated. Again a variety of crops is grown, with groundnuts considered the most valuable cash crop because of favourable marketing conditions. Field size varies, with some 1000 farmers cultivating holdings that vary from 200 to 5000m². Local leaders and officials showed initiative 'in setting up a mechanism of control for collecting taxes and settling conflicts among drawdown users' (Tjitradjaja, personal communication).

No doubt influenced by such studies as Tjitradjaja's and Winarto's, more recent resettlement planning for the Cirata and Saguling Dams has considered drawdown cultivation as well as cage culture.[10] Again responding to local initiative, some government authorities in India have also begun to recognize the need for, and value of, drawdown agriculture. The Bargi Dam in the Narmada Valley provides one example, though only after an unacceptable resettlement programme for 162 villages, some of which had to move more than once as a result of misinformation about the reservoir's full storage level, and none of which received compensation land. After many complaints and two major demonstrations following the dam's completion in 1990, government officials finally agreed in 1998 'to lower the reservoir by four meters every December thus making a relatively large and fertile area of land available for cultivation' (IRN, December 1999a, p9).

Because conditions do vary from one reservoir to another, zoning for different land uses is important. Otherwise conflicts can occur among local users who wish to use the drawdown area for different purposes and between local people and immigrants.

Access to common property resources

Whether resettlers relocate within a reservoir basin or elsewhere, a major cost of large dams to indigenous people, many ethnic minorities and other households without land or major assets is loss of common property resources – access to which had been restricted to community members under systems of customary tenure. In dam projects, as well as in other projects causing involuntary community resettlement, this loss to already-poor people 'is systematically overlooked and uncompensated in government recovery schemes' (Cernea and McDowell, 2000, p291). A major reason is the common failure of governments to provide legal protection to common property rights with the result that their loss may be uncompensated (Koenig and Diarra, 2000, pp337–338).

Especially detrimental is loss of access to floodplains and riverine and inland forests. In addition to providing nurseries for increased fish production, wetlands provide grazing. Riverine and inland forests and associated vegetation also provide grazing and browse as well as a wide range of natural products of which building materials, fuel and edible and medicinal plants are especially important. Whether people are resettled within reservoir basins or elsewhere, I am aware of no cases where equivalent access to common property resources has occurred. Not only is access reduced, but increased population densities, as in India, West Africa and the Sudan, can lead to serious conflicts between resettling communities and hosts.

In India, tribal people farming and otherwise using forest lands on which they have lived for centuries are often considered 'encroachers' by project authorities, as in the Sardar Sarovar case. For those tribal households shifted to the plains below the dam, loss of grazing, fuel, building materials and other forest products caused hardship. Because of loss of grazing, livestock numbers fell as families sold at deflated prices (because of the quantity of stock involved) cattle and other livestock that they could no longer feed. What stock they took with them led to complaints from host villages.

In Africa, many examples exist of hardship especially during the initial years following removal. At Akosombo, Ghanaian authorities made no provision for livestock in the 52 planned communities into which over 80,000 resettlers from 740 villages were expected to move with or without their livestock. Because the government was able to acquire from host areas only one-third of the land intended for mechanized agricultural development, it is not hard to imagine why a major loss of resettler stock occurred as a result of non-availability of common property resources and non-provision of the necessary fodder. A similar loss of stock, accompanied by low priced sales, occurred at Kom Ombo when Egyptian Nubians were relocated to what was still a desert plain in which land for the planned irrigation scheme had yet to be reclaimed, let alone watered so that fodder could be grown. While lessons were learned by the Ghanaian authorities from the Akosombo experience that were to be applied to Kpong-related resettlement further downstream, violent conflicts occurred over land and common property resources that led to host and resettler deaths. Conflict also occurred at Khashm el-Girba when Shukriya grazing lands were incorporated within an irrigation scheme for Sudanese Nubians relocated in connection with the Aswan High Dam scheme. That too led to inter-ethnic conflict (Salem-Murdock, 1989).

There are no easy solutions for the restoration of, or substitution for, common property resources. As a first step, customary property rights to common property resources should be acknowledged by project authorities and properly compensated for, as the Lesotho Highlands Development Authority is attempting to do with Katse and Mohale Dam resettlement and the Government of Swaziland is attempting with the Maguga Dam project. In the Lesotho case, following a well-meaning but unsuccessful attempt to provide fodder purchased in South Africa for a limited number of years, cash compensation has been placed in community trust funds to use for development purposes that require a business plan before funds are disbursed. Although a commendable effort, the problem is that it will be difficult, if not impossible, to reproduce lost grazing and other common property resources because community households are opting to relocate in different areas. As a result, livestock numbers already are falling as people move into heavily grazed host areas. The Maguga situation is better for that majority of households opting to resettle in a designated downstream resettlement area where a major attempt is being made to designate and develop appropriate common property grazing areas. Those who opt to remain within the reservoir basin can expect to lose out, however, since they will not only lose valuable grazing to the reservoir but may be denied access to it.

One reason why I favour resettlement within reservoir basins if resettlers prefer that option relates to the grazing potential of the drawdown area. Although governments, as in the US and Europe, frequently create green belts around reservoirs above full storage levels, rarely are resettlers involved in their planning let alone their utilization. Yet such zones have considerable potential for a wider range of tree crops to provide fodder, fuel, building material and fruits and nuts.

Reservoir fisheries

Although reservoir fisheries provide another major opportunity for improving the living standards of resettlers, hosts and immigrants in Africa, Asia, Latin America and the Middle East, considerable confusion exists among planners and even fisheries experts as to the nature of the potential. With the exception of 'run-of-the-river' projects, reservoir impoundment is followed by an explosion of biological productivity as nutrients are released from the soil and inundated vegetation. As impounding proceeds, predators are also dispersed providing temporary protection to spawning fish and fry. Once stabilization occurs, productivity drops off rapidly as in the case of Kariba where catches declined from over 7000 tonnes to approximately 2000. Declines of 50 per cent or more have also occurred elsewhere, with productivity in Lake Volta dropping from an estimated 60,000 tonnes to 30,000. What has been characterized as a 'boom and bust' phenomenon (to which I also subscribed in the late 1960s) has tended to 'blind' planners to the potential that remains. Rightly concerned about the inability of a reservoir fishery to replace losses in productivity below dams and above reservoirs, even experts tend to underestimate the importance of a reservoir fishery for resettlers and its ability to increase yields as techniques are improved to catch a wider variety of species.

So that the initial increase in productivity is not lost to natural mortality, every effort should be made to prepare resettlers and hosts to commence fishing as soon as the reservoir begins to fill. It is also important to protect them from immigrant fishers who already have the skills and gear to fish large bodies of water.[11] Both approaches were successfully implemented by the colonial authorities on the north bank of Kariba. Even before the dam was sealed, gill nets were issued to schools and select individuals, with extension personnel training them in their use and upkeep.

The reservoir was also closed to outsiders for a five-year period when filling began in late 1958. Resettler and host fishers began to respond to the new opportunity almost immediately. By 1963–1964 approximately 2000 north bank fishers using 5000 nets were landing 4000 tonnes of fish, with south bank fishers netting perhaps 3000 tonnes. By the time that total north bank landings and catch per unit effort dropped off rapidly to below 2000 tonnes, a majority of those fishers had saved enough to purchase oxen for the cash cropping of cotton, the starting of small businesses, and the secondary and tertiary education of kin. Although the war for Zimbabwe's independence brought the fishery to a standstill during the 1970s, since 1980 the artisanal fishery has been gradually recovering, with yields over 5000 tonnes by the 1980s.

At Lake Volta, current catches vary between 30,000 and 40,000 tonnes, with a drop-off when reservoir levels recede in drought years. Although the high point of 60,000 tonnes was reached in 1969, in 1975 Coppola and Agadzi (1977) estimate that the fisheries were supporting 87,000 people living in 1479 settlements scattered around the reservoir. In 1977 the value of fish landings actually exceeded the sale of electricity (though for one year only), which had been the primary purpose for the dam's construction. At the 1993 Egyptian National Committee on Large Dams workshop on the High Dam at Aswan, participants referred to catches from Lake Nasser varying between 30,000 and 35,000 tonnes in the early 1990s. In that case, most of the 7000 fishers were immigrants from Upper Egypt.

Because the above figures are taken from the three largest artificial reservoirs in the tropics and subtropics, it is important not to overestimate the importance of fisheries in comparison to other opportunities for resettlers. Artisanal fishing is, after all, a hunting and gathering activity. Where large numbers of people are resettled, such a fishery usually can only support a minority of resettlers, as is the case for Kariba. It is also true for the Volta and Aswan High Dam reservoirs since the large majority of fishers there are immigrants. Immigrants also compose the majority of fishers at Kariba following the opening of the reservoir to outsiders. In all three cases, fishers with families tend to complement fishing with other activities such as cultivation of the drawdown area.

Because fish tend to be the most important source of animal protein for many river basin residents, the global experience is that local networks soon appear for marketing the catch. At Kariba, for example, traders using bicycles and small pickup trucks loaded with sawdust and ice appeared almost immediately; the same was true in connection with the marketing of fish from Sri Lanka's Mahaweli reservoirs and tanks. So as to provide another source of employment and income generation, project authorities and governments should resist the temptation to step in to organize and run marketing activities, or to contract or auction fishing rights as monopolies to influential politicians or well-connected entrepreneurs, as has happened in India as well as in Laos. In India, resettlers at Bargi initially were not even allowed to fish the reservoir, let alone market the catch. Only after major resistance were they finally permitted to form their own fishing cooperative, the future of which remains uncertain since 'others try to bribe officials to get their cooperative out' (Black, 2001, p14).

In Laos' Nam Ngum reservoir a politically influential entrepreneur from the capital continues to have a marketing monopoly that has an adverse effect on producer prices as well as on timely pickup of the catch in an environment where quality is soon compromised. There are at least partial exceptions to such criticism. One is the Lake Nubia fishery, located in a Saharan environment where the catch can soon rot. There is a high demand for fresh fish in Cairo and the government operates refrigerated water transport that purchases fish at the source, 10,000 tonnes of which are processed in Aswan for export to Cairo and the Delta.

Properly located ice plants are another way in which project authorities, governments and the private sector can assist fishery development. Also essential is a carefully designed research programme for management purposes that stipulates what types of gear and catching techniques are acceptable and what types are not, as well as the location of sanctuaries where fishing is prohibited. Research is also necessary to assess the pros and cons of a closed season and stocking the reservoir with indigenous and/or exotic species. In addition, research is needed for analysing the utility of more intensive fishing techniques and aquaculture. Examples include stocking cages in reservoir water with appropriate species that are fed prepared foods or local crop residues and wastes. Cage culture has provided an important source of income and employment to resettlers in China and Vietnam, while recent experimentation has also begun in Lake Kariba. Caution is needed, however, so as to avoid the type of pollution and immigration that undermined an initially promising cage culture fishery for resettlers behind Indonesia's Cirata and Saguling Dams.[12] Other fishery options might include building simple weirs across reservoir inlets within the drawdown area that hold water for stocking when reservoir levels rise. If stocking is advocated, construction and operation of hatcheries is another example where outside assistance is needed to support the development of a more productive reservoir fishery.

Natural resource management and tourism

Resettlers, hosts and downstream and upstream residents have rarely been asked to play a major role in developing plans for managing reservoirs, reservoir basins and adjacent areas as resources for the development of national and regional parks and reserves, recreation and tourism. On the contrary, governments have tended to ignore resettlers' customary land use and land tenure rights in establishing reserves, examples including the Zimbabwe foreshore of Lake Kariba, various reservoirs in Thailand and Costa Rica's Arenal. The same applies to influential immigrants, as on the Zambian side of Lake Kariba, Lesotho's Mohale Reservoir and Thailand's Khao Laem.

A partial exception is the Lesotho Highlands Development Project. In connection with the construction of the 'Muela Dam and downstream development, a contract was given to a South African firm to involve affected people in the planning and management of two reserves.[13] One, Ts'ehlanyane, would be for the protection of a unique forest ecosystem. The second, Lephofung Cave, would protect the cave's rich cultural heritage as a sheltered site for Bushmen and, more recently, for Basotho herd boys and their livestock. In both cases communities could see potential income- and employment-generating advantages and participated in planning for a reserve. Although the Ts'ehlanyane Reserve would involve excising a relatively large land area, 'Community representatives believed that there was a prospect that they might derive more benefits from their land turned into a reserve than under the former agro-pastoral land-use' (LHDA POE, 1999, p20). Such a trade-off appeared even more advantageous with Lephofung because only a small area was needed and because local people would be employed at the associated cultural centre where local craftspeople could sell their products.

On the other hand, as in the case with most other dams, involvement of local communities has been ignored in the planning of reserves and tourism in connection with the much larger Katse and Mohale Dams and reservoirs. While outsiders push their own interests with project and government officials, the project authority, with the Lesotho Tourism Board, commissioned a video to illustrate possible sites for hotels, resorts and an 18-hole golf course. Ways in which the reservoirs and surrounding areas could be zoned and developed for the benefit of local communities have received little attention in spite of various suggestions and recommendations. The POE's position is clear: because the dams are built on community lands, 'local communities must perceive that they have ownership over all processes' relating to their development whether that involves fisheries, or land-based reserves and tourist facilities. What is being advocated is greater community empowerment so that local people do not lose out on income earning possibilities or be further impoverished by ventures that use their resource base yet bypass their members. In addition there is the risk of tourist developments emerging 'as "islands" of luxury and wealth in a "sea" of rural poverty. Profits will be exported and there will be little trickle down to local communities' whose main benefit will be employment in low-paid 'menial tasks' (ibid, p15). Under such circumstances community hostility might also adversely affect profits.

Other than reserves and tourism, another example of a way in which communities could be involved would include 'ownership' of the reservoir fishery. While the Lesotho project authority has funded a contract to train a small number of community fishers to set gill nets from boats and are encouraging villagers to fish from the shoreline, local communities receive few benefits from South Africans who come on weekends and holidays to fish and camp. As recommended by the panel, there is a need for the project authority to facilitate 'community participation in developing a fishing resource right system around Katse reservoir, and around the future Mohale reservoir. This would be part of a bigger resource right system ... where local communities exploit, manage and police the resources over which they have rights' (ibid, p17). As for involvement in resort development, the rights that local communities bring to possible joint ventures with the private sector and government should include both land and water access. Because cash compensation is being given to communities for loss of common property resources such as grazing, fuel, thatching and other plant products, they could also bring their own finance to negotiations.

Such an approach is not mere wishful thinking if the kind of 'rights and risks' based approach to a more equitable and sustainable development process is followed as WCD has recommended. Even at Kariba, where the lucrative open-water fishery is dominated by outsiders, as are tourist facilities on islands and along the reservoir fringe, and where chiefs can still be bribed to give up valuable lakeshore frontage, local councils are beginning to insist on their rights to reservoir basin resources. On the Zimbabwe side, the Communal Areas Management Programme for Indigenous Resources (CAMPFIRE) provides funds from safari hunting and resorts to district councils and council units for the building of schools and clinics. On the Zambian side, local councils lease out rights to outsiders to develop game parks and tourist chalets on islands. Such a beginning, however, is still a far cry from local residents being co-investors in such facilities and operations.

Job training

Generally speaking the record with job training to provide employment has been disappointing for two major reasons. First, the large majority of resettlers are poorly educated farmers. Although the household economy of many involves migratory wage labour when agricultural activities are less demanding, jobs available usually involve low paid, unskilled work. Another problem is the demands on the time of resettlers immediately before and after physical removal. Before removal, adult members may actually leave their jobs to help the household prepare for the move, while after removal inadequate family labour can be a constraint for adapting to new conditions. What jobs are available do not carry rights of inheritance for other family members unlike legal or use rights to land and common property resources – an important point that is often ignored when cash compensation and jobs are promised as a substitute for land.

As the second major reason, there tends to be a poor fit between job training and the market for those so trained. What jobs are available, such as unskilled jobs during a dam's construction, are usually temporary – a factor that planners tend to downplay when calculating employment benefits. Once construction is over, the size of the labour force is drastically reduced and replaced by a much smaller and more highly skilled operations and maintenance crew that provides little opportunity for resettlers. During periods of economic downturn, retrenchment is another problem as in the case of Thailand's Pak Mun Dam where resettlers lost newly found jobs in Bangkok during the mid-1990s recession.

In Lesotho's Highlands Water Project, the project authority's rural development centre made an effort to train local people in skills needed during the construction phase as well as for starting small rural industries. Contractors hired only a few, claiming that their hastily acquired skills were insufficient or non-competitive with those of immigrants. There is also a tendency for contractors within a region or country to bring with them a significant portion of their own labour force. Or, as in China, resettlers and hosts cannot compete with workers who move from one dam site to another.

More successful in the Lesotho case has been a policy developed for the Mohale Dam where contractors are required to hire locally what unskilled labour is needed. In that case, local chiefs compile registers of those seeking employment from which contractors must recruit unskilled labour when needed. The system has worked well and if appropriate training was provided at an earlier date might also be applicable to semi-skilled labour. Another approach, especially applicable with relatively small numbers of resettlers, is to train and provide employment for one member of each household – an approach that the Asian Development Bank's expert panel reports has been a success in connection with Nepal's Kali Gandaki Project (communication from Michael Cernea).

Rural industries and urban resettlement with development

Rural industries

As part of a national policy to stop rural to urban migration, the Chinese have been the most successful in shifting farming households into non-farming village industries. Their approach requires careful examination in regard to its sustainability, adaptability to dam resettlement and applicability to other countries. Results to date in villages not required to resettle have been impressive. In the 1980s, I visited several villages in the middle and lower Yangtze basin in which a purely agricultural economy had been converted within a single decade to one in which a wide range of village industries had become the major source of employment. Employed youth, now better educated than their parents, were said to prefer such non-farming work within their communities. Out-migration was minimal to non-existent at that time, although the situation may have changed as urban influx control policies have been moderated.

A wide range of goods was being manufactured in the villages that I visited, with a minimal requirement for credit. Rather, 'barter type' arrangements were made with potential buyers such as companies needing bricks for building expansion, parks needing iron fixtures such as benches, or the Red Army needing hats and other clothing. In return for helping a village industry establish itself, the buyer was repaid in produce. Insufficient time has gone by, however, to know how competitive such industries will be over the longer term given the conventional wisdom that half of small businesses worldwide can be expected to fail, and the relatively low quality of what is produced. Even less time has gone by to assess the ability of the Chinese to apply the same policy to dam-induced resettlement. Early evaluations of their record with village industries in connection with Shuikou are encouraging but too early to be convincing. Intentions of resettling large numbers of Three Gorges farming families in non-farming enterprises are just that – intentions only. One problem that I anticipate will be competition from pre-existing enterprises in host areas.

Commoner is the approach in Lesotho where job training was also intended to help resettlers learn such crafts as carpentry, masonry and tailoring as well as acquire training for poultry rearing and baking. To date, results in connection with the Katse project are not encouraging. A major problem is that most of those trained have not been able to establish commercially viable businesses for marketing their new skills. Another problem, common to all sorts of training institutions, has been failure of training staff to follow up trainees in the field to help them deal with problems, unanticipated or otherwise. A further constraint has been the persistent failure of project authorities or other agencies to institutionalize the necessary credit facilities. Such problems have global applicability.

Urban resettlement with development

Two types of urban resettlement need to be distinguished. The first is where rural resettlers chose to migrate to cities. The second is where urban populations themselves must be resettled. What should be avoided with the first type are situations, as have occurred in India, where rural resettlers without skills are forced to move to large cities because of a failed rural resettlement programme. Gujarat's Ukai Dam is an example where entire families, made destitute by resettlement, close up their homes to seek employment in Mumbai and other cities (Mankodi and Gangopadhyay, 1983). China's record shows much better planning, although insufficient time has gone by to analyse outcomes. In more recent projects such as Gezhouba, Shuikou and Three Gorges, a major effort has been made to resettle rural youth in urban industries because of the lack of arable land and the inability of rural industries to employ the numbers involved. The key will be whether or not new urban industries can be created which remain competitive. It will not be easy, in part because the irrigation of labour intensive, high value crops, with the type of multipliers that could be associated with the development of agro-industries, is not a major component of these three projects.

Although urban resettlers continue to form a small minority of communities undergoing involuntary relocation, a number of dams have displaced towns and small cities. Examples include the flooding of Posadas (Argentina) and Encarnacion (Paraguay) in connection with the binational Yacyretá Dam, Wadi Halfa (Sudan) in connection with the High Dam at Aswan, and Teldenniya (Sri Lanka) in connection with Sri Lanka's Victoria Dam. China's Three Gorges Dam will flood a number of towns and cities along the Yangtze; indeed, in this case the number of urban residents to be relocated may well exceed the number of rural resettlers. Urban development opportunities are important not just for such urban resettlers and rural resettlers but also for downstream residents who move to cities because of the lack of rural opportunities following dam construction.

While many studies have been made of rural resettlement, unfortunately few have involved urban resettlers – involuntary urban resettlement remaining a 'vast "field-in-waiting" ' (Cernea, ed, 1999, p147). What knowledge is available comes largely from studies of urban redevelopment projects in Europe and the US, complemented by some in developing countries such as Perlman's in Brazil (1976). As for research on urban communities inundated by dams, Bartolomé has published on Posadas (1991) and Mejía has discussed economic dimensions of various types of urban resettlement (some dam related) in Latin America (1999). Few other case studies are available, the work on urban resettlers in China dealing primarily with the first two stages of the resettlement process. For that reason one does not know how successful job training programmes, credit programmes for the establishment of single-family businesses, and industries for larger numbers of resettlers will be there.

Because of the paucity of case studies, I am uncertain as to the extent that the four-stage framework is applicable to urban resettlers. My reading of the literature on urban redevelopment in the US, including work by Fried (1963) and Hartman (1974), suggests that it is, but further case material is needed. One problem relates to whether low-income urban communities contain households that are more entrepreneurial and adaptable in coping with disturbance than rural communities. Publications on rural to urban migration suggest that a degree of self-selection is operative, with recent urban migrants being more entrepreneurial than those who remain behind in rural areas. On the other hand, increasingly long-term studies of rural communities (Kemper and Royce, 2002) show that the majority there are also more willing to experiment with new opportunities than was previously thought, while the type of migrants to cities has become less selective in recent years because of increasing land scarcity for farming and other impoverishing factors in rural areas.

While there are important differences between urban and rural resettlers (Mejía, 1996, 1999), their resettlement experience and the resettlement process are not that different. This is because the same constraints of inadequate commitment and capacity, including financial capacity, on the part of those responsible for planning and implementation afflict both types of resettlement. Lack of attention to economic development is an especially glaring constraint, starting with the current 'rudimentary' knowledge 'of the economic dimensions of urban resettlement' (Mejía, 1999, p148).

As for differences, Mejía's characterization of urban resettlers moved in connection with all sorts of World Bank-financed projects in Latin America, including Yacyretá, is a good starting point (1996, pp5–7; 1999, pp152–154). So too is her discussion of 'Economic Reconstruction and Participation' and 'Economic Issues in House Replacement Alternatives' in her 1999 publication. Although the large majority is poor in both rural and urban removal, urban residents tend to be more dependent on the informal economy. Those threatened by inundation or urban redevelopment in Latin America also tend to be relatively recent immigrants, with 65 per cent of those in Mejía's project sample having lived in an affected area for less than five years and only about 15 per cent resident for 20 years or more. In searching for housing and job opportunities they also tend to be more mobile than rural residents; hence, I would suspect that a proportion of Mejía's 65 per cent have longer urban histories. That would certainly be the case in other parts of the world; indeed in Asia, and especially in China, affected urban populations would be longer-term residents, including multigenerational families.

Another major difference has been the tendency of planners to see urban resettlement as a process dealing with an aggregate of separate households rather than with communities. As a result, the focus has been on housing as opposed to helping resettlers move in social and community units of their choice and as opposed to social services and economic development. More is known about what 'not to do' than about what 'to do'. Pejorative terms such as 'slums' should be avoided as they downgrade low-income communities as functional systems. Where housing is provided it must not be at an inconvenient (in terms of travel time and expense) distance from resettlers' places of work, which frequently lie outside an inundated area. Community participation to deal with all issues is crucial and should be initiated in the early stages of the options assessment process and, should the dam option be selected, throughout the resettlement process.

Community and marketing services

Mahapatra has emphasized that a major impoverishment risk in India is the non-provision of the educational services that are so important for poverty alleviation (1999a, pp72–74). Equally important are medical services, systems for the provision of potable water, and a wide range of other government services. A frequent omission of resettlement planning, and indeed of general planning even for irrigation projects, is how farming and non-farming production is to be marketed. Reynolds (1981, 1992) has addressed ways in which government and other services, including provision of credit, could be provided to local communities through a hierarchy of markets such as those described in Chapter 6.

The record is not good in regard to the provision of such services. Marketing tends to be neglected in the large majority of cases. Although the record is better with schools and medical services, these were not provided in 17 (37 per cent) of the 46 cases in the 50 dam survey where data were sufficient, while in another seven cases (15 per cent) defects persisted. As for critically important water and sanitation facilities, they frequently worsen following removal. In the 50 dam survey, for example, they were not completed adequately in two-thirds of 46 cases. For people used to drawing water from free-flowing rivers to become dependent on poorly constructed wells and piped water – supplies that often are irregular and of poor quality – is a frequent and unacceptable outcome. It is also paradoxical, given that people have been shifted because of reservoir formation. As for sanitary facilities, they tend to be inadequate in part because people are often resettled in larger communities.

One of the worse cases of inadequate water supplies and sanitation continues to afflict the Lusitu area where 6000 Kariba resettlers were moved in the late 1950s. With the majority resettled at a distance from the Zambezi River, initially they were dependent on an inadequate number of boreholes that produced at best low-quality water. When a pipeline pumping water from the Zambezi was installed several years later to serve most of the resettlers, it experienced many subsequent breakdowns. Now over 40 years later, with the population in the area having doubled, a recent groundwater and tributary water study concluded that 'provision of adequate good quality water for the Lusitu community is the biggest social problem the people are currently facing' (Yambayamba et al, 2001, pviii). The concentration of minerals such as sodium, fluoride, iron, lead and chromium in borehole water was found, more often than not, to exceed World Health Organization standards, while standing water and the water in the Lusitu River was contaminated with faecal coliforms. Such pollution was associated with dysentery and diarrhoea. Presumably it is also a factor in periodic outbreaks of cholera that first occurred in the 1980s.

While the Lusitu case may be extreme, it is not uncommon for resettlement sites to overlie poor aquifers. That is one reason why they are available in the first place. Five years after the filling of the Katse Reservoir in the mid-1990s, over 50 per cent of the surrounding Basotho communities had still to receive their promised water and sanitation supplies. The same applies two years after removal to the first planned community in the foothills from the recently completed Mohale Dam.

AVOIDING INVOLUNTARY RESETTLEMENT

Introduction

In spite of serious weaknesses (Chapter 8), the World Bank's current Operational Policies dealing with involuntary resettlement have two major strengths. The most important, listed as point (a) on the first page under Policy Objectives, is that 'Involuntary Resettlement should be avoided where feasible, or minimized, exploring all viable alternative project designs.'[14]

Selecting other options to avoid involuntary resettlement

As awareness increased of problems associated with dam construction, those concerned with water resource and energy development were already emphasizing by the 1960s that dams should be considered as only one of a number of possible options.[15] Yet as WCD documented in detail in its Final Report, inadequate attention to options assessment has continued down to the present. A major reason, dealt with in more detail in Chapter 8, relates to the type of institutions responsible for water resource and energy development. In the majority of cases, especially in China, India and throughout Africa, such institutions tend to be a single ministry with a single priority – more often than not the priority being energy or irrigation.

In the case of energy, a ministry of power or a parastatal (the Federal Power Board in the case of Kariba or Thailand's EGAT) responsible for meeting a rising national power demand looks for a least-cost solution to its problem in which the costs of infrastructure construction and operation and maintenance of different facilities are compared as if they existed in a vacuum. This approach may not be problematic when dealing with a thermal station, but dealing with a free-flowing river where construction of a dam can be expected to have major upstream and downstream impacts is a very different matter. Tunnel vision is also apt to characterize ministries of irrigation, as is the case in India. There the single responsibility for increasing food production dominates, with scant attention paid to downstream impacts or numbers of people requiring resettlement. In both cases, the projects selected are also large scale, with their budgets perpetuating the ministries concerned as well as increasing the opportunity for corruption.

FUNDING RESETTLEMENT

Introduction

Along with ensuring that adequate funds are budgeted for resettlement with development and that the funds budgeted are actually used for resettlement purposes, there are two other key financial issues. One is that the budget should reflect the actual number of resettlers rather than initial estimates. The other is that funding must be available throughout the physical removal and development phases, which can be expected to extend well beyond the end of dam construction.

A separate and protected resettlement with development budget

In the case of dams involving large numbers of people such as Brazil's Itaparica and China's Three Gorges, resettlement costs can exceed 30 per cent of the total. The magnitude of such costs is one reason why the resettlement component requires its own budget. Resettlement budgets must cover *all* expected resettlement costs for ensuring improvement. While that would appear to be self-evident, the current World Bank's Guidelines, which have been so influential since their formulation in 1980, 'arbitrarily limits the cost of resettlement to "direct economic and social impacts" ' (Downing, 2002a, p14). In so doing, the guidelines 'exclude the critical costs of reintegrating and restarting disrupted economies, social institutions, and educational systems' (ibid) as well as ignore the physiological, psychological and socio-cultural stress that accompanies involuntary resettlement.

Just as project authorities are able to find funding to complete construction where cost overruns occur, so too must they have the flexibility to deal with increasing resettlement costs. It will not be easy to build into the budgetary process the necessary flexibility to revise budgets upward as the numbers of people requiring resettlement or other costs increase. Even where treaties and guidelines require adequate attention to be paid to resettlement, and where political will is present to observe such requirements, project authorities tend to resist, for budgetary reasons, subsequent attempts to increase initial estimates of resettler numbers or to widen the conditions under which affected people can choose project-financed resettlement. A recent and ongoing example is the Lesotho Highlands Water Project. In that case, the binational commission that oversees the project needed considerable prodding from the POE and the World Bank to acknowledge the increased number of resettlers affected by the Mohale Dam project.[16] In the case of the previously built Katse Dam, the project authority and the Commission were unwilling at a later date to provide resettlement benefits to households at risk from the project because of their proximity to the reservoir once it reached full storage level.

Resettlement budgets must also be protected so that they are not raided to finance the cost overruns that all too frequently have characterized a dam's construction phase (WCD, 2000, p39). Ghana's Kpong Dam provides a warning. While planners learned much from the failure of Ghana's previous Volta Dam at Akosombo to realize its broader development goals, when the time came to finance the development portion of Kpong resettlement, Brokensha and I were told during a 1989 visit that the necessary funds had been used for other activities. Because resettlement will continue to be considered a by-product of a larger project when the dam option is selected, it may be necessary to 'protect' the budget in a special way.

Setting up a trust fund is one possibility that warrants serious consideration. Absolutely essential for contractors with resettlement responsibilities are performance bonds. Also needed are 'safety net' mechanisms that ensure a basic-needs standard of living if plans for resettlers to become project beneficiaries fail. Downing labels such a mechanism 'as induced-displacement insurance... This innovation would lead underwriters and the market to nudge borrowers to mitigate and avoid known risks' (Downing, 2002a, p14). Goodland also emphasizes the need for resettlement insurance that 'provides finance as soon as it is detected that livelihoods are not improving' (2003, p3). Although time-bound, one 'safety net' operation that warrants study is the 'minimum threshold allowance' that the Lesotho Highlands Development Authority is giving to vulnerable families.

Ways for financing the extended resettlement with development process

The development phase associated with a new dam obviously extends well beyond the construction phase. This is as true for resettling communities as it is for the society at large that is intended to benefit from the development that follows the completion of construction. The large majority of resettlers, however, are poor people. If they are to benefit from fishing the reservoir, for example, they are going to need extension (for fishing a large reservoir is different from fishing a free-flowing river) and they are going to need credit for purchasing appropriate gear including more stable boats. Where is the financial assistance to meet such needs going to come from?

The best way to provide the necessary funding is to allocate a portion of project revenue for resettlement with development and for environmental purposes. Two countries, China and Brazil, have pioneered such an approach; others are experimenting with it. In the case of China, starting in the 1980s a percentage of revenue from the sale of electricity is set aside not just for financing resettlement costs but also for attempting to rectify problems associated with previous resettlement. The Danjiangkou Dam provides an excellent example. In the 1980s, revenue from hydropower generation was placed in a 'remaining problems fund' available for helping households, kin groups and communities that had been resettled around the reservoir margin to fund income-generating enterprises. During a visit in the late 1980s I was impressed by the range of enterprises being funded and the good repayment rate that ensured the funds continuity.

Brazil's approach expands revenue sharing beyond resettling communities to municipal districts surrounding a reservoir, to the relevant state and to the federal government. Rather than placing a tax on revenue received from the sale of energy, a 1989 law taxes water that is used to generate electricity. In the form of royalties, 45 per cent of the income generated goes to the relevant municipalities, with their share based on the size of the area under their jurisdiction; 45 per cent goes to the state; and 10 per cent to the federal government.

At the suggestion of the World Bank, the Government of Lesotho is also setting aside revenue from project income (in this case from the sale of water to South Africa) in a trust fund for development purposes, while the Government of Laos has established a separate account for income from the sale of NT2 power to Thailand. In both cases, however, the funds received are to be used for purposes of poverty alleviation at the national level rather than just for resettlement.

Whether a tax on electricity or on water, such approaches, important as they are, do not provide a sufficient source of funds for resettlement with development purposes. For one thing, the funds only become available once the project becomes operational. Where will funds come from before that time? During the Canadian evaluation of China's Three Gorges Project in the 1980s, on which I was resettlement adviser, the question of where the funds were to come from for the physical relocation and initial development of hundreds of thousands of people was never satisfactorily answered. In the Brazilian, Lesotho and Laotian cases, revenue available for resettlement purposes was or will be only a relatively small proportion of the total royalty and of the necessary budget. Furthermore, funds in all four cases are tied to specific project components such as energy generation and sale of water. They illustrate, however, the type of innovative approach that is necessary for ensuring a continuity of funding for development purposes beyond the completion of dam construction.

SELECTION OF SITES AND RESETTLING UNITS

Introduction

Involving resettling communities in the decision-making process about where to move and with whom to move is an important procedure for reducing the stress that follows removal and speeding subsequent community formation and economic development.

Predictably, a majority of resettling households and communities can be expected to prefer moving to a familiar area with a known host population. Based on case histories, the preferred locale is resettlement within the reservoir basin, followed by the area below the dam. In 30 (63 per cent) of the 48 cases in the 50 dam survey where resettlement from the reservoir basin was necessary, the largest number of resettlers were relocated within the basin. In 12 of the remaining 18 cases, resettlers were dispersed to various locations, while in six they were resettled downstream from the dam.

Picking resettlement sites

In only one-third of 47 cases in the 50 dam survey were resettlers actively involved in site selection, with involvement including consent to the site or sites picked. In another one-third of the cases, resettlers had no involvement in the site selection process. In five other cases (11 per cent), self-resettlement occurred. In the remaining cases resettlers were either consulted or involved in the planning process but without consent.

Even when policies actively involve resettling communities in site selection, as is increasingly the case, and the political will exists to implement those policies, two major types of difficulty should be anticipated. One is that the preferred sites are problem-prone. The other is that members of households and communities have different opinions as to where they want to move and with whom. As global populations have increased and spread over the landscape, it is to be expected that areas that remain sparsely populated, or otherwise available as resettlement sites, are problem-prone. That is reason in itself for resettlement planning to be integrated early on into the assessment of options as to whether a dam should be built. Following soil, water, other natural resource and host population surveys, it may be possible to overcome some problems. In arid and semi-arid areas, irrigation may prove a solution, as it did in Egypt's Kom Ombo area. In other ecological zones the Chinese have had success in developing non-farming employment in village industries as well as fish cages in reservoirs. But other problems, such as too large a host population and poor soils and water supplies, may be insurmountable, in which case either the dam option should be dropped or alternative resettlement areas discussed with resettling communities. If communities have been involved in the initial surveys, it should be easier – though still difficult – to work with them in the selection of alternative areas.

Deciding who resettles with whom

As communities become more complex, the risks increase that members will disagree not only about the advantages and disadvantages of a dam and a resettlement programme, but also about how compensation and development opportunities should be split among members of households and kin groups and who should resettle with whom and where. Although little has yet been written on such disagreements, what evidence is available suggests that they are not uncommon, that they can have a detrimental effect on how people reconstitute their lives, and that their frequency is related not just to community complexity and heterogeneity but also to the adequacy of resettlement programmes. Such disagreements within families and kin groups, and the conflicts that may arise from them, are yet another cost of resettlement of which most policy-makers tend to be unaware.

The most destabilizing cases that I have observed were in India in connection with the Sardar Sarovar Project. A worst-case example was where one of 22 households formerly dependent on joint land use sought total control of resettlement land. While working together, Mahapatra and I also noted cases where household members differed and conflicts arose as to where family members should relocate and how cash compensation should be divided. Such conflicts were exacerbated because project authorities in Gujarat were unwilling to resettle communities, kin groups and even households of extended families in social units of their choice. Also, contrary to the stipulations of the Narmada Water Disputes Tribunal, efforts in Madhya Pradesh to replace a land for land strategy with cash compensation can be expected to lead to similar conflicts.

Conflicts, however, are not restricted to poorly planned and implemented resettlement. In Lesotho where Mohale Dam resettlers have the option of moving with project benefits anywhere within the country, in a number of cases younger family members wish to relocate from the mountains to the lowlands, whereas a widowed mother or other elderly relative may wish to remain within the reservoir basin. This is especially the case where the policy option exists for extended families to split into separate nuclear families, hence separating elderly parents from their married children and grandchildren. The same problem exists in connection with Swaziland's Maguga Dam project where the desires of an elderly relative may vary from those on whom that relative is dependent.

Housing

As defined here, housing includes all structures utilized by household members including outbuildings such as kitchens, granaries, corrals and other livestock structures. Throughout the world, project authorities have dealt more effectively with replacing housing than with income generation and economic development. Where they are more likely to fall short is in the extent to which resettlers are involved in the selection of house types and in considering the pros and cons of resettlers participating in their construction. In the 50 dam survey, resettlers built or bought their own housing in 21 (45 per cent) of 47 cases. In 13 (27 per cent) cases they were actively involved in the planning process including approval of the final design. Their involvement was less active in five (11 per cent) other cases, and in the remaining eight cases (17 per cent) they had no involvement.

Project authorities tend to be especially weak in their understanding of the environmental and sociological benefits of existing household structures, including reasons for their spatial distribution not just within a particular homestead but in the relationship of homesteads to each other. This deficiency makes it difficult for resettlement staff to design alternative housing or to explain to resettlers the cultural implications of other 'more modern' housing types that resettlers may opt for if they have a choice. It may also make reconstituting social units more difficult. Such deficiencies are best corrected through active resettler participation in all housing issues.

In the case of the Lesotho Highlands Water Project, resettling households could choose either customary replacement housing or modern housing. The latter was most frequently selected with resettlers in the mountains not realizing until they moved how much warmer their customary housing had been. Although eventually the project provided stoves, that was only a partial solution as was the construction of a separate, customary kitchen in which to cook, eat and visit. In the Aswan High Dam case, for reasons of cost and efficiency, project-designed houses were fused together in rows according to the number of rooms. Not only did that violate Nubian concepts of privacy but it also separated the single-room project housing for elderly parents from the multiple room housing of their descendents. In China, the government preference for apartment buildings resulted in some ground-dwelling ethnic minorities in the Ertan Dam case finding themselves on the top floors (communication from Robert Goodland).

For housing, as with so many other resettlement decisions, there is no best policy other than having sufficient time actively to involve resettlers in all major decisions, including decisions related to future household expansion. Although both men and women need to be involved, the active involvement of women is essential since they will be spending disproportionately more time in whatever housing is built. Sufficient time is especially important if the decision is made for resettlers to participate in construction.

COMPENSATION

Introduction

Policies based on compensation alone are not an acceptable option because they replicate poverty. Even attempts merely to restore income and living standards require a combination of compensation and development. This conclusion is one of two that I have had the most difficulty explaining to those in project authorities and donor agencies such as the World Bank who have not had direct experience with resettlement issues. The other conclusion is that policies that focus on restoration alone, such as those emphasizing compensation, worsen rather than restore living standards.

The Lesotho Highlands Water Project provides an excellent example for illustrating how overemphasizing the role and adequacy of compensation can have an adverse effect on project outcomes even where the political will exists to implement policy goals. It is a contemporary project as well as one of the five largest infrastructure projects in the world involving dam construction. Although it is a World Bank-funded project, policy-makers in the Bank tend to overemphasize compensation at the expense of development. The same can be said of the Bank's 2001 resettlement guidelines.[17] While they state up front that resettlement projects should be development projects, the text that follows mentions 'compensation' 19 times and 'development' only 4 times, and places far more emphasis on compensation issues than on the necessary development issues.

The Highlands Water Project came into being with a 1986 treaty between Lesotho and South Africa and the 1986 Order establishing a Lesotho Highlands Development Authority (LHDA). Both documents required only a restoration approach. As the main beneficiary, South Africa is responsible for financing the treaty's resettlement requirements. From 1989 through April 2002 I was a member of the World Bank-required POE whose reports were submitted to LHDA, to the binational Lesotho Highlands Water Commission that oversees policy and financial issues, and to the World Bank before becoming public documents.

Most of the POE's responsibilities relate to impacts arising from the construction of the Katse and Mohale Dams and subsidiary works. Katse was completed in 1995 with the reservoir filling during the 1995/96 rainy season; the Mohale reservoir began to fill during the 2001/02 rainy season. Throughout the planning and implementation of Katse resettlement our panel explained in report after report why income and living standard restoration required both compensation and development. Yet we were unable to convince the South African members of the Commission and expatriate delegates representing Lesotho of this requirement. Time and again Commission delegates, who were mainly engineers, believed that treaty requirements could be met by implementing only a compensation policy. They were unable to distinguish between development initiatives necessary for restoration and those which went beyond a restoration policy and which, if implemented, should indeed be financed by the Government of Lesotho. As an example of the lack of balance, land to be acquired from resettlers for the Katse project was carefully mapped for compensation purposes. No funds, in spite of panel recommendations, were spent to map their remaining land resources as part of the necessary planning to achieve resettlement goals. As a result of such biases, the majority of resettling households continue to be worse off today.

Many lessons were learned by the Commission and the Project Authority from the Katse experience that are now being applied constructively to the Mohale project. Nonetheless, periodically the same confusion continued over the extent to which development opportunities are essential for meeting treaty requirements. As Mohale resettlement activities got underway, the POE reiterated its concern. In the first recommendation of its 1999 report on the Mohale Environmental Action Plan, the panel stated that 'Without de-emphasizing compensation, a better balance between compensation and development activities is required if the obligation in the 1986 LHWP Treaty to restore living standards is to be met.' In the accompanying text the report then stated, 'While early POE reports (1990, 1991) explained in detail why restoration of living standards required more development activities as legitimate project costs, the imbalance between physical resettlement, compensation, and development activities has continued to this day' (LHDA POE, 1999, pp5–6).

Replacement (as opposed to market) value compensation in cash and kind is, of course, essential for dealing with such tangible, physical assets as houses and household structures, land, field and other crops, and common property resources. But how to fairly compensate people for the multidimensional stress associated with removal? For the possible increases in morbidity and mortality rates? For the anxiety of leaving a homeland, especially when the majority of those involved have strong psychological and religious, as well as economic, ties to that land? For the loss of knowledge and customs that cannot be transferred to resettlement sites? It cannot be done. Even in regard to occupational compensation, how does one compensate an agricultural labourer, sharecropper or leaseholder who is unable to find land to work following removal? Or a business that cannot be transferred because host rivals dominate the market for the goods and services provided? The only equitable procedure is to provide new development opportunities.

Cash compensation

An over-reliance on cash compensation by project authorities has been an impoverishing factor in many cases. Besides the limitations of any policy based on compensation alone, compensation in cash has other limitations. One is the difficulty of assessing the replacement value of the items for which cash compensation is being given. Even where careful pre-project surveys are completed on time, they tend to underestimate the value of existing production systems. Fearing taxation issues, those interviewed may minimize cash income or herd size. Even if heads of households try to provide accurate data, recall difficulties can be expected about previous transactions as well as about income and economic resources provided by other family members.

Another major problem documented in case after case is inexperience in using compensation monies received, with the result that they too often are spent on consumer goods or on marriages, funerals and other ceremonies rather than on income restoration and improvement activities. There is also the problem of 'to whom and how to give the money' so that it is used to meet household needs as opposed to those of the recipient who tends to be the household head. Even where wives must approve and/or sign for major uses of cash compensation received, their unequal status in the household may make them fearful to oppose a husband's wishes. Similarly, funds given to widows and elderly couples may be expropriated by younger relatives. There is also always the risk of corruption on the part of those responsible for implementing a compensation policy, as has recently been documented in connection with China's Three Gorges Project.

Thailand's Pak Mun case, discussed in Chapter 3, is an excellent example of the risks involved in a resettlement programme that relies primarily on cash compensation. Initially the project authority planned to cash compensate arable land at its replacement value. When local people complained, 'land compensation rates were quintupled, to seven to eight times the market value of unaffected land in the vicinity' (Picciotto et al, 2001, p63) with further adjustments made later. Unfortunately, 'less than six per cent of the total compensation received was spent on buying land' (ibid, p64). Rather, many of those involved left their rural occupations and went to Bangkok to find employment. When many lost their urban jobs during the Asian economic downturn, however, they had no natural resources to fall back on since the project also had had a devastating effect on the previously existing fishery. For that reason, cash compensation given subsequently to those for whom fishing was the primary source of income also failed, with many of those involved unable to find alternate employment (Amornsakchai et al, 2000, p64).

Although over-reliance on cash compensation must be avoided, some compensation in cash is necessary to deal with new as well as unexpected costs associated with physical removal and its aftermath. Where access is lost to common property resources such as wild food and medicinal plants, fuel and grazing, cash will be needed for purchasing equivalent resources. Because of the greater fertility of riverine soils, replacement land within reservoir basins and elsewhere is likely to require cash to purchase fertilizers and other inputs for producing equivalent yields. Even where fertility and size of arable holdings is the same, it may take time to bring them into full production, time during which cash will be needed for food purchases.

Cash compensation should also be seriously considered for the minority of entrepreneurs who wish to use it for business purposes wherever they plan to relocate. There too, however, caution is needed. Just as a large number of resettlers who wish to continue farming elsewhere can be expected to inflate land prices, so too can entrepreneurs underestimate the competitive difficulties of shifting an old business or starting a new one in a host area where local demand may already be met. At the very minimum it should be the responsibility of the resettlement unit to work closely with such people in fashioning a business plan that has a reasonable chance for success as a production and marketing entity.

Land for land, food relief, and other compensation in kind

Land for land

Although reservoir formation may flood towns, as was the case with Yacyretá in Argentina/Paraguay and Victoria in Sri Lanka, the large majority of resettlers in the major dam-building countries continue to be members of rural communities. During the 1990s, for example, four-fifths of the US$32–45 billion spent on large dams annually was in 'developing countries' (WCD, 2000, p11). Not only is agriculture the basis of the rural economy in the majority of such countries, but in the early stages of industrialization it is the rising income and living standards of their farming households that is the engine that can be expected to drive development (Johnston and Kilby, 1975).

While the World Bank is correct in stating that a land for land strategy 'should not be adopted regardless of costs' (Picciotto et al, 2001, p134), more attention needs to be paid to accessing ways in which land might be made available. This is especially important where governments and project authorities attempt to justify reliance on a cash compensation policy by claiming that arable land is unavailable. On the face of it, such a claim may seem reasonable, especially in densely populated countries in which rural populations predominate. Egypt is such a country, but there the government saw resettlement in connection with the High Dam at Aswan as a development opportunity and brought irrigation to new lands for the resettled population. A contrary case is India's Sardar Sarovar Project. There the project authorities in Gujarat informed the World Bank that much as they would have liked to implement a land-based strategy as opposed to one based on cash compensation, the necessary land was just not available. In fact, landlords were willing to sell thousands of hectares for an affordable price.[18] Even if the Gujarat landlords had been unwilling to sell land, other options would have been available. One option would have been to implement existing laws such as India's *Land Ceiling Act*. Another – practised in China – would have been to use project resources, especially irrigation, to increase the productivity of host land by a factor of two or more and then divide that land between hosts and resettlers. In addition to incorporating resettlers in old or new irrigation projects, yet another option would be to zone the reservoir drawdown area for their cultivation.

Another case where land-based strategies initially were ignored because available arable land was said to be scarce was the Lesotho Highlands Water Project. As in India, one might see that claim as reasonable although for different reasons. While India's arable landscape was densely populated, the Lesotho argument that land for resettlement was unavailable was based on historical factors, the farming population having been forced into highland areas by the expansion of European settlers in South Africa. Even there, however, two types of arable land were available. One was the large holdings of chiefs. Another, more available, was lowland fields that lay fallow because poor families did not have the capital and labour resources to cultivate them. As a result they were willing to allow resettlers to share crop, lease and, in some cases, purchase such land. Areas available were sufficient, for example, for over 20 households shifted from the Mohale Dam reservoir basin to the host community of Makotoko in the foothills.

In all cases where a land for land strategy exists it is the responsibility of the project authorities to negotiate legal transfers that are acceptable to the host population. Unacceptable is the type of situation that the Sardar Sarovar authorities practised in Gujarat where they expected individual resettling households to use cash compensation to purchase replacement lands. Such an approach was unacceptable for several reasons. For one, it did not allow resettlers to move as social units of their choice, as required by the policy stipulations of the Narmada Water Disputes Tribunal. For another, large numbers of resettlers looking for land inflated prices beyond the compensation that resettlers had been given to purchase equivalent land. Even where lands were purchased, resettlers often found legal restrictions on their use.

Also unacceptable is the type of situation that characterized the acquisition of land for 22 Mohale households that were the first to resettle in the lowlands of Lesotho. In that case, the Lesotho Highlands Development Authority acquired land legally from the relevant municipal council. They neglected, however, to discuss the purchase with the host community from whom the municipal council had originally acquired the land. That oversight led to an unnecessary dispute between the resettlers and the hosts that was fostered by a government minister from the host community as a way to pressure the project authority to provide excessive benefits to his political constituency. While the dispute was exacerbated by complex political issues at the national level – the minister's house had been burned down by non-resettler opponents at an earlier date – the victims were the resettlers. Initially, the host community refused to allow the resettlers to use their burial area. Subsequently the minister demanded that the 22 resettler households be moved elsewhere. Because they were some of the first households to resettle from the Mohale basin, that demand jeopardized the entire resettlement programme since those who had yet to move suspected that even the project authority could not protect their rights. Eventually resolved at the cabinet level, the Mohale case illustrates the type of complexity that project authorities must be prepared to handle.

Food and other forms of relief

During the difficult Stage 2 years that immediately follow physical resettlement, food relief, a disturbance allowance and other forms of relief such as temporary cessation of taxation may be necessary while resettlers are re-establishing their livelihoods. The need for, and nature of, such relief should be discussed with affected people during the initial planning process. Where elaborate development plans are intended, as in the Akosombo case and the High Dam at Aswan, the possibility of major delays – such as occurred in both cases – needs to be built into planning. In both of those cases, which also involved large numbers of resettlers, assistance was provided by the World Food Programme – the need for which should be considered well ahead of time. Where to store food relief prior to use and how to transport it also requires careful attention, especially during the rainy season or seasons when road access may be difficult.

Other compensation in kind

While land for agricultural and other livelihood purposes is the most important resource requiring compensation in kind, it should always be the responsibility of the project authority to provide adequate water and sanitation facilities and social services such as schools and clinics. Other resources requiring similar treatment should be dealt with on a case-by-case basis. With fruit trees and wood lots, the best approach is replacement in kind if the household so wishes. On the other hand, provided adequate information is given on the implications of different options, resettlers may wish replacement value cash for building their own houses and associated structures as opposed to having project-financed contractors do the job or sharing different aspects of the work with the project authorities.

Cultural continuity and change

At the time of writing this section in October 2001, the World Bank's Board of Directors had recently approved, with no negative votes and only one abstention, a revised and weakened version of the Bank's guidelines on involuntary resettlement. Still allowing borrowers the fallback position of income and living standard restoration, those guidelines continue to show an unacceptable ignorance of the resettlement process since a restoration policy can be predicted to impoverish many, if not the majority, of those involved. Covering only 'direct economic and social impacts', it leaves out a range of important indirect and intangible cultural means for dealing with such important questions as 'Who are we? Where are we? Why do people live and die? What are our responsibilities to others and ourselves?' (Downing, 1996, p36).

Replying to such fundamental questions are cultural concepts of space and time, or what Downing calls social geometry, which are often tied to the place where rural people live. As my colleague George Appell theorized when we were graduate students, love of natal environment would appear to be a cultural universal, with Downing (after Marcus, 1994) pointing out that 'Research on environmental memories has discovered the near universality of fondly remembered childhood places, representing the intersection of culturally constructed time and place' (op cit, p40). For those forced to move, dam resettlement is especially stressful since places of origin and cultural meaning, once inundated, cannot be revisited.

Economic, political, social and religious attachment to natal environment is especially strong for those indigenous people, ethnic minorities and peasants who make up the majority of peoples evicted because of dam development. In the Gwembe Tonga case, rituals dealing with risks and uncertainty in making a living in a drought-prone and difficult environment (where people were dependent not just on agriculture but also on wild food plants, fish and game) were tied to sacred sites that were inundated by the Kariba reservoir and could not be transferred. Even if transference had been possible, it would have created conflict with the host communities in regard to existing ritual authority. In India, members of a Vasava community who were shifted from a forest habitat to five sites on the lower Narmada plain in connection with India's Sardar Sarovar project suffered major hardships from loss of grazing, fuel, building materials and other forest products. Those losses could be resolved through direct development means. Loss of forest access, however, also influenced Vasava 'religion, myths, social behaviour and their understanding of such concepts as space, distance and possession' (Hakim, 2000, p236).

Such losses can be mitigated but they cannot be restored. Mitigation can take the form of allowing resettlers to harvest their crops before inundation and to carry out harvest and other important ceremonies that are tied to specific locales. It should also involve ritually appropriate relocation of cemeteries and individual graves should resettlers so desire. A dispute during the Lesotho Highlands Water Project was whether miscarried foetuses that do not receive full burial rights should also be relocated as a project cost.

Another positive mitigation is to encourage and assist resettlers to complete appropriate departure and new site arrival rituals. In the Mahaweli case, these were officiated by Buddhist priests. In the case of Mexico's Zimapan Dam, festivals in the community of origin and the new settlement were coordinated (Downing, 1996, p46). Downing (after Guggenheim, 1993) also notes how Huichol resettlers in connection with the Aquamilpa Dam in Western Mexico worked with anthropologists in a census of village of origin sites and 'to create a symbolic reference map for the new sites' (op cit, p45). In all such cases active participation of resettling communities obviously is essential.

Mitigation can only go so far since some losses are irreversible. They are best addressed by providing opportunities that will allow resettlers to improve their living standards, including their capacity to incorporate their new sites and lives into an evolving cultural context. In this regard, one of the indicators of successful community formation associated with Stage 3 is the appearance of appropriate ritual, with religious leaders and structures. In the Gwembe Tonga case some resettlers began to participate in the agricultural rituals of the hosts. They also joined newly introduced fundamentalist Christian cults as well as acknowledging the ability of a cult developed locally, and combining customary aspects with new Christian ones, to deal with a range of resettlement-associated afflictions. Important in the Egyptian Nubian case was the reappearance of tombs associated with Muslim personages with associated ritual, and in the Sri Lankan Mahaweli case, the construction of Buddhist temples.

THE ISSUE OF REPARATIONS

In 1994, 326 signatories from 44 countries signed the Manibeli Declaration that requested the World Bank to stop funding dams until various corrective actions had been carried out. One of those actions was for the Bank to establish 'a fund to provide reparations to the people forcibly evicted from their homes and lands ... without adequate compensations and rehabilitation'. Involving the first international meeting of dam-affected people, the Curitiba Declaration extended that request in 1997 to all governments, donors and other agencies involved in dam construction. As with the Manibeli Declaration, one of the conditions for lifting the recommended moratorium involved 'reparations'. While the authors of the Bank's 1994 *Resettlement and Development* recommended 'remedial and retrofitting actions' (World Bank, 1994a, pp 8/2–8/3), the issue of reparations has yet to be systematically addressed by the Bank.

Defining reparations as 'action or processes that repair, make amends, or compensate for damages', Johnston notes that three types tend to be recognized: 'restitution, indemnity (or compensation), and satisfaction' (2000, pp39–40). In relation to dams, the first could involve restoration of living standards through the development of fisheries or drawdown agriculture, while the second tends to involve financial compensation for loss of physical assets. Satisfaction, in the form of public acknowledgement of a wrong and formal apologies, 'is meant to address any non-material damage' (ibid, p40). The emphasis throughout is on restoration following what may have been many years of impoverishment – hardly an unjustified request on the part of affected people!

Fortunately, precedent already exists where governments, and more recently donors, have begun to take action. In 1981 China's Reservoir Resettlement Law established a Maintenance Fund whereby dams with hydropower components set aside a proportion of revenue for the benefit of resettlers (Bartolomé et al, 2000, p24). In 1986 China's Ministry of Water Resources and Electric Power initiated a major programme to improve the living standards of approximately 5 million reservoir resettlers in 46 different areas (WCD, 2000, p129).

Although over 40 years after the initial claims were made, in 1994 the US paid US$54 million as reparations to Native Americans who had been impoverished by the construction of the Grand Coulee Dam in the 1940s. In 1995 the World Bank tied a loan to the Government of Pakistan for the Ghazi Barotha hydro project to dispute resolution for resettlers displaced by the Tarbela Dam 20 years earlier. Later in the 1990s the World Bank and the Development Bank of Southern Africa launched a reparations programme for the 34,000 Zambians who had been resettled in the late 1950s when the

Kariba Dam was built on the Zambezi (WCD, 2000, p128).

Establishing a precedent, however, is not enough. Nor is it sufficient to show how international covenants signed by most countries support the demands of resettlers for reparations, as WCD has done in its Final Report and supporting documents. A more proactive approach is necessary that must involve a wide range of actors in addition to affected people and their governments. That will require the assistance of research institutions better to monitor and evaluate the impacts of removal on resettlers and their hosts. It will also require more institution-building assistance from NGOs to help affected people better advance their own interests. Donors also have a responsibility to get involved. How then to coordinate the necessary participants?

As Bartolomé and his colleagues emphasized in their Social Issues submission to WCD, 'making reparations to displaced people requires considerable political will not just from national and regional governments but also from international development and infrastructure financing agencies as well as governments in the industrialized countries' (2000, p44). Lack of political will, however, has been an all too frequent failing, especially on the part of nations in which dams have been built, with affected people at every WCD public consultation telling the Commission 'about the ongoing problems, broken promises, and human rights abuses associated with the involuntary resettlement and environmental impacts from dams' (WCD, 2000, p228).

As a way forward, Johnston recommends as 'an essential first step ... the creation of an independent panel or commission charged with determining the shape and feasibility of an international reparations mechanism – a commission, tribunal, or other entity created through international agreement, treaty or other process' (Johnston, 2000, p42). Although that would appear to be a minimal international component, the sovereignty and other sensitivities involved make a more direct approach unlikely. How to approach the issue of reparations could also be a responsibility of the International Adjudication and Compliance Board recommended in Chapter 9.

5

Sri Lanka's Mahaweli Development Project

INTRODUCTION

In the initial draft of *The Future of Large Dams*, analysis of the Mahaweli Project was one of eight detailed case histories. It has been retained in its original form because it best illustrates the complexities and unexpected events that accompany the often lengthy planning and implementation of major projects involving large dams. Issue-relevant data from the other seven case histories have been incorporated elsewhere within the text, and especially in Chapters 3 and 6. The case histories are the Kariba (Zambia–Zimbabwe), Aswan High(Egypt–Sudan), Sardar Sarovar (India), Lesotho Highlands Water, Okavango (Botswana), Grande Baleine (Canada), and Nam Theun 2 (Laos) Projects. Readers interested in longer versions of these case studies that include a general analysis of each project, can download them from my website (http://www.hss.caltech.edu/~tzs).

During implementation in the late 1970s and throughout the 1980s, what was called the Accelerated Mahaweli Project (AMP or the Project) was one of the largest integrated river basin development projects under construction in the world. A national project in its potential impact, the government in power declared the AMP its lead project in its 'statement of political will' to which initially 30 per cent of national capital development funds were allocated. According to the Minister of Mahaweli Development, 'The Prime Minister, having given the utmost priority to this scheme, requested me to galvanize all the energies available in Sri Lanka to complete the Mahaweli Ganga Development Scheme within the lifetime of the present government' (MDB, 1977). That would be within seven years and before the next election, although the minister saw completion in five to six years.

The scope of the Project included four major dams on Sri Lanka's major river, the Mahaweli, and one on the Maduru Oya, with diversions into other river basins in north-eastern and north-western Sri Lanka (see Figure 5.1). As conceived by its advocates, the Project had the potential for catalysing a process of regional development, the multiplier effects of which would radiate throughout the country. Principal goals were employment generation and

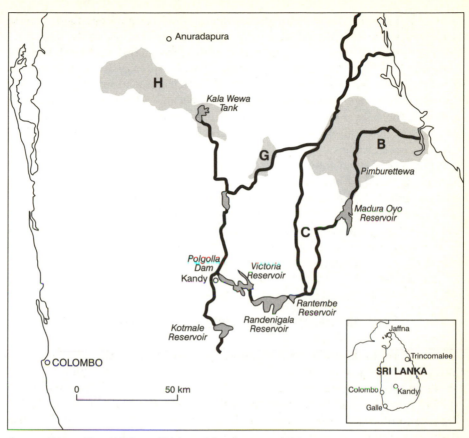

Source: Adapted from Ministry of Mahaweli Development, 1983

Figure 5.1 *The Accelerated Mahaweli Project*

achieving self-sufficiency in electricity generation and rice production. Rice and other field crops were to be cultivated by 225,000 peasant families to be settled on 0.2ha home lots and double cropping annually 1ha fields. The Project also had the potential for integrating into the various Mahaweli systems the Tamil-speaking Hindu and Muslim minorities.

None of these major goals were achieved for a range of reasons. One was organizational, with the hierarchical Mahaweli Authority unwilling to share implementation responsibilities with other agencies or to encourage settler participation during the important initial years of the project. Also important was the inability of Mahaweli planners to design a project that could stimulate a process of regional development. Far too much emphasis, for example, was placed on the double cropping of irrigated rice (paddy), with the result that the disposable income of thousands of Mahaweli Project households was insufficient to have major multiplier effects. Tamil-speaking Hindus were not selected as Mahaweli settlers according to their percentage of the national population – a situation that contributed to a continuation, and intensification, of the Sri Lankan civil war. By 1988, when a newly elected president shifted priorities away from the AMP, approximately 75,000 households, only one-third of those intended, had been settled in the three major Mahaweli systems (Systems H, C and B in order of development). Approximately 30,000 were host households. They had priority of settlement along with 10,000 households that were involuntarily displaced because of project infrastructure and had the option of choosing resettlement in one of the three systems.[1] Another 30,000 households were selected by members of parliament from their various constituencies.

The sections that follow begin with a brief description of the project area and people and of the nature of my involvement. Next comes a detailed analysis of the origin and history of Mahaweli development from the 1960s to the present. It includes major constraints that have kept the Mahaweli Project from catalysing a process of regional development. Benefits, and there are real benefits, are then discussed. Thereafter the settlement component, including our survey methodology, is analysed using data from the late 1970s to 2001. A final section deals with the major lessons learned.

THE PROJECT AREA AND ITS INHABITANTS

It is not easy to describe the area and people affected by the AMP since its influence extends over the entire country. Approximately 65,000km² in size, Sri Lanka contains five topographical regions that include 17 agro-ecological zones. Twice as long as the country's other rivers, the Mahaweli rises in the high-rainfall area of the central highlands where the Kotmale and Victoria Dams were built. It flows predominantly north through the lowlands that contain the various Mahaweli irrigation systems, to exit into the large natural harbour at Trincomalee. Rainfall in the northern lowlands falls largely during the northeast monsoon (December through February) and can be irregular, whereas the high-rainfall southwest region receives rain during both the northeast monsoon and the southwest monsoon (mid-May through September). While rainfall is ample in the southwest region, throughout the northern lowlands it is water rather than land that is scarce for what was predominantly a population of farmers at the commencement of the AMP.

Incoming Indo-Aryan migrants settled first in the northern lowlands prior to the beginning of the Christian era. During the first millennium, Singala-speaking Buddhist kings unified the predominantly Sinhalese population and built what archaeologists and historians consider to be some of the world's most impressive irrigation works and cities. Decline came during the 12th century, after which reforestation reclaimed much of the land. Reasons for decline vary with the interpreter. They include a combination of disease (especially malaria), warfare and irrigation decline because of problems such as salinity and water logging. When the Mahaweli Project began, the so-called dry zone of the country, though covering roughly 75 per cent of the country, contained only about 25 per cent of the population.

The dry zone population lived primarily in scattered villages. The large majority of villagers grew both rain-fed and irrigated crops, with irrigation provided by small reservoirs (tanks in South Asia) backed up behind earthen dams. As Leach notes in his classic study of a northern lowland village, it was the available supply of water that 'sets a limit to the area of land that may be cultivated and hence to the size of the population that may survive through subsistence agriculture' (1961, p17). Water also figured prominently in cultural symbolism. Dealing with the Buddhist majority, Disanayaka, in a section on Water in Nature and Culture, refers to 'Water, the Purifier, Water, the Life Giver, Water, the Symbol of Transfer, and Water, the Destroyer of Evil' (2000, pp31–48).

In the north-eastern area that was to be incorporated within the Project's System B, the majority of the population were Tamil-speaking[2] Hindu and Muslim villagers, who had been later immigrants into Sri Lanka, plus a small minority of the indigenous Veddah. What became System C was mainly forest, while what became System H contained mainly Sinhalese villages plus a minority of Hindu and Muslim villages. Throughout, villagers were predominantly farmers cultivating irrigated rice for consumption and rain-fed upland (*chena*) crops such as legumes, cucurbits, chillies and tobacco.

MY INVOLVEMENT IN THE MAHAWELI PROJECT

I first visited Sri Lanka in 1979, at the request of the US Agency for International Development (USAID) office in Colombo, as a consultant adviser on possible US assistance to ongoing Mahaweli development initiatives, with special emphasis on the settlement of new lands. After arrival I was very fortunate to be joined during the field portion of my visit by Kapila P. Vimaladharma (spelt Wimaladharma during the 1980s), which started a partnership and friendship that continued until his death in 2005.

Whereas I brought an international perspective to the study, Vimaladharma had the necessary knowledge of Sri Lankan cultures and culture history, administration and politics, and land settlement. A sociologist and senior official in the Ceylon Administrative Service, prior to our joining forces he had been the government agent responsible for one of Sri Lanka's 24 districts as well as the first Secretary and sociologist of the Mahaweli Development Board (MDB) in the early 1970s. When we first met he was Additional General Manager, Mahaweli Development Board, responsible for all aspects of policy planning for, and administrative direction of, land settlement activities in the Mahaweli systems. After approximately a year in that position, he became the head of the Ministry of Lands and Land Development's Land Settlement Department until August 1983, followed by three years as the National Adviser on the UNDP Project for Advancing Settler Expertise. Appointments since then had increasingly included consultancies with bilateral and multilateral agencies dealing with land settlement issues.

Our emphasis during my first visit was to familiarize me with Sri Lanka's experience with previous irrigated land settlement projects, some of which dated back to before World War II. We were especially interested in the Minneriya Project that Vimaladharma considered to be the most successful settlement scheme in Sri Lanka. Rising settler incomes caused major multiplier effects with non-farming employment generation and enterprise development stimulating the growth of a thriving commercial centre and town within the scheme. Thereafter we collaborated in the writing of five reports between 1980 and 1989. Funded by USAID, they evaluated the settlement component of the AMP through repeated interviews with a small sample of settler households, the number of which we gradually increased to 45.

USAID funding for our surveys ended after the 1989 visit. When I returned to Sri Lanka in 1998 for the first WCD consultation, Vimaladharma and I were able briefly to revisit a third of the sample households accompanied by Randolph Barker of the International Water Management Institute (IWMI) and Ranjit Wanigaratne, who was then the director of the Mahaweli Authority's Planning and Monitoring Unit (PMU). Sponsored by IWMI, in May–June 2001 Vimaladharma and Wanigaratne re-interviewed all 45 sample households in the three major Mahaweli systems as well as several others in a fourth system. They reported their results at the special Mahaweli Session of the Annual Meeting of the US Committee on Irrigation and Drainage that met in late June 2001 in Denver, Colorado.

Although our conviction that periodic re-interviews with small samples of households could evaluate a settlement process that eventually involved over 500,000 people aroused considerable scepticism (Scudder, 1993b), none of our major conclusions have subsequently been shown to be wrong. As a result, over the years we developed close professional ties with the late Gamini Dissanayake, who was the Minister in charge of both the Ministry of Mahaweli Development and the Ministry of Lands and Land Development. He in turn allowed us free access to officials in both ministries and arranged meetings with the Director General of the Mahaweli Authority of Sri Lanka and the President of Sri Lanka. Such access was invaluable and deeply appreciated since it allowed us to complement our field investigations with the knowledge and reports of officials in the key planning and implementation agencies.

I was personally excited to be involved in such a project. During our initial surveys, Vimaladharma and I made frequent mention of the AMP's development potential. I now realize that I was overoptimistic and naïve. Although my Kariba, Aswan High Dam and West African research and consultancies had made me aware of the complexities and difficulties associated with the successful implementation of projects involving large dams, I had yet to identify and think through the implications of the entire range of likely constraints. In the Mahaweli case, the subsequent failure of the settlement component to reach the third stage of economic development included various economic, political and religious issues. Most were derived from forces operating outside the project at a national level. Not arising from the way the project had been conceived and planned, they posed major implementation constraints because the project's size and national prominence drew the attention of powerful national figures with a range of very diverse, and often contradictory, agendas. If the Mahaweli case has significance for projects outside Sri Lanka, and I believe it does, that significance is that bigness in itself is a constraint to the realization of even well planned, government-implemented development (Scott, 1998).

Although still enamoured by the AMP, Vimaladharma and I began to have doubts in 1983 about it realizing its potential. In our report submitted that November we wrote: 'The Accelerated Mahaweli Programme is a grand concept; indeed it may well be the most ambitious program of its kind currently being implemented in the tropics and subtropics. It is a program that we fully support because it has such potential for improving the living standards of Sri Lankans at the household, village, district, regional, and national levels. *We believe, however, that there is a very real danger that this potential is not being realized, and will not be realized in the future*' (our italics, page 2).

Subsequently, at a time when others were emphasizing the project's ongoing success, we were the first to inform the Minister that the AMP risked replicating poverty within the Mahaweli systems. I remember the occasion well. The Minister had invited us to his Colombo residence to brief him on the results of our latest survey (one of the benefits of which was a written report within a fortnight of completion). As his unofficial advisers we had to inform him of our belief that the settlement component of the country's largest ever project was failing. A shocked silence followed – the Minister's initial reaction being that if such was the case he would have to resign. Since then our negative assessment has intensified and Vimaladharma and Wanigaratne's recent survey has further documented settler poverty and lack of multiplier effects. That conclusion is one reason why it is so important to carefully analyse and learn from the Mahaweli case.

EVALUATION OF THE MAHAWELI DEVELOPMENT PROJECT OVER TIME

Background

If any country had the capacity to plan and implement a large irrigated land settlement project, it was Sri Lanka. For a period extending over 2000 years, a series of civilizations had built dam-supplied irrigation works throughout the country's dry zone.[3] To provide water to the city of Anuradhapura the Abaya tank, or reservoir (*wewa* in Singala), covering 250 acres was built in the fifth century BC. The city's water supply was augmented during the third century BC by the construction of the 550 acre Tissa Wewa. Eight centuries later the 6000 acre Kala Wewa, which plays the major role today in supplying water to the Mahaweli Project's System H, was built to store water from the Kala Oya

River Basin and then channel it by a 54 mile canal into the Tissa Wewa. According to De Silva, 'This canal was an amazing technological feat, for the gradient in the first 17 miles of its length was a mere six inches to a mile' (1981, p30).

De Silva is not the only 20th century historian to eulogize the hydraulic technology of the early Sri Lanka kingdoms. According to Parker, ancient Sri Lankan reservoirs are 'among the finest and greatest works of the kind in the world' (1984, p382), while Disanayaka states that Toynbee considered Sri Lankans to have produced one of the world's 'foremost hydraulic civilizations' (2000, p77). Especially impressive in regard to sustainability over centuries were sluices, sometimes carved from the granite bed of a reservoir, which could have a double function – still spilling irrigation water when reservoir levels dropped and desilting them and fertilizing downstream fields.

Previous engineering capabilities were such that in a number of cases remains of dams and canals were found under excavations made for Mahaweli and earlier 20th century structures. One was found by the Canadians at the spot that they had identified for building the Maduru Oya Dam. So that it could become a national shrine, the modern dam site was shifted a short distance upstream. Sri Lanka's contemporary expertise was also impressive, having been honed during the completion of more recent projects, the impacts of which had been evaluated by countless studies including various PhD dissertations.

Mahaweli Project origins and initial planning

Origins

The first major proposal for diverting Mahaweli waters for development purposes was submitted by the US Overseas Mission (the precursor to the current Agency for International Development) in 1962. It dealt primarily with development in the upper basin and was rejected by Parliament for fear that it would reduce water availability for future projects in the lower basin.

In 1963 UNDP signed a master planning agreement with the Government of Sri Lanka for the Mahaweli River Basin. FAO was the Executing Agency. An Engineering Services Organization was established within the Department of Irrigation as the government's counterpart agency. In 1970 it was incorporated within the newly formed Mahaweli Development Board (MDB) 'together with most of the officials, equipment, vehicles and buildings' (Wimaladharma, 1984).

Also in 1970 the government changed, with the United Left Front taking over from the Sri Lankan Freedom Party that had laid the foundations for the Polgolla Project a month before the elections. With a socialist orientation, the policy of the United Left Front government was to favour a centrally planned economy with minimum foreign aid and maximum use of local contractors. Emphasis was placed on completing the major works at Polgolla that would enable water from the Mahaweli to be distributed to two major areas after passing through the 40MW Ukuwela power station en route to the Bowatenna reservoir. Distribution to the north-eastern area involved another 40MW power station that channelled Mahaweli waters via a tributary and various canals into a number of older irrigation schemes including Minneriya. The other would involve another trans-basin transfer whereby water would flow northwest from the Bowatenna reservoir to what became Mahaweli System H in the Kala Oya Basin. Completed in 1976, the Polgolla Project allowed 132,000 acres of previously irrigated land to be double cropped for the first time. Donors were unwilling, however, to provide funds for the development of new lands in System H because of the 'ultra-socialistic policies of the Government at the time' (Cooke, 1992, p67).

Planning

A Master Plan was completed in 1969. It covered 39 per cent of the entire country and 55 per cent of the dry zone. Three phases involving 15 separate projects were recommended to be implemented over a 30-year period under the MDB. The two major components were hydropower generation and irrigated production of paddy rice, to achieve national self-sufficiency, plus various other field crops. Headworks and canals were to channel water to 365,000ha, 100,000 of which were already irrigated but suffered water scarcity. An interesting aspect of the Master Plan was the incorporation of the Northern Province, which was largely inhabited by Tamil-speakers. Although subsequently dropped from the AMP, it could have played an important role in showing that Mahaweli development was for all Sri Lankans irrespective of ethnicity, language or religion. As for environmental issues, they were ignored in the Master Plan, while emphasis on agriculture stressed production as opposed to income generation, enterprise development and creation of non-farming employment.

After the MDB's formation, planning was directed by a cluster of experts around the Board Chairman with continued input from UNDP as well as the World Bank. Lasting only a few months, the first chairman was replaced by the Director of Irrigation. Although he had a broad view of the purposes of the Mahaweli Project, that did not prevent an irrigation and engineering bias from dominating the planning process throughout the 1970s. Just as the tendency in sub-Saharan Africa is to identify river basin planning with energy ministries, so the tendency in South Asia to make irrigation the responsible agency has created an obstacle to the implementation of integrated river basin development. Strengthening a technical planning approach was the disproportionate influence of senior engineers whose primary interest was the construction of the major headworks (Wickremaratne, 1995). The irrigation–engineering combination focused attention on individual Mahaweli irrigation systems rather than on the relationship – in terms of regional development – of the systems to each other and to adjacent towns and rural areas.

In 1978 UNDP published a lengthy document containing a rather remarkable set of recommendations for 36 planning studies based on the collective wisdom of an impressive set of international consultants working with three Sri Lankan colleagues, including Vimaladharma. Adviser and coordinator was W. J. van der Oord, who had previously played a key role in setting up the Mekong River Committee and Secretariat. The justifications presented for why the 36 studies were considered necessary provides an authoritative criticism of planning weaknesses at the AMP's very beginning. Estimated to cost about US$20 million, the studies were unfortunately not prioritized. That plus the massive nature of the report and its lack of sequential pagination no doubt contributed to its lack of influence on further government planning.

Especially significant was the report's concern about the inadequate attention paid by Mahaweli planners to marketing and to regional planning. In regard to marketing, 'there has yet to be a comprehensive marketing and price study of crop and livestock commodities physically suited to the various agro-ecological zones of the Mahaweli development area... The enormous production potential ... may not be realized unless an orderly commodity marketing and price structure is established' (UNDP, 1978, p1.4.1). The authors went on to note the lack of coordination between the different agencies responsible for such specific crops as tea and coconuts – there being no institutional capacity to deal with 'the market sector as a whole. This is a major and urgent undertaking' (ibid, p1.4.4). A related concern was the lack of attention being paid to agro-industries as well as the need for more attention to planning for the incorporation and upgrading of existing towns which, among other attributes, could provide sites for agro-business.

The government's lack of capacity for dealing with regional development is a topic that will recur throughout this chapter. In seeking an explanation, the authors noted that 'MDB's terms of reference, area of authority, composition, functions, and power as established in its constituting act limit the ability of the Board to examine the interfaces and relationships between the Mahaweli development area and the rest of the country and to measure the impacts of the settlement scheme on the regional structure of Sri Lanka' (ibid, p4.1.1). Although the government had a limited town and country planning capacity, its parent ministry was not represented on the Board. Worse yet, because 'comprehensive physical planning at various geographical levels remains unfulfilled' (ibid, p4.1.2), the only solution the authors saw was creation of a new institution (ibid, p4.1.5).

Within the different Mahaweli systems and agro-ecological zones another recommended study dealt with the need for, and lack of, appropriate soil surveys. While that is a major indictment of an agricultural development project, the absence, or poor quality, of soil surveys is a major inadequacy of land settlement schemes throughout the tropics and subtropics (Scudder, 1981b, pp215–216). In the Mahaweli case a partial excuse may have been the assumption that only one major cropping system – paddy – was anticipated. An obsession with paddy dates back to the 1930s. To reduce the necessity to import 50 per cent of the country's demand for rice, a policy decision was made to grow rice on all soil types regardless of suitability. While that requirement was dropped after 1965 in order to encourage cultivation of other food crops, emphasis on paddy by both the government and farmers has continued to the present.

The UNDP report was equally critical of the lack of emphasis on diversification that the authors emphasized should include livestock and fisheries as important components. While the Mahaweli Project presented a 'vast scope' for livestock production, that potential was being ignored even though national demand in recent years had resulted in the importation of beef and chicken (UNDP, 1978, p1.3.1). As for fish, the authors realized the great potential offered by the various sized tanks that would be incorporated within the Mahaweli Project.

1977–1988: The Accelerated Mahaweli Project

Introduction

Increasing unemployment estimated at 15–20 per cent and power deficits caused a change in government in July 1977, when the West-oriented United National Party (UNP) came to power. Their major development policy was to accelerate the completion of major components of the Mahaweli Master Plan before the next election. At this point a major policy contradiction occurred. On the one hand, as was stated by the Prime Minister shortly after the election, the main purposes of the AMP were 'employment first, employment second, and employment third' followed by hydropower and agricultural production. On the other hand, to speed construction and further the government's other liberalizing economic goals, international donors were invited to finance the major headworks. That decision led to international competitive bidding where World Bank and Asian Development Bank aid was involved, and to tied aid favouring home firms, as well as capital intensive construction, where bilateral aid was involved. Major dams became in effect donor projects. Kotmale, for example, on the upper Mahaweli was largely financed and built by the Swedes, while Victoria on the middle Mahaweli was a 'British' Dam, Randenigala on the lower Mahaweli 'German', and the trans-basin Maduru Oya Dam 'Canadian'.

Capital intensive development was favoured in all such cases undermining, for the construction phase of major structures, the UNP employment generation goal. Rather than 100,000 to 200,000 local jobs, the final tally was 'only 12,000 persons at times of peak activity' (Wickremaratne, 1995, p109). Acceleration also had adverse effects on the downstream development of the distributary system for irrigated settlement. Affecting large numbers of settlers, it resulted in inadequate contractor qualifications, poorly constructed canals as a result of haste, poor land preparation, and corruption (especially use of sub-standard materials or use of insufficient quantities). Employment generation failed to realize expectations in another way. Because the number of involuntary relocatees from reservoir basins, canal and other works had been underestimated, as well as the number of households already resident in the Mahaweli systems, the number of newly recruited households from outside project areas was only about 35,000 as opposed to the 225,000 peasant households mentioned in 1977! As for multiplier effects creating the type of non-farming employment and enterprise development that Vimaladharma had found at Minneriya, not only has that yet to occur, but it may be too late to occur for reasons explained in later sections.

Major AMP players and institutions

The key political players for implementing the AMP were N. G. P. Panditharatne and Gamini Dissanayake. The second most important member of the government after President Jayewardene, Panditharatne was the Chairman of the United National Party, Chairman of Hatton's National Bank and a member of the Monetary Board. In 1978 he became the Chief Coordinator of the AMP and then in 1979 was appointed the Director General of the new Mahaweli Authority of Sri Lanka (MASL or the Authority). With the Secretaries of the Ministries of Finance and Mahaweli Development as ex officio directors and an administrative Executive Director, the Authority incorporated the former MDB which was reorganized (and subsequently renamed the Mahaweli Engineering and Construction Agency) to handle downstream infrastructure development, while the Central Engineering Consultancy Bureau, which also had wider national responsibilities, became the government counterpart agency responsible for the various headworks. Subsequently a Mahaweli Economic Agency (MEA) was established as the third key institution within the Authority with responsibility for land settlement and related development in the Mahaweli systems.

Dissanayake had been a younger but rapidly rising Member of Parliament with a close personal relationship with Panditharatne (who had no children), and was looked on with favour by President Jayewardene. A lawyer, he was first elected to Parliament in 1970 at the age of 28. After the 1977 election he was appointed Minister of Irrigation, Power and Highways and then was assigned in 1978 to head the two key ministries assigned AMP responsibilities. Both staffed with exceptional Secretaries, these were the newly formed Ministry of Mahaweli Development and the old Ministry of Lands and Land Development that had previously overseen Mahaweli development activities. That same year Dissanayake appointed an interdisciplinary Advisory Committee on the AMP that Panditharatne chaired and which played a key role during the remainder of the 1970s in reducing the scope of the AMP from the overly ambitious and highly politicized 1977 version to the version that was to be implemented.

While they shared a close personal relationship and were both completely committed to the accelerated programme, Panditharatne and Dissanayake had very different views as to how to deal with the AMP as a land settlement project. Panditharatne's view was that settlers not only needed to be told what to do but must also be protected from outside influences. Dissanayake's view for all Sri Lanka's settlement schemes was well stated in his foreword to the 1978 Report of the Ministry of Lands and Land Development: 'I must emphasize the need for our officers to learn from the experience and age-old wisdom of our rural farmer so that all plans and programmes are in consenance [sic] with the existing farming systems which then should be fortified with new techniques and innovations for enhanced productivity after careful dialogue.' Unfortunately, Panditharatne's view dominated until his retirement in 1984, thus delaying for seven critical years more emphasis on the type of diversification and participatory development that was essential if the AMP was to realize its development potential.

Without doubt, putting people such as Panditharatne and Dissanayake in charge of key agencies played a significant role, along with the government's macro-economic policies, in bringing over one billion dollars of donor funding into the AMP in record time. In a tribute to Gamini Dissanayake on his 50th birthday, Cooke (a former chairman of the MDB and Special Adviser to the Minister in the late 1970s) gives a fascinating review of the fund raising process during a single visit to Europe on which Dissanayake was accompanied by Cooke and the Secretary of the Ministry of Finance.

The first stop was London, where Cooke credits Dissanayake's ability with convincing the British shortly thereafter to commit not just to the Victoria Dam Project but to downstream development in Mahaweli System C as well. In Stockholm a few days later, the Swedes had rejected several prioritized suggestions for funding when Cooke whispered to Dissanayake that the Kotmale Dam involved the type of hydropower project that the Swedes favoured. Although the Kotmale Dam was not high on the government's priority list at that time, 'Minister Dissanayake did not want to lose this opportunity for Swedish aid and offered this project to the Swedes who were happy to take it up' (Cooke, 1992, p71). This is the way that donor finance was acquired and project priorities established!

Yet the story continues. While in Stockholm the fund raisers received an invitation from a group of private sector firms in Germany who were interested in a Sri Lankan project because 'their expertise was lying idle due to a recession in their activities' (ibid). Itineraries were changed, with a visit to Bonn leading to a German visit to Sri Lanka and a financial agreement with the Government of Germany for those firms to build the Randenigala Project. So persuasive was Dissanayake that he was even able to convince the previous government's elderly and about-to-retire ambassador to the United Nations to assist him in seeking further funds (Coomaraswamy, 1992, p49). Subsequently the Asian Development Bank and the World Bank provided further aid with the World Bank also playing the role of coordinator of development assistance, a role that leveraged more bilateral aid.

Planning changes

Partly to address donor concerns about overambitious goals, NEDECO, a respected Dutch firm with international irrigation experience, was asked to review both the 1969 Master Plan and the government's 1977 acceleration goals. Apart from shifting later phase projects to the accelerated phase and lengthening the time to achieve AMP goals, the major headworks change from the 1969 Mahaweli Master Plan in NEDECO's 1979 report was to drop the Moragahakanda Dam. That eliminated, at least until the present, all possibility of further extending inter-basin transfers into northern areas with a larger Tamil-speaking rural population. As for downstream development, that was to focus on three major irrigation systems – H, C, and B, in order of development.

Even if the necessary infrastructure in the Master Plan had been built, it is far from certain that water in the Mahaweli system would be sufficient to irrigate available land. Partly this is because of other AMP changes relating to the height of the upper basin dam at Kotmale and the middle basin Victoria Dam. Although the Master Plan had envisioned a high dam at Kotmale to store additional water for downstream irrigation, cost overruns and the need to shift the dam site resulted in a lower Kotmale Dam being built. The problem was compounded by a decision, encouraged by British experts, to build a high dam at Victoria in order to increase the output of electricity. Implementation of that decision meant that more cost-effective electricity generation would be at the expense of agriculture when water was scarce since the Victoria Dam was located downstream from where the Polgolla Project diverted water north for irrigation. One result is that the H system has suffered seasonal periodic water shortages.

Major AMP implementation constraints

AMP activities favouring the Buddhist majority at the expense of Tamil-speaking Hindus

Although proud of its ancient Buddhist and Hindu civilizations, since independence successive majority-elected governments have discriminated against the Tamil-speaking Hindu minority in a number of ways. Hindu entry into the civil service, the army and the university system was constrained, for example, while the Tamil language was marginalized in the educational system and at the national political level. The independence years have also been clouded by periodic and bloody clashes between Singala-speaking Buddhists (Sinhalese) and the Tamil-speaking Hindu minority, with worsening attacks on Hindus in Colombo and other urban centres as well as in rural areas during the 1980s.

In spite of numerous attempts to explain increasing ethnic strife by such reasons as ancient warfare between Sinhalese and Hindu civilizations, the favouritism shown to the better-educated Hindu minority by the colonial authorities, and post-independence paranoia because of the close proximity of hundred of millions of Tamil-speaking Hindu across the Palk Straits in South India, it is hard to explain the depth of antagonism behind Sri Lankan ethnic strife. Eventually erupting into a civil war between the government and the Liberation Tigers of Tamil Eelam (LTTE or the Tamil Tigers), certainly it has boomeranged not just against successive discriminating governments but also against all Sri Lankans.

During our interviews in the northern portion of System B, Vimaladharma and I were well aware that some of our interviews were attended by well-dressed youth of both genders who we knew to be Tamil Tigers. As in conflict-ridden African countries where educated youth are kept by government policies from participating in national development, I could understand why such Hindu youth would eventually come to believe that they had little to lose by taking up arms in an ill-fated attempt to hive off an independent Tamil-speaking homeland.

One reason why I was initially so enthusiastic about the AMP was that initial plans were to incorporate Sri Lanka's various ethnic groups according to their proportion in the population. In 1981, Sinhalese constituted 74 per cent of the total, indigenous Tamil-speaking Hindu 12.6 per cent, Tamil-speaking Hindu recently arrived from India to work the tea estates (and not active in the LTTE) 5.5 per cent, and others (mainly Muslims) 7.9 per cent (Central Bank of Ceylon, 1981). I had hoped that implementation of the government's lead project for the benefit of all Sri Lankans would play a role not just in reducing communal strife but in helping with ethnic integration.

Such was not to be the case. Whether intentional or not, Wickremaratne notes that the President's 1979 policy on the selection of AMP settlers 'increased ethnic discontent' (1995, p39). First priority was given to families already living within the various project areas, including descendants of the original pioneers (hosts) and more recent families (spontaneous settlers) that had in-migrated before AMP cut-off dates. Priority was also given to those uprooted by headworks, other infrastructure and reservoir formation. While these priorities would meet international 'best practice' today, those that followed would not. Spreading out in concentric circles, they favoured applicants from adjoining electorates followed by 'wet zone districts with the most adverse man-land ratio'. As those districts contained few Tamil-speakers, the AMP was biased against Hindus from the start. By the end of the AMP, of the more than 75,000 households settled in the various Mahaweli systems, only 1.9 per cent were Hindu and 2.9 per cent Muslim (Wickremaratne, 1995, p40).

Even in system B where Tamil-speakers lived in adjoining electorates, none were selected as Mahaweli Project households. In fact, a cabal within the Mahaweli Authority, working with a nationally prominent ultra-nationalistic Buddhist priest who was subsequently killed by the Tamil Tigers, organized a land-invasion in 1983 during which they claimed to have imported 45,000 poor Sinhalese settlers from the Kagalle District at the southern end of the island (Gunaratna, 1988). Surely that figure was an exaggeration; nonetheless many thousands were said to have been involved.

By creating a corridor of Singala-speaking Buddhist settlers in a Tamil-speaking homeland between the northern portion of System B and Trincomalee, the plotters' intention was to split the major Tamil-speaking areas in the Northern Province from those along the east coast in the Eastern Province south of Trincomalee. The land invasion was ill-timed, with the government forced to remove the immigrants because of complaints from the Canadian Government, which was the principal donor in System B, and the Indian Government, whose Minister of Foreign Affairs happened to be in Sri Lanka at the time. Presumably because he had, at the very least, been aware of the impending land invasion, Panditharatne was also affected by the fiasco, resigning in 1984 as the Authority's Director General as well as Chair of the United National Party.

Immediately thereafter the government continued to follow its policy of favouring the selection of poor Sinhalese from the Kagalle District at the south end of the island as new settlers in the northern portion of System B. In so obviously discriminating against the area's Tamil-speaking majority, that politically inspired policy, as with the land invasion, placed Sinhalese settlers at risk from LTTE retaliation. My criticism does not reflect the wisdom of hindsight; in a lengthy 1985 memo to the US Agency for International Development I stated my concern that the AMP's settler selection policies were responsible for increasing communal strife by bringing poor Sinhalese settlers into a Tamil homeland.

Arguing that the situation showed the government's bad faith in a number of respects, I wrote that 'Mixing Singala- and Tamil-speakers in the same community is not only a blueprint for future ethnic strife, but it also places the lives of those Kagalle settlers at risk. They, not the security forces, are manning the frontier between the Singala- and Tamil-speaking areas. Should militant Tamil youths decide to retaliate against AMP settlement policy, it is likely to be those isolated ... settlers who would be attacked.'

In the same memo I noted the extent to which the government's security forces were harassing (and, as I learned during our 1989 visit, torturing) Tamil-speakers in two villages that Vimaladharma and I had incorporated in 1979 into our ongoing evaluation. From one of those villages the security forces had removed over half of the young men. Weeks later none had returned, 'nor had their parents, relatives and friends received any news as to where they were, what had happened to them, or when they might be coming back' (ibid). Subsequently I received a letter from one resident in which he said that the youths were still in detention and that 'mothers also still crying continuously'. I knew that he was not exaggerating because on our earlier arrival at the village one mother had thrown herself to the ground, clasped my feet and begged us to help restore her children. So fearful were some families that they were fleeing the village to the relative safety of Trincomalee, hence reducing the odds that they would eventually be incorporated within System B as Mahaweli settlers. And indeed the proportion of legitimate households that did not eventually receive Mahaweli holdings was larger than in Sinhalese host communities.

USAID did not reply to that 1985 memo. Indeed, its only impact appears to have been a decision on the part of USAID not to renew funding for further reviews until 1989 after new personnel had staffed the Colombo office. In 1987, however, I received a memo from a colleague in Washington stating that 'the US embassy reported on June 1, 1987 that a village in System B was attacked on May 29, 1987 by an insurgent band that killed two men, five women and a baby and wounded four other persons... Embassy analysis ... believe that this village may have been singled out because it is home to one of the largest Sinhalese 'selectee' groups in the Mahaweli. Those settlers came from the Kagalle District.' Subsequent massacres of both Sinhalese and Tamil settlers have continued to occur with at least 20 people killed in our two study villages and at least 74 killed in a 1992 attack on other System B villages. In all such cases, I believe that the government's subversion of its own settlement policies to foster political goals has been a major causative factor. Some blame must also be assigned to the donor community including USAID and the World Bank who failed to take a strong stand against the government's violation of its policies. Although it was agreed during 1986 negotiations in Bhutan that yet-to-be-initiated settlement on the right bank of the Maduru Oya in System B would be restricted to Tamil-speakers, ongoing communal strife continues to preclude the implementation of that decision.

Construction bias

In addition to the various problems associated with acceleration was a construction bias on the part of key senior Mahaweli Authority officials that has adversely affected downstream development. Especially influential was D. D. G. P Ladduwahetty, an engineer and last chair of the MDB before its 1979 incorporation within the Authority. He was responsible for accelerating the construction of headworks. In a 1983 World Bank Staff Working Paper, Richard Heaver noted how Ladduwahetty's construction bias adversely affected the settler population as a result of 'the poor articulation between the construction and development phases of the project'. Heaver was also concerned about a decreasing willingness to accept criticism: 'Monitoring and evaluation (M&E) also suffered. Although initially the chairman supported M&E, he subsequently brought it under his direct control after monitors began to document implementation inadequacies. With both planning and monitoring dominated by the chairman, the better staff resigned – with M&E deteriorating over time' (World Bank, 1985a, p31 based on Heaver, 1983).

Irrigation system bias at the expense of a diversified settler household production system, non-farming employment generation, and regional development

As stated in our second Mahaweli report in 1980, 'the greatest single weakness of Mahaweli planning is the longstanding tendency to focus on separate areas under irrigation command ... as opposed to the integrated river basin and inter-basin development of larger areas' (Scudder, 1980, p2). At the time, I was in the process of completing a global review of large-scale government-sponsored irrigated and rain-fed settlement schemes. Their analysis had convinced me that projects such as the AMP had the potential of creating at least one non-farming job for every farming household, provided the rising disposable income of the farming community stimulated increasing purchases of goods and services, and provided the necessary marketing services and commercial centres were available. Although not yet affecting my enthusiasm for the AMP, my concern, even in 1979, was that the necessary planning for achieving major multiplier effects was not occurring. That year I had recommended that a high-level Mahaweli workshop be convened to deal with a range of critical issues. They included a regional perspective that incorporates current urban centres; marketing networks and nearby villages; occupational specialization within settler communities; crop diversification; and integration of crop agriculture with livestock management, fisheries and forestry. With the partial exception of crop diversification, all were neglected during the 1970s and well into the 1980s.

These weaknesses dated back to the very beginning of the MDB that grew out of, and was housed in, the Department of Irrigation. Although officials talked about the importance of the Mahaweli Project fostering a process of regional development, actual planning for such development did not exist. Rather, development of the three major Mahaweli systems proceeded as if they existed in a vacuum. Even adjacent towns and commercial centres were ignored, with the Mahaweli agencies increasing project costs by creating one or two expensive new towns in each system. A case in point was the new town of Girandukotte in the southern portion of System C that was less than 20km from a thriving old town which at that time was undergoing a major process of renewal in anticipation of becoming the headquarters of a new district. As part of our methodology, we had followed the development of such new towns by enumerating the number and type of commercial activities. When Vimaladharma and Wanigaratne revisited Girandukotte in 2001, commercial activities catering to larger numbers of people were noticeable only on the day of the weekly market. Even then, a significant number of shops remained shut. After the market closed down, with vendors moving off to other locations in the market circuit, 'the town literally "closed shop" ' (Wanigaratne and Vimaladharma, 2001, p17).

Although the fact that Sri Lanka was on a 'war footing' must be taken into consideration, they also found drains clogged up with refuse, while the only public water tap near the bus station had been closed by the local authorities 'as an uneconomic public utility' in spite of the fact that school children passing through the town would have benefited from a safe water supply. Public health was further jeopardized because of inadequate servicing of the public toilets. As traffic dwindled, 'the bus stand serves as an informal stray cattle shed during evening and night times... The overall town scenario is one of total neglect.'

Galnewa, a similar new town, had been built with similar fanfare in System H despite the existence of one old town on the northern fringe with another situated on a main route near the western boundary. When opened for business, optimistic shopkeepers stocked their new stores with the type of goods found in the thriving commercial centre that served the highly successful Minneriya scheme. By 1985, some shops had already gone out of business, while others had scaled down the quality of their merchandise. Apart from vendors attending the weekly market, in 1989 we found the only successful businesses were coffin-making funeral directors, the number of which had increased from one to two. In 2001 Vimaladharma and Wanigaratne found that for every five shops at least one was closed and shuttered.

Policies of the Mahaweli Authority's Director General

N. G. P. Panditharatne was a dynamic, self-assured, successful businessman and politician whom I liked and respected while disagreeing with those of his policies which I believed were keeping the AMP from realizing its development potential. While his presence illustrated for donors the importance that the government placed on Mahaweli development and facilitated acquisition of the necessary donor finance, 'his appointment accelerated the politicization of the AMP in ways that imposed further constraints on the development of settler institutions. At the same time Panditharatne's strong religious views adversely affected settler living standards by constraining diversification of production at household and village levels' (Scudder, 1995a, p154).

Vimaladharma and I were especially critical of two policies that we saw as serious constraints. The first arose from Panditharatne's conviction that peasants were easily confused and hence required strong top-down leadership from a single government organization. On at least one occasion, he told me that because of his own rural background, he 'knew' peasants, he 'knew' what was good for them, and he 'knew' they would do what he told them. To provide the necessary leadership, MASL Act No. 23 of 1979 required all activities within AMP areas, with the exception of policing, national security and banking, to be carried out by the Authority. This effectively restricted access of such ministries as agriculture and public works as well as of the private sector and NGOs. Even marketing was to be strictly an Authority function, while development activities, such as fisheries, where the Authority had no capacity, were initially ignored.

Land settlement is too complicated a development process to be restricted to government agencies, let alone officials of a single agency with top-down priorities. The active involvement of settler-led institutions, the private sector and NGOs as well as other government agencies is also necessary (Scudder, 1995a, p151 and Chapter 8, this volume). In the Mahaweli case, all such agencies were shut out of the AMP during the 1980s.

Undermining the emergence of settler-led organizations in the late 1970s and early 1980s was Panditharatne's insistence in 1983 that henceforth the principal settler organization must be headed by junior Mahaweli Authority officials who increasingly were being recruited from university graduates, who were government party members and who had little experience with rural development. Vimaladharma and I were especially critical of this policy in our 1983 report. It caused settlers to view so-called farmers' organizations as belonging to the Mahaweli Authority rather than as their own institutions. Some settlers also believed that the officials in charge intentionally ignored settlers' project-related complaints for fear that such complaints would reflect negatively on their reputation if they were forwarded to a higher level in the Mahaweli Authority hierarchy (Scudder and Wimaladharma, 1983, p14).

Restricting the private sector from institution building and marketing activities also had negative impacts. Starting in 1981, Vimaladharma and I began monitoring a very interesting experiment that the Ceylon Tobacco

Corporation (CTC) had initiated in a zone of H System at the request of the Mahaweli Authority.

CTC already had had ample experience with small-scale farmers. In addition to a large population of contract farmers growing rain-fed tobacco, the company had also started its own small-scale irrigated settlement scheme in the mid-1960s for 60 families. Ahead of the times, in their System H zone they were attempting to involve settler-led organizations in the operation and maintenance of irrigation distributary canals. They were also trying to diversify household production systems into higher value crops that CTC then helped to market. In comparison to the Authority's MEA, settlers informed us that the CTC also did a superior job in providing extension services, being more likely to meet with farmers in their fields rather than in the class room. Yet in 1983, MASL terminated CTC involvement without explanation.

The second seriously constraining policy arose from Panditharatne's strong, indeed fundamentalist, Buddhist beliefs. In addition to de-emphasizing crop diversification in favour of paddy production, initially he strongly opposed incorporation of livestock into the settler farming system as well as the development of fisheries on AMP reservoirs and the many older tanks that had been incorporated within the Mahaweli systems. Although he eventually agreed to a dairy programme, and fowl and egg production increased in importance after his 1984 retirement, the opportunity of incorporating livestock management from the start had been lost.

When a dairy programme was finally developed under Chris de Saram, who subsequently became a MASL Director General in the second half of the 1980s, it played an important role in the settler community. As wealthier settlers increased their number of cows, lack of grazing encouraged them to herd out cattle to the care of poorer farmers on a share-cropping system through which caretakers were paid in calves so that they too could become dairy farmers in time. As numbers of dairy producers slowly increased, cooperatives were formed in which the daughters of settlers found employment as managing secretaries.

Although restricted primarily to the larger reservoirs, fisheries development also was finally encouraged after Panditharatne's 1984 resignation from the Mahaweli Authority, with the Department of Fisheries allowed to provide improved boats on credit. However, it was only in the second half of the 1990s that a major programme was initiated to increase production and employment. As with dairy, the development potential that could have been realized from the start is illustrated by a 1997 estimate that the total potential productivity of the fishery is 22,400 tonnes per annum (MASL, 1997, pv). While this includes the currently expanded Mahaweli system that includes the Uda Walawe Reservoir outside the Mahaweli basin, most of that production would come from the three major Mahaweli systems. As for dairy, the opportunity lost by not emphasizing livestock management from the start is also illustrated by 1997 statistics. At the time of Vimaladharma's and my last report in 1989, dairy production fell just below 600,000 litres. By 1997 it has risen to nearly 2.4 million litres, with a 14.9 per cent growth rate per annum.

Inconsistent implementation of policies

Especially damaging was the ambivalence within the Mahaweli family of agencies toward institutions run by settlers. While burial and temple societies were acceptable, attitudes toward village or water user associations run by settlers changed during the early years of the AMP. Partly responsible was the history of development-oriented local societies since independence. While a successful participatory cooperative movement had existed in the 1950s, thereafter the most prominent local organizations had been created by the government in power for the control rather than the participation of the farming community. Viewed by farmers as government organizations, they responded in a non-participatory way.

On coming to power in 1977, the UNP abolished the previous government's Agricultural Production Committees and Cultivation Committees. Because new AMP replacement policies had yet to be initiated, various officials in the field experimented with several interesting participatory approaches. Anticipated by planners in the early 1970s, in System H Mahaweli agencies were experimenting with water user associations focused on each irrigation turnout,[4] while CTC was experimenting with similar organizations at both the turnout and distributary canal level. In System C, experiments were underway with worker/settler groups that worked together building both houses and the irrigation system that they would subsequently be using.

We were impressed by the initial results of such experiments, noting in our 1980 report that 'the current organization of turnout groups is tremendously important and should be encouraged', while worker/settler groups in System C, we believed, presented 'an excellent opportunity to federate turnout units at the D channel level soon after they were formed' (Scudder, 1980, p22). Where institutional difficulties occurred in a minority of turnout groups, observed that year and in 1981, we were inclined to blame them on too heterogeneous a membership caused by the mixing of very different categories of people, such as upcountry reservoir evacuees with local dry zone villagers (hosts). Such cases were in the minority, however. Generally speaking we found that members of turnout groups were working increasingly well together and that water distribution and general management was improving.

On our return in 1983 we found that participatory institutions had suffered a major setback because of Panditharatne's new policy that the key settler organization must be chaired by an MASL official. The emphasis then was on setting up Authority-headed hamlet associations that were organized to include turnout representatives, women, youth and other MASL-stipulated categories. Those representatives, including turnout leaders, in some cases were even appointed by Mahaweli officials, with observable impacts on reduced water management cooperation. Two years later, while elsewhere in Sri Lanka other government agencies were beginning to put greater emphasis on settler-run water user associations, we found no effective settler-run institutions dealing with irrigated agriculture in the Mahaweli systems. It was already apparent that MASL-dominated hamlet associations were having an adverse impact on community formation and economic development. Moreover, rather than controlling settlers as intended, hamlet associations were having the exact opposite effect with settlers beginning to join other types of organizations for better meeting their social, economic and political needs (Scudder and Wimaladharma, 1985, p30).

With Panditharatne no longer Director General after 1984, interest within MASL in a widening range of settler-run organizations increased. As Panditharatne's replacement, Chris de Saram was pushing individual dairy societies and their federation within a dairy union, while Jayantha Jayewardene, in charge of the MEA, was a strong supporter of turnout organizations and their federation at the distributary canal level. A 1989 Cabinet decision to push water user associations throughout Sri Lanka provided further stimulus which Wanigaratne and Vimaladharma reported continues today, although the tendency for individual Mahaweli officials to superimpose their authority on settler activities continues.

Other external events
POLITICS WITHIN THE UNP When President Jayewardene decided not to stand for re-election in 1988, three UNP ministers competed to replace him, one of this group being Gamini Dissanayake. However, R. Premadasa, the Prime Minister at the time, was selected, becoming President when the UNP was returned to power. Seeing Dissanayake as his principal rival within the UNP, Premadasa's efforts to marginalize him included, in my opinion, downgrading the AMP at the very time that additional finance and effort were needed to complete the project. Using more diplomatic language, we generalized the problem in our 1989 report by stating 'Within Sri Lanka we see lack of strong political support for the AMP as a very serious problem... (F)armers now point to a lack of attention to, and concern for, their problems. As for high government officials and donors, both seem to have forgotten that the AMP continues to be Sri Lanka's largest and most important single development project. To reduce commitment and funding at this time ... makes no sense whatsoever' (Scudder and Wimaladharma, 1989, p19).

Although implementation would have been difficult because of the ongoing civil war in the area, especially important would have been allocating funds and initiating construction for Tamil settlement on the right bank of System B, as agreed upon during the 1986 Bhutan negotiations. While risks would have been involved, we noted in our 1985 report that there was no evidence that the LTTE had any intention of damaging irrigation structures on either the left or the right bank. In support of such an interpretation we noted how planning for Mekong River development continued during the Vietnam war, while Zambia and Rhodesia continued to operate joint facilities at Kariba during the war for Zimbabwe's independence.

Instead of following through on necessary AMP development, Premadasa pushed his own project – 100 new houses for low-income Sri Lankans in every electoral district – which was more designed for getting votes than for development. No longer Minister of Mahaweli Development, Dissanayake was shunted aside as Minister of Plantations, a position that he held for 14 months, before Premadasa removed him from the Cabinet without explanation. After a recuperating period at Cambridge University where he did Development Studies, Dissanayake returned to Sri Lanka to play an active role with UNP parliamentary colleagues in an unsuccessful attempt to impeach the President. Their goal was to 'curb the Powers of an Executive Presidency which had encroached on the rights of individual MPs, as well as the larger civil society... Five months later, Gamini was no longer an MP, and he together with nine others, formed a new political party' (Hullugalle, 1992, p5). Subsequently both Dissanayake and Premadasa were killed in separate suicide bombing attacks.

THE SRI LANKAN JANATHA VIMUKTHI PERAMUNA (JVP) INSURGENCY Sri Lankan governments have suffered the insurgency of Sinhalese youth as well as Tamil youth. Lack of employment and lack of involvement in the governing process are common causes. Although currently a legitimate political party, the JVP rebelled in both 1971 and during the 1980s. In the 1980s they targeted the AMP, including settlers who were UNP members, as representative of the government in power. Especially active in System H but also active in System C, they killed local government officials as well as settlers including one household head in our sample. In addition to creating a sense of insecurity throughout the area, JVP actions also had an adverse effect on participatory institutions since settler leaders were especially at risk.

JVP attacks and government retaliation were vicious. In 1985 we were interviewing beside a major road in System H when several security vehicles went by. In response to our queries, we were told that a JVP landmine had detonated under a jeep, killing five security personnel. Wanting to assess the validity of rumours that security force retaliation targeted anyone in the immediate vicinity of an attack, including Mahaweli settlers, we visited the site the next day after travelling through several road blocks. Tragically, the rumours were correct. An elderly settler living beside the road where the landmine exploded told us how the security forces came to his house at night, piled up his furnishings in one room and torched the house. In the vicinity, I counted over 20 settler homes that were similarly burned.

Also told that the security forces further retaliated by killing youths at nearby crossroads to terrorize the settler population, we drove to one of the sites mentioned. The victims had been decapitated, necklaced with tyres and burned with gasoline. When we arrived, only ashes, the metal reinforcing of the tyres, pelvic bones and vertebrae remained. I counted the number of victims by counting the pelvic bones. Five people had been burned. Subsequently I was told by reliable sources that the total number killed in retaliation was 70 people, although I had no way of confirming that figure.

1988–2001: The post-AMP years

Although 1988 is an arbitrary date for considering the national influence of the AMP to have ended, it is as good as any. Since the 1980s no further major headworks have been completed, although a recent feasibility study has re-

examined the Moragahakanda Dam. As for the specific date of 1988, that was
the year of Premadasa's election as president when he de-emphasized not just
the AMP but the entire Mahaweli Project. It was also the year that Gamini
Dissanayake's dynamic leadership of the AMP came to an end.

Since then further settlement has continued in the northern portion of
System C where a second new town was completed at Dehiattakandiya. During
their 2001 visit Vimaladharma and Wanigaratne found Dehiattakandiya to be
more active than the larger Girandurukotte, due partly to the distance from
other commercial centres and to the Resident Project Manager having shifted
his administration there. In System B the ongoing civil war had slowed further
expansion. In 1998 when we visited one village late in the afternoon, we met
the villagers leaving their homes in order to spend the night behind the
government security forces. That was the pattern in other villages as well.
During the daylight hours the settlers visited their homes and fields; at night
the LTTE took over.

The biggest changes in the Mahaweli Project have been in the past five
years during which the MASL has undergone a major restructuring, while
rehabilitation efforts have been ongoing in all systems. Restructuring was a
requirement for a further World Bank loan in 1997 of US$57 million that
also included rehabilitation of canal networks in System H. It involved several
major initiatives including downsizing the staff from 10,918 to 4968 through
use of a Voluntary Service Relinquishment Payment. By early 2001, about
5500 employees had left (Niyangoda, 2001, p9). Other initiatives linked a
strengthening of settler participation with private sector activities,
commercialization of activities and staff redeployment to support those
efforts.

Thirty years too late, a further initiative was referred to by the President in
her budget presentation in February 2001. As part of the World Bank loan,
this initiative is a proposal, still to be implemented, to convert the MASL 'from
a project implementing agency to a River Basin Management Agency in order
to revitalize the role of the agency' (Sri Lanka, 2001). As Niyangoda succinctly
words it, 'The Mahaweli Authority itself is a River Basin Management Agency
but no proper River Basin Management is being practiced' (2001, p10,
footnote 6). He also notes that conversion, as with the other initiatives, will
not be easily achieved since most of the more experienced technical staff have
resigned, while many of those that remain do not have the necessary training.

When formed, the new agency will be called the Mahaweli River Basin
Management Agency. As one of a number of agencies responsible for
implementing the new National Water Resources Policy throughout the
country, it must take the lead 'in planning, developing, and managing in a
participatory manner, current and remaining economic water resources,
development opportunities in the Mahaweli and connected river basins, fully
integrating environmental, soil, technical and resource sustainability
considerations' (ibid, p10).

System rehabilitation is the infrastructural and developmental initiative
designed to increase settler participation and raise the disposable income of

settler households in all systems. In System H, the rehabilitation of '893km of canal network through farmer participation benefiting 31,500ha and over 20,000 families' (MASL, 1997, piii) is underway. Also being implemented in System G and part of System C under donor funding is a project linking irrigation and road rehabilitation with extension, credit (primarily for paddy cultivation) and strengthening of settler institutions. In System B, the Saudi government is following up on previous left bank assistance with further funding for social development. Those are the goals. Whether or not they can be achieved remains to be seen. According to Vimaladharma (personal communication), an ongoing problem continues to be staff attempts to control and/or undermine settler initiative and institutions seen as threatening staff authority.

BENEFITS ACHIEVED: 1977–2001[5]

Overall project benefits

Before detailing the constraints which I consider responsible for the failure of the Mahaweli Project, not just as a land settlement scheme but as a project for integrated river basin development, it is important to acknowledge the benefits that were realized during the years of Jayewardene's presidency (1977–1988) and thereafter.

Installed AMP generating capacity is 671 MW, which exceeds the projected output from the 30-year Master Plan. During the ten-year period between 1988 and 1997 the percentage of AMP output to national energy production ranged between 36 per cent and 56 per cent. A total of 75,609 households were settled on a similar area of irrigated new lands in the three major Mahaweli systems plus System G, with an unknown proportion of the second generation receiving home lots after marriage. Approximately 100,000ha of previously irrigated land received Mahaweli waters for double cropping. During the 1994–1997 period, the share of national paddy production provided by the Mahaweli Project varied between 20 and 26 per cent. The similar share of chillies ranged between 20 and 59 per cent, Bombay onions 38 to 79 per cent, soya beans 20 to 52 per cent, and green gram – by far the most important legume consumed in Sri Lanka – between 10 and 16 per cent. While these are impressive figures, until the present, the Mahaweli Project's land settlement component has continued to emphasize the double cropping of paddy.

Of a crop production output of over 800,000 tonnes in 1999, 81 per cent was paddy. While this emphasis has helped Sri Lanka approach self-sufficiency in rice production, the land settlement component of the Mahaweli Project, the largest project of its kind in Sri Lanka and one of the largest in the world, which told over 600,000 people where to live and what to do, still remains in the adjustment and coping stage (Stage 2) of the four-stage framework after more than 20 years of implementation. Furthermore, at this late date, I have serious doubts as to the ability of the majority of settler households to move beyond subsistence, hence limiting the project's potential multiplier effects.

Through 1997, approximately 53 per cent of financing had been used for headworks, power stations and construction, and operation and maintenance of the trans-basin water diversion system. The other 47 per cent financed downstream development. In terms of output, 52 per cent came from crop production, 3 per cent from livestock, 11 per cent from non-farming activities and 34 per cent from power (MASL, 1997). According to Wanigaratne, by the end of 1999 the sale of power alone had exceeded the investment cost of the project up until that time. Adding on the value of crop production, he calculated a cost–benefit ratio of 1:2 (Wanigaratne and Vimaladharma, 2001, p3).

Settlement benefits

Although acceleration caused delays, with construction of health services and schools poorly synchronized with the pacing of settlement, settlers have benefited from improved social services. In two of the older System H settlement zones, Bandaragoda notes that they appeared higher than the national average. For a population of about 25,000, the MASL had built 23 primary schools, 17 junior secondary schools and one senior secondary school. A network of family health workers had been established and two new hospitals had been built with four medical officers between them (Bandaragoda, 1987, p167).

While the majority of settlers were still poor in 2001, most were less poor than they had been before the Mahaweli Project began. In three System H villages studied during 1985–1986 and revisited in 1989, Rodrigo categorized one-third of the households as failing, one-third on a plateau and one-third successful. Based on a 1000 household sample surveyed in 1997, Wanigaratne and Vimaladharma referred to about 38 per cent of households in Systems C and G as being at a subsistence poverty level (2001, p68). When Vimaladharma and I asked households in our 1989 sample in what way they had benefited from the AMP, a frequent answer was that 'now we have irrigated land whereas before we had none'. In addition to land, the majority of settlers also have been able to slowly improve their housing and to furnish it, TVs being common in 2001.

Throughout the 1979–2001 period our data illustrates the ingenuity and enterprise of the large majority of settlers. Both were specifically mentioned in the 1981 report and again in the 2001 report. Nonetheless, variations in income distribution became apparent in all systems within a few years. Other studies also suggest that approximately one-third of settler households have been able to improve their income, with perhaps 10 per cent improving their income and their living standards significantly. Based on processed data from 2000/01 base-line socio-economic studies, Wanigaratne and Vimaladharma report that the bottom 40 per cent of households controlled approximately 18 per cent and 15 per cent of income in Systems G and C, respectively, while the top 20 per cent controlled 43 and 45 per cent. In System B in 1991/92 the proportion for the bottom 40 per cent was 15 per cent and for the top 20 per cent of households 42 per cent. Along with similar 1991/92 data from System C, Wanigaratne and Vimaladharma suggest that differentiation had plateaued out: 'Overall, the income shares of all deciles in System C appear to have remained frozen over the last decade ... probably reflecting the vagaries of the underlying paddy system which seems to perpetuate existing income disparities and tends to keep the majority of producers who are poor in a perpetual "poverty sharing" situation' (2001, p66).

The differentiation that has occurred is contrary to the intentions of planners who had assumed that similar sized field and home allotments would produce similar small-scale commercial farmers who would still be peasants. As Rodrigo emphasizes, entrepreneurial ability is an important cause of differentiation. Also important was a different resource base and set of experiences that settlers brought with them. Some of those displaced by project infrastructure[6] arrived with considerable sums of compensation, while other settlers received help from off-scheme relatives. Once established, especially important for a family's income generation were small commercial businesses, whereas those who continued to rely more on agriculture improved their income by acquiring access to additional field allotments with the costs of production dropping as the cropped field size increased. Through the informal land market (for such exchanges were illegal under Sri Lankan law) such access included various share-cropping arrangements, leasing, and acquisition of mortgages and purchase of field allotments from the less fortunate. Frequency of land acquisition is high. It characterizes 55 per cent of households in System H and 40 per cent in System B (Wanigaratne and Vimaladharma, 2001, p33).

An important question is whether this differentiation will allow the living standards of the wealthier minority to increase to the point where multiplier effects can be expected. The number of households involved is not insignificant; the top 20 per cent of the original 75,000 settler households totalled 15,000 households, or 82,500 individuals at 5.5 members per household.

ASSESSING MAHAWELI AS A SETTLEMENT SCHEME

Introduction

Very little has been written about the displaced households who were required to relocate because of headworks and other project construction and who opted against resettlement in the downstream Mahaweli systems. They are ignored, for example, in statistics provided by the MASL's Planning and Monitoring Unit. Although totalling no more than 5 per cent of project-affected households, nonetheless up to 4000 households were involved. The large majority was displaced from the fertile lands within the future Kotmale and Victoria reservoir basins; most were resettled in old government plantations and other government-supplied lands on slopes above the reservoirs. What evidence is available (see, for example, Softestad, 1990) indicates that the majority are worse off today than they were before resettlement. Environmental degradation has also become a major problem within the Kotmale basin. Although these two negative effects are costs of the Mahaweli Project, the analysis of Mahaweli as a settlement scheme that follows deals only with the organized settlement of the 75,609 households that were settled in the major downstream Mahaweli systems.

Assessment methodology

Vimaladharma and I designed a methodology in 1980 that we believed would allow us to generalize about the land settlement process in the three main systems (Scudder, 1993b). Its purpose was to provide information for policy-makers as opposed to academics and other researchers. I describe it here in some detail because it represents the type of cost-effective longitudinal monitoring that is needed, but seldom done, for assessing project impacts on resettlers and other project-affected people.

We decided to centre our attention on a small opportunity sample of households that would be re-interviewed during a series of annual visits. Opportunity sampling was an approach used extensively in 1979 and 1980. While in the field, whenever we noticed anything that appeared relevant we stopped to investigate. Included were construction activities, meetings, groups of people such as worker/settlers and members of a turnout, and individuals and households (several of whom we incorporated during 1980 in our household sample) involved in a wide range of activities.

Based on a number of selection criteria, we picked households where people were present as we travelled about. Table 5.1 shows the final 1989 sample according to type of settler household, location, and language and religion.[7] Those forced to move (evacuees) because of project works including canals and reservoirs were emphasized because of my interest in dam-induced involuntary resettlement. While most hosts were residents of longstanding villages that had been incorporated within a Mahaweli system, they also included four households brought into the area in the 1970s during government-sponsored land settlement. Selectees were those picked in each electorate by government party members of parliament from lists, prepared by technical departments, of poor households with supposedly relevant experience, while spontaneous settlers were those who had migrated into the area and established households and fields on their own initiative. Not shown in the table, but perhaps our most important criterion, was the selection of a disproportionate number of households with more resources in terms of capital, kinship networks, labour resources and experience. That was because we assumed that if those households in aggregate had production and income-generating problems, the larger majority with fewer resources would also be problem-prone.

Table 5.1 *Household sample*

Category	1981	1985	1989
Sample size	19	33	45
Type of settler household			
Host	5	9	13
Evacuee	8	12	14
Selectee	3	7	12
Spontaneous	3	5	6
Location			
System H	13	15	15
System C	5	8	10
System B	1	10	20
System G	0	0	0
Language and religion			
Singala (Buddhist)	19	33	40
Singala (Muslim)	0	0	1
Tamil (Hindu)	0	0	3
Tamil (Muslim)	0	0	1

During each visit a detailed questionnaire, initially taking about an hour but lasting up to three hours in special cases, was completed. In addition to whatever open-ended questions that we might ask household members or that they might bring up themselves, topics included family demographic and economic history; nature of land, livestock and other economic resources; water management at the turnout level; household income and expenditures with special emphasis on agricultural income and expenses and major purchases of consumption and production goods; education, health and sanitation; travel; changes in household affairs since the last interview and plans for the future; and settler/Authority relationships. Questions were also included on assessment by household members of whether they and other households in their closest reference groups were improving their living standards, standing still or going downhill.

Varying from household to household, reference groups included such categories as settlers from the same electorate, on the same turnout and/or evacuated or resettled from the same community. In addition to asking household members how their peers were doing, a later group meeting was often held with neighbours, during which further information was sought on key issues raised during the household interview.

A simple wealth index was also used during each visit that involved inspection of housing; household furnishing; water and sanitation facilities; fuel and lighting; and agricultural and other income-generating equipment. Zero to five points were given in each of the five categories. One of the benefits of repeated interviews is that completion of the wealth index alone would give us a good idea of how the household had fared since the previous interview.

Such impressions would then generate more specific questions as to how, for example, the members had obtained the capital to replace a thatched with a tile roof or purchase new furnishings.

Because the wealth index dealt more with consumption than productive activities we considered it a part of the longer interview rather than a stand-alone assessment. Although initially we had expected to complete detailed agricultural income and expenditure questions for each crop harvested during the past irrigation cycle and more general information for other cropping periods since the last interview, similarities in the information given caused us to ask those questions to a smaller number of households during the 1985 and 1989 interviews.

Over the years, generally speaking, household members appeared pleased to see us. In 1989, after a three-year absence, we were warmly welcomed by most households. That year, and in 2001, only one household head – probably the wealthiest in our sample – refused to be interviewed. While others may have seen our reappearance as a nuisance, we were still welcomed back 'not so much as friends but as influential outsiders who were familiar with the difficult lives of settler households' (Scudder, 1993b, p36). While no regular payments were given, we did provide advice and assistance in six cases, when household members discussed specific problems with us. Although we should have been more systematic we also presented some households with coloured photographs of family members that we had taken on a previous occasion.

Nonetheless, while the World Bank published a chapter on our methodology in a 1993 publication on *Rapid Appraisal Methods*, scepticism remains. Dennis Casley, a statistician and former chief of the Bank's Operations Monitoring Unit, wrote in the book's introduction that of all of the chapters 'I consider the first by Scudder to be one of the most important and one of the most controversial... It is controversial, in that the small sample was selected in about as non-random a way as would be possible to devise and was then maintained almost without rotation over a number of years' (Scudder, 1993b, p4). More specifically, the editor (Krishna Kumar) refers to three limitations: 'First, since the sample is both small and opportunistic, there exists a high probability of bias in the findings. In our judgment, the sample seems more appropriate for highlighting problem areas to be further explored than for making generalizations about an entire population. Second, the researchers' familiarity with the respondents – and the latter's expectations of help from them – might have influenced their responses. Third, a time interval of one or two years is too long for accurate recall. Despite these limitations ... this methodology has great potential for monitoring and evaluation' (ibid, p24).

That potential, I believe, justifies the risks. In regard to the risks, I believe that they are overstated. When one is dealing with large numbers of low-income households pioneering a new form of development in a problem-prone area, I found that most households respond in relatively similar ways about which one can generalize. If, for example, 30 per cent of a small sample in widely scattered locales suffers from malaria or malnutrition, one can assume that malaria and malnutrition are wider problems. The same applies if one-third or more of the sample suffer from land preparation and/or water delivery problems, or 50 per cent cannot repay their loans.

To reduce the methodology's weakness as a 'stand-alone' assessment procedure, interviews with settler households and groups were complemented by a wide range of other methods. During each visit we discussed our findings with all levels of Mahaweli Authority officials as well as with officials in various ministries. In commercial centres we also interviewed banks providing credit, suppliers of agricultural equipment (to get information, for example, on numbers of tractors sold), crop and livestock research centres, and shopkeepers. In several of those centres we also counted and categorized shops and their merchandise. We also checked our findings with available research reports (including detailed and time-consuming reports based on large, random samples) by the Mahaweli family of agencies, donors, and individual researchers, including a number involved in PhD programmes.

Four to seven weeks was the average time spent on each occasion with a report submitted to USAID and the Mahaweli family of agencies before my departure from Sri Lanka. The methodology and rapid report submission provided USAID and the government with policy-relevant information within a month at a cost of US$20,000–40,000 for each report. Although some conclusions met with considerable scepticism at the time, we have yet to learn of cases where they were subsequently shown to be wrong.

On the other hand, while we believe the methodology should be used elsewhere, caution is necessary. Although not mentioned in the Kumar book, we believe that its use requires experienced interviewers. In our case, Vimaladharma was one of Sri Lanka's foremost scholars and administrators dealing with land settlement throughout the country. Although I had never worked in Sri Lanka before 1979, I brought to our team an international perspective on land settlement. Together I believe that we were able to avoid the type of pitfalls that might have affected the judgment of younger and less-experienced evaluators.

There are, of course, many ways that we could have improved the methodology with the wisdom of hindsight. The sampling process could have been less opportunistic. If we had had more time, we would have added network analysis to assess resource flows into, and out of, settler households from, and to, kin and others, as well as to and from economic activities elsewhere within and without the project area. Although we discussed this need and piloted it with one family in the Victoria reservoir basin, this happened in the year our USAID funding ended. Also important would be to build into the overall evaluation process complementary means for checking results. In addition to more routine studies based on large random samples that were carried out by the PMU in the 1990s, far more use should be made of university resources including dissertations by Masters and PhD candidates.

Stage 1: Planning and recruitment

Introduction

Initial planning for the settlement component in the early 1970s impressed me since it drew on the expertise of an interdisciplinary group of experienced officials, including Vimaladharma. One benefit was the use of university-implemented surveys that came up with important and novel recommendations. Whereas previous Sri Lankan settlement schemes, for example, had favoured the selection of government-sponsored households from without the settlement zone at the expense of host communities, one such survey resulted in an agreement to give first priority to those already living in each Mahaweli system. That was a major innovation, for, as Vimaladharma notes, previous planners 'were concerned with the setting up of new settlements, and there was no excitement in redeveloping existing villages' (Wimaladharma, 1984, p5). I was also impressed by the implementation of one of the major land reforms of the 20th century whereby eventually over 75,000 families, the large majority of whom were poor, received similar field and homestead allotments. There were many other attractive features as well as problem areas, as illustrated by the selection of settlers.

Strengths and weaknesses

Strengths

SELECTION In selecting households for settlement, first priority was given to current residents within the various settlement areas and to those who must make way for project works such as dams, reservoirs and canals. Although government party MPs made the final selection of all others, those selectees were drawn from lists made up by technical departments. As a result the large majority of households selected were relatively poor and relatively landless.

COMMUNITY PLANNING Just as Mahaweli planners rejected long distributary canals in favour of irrigation turnouts, so too did they reject the 'ribbon' form of settlements that was characteristic of earlier settlement schemes. Instead they clustered settlers in hamlets, four to six of which were articulated to a village centre. Village centres in turn were planned in relationship to new towns. The cluster approach made sense under Sri Lankan conditions since social services could be improved, as could cooperation between households, while the small size of field allotments meant that they were within walking distance from home lots for the large majority of settlers.

Although not as systematically implemented as it should have been, another major policy decision was to locate people of similar background in the same hamlet. This meant that evacuees and host villages were shifted to new sites as units, while an effort was also made to group together selectees from the same constituencies. Because of the country's history of communal strife it was also agreed not to mix Hindu, Muslims and Sinhalese in the same hamlet. Rather, the expectation was that nation building would occur among youth of different ethnicity and religion when they moved from their hamlet primary school to secondary schools in village and town centres.

The major weakness was that the planners ignored the relationship between the proposed Mahaweli settlements and existing villages and communities in adjacent areas. We commented on this deficiency in our first report, noting that insufficient attention had been paid to articulation of settlement areas to 'villages outside the area under command and especially to established urban and commercial centres' (Scudder, 1979, pp11–12).

As planned and implemented, hamlets were to cater to 100–125 households and would include a primary school, a cooperative store and a visiting dispensary and health centre. Other shared facilities included a site for a sporting field, a religious structure and a cemetery. Village centres would provide 500–600 households with a junior secondary school, a health centre with resident personnel, a cooperative depot and store for provision of agricultural inputs and bulking of produce, a bus stop, a community centre and a small police station. At the top of the hierarchy would be a new town serving 2500–3000 households with a multibed hospital, senior secondary school, MASL administrative offices, one or more banks, a market site and commercial businesses. We were most critical in early reports of new towns that we thought were being overbuilt and should be restricted to remote areas without established services. Otherwise, we suspected that growth rates would be slower than expected, which proved to be the case, and that 'their location near existing commercial centres may interfere with the development of either type' (Scudder, 1981c).

ADMINISTRATION As a former head of the Mahaweli Economic Agency, Bandaragoda emphasized two characteristics of the MASL approach to settlement as major innovations. One was the settlement cluster system. The other was the MASL approach to extension at the hamlet level where 'a multitude of village-level officers representing different functional responsibilities are replaced by a single officer' (Bandaragoda, 1987, p181). Piloted first in late 1979 in System H, the key official was called the Unit Manager. He or she (for there were a few women appointed) then drew on the expertise of specialists in fields such as water management, agriculture production, marketing and community development who served under a Block Manager at the next level in the hierarchy. At the top were a Deputy Resident and a Resident Project Manager with their own senior specialist and administrative staff.

In spite of policies handed down from the top of the MASL, there was sufficient flexibility within this system to allow resident project managers and their staff to experiment with different approaches to development in the different systems. Hence in System H, Bandaragoda notes how drought and project-induced water scarcity, along with a growing realization of the shortcoming of over-reliance on paddy, led to increasing emphasis on other field crops such as chillies as well as some emphasis on 'off-farm opportunities' (ibid, p182). Although senior officials also experimented with different approaches to settler involvement within water management activities, the bias of far too many officials against devolution of responsibility to settler organizations has continued to this day.

As designed, the system was no stronger than the experience and character of the Unit Manager. While good ones could facilitate development, the system's potential was weakened in the early 1980s by the decision of the Authority's Director General increasingly to recruit university graduates who were government party members as Unit Managers. Too many of the new recruits had insufficient experience, and perhaps motivation, for such an important position.

Weaknesses

SETTLER SELECTION A major weakness was the bias against selection of Tamil households, Sri Lanka's largest minority. My initial hope that the project could serve as a unifying mechanism was based on ignorance of the history of land settlement in Sri Lanka and on statements and policy documents that the different ethnic groups would be selected according to their numbers in the national population. One document had particular influence, although no doubt I should have been suspicious of the fact that it was undated and with the source not identified. Appended to our 1989 seventh report it stated that of 101,483 allotments in six planned systems, approximately 25 per cent would go to Hindus and Muslims. The specific breakdown was 12,787 to Sri Lankan Tamils, 7509 to Muslims, and 5683 to Indian Tamils. I suspect that I was also influenced by a 1985 quotation that I had clipped from the *Los Angeles Times* of a speech by President Jayewardene. There he stated 'we consider Sri Lanka as one land belonging to all citizens, consisting of 75% of Sinhalese and 25% of other races. As such, we will settle Sri Lankans in this proportion throughout the island on state land' (*LA Times*, 1985).

I should have been more influenced by the implementation of past policies for other land settlements where government policy was to use settlement as a means for reintroducing Sinhalese into those portions of the dry zone in which Tamil-speakers were currently in the majority. Bandara (1985, p276) quotes a speech of Gamini Dissanayake in which the Minister states that 'what the men of vision envisaged was the "dawn of a Mahaweli Era" ' whereby Singala-speaking Buddhists would return to their ancient homeland where they 'would reawaken to their cultural ethos and build a new civilization like that which flourished in the ancient kingdoms of Anuradhapura and Polonnaruwa'. As for President Jayewardene's speech, I should have compared his statement of intent with the insignificant proportion of Tamils that had actually been settled by that date in the major Mahaweli systems.

As for other weaknesses, a serious miscalculation on the part of settlement planners was the assumption that families consisting of younger settlers (with one or two young children) selected by members of parliament from electorates outside the Mahaweli systems would be in the majority. In fact they are a minority as a result of the underestimating of the number of evacuees as well as hosts already living in the various systems. Not only were evacuee and host households 53 per cent of the 75,000 resettled households, but they had more children than the younger selectee households, including older children ready to marry.

In 1989, an official responsible for one of the villages in our sample informed us that 40–50 new second generation families had already been added to the original 141 allottees. Elsewhere, our information suggested that 50 per cent or more of first generation families in communities dominated by existing villages and evacuees had already married off one child. As a result, the second generation problem arose much more rapidly than expected with its impact, in terms of land subdivision and lack of employment, worsened by the failure of the AMP to plan for non-farming employment. In his 1984 PhD dissertation on the Kaltota settlement scheme, Wanigaratne had shown that families farming small holdings tended to increase the area devoted to paddy production for home consumption, as opposed to growing higher value crops for sale, as the number of family members dependent on the holding increased. We expected the same to characterize the Mahaweli Project once it was clear that the diversification of household economic activities necessary to raise living standards, and help generate new jobs for second generation households, was not occurring.

Another major weakness was the lack of attention paid to women in the interviewing of prospective settler households and to gender-based recruitment for leadership capacity, entrepreneurial activities and non-farming skills such as masonry and midwifery. Where female household members were involved, the assumption of interviewers was that the women's role would be largely restricted to child rearing and home economics. As Rodrigo emphasized in her PhD dissertation, women's high labour participation is, in fact, essential if living standards are to increase, the labour of men alone being insufficient 'to attend to the land or support the family' (1991, p325). Yet MASL staff did not incorporate women as co-producers – rather as 'dependent wives and daughters of male farmer/producers' (ibid, p327). This was a serious mistake which we emphasized in our second report (Scudder, 1980) where we referred approvingly to the policy of Malaysia's Federal Land Development Authority in which selection interviews involved both husband and wife. Otherwise we noted the danger of wives being reluctant settlers, a situation which later made one of our sample households dysfunctional.

As for widening the pool of externally recruited settlers, which we had also stressed in our 1980 report, the emphasis continued to be on young couples and on the husband's agricultural experience. They would be expected to follow MASL orders. Because such settlers were in the minority, the impact of their restricted skills and experience was less serious than might otherwise have been the case; nonetheless, it was potentially serious for the households involved. As Rodrigo noted in her case study in System H, entrepreneurial skills tended to characterize the most successful third of households in her sample (1991, p311).

In regard to categories of settlers, most problems during the selection process occurred among those selected by Members of Parliament. Throughout, MPs were tempted to add party members and other loyalists to the selection lists that they had received from civil servants. One selectee in our sample, for example, explained how the MP and party officials added about ten wealthy loyalists to the list. Although we were provided with other similar examples, nonetheless my impression is that during the initial years of the AMP less than 10 per cent of settlers were inappropriately selected. Selection deteriorated in the mid-1980s, however. Then the problem was not so much recruitment of higher-income loyalists as the selection of very poor people with no agricultural experience. In 1989 we found for the first time that selectees were having more difficulty in adjusting to Mahaweli conditions than evacuees or host villagers. After suggesting ways to improve selection, such as interviewing both spouses and involving community members more in the selection process, we added that the selection of settlers, especially in System B, should no longer 'use settlers as a mechanism for the realization of short-sighted political goals'. Contrary to stated policies, we were referring here to settling 'desperately poor' Sinhalese in Tamil-speaking areas where LTTE attacks could put their lives in danger (Scudder and Wimaladharma, 1989, p16).

Initially no provision was made for farm labourers and non-farming settlers in the various Mahaweli systems, that being yet another example of the lack of attention paid to possible multiplier effects. Although a corrective policy decision was made in 1979/80 to allocate 20 per cent of 0.2ha home lots to other categories of settlers, that too underestimated the non-farming employment potential based on the Minneriya experience and on the experience of a number of other well-planned and implemented large-scale irrigation projects around the world (Scudder, 1981c; Chapter 4 this volume). Vimaladharma's calculations in the Minneriya case had farming settlers constituting 40 per cent of employment; those in government services, business and trade, and other non-farming occupations 38 per cent; and labourers (including agricultural as well as non-farming) 21 per cent. Casual migrant labour was excluded (Wimaladharma, 1982, p29).

SIZE OF THE HOME LOT AND THE FIELD ALLOTMENT Between the 1940s and the commencement of the AMP in the late 1970s the size of the home lot had been gradually reduced on government settlement schemes from 1.2 to 0.2ha (Abeygunawardena, 1980). One reason was to increase the number of settlers and another related to the lack of attention paid to agricultural diversification as opposed to paddy cultivation. Because in the early years of AMP the keeping of livestock was ignored, as were home lot gardens, planners assumed that a 0.2ha home lot would be sufficient for housing a young family. Influenced by the Minneriya project where home lots, 1.2ha in size (field allotments were 2ha), played an important role in family nutrition and income generation, we concluded in 1979 that 0.2ha was too small. We subsequently recommended a doubling in size. Although doubling was later recommended for Systems C and B, I am unaware of the extent to which that policy change was implemented.

Initially I was also concerned that a 1ha field allotment might also be too small to enable settler households to generate the income necessary for stimulating multiplier effects. With the earlier-than-expected commencement of the second generation problem, and the inadequacy of on-farm diversification and off-farm employment, that concern appears to have been reinforced by Vimaladharma and Wanigaratne's 2001 survey which reports an increasing emphasis on paddy cultivation.

The decision to allocate a 1ha field allotment to each household was based on a number of factors. One was ideological – a policy decision to maintain, indeed nurture, a Sri Lankan peasantry (Wimaladharma, 1984, p14) that would work its own land without the need for hired labour. Another, however, was based on the best expert advice available in Sri Lanka backed up by results from experimental plots farmed by labourers on the country's leading dry zone agricultural research station. Those results tended to reinforce the 1ha size that had already been proposed as the maximum that could be farmed by a small family with two labour units. For the cultivation of paddy that assumption was wrong, however, since most settler households hire labour when seasonal requirements, such as transplanting, become heavy, while at other times they are underemployed. Expected to be both peasants and small-scale commercial farmers, settlers were unable to convene for labour intensive tasks historically important communal work parties because rigid irrigation timetables required all households to initiate critical tasks at the same time.

DIVERSIFICATION OF HOUSEHOLD PRODUCTION I have already emphasized throughout this chapter the planning obsession with paddy cultivation at the expense of diversification and income generation. The need for diversification was a major theme in our 1979 report. Referring to Sri Lanka's 17 agro-ecological zones, I wrote that 'Overemphasis on one crop (no matter how important that crop is) in terms of acreage, marketing facilities and price policy reduces the nation's ability to capitalize on the productive capacity of these zones' (Scudder, 1979, pp19–20). In regard to Mahaweli, three of the topics that we prioritized for the 1979 workshop dealt with crop diversification on settler fields and home lots, integration of crop agriculture with livestock management, fisheries and forestry, and occupational specialization within settler communities. While we emphasized forestry less than livestock and fisheries, woodlots were a major concern of the Forest Department. Worried about future settler fuel supplies, they reported that the MDB 'has not paid adequate attention to the important question of energy supplies for the large increase of settlers in the area.' (Sri Lanka, 1978, p11). Because such topics lay outside the expertise of the MASL, during the critical initial years they were ignored. As for the folly of planning all three systems for the double cropping of paddy, we returned to that theme in each subsequent report stating our inability to understand 'the rationale of this emphasis' in the 1981 report.

SETTLER PARTICIPATION IN MAHAWELI PLANNING, IMPLEMENTATION AND EVALUATION Local participatory organizations for economic purposes were not given legal standing in Sri Lanka until after 1989 (Wickremaratne, 1995, p50). In the Mahaweli case, there were no policies to involve settlers in the decision-making process nor was there any 'current or proposed study to ascertain settler preferences' (UNDP, 1978, p5.1.2). International consultants such as Canada's Acres International, England's Hunting Technical Services and Holland's NEDECO also failed to emphasize the importance of settler participatory organizations. A former Director General of the Authority, Wickremaratne explains that gap as a result of the government's emphasis on acceleration and the Authority's top-down, centralized management system, although he also suspects that the government's fear of any sort of devolution might be related to Tamil demands for increasing autonomy.

During the planning process, the one exception was a decision early in the 1970s to pioneer a small settler organization focused on an irrigation turnout involving 10–18 settler households. Each turnout would have two leaders: one to deal with water management and the other to cooperate with the government extension worker dealing with crop production. Previous irrigation settlements tended to be served by long distributary canals from which water was distributed to individual farmers. Such canals 'allowed little room for collective organization for water distribution' (Wimaladharma, 1984, p11). Turnout organizations, on the other hand, were compared with indigenous cooperative units at the village hamlet level.

Stage 2: Initial coping and adjustment

Introduction

In 1989 we asked most of our settler households in Systems B and C what time period had been the most difficult for them. We expected the large majority to mention years characterized by the most communal strife and terrorism. In System C the JVP had been implicated in a number of killings followed by retaliation by the security forces on Mahaweli settlers living in surrounding areas. In System B, all of our Sinhalese households lived in fear of LTTE attacks that had already resulted in massacres in neighbouring villages, while Tamil-speakers feared the government security forces, which had detained and tortured Tamil youths.

As expected some households did identify the most difficult year as the one in which communal strife most directly affected their community. But communal strife was only the second most frequent answer. The first dealt with problems encountered during the initial year or two following their incorporation within the Project. That answer included not just evacuees, as might be expected from the history of dam-induced involuntary resettlement, but host and selectee households as well.

Of our nine sample households in System C, four referred to the first year or the first and the second as the worst, three referred to a year in which communal strife affected them, and one referred to a year when crops failed. The ninth family was not asked the question. Although the problems mentioned during the initial year or two varied from household to household they all were AMP-related. Of the four households, one involved an evacuee household head from the trans-basin canal who came to System C as a worker/settler in August 1980. Because of the lack of suitable land in the vicinity, he was shifted to a second worker/settler camp and then a third. It was only after nearly a year that he finally received a home lot on which he built a house with the help of his two oldest children. The remainder of his large family came three months later, after which the MASL provided him with a temporary field for rain-fed cultivation. He told us that the first year was the most difficult, with problems including his separation from his family and the high transport costs to visit them.

The history of a second trans-basin canal evacuee was more complicated. Like the first he was a worker/settler housed in a dormitory with a zinc roof that was so hot that he characterized living there as 'hell on earth'. Water was brought by tanker only twice weekly and was so bad in quality that you 'wouldn't use it for the latrine'. Although he received his home lot and his field within a reasonable time, after building his house he was told that he must tear it down and move elsewhere since Authority officials mistakenly had given him land that was meant for other purposes. When asked in 1989 which year or years had been the worst, he replied the first two. The third household head, a host, mentioned the first two years because the tank on which his family depended for irrigation water was being renovated during that time. The fourth family, a selectee household, found the first year the hardest because they did not receive their paddy allotment until the following year. They also mentioned malaria and lack of transport. Answers from System B households were similar. An evacuee household from the Victoria reservoir basin mentioned the first year because of cultivation difficulties and lack of advice on how to handle them. A Tamil-speaking host emphasized lack of water, while another Tamil host went into more detail by noting not just lack of irrigation water but also the need to tear down his house prior to rebuilding on his new home lot, to clear new land and to cope with malaria.

For the three System C households that mentioned communal strife, either 1988 or 1989 was noted as the worst year. During 1988, communal strife kept settlers from cultivating their fields during one or more weeks. Shops were closed and prices went up; transport was not available for those with medical emergencies. During 1989, the reason given was retaliation by government security forces. After five of their members were killed by the JVP, we were told that security personnel killed and burned four boys and girls from the neighbouring area and returned the next day to blindfold and take away 18 more settler youths.

Whether researchers or officials, it is very difficult for an outsider to understand the hardships that settler households must undergo during the initial year to pioneer new lands. In the Mahaweli systems, the most difficult pioneering fell to those worker/settlers who had to live in dormitories without their families for up to a year while constructing irrigation channels. After receiving their home lot and field allotment, they had to provide themselves with temporary shelter while completing their house. Since the large majority of all settlers did not receive irrigation water until a year (and for some two years) after receiving a home lot, they were also expected to undertake dry-land farming during their first cultivation seasons in a problem-prone environment characterized by drought, malaria, and crop-destroying elephants and wild boars. In addition they were expected to learn to live with new neighbours and adapt to an unfamiliar government bureaucracy. Once paddy fields were received, they were expected to farm them commercially, with inputs purchased with, for many, the first loans that they had ever received from banks. Additional to such hardships, at least 15 per cent of households, and perhaps considerably more, had to cope with improperly constructed irrigation facilities and/or improperly prepared field allotments, while a greater proportion became indebted following their first season of irrigated agriculture because yields were inadequate to pay off the cultivation loans received for purchase of inputs.

Improperly prepared irrigation facilities and field allotments

To check out settler complaints in System H that water management problems affected from 48 per cent to 61 per cent of households in different zones, the Water Management Division carried out a 1979 survey in the Galnewa area three years after the first irrigation releases had occurred. Results showed that 33 per cent of field irrigation turnouts had either not been provided or needed to be reconstructed or otherwise improved. As for field irrigation channels, 33 per cent had problems. Drainage was found to be even worse – of 558 turnout areas inspected, 46 per cent had problems.

Even as late as 1989, far too few irrigation and field allotment defects had been corrected. According to a Mahaweli Economic Agency survey, 8500 fields could only be partially cultivated because of various defects. Although probably an underestimate, that figure was over 10 per cent of the total number of allotments. Urgent attention was recommended in various problem hamlets where a larger proportion of households were affected. In 2001 Wanigaratne and Vimaladharma reported that some defects among sample households had yet to be corrected.

Indebtedness

AMP planners wanted settlers to behave as small-scale commercial farmers most of whose production would be marketed. Commercial banks were each allocated one or more Mahaweli zones in which they were expected to provide annual cultivation loans starting with a settler's first irrigation release. At that time, few settlers had the experience to harvest and sell sufficient produce to repay their loans, with the result that indebtedness was added to the stress characteristic of the early years of a pioneer settlement project.

Since a new loan required the repayment of the previous one, over the years the proportion of settlers who qualified for further loans gradually dropped. The bank with the best repayment rate was Hatton's National Bank, which pioneered commercial credit in an H System zone. Hatton's, like the Ceylon Tobacco Corporation, also had had previous experience with smallholders, including providing agricultural credit since 1973 to households on another irrigation settlement scheme. In System H they hired their own agricultural staff and facilitated the emergence of settler institutions for water management at turnout and distributary canal levels. Their first loans were given in 1980. The repayment rate was 99 per cent with only two loans outstanding. The next season 876 cultivation loans were issued and had a recovery rate of over 85 per cent at the time Vimaladharma and I visited the area before the end of the repayment period. However, for reasons beyond their control, including inadequate irrigation water supplied by the Authority, the proportion of settlers receiving loans decreased from approximately 40 per cent in 1985/86 to only 9 per cent in 1988/89.

The Bank of Ceylon serviced 7000 households in System B and only 18 per cent received loans in 1985/86, with the proportion dropping to 13 per cent in 1988/89. During that period, repayment rates dropped from 80 per cent to 60 per cent (Scudder and Wimaladharma, 1989, Appendix 4). Although a minority of households in our sample of 47 refused to take out bank loans as a matter of principle, the majority were no longer eligible because they had been unable to repay their first loan or a subsequent one because of crop failure for reasons largely beyond their control.

Health

In her 1978 report on System H, Lund referred to malnutrition, as did Vimaladharma and I in 1981. We thought that malnutrition might be associated with home lots that were too small for the keeping of livestock and for a household garden large enough to provide for domestic consumption and income generation. Malnutrition has continued to be a major problem until the present. According to a 1997 survey, only 26 per cent of children under five who were weighed were adequately nourished. A total of 42 per cent were acutely malnourished and 32 per cent malnourished (Wanigaratne, 1998, p12).

In the first half of the 1980s, Vimaladharma and I were also critical of the lack of health facilities provided during the early years in Systems B and C, which were more isolated and less well provided with social services than System H. Especially vulnerable were evacuees and selectees coming from malaria-free highland areas into a malarial zone. Failure to provide adequate potable water supplies to settlers during the initial settling-in period also led to an increase in water-borne diseases, as did the Authority's erroneous expectation that settlers would be able to dig productive wells on their home lots. Snake bites were also a serious problem with adults in two of our households dying from bites.

During the first half of the 1980s we also stated that the Authority was paying inadequate attention to the type of stress that tends to be associated with all types of pioneering settlement. We were particularly concerned in our 1984 report that the lengthy transition period between the stages of coping (Stage 2) and development (Stage 3) 'may be having an adverse effect on the mental health of some settler households' (Scudder and Wimaladharma, 1985, p38). We noted as examples tensions between related households that had moved together leading to 'a severing of relationships' as well as to 'charges and suspicions of sorcery'. We were especially alarmed by 'a disturbing number of reported suicides' (ibid).

We now know as a result of subsequent studies that the Mahaweli settlements have the highest level of suicide in Sri Lanka. In an undated paper from the second half of the 1980s, Silva and Kumara (undated) reported on a study of suicide trends in System C from 1983 through 1987. They found that suicide, not illness, was the leading cause of mortality, causing 70 per cent of hospital-reported deaths during that period, with a suicide rate of 43.7 per 100,000 people. Approximately 70 per cent of those who killed themselves were males, with the 20–30 age bracket being the most at risk. In a 1998 paper Van der Hoek and colleagues reported on a detailed study of insecticide poisoning, the drinking of insecticide being the main means for committing suicide. Based on records of death from two hospitals in System H, 50 per cent of deaths from one were the result of insecticide poisoning and 29 per cent of deaths from the other. As for the suicides, they concluded that 'the incidence of acute insecticide poisoning in this settlement area is the highest ever reported in Sri Lanka or elsewhere' (Van der Hoek et al, 1998, p500).

Replication of poverty

Vimaladharma's and my optimism about the Project's potential was such that we believed that the economic development that characterizes Stage 3 might have begun by 1981 in System H, five years after the incorporation of the first settlers. Two years later, however, we reported that the shift toward Stage 3 was no longer occurring, while poverty was being replicated in System C and System B. While drought and inadequate delivery of irrigation releases were certainly major constraints in System H, there and elsewhere other factors were important. One was insufficient Mahaweli Authority emphasis on settler well-being and incomes as opposed to paddy production. Another was the earlier-than-expected commencement of the second generation problem. Also criticized was the undermining of settler institutions caused by the Authority decision to appoint officials as their leaders. In the older zones of System H, we reported that settlers were becoming disillusioned because their living standards were growing at a slower rate than expected. Supporting our concerns was a 1983 study in the older areas of System H directed by Vidanapathirana. In a sample of 406 households, approximately 75 per cent of total income came from paddy. He considered that dependence 'excessive … since the producer margin and profitability of paddy as a crop has been shrinking from a level of 72 per cent of total income in 1972 to 49 per cent in the 1982/83 cultivation season' (Vidanapathirana, 1984, p39). His conclusion: 'almost 80 per cent of the settlers are below the break even point' (ibid, p44).

Our 1984 report was even more emphatic about unsatisfactory development in all three systems. Net incomes of 'the large majority … in even the oldest Mahaweli settlement areas have not yet moved beyond the subsistence level'. Indeed, we believed that they actually may have been dropping in a significant number of cases. System H provided an example where living standards of 7 of our 15 households appear to have dropped while those of another 2 have stagnated; and that despite our sample containing a larger proportion of leaders and wealthier households than in the general settler population. As for the other six households, the upturn was 'only very slight' in four cases, while off-farm income was the major reason for the improved living standard of the other two. While water scarcity continued to be a serious problem, among the seven households in our System C sample that had adequate water supplies at that time, living standards had risen significantly in only two – again due primarily to off-farm income. The following year we reported that the majority of System H settlers continued to live in poverty as did settlers in Systems C and B.

The main cause of continuing poverty among a majority of settlers was the ongoing, indeed increasing, reliance on the double cropping of paddy. Because of low producer prices for rice and escalating prices for inputs and a wide range of basic-needs consumption goods, our earlier conclusion that paddy production could not move the settler community beyond subsistence was generally accepted by the mid-1980s. During a 1985 seminar on land settlement in Sri Lanka, the Executive Director of the MEA reported that between 1977 and 1984 'open market rice prices increased by only 158 per cent, whereas the price of [such basic-needs items as] kerosene increased during the same period by 733 per cent, coconut oil by 399 per cent, milk powder by 346 per cent' (MEA, 1985). Trying to improve settler incomes in the late 1980s through crop diversification, agricultural economists working on the Mahaweli Agriculture Research and Development (MARD) project in System B referred to the double cropping of paddy as 'the paddy trap' (Gleason et al, 1990).

Because of belated policy improvements following Panditharatne's resignation as the Authority's Director General, the situation had improved 'incrementally' by 1989. We still noted impediments, however, 'which will lead to a replication of poverty during the next five years in System H and the older settlement areas of System C and B unless urgent action is taken' (Scudder and Wimaladharma, 1989, pii). This was because average incomes for the majority were still inadequate to catalyse a process of integrated area development. Indeed in System H, a downward spiral had occurred during the previous 12 months in the living standards of thousands of households caused by a shortage of irrigation water, while elephant damage and malaria continued as problems in Systems C and B where increases in living standards were not yet sufficient to generate multiplier effects.

During our 1989 survey, we concentrated on asking household members detailed questions about their 'basic-needs' annual expenditures. Answers from the three Mahaweli systems were quite similar. Average gross expenditure was 46,566 rupees[8] (Table 5.2). This did not include the purchase of rice, even though crop failure requiring rice purchase was a constant risk for many for such reasons as irregular water supplies, damage by elephants and other pests, family illness and crop disease, and a range of field allotment problems. Also not included was the cost of crop insurance or interest on loan repayments. Omitted were costs for income-increasing purchases, such as dairy cows, sewing machines and two-wheeled tractors or plough animals. The same applied to costs for housing improvement and the purchase of major

Table 5.2 *Household expenditure for basic needs 1988/89 (averaged over a 12-month period)*

Item	Number of households	Amount in Rupees
Food expenditure	33	20,449
Paddy costs of production	17	18,558
Clothing (family of five)	37	4400
Travel expenses	37	946
Social and ritual	38	943
Medicinal	39	800
Minor household items (pots, pans etc.)	35	470
Total		46,566

household furnishings. Major expenses that could increase indebtedness such as serious illness, weddings and funerals were also omitted.

The Authority's Planning and Monitoring Unit surveyed settler farming budgets in System C during the 1989/90 agricultural year. Gross income was 52,284 rupees, gross expenditures 29,136 rupees and net farming income 28,404 rupees. Our data suggests that the Unit's expenditure figures were seriously underestimated. If ours are used (and it is important to remember that we did not find major expenditure differences between the three systems), then net income would only be 5718 rupees – hardly sufficient to achieve multiplier effects.

In our 1989 report we estimated that a gross annual income of 70,000 rupees for the majority was necessary if land settlements such as the Accelerated Mahaweli Project were to produce multiplier effects in terms of non-farming employment generation and enterprise development. Such an income requires that the cultivation of rice be complemented by other major activities such as home lot development (as with a fish pond, cultivation of medicinal plants and room rental), cultivation of other field crops, livestock management, wage labour and various commercial activities. The wealthiest six families among our 36 households who became Mahaweli settlers before 1986 all had diversified their economies. Supplementing income from the cultivation of paddy and other field crops, one was experimenting with prawn farming while three others had small general stores. All but one had either a two-wheeled tractor or plough animals. Of significance, all except one had resources other than a 1ha field allotment when they arrived, and in the one exception, the settler was assisted by an enterprising son who by 1989 was experimenting with pig and poultry production. Of the other five wealthiest families, one came with capital as well as seven sons, two were able to acquire capital for diversification from off-scheme relatives, and two acquired capital as small-scale contractors during the Project's construction phase.

Twelve years later in 2001, Wanigaratne and Vimaladharma reported that further deterioration in settler incomes had occurred, a conclusion that was based on broader sample surveys as well as re-interviews of our sample households. Generalizing for all three systems as well as for System G, they reported that 'In real terms the 1999 Mahaweli settler household income represented a decline by 5% over a relatively higher position reached in 1990... Seemingly, producers in the Mahaweli are being pushed by price inflationary conditions to produce more to derive higher nominal incomes, merely to maintain their real purchasing power at a low and stagnant position over the 1990 decade' (Wanigaratne and Vimaladharma, 2001, p62). The result is that 'the agricultural production base ... at present does not reveal any symptoms of initiating a major economic transformation in settler incomes and living standards from what they were in 1989' (ibid, p17).

Not only did they find that the Mahaweli system of agriculture at best could only maintain 'the majority of settlers in subsistence poverty' (ibid, p35), but the nature of the farming system was also becoming less intensive. Although partly a private sector and government supply failure, only 15 per cent of paddy was produced from improved seed. More farmers than in the past were broadcasting their seed as opposed to practising transplanting, while fertilizer recommendations were less likely to be followed. Yields had plateaued out with farmers reporting an increase in the resistance of plant pests and disease to available agro-chemicals. Increases in the ownership of two-wheeled tractors was explained more as a labour saving device because of rising labour costs than as an income-generating resource to be rented out. To reduce labour costs, farmers had also increased their use of customary cooperative community labour, an institution the use of which we had not observed during the 1979–1989 period.

Poverty would have been even worse if settler households had not been able to increase the proportion of their income from non-farming sources. While a number of studies had indicated that nearly 80 per cent of total household income had come from own cultivation (76 per cent) or agricultural wage labour (3 per cent) from 1990 to 1998, major increases in non-farming income were occurring toward the end of that period. In Systems C and G a sample survey of 1000 households showed the proportion of income from own cultivation (as opposed to agricultural wage labour) dropping to 43 per cent from 1996/97 to 2000/01. The beginning of such a rapid change was reported also from System H, while re-interviews of our households in System B 'showed a growing importance of non-farming sources of household incomes' (Wanigaratne and Vimaladharma, 2001, pp62–63).

Of obvious importance to the households involved, the major sources of non-farming income were not generated by the Mahaweli Project. The most important sources, especially in Systems B and C, were wages received after joining the home guard and the army – both related to the ongoing civil war. These were important for 24 per cent of our sample households. Next in importance (11 per cent of households) was employment of daughters in the Sri Lankan garment industry, whereas the major source of income for several households was wage employment in the Middle East.

Why poverty replication?

Many of the reasons why the Mahaweli Project had failed to move the majority of the settler population beyond poverty were similar throughout the 1977–2001 period. The absence of national policies favouring agriculture was especially important. So too were adverse terms of trade with costs of inputs, agricultural equipment and basic-needs household expenses rising faster than agricultural prices and especially prices for paddy. Absence throughout of a supportive and consistent marketing policy was a major constraint. In 1999, for example, the government reduced the rice import duty from 35 per cent to 10 per cent while importing 50,000 tonnes of rice on concessionary terms. At a time when domestic production was increasing, rice imports were increased by 28 per cent (Wanigaratne and Vimaladharma, 2001, p4). Farm gate prices for Mahaweli settlers fell during the next two cultivation seasons. Sporadic changes in import policies also have had a negative impact on other food crops. Because the greater risk involved in other food crops offset their higher value, Wanigaratne and Vimaladharma noticed an increase in the double cropping of paddy even in systems where water periodically was scarce.

Within the Mahaweli family of agencies, one constraint, a product of acceleration, was caused by the poor linkage between simultaneous construction and settlement activities adversely affecting settler well-being. In addition to the Project's construction bias, there was insufficient time to evaluate and extend a number of successful pilot projects which were initiated in System H where the first settlement occurred. An example included the excellent primary health care approach implemented in one System H zone that should have been implemented during the initial settlement years in Systems C and B. Another example was an innovative orientation programme developed for selectees that should have been extended to all settlers.

Already emphasized as a major constraint was initial Mahaweli Authority emphasis on the double cropping of paddy as opposed to a diversified production system at the household level. While diversification received more emphasis after 1984, the small size of the home lot and the lack of grazing restrained livestock production, whereas price and marketing constraints adversely affected settler efforts to grow other food crops. As for useful donor-funded efforts to diversify agriculture and stimulate non-farming enterprise development, such as USAID's MARD and Micro Enterprise Development Projects, they collapsed after donor funding ceased because of the lack of effective handing over. Meanwhile, the early appearance of the second generation problem put increasing pressure on the 1ha field allotment to feed not just one but two or more families. By 1999 paddy constituted 81 per cent of Mahaweli food crop production. With settlers unable to move beyond subsistence, Wanigaratne and Vimaladharma blamed the two season paddy economy for the 'low and erratic demand' that produced the low level of commercial activity in Mahaweli towns and along roads running through Mahaweli systems (2001, p20).

Yet another constraining factor was the hierarchical structure of the Authority that various observers compared with the top-down management of

Sri Lankan tea plantations. In addition to Authority constraints placed on the development of the necessary settler-run institutions, the gap between officials and settlers was such that critical problems relating to settler well-being were neglected. In addition to ongoing irrigation and field defects and the problem of indebtedness were high levels of malnutrition and suicide. A settler service unit to address such issues was not established until 1989.

After the 1988 election, Wanigaratne and Vimaladharma also noted a de-emphasis on irrigation and especially a reduced budget for extension and irrigation management within the Mahaweli Authority. These authors were also highly critical of constraints associated with the World Bank-required restructuring of the Authority and of national agricultural policies. During the restructuring process not only were key staff members lost but institutional capacity to deal with critical areas such as non-farming enterprise development was weakened. As for changes in agricultural policy, they have resulted in a much weakened government research capacity and a radical reduction in numbers of agricultural field workers who, starting in 1989, were transferred to the Ministry of Public Administration to carry out a wider range of services. No longer provided by field officers, extension was to be provided by radio and TV programmes and demonstration plots, further reducing the ability of the Department of Agriculture to deliver what research was available to farmers, or to instruct farmers in the proper use of such inputs as insecticides (Van der Hoek et al, 1998, p501) Although new policies were supposed to bring the private sector into agriculture to substitute for reduced government services, by 2001 private sector impact on critical activities such as seed production and extension was minimal.

Stage 3: Community formation and economic development

Based on a 1986 survey and earlier data, Bandaragoda[9] (1987) concluded that the settlement of 6000 households in the older portions of System H was a success story, based on productivity, income and social services. That was a reasonable conclusion based on the data available to him. Prior to the arrival of Mahaweli waters, irrigated paddy production in existing villages was below the national average. Ten years later in 1983 System H yields not only exceeded the national average, but 'increasing crop production generally has been impressive, and the area holds great promise for sustained, high agricultural production'. (World Bank, 1983b, Annex 1, p1). Household incomes also exceeded national averages, as did social services.

On the other hand, were the incomes recorded high enough to stimulate the type of household consumption necessary to move the majority of households beyond subsistence and to have multiplier effects – in other words to allow the majority to move from Stage 2 to Stage 3? And in the oldest AMP zones were they high enough to justify annual government capital expenditure of from 32 to 45 per cent on the AMP during the 1981–1985 period (Jogaratnam, 1995, p112) and the foregone opportunities that other uses of that capital could have realized? Although the second question, while important, is unanswerable, the data that Vimaladharma and I collected from our sample and other sources indicate that the majority of settlers at that time had yet to move beyond subsistence. We found that still to be the case in 1989 and Wanigaratne and Vimaladharma found a similar situation in 2001.

If economic development had not occurred, community formation – the other major characteristic of Stage 3 – had. By the mid-1980s, funeral societies had been formed with good membership. Although the Mahaweli Authority provided sites and some help, settlers were also active in building temples and seeking resident priests. They also responded favourably to Authority attempts to form turnout groups in the early 1980s, losing interest only in the mid-1980s when the Authority filled leadership positions with officials.

Although we have few data on trends during the 1990s on how settlers responded to the 1989 cabinet decision to foster participatory organization for development purposes throughout the country, in 2001 Vimaladharma and Wanigaratne found a range of active, settler-run irrigation system and community organizations. This increased activity they attributed partly to involvement of a better-educated second generation that gradually was taking over the management of their parents' allotments as well as to more participatory changes in government policies. In general they found a new assertiveness emerging 'where a new sense of destiny, discipline and public service is being established' (Wanigaratne and Vimaladharma, 2001, p53). Throughout, turnout organizations had been federated to undertake the operation and maintenance of distributary canals. While an important step forward, according to an Authority 2000 survey of 585 farmers' organizations in the four systems, only 23 per cent were actually strong enough to take over the operation and maintenance of distributary and field channels, which was a reason why donor-funded rehabilitation projects at this time were emphasizing the training of farmer organizations (Niyangoda, 2001, pp7–8).

In several systems some farmers' organizations had begun to take on additional activities including operating as credit-providing funeral associations. Separate funeral and credit associations also existed with small groups, especially of women, encouraged to form small rotating credit associations (tontines). Vimaladharma and Wanigaratne were especially impressed by several settler-run farmers' companies. Registered in 1996, one that rose spontaneously in System G had formed its board from members of the various political parties. By 2001 it was acting as an agent for different agencies selling agro-chemicals and agricultural equipment and had received preferred customer status from a commercial bank. It also provided a community service by helping poor households pay off mortgages on their field allotments. Future plans included production of improved paddy and other seed, although realization of that goal had brought it into conflict with a senior Mahaweli official who – as with Mahaweli Authority officials in the 1980s – was still trying to maintain, rather than hand over, authority.

Stage 4: Handing over and incorporation

Like a majority of older settlement schemes throughout the tropics and subtropics, the Mahaweli Project has bypassed the stage of economic growth by moving directly from Stage 2 to Stage 4. By 2001, 42 per cent of our sample households had either handed over the management of their economy to the second generation or were in the process of doing so. Although official resistance continued, even the Authority was now beginning to hand over irrigation system and community development responsibilities to the settler community.

The question for the future is whether or not income levels of a sufficient number of settlers can rise enough to have the type of multiplier effects that characterize the Minneriya scheme. No longer optimistic, I am inclined to doubt it. Wanigaratne and Vimaladharma remain relatively optimistic 'if the right blend of market oriented crops and livestock enterprise' develop (2001, p64). They also mention five priority actions currently being planned and implemented by the authorities that have promise. Four of those mentioned, however, have merely been recycled from the past while the fifth – the restructuring of the Authority – to date has proved to be more a constraint than a benefit. Other factors that become more constraining as time goes by are the small size of the field allotment coupled with subdivision because of the second generation problem.

Major lessons learned

- To justify their increasing cost per hectare and per household, large multipurpose schemes with a major land settlement component must generate major multiplier effects. The Mahaweli Project did not.
- Large multipurpose projects require a regional planning capacity that the Mahaweli Project has yet to develop within its Planning and Monitoring Unit (PMU). As a result, the individual irrigation systems were planned and implemented as if they existed in a vacuum. They were neither related to each other nor to surrounding towns and villages and the national economy.
- Where seemingly good policies and plans are presented to affected people, to national governing bodies and to donors, a major problem throughout the world continues to be their implementation. A common problem is an implementing agency with inadequate authority, finance and personnel. Prior to the 1988 election, that was not a problem with the Mahaweli Project, where initially the President chaired a cabinet committee on the AMP and key people were appointed to run the Mahaweli family of agencies. Rather, the problem was the failure of those agencies to implement their policies and of the donors to intervene when policies agreed upon in negotiated documents were ignored.
- Special attention must be paid to the balance and linkages between the construction and development phases. The development phase in the AMP

case suffered because of acceleration, a major bias toward physical infrastructure and inadequate monitoring. Not only did the balance between the two phases favour construction at the expense of development but the linkage between the two was inadequate. There was either too much overlap or the construction phase ended before the development phase began to show results in terms of higher income and improved living standards. Too much overlap resulting from the authorities trying to force the pace of implementation resulted in too many irrigation and land preparation defects as well as too little attention paid to settler health and well-being. Poor articulation between the two phases meant that agricultural development had not reached the point at which it could provide an improved standard of living for those households that had depended on wage labour and small contracts while construction was underway.

• A monitoring and evaluation (M&E) capacity independent of the project authorities is essential. In the Mahaweli case, rather than encouraging identification of implementation problems brought to his attention, the chair of the MDB at the time acceleration began undermined the quality of M&E by bringing it under his direct control, with the result that the better staff resigned. On the other hand, project authorities do need a capacity to evaluate the results of independent monitoring. In that regard the MASL's Planning and Monitoring Unit was effective.

• While the local initiative of settler households is essential, it must be complemented by appropriate assistance from whatever planning and implementing agencies are involved. In the Mahaweli case the gap between MASL policy and settler initiative, experience, capacities and interest was far too great. An exception indicating the type of greater potential that could have been realized was dairy development starting in the mid-1980s. Conceived and overseen by a senior MASL official, this included a credit component for those households that could meet some of the cost for dairy cows and marketing cooperatives. Both wealthier and poorer households benefited since purchasers herded out cows because of lack of grazing or labour to poorer settlers on a share-cropping arrangement whereby the herder built up her or his herd by keeping every other calf. Daughters of settlers ran the cooperatives. Participation was so great that between 1989 and 1997 milk collection increased at 15 per cent per year.

• Settler dependency is not a problem provided opportunities are available for raising living standards. Because of the multiple demands on settler households during the initial years, however, close attention needs to be paid to settler well-being during that time period. In the Mahaweli case the settler service unit that was finally established in 1989 should have been institutionalized over ten years earlier to identify and deal with irrigation system and field preparation defects, household water supply, malnutrition, malaria and other health issues, indebtedness and other major problem areas

- The balance between housing, social services and a household economy that can raise living standards and stimulate multiplier effects should favour economic opportunities. In the Mahaweli case, it was not that too much attention was paid to settler housing and social services but that too little attention was paid during the planning process to income generation.

6

Further Case Studies

INTRODUCTION

A total of 7 of the 14 chapters in the initial draft of *The Future of Large Dams* were devoted to detailed case histories. Each provided a general description of the project as well as analysis of the project authorities, the resettlement process and, to a lesser extent, selected environmental impacts. At over 650 pages, the resulting manuscript required shortening. Revision focused largely on the case studies. One case study, Sri Lanka's Accelerated Mahaweli Project, has been retained (Chapter 5) as originally drafted. Four case studies – Kariba (Zambia–Zimbabwe), Sardar Sarovar (India), Southern Okavango Integrated Water Development Project (Botswana) and Grande Baleine (Canada) – follow in this chapter, with emphasis on specific issues of wider relevance. The other three (the High Dam at Aswan, the Lesotho Highlands Water Project, and Laos' Nam Theun 2) have been used throughout the text to illustrate specific points. Readers interested in the full case histories can download them from my website (http://www.hss.caltech.edu/~tzs).

THE KARIBA CASE STUDY[1]

Introduction

Built in British colonial Africa in the 1950s, the Kariba Dam provides an important case study for numerous reasons. It was the first mainstream dam on the Zambezi River. It was the first large dam financed by the World Bank in Africa and involved the Bank's largest loan at that time. It was the first dam in the tropics and subtropics studied by independent researchers throughout the project cycle, with that research providing planners with important information and lessons.

Considered a successful dam even by affected people based on conventional cost–benefit analysis, Kariba also involved unacceptable environmental and social impacts. Especially unacceptable were adverse impacts on 57,000 resettlers (most of whom were resettled within the Kariba Lake Basin) and irreversible impacts on the delta and other wetlands of the Zambezi River. On the other hand, Kariba provided a number of important benefits for resettlers that warrant analysis and replication as well as important lessons that have yet to be adequately applied to more recent large dam projects. In the Zambian portion of the Kariba Lake Basin, which is emphasized in this case history, examples include a successful inshore fisheries programme and effective utilization of the reservoir's extensive drawdown area. Implemented in the 1990s, another example includes the first reparations projects for offsetting at least some of the impoverishing aspects of the resettlement programme. On the Zimbabwe side, reparations have been pushed by the binational Zambezi River Authority and on the Zambian side by the government's electricity parastatal with funding from the World Bank and the Development Bank of Southern Africa.

The major international benefit: Generation of electricity

In evaluating the development effectiveness of the Kariba project, it is important to keep in mind the growing energy crisis in the Northern Rhodesian copper belt during the 1950s, Zambia's increasing demand for energy between 1964 and 1974, and Zimbabwe's requirements after 1980. Stage 1 construction in the 1950s brought on line a maximum capacity of 705MW provided by six turbines located on the south bank of the Zambezi. Stage 2 followed in the 1970s with four north bank turbines that brought total capacity to 1320MW.

Direct beneficiaries were the mining industries and other industries in both countries as well as their employees. Zimbabwe in particular was able to develop a wider range of electricity intensive industries including fertilizer production. Governments also benefited, with over 80 per cent of Zambia's foreign exchange coming from copper from the second half of the 1960s until the end of the 1980s.

Opportunities and constraints of relevance to other large dam projects

Fisheries

Yet to be extensively applied elsewhere, a major lesson from Kariba concerns the fisheries potential that dam reservoirs have for subsistence and commercial fishing by immigrants and local residents, and for recreational fishing. Immigrants are noted first in the preceding sentence since they, like the urban users of Kariba's electricity, were the main beneficiaries at the expense of local residents. The major exception was the inshore fishery on the Zambian side that provided substantial benefits to thousands of resettlers and hosts, and has major implications for large dams elsewhere.

A characteristic of all man-made reservoirs is an initial explosion of primary and secondary productivity following impoundment as a result of release of nutrients from flooded soil and vegetation. In the Kariba case nutrient content as measured by total dissolved solids increased from a pre-project 26 parts per million (ppm) to 65ppm by 1963 and dropping to 42ppm after 1964–1965 (Balon, 1974, p139). During the 1959–1963 period, not only did commercial species of fish such as tilapia find an ample food supply and exceptional breeding conditions, but predators such as tiger fish (*Hydrocynus vittatus*) and crocodiles, which had dominated the Zambezi's primary channel, were spread over a much wider area. Resident species also increased from 28 before Kariba to 41, of which 13 were 'economically preferred species' in the artisanal fishery (ibid, p14).

Because such a rapid initial increase in productivity cannot be expected to last as nutrient levels decline and predators extend their range, a commercial fishery must be available to exploit it from the start; otherwise natural mortality will reap the harvest. In the Kariba case the reservoir did not reach full storage level until the 1963 dry season, so that the period of highest productivity lasted for over five years.

Careful planning by the north bank administration, with features that are transferable to other reservoirs in the tropics and subtropics, meant that the Gwembe Tonga resettlers and hosts had the opportunity to benefit from that surge of productivity. Initially the fishery was restricted to lake basin residents so as to protect them from more experienced immigrant fishers. Even before the dam was built, the District Commissioner distributed gill nets to schools and selected individuals, with training provided by the Department of Game and Fisheries. As the reservoir began filling during 1959, the first resettler and host fishers were already at work, with the first government survey that August reporting 407 fishers using 748 gill nets and 93 boats.

Starting in 1959, standardized equipment was sold through the offices of the Gwembe District administration until handed over to two local cooperatives. When increasingly sophisticated Tonga fisherman began to complain about inadequate inventory, the District Council complemented the cooperatives with licensed private traders. During 1961 a fisheries training centre was opened that offered short courses and included a section for building improved boats. A successful credit programme with a repayment rate of over 90 per cent was also introduced to cover the cost of nets and boats.

By the beginning of 1963 over 2000 north bank fishers were using over 5000 gill nets and were catching 3000–4000 tonnes of fish per annum. Resettlers were more actively involved than hosts. They had dispersed over the entire length of the reservoir establishing camps along the shoreline and on islands. Although women were not actively involved in catching fish or mending nets, the fishery also played an important role in their further incorporation into a market economy. While a few settled in the fish camps or became fish traders, the majority came from their villages to sell beer and agricultural produce such as eggs, fowl, cereal stables and vegetables. As for fishers, most financed the education of relatives and purchased cattle – as did many of the relatives whose education they had financed.

Within several years of the reservoir's formation, most of the drawdown area was colonized by an extensive sward of *Panicum repens* – a very nutritious grass for domestic stock on the Zambian foreshore and wildlife such as elephant, buffalo and antelope on the Zimbabwe side. Realizing that they had access to one of the best and healthiest (because of initial absence of the liver fluke) grazing areas in the country, resettlers used fishing profits and other funds from the early 1960s to build up herds of cattle. Between 1962 and 1972 herd size more than doubled from 24,000 cattle to over 52,000. In the villages, the large majority of farming families were able to switch from hoe cultivation to ox traction, which in turn expedited the growing of cash crops when the fishery began to decline. Cotton, brewing sorghum and maize were the principal cash crops.

In 1963 there were only 43 cotton growers. By the 1966/67 season there were over 350 with the total increasing to over 600 in the early 1970s. By then, more smallholder cotton was being grown than in any other Zambian district. Capital from fishing also played an important role in funding the proliferation of beer halls as well as small general stores for serving an increasing demand for a greater variety of consumer goods. Bicycles, transistor radios, and paraffin lanterns were no longer rare. Diets were improved with more consumption of animal protein. Improved village housing was furnished with folding and other chairs, small tables and spring beds and mattresses with blankets and sheets. Kitchenware improved as did clothing for men, women, and children.

The reservoir drawdown zone

Prior to Kariba's construction, the distribution and density of the 57,000 people who were subsequently resettled was determined by the availability of fertile alluvial soils along the banks of the Zambezi and the lower reaches of its major tributaries. When the people were resettled the large majority were moved inland to much less fertile Karroo sediments that could be cultivated only once annually if rains were sufficient and which also required periodic fallowing. The Gwembe Tonga situation is characteristic of most farming populations that must resettle because of large dam construction. Such resettlement to less fertile land is a major reason why new opportunities are so crucial if people are to benefit from the resettlement process.

Requiring less change for the majority than either commercial fishing or irrigation, utilization of the reservoir drawdown area is a seldom used option that requires much more consideration by planners. Fortunately for the Gwembe Tonga living on the north bank, their local council had negotiated with the colonial government that resettlers and hosts could occupy the edges of the reservoir and utilize its drawdown area once Kariba Lake reached full storage level. In most years reservoir levels begin to draw down in June–July, remaining down until after substantial inflows begin after the commencement of the rainy season in November–December. That gives at least four to five months during which crops can be grown in the upper drawdown zones, which are more than sufficient to grow early maturing maize and horticultural crops.

The WCD Kariba Case Study estimated the area available for drawdown cultivation on the north bank to be approximately 2450ha, over half of which was available in the upper third of the reservoir basin (Soils Inc, 2000, p59).

While I consider that an underestimate, it is still a significant area of arable land that has played an important role in helping the Gwembe Tonga survive a seriously flawed resettlement programme. That has been the case especially during the increasingly frequent drought years that characterized Central Africa during the 1980s and 1990s. Then the drawdown areas became even more extensive when reservoir levels fell significantly between the 1981/82–1998/99 rainy seasons when Zambezi flows were only half of what they had been during the previous two generations.

In recent years more and more households have moved down to the edge of the reservoir to cultivate the drawdown area, graze and water their cattle and other livestock and to fish. The opportunity provided by the drawdown area could be significantly improved in two ways. One would require formulation of a simple hydrological model that would allow the government annually to advise farmers when drawdown could reliably be expected to begin and to experiment with potential food and cash crops for the drawdown area. The other would involve two types of zoning. The first would legalize Gwembe Tonga communal ownership of the drawdown area so as to restrict its privatization by both immigrant entrepreneurs and local elite. The second, within each village area, would zone the land for agriculture and grazing and in some areas perhaps for joint ventures with the private sector for tourism and game management.

Water supplies

Provision of adequate water supplies prior to resettlement was a failure that can also be generalized for dam-related resettlement in other parts of the world. In the Kariba case, the problem began when the first four villages were moved in 1956 because of proximity to the dam site. As noted in the 1956 Annual Report of the District Council, the delay in providing water supplies there was unfortunate. Not only did similar delays occur in other villages subsequently moved inland from the future reservoir, but inadequate supplies continue to this day in many areas. Initial water supply problems also plagued a majority of the people moved to the Lusitu area below the dam site. There the boreholes drilled either came up dry or were saline, with inadequate supplies remaining until a reticulation scheme of piped water pumped from the Zambezi was built in 1960. Providing unpurified water, that scheme remains the major source of water today for a majority, although periodically the system breaks down.

Today the two resettlement areas with the densest population of resettlers are the Lusitu area and the Siameja area at the upper end of Kariba Lake. Inadequate water supplies in both areas are a contributing factor to dysentery and diarrhoea (Yambayamba et al, 2001) and ongoing outbreaks of cholera (previously non-existent in the Valley). Inadequate water supplies also remain a major problem within the Zimbabwe portion of the Valley. In Binga District, 'It remains an irony to the River Tonga that most of them do not yet benefit from the great resource of Kariba Lake, their former waters.' Despite a growing population, and 'despite all the efforts that have been made in the past, there remains a serious problem in Binga District regarding the availability of safe drinking water' (Tremmel, 1994, pp48–49).

Degradation of resettlement areas above and below the dam site

Because of inadequate land for resettlement purposes on the north bank and the continuation of the resettlers pre-dam system of land use, serious degradation has occurred in the most densely populated resettlement areas. Most seriously affected is the Lusitu area where 6000 resettlers were shifted to an area with an existing population of less than 2000. At the time I estimated that the carrying capacity of the area under the existing system of land use had been exceeded threefold. While I suspect that was an exaggeration, there is no question that too many people were relocated there. At the time of resettlement only a small area was under cultivation by the host population. Remote sensing showed increasing land-cover change from forest to cultivation and bare soils during the 1980s and 1990s (Petit et al, 2001).

Expanding areas designated as bare soils on remote sensing images from 1986 and 1992 are truly bare soils. In drought years the area takes on a Sahelian appearance, with wind-swept dust sweeping across the landscape. Topsoil has been removed to the extent that formerly buried lateral roots of giant baobab trees are now exposed on the surface, with some trees actually toppling over. During recent drought years, livestock either die or must be herded elsewhere – there being neither sufficient grazing nor browse to sustain them. Based on our ground surveys, a similar situation has been developing in the Siameja resettlement area at the upper end of Lake Kariba and in the Chezia resettlement area in the middle reaches of the reservoir. The situation is truly horrifying for it is, in my opinion, an illustration of what is currently underway, though at a much slower rate of degradation, throughout Africa's woodland savannahs – which cover approximately one-third of the continent.

INDIA'S SARDAR SAROVAR PROJECT (SSP)

Introduction

So complex and controversial is SSP that interested readers should download the case history (38pp) from my website. The Sardar Sarovar Dam was planned as the largest single component of a Narmada River Basin programme involving 30 large dams of which 4 were to be multipurpose, 5 were for hydropower and 21 were for irrigation. A total of 125 medium irrigation projects were also intended along with thousands of small-scale schemes as well as trans-basin transfers. Including benefits attributed to SSP, the area to be brought under irrigation could reach five million hectares. The intended installed capacity of hydropower was 2700MW.

The key feature of SSP was to be a dam 138m high to provide irrigation water for 1.8 million hectares and to have a hydropower installed capacity of

1450MW. Major actors involved hundreds of thousands of resettlers, the state of Gujarat as the main beneficiary, three other states, the Government of India including its Supreme Court, the World Bank and a number of national and international NGOs.

The project was controversial from the start. Because the three riverine states were unable to agree on how to share the expected benefits and financial costs, the Government of India established a Narmada Water Disputes Tribunal whose 1979 report was accepted as a basis for future planning. From the start other options were ignored such as those that recognized the cultural symbolism associated with a free-flowing river. Within the Hindu religion, the Narmada is considered India's most sacred river. Whereas the Ganges is 'regarded as the head and hands of the country', the Narmada 'is its heart and soul' (Paranjpye, 1990, p1). Such beliefs took on reality in the country's holiest pilgrimage route whereby pilgrims are supposed to take three years, three months and three days to circle the length of the river.

The site for the SSP dam is located where the Narmada breaks through the final set of hills before flowing onto the coastal plain. In that area, the pilgrim would pass through tribal villages in which the river, its banks and the adjacent forest zone support a diversified production system similar to that along the Zambezi and the lower Mahaweli. Further upriver, but still within the proposed SSP reservoir basin, the narrow but fertile alluvial floodplains supported over a hundred peasant villages. Those requiring resettlement are estimated to number over 200,000. As many as 200,000 others could require resettlement during construction of the 460km main canal and associated irrigation distribution system, implementation of compensatory forestation and other project-related features.

World Bank involvement also began in the late 1970s. World Bank interest was primarily focused on the SSP's irrigation potential. Irrigation was stressed because of Gujarat's history of drought and famine; because realizing the benefits of the 'green revolution' required a reliable water supply; and because the Bank estimated that three-quarters of India's increase in agricultural productivity between 1960 and 1980 came from irrigation. There was also the appeal of getting in on the ground floor not just in controlling a major 'undeveloped' river but also of getting in on 'the largest Indian irrigation project ever planned and implemented as one unit' (World Bank, 1984).

Throughout the project appraisal process during the early 1980s Bank officials failed to observe their own environmental and resettlement guidelines. When the Bank's sociological adviser (Michael Cernea) discovered this, he pointed out that 'detailed resettlement planning' (World Bank, 1980) was an appraisal requirement. He suggested my recruitment as a consultant to work with Indian officials in drawing up the necessary resettlement plan. I made four visits to India, the first in 1983 and the last in 1989.

India's record with development-induced resettlement I consider to be the worst of any democratically elected government. Not counting those forced to move because of irrigation infrastructure, which Parasuraman estimates might exceed ten million people (1999, p50), Indian researchers Fernandes and Raj

(1992) estimate that the total moved in India because of dams and other infrastructure projects, mines and industries falls between 18.5 and 30 million. Estimates of those moved because of dams alone exceed ten million.[2]

In *The Development Dilemma: Displacement in India,* Parasuraman states that 'the resettlement and rehabilitation of displaced people remains highly unsatisfactory. Fewer than 30 per cent of those displaced in the 1950s and 1960s have been resettled; the situation for people displaced after 1970 is no different... Over 50 per cent of the people displaced by development projects are tribals, who account for 7.85 per cent of the total population of India' (Parasuraman, 1999, pp50–51). In its *Mid-Term Appraisal 2000*, no less an authority than India's Planning Commission stated that approximately 40 per cent of an estimated 25 million people displaced by development projects since 1950 were tribal people: 'Less than 50 per cent have been rehabilitated – the rest pauperized by the development process.'[3]

Even today Parliament has not approved an adequate national resettlement policy despite the efforts of civil society, as well as some in government, to legislate one. Although policy statements and publications refer to 'resettlement and rehabilitation', the planning, staffing and implementation emphasis is on 'resettlement' by which the Indians mean physical removal and compensation of people as required by the construction timetable.

For the SSP, all five of the major reasons for unacceptable resettlement outcomes apply. These are lack of political will, lack of planning and implementation capacity, lack of funds, lack of resettler participation and lack of opportunities for enabling resettlers to become project beneficiaries (Chapter 3). Moreover, the way resettlement is being carried out involves major human rights violations while the growing controversy over the project has delayed its implementation and sullied India's reputation, including that of its Supreme Court.[4]

To document the lack of political will of SSP authorities at both the state and central levels it was necessary to analyse in detail the resettlement planning and implementation process and the opposition to that process of affected people, of other concerned Indian citizens and of NGOs over a 40-year period. The analysis can be downloaded from my website. Here one issue is pulled out for separate analysis. It illustrates the lengths to which the Government of Gujarat went to discourage resettlers from the other two riverine states (Maharashtra and Madhya Pradesh), which contained the large majority of those facing inundation, from resettling within the SSP command area – an option that was required by the Tribunal to spread irrigation benefits beyond Gujarat. It is just one illustration from the SSP case history that shows not only the extent to which the project authorities ignored Tribunal and World Bank resettlement guidelines and their own courts but also how the project authorities suffered a financial cost of over a billion dollars (World Bank, 2003) because of the controversies that have delayed SSP construction.

The Parveta and Guttal pilot projects

Introduction

Parveta and Guttal are by far the most important resettlement sites associated with the Sardar Sarovar Project. They are so important because Parveta was the pilot site in the SSP command area for resettlers from Maharashtra, while Guttal was the site for Madhya Pradesh (MP) resettlers. If Gujarat had attempted to make Parveta and Guttal a success from the start, quite possibly still ongoing dam construction would have been completed within the 1990s. But Gujarat chose, intentionally I believe, to implement the initial resettlement in a way that would discourage resettlement within the SSP command area from the other two states.

The land was there. Our World Bank mission documented that fact in 1985 after receiving from the NGO Action Research in Community Health and Development (ARCH)-Vahini a listing of Gujarat landlords willing to sell nearly 4000ha at reasonable prices. Based on that information I recommended a 'cluster approach' whereby resettlers would be more able to move in social units of their choice by acquiring blocks of land in adjacent areas. Gujarat government field staff agreed that such an approach was feasible. It would have required, however, a willingness on the part of the Gujarat authorities to play a much more active coordination and acquisition role based on the purchase of private land. Unwilling to play such a role, they lost the opportunity at the expense of their own project. Ironically, after 1988 a reorganized Gujarat project authority began to pursue just such a strategy, but by then opposition to the dam had crystallized among resettlers in both Madhya Pradesh and Maharashtra.

Parveta

I first visited the Parveta site in August 1984 before resettlement had begun. Not only was the neighbouring host village of similar background, but some families in the first three Maharashtra villages to be moved had relatives in the vicinity. Presumably that was one reason why 564 families from those villages were willing initially to come to Parveta. The host village of about 130 families, most of whom worked largely as agricultural labourers in neighbouring villages, would also have benefited from a well-implemented resettlement programme. Although well connected to a tarred road and with access to electricity, they also would have benefited from irrigation and a much-needed middle school for boys and girls.

By our September 1985 visit, 10 resettled families had been in residence for nearly six months while another 30 were moving back and forth between the two sites. In my report I wrote 'The current resettlement and rehabilitation … is not adequate.' Moreover, those who had already moved suggested to those yet to move to wait until, for example, the Gujarat authorities had 'announced what the price is that they must pay for Parveta land since preparing Parveta lands for cultivation has already cost the oustees more than they received for their lands in Maharashtra. The situation at Parveta may well discourage any further oustees from Maharashtra from coming to that site. Since Maharashtra oustees may well be communicating with MP oustees, similar difficulties can be expected at Guttal.'

Resettler concerns about land prices were legitimate. They had received only 1400–2200 rupees per hectare for their own land, and rumours circulated that the cost of Parveta land would be at least 4600 rupees. The problem was that Gujarat, which must pay all resettlement costs, and Maharashtra had not yet agreed on land compensation prices. Living conditions were also poor. Resident families were living in inadequate government-supplied temporary shelters that were ten by ten feet in dimension and made of iron sheeting. Drinking water was polluted and social services were yet to be provided.

Nearly four years later, in May 1989, not only did the same legitimate complaints exist, but in some respects the situation had deteriorated. Although recent Gujarat resolutions now advocated the purchase of private arable land, no such land had been purchased in the vicinity for resettlers previously willing to come from other villages if farmland was available. In spite of requests for clarification, resettlers had yet to be informed how much they would have to pay for arable land received. As for housing, they did not have the funds to build their own housing and were still living in the 'temporary' iron sheeting shelters that 'periodically blew down in high winds' and were 'too cold in the cold season and too hot in the dry season' (Scudder, 1989, p21).

People's health over the years had actually deteriorated, with the Tata Institute for Social Science reporting exceptionally high mortality rates in young children in 1986/87 and 1987/88, during which deaths among children under four equalled new births. As I wrote in my 1989 report, the large number of deaths among children from dysentery was 'also consistent with the polluted water supplies noted in 1985', not to mention the crowded temporary living conditions.

I also reported that a World Bank mission that visited Parveta in 1987 found 'severe R&R problems, grievances at the time relating to incomplete compensation, uncultivable or uncleared lands, and insufficient grazing for livestock'. Having coped with such conditions over a four-year period it was 'hardly surprising that the other nine Maharashtra villages are now refusing to come to Gujarat' (Scudder, 1989, p22).

Based on monitoring activities, Parasuraman reports a similar situation among resettlers from the first village that moved – a majority of whom had moved by the end of 1986. They 'went through serious hardship. Until 1987 ... the resettlement site was barren, without basic provisions. Only a few tin sheds had been erected. People suffered serious health problems due to nutritional deficiency and lack of proper water and medical facilities... The host villages were hostile... Food shortages, a lack of proper cooking facilities, and difficulties in obtaining potable water compounded the difficulties... People have had to fight for each and every basic service provided... Without determined struggle, Parveta would not have received any basic facilities' (Parasuraman, 1999, p102).

Since the late 1980s, Parasuraman reports that incomes have 'increased considerably,' while 'the overall economic performance of the Parveta households appears to be good' (ibid, pp196–197), although I am not sure that he pays sufficient attention to significant increases in expenses, with his later statement that 'the proportion of households facing economic hardship has been increasing since 1989' (ibid, p206) perhaps supporting that possibility. Nonetheless, the situation for resettlers certainly has improved. A major factor was the final willingness of Gujarat to provide rehabilitation assistance in the form of plough animals, agricultural equipment and institutional credit. Potable water is now available throughout the year. Educational facilities have been greatly improved with '70 per cent of children between 6 and 14 in school'. Living standards can be expected to improve further if the promised irrigation arrives.

One cannot help but wonder how the SSP might have fared if that kind of resettlement with development had been available from the start for resettlers from Maharashtra and Madhya Pradesh rather than emerging on an 'ad hoc' basis, as Parasuraman puts it, in response to increasing opposition to the project. The same question applies equally to Gujarat's resettlement of its own inundated villages. If land for the landless had been agreed upon in the early 1980s rather than in 1987, if land for major sons had been agreed upon then rather than in 1988, and if Gujarat had been willing to purchase private land from the start, it might have been possible to settle villagers in social units of their choice rather than scattering resettlers from the 19 Gujarat villages at 175 different sites!

Guttal

By 1984 Guttal was the only site within the SSP command area that Gujarat had made available to resettlers from Madhya Pradesh. Land there was limited to less than a 100ha. When our World Bank Mission visited the site in August, 84 families from the first 14 MP villages to be flooded had stated a willingness to come if promised facilities were available by January 1986. A year later during our September visit, officials in Madhya Pradesh told us that those families, and others, were no longer willing to go there because they had heard about the problems at Parveta!

Even if those families had been willing to move to Guttal, the Gujarat authorities had only slightly increased the available land. That situation did not change until June 1988 when the authorities agreed to offer privately purchased land in areas surrounding Guttal and elsewhere. Ten months later, however, we found that no MP resettlers had yet come to Guttal, where no potable water was yet available nor had construction been completed on a school. As I reported to the Bank, 'In delaying Guttal preparation for over nine years, the Government of Gujarat (GOG) has lost the opportunity for planning and implementing a worthwhile pilot project that could have played a major role in attracting a significant number of MP oustees to SSP command areas during the 1980s. As a result of these delays, GOG has placed in jeopardy the entire R&R component of the SSP' (Scudder, 1989, p21).

On the basis of admittedly fragmented information, it is my understanding that the willingness of MP resettlers to go to Guttal decreased further in the 1990s. Following her 1999 revisit to Anjanvara (an MP village threatened with inundation during the 1999 monsoon because of the renewal of construction on the Sardar Sarovar Dam), Amita Baviskar wrote 'If there is one thing that Anjanvara is sure about, it is this: they don't want to go to Gujarat. They have visited resettlement sites there and they have seen the misery. Waterlogged fields, no livestock, fragmented families, hostile neighbours, no commons to collect fuel or fodder – this sums up the experience of most adivasis [tribals] from MP who were given land in Gujarat' (Baviskar, 1999).

BOTSWANA'S SOUTHERN OKAVANGO INTEGRATED WATER DEVELOPMENT PROJECT AND HYDRO-QUEBEC'S GRANDE BALEINE PROJECT

Introduction

Two projects are dealt with in which the construction of large water development projects was 'stopped' – at least temporarily. The Southern Okavango Integrated Water Development Project was 'cancelled' by the Government of Botswana, whereas the Grande Baleine Project was suspended by Hydro-Quebec. I use the words 'stopped' and 'cancelled' with caution. As Harvard's Peter Rogers told me in regard to the Botswana project, large dams are like vampires in their ability to rise from the dead. For dams, however, there is no equivalent to a wooden stake through the heart. As circumstances change, they can always be resurrected at some future time. Civil society must be constantly on the alert to ensure that its best interests are not neglected.

Analysis of the two cases illustrates a number of important lessons. One points up the importance of a decision-making process that considers a wider range of alternatives from the start. In both cases such an approach would have resulted in better outcomes at a lower financial cost to the project authorities and reduced stress and uncertainty for affected communities. A related lesson illustrates the danger of leaving project planning exclusively in the hands of dam advocates. No matter how competent, and in both cases technical competence was high, such advocates run the risk of losing their perspective. That was especially the case with the Botswana project where members of the responsible ministry became project 'boosters' to the extent that they stigmatized critics and refused to acknowledge project defects or consider alternatives.

Another lesson illustrates the importance of incorporating local involvement in decision-making from the start and the key role that local communities must play if badly planned dams are to be stopped. A fourth lesson illustrates the wide range of unexpected events than can influence outcomes. The likelihood of such events increases because of the relatively long planning process that characterizes most major water development projects. A fifth lesson concerns the likelihood that conditions will change during the planning process that will influence the assumptions on which a particular option was selected. In the Okavango case, elimination of the flood recession agriculture component and reduction of the area to be irrigated should have led to a re-evaluation of the project's cost effectiveness. The same applies to the successful drilling for groundwater to serve the needs of the diamond mines. Yet no such re-evaluation occurred. In the Grande Baleine case, reduction in energy demand should have had a similar effect on the project but did not.

While both the Botswanan and Canadian authorities can be faulted, it is important to emphasize that the favourable outcomes that eventually occurred would not have happened if those authorities had not been willing eventually to make pioneering decisions. In the Okavango case, the government deserves praise for two important reasons. The first was its willingness to be the first government to invite an outside agency, in this case IUCN, to evaluate a major but controversial water development project. The second was the government's 1997 declaration that made the Okavango the world's largest Ramsar site – a decision that makes the initiation of future large-scale infrastructure projects in the delta more difficult.[5] In the Canadian case, Hydro-Quebec's decision to make the informed consent of indigenous people a prerequisite for future projects, including any attempt to resurrect the Grande Baleine Project, warrants praise.

That said, the habitat and local communities remain at risk in both cases. Even without potentially adverse effects of global warming on Botswana's pastures, the country's elite community of ranchers would welcome access to the Okavango's grasslands and water supplies. As recent events have shown, the Government of Quebec, while willing to involve the Cree Nation in the realization of its goals, wants to develop – on its own terms to the extent possible – the hydropower, mining and timber resources of Central and Northern Quebec. While individual projects have been stopped, in both cases expanding human populations continue to threaten the natural resource base.

In the sections that follow, two issues are dealt with in more detail. The first, in the Okavango case, is the government's precedent-setting decision to ask an international agency to evaluate a major water resource development project. That decision is important, for its sets a partial precedent for the type of international adjudication and compliance board that I believe is necessary for dealing with contentious projects at local, national and international levels. The second issue, relevant to both cases, deals with the role of local communities in stopping, or at least suspending, controversial projects. As with the other cases presented in this chapter, interested readers can download a more detailed analysis of both projects from my website.

The Southern Okavango Integrated Water Development Project (SOIWDP)[6]

The Okavango Delta is advertised as the largest oasis in the world and is 'one of the world's premier wildlands, with magnificent scenery, game-viewing and bird-watching' (Scudder et al, 1993, p51). Located in north-western Botswana, the delta 'is not a true delta but an alluvial fan whose primarily origin and, to some extent, evolution has been controlled by regional earth movements and land subsidence' (Manley and Wright, 1996, p213). The second of two major faults, running at right angles to the fan's lower margin, receives inflowing water and channels it to the Boteti River that flows only during the annual flood. As mapped by the 1991–92 IUCN Review, the size of the delta is approximately 15,846km². The largest of its five zones is perennial swamp that covers 31 per cent of the surface area. Next in size is seasonally flooded swamp (24 per cent), followed by seasonally flooded grassland (17 per cent), intermittently flooded land (16 per cent) and dry land (12 per cent). A major characteristic of the delta, unlike the situation in most other Africa wetlands, is the existence of hundreds of islands that are scattered throughout the flooded area. They greatly enhance the delta's world famous biological diversity of plants and wildlife. Including over 350 species, birdlife is prolific in the delta and immediately surrounding fringes. During the dry season, large mammals, including herds of elephant and buffalo and thousands of antelope, come to the delta from elsewhere in Botswana and from surrounding countries. Lions swim from island to island seeking prey.

Approximately 100,000 people lived in the Okavango Region in 1991, of whom about one-quarter lived in the administrative centre of Maun located just inside the lower margin of the delta. At that time about half of the population lived in settlements of less than 500 people. Living standards were among the lowest in Botswana, with at least 80 per cent of households living below the country poverty datum line in the late 1980s.

Following independence in 1966, the government requested assistance from the United Nations as well as from bilateral donors in assessing how to use Okavango waters. Most important were two sets of studies completed under UNDP/FAO auspices. Sixteen schemes were evaluated, one of which led to the SOIWDP. Implementation was approved in late 1988.

Designed as an integrated project, SOIWDP was intended to increase food production through 10,000ha of commercial irrigation and 5000ha of improved flood recession agriculture; raise the living standards of the local population; and deliver water to the administrative centre of Maun, riverine villages, the town of Rakops on the Lower Boteti and the Orapa mines and mining community. Those goals were to be achieved by channelizing the delta's main outflowing river and by the construction of two large dams and two smaller dams to receive the increased flow in three reservoirs (see Figure 6.1).

When the contractor selected to initiate the project began to mobilize in November 1990, the local and international environmental movement along with local villagers and safari operators were incensed. The strongest initial response came from Greenpeace whose Amsterdam office threatened to launch an international campaign in which the DeBeers' slogan, 'Diamonds are for Ever,' would become 'Diamonds are for Death'. The speed with which grass-roots opposition was organized was due in good part to the efforts of two NGOs. One was the Maun Branch of the Kalahari Conservation Society –

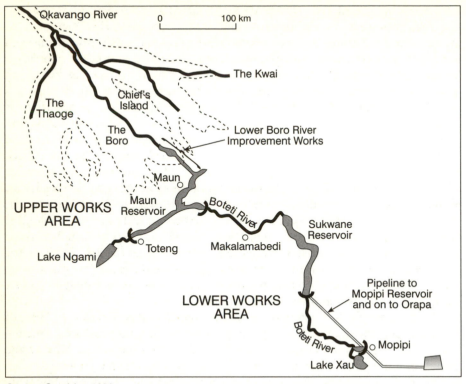

Source: Scudder, 1993c

Figure 6.1 *Botswana's Okavango River System and the Southern Okavango Integrated Water Development Project*

Botswana's largest and most important environmental NGO. The other was Tshomarelo – a local NGO founded for the purpose of opposing SOIWDP.

To respond to growing criticism, the government organized a meeting in Maun on 11 January 1991 – just several days before project construction was to start. At least 700 people participated, most of who were local villagers. The outpouring of opposition to the government's position may well have been the strongest attack on any government policy since independence in 1966. The government's reaction to the outpouring of opposition was exceptional and pioneering. Not only was the project temporarily suspended, but the government requested IUCN to complete a detailed evaluation.

During the summer of 1991 IUCN put together under my leadership an exceptional team of 13 members of four different nationalities recruited from 12 different organizations. The SOIWDP evaluation began that October. A Draft Final Report released on 21 May 1992 recommended that the SOIWDP be terminated. A wide range of deficiencies was presented relating 'both to the project itself and to the process whereby it was planned and designed' (IUCN, 1992a, Exec. Sum.). Neither of the two major goals of the project to increase food production or raise living standards would be met; nor was the project necessary for meeting the water demand of Maun and the Orapa mining complex. The team's conclusions justified and supported local opposition. Although villagers tended to ignore the negative impact on their lives of factors that had nothing to do with the project, such as drought and population increase, their assessment of the negative impact on their living standards of previous government and private sector efforts to manipulate Okavango flows was correct. As they suspected, SOIWDP's implementation would have had an even more serious impact.

Accepting the government's major development goals for the Okavango region and the delta's outflow areas, which included important diamond mines, the longest chapter in the IUCN report dealt with a better-designed and more cost-effective alternative to realize those goals. Consistent with policies presented in the government's recent Seventh National Development Plan (Botswana, 1991), emphasis was on the nature of the natural resource base in the Okavango region; existing economies at village and district/sub-district levels; and current planning by the local Land Use Planning Unit, Land Board and District Council. Special attention was paid to ensuring that the IUCN alternative was strongly participatory and that it built on the multi-stranded initiatives that villagers used to maintain and improve their living standards.

To evaluate economic activities at the household level, the IUCN team dealt with rain-fed and flood recession agriculture, livestock management, wage labour, gathering, fishing, hunting and craft manufacture, and small business enterprises such as tea rooms, cafes and shops. New development initiatives were also recommended. The team recommended, for example, that productive activities and administrative services be linked to a hierarchy of markets for the better integration of rural and urban areas (Reynolds, 1992). To meet Maun's increasing demand for water, the conjunctive use of surface and groundwater was emphasized, while groundwater was seen as sufficient for meeting the needs of the diamond mines.

The results of IUCN's 1992 Draft Final Report were presented during a public lecture in Botswana's capital in late May 1992. Approximately 30 minutes before it began, the government announced on the radio that the SOIWDP had been suspended. The announcement was made both to save face and to emphasize the government's democratic procedures. No mention was made of IUCN or the IUCN report. The project had been cancelled, according to the government announcement, because of the strength of local opposition.

Between May 1992 and the present, several events have occurred that reduce but do not eliminate the possibility of SOIWDP's return or implementation of another project involving dams and major manipulation of Okavango flows. A tripartite Okavango River Basin Commission (OKACOM) was established in the mid-1990s with Angola, Botswana and Namibia as members. Its existence reduces the possibility of member countries unilaterally implementing a major water resource development project. It also increases the opportunity for comprehensive environmental, social and health impact studies being completed for any options that all three members might approve.

Also during the mid-1990s, Botswana's Department of Water Affairs drew up terms of reference for two phases of hydro-geological studies in the lower reaches of the delta that would investigate the IUCN belief that conjunctive use of groundwater and natural surface flows would be sufficient to meet the water resource needs of the Okavango region. By 1997, 111 boreholes had been drilled during the first phase, with test pumping from 46. Supporting the conclusions of the IUCN review, the consultants concluded 'that groundwater utilization is a viable option to meet the medium and longer term water supply needs for Maun. Surface water, when available, can be used conjunctively to artificially recharge the Shashe River Valley and for direct supply utilizing the present surface water treatment plant' (Eastend Investments, 1997, p16).

Also in 1997 the Government of Botswana agreed for the Okavango Delta to become the world's largest Ramsar site, another recommendation in the IUCN report. Contracted during 2001, the terms of reference for the second phase of the hydro-geological work included siting and installation of 'at least two wellfields to provide water to the town of Maun and surroundings through the year 2015' (www.vuawater.com).

Hydro-Quebec, the Grande Baleine component of the James Bay Project and the James Bay Cree

The history of Hydro-Quebec's James Bay Project is important because it illustrates how an indigenous people, initially exploited and weak institutionally, were able to organize themselves to the extent that they stopped the construction of the Grande Baleine Project and became partners with Hydro-Quebec in the future development of their homeland.

Hydro-Quebec is a powerful Canadian parastatal owned by the Provincial Government of Quebec for the generation and distribution of electricity. During 1999 it was responsible for 29 per cent of the electricity generated in Canada. It also sells high-cost peaking power to the north-eastern US during hot summer months. As is so often the case with large dams and large-scale river basin development, the James Bay Project was pushed forward by a single powerful politician – in this case by Quebec's Premier Robert Bourassa – when his Liberal Party was in power. As announced by Bourassa on 30 April 1971, the James Bay Project was to be implemented in three stages – each of which would have cost billions of dollars. Referred to as the NBR Project after the Nottaway–Broadback–Rupert system of rivers, the first stage would divert water from the other rivers into the Broadback where up to eight power plants could produce 8400MW. The second La Grande stage comprised two phases. The first would involve three dams on the La Grande River with a generating capacity of 10,282MW. The second, involving diversions to the La Grande from three other rivers, would produce 5537MW from six power plants. The third stage was called Grande Baleine (Great Whale). It would involve three dams on the Grande Baleine River. By increasing flows with diversions from two tributaries of a second river, 3212MW could be generated.

As announced in April 1971, the James Bay Project would have been one of the largest river basin development projects in the world under single management. Implementation of as many as 20 dams affecting nine major river systems would have unforeseen cumulative impacts on the entire homeland of the indigenous Cree Indians (Scudder, 1996), yet no attempt was made to consult with, let alone involve, the Cree. They lived in nine small communities that were relatively isolated because of lack of roads. In each, inhabitants had been able to maintain a preferred lifestyle and culture dominated by hunting and fishing with some gathering and some wage labour. It was a lifestyle that the large majority believed to be threatened by the James Bay Project. But the Cree also had a problem – a rapidly increasing population that had grown from 5500 when the James Bay Project was announced to 11,000 in the mid-1990s and to 13,000 by 2002. With over 50 per cent under the age of 20, the Cree had a serious unemployment problem that would require them to make compromises that could further degrade their habitat and threaten their culture.

The Cree, including local leaders, first heard about the project after it was announced to the public. Billy Diamond, who subsequently led initial opposition to the James Bay Project as the first president of the Grand Council of the Crees, heard about the Project from his wife who heard about it over the radio. Cree involvement was also ignored when the James Bay Development Company, a Hydro-Quebec subsidiary, was formed several months later to implement a project which, with or without their involvement, would integrate their previously isolated society into Quebec's. The Cree response was to organize themselves into what has become perhaps the most effective political entity among affected local people trying to stop or otherwise influence the construction of large-scale dams. That entity is the Grand Council of the Crees that brought together nine isolated communities in 1974 into an increasingly effective negotiating organization.

Initially confused as to their options, community leaders did not meet together until July 1971, at which time they decided to protest the project to the provincial minister of Indian Affairs. Financial help from the Arctic Institute of North America started a coalition between the Cree and non-Cree experts and institutions that has proved so important in the people's ability to influence events. Because of protests from ecologists, as well as from anthropologists at McGill University who had been working in Cree communities, in January 1972 the project authorities announced that they would start with the central (La Grande) component of the project rather than the southernmost one. Grande Baleine would follow.

Initially the Indians of Quebec Association, based on the testimony of experts recruited to document how the project could cause irreparable harm to the Cree, sought a court injunction against the project toward the end of 1972. While the court deliberated, the project authorities proceeded with road construction to the major La Grande Dam site. During a seven-day period in November 1973, the court ruled in favour of the Cree and work on the project stopped. Four days later Quebec's Premier offered to negotiate on what he felt were generous terms. When, on appeal, the initial judgment to stop work was overturned a few days later, the Cree agreed in 1974 to negotiate a settlement of their aboriginal land claims that had been the focus of their law suit. An Agreement in Principle was signed in November 1974 and after a year's attention to details, the James Bay and Northern Quebec Agreement (JBNQA) was signed on 11 November 1975.

Opinions vary as to the extent to which the JBNQA was actually in the interests of the Cree. Given that the Cree lost their case on appeal and the project authorities proceeded with construction on the main La Grande Dam, the prevailing view is that the Agreement represented the best outcome that the Cree could expect at the time. Negative aspects included stopping their legal actions against the project authorities, agreeing to not base future claims to land on 'aboriginal rights' and acknowledging Quebec's sovereign rights as opposed to the federal government's.

Benefits would include a greater degree of self-government including greater control over education and health, formation of a police force, and cash compensation in instalments and receipt of a share of revenue from electricity generation. Institutions of self-government improved rapidly. By 1977 the Cree Regional Board of Health and Social Services had developed to the point that it took over the hospital and nursing stations formerly run by federal and provincial agencies, while the Cree School Board took over the running of schools the following year. For the nearly one-third of Cree families that wished to maintain their pre-project lifestyle, the most innovative programme in the Agreement was 'an Income Security Programme for Hunters and Trappers (ISP), which guaranteed full-time hunters a minimum cash income (indexed and variable by family size) each year, plus an allowance for each day spent in hunting' (Salisbury, 1986, p57). Implementation of that component has been a success with Feit (1995) noting how the number of families or individuals hunting intensively rose from about 700 in 1975 to about 1200 after the ISP was implemented. In the northernmost community, for example, 35 per cent of Cree were reported to benefit during 1991–1992 (Hydro-Quebec, 1993, Part 2, Book 8). The time spent hunting also increased, with most families now spending seven or more months in their bush camps.

More controversial as a benefit or a cost was the land allocation process. To compensate for loss of control over 80 per cent of their homeland, eight of the nine Cree communities received 'ownership' of surface resources in the immediate vicinity of each community (the ninth would receive land once legally incorporated). Altogether only about 5 per cent of their homeland was involved. In buffer zones around each community that totalled 15 per cent, they were given exclusive hunting, fishing and gathering rights. The remaining 80 per cent was open to everyone, although hunting and trapping of certain animals was restricted to the Cree. In 1993, for example, those lands were utilized by approximately 1000 non-resident hunters and 4500 non-resident fishers (Dickson et al, 1994, p30); quite an incursion into the Cree homeland.

When Hydro-Quebec accelerated planning for the Grande Baleine Stage in 1985, the Cree were in a much stronger position to negotiate outcomes. Unlike the La Grande stage of the project, the Cree claimed that the 1975 JBNQA did not allow the Grande Baleine stage to proceed without negotiations leading to a separate agreement. The Cree, through their Grand Council, were also increasingly critical of what they considered to be the failure of the project authorities to incorporate the Cree into the development of the James Bay region.

In trying first to stop and then to influence the La Grande stage, the Cree relied primarily on Canadian expertise. They soon realized its value. As Billy Diamond summed it up later, 'These scientists played a very valuable role. Our people knew where the data was – the animals, what they did – but we needed the scientists to write it down so it would become scientific evidence' (MacGregor, 1990, p75). During the first half of the 1980s, the Cree expanded the universe in which they sought both expertise and support of their position beyond Canada to include, eventually, the United Nations and the Pope.

When serious planning began in the mid-1980s for Grande Baleine, the Cree had ample reason to question the political will of the project authorities to implement negotiated outcomes. As opposition within the nine communities toward the project increased, the Grand Council of the Crees withdrew from negotiations in 1988. Between 1988 and 1994, when the Premier announced that Grande Baleine had been 'put on ice', the Cree spearheaded a successful process of opposition. On the one hand, they successfully required the project authorities to carry out what may well be the most expensive dam-related environmental impact assessment undertaken to date as well as an elaborate review process at federal and provincial levels as to its adequacy. On the other hand, they worked closely with environmental organizations in Canada and the US to stop the project.

At a cost of CAN$256 million, the Environmental Impact Statement was published in August 1993 in 30 volumes, a total of 5000 pages in length. The review process involved five panels, including Cree members, which issued a joint 119-page Conformity Report on 18 November 1994. Hydro-Quebec recruited its own review panel on which I was one of five members. Based on a much shorter assessment, our report was made public on 26 July 1994 (Dickson et al, 1994). Both the Conformity Report and the Hydro-Quebec panel found the Environmental Impact Statement inadequate.

In their opposition to the project, the Cree launched a multi-stranded approach. One strand was to foster joint action with NGOs such as Canada's Probe International and, in the US, Cultural Survival, the International Rivers Network, the National Audubon Society, the Natural Resources Defense Council and the Sierra Club. Activities included placing a full-page advertisement in a 1991 issue of the *New York Times* that showed caribou being drowned by waters released from a Hydro-Quebec Dam. In 1992 Cree representatives – joined by Inuit who were also against the project – travelled by canoe through the north-eastern US to New York City. Along the way they held meetings to explain why they were opposed to Hydro-Quebec's plans to export power to the State of New York and to the New England States. The finale of the voyage was on Earth Day 1992 when the Cree Grand Chief addressed a crowd estimated at 10,000 in New York's Times Square, an event that generated good media coverage. Such activities were instrumental in the

State of New York cancelling that year a contract with Hydro-Quebec involving 1000MW, with a seasonal contract for another 800MW not renegotiated two years later (Niezen, 1998, p120). State governments in Vermont and Maine also refused to take electricity from the Grande Baleine Project if built.

The day after the Conformity Report from the five federal and provincial review panels was published, Quebec's Premier, who had recently been elected, publicly announced that the Grande Baleine Project 'is on ice for a good long while... We don't need Great Whale' (*The Gazette*, 1994). In trying to explain that decision, I believe first in importance was the active opposition to the project in which the Cree played the key role.

Following the suspension of the Grande Baleine Project, the federal government and the Grand Council of the Crees appointed negotiators to explore more cooperative ways for implementing the 1975 James Bay Agreement. In June 1998 the Cree and the federal government launched a Cree–Canada Round Table with six ministers and 11 Cree present (including the Grand Chief, the deputy Grand Chief and the chiefs of all nine communities). During the same time period, Hydro-Quebec established new policies relating to affected populations of Native Americans and other Canadians as well as to the environment. In 1997 implementation began of an environmental management system in compliance with ISO standard 14001. Released the next year, their 1998–2002 five-year plan stated that new projects must not only be acceptable economically and environmentally, but also be approved by affected people. Hydro-Quebec also 'proposed partnership agreements to local communities for all new hydropower projects' (WCD, 2000, p128).[7]

In a speech before Quebec's electricity industry association (AIEQ) on 18 March 1999, the Grand Council's Director of Relations with Quebec responded positively to Hydro-Quebec's new approach.[8] More specifically he noted that Hydro-Quebec's 'consent element in the new approach is something that is worthwhile for us'. The problem for the Cree, he noted, is that 'We have always known what we do not want, but have never reflected on what we want for our future' that includes a situation where, on the one hand, 500 youths enter the job market annually, and, on the other hand, the livelihood of 30 per cent of the population is still based on hunting and fishing. For those youths new jobs are essential, jobs such as the 75 provided in one community two years earlier by a Cree-constructed sawmill. He added, 'I think more and more we will be seeing that type of development initiative taking place in Cree communities. We have no choice.'

Perhaps during 1999 the Grand Council began to negotiate in secret with the Government of Quebec and Hydro-Quebec an agreement that would include a partnership to divert the Rupert River into the Eastmain to generate 1200MW. Again in secret, an Agreement in Principle was signed on 23 October by the Grand Chief of the Grand Council and two of the nine community chiefs for the Cree and by the Premier and two Ministers for Quebec Province. Five major purposes were outlined. The first was 'The establishment of a new nation-to-nation relationship, based on the common will of the parties to continue the development of the James Bay territory and to seek the flourishing of the Crees within a context of growing modernization.' Interesting and relevant was that it referred to the Cree as a 'nation'. The second was 'The assumption of greater responsibility on the part of the Cree Nation in relation to its economic and community development and, in so doing, the achievement of increased autonomy with a greater capacity to respond, in partnership with Quebec, to the needs of the Cree population.' That purpose of responsibility for self-government would be financed by Quebec with annual contributions starting at CAN$26 million in 2002 to increase to CAN$70 million in 2005. Thereafter for 45 years the CAN$70 million would be indexed to reflect revenue from hydropower, mining and forestry development.

The third purpose was to settle all questions relating to Quebec's responsibilities in regard to 'the development of mining, forestry and hydroelectric resources on the James Bay territory' and to 'the provisions pertaining to the economic and community development of the Crees found in the JBNQA and in the complementary agreements, including those dealing with the nature, scope and implementation of Quebec's commitments in this respect'. To deal with the contentious issue of adverse logging impacts on Cree hunting territories, new regulations would be institutionalized, a Cree–Quebec Forestry Board would be created, and the Cree would be able to make non-binding recommendations as to how hunting territories were logged. As for the fourth purpose, that involved 'The definitive settlement or withdrawal of the legal proceedings opposing the Crees and Quebec in accordance with the provisions of the present agreement.' And last, but not least, 'the consent of the Crees to the carrying out of the Eastmain hydroelectric project and the Rupert River diversion project' at an estimated cost of CAN$3.8 billion. During January 2002 Hydro-Quebec offered the Cree CAN$862 million more in contracts in connection with constructing the Rupert–Eastmain project.

On 18 December 2001 in a talk to Quebec's Electricity Industry Association, Ted Moses, at that time Grand Chief, stated his support in largely symbolic terms. The key symbol was the concept of informed consent – applied for the first time in Canada not just to the James Bay Cree, but to any Native American group. 'It is this consent that is at the heart of our new relationship with Quebec. Consent requires two parties: the one who seeks consent, and the other who gives or withholds consent. **That essential fact, that Quebec chooses to obtain Cree consent, allows the Cree people and the Cree Nation to enter into a new relationship with Quebec... What we must understand is that the James Bay and Northern Quebec Agreement is essentially a development agreement for Quebec... The Cree Nation is no longer seen as being in the way of development. Instead the Crees are recognized as essential to development – the logical centre for development in the territory'** (Bold print as in Grand Chief Ted Moses' statement).

On 31 January 2002 a referendum was held. With high voter turnout, 70 per cent approved the Agreement with only one of the nine communities in opposition, and there the vote was close with 48 per cent for approval. The Agreement was signed by the Cree and the government on 7 February 2002.

It remains to be seen if the spirit of the 2002 Agreement is implemented or the history of the James Bay Agreement between 1975 and 2001 is repeated. It also remains to be seen if the desired results – jobs and higher living standards for the Cree combined with a desired culture – are achieved if the agreement is implemented. As with the 2002 agreement, whatever agreements that the Cree sign in the future will add to the ongoing, and perhaps inevitable, environmental degradation caused by an expanding human population in search of higher living standards.

7

Addressing Downstream and Upper Catchments: Social and Environmental Impacts

INTRODUCTION

Few attempts have been made to determine the ecological, economic and cultural importance of rivers before they have been dammed. Even fewer before-and-after studies exist. This is especially the case in regard to environmental and social impacts below dams. What is known is that such impacts will be more serious in the future than in the past, which adds an additional burden to late-industrializing countries in which the majority of future dams will be built. Impacts on people will be more serious for two major reasons. One is that downstream populations are larger as a result of population increase. The other is that, in comparison to downstream populations in North America, Europe and Japan, their livelihoods are more dependent on natural flood regimes because of the greater importance of flood recession agriculture, floodplain grazing, fishing, foraging and aquifer recharge for domestic water supplies and reforestation.

Ecological impacts on offshore resources, deltas and wetlands below dams also will tend to be more serious. This is especially the case with tropical and subtropical rivers because of their greater biological diversity and productivity. The dam-related destruction of mangroves in such deltas as the Indus and the Zambezi has been especially detrimental to offshore fisheries. In this chapter special emphasis is placed on the need to consider environmental flows, the purpose of which is to mimic the natural flow regime of a river, including flood pulses and low season flows, in any water resources options assessment process that includes large dams. There are, of course, other environmental issues that also need consideration, but are omitted because of lack of space. Global warming[1] is one, where the uncertainty associated with extreme events makes water storage behind dams especially vulnerable to drought and flood. Another issue concerns the deterioration of water quality[2] that may be associated with large dams and which currently is of major concern in connection with the reservoir forming behind China's Three Gorges Dam.

In this chapter the focus is on the many millions of river basin residents whose economies and lifestyles are dependent on free-flowing rivers or were so dependent before dam construction. The large majority of such river basin residents live in Latin America, Africa and Asia. While their predominantly rural communities are low income, the development potential of their economies continues to be seriously underestimated. In the first section of this chapter, the importance of natural flood regimes for tens of millions of people and for development is examined. Two case studies – one in Nigeria and one in Senegal – show how returns per unit of water, labour and capital can exceed those from a primary focus on dam-supplied irrigation. The next section further examines the adverse impact of large dams on downstream ecosystems and rural livelihoods caused by regularization and reduction (as through trans-basin transfers) of annual flows as well as operational inefficiencies, which can significantly reduce overall economic benefits while increasing costs to local communities. Ecosystem and social effects caused by reduced flows and increased pollution are illustrated by examining the current state of four major deltas.

The third section deals with efforts of restoration once large dams have been built. The advantages and disadvantages of environmental flows, synchronized with reservoir drawdown, should be assessed during the planning process as a means for reducing otherwise irreversible ecological impacts downstream, and for the benefit of those living downstream and those living and resettled within reservoir basins. Such methods, however, require an experimental or adaptive management approach because of the uncertainties involved. The necessary monitoring and adjustments based on that monitoring are expensive in time, personnel and money. Their implementation must also face vested economic and political interests favouring the status quo as shown by reluctance in the US to release environmental flows from dams on the Missouri River or to restore the Everglades in Florida. Moreover, restoration measures are not panaceas; what has been lost cannot be completely recovered since large dams cause irreversible damage to offshore marine resources, coastlines, deltas and wetlands. These impacts need be seriously considered during the options assessment process because they can be a major reason why some mainstream dams should not be built. The fourth section, followed by a short summary, deals with upstream habitats and users.

This chapter conveys my sense of anger at the extent to which downstream communities in developing countries have been, and are being, unnecessarily impoverished as a result of dam construction. It is important to realize that this conclusion is based on case studies as well as on the work of the WCD. The Commission's November 2000 Final Report emphasized negative impacts on ecosystems and project-affected communities as two of the most serious failings of existing dams. Downstream impacts include biodiversity impacts that are irreversible as well as the 'loss of ... the services of downstream floodplains, wetlands and riverine estuarine and adjacent marine ecosystems' (WCD, 2000, pp92–93). As for downstream people, 'millions ... have also suffered serious harm to their livelihoods and had the future productivity of their resources put at risk' (ibid, p129).

While WCD considered the adverse impacts of dam construction on riverine communities as 'unacceptable', planners and project authorities pay the least attention to downstream impacts. WCD noted that 'even in the 1990s, impacts on downstream livelihoods were not adequately assessed or accounted for in the planning and designing of large dams' (ibid). With a few major exceptions dealing with tropical Africa, the scientific community has been equally remiss. Natural flood-dependent people are usually ignored when academics assess downstream impacts of dams and other infrastructure. This deficiency applies to the literature as well as to methodologies. For example, issues of *Bioscience* in 1995, 1998 and 2000 had special sections on the 'The Ecology of Large Rivers', 'Flooding: Natural and Managed Disturbances', and 'Hydrological Alterations Cause Global Environmental Change', but made no mention of the dependence of millions of people on natural flood regimes aside from the odd mention in passing of the importance of riverine fisheries. Perhaps because instream flow requirement (IFR) methodologies were developed in countries with few such human populations, planners and scientists continue to leave out people as part of riverine ecosystems. The major exceptions are the DRIFT methodology developed by Jackie King and her colleagues at the University of Cape Town; METSI Consultants' recent study of the Lesotho Highlands Water Project (2000), which utilized the DRIFT methodology; IUCN's 2003 *Flow: The Essentials of Environmental Flows* (Dyson et al, 2003); and Postel and Richter's *Rivers for Life: Managing Water for People and Nature* (2003).

THE IMPORTANCE OF NATURAL FLOOD REGIMES FOR RIVERINE COMMUNITIES AND FOR DEVELOPMENT PURPOSES

Importance for riverine communities

Archaeologists and social scientists have documented the importance of natural flood regimes for the rise of civilizations and for millions of contemporary people in the tropics and subtropics and in sub-temperate habitats. How floodplains nurtured the rise of early civilizations is best documented for arid and semi-arid areas in the Middle East, including the floodplains of the Nile, the Euphrates and Tigris system above and below their junction, and the Indus. South of the Sahara, the annual flooding of the inland delta of the Niger sustained kingdoms and civilizations during the European Dark Ages and continues to sustain the ancient city of Djenne.

But floodplains have also played an important role in the rise of ancient civilizations and the lifestyles of millions of contemporary people in the monsoon climates of East, Southeast and South Asia. Examples in China include the floodplains of the Yangtze and Huang Ho (Yellow) Rivers. In

Cambodia, the annual flooding and recession of the Tonle Sap or Great Lake from, and back to, the Mekong River supported the dense population associated with Angkor Wat and surrounding centres, while millions in riverine communities along the middle and lower reaches of the Mekong continue to depend on flood recession agriculture and fishing (McElwee and Horowitz, 1999).

Although I have no figures for the number of people dependent on natural flood regimes in the combined delta of the Ganges, Brahmaputra and Meghna systems prior to the commencement of major levee construction in the second half of the 20th century and the movement of an expanding population into more flood-prone areas, well over ten million can be assumed. During the type of normal flood (*borsha*) on which Bangladesh villagers depend, 25,000 to 45,000km^2 would be flooded. 'Such normal annual flooding is a desirable event since it commences at the right time for cultivation, lasts for an appropriate duration for paddy rice and other major crops, and is of a limited severity which the local conditions of settlement and housing, agriculture, and physical infrastructure can normally withstand' (Curry, 1993a, p3). With a national population density exceeding 800 per square kilometre in the late 1980s, 20–36 million people might depend directly on that area. During extreme floods (*bonna*), such as the 100-year flood in 1988, 66,360km^2 was inundated, or approximately 46 per cent of the country, with 45 million people displaced. Deaths, however, were kept to about 2000, which illustrates how well residents have adapted to floods, as opposed to cyclones, which were responsible for the deaths of over 200,000 people in 1970 and 70,000 in 1985 (ibid, p9).

Because of the magnitude of flooding and associated erosion, the Bangladesh delta area is a riskier environment for flood-dependent villagers than elsewhere, with river channels shifting as much as 100km and natural levees and islands being constantly formed and reformed. The flood-enhanced productivity of the area, however, is the compensating factor for local residents who are accustomed to mobilizing kin groups to build homesteads on mounds which may be more than 2m high and to seek safety at mosques and other community and government buildings that have been built on still higher natural levees that community members have further heightened (ibid, p16). All such mounds have been further 'buttressed by homestead trees and bamboo groves, which have allowed the dissipation of energy from cyclonic storms ... and have also provided fuel for cooking' (Curry, 1993b, p5).

Food production is dominated by varieties of rice. Some are planted on higher slopes and floating rice is planted in deeper depressions in anticipation of the arrival of the annual flood. Some varieties are able to grow more than 15cm a day as water levels rise, with the crop harvested when the flood recedes (Curry, 1993a, p17). Next in dietary importance is fish, which constituted 80 per cent of animal protein consumption in the second half of the 1990s. Even though by then 50 per cent of Bangladesh's wetlands had been lost as a result of large-scale construction of man-made levees and other infrastructure, 'nearly one million people are directly employed in fishing and another ten million in fish marketing and processing. At least 80 per cent of all rural households engage in seasonal fishing...' (Capistrano and Stackhouse, 1997, p31).

In Latin America, recent archaeological research on Marajó Island, at the mouth of the Amazon, and throughout the Amazon Basin, has demonstrated the importance of floodplains for a series of cultures over more than 10,000 years (Roosevelt, 1999). Estimates of floodplain extent vary from 40,000 to 200,000km^2 (ibid, p284). Palaeo-Indians combined floodplain fishing, gathering of tree fruits and seeds, and hunting with inland foraging. More recent Holocene foragers (the terminology is Roosevelt's) settled down along the Amazon over 7000 years ago; excavation of their large shell middens showing their primary dependence on fish and shellfish. The dry land cultivation of cassava was added to fishing, gathering and hunting 'at least 4,000 years ago and cropping of a number of crops probably was widespread by 2,000 years ago' (ibid, p379) including 'primitive popcorn maize, tropical beans, and some native seed-bearing herbs that we know little about' (ibid, pp379–380). Although identification of materials is difficult, some of those crops presumably were cultivated on seasonally flooded alluvium.

Such diversified production systems supported the rise of complex Amazon floodplain societies during the first millennium of the Christian era. Most impressive were the mound-building societies of Marajó Island during the period A.D. 400–1100. They had permanent populations as large as 200,000 people, estimated from published sites alone, with individual mounds supporting up to 5000 people and multi-mound sites '5,000 and upward' (Roosevelt, 1991, pp38–39). The exploited habitat of the eastern central portion of the 50,000km^2 island was 'a seasonal floodplain with heavy nutrient-rich soils and savanna and galley forest vegetation' that supported a household economy 'based on annual cropping of seed crops, plant collection, and intensive seasonal fishing' (ibid, p404). Tree fruits and seeds were especially important, with trees such as açai, a riverine palm (*Euterpe oleracea*), and a number of leguminous species being protected and perhaps cultivated. Maize was also present but apparently only as 'an accessory crop' (ibid, p377).

The fact that such densely populated floodplain societies had vanished by European colonial times contributed to the still current misconception that the Amazon basin was a 'backwater' unable to support complex societies and cultures. As for current floodplain-dependent communities, they have been best described from the Upper Amazon Basin in Peru where mixed populations of indigenous people and post-colonial immigrants continue to rely on the flood recession cultivation of rice, vegetables and other crops, and on fishing and gathering (Chibnik, 1994; Padoch et al, 1999). While crops are planted on all floodplain features, locales preferred by villagers are, in order of importance, natural levees from top to bottom; the back slopes of levees where jute, in particular, is planted; and silt bars and mud flats for rice cultivation (Pinedo-Vasquez, 1999).

In the Central Amazon floodplain, intensive vegetable and horticultural production provides the highest returns on land and labour, data suggesting that 'a farmer can achieve a high income on a relatively small area using such intensive methods' (Ohly and Junk, 1999, p289). While bananas, mangos and other fruit trees are also grown on upper slopes, they are susceptible to flood damage, unlike the various flood water forest species whose fruits and seeds were so important to pre-colonial populations. The major source of protein for Brazil's low-income majority is fish. The annual potential of the Amazon fishery is estimated at one million tonnes (Bayley and Petrere, 1989), of which only 20–25 per cent is currently exploited (Ohly and Junk, 1999, p293). Livestock management involving cattle, swine and water buffalo has also become important along the length of the river. As in Africa, a species of *Echinochloa* provides an important source of floodplain grazing and is used for the stall-feeding of dairy cows (ibid, p289).

Throughout the world today, floodplain utilization is part of a wider production system that includes rain-fed agriculture on upland soils, localized and transhumant pastoralism, and wage labour. As for the floodplain component, floodwaters are used in a number of economically valuable and ecologically sustainable ways. Some societies use them to support complex and diversified economic systems based on crops, livestock, fishing and other natural resources; others concentrate on a single flood-dependent resource. Most important is flood recession agriculture, in which farmers plant a succession of crops in river basins, tributary deltas and connected basins and pans as floodwaters recede. Distribution of flood recession agriculture is global and is of continued importance in major river basins such as the Amazon in Latin America; the Senegal, Niger, Lake Chad and Zambezi basins in Africa; and the Ganges–Brahmaputra–Meghna, Mekong and Yangtze River Basins in Asia. In both West and East Africa, ingenious systems have been developed in deltas whereby tidal flows are used to push fresh water into arable areas or floodwaters are used to flush saline deposits from tidal flats. Less commonly, farmers in the Niger Basin have adapted species of African rice (*Oryza glaberrima*) to grow with the rising flood. Floating varieties of rice are also sown in Bangladesh, Myanmar and Vietnam.

It is hard to overemphasize the importance of floodplains that border rivers flowing through arid and semi-arid habitats (Adams, 1996, p5). In such habitats, floodplains also provide critical grazing at the end of the dry season for herds of cattle and small stock that otherwise could not exist. In the late 1970s Bingham estimated that there were approximately half a million cattle in Zambia's Kafue Basin, of which at least half probably depended on the floodplains of the Kafue Flats for dry season grazing. He considered the Kafue Flats to be Zambia's 'most valuable agricultural entity' (Bingham, 1982). These conclusions are based only on use of the floodplains by people. When their total biological productivity is taken into consideration, the contrast is even more glaring. According to Williams and Howard 'the biological productivity of an area such as the Kafue Flats may in the long run prove to be vastly more important to mankind than its short term value as a modified water storage for the generation of electrical power' (1977, p6). In the Niger Basin, Fulani and other pastoralists also are dependent on such grazing, driving their stock through the water to preferred areas on river banks and islands. As the dry season progresses, several million Nilotic cattle and small stock were equally dependent on grazing grasslands behind receding White Nile floods in the Sudd region of the Central Sudan before the recent civil war.

Riverine fisheries throughout the tropics also depend on annual flooding for maintaining productivity. Fish migrations are influenced by flood regimes, while wetlands are important for spawning and for protecting and feeding fry which would be easy prey in the primary channel. It is the annual flooding of the Mekong that increases the productivity of Cambodia's freshwater fishery by up to 450,000 tonnes per annum (Ahmed et al, 1998, p3). As a source of protein for the poor, it is hard to overestimate the importance of such fisheries. Other benefits from the flood include aquifer recharge with water for wells and for riverine forest and associated vegetation with their multifunctional uses for riverine communities.

One or more ethnic communities may combine several of the above activities to sustain larger populations. In Kenya's lower Tana River Basin, 115,000 people are dependent on flood recession agriculture while a significant number of 176,000 transhumant pastoralists are dependent on floodplain grazing (Acreman et al, 2000, p14). In the inland delta of the Niger, as in the Tana River Basin, ethnic specialization has taken place with some communities more dependent on flood recession and flood rise agriculture while others fish or are transhumant pastoralists. In the 1960s, flood-dependent people included over 300,000 pastoralists, 80,000 fishers and 70,000 farmers (Gallais, 1967) with interdependent economies.

The farmers of the Niger, who are believed to have been the domesticators of African rice over 3000 years ago (Portères, 1976), cultivated 100,000ha of seasonally flooded land in the 1960s. On the lower floodplains, floating varieties of rice would be planted prior to the flood; lengthening their stem as the floodwaters rose, they would be harvested from dugout canoes. Later, non-floating varieties would be planted on the more elevated floodplains and would be harvested as the flood water receded. A second crop would be planted behind the receding flood with more drought-resistant varieties of millet and sorghum planted first on the higher slopes. The farmers also planted rain-fed crops, with their upland fields benefiting from manure from the thousands of cattle and small stock returning to the floodplains during the dry season and hence after the harvest. Once on the floodplains, their manure also contributes to a more productive fishery.

With thousands of cattle grazing crop residues in rain-fed fields and on floodplains, large amounts of manure are deposited. W. A. Payne estimated that 2–3 tonnes per hectare was being deposited by the cattle of the Western Dinka in the fields and floodplains fringing the White Nile when the two of us travelled through the area just before the arrival of the rains in the late 1970s.

While floodplains cover a much smaller area than rainy season pastures, not only are they available when the latter can no longer support the herds, but they can be more heavily stocked by herds grazing on such genera of grasses as *Echinochloa, Eragrostis, Panicum* and *Vossia*. According to Buchan (1988, p16), stocking densities on the floodplains of the Phongolo in Southern Africa were 0.78 animal units per hectare, as opposed to only 0.24 in adjacent dry land areas. Diarra reports similar stocking rates on *Eragrostis* grasslands in the inland delta of the Niger (1988).

Importance for development

Introduction

I believe that a major reason why flood-dependent economies have been ignored or belittled by planners is a misconception about their productivity. Early comparisons dealt mainly with productivity per unit of land. Irrigation based on modern inputs was considered far superior to flood recession and flood rise cultivation. But consideration should be given to productivity per unit of water, capital and labour. Recent research by Barbier and colleagues in Nigeria and by the Institute for Development Anthropology in Senegal shows irrigation to have returns inferior to those of floodplain and wetland utilization when scarcity values are assigned to water and to local capital and labour resources. Furthermore, the increased productivity per unit of land of modern irrigation does not take into consideration the time factor. Double cropping of frequently inundated floodplains along the Middle Zambezi and within the deltas of its tributaries have probably been practised for hundreds of years without degradation, while similar floodplains along the Senegal, Niger and Nile rivers have supported flood recession agriculture for millennia.

As in the past, large-scale irrigation continues to be threatened by salinity, water logging and a variety of other inefficiencies. Take, for example, irrigation initiated along the left bank of the Senegal River's Lower Valley since the completion of the Diama and Manantali Dams in 1986 and 1988. Of 71,751ha 'laid out' for irrigation by 1995, only 29,792ha was actually irrigated that year. Although only placed under cultivation within the past ten years, part of the remaining 42,000ha was no longer cultivated because of water logging and salinity, whereas other plots were fallow because productivity was insufficient to cover loan repayments (Adams, 1999).

The Hadejia-Nguru case

Of the two recent West African studies that show the greater efficiency of customary floodplain production systems in terms of water use as well as of local capital and labour resources, one deals with the flood-dependent Hadejia-Nguru wetlands in Eastern Nigeria and the other with the left bank of the Middle Valley of the Senegal River. As with other floodplains in semi-arid and arid areas, the Hadejia-Nguru wetlands have enabled a much larger population to exist than would otherwise be the case. Spreading out from the junction of the Hadejia and Jama'are Rivers, maximum flooding covered 250,000–300,000ha in the 1960s and 1970s and 70,000–100,000ha in the 1980s and 1990s following the construction of two upstream dams on the Hadejia. As a result of aquifer recharge, the floodplain production area was much greater. In 1989/90, for example, it was estimated at 730,000ha, including 100,000ha fished, 230,000ha cultivated, and 400,000ha providing fuel wood. That season the area inundated was 112,817ha, so the productive area was 'around 6.5 times greater than the actual area flooded' (Barbier and Thompson, 1996, p12).

The dependent, multi-ethnic population, including those living in three towns, was estimated to be more than one million people. As in the inland delta of the Niger, ethnic specialization has occurred. Areas were farmed, fished and grazed by different people at different seasons. As part of a multi-donor research and development effort, Barbier and colleagues compared floodplain water use by local people with an upstream irrigation project that received water from the Tiga Dam at the expense of downstream people and wetlands (Barbier et al, 1997, pp48–51). Although the authors admit that their calculations did not include the value of urban water from the Tiga Dam to the city of Kano, which restricts their analysis to the irrigation portion of the Tiga Dam project as opposed to the dam itself, neither did they include the full range of floodplain benefits to local people – grazing, for example, was not included nor was wildlife.

According to the estimates of Barbier and his colleagues, the net present values of weighted benefits from floodplain agriculture, fisheries and fuel wood were 'US$34 to US$51 per ha ... of annual floodwater input determined from river gauging records' (ibid, p6). That contrasted with values of US$21–31 per hectare for Tiga Dam irrigation. Even more glaring was the contrast between the two users when values per $10^3 m^3$ of water were compared. These values were US$9.6–14.5 for floodplain use versus US$0.03–0.04 for the Tiga irrigation scheme. Their research also showed that it would be 'uneconomic' to increase the current area under irrigation because of increased downstream costs. Given 'sunk' costs in infrastructure, the most economic strategy would be to combine existing irrigation with environmental flows to reduce existing costs to the Hadejia-Nguru floodplains.

The Senegal River case

Over half a million people in Senegal and Mauritania inhabit the middle and lower regions of the Senegal River Basin. When rainfall is good, the annual flood can cover a floodplain of about 5000km² with coverage reduced as the flood recedes to 500km². The majority of the population practise a diversified production system that includes the rain-fed cultivation of uplands, small-scale pump irrigation, wage labour and various flood-dependent activities that were essential for community well-being. In addition to supporting flood recession agriculture, dry season grazing and a more productive fishery, annual flood pulses also recharged an aquifer that supplied village wells and maintained acacia-dominated woodlands that provided building materials, fuel and various non-timber forest products.

In the early 1970s the governments of Mali, Mauritania and Senegal established the Senegal River Authority (Organization Pour La Mise En Valeur Du Fleuve Senegal or OMVS) to develop the river basin. As planning proceeded, three major goals (requiring two dams to be built) emerged: hydropower generation, irrigation of up to 375,000ha, and navigation that would give land-locked Mali access to the ocean. Completed in 1986 and situated 23km from the ocean, the Diama Dam was intended to stop saltwater intrusion as well as to provide storage for lower basin irrigation. The Manantali Dam, situated nearly 1200km upriver in Mali and completed in 1988, was designed to provide hydropower as well as to even out downstream flows for the benefit of irrigation and navigation.

During the second half of the 1970s, the consultancy firm Gannett Fleming completed a number of reports assessing environmental impacts in which the adverse effects of the three goals on the flood-dependent economies of affected communities were noted. The release of a managed flood was suggested as a mitigating option that warranted attention. That option was further evaluated by Alexander Gibb and Partners in the mid-1980s. Restricting their analysis to the value of flood recession cultivation of sorghum that would produce only FCFA[3] 34,000 per hectare versus 71,820 for irrigation, Gibb concluded that environmental flows were not an economic option over the longer term. Recognizing, however, their importance for local communities, flood releases were recommended over a ten-year period following dam construction during which farmers should be encouraged to shift to full-time irrigation; thereafter environmental flows should be stopped.

Convinced that a stronger case could be made for environmental flows, the Institute for Development Anthropology (IDA) persuaded USAID to fund an ambitious six-year research programme that started in 1987. At a November 1990 workshop in Dakar, data were presented from studies of three left bank villages that showed that Gibb had underestimated flood-related benefits to local producers. Flood-dependent fishing, according to the IDA study, added another FCFA 35,000 per hectare while the value of grazing added 17,500 more. Even without the benefits of aquifer recharge to village wells and forest products the total exceeded that for irrigation by nearly FCFA 15,000 (Horowitz and Salem-Murdock, 1990; Salem-Murdock, 1996).

Furthermore, the IDA studies showed that labour and capital, and not land, were the scarce factors of production within local communities. While irrigated fields might have higher yields per unit of land, not only did they have higher capital and labour requirements, but capital returns on investment of labour favoured work for wages in Dakar and other urban centres. These results did not mean, however, that small-scale irrigation should be dropped. On the contrary; villagers valued irrigation as an important part-time component in their diversified household economy because it tended to produce more reliable yields in a semi-arid, problem-prone environment than rain-fed and flood recession agriculture.

The IDA team also addressed the argument that a managed flood would be at the expense of the generation of electricity. If so, that could be an important constraint, because the three governments intended to rely on revenue from power sales to pay off OMVS project debts. Research by hydrologist Hollis showed that during 62 years of an 81-year period

(1904–1984), a Manantali-type reservoir would have held enough water to provide both the intended output of electricity and controlled flood releases sufficient for the flood recession cultivation of 50,000ha. During the remaining 19 years, the needs of flood recession cultivators during a ten-day August period would require releases over 100–200m^3 per second in only three of those years. In effect, flood recession agriculture and hydropower generation were not incompatible. Moreover, should major trade-offs be necessary, environmental flows could always be withheld during any particular year. Local communities, after all, were accustomed to drought years when natural flooding had been greatly reduced at the expense of flood recession cultivation, grazing and fishing. Such a trade-off would be more than compensated for by more reliable managed flood releases in most other years for which farmers could plan ahead. As for extreme events requiring much larger releases, Hollis pointed out that a well-maintained hydromet system should be able to provide forecasts to downstream users 'at least 14 days in advance' (Hollis, 1996, p184).

THE IMPACT OF DAMS ON NATURAL FLOOD REGIMES AND ASSOCIATED ECONOMIES

Introduction

Downstream communities are adversely affected by large dams in several ways. The most frequent adverse effect is where dams are intended to regularize river flows for hydropower, irrigation, navigation and other purposes by reducing flood pulses and increasing low season flows. Impacts are most serious where major water diversions are also involved. Transfer to a major irrigation project is one example of such a diversion, which is the intended purpose of India's Sardar Sarovar Project. Inter-basin transfers that adversely affect downstream communities in two-river systems are another. In all cases, operational inefficiencies at the dam site can worsen impacts, as can favouring inappropriate political considerations over economic considerations.

Regularizing natural flood regimes

As in the Hadejia-Nguru and Senegal River cases, regularizing natural flood regimes reduces land available for flood recession agriculture and grazing. In addition to the effect of all large dams on fish migration, it also adversely affects fisheries by reducing the extent of floodplain inundation. Nigeria's Kainji Dam on the Middle Niger, Bakolori on a Middle Niger tributary and Ghana's dam at Akosombo are three other West African cases that illustrate how serious such impacts can be.

Built in the 1960s largely for power generation, Kainji has evened out the Niger's natural flood regime. Drawing his information from three separate villages, the furthest of which was 200km downstream, Adeniyi (1973) reported incomes from fishing decreasing from 47 to 73 per cent as a result of lower productivity, while the Kainji Lake Research Institute showed declines in catch statistics of more than 50 per cent. Adeniyi also reported that the three villages had 44–70 per cent declines in dry season rice harvests from seasonally flooded areas (*fadamas*), while Roder refers to a 30 per cent reduction of *fadama* causing an 18 per cent reduction in swamp rice harvests (1994, p10).

Awachi reports even more extreme impacts that stretched as far downstream as the apex of the Niger. Over a three-year period following dam closure 'Fishermen and farmers watched helplessly as their yields fell. By 1970, the lower Anambra Basin which hitherto had been responsible for 70% of freshwater fish and yam production in Eastern Nigeria had lost both 60% of its fish output and yam production running into 100 thousand tons' (Awachi, 1979, p21). Although Adeniyi's and Awachi's survey results presumably were influenced by the 1968–1974 Sahelian drought, Adams' Bakolori research (1985, 1993) was undertaken after the drought had ended. Following dam completion, flood recession agriculture in one of his study villages declined from 100 per cent participation to 27 per cent and from 93 per cent to 59 per cent in another. 'Wet-season cultivation of rice declined... The economically cultivated dry season vegetable cultivation was reduced, and farmers turned to dry season labour migration, a traditional response to periods of drought and hardship' (Adams, 1985).

In the Ghanaian case, Hilton and Kowu-Tsri report that Akosombo's construction 'brought severe hardship to the people of a narrow and rather crowded zone below the dam' (1973). Reductions in flood recession agriculture led to increased out-migration, as occurred in Nigeria's Bakolori case. Adverse impacts, however, extended well beyond the river's lower reaches. In the neighbouring countries of Togo and Benin, annual coastline erosion was estimated at 10–15m (Bourke, 1988, p117).[4] In Ghana itself, *New Africa* (1985) reported that 10,000 people were displaced when the coastal town of Keta was destroyed with another 10,000 at threat in the town of Aneho. Such coastal erosion is a global problem associated with dams, including those on the Colorado and Mississippi in the US, the Nile in Egypt, the Zambezi in Mozambique and the Indus in Pakistan.

The WCD found comparable impacts throughout Latin America and Asia (2000, p102). In Brazil, the Tucurui Dam has had negative impacts on fisheries and floodplain agriculture of the lower Tocantins, while the Sobradinho Dam adversely affected the flood recession agriculture of 11,000 downstream families (ibid, p112). In Asia, Pakistan's Mangla and Tarbela Dams on the Indus have adversely affected downstream habitats, the delta especially, and associated communities. The same applies to the Yellow River, which increasingly no longer reaches the South China Sea. In North America the flood recession agriculture and fisheries of the Cocopa and other Native Americans along the Lower Colorado River were adversely affected by the Hoover Dam.

Diversions and inter-basin transfers

Far too little research has been completed on the impact of diversions and inter-basin transfers on affected people and riverine ecosystems (Snaddon, et al, 1999). This is true even for transfers from the Colorado River and from Central California to the Los Angeles basin. The lack of research is especially glaring in densely populated developing countries in regard to both channelized transfers and those routed through rivers. One of the biggest transfers under consideration is China's intention to route water from the Yangtze to the North China plain by one of three possible routes. Use of the central route could require the resettlement of 100,000 people. It could also be expected to require the destruction of fields of a still larger number who would not have to physically relocate.

India's Farraka Barrage, diverting water from the Ganges to Calcutta, has adversely affected the production systems of countless communities further downstream in Bangladesh. Should India proceed with current plans to divert its northern rivers to Southern India, officials in Bangladesh fear that more than 100 million citizens will be adversely affected. As reported by John Vidal in *The Guardian* on 24 July 2003, Bangladesh's Water Resources Minister stated that India's proposal 'could affect the whole of Bangladesh and be disastrous'. Referring to the Farraka Barrage, he also stated that part 'of Bangladesh is already drying out after the Ganges was dammed by India in 1976'.

In Africa, diversions to Gauteng, South Africa, from the Katse and Mohale Dams will adversely affect approximately 150,000 people in Lesotho below the two dams. That conclusion (METSI, 2000) was based on the type of study of environmental flows that should have been completed during the original feasibility studies, but was done only after the Katse reservoir had been filled and construction on the Mohale Dam begun. Then it was too late to follow the preferred METSI scenarios since their implementation would significantly reduce the project's financial returns.

Where the lack of research is especially unfortunate is where transferred flows augment the flow of existing rivers. Illustrating the costs of ignorance are two recent cases in South Africa and Laos. Water diverted from Lesotho's Katse Dam was piped into South Africa where it was dumped into the Ash River en route to Gauteng Province. Little attention was paid to significantly increased flows until serious erosion was reported that also reduced the quality of what was supposed to be high quality water for urban use. Currently feasibility studies are underway as to the possibility of bypassing the Ash River with a pipeline. Obviously it would have been far better if such studies had been completed in time to influence the original project design.

The Theun Hinboun project in Laos, unlike the South African case, affected a large human population whose livelihood was dependent on a free-flowing river. In addition to serious environmental impacts, Theun Hinboun adversely affected fisheries and flood recession agriculture as well as village water supplies and communications. It will be analysed in detail because of its relevance to projects elsewhere where people depend on natural flood regimes.

The purpose of the Theun Hinboun project was to export hydropower for peaking purposes to Thailand. A joint venture between Laos' electricity parastatal and private sector companies in Thailand and Scandinavia, its funding involved a major loan from the Asian Development Bank (ADB). As designed, water backed up in a reservoir behind the Theun Hinboun Dam on the Nam Theun River would be diverted down an escarpment to a power station from which it would exit into a tributary (the Nam Hia) of the Nam Hinboun via a regulating reservoir. Construction began in 1994 and was finished in 1997. Perhaps influenced by inappropriate designation as a run-of-the-river project that would involve no involuntary resettlement, feasibility studies, as well as an environmental impact assessment by a Norwegian firm, seriously underestimated the environmental and socio-economic impacts of diverting flows from the upland Nam Theun to the lowland Nam Hinboun system. A major error was to restrict the area of project impact. Not only was inadequate attention paid to downstream impacts on the Nam Theun below the dam, but impacts of trans-basin flows were also ignored.

Almost immediately communities along the Nam Hia and the Nam Hinboun from its junction with the Nam Hia to its outflow into the Mekong complained about the assault on their livelihoods. The Asian Development Bank sent out a mission in late 1998. This found increased flows throughout the year had eliminated a large but unknown number of flood recession riverbank gardens. They also noted that severe erosion had cut back river banks as much as 3m: 'this has resulted in high sedimentation of the Nam Hia and the Nam Hinboun, with resulting secondary impacts on fish and fish habitat, fish capture, water use, river aesthetics, and in isolated instances, boat passage' (ADB, 1998, p5).

Although the ADB report recommended a timely and comprehensive mitigation programme, previous surveys already had shown that, as with resettlement programmes, mitigation must be combined with development to avoid impoverishment of an unacceptable number of people. During a brief visit in March 1998, Shoemaker was informed that villagers along both the Nam Theun and Nam Hinboun were experiencing losses. Throughout that year Warren had been contracted to identify impacts on the biology and socio-economics of the existing fishery. In a report of June 1999 and subsequent reports he noted probable reduction in fish populations caused by migratory disruption and habitat alteration including a reduction of breeding sites in rapids, a silting up of deep-hole fishing grounds, and unstable habitats and scouring caused by operating the dam as a peaking installation. In noting reduced catches, fishers reported loss of gill nets as a result of increased and irregular flows, and the unsuitability of their gear under the new conditions.

Belatedly responding to ADB and increasing NGO criticism, the project authority presented its Mitigation and Compensation Program in September 2000. It addressed a number of issues along the reservoir, the Nam Theun and the Nam Hinboun, but continues to be inadequate (Shoemaker, 2000; Sparkes, 2000), with Sparkes noting that the 'emphasis should be on rural development rather than compensation issues from 5–6 years ago' (Sparkes, ibid, p16).

More specifically he recommends improving food production through increased use of electrified irrigation pumps. Proper use and maintenance would require improved training and perhaps oversight and assistance from the project authority. Local government capacity should also be strengthened to assist with longer term development initiatives.

The Theun Hinboun experience provides major lessons for the larger upriver Nam Theun 2 project which will involve an ever-greater river basin transfer. A joint venture like the Theun Hinboun project that also involves the Government of Laos, NT2 will have a plant capacity of 1070MW for export of 'peaking' power to Thailand as opposed to Theun Hinborn's 210MW capacity. Doubling its annual flow, 6975 million cubic metres will be diverted annually down an escarpment and through the turbines into the Xe Bang Fai River via a regulating reservoir and the Nam Prit tributary. Unlike the planning for Theun Hinboun, the project impact area has been expanded to include the length of the Xe Bang Fai from the confluence with the Nam Prit to the Mekong. In the uppermost of three project zones, the capacity of the regulating reservoir will be increased so as to release a constant flow down the Nam Prit. To keep downstream flooding within historical limits, the flows will be stopped and the turbines shut down when necessary. Although funds will be available for compensation and mitigation purposes, increased flows will also be used for irrigation development within the upper zone. En route to the Nam Prit, water will be released into an existing community irrigation scheme to allow its extension as well as double cropping. Flows from the regulating reservoir can also be diverted down another tributary to bring irrigation and improved fishing to 20 other villages.

Although the project authority believed at the time that increased flows would actually increase the productivity of the Xe Bang Fai fishery, it agreed to fund in 2001 a comprehensive five-year pre-project study of the existing fishery by Warren and Laotian colleagues. The study will continue after operations commence so that whatever impacts occur can be dealt with on a sounder basis. The biggest challenge, however, will be in the lower zone where up to 50,000 people are said to utilize the floodplains and where currently the biggest constraint to development is reduced water levels in the Xe Bang Fai, which interferes with pumping water for irrigation. Since the project will eliminate that constraint, the logical solution to avoid possible adverse impacts on the fishery and flood water irrigation would be to coordinate the implementation of the NT2 project to combine fishery development activities, including aquaculture, with existing plans to extend irrigation.

Operational inefficiencies

Failure to operate dams to optimize a wider range of development benefits can be especially destructive to downstream communities, some of which may have moved onto the floodplain following construction under the false assumption that all flood risks had been eliminated. In both 1999 and 2000, poorly managed flood releases from Vietnam's Yali Dam killed and injured downstream villagers and destroyed livestock and crops in both Vietnam and Cambodia.[5] The Asian Development Bank, as a donor to Vietnam's electricity parastatal, asked the private sector firm Worley International to evaluate the situation. Citing 'management recklessness,' Worley's recommendations were intended to ensure that the Yali Dam was 'operated safely and responsibly, meeting international standards'.

Recent African examples of flood mismanagement involve Nigeria's Tiga, Challawa Gorge, Kainji, and Shiriro Dams; Kariba and Cahora Bassa on the Zambezi; and Manantali on the Senegal River. To maximize water for irrigation and urban use (Tiga and Challawa Gorge) or hydropower (the other cases), operators of the first six dams were unwilling to draw down reservoirs as a flood management mechanism before the annual rainy season. As a result large volumes of water have had to be released at the last moment when recent major floods threatened dam safety. Downstream impacts in each case were devastating.

Downstream of Tiga and Challawa Gorge, 350 Nigerian communities and their arable lands were inundated during 2001 flooding, with initial reports of over 100 deaths and up to US$100 million of damage. According to Nigeria's African Network for Environmental and Economic Justice, the consequences have been disastrous – 'the worst in the history of dams in Nigeria' (IRN, 2001a). Such damage was avoidable according to the governor of one of the three states involved who noted that reservoir levels were already quite high when the floodwaters arrived (ibid).

In the Kainji case, the most damaging Nigerian floods were in 1999, whereas those caused by mismanagement of the Shiriro Dam were in 2003. Downstream flood damage exacerbated by the Kariba and Cahora Bassa Dams occurred in February 2001 and February 2002. Without proper warning from dam operators the 2001 floods had different impacts in Zambia and Mozambique. In Zambia untimely releases from Kariba destroyed the crops of thousands of farmers a month before they were to be harvested (Bond and Ndubani, 2001). In Mozambique, far more people were involved, some of whom had moved onto the floodplain and islands following Cahora Bassa's construction. Initial reports from Mozambican officials and the Mozambique News Agency reported that 81,000 people had been evacuated and that over 400,000 had been affected, with loss of crops estimated at 27,000ha. The deaths of over 100 people were reported. Even cities were affected by floodwaters. Eight months later and just prior to the commencement of the 2001/02 rainy season, the University of Cape Town's Bryan Davies (2001) repeated a warning that he had first given in 1998 'that unless coordinated management of the Zambezi reservoirs occurred, then loss of life and infrastructure would be a fact of life in the Middle and Lower Zambezi reaches'. In that November 2001 warning, Davies also noted that 250,000 people flooded out by the Zambezi flooding in March were still homeless.

The Manantali Dam situation in the Senegal River Basin is different. There operators at the dam and the project authorities (OMVS) have been unwilling to honour agreements to release environmental flows even during the

1987–2002 period before turbines for generating hydropower were operational. Although their argument was that the reservoir must remain full for testing the dam infrastructure during those years, the timing of what releases were made showed disregard for the interests of over half a million people downstream. In 1989 and 1991 the agreed environmental flows released in September were followed by a second unannounced flood the following month that destroyed crops planted after the earlier flood had begun to recede. Then in 1992 and 1993, the duration of the September releases was insufficient for allowing, on the left bank, the recommended environmental flows for the flood recession cultivation of 50,000ha.

Political impacts

During their planning and construction, large dams often are a country's largest single project, often having the backing of a powerful coalition that may reach up to the office of the head of state. Especially in countries with a small number of major rivers, such projects may also be in national heartlands. Given the funds for construction, which may reach into billions of dollars, and anticipated benefits, powerful individuals and agencies compete for project involvement. Victims of such competition are most likely to be riverine communities dependent on natural flood regimes. Dam-supplied upstream irrigation projects in semi-arid areas, as in India and in Nigeria with the Bakolori, Challawa Gorge and Tiga Dams, have been especially detrimental to downstream communities.

As water becomes scarcer, it is likely that legitimate and illegitimate political considerations, for which the term 'hydropolitics' has been coined, will become more important. Past examples include Egypt's Aswan High Dam (Waterbury, 1979) and the binational Itaipu (Brazil–Paraguay) and Yacyretá (Argentina–Paraguay) dams on the Parana River (Ribeiro, 1994). Ribeiro's analysis of the decision-making that led to the construction of Yacyretá is especially relevant. Noting that Argentine experts knew of better alternatives such as the use of natural gas, smaller dams and better sites for high dams, Ribeiro concluded that political considerations played the dominant decision-making role. Rather than as a development project, he saw Yacyretá as 'a form of production linked to economic expansion' into an 'outpost' area (ibid, p163), the siting of which was influenced in competition with Brazil over 'regional hegemony' (ibid, p45). Such a definition could also be applied to Hydro-Quebec's James Bay Project and more specifically to the currently suspended Grande Baleine Project. In the latter case, further dam construction would give the Province of Quebec 'increased control over indigenous lands of ambiguous legal status' (Scudder, 1997b, p660). One could also speculate that provincial officials favouring Quebec's independence may well have viewed additional hydropower dams as a means for providing the necessary economic underpinning for a new nation.

In these cases it can be argued that hydropolitics played a legitimate role within the context of each nation's political economy. Illegitimate and unacceptable cases are where dams and other river basin initiatives have been used by governing elites and their supporters to force local households and communities off their land. Examples in which I have been directly involved include the proposed Baardheere Dam on the Juba River (Somalia), the Manantali Dam on the Senegal River (Mauritania) and the Accelerated Mahaweli Project (Sri Lanka). The latter two cases also involved ethnic cleansing.

The Mahaweli case was described in Chapter 5. In the 1970s the Somali Government of Siad Barre committed itself to building the Baardheere Dam downstream from the Ethiopian border. Designed to irrigate 100,000ha, the dam was seen as a means for converting the Juba Valley into a national heartland. To open up the area to influential outsiders, the government legitimized the takeover of riverine community lands held under customary tenure by passing the 1975 *Agricultural Land Law* that gave the Ministry of Agriculture the authority to lease land to agencies and individuals. Because remote and poorly educated riverine villagers were slow to register their use rights, the 1975 law gave government officials and immigrant entrepreneurs the opportunity to acquire legal land rights. As a result, by the end of the 1980s 'large tracts of valley land have been registered in what appears to be a land rush... Land, for generations a nearly limitless commodity, is scarce. Expropriation of thousands of hectares of land by state farms ... and the recent "rush for land" by outside investors and speculators have put tremendous pressure on land access for villagers' (ARD, 1989, Vol. III, pA-29; see also Besteman and Roth, 1988). That 'rush for land' is also believed to be a contributing factor to the inter-clan and inter-ethnic warfare of the 1990s (Besteman and Cassanelli, 1996).

As in Somalia, governing elites in Mauritania used national legislation in 1983 as a means for driving tens of thousands of Senegal River villagers from their land. Again, the ability of a dam, in this case the upstream Manantali Dam, to deliver water for irrigation in a drought-prone, arid land, was responsible for a major land grab as well as an undeclared war of a state against its own citizens that involved ethnic cleansing (Amnesty International, 1990). The necessary legislation was Ordinance No. 83-127 of 5 June 1983 that 'provided a legal justification whereby the white elite ... might seize floodplain holdings from black recession cultivators whose customary titles to the land were no longer recognized' (Horowitz, 1991, p170). The governing elites were Arabic-speaking Bidan, or White Moors, who also dominated the military, the private sector and the Islamic religious hierarchy (Horowitz, 1989, p4), whereas the riverine villagers, also Muslims, were black Pulaar-speakers whose livelihood was based on the type of previously described flood-dependent economy.

The situation was exacerbated by increasing drought that, on the one hand, had undermined the Bidan's customary pastoral and oasis-based economy and, on the other hand, had made the Manantali-based irrigation potential of the Senegal River valley more attractive to the Bidan. Using their black Haratine dependents who were primarily Arabic-speaking former captives, 'The army, security forces, and the Haratine militia arrest, torture, or kill unarmed villagers without fear of any disciplinary action or legal proceedings… What is taking place in southern Mauritania is, in effect, an undeclared war, in which one community is using the resources and power of the state against another community' (Amnesty International, 1990). That undeclared war nearly led to war between Mauritania and Senegal as over 50,000 north bank villagers fled as refugees to the Senegalese south bank where most remain today. Some 70,000 Senegalese citizens were also expelled from Mauritania while Senegal expelled more than 100,000 Mauritanian citizens (Horowitz, 1991, p171).

Impacts on deltas

Introduction

Deltas are complex and highly productive ecosystems. They are built up by natural processes, including the deposition of silt held in place by salt marshes, mangrove forests and other emergent vegetation. Although influenced by other factors such as subsidence, the effects of which will be compounded by any rises in sea level as a result of global warming, the natural processes involved 'are severely hampered by modifications in the river basin, especially by the construction of dams, by the water abstraction for irrigated agriculture (Nile, Indus) and by other schemes of "overregulation" of river flows' (IUCN, 2000b, pp1–2).[6] Such adverse modifications are underway throughout the world and have long-term consequences for life support systems. Such consequences have yet to be built into the water resource and energy development options assessment process and, more specifically, into feasibility studies for large dams. The three examples of adverse impacts that follow deal with the deltas of the Nile in Egypt, the Zambezi in Mozambique and the Indus in Pakistan.

The Nile Delta

Mohammad Kassas, a science professor at the University of Cairo, was concerned about delta retreat in the early 1970s. Like other researchers he pointed out that an extended period of delta building had slacked off during the 19th and 20th centuries because of the construction of barrages and the original Aswan Dam. The completion of the High Dam in 1967 brought 'the delta building process to an end' (Kassas, 1972, p179). Although Mediterranean-induced erosion varied locally, Kassas was concerned 'with coastal retreat that is actively taking place now at the alarming rate of several meters per year' (ibid, p186) and with the likely collapse of the narrow bars separating the two major deltaic lakes from the sea – the transformation of these 'into marine bays will endanger the hydrology of the northern Delta drainage systems' (ibid, p187).

In an overview of the High Dam project 16 years later, White noted that latest estimates suggested that 'the actual losses of coastal land were severe in only a few sectors' (1988, p37). Five years after that, in an article in *Science* titled 'Nile Delta: Recent Geological Evolution and Human Impact,' Stanley and Warne 'envisioned' that declining conditions might be reversed by 'coastal protection structures on the scale of Netherlands' Great Delta Works..., strict regulation of the limited Nile water supply, increased groundwater exploitation along the delta margins, and construction of artificial wetlands and treatment facilities for recycling wastewater. At current rates of population growth, however, these measures will be inadequate' (Stanley and Warne, 1993, p634).

In 1999 Shenouda at ICOLD's annual meeting quoted Waterbury's statement that 'With or without the High Dam, the northern delta would be under attack' and implied that whatever problem of shore erosion existed was being overcome since the establishment of the Shore Protection Authority (1999, p316). In 2000, IUCN noted current delta retreat at the annual rate of 240 metres (op cit, p1). How does one evaluate these differing viewpoints that, on the one hand, refer to a controllable problem and, on the other hand, suggest that a project that is considered a major success is contributing, at an unknown rate, to the eventual degradation of Egypt's most valuable piece of agricultural real estate?

The Zambezi Delta

Because of two major mainstream dams, the Zambezi Delta – the largest and most valuable on Africa's East Coast – has slowly been drying out. While overflying it in 1996, Davies pointed out to me the increasing destruction of mangroves. Also obvious was the reduction of open-water areas and wetlands and the clogging of channels with aquatic vegetation. More recently Beilfuss and colleagues (2000) have shown how upland plant communities have been replacing wetlands, with savannah woodland species encroaching on open floodplains. Desiccation has also increased access for poachers with Tinley (1994) reporting a reduction of 95 per cent and more in large mammals such as cape buffalo, waterbuck, zebra and hippopotamus. Grassland fires have increased (Beilfuss et al, 2001), while the breeding area of wattled cranes, an indicator species for flood water birds, has been restricted (Bento, 2002). In sum, the delta is 'rapidly losing ground' (Beilfuss, 2003).

The delta and lower reaches of the Indus

The Indus Delta is the seventh largest in the world, covering an estimated 600,000ha. Its dynamics and nature, however, have been radically altered by human activities since the 1950s, which have changed it from a growing delta with five channels to a much smaller one dependent on a single channel (Khwaja, 1998, p1). As a result of 22 upstream dams and barrages that supply water to vast areas under irrigation in both India and Pakistan, and exacerbated by drought, annual flooding increasingly covers less than 25 per cent of the delta's historic floodplain, with water extraction and the construction of flood bunds restricting the active delta to 'only 10 per cent of its original area' (Asianics, 2000, p107).

Since the construction of the Kotri Barrage on the lower Indus and upstream barrages and dams, the annual average number of days during the 1962–1997 period with no downstream flows below Kotri has increased from zero to 85 (WCD, 2000, p88). One result, exacerbated by unsustainable use, has been the reduction in the area of mangrove cover from an estimated 300,000ha in the mid-1960s (Bakhsh et al, 1999) to 263,000ha in 1978 following the construction of the Mangla Dam and then to around 158,000ha in 1990 (Asianics, op cit). Habitat degradation has also reduced the number of mangrove species from eight to one (Khwaja, 1998).[7] Current losses are estimated at about 2 per cent per annum (Asianics, 2000, pxiii).

According to *Dawn's* internet edition for February 2003, the delta currently is facing 'an environmental disaster' which is 'having disastrous consequences for agriculture, forests, livestock, wild life, fisheries and the lives of people'.[8] Two months later, an article in the *International Herald Tribune* reported that 'at least 1.2 million acres of farmland have been covered by seawater' and that losses of land and water shortages have been devastating for 'millions of smaller-scale land owners, tenant farmers and river fishermen'.[9] No longer are cattle, sheep and goats herded in the delta; 'only herds of camels are still found there' (Asianics, 2000, p118).

Increasing salinity upriver in the Indus' agriculturally important meander belt has also become a serious problem as a result of reduced flooding and reduced silt deposition combined with strong marine wave action[10] and saltwater intrusion that reaches 25–30km inland. Before dam and barrage construction, the annual flood covered a lower Indus floodplain that could be 8km wide. Approximately half the better flooded area, estimated at 240,000ha, was well forested but currently is undergoing desertification. Desertification is also adversely affecting farmers that use the other 240,000ha. The same is true for herders whose estimated 900,000 cattle and buffalos, plus small ruminants, graze and browse the entire floodplain. For the people involved, estimated at a million, 'the vital source of subsistence ... have [sic] declined in quality and number from degraded forests and pastures and emaciated flocks of livestock' (Asianics, 2000, p109). As poverty has worsened, increasing numbers of villagers have left for Karachi and other cities.

ENVIRONMENTAL FLOWS

Introduction

Where river flows have been regularized for competing uses of water, environmental flows would attempt to restore previous flood pulses as well as periods of low flows. Both flood pulses and low flows are necessary to maintain not only ecosystem services but also community livelihood systems dependent on flood recession agriculture, floodplain grazing, aquifer recharge and fishing. Currently environmental flows are being implemented in only 25 countries, which is far short of their universal use as recommended in two reports by scientists associated with the World Conservation Union. The first (Bergkamp et al, 2000) was prepared as the lead paper for the World Commission on Dam's Thematic Review II.1 on Dams, Ecosystem Functions and Environmental Restoration. It was supported by a contributing paper from colleagues elsewhere on *Managed Flood Releases from Reservoirs – Issues and Guidance* (Acreman et al, 2000). The second IUCN paper (Dyson et al, 2003) was published under the title *Flow: the Essentials of Environmental Flows*.

Dyson, Bergkamp and Scanlon see environmental flows as 'part of a broader notion of taking an ecosystem approach to integrated water resources management' (ibid, p74). More specifically 'they are absolutely essential to maintaining healthy river systems' (ibid, p87) and 'today serve as the single most important tool for managing the ecosystem and associated impacts of dams. [They] should be a requirement for all future dams' (Bergkamp et al, 2000, p86). That said, the authors of *Flow* realize that their implementation 'will require a long and sustained effort' (Dyson et al, 2003, p87) involving a legal framework at the national level and political will and capacity to implement it. Capacity is important because there is no science that can be extrapolated to meet different river requirements, with estimates varying between 65 per cent and 95 per cent as to the volume of the natural flow regime (with natural flood pulses and low flows retained) needed to maintain ecosystems (ibid, p3).

The sections that follow deal first with the benefits of environmental flows for downstream ecosystems and users. Such benefits are limited, however, not only because some dam-induced impacts, such as those on deltas, are irreversible, but also because of a range of other limitations and difficulties that are considered in the sections that follow. The last section deals with the possibility of linking or synchronizing environmental flows with reservoir drawdown for the benefit of reservoir basin and downstream communities.

Downstream users and environmental flows

Where dams are built, the two most important interventions for the benefit of downstream communities are to involve them in irrigation, rural electrification, and whatever other development opportunities are available and to release environmental flows, which have the potential to improve downstream living standards by providing a better timed and more reliable annual flood and drawdown during most years. Although the concept of environmental flows has existed for a long time, only in the past 30 years have researchers and practitioners begun to advocate them as a mitigation and development option for human settlements in addition to riverine ecosystems – first in connection with individual projects and then as a strategy with global relevance.

From the time of its construction in 1902 to the completion of the High Dam at Aswan, the original Aswan Dam was designed to pass most of the silt-laden Nile flood downstream, accomplishing two major goals in the process. One was to reduce siltation in the reservoir, the gates being closed to capture the relatively silt-free waters toward the end of the annual flood. The other was to renew the downstream fertility of land where flood recession agriculture (called basin irrigation in Egypt) had been practised for thousands of years.

Dams in China and Sri Lanka had been operated in a similar fashion for an even longer period of time.

Starting in the 1970s, most project-specific experimentation with environmental flows for the benefit of local communities has been in Africa south of the Sahara. The management of the Pongolapoort Dam in KwaZulu/Natal, the IUCN Waza-Logone Project in Cameroon, the Tiga Dam and Bakolori Dams in Nigeria, the Manantali Dam in Mali and the Itezhitezhi Dam in Zambia, is instructive. The first two illustrate the potential of environmental flows; the other three the difficulties involved in realizing their potential.

With impoundment in 1970, the Pongolapoort Dam was built by the South African government to irrigate 40,000ha for 4000 white settlers who the authorities hoped would move to a region close to the border with Mozambique and Swaziland. When settlers failed to come, scientists who had been studying the downstream floodplain (Coke and Pott, 1970), and had anticipated the adverse impact of the dam on floodplain biodiversity, influenced the government's Department of Water Affairs and Forestry (DWAF) to experiment with environmental flows starting in the early 1980s. Although initially floodplain villagers were not involved, during the 1980s they were drawn increasingly into the planning process with a Water Committees Programme designed and approved by the regional and local authorities in 1987. Based on local wards, 14 water committees were formed with an overarching union. The result has been 'joint management of the dam by the DWAF and resident communities' for the benefit of biodiversity and local communities, whose population had increased to 70,000 people (Bruwer et al, 1996, p207).

As a result of this experiment, Bruwer, Nyathi and Poultney believe that 'Such floodplain management could be emulated elsewhere' (ibid, p210), with Poultney more recently discussing possibilities for expanding the benefits to communities further downriver in Mozambique. Even this successful experiment, however, is at risk because of a revival by politicians and elites of the original irrigation plan for the Makatini Flats immediately below the dam. Any attempt to maximize water use and production there could be at the expense of the downstream ecosystem and its users (Poultney, 2001).

The IUCN Waza-Logone Project in Northern Cameroon has the potential to be another success story,[11] while its receipt of an award for excellence at EXPO 2000 in Hanover, Germany, in the 'Environment' category reflects its importance for implementing an ecosystem approach for floodplain restoration. During the 1970s, the Mega Dam and further embankments were built in the Logone River Basin to provide irrigation water to the Semry rice project. Reduced downstream flooding had an adverse effect on the biodiversity of the Waza National Park and the livelihood of about 150,000 villagers, some of whom had to seek opportunities elsewhere. The IUCN project began in 1988 with the goal of improving conditions in the national park and the people's flood-dependent economy. In the planning of two pilot flows and future environmental flows all relevant users were involved including local communities, local government, management of the rice project and park staff. Surveys involving participatory rural appraisal were completed to assess just how a reduction in flooding had affected local communities, and to encourage their involvement in flood management planning. Local communities were also helped to develop their own environmental and socio-economic monitoring systems.

Pilot flows were released from the Logone River in 1994 and 1997 by breaching the embankments. They covered about 20 per cent of the floodplain that had been deprived of water by the Semry works. Researchers and villagers alike agreed that habitat recovery was associated with improved grazing, fishing and agriculture. Especially impressive was a 'recovery of the vegetation from annual grass species back to perennial species... An indicator of the rangelands' improvement was the increase of 260% in the number of cattle in the floodplain since 1994, without any sign of degradation to the grasslands' (Loth, 2004, p94).

A hydrological model was used to simulate the effects of the pilot releases and of the necessary releases for further restoration of the floodplain, which an economic evaluation had shown would provide 'substantial economic benefits' (ibid, p83). Success was such that the project is currently seeking donor support to rehabilitate the entire floodplain. That will also require releasing environmental flows from the reservoir, an additional benefit of which will be more agriculture within the drawdown area (ibid, p107).

Positive results from such cases are having an impact elsewhere for planning environmental flows. In Mozambique current research under the auspices of the International Crane Foundation on potential benefits of environmental flows from the Cahora Bassa Dam on the Zambezi has caught the attention of the President and the Lower Zambezi River Authority (communication from R. D. Beilfuss). In Kenya, project authorities are considering designing the Grand Falls Dam on the Tana River to permit environmental flows that could benefit approximately 150,000 villagers practising flood recession agriculture and 176,000 transhumant pastoralists whose livestock are dependent during the dry season on floodplain grazing (Acreman et al, 2000, p8 and p14).

Restoration limitations and difficulties

Introduction

No matter how well environmental flows and other restoration mechanisms are planned and implemented, they will be unable to restore the extent of previous downstream ecosystems and livelihood systems because some dam-induced losses, such as those to deltas, are irreversible. Such losses include extractions for irrigation and urban water supplies that inevitably reduce the quantity of water, as does evaporation from reservoirs, whereas use of water for hydropower generation, irrigation and navigation reduces the variability of natural flows. Such constraints to restoration require that decision-making for river basin development includes the non-dam option.

Successful implementation of environmental flows also faces other limitations and difficulties. One is uncertainty about outcomes as a result of the complexity and dynamics of river basin ecosystems and inadequate knowledge about the nature of such systems. That uncertainty requires an adaptive management approach that is expensive in terms of finance, staff and time. Operational limits also exist, as do entrenched economic and political interests.

Uncertainty and the need for adaptive management

Adaptive management, as a concept and a strategy, developed in recent decades as a corrective to traditional approaches to design that stuck to a single least-cost option once selected during feasibility studies. It is a concept that admits the limits to scientific knowledge and acknowledges uncertainty as an inherent feature of a project or programme. It is a strategy for dealing with projects and programmes associated with uncertain outcomes and is especially suitable for large-scale water resource projects. Its purpose is to encourage formulation of a management approach based on an ongoing consideration of alternative models and is flexible enough to allow adjustments based not only on the results of long-term project monitoring but also on changes in societal values and preferences.

Adaptive management is complex, expensive, and time consuming because it is interdisciplinary and requires long-term monitoring with policy readjustment based on the results of that monitoring. For such reasons it is best used for projects, such as large dams, known to be associated with uncertain outcomes that could cause irreversible and adverse environmental, economic and social impacts.

Policy constraints

Policy constraints involve project authorities, national governments and donors. The extent of trade-offs between the benefits of regularizing river flows for hydropower generation and irrigation and the release of environmental flows has seldom been analysed. Beilfuss (2001) and Gammelsrød (1992) have shown that environmental flows can be released from Mozambique's Cahora Bassa Dam without sacrificing generation of hydropower, while the Institute for Development Anthropology team has shown the same to be the case for Mali's Manantali Dam. While this may also be the case elsewhere, environmental flows often involve losers as well as winners. Reducing flows from dams along the Missouri River in the US to mimic natural flows during summer months for environmental benefits will disadvantage navigation along the river's lower reaches. Reduced flows will also increase pumping costs for irrigation.

Elsewhere there may well be trade-offs between hydropower generation and environmental flows that could have major financial implications. Over the longer term, environmental flows coupled with rural electrification make economic and political sense. On the other hand, it is sale of electricity that is the main determinant over the short run of a project's cost effectiveness and ability to pay off donors. Maximizing the distribution and sale of electricity to urban consumers is a faster way of paying off debts than taxation of, and electricity payments from, hundreds of thousands of lower income and slowly developing river basin households.

Policy-makers are faced with other short-term versus longer-term development dilemmas. Without environmental flows and other development opportunities, rural poverty in river basins can be expected to increase labour migration to cities – as continues to be the case with Kariba in Zambia and also is the case in Senegal in regard to migration from the Senegal River Basin to Dakar. Policy-makers have yet to think though the economic and political implications of more rapid urban inflows in relationship to greater pressure on urban infrastructure and services as well as to unemployment and crime.

Operational difficulties

Operating a dam for multiple purposes is a difficult management task in any country. It will be more difficult in many late-industrializing countries because of the lack of instrumentation, data and staffing capacity. For an effective programme of environmental flows, adequate upstream hydrological and meteorological stations are necessary along with the ability to interpret the data provided. Such skills are in short supply and where present may require expatriate expertise, which adds to their costs (Scudder, 1991, p106). For downstream residents to benefit, the scheduling and nature of each year's environmental flows must be effectively communicated.

The Bakolori (Nigeria) and Itezhitezhi (Zambia) cases illustrate difficulties concerning the timing, duration and volume of flows. After the adverse effects of the Bakolori Dam on downstream communities had been demonstrated, complaints to the political authorities did result in some releases at the appropriate time. But their duration and magnitude was inadequate. Whereas the Bakolori Dam was not planned with such releases in mind, the Itezhitezhi Dam was heightened at considerable cost to increase environmental flows, which proved to be not as beneficial as expected (Acreman et al, 2000).

Dealing with economic and political vested interests

Interest, and even commitment to the timely release of environmental flows, is not sufficient, nor is their implementation on an off-and-on basis. Such commitments supposedly exist for the dams on the Hadejia in Nigeria, where project authorities were willing to experiment with releases 'to augment the annual flood' (Acreman et al, 2000, p7). The same was supposed to apply to Mali's Manantali Dam on the Senegal River. Yet in both of these cases, other interests have dominated that not only stop the release of the agreed flows but also allow dams to be operated in ways that create additional costs to downstream communities.

The impasse over environmental flows on the Missouri River illustrates how social values are changing and how a combination of economic and political interests can interfere with acknowledging those values by prohibiting releases recommended by teams of scientists. Over the past 70 years, the geomorphology, hydrology, wetlands and biodiversity of the Missouri River have been extensively altered by engineering activities including the construction of a cascade of seven mainstream dams. In 1999 the National Research Council was requested by the US Corps of Army Engineers and the Environmental Protection Agency to produce a report that could 'provide a better scientific basis for river management decisions' (NRC, 2002, p14). Summing up their findings, the authors of the Council's 2002 report concluded 'Degradation of the natural Missouri ecosystem is clear and is continuing.' It will continue in the future 'unless some portion of the hydrologic and geomorphic processes that sustained the pre-regulation Missouri River and floodplain ecosystem are restored – including flow pulses that emulate the natural hydrograph... The ecosystem also faces the prospect of irreversible extinction of species' (ibid, pp3–4).

The seven mainstream dams built on the Missouri River were designed and operated to control floods, generate electricity, and stimulate irrigation and, in the lower basin, navigation. Not only were those goals only partially realized (navigation in particular failed to meet expectations), but society's values subsequently changed – interest in additional large-scale projects in the US was being replaced by a concern about dam-related environmental degradation within the country's river basins and an increasing emphasis on their use for recreation and tourism. The upper basin states along the Missouri benefited most from recreation and tourism. They wanted to improve ecological conditions by releasing environmental flows that would mimic the seasonality of the Missouri's natural regime. The lower basin states wanted to maintain the existing regularized regime for the benefit of agriculture and navigation.

After assessing the current state of the Missouri River ecosystem, the previously cited 2002 report of the National Research Council recommended environmental flows. They made economic as well as environmental sense, the report noted, since recreation benefits in the upper basin states exceeded downstream agricultural and navigation benefits. There the issue lies since there is no mechanism for arbitrating the disagreements between the upper and lower basin states (Chapter 9).

Synchronizing managed floods with reservoir drawdown

Not only should future planning for dams include the environmental flows option but the potential benefits of linking that option to reservoir drawdown should also be included (Scudder, 1980). As detailed in Chapter 4, cultivation of the drawdown area is of importance to countless thousands of those resettled or otherwise living within reservoir basins. Regularizing drawdown could significantly increase the productivity of crops grown and increase the area farmed. It could also provide a method for lowering the incidence of malaria and schistosomiasis by altering the habitat of larvae and snails.

Test cases for synchronizing environmental flows with drawdown of existing reservoirs

Manantali and Cahora Bassa are examples in which synchronizing environmental flows with reservoir drawdown might have major benefits for both downstream communities and resettler and host communities within the reservoir basin. For Manantali we know that environmental flows in September would greatly benefit half a million people downstream. Hydrological studies would be necessary to see if the recommended releases would also draw down the reservoir sufficiently to allow several thousand farmers and fishers living in the reservoir basin also to practise drawdown cultivation.

The potential of such synchronization would appear to be much greater for Cahora Bassa because tens of thousands of people live within the reservoir basin. When the drawdown would begin would depend on the best timing for environmental flows for the benefit of the much larger number of downstream residents (Beilfuss, personal communication). Before Kariba and Cahora Bassa were built, natural flood pulses reached the middle Zambezi in March and the lower river in April. Today the two reservoirs are still filling at that time, with Kariba drawdown beginning in July and Cahora Bassa several weeks later in most years. Even without environmental flows, villagers around both reservoirs are able to plant thousands of hectares in drawdown crops for harvesting before the arrival of the rains and the commencement of reservoir refilling in November. Releasing environmental flows during the August–October period for downstream benefits and flood management purposes would also increase the area within the reservoir for flood recession agriculture. Especially in drought years or years of poor rainy season harvests, that would provide a major benefit to farmers.

UPSTREAM USERS AND CATCHMENT PROTECTION

Inadequate attention also has been paid to the impact of large dams on river basin communities living upstream from reservoir basins, and to the impact of upstream activities on reservoirs. Negative and positive impacts can vary from negligible to major. The Kariba Dam on the Zambezi, for example, had virtually no impact on upstream residents. That was because few people lived in the gorges immediately above the reservoir, while the Victoria Falls at the end of those gorges restricted upriver migration of fish. Thailand's Pak Mun Dam, located on the Mun River only 5.5km upriver from its junction with the Mekong, on the other hand, has had a serious negative impact on thousands of fishers living upriver from the Pak Mun reservoir (Chapter 3).

Of increasing concern to Chinese planners is deforestation, which is causing increased silt loads in the Yangtze and Yellow Rivers. Where protection strategies are implemented they can either cause additional involuntary resettlement or be designed to protect catchment ecosystems and raise local living standards, as is being attempted with pilot projects in China, Laos, South Africa and Zimbabwe.

Upstream catchment management for the benefit of ecosystems and people as well as for controlling sedimentation in reservoirs is seldom incorporated within feasibility studies for dams. An exception is Laos' NT2 project. More frequently, though still uncommon and usually a response to increasing reservoir sedimentation, management efforts commence following dam completion. Two World Bank-funded projects in China provide examples.

The Chinese projects in small tributary watersheds of the Yellow River's middle and upper basin, as with the one in Laos, are multifunctional. The setting is the Loess Plateau, which is 'the most erosive area in China' (World Bank, 2003, pp 131–139). Together large numbers of village projects on small watersheds will reduce sediment flows into reservoirs behind mainstream dams, but their main function is to improve land and water management for thousands of village residents. Government officials have worked with farm communities in two projects (Loess I 1994–1998 and Loess II 1999–2004) to build over 450 small, medium and large dams (most 5–15m in height but a few up to 30m). Together the two projects are intended to incorporate an area of 19,500km^2 that includes 12 tributaries of the Yellow River for the benefit of two million people living in 3350 villages. Such a programme of integrated rehabilitation and development in a large number of sub-catchments required the Chinese to plan and implement an effort requiring input from many disciplines and the cooperation of different levels of government with local communities.

Prior to infrastructure construction, individual communities are provided with 'a menu of options and support services' (ibid) that they believe will best meet their needs. Loess II options included sediment control dams that could be designed also to provide flood control, build new land for agriculture, or store water for irrigation and household supply. Other options were rainwater harvesting, conjunctive use of surface and groundwater, and a variety of crop and sideline activities based on analysis of farm models that took into consideration the sensitivity of produce to drought and price changes. Institutional changes were also included. One of the more important addressed insecurity of tenure, with farm households given contracts for using new arable land that were no less than 30 years. Depending on the options selected, credit was available to participating communities down to individual farmers, with repayment geared to output. Results were impressive, with counties competing to participate in the expanded programme under Loess II. Farm incomes were shown to rise appreciably, while the system of dams 'was able to provide a 100 percent control of course sediment runoff in small watersheds' (ibid).

The upper catchment project in Laos is a direct result of feasibility planning for the Nam Theun 2 Dam. An upper catchment of over 3500km^2 is set off from the future reservoir by a line of hills that on one side curves around to the border with Vietnam and on the other side falls away via a steep escarpment to the plains below. The upper border is the crest of the Annamite Mountains that form the boundary between Laos and Vietnam. In terms of biodiversity of both flora and fauna, the upper catchment is outstanding, being 'probably the richest and largest wild area remaining in Lao PDR, and one of the largest in South East Asia' (NT2 POE, 1997, p12). As the catchment ascends from about 600m in elevation to over 2000m, the vegetation varies from pine to evergreen broadleaf forest types to upper montane forest that includes one and perhaps two relict genera. Wildlife includes not only elephant and tiger and a rich bird fauna but also four new species of mammals. Six perennial tributaries that rise in the Annamite Mountains link the upper catchment to the future reservoir basin after they cut through the lower hills en route to the Nam Theun River. They are inhabited by approximately 6000 indigenous people belonging to a number of different and poorly described ethnic and linguistic communities, one of which only recently shifted from a foraging economy to one dominated by bush fallow agriculture.

The biodiversity of this entire area is at risk, however, with the risk expected to accelerate if the NT2 project does not go ahead as planned. Until the mid-1990s, a government parastatal controlled by the military was responsible for developing the area. To cover costs and to bring development to local residents who are clustered in three sub-districts, the military had begun building a road to traverse the area with an offshoot into the Annamite range for logging purposes. In the meantime, helicopters were being used to remove the most valuable timber. All such activities were stopped at the request of the World Bank.

From 1995 to 1998 IUCN worked on an Environmental and Social Management Plan for the upper catchment. During 2000 the government released a blueprint for the establishment of a Watershed Management and Protection Authority to implement the plan. Meanwhile, the administration of communities along the tributaries has been transferred from the military to the relevant district and provincial authorities with IUCN and World Bank assistance. That has brought both the upper catchment and the reservoir basin under the administration of a single district whose headquarters are close to the future reservoir, whereas formerly the military's administrative centre was in another province. Communications will be based on routes ascending the tributaries rather than on a military road traversing the whole area at right angles to those tributaries.

All the above activities have been an outcome of planning for World Bank involvement in the funding of the NT2 Dam. If the dam is cancelled for any reason or donor funding ceases to be available for the watershed planning that has already occurred, government institutions will have little option but to renew logging. Quite possibly the government's previous policy, also stopped at the World Bank's request with strong POE support, to consolidate the various ethnic communities in centralized villages, or even to relocate them to the lowlands as done in other portions of the country, would be reintroduced at the expense of the current villagers' cultural integrity and health.

SUMMARY

What is becoming increasingly evident is that the ecological services provided by natural river flow regimes and their socio-economic importance, in late-industrializing countries especially, have been seriously overlooked by planners, donors and academics. Where dams have been built, inadequate attention has been paid to management of their catchments and to adverse downstream environmental and socio-economic impacts. While some attention is now being paid to catchment management to reduce the deforestation and erosion that pose a threat to the benefits of dams because of increasing siltation, less attention continues to be paid to downstream impacts.

Far more downstream people tend to be adversely affected when dams are built than the number requiring resettlement from future reservoir basins. Yet bilateral and multilateral donors and national governments have still to develop specific guidelines for their incorporation in dam-related feasibility studies. Building up local institutions for participation in the decision-making process presents a problem, especially where communities are spread out over a long distance and are unaware of how their futures may be affected by dams that can be hundreds of kilometres upstream. A further problem to building capacity is lack of involvement of supportive NGOs. If proper attention were paid to the productivity of downstream floodplains and communities and to the adverse effect of dams on that productivity, that in itself should lead to consideration of a wider range of options than dams for meeting water and energy requirements. And where dams are selected, greater awareness of that productivity should lead to a more serious consideration of environmental flows and synchronized reservoir drawdown.

While the examples described in this chapter, as well as experiments with environmental flows in the US for the benefit of fisheries and riverine habitats, increasingly have shown their importance and potential for habitats and dependent communities, they are not a panacea for curing the adverse downstream impacts of dams. Policy, management and environmental constraints also must be acknowledged and dealt with. Environmental flows and regularized flow regimes for hydropower generation and irrigation benefit different constituencies with a multiplicity of goals. Working out acceptable sub-optimization or other strategies will not be easy, especially in Africa and other developing countries with little experience in more open systems of planning that involve all the important users. Where there will be trade-offs between environmental flows and hydropower generation, financiers may be concerned about debt repayment, since it is the sale of electricity to urban areas, mines and other large-scale industries that is the main source of revenue. Although the economic benefits of a managed flood from the Manantali reservoir to over half a million Senegalese villagers will exceed any economic loss from reduced electricity generation, how do you tax those villagers, or villagers who are beneficiaries of other projects, for debt repayment purposes?

While management constraints may be the most easily overcome, they require committed operators, a sophisticated hydromet network and modelling capacity, and an effective communication system to inform downstream farmers and other residents about the timing, duration and magnitude of releases. Environmental constraints can be expected to be the most intractable, with some impacts of dam construction irreversible. Although we need to know far more about the role of natural flooding and of dam-regulated regimes on ecosystems, the reduction of flood events as water is syphoned off and/or stored is known to have an adverse effect on the size of deltas and wetlands and on their productivity, as illustrated by experience on the Nile, Zambezi and Indus.

8

Institutional Arrangements

INTRODUCTION

The purpose of this chapter is to discuss the range of institutions that needs to be involved if sustainable water resource development is to occur. In addition to central governments and project authorities, other government institutions are needed as well as private sector contractors, consultants and other firms and local institutions, including those of affected peoples, NGOs, donors, financial institutions, independent panels, and universities and non-profit research institutions. Following an introductory section on hydropolitics, the historical strengths and weaknesses of each type of institution are assessed.

HYDROPOLITICS AND THE POLITICAL FACTOR

The importance of the political factor, and more specifically of hydropolitics (Chapter 7), should not come as a surprise in a world of national political economies. As Frederiksen notes in the World Bank's report *Water Resources Institutions* 'Goals, resource allocation and programmes are formulated through the political process' (1992, p4). The strong backing of politicians is also needed to see major projects implemented, a point stressed by the Chief Executive of the Zambezi River Authority (Tumbare, 2000, pp97–111).[1]

Problems arise when 'political considerations supersede all else, in institutional and programme matters' (Okidi, 1987b, p20). This situation can result in decisions to proceed before the necessary options are assessed and can result in institutional capacity being undermined by staff appointments based on 'political patronage to the exclusion of merits and expertise' (ibid). Large dams, indeed large projects in general, involve powerful project authorities and public and private engineering institutions, usually with strong state backing. More often than not they are planned and implemented for political and ideological purposes as well as macro-economic ones. Heads of state are frequently involved as both originators and strong supporters (Chapter 1). When Fahim reports Nasser as exclaiming 'In antiquity we built pyramids for the dead. Now we will build new pyramids for the living,'[2] Nasser was referring to the High Dam at Aswan, the history of which

Waterbury states 'is testimony to the primacy of political considerations determining virtually all technical choices with the predicted result that a host of unanticipated technical and ecological crises have emerged that now entail more political decisions' (1979, p6).

Waterbury's book is aptly titled *Hydropolitics of the Nile Valley*. The word 'hydropolitics' also is prominently displayed in the title of Ribeiro's 1994 study of Argentina and Paraguay's Yacyretá Dam.[3] In other cases, a presidential decision was made to proceed with a large dam, and fund raising initiated, even before the necessary feasibility studies had been completed or, if completed, were unfavourable. Kenya's Turkwell Dam is one example. Although construction has been delayed, Gambia's Balingho Dam and Somalia's Baardheere Dam are two other examples (Scudder, 1981b, p192).

The ideological component is perhaps equally significant. Scott argues that decisions are influenced by the utopian character of large projects, with planners utilizing what he calls 'a high-modernist ideology' emphasizing science and technology for the 'ordering of nature and society' (1998, p4). Large dams are especially susceptible to such an approach, which superimposes a controlling and simplifying vision onto a complex, poorly understood river basin at the expense, usually, of the socio-cultural systems of local communities and the ecological health of the basin. Outcomes, according to Scott, can be especially destructive in late-industrializing countries where an authoritarian state is able to superimpose an untested vision upon a weak civil society.

PROJECT AUTHORITIES

Introduction

Project authorities historically have been dominated by parastatals[4] or by single-purpose government ministries. They also include a small number of international river basin authorities. Important as the latter are for dealing with equitable use of international waters, I pass over them quickly because water resource development continues to be viewed by governments as a national issue. For the same reason I do not deal with treaties between nations that cooperate in a river's joint use as with the Columbia River Treaty between Canada and the US.[5]

Where evaluations have been made of international river basin authorities, the authors tend to be more interested in enabling legislation and institutional performance than with development outcomes. Examples include Africa's Senegal, Gambia, Niger, Lake Chad and Kagera authorities. Lawyers, for example, are interested in the circumstances under which states are willing to delegate certain prerogatives to such agencies and then to allow them to actually exercise those prerogatives. In commending the tripartite Organization for the Development of the Senegal River Valley (OMVS), LeMarquand, for example, praises it more as a model of what an international authority should be in a statuary sense than in regard to its actual accomplishments (1982).

Although there is insufficient data to test the hypothesis, what data I have suggest that affected people and the environment may be at a greater risk when affected by international river basin authorities because an additional level of hierarchy has been added to what are already highly centralized organizations. OMVS, for example, has resisted controlled releases from the Manantali Dam for the benefit of over 500,000 downstream users despite research demonstrating their socio-economic and environmental benefits and the support of Senegal as one of OMVS's three members.

Parastatals vary widely in regard to functions as well as location in government structures. National river basin authorities tend to be multipurpose agencies, although the terminology used can be deceiving. The Tennessee Valley Authority is multipurpose and falls under the Office of the President. Ghana's Volta River Authority is also an autonomous agency, with its chief executive nominated by the government and appointed by the board (with President Nkrumah the first chair) after approval by international lenders. Although it was established as a multipurpose agency, lenders' influence resulted in hydropower generation being favoured. The primary concern of Zambia–Zimbabwe's Zambezi River Authority is hydropower, while the Lesotho Highlands Development Authority gives priority to two tasks – water transfer to South Africa and hydropower generation for domestic consumption. Both authorities fall under ministerial control, energy in the Zambia–Zimbabwe case and natural resources in the case of Lesotho. In Sri Lanka the Mahaweli Authority (MASL) is under the Ministry of Mahaweli Development.

Other types of parastatals can be multifunctional, although the large majority has a dominant purpose such as dam construction for the generation of electricity. In Canada examples include Hydro-Quebec, Ontario Hydro and BC (British Columbia) Hydro and in China the South China Electric Power Joint Venture Corporation. Although responsible primarily for dam construction for irrigation, the US Bureau of Reclamation's responsibilities also include hydropower generation, as is the case with the US Corps of Army Engineers, whose initial mandate stressed flood control and navigation. In recent years both US parastatals have been instructed to deal with environmental issues including adaptive management and, more specifically, habitat restoration. Turkey's State Hydraulics Works (DSI) has a broad multipurpose mandate that includes the ambitious Southeastern Anatolia Project (GAP).

Single-purpose ministries dealing with irrigation or hydropower are the dominant project authorities in countries where the largest number of dams are currently being built. That is irrespective of whether the project is primarily single or multipurpose. In India the responsible ministries tend to be irrigation. Gujarat's Ministry of Irrigation played the dominant role in connection with the Sardar Sarovar Project (SSP) until a subsequently created parastatal took over. In China, the Ministry of Energy has responsibility for the Xiaolangdi Dam on the Yellow River and Three Gorges Dam on the Yangtze – both of which are designed as multipurpose facilities.

Parastatals

Strengths and weaknesses

At first glance, one might think that parastatals are the logical institutional mechanism for planning and implementing large dams and other large-scale river basin infrastructure. They are among a country's largest projects, if not the largest, and have strong backing from the centre. Roosevelt saw TVA as a means for bringing regional development to a poverty-stricken section of the US. Nkrumah, influenced by the TVA model, pushed the Volta River Authority as a grand experiment that would show Ghanaians how to industrialize both the rural and urban sectors of the economy. Sri Lanka's president had a direct interest in the MASL, appointing the chairman of his political party, who was one of the most powerful men in the country, as the chief executive. He also appointed one of the rising younger politicians in the party to be in charge of the overseeing ministry.

In addition to political backing, such organizations are also able to attract the best available staff, who are drawn by what are usually higher salaries and better conditions of service as well as by the development vision that brought the agency into existence. Such strengths are especially important during the planning and early implementation stages of a project and for fund raising, as was illustrated by the success of the MASL in funding the acceleration of the Mahaweli project during the 1970s (Chapter 5).

While parastatals get infrastructure built, their strengths are also weaknesses. The weaknesses are most likely to appear during the later stages of a project's cycle. They are associated with the parastatals' centralized and hierarchical organization and the nature of their staffing as well as with their visionary mandate. Staff are dominated by engineers whose main responsibility to is build infrastructure. This can come to be seen as an end in itself rather than as a means for development. A parastatal's centralized and hierarchical organization and visionary mandate to reorder society and nature tends to ignore, or at best de-emphasize, local knowledge (Scott, 1998), participation of affected people and the poorly understood complexity of social and environmental conditions; a tendency reinforced by reluctance of senior staff to live on site and the frequently lower status of staff dealing with social and environmental issues.

Lack of political will, lack of capacity and ignorance are three reasons why socio-economic costs to local communities and environmental costs to river basin ecosystems continue to be seriously underestimated by parastatals as well as by other project authorities. Contemporary examples include Yacyretá in Argentina–Paraguay, India's SSP and Lesotho's Highlands Water Project (LHWP). In the first two cases construction began in the face of ignorance of, and an absence of concern for, social and environmental issues. When such issues were dealt with, it was largely a response, and an inadequate one at that, to World Bank requirements.

In the Yacyretá case, the project authority reduced staffing and de-emphasized social planning when only a minority of resettlers had moved.

Subsequent upgrading occurred because it was a requirement for receiving additional donor funding. As for the SSP, the project authority's inability to deal with social and environmental issues led to World Bank withdrawal from the project.

During LHWP feasibility studies not only was the number of resettlers underemphasized, but projected minimal flow releases from both the major dams were based on the unwarranted assumption (METSI, 2000) that downstream social and ecological impacts would be minimal. When the Lesotho Highlands Development Authority (LHDA) was subsequently established to implement the relevant portions of the project within Lesotho, what became the Environment and Social Services Group (ESSG) was seriously understaffed, underfinanced and under-equipped (LHDA POE, 1991). Even today the status of ESSG staff is the lowest in the organization, one indicator being the continued micromanagement of its affairs by the policy-responsible Lesotho Highlands Water Commission.

Another parastatal weakness is a tendency for its leadership to 'go it alone' by not involving other government agencies, the private sector, NGOs and local institutions in decision-making and implementation. Recent examples include MASL and LHDA. In the Mahaweli case, the authority's establishment act restricted activities of other government agencies to the provision of credit and to policing and national security. Key NGOs, such as Sarvodya, were prohibited from working with tens of thousands of incoming settlers.

LHDA eventually took a pioneering approach to involving local NGOs, but it took nearly ten years to institutionalize their involvement. The Authority has also been slow in regard to utilizing the facilities and staff of various government institutions. One such institution is the existing farmers' training centre in the foothills where a majority of Mohale Dam resettlers wished to move to continue agricultural activities in an area where LHDA has little institutional capability and expertise. Only after asset handing over became a major issue did the Authority begin a hesitant and small-scale use of the training centre's facilities.

It can be argued that the weakness of other institutions is a justification for not involving them. The flip side of that argument, however, is the necessity, in most cases, sooner or later to hand over assets and services to line ministries and other institutions. Their very weakness becomes an argument for parastatals such as the Mahaweli Authority to help upgrade their capacity. Again the Lesotho farmers' training centre provides an example. When I first visited it in the mid-1990s the centre's physical infrastructure needed rehabilitation while the motivated staff needed equipment and other facilities. For example, for training farmers in livestock management they lacked the necessary domestic stock. They also lacked such essential equipment as a working tractor and oxen and parts for the use of animal traction. Once it became obvious that a majority of Mohale resettlers wished to move to the foothills and that the Authority did not have the facilities and staff to service them, a strong case existed, but was neglected until recently, for funding the necessary upgrading of the training centre.

Strong, centralized parastatals also run the risk of riding roughshod over the interests of resettling communities. Two contemporary examples are the actions of Chile's ENDESA in relationship to indigenous communities involved in the Pangue and Ralco Dam projects on the Biobio River (Downing, 1996; Hair et al, 1997). Still worse because of the tens of thousands of people involved, are parastatal actions in Madhya Pradesh in regard to resettling communities in connection with India's Sardar Sarovar Dam.

Parastatals also are slow to hand over project assets to settler households and communities. Until recently project after project showed an unwillingness to sponsor and facilitate the emergence of local water user associations for maintaining dam-supplied irrigation projects. Still a problem with many projects is an unwillingness on the part of the project authority to hand over to settler/resettler households promised title documents to their house plots and fields despite their importance for obtaining credit and for providing households with the type of security needed for making permanent improvements.

Another common weakness associated with parastatals is the often difficult relationships between a strong parastatal and line government agencies such as ministries of agriculture, education, health and public works to which eventually responsibilities must be handed over. Hostilities and jealousies can date back to the parastatal's hiring staff away from other government institutions with lower salaries and poorer terms of service, as happened when LHDA hired staff from the Ministry of Agriculture. Even where difficult relations do not exist, line government institutions may refuse to take over assets in which they had no preceding involvement. Or they may not have the necessary budgetary, staffing and equipment resources, with the result that infrastructure and services decline after handover.

Strong parastatals are also more vulnerable to political events than line ministries, including changes in regime and leadership. Once Premadasa became President of Sri Lanka he downgraded the Mahaweli project because of his rivalry with that project's minister. Parastatals also are probably more easily corrupted because of their relative autonomy. The 2002 conviction of LHDA's first chief executive for taking bribes from some of the world's most prominent engineering firms is a recent and flagrant example of individual and corporate corruption.

What I call 'institutional corruption' includes intentional inflation of benefits in order to proceed with new projects. When the lead US Army Corps of Engineers' economist concluded after a five-year study that Upper Mississippi River lock expansion was not economic, he was replaced and the Corps circulated e-mails to launch 'a campaign "to develop evidence or data to support a defensible set ... of projects", announcing that if the economics did not "capture the need for navigation improvements, then we have to find some other way to do it" ' (as quoted in the *Washington Post*, 2000). Another recent example was documented in an April 2002 report of the General Accounting Office that 'found that the corps had vastly overestimated the economic payoff of a US$300 million dredging project in the Delaware River

– the latest in a serious of projects where the corps seem to have cooked the books to justify huge budget outlays' (*New York Times*, 2002).

'Institutional corruption' is fostered in the US Army Corps of Engineers case by the Corps' close association with Congress. Although the Corps falls under the executive branch of the government, its funding comes from Congress. Over the years, members of Congress have used the Corps, which is the largest construction institution in the US, to build self-serving 'pork-barrel projects' whereby they 'bring home the bacon' to constituents in their various districts and states. Such projects have so inflated the Corps' budget with taxpayer dollars that finally a number of Democratic and Republic senators 'are determined to challenge the self-interest of many of their colleagues by instituting a top-to-bottom overhaul of the Army Corps of Engineers. Their objectives are twofold. One is to make sure the Army Corps' multibillion-dollar construction budget is spent on vital infrastructure, not wasteful pork-barrel projects... The other is to make sure that the corps proceeds in an environmentally responsible manner' (ibid).

Ways for anticipating weaknesses of parastatals where governments intend them to eventually hand over activities to line ministries and other institutions include incorporating a 'twilight clause' in articles of incorporation. 'Twilight clauses' should be complemented by specific, time-bound requirements for commencing the handing over process. Flexibility, however, must also be built into acts of incorporation to deal with unexpected events that may delay or speed up construction and other activities. For both time-bound parastatals and 'permanent' ones such as the Tennessee Valley Authority, budgets should reflect project-related impacts and requirements that can be expected or that may arise unexpectedly late in the project cycle or after handing over. Examples include upgrading during the implementation process institutions to which functions will be handed over, dealing with 'remaining problems' of project-affected people and with environmental impacts such as downstream erosion. Because large dams on mainstreams and major tributaries can have serious adverse impacts over extended time periods, their nature, and the capacity (including budgetary) of governments to deal with them, should be considered during the options assessment process. Trust funds funded from project revenue should be created for such purposes, including eventual decommissioning.

Line ministries as project authorities

It is hard to make a strong case for making a line ministry the sole project authority. Even in the case of a single-purpose project for irrigation, hydropower generation or flood control, it is legitimate to ask whether the involvement of a broader set of actors would have resulted in a very different outcome, or, if a dam was selected, in a different set of priorities. On the other hand, a single ministry as a lead agency may work provided mechanisms exist to provide other agencies with sufficient clout and finance to influence key decisions and carry out their responsibilities. In my experience the best way to ensure that this happens is to place the necessary council of ministers or other interagency body under the chairmanship of an actively involved president, prime minister or deputy prime minister who has the clout, and willingness to use it, to ensure that an interagency approach works. Such a politician should be actively involved during the initial stages of the project and sufficiently involved thereafter so that the lead ministry and other agencies remain aware of his or her interest and presence.

In India project after project planned and implemented by the Ministry of Irrigation has failed both to deal adequately with resettlement and environmental issues and to achieve the irrigation benefits claimed during project appraisal (WCD, 2000; Banerji et al, 2000). In Botswana, a major problem with the Southern Okavango Integrated Water Development Project was that the Ministry of Mineral Resources and Water Affairs, and more particularly the Department of Water Affairs, dominated working group meetings and ignored the concerns of other participants, weakening the project in the process.

A lead ministry with strong support from the centre and other ministries can, on the other hand, work effectively. China provides one example in which the Ministry of Energy (since the 1980s), with strong support from the central government, worked effectively with other government agencies to implement at least some major dam projects. Resettlement and environmental costs, for example, are considered project costs, with resettlement costs at Xiaolangdi estimated at 20 per cent of total costs and those for Three Gorges approximately one-third of costs. The responsibility for resettlement is then handed over to the provincial governments involved, which in turn directly involve district governments and resettler and host community institutions. Not only is resettlement considered a project cost, but a portion of revenue from hydropower generation is placed in a fund for dealing with further environmental and affected community needs.

Egypt provides another example. A separate ministry was created as the project authority for the Aswan High Dam once the decision was made to proceed by Egypt's Revolutionary Council. The eventually successful resettlement of the Egyptian Nubian population was the responsibility of the Ministry of Social Affairs, whereas the return of Nubians to the shores of Lake Nubia fell under the Aswan Regional Planning Authority. In Laos, with the active support of the First Deputy Prime Minister, the Ministry of Industry and Handicrafts has played a relatively effective role to date in pushing forward and coordinating planning for the Nam Theun 2 project.

Private engineering firms as project authorities

In recent years the role of private sector engineering firms has been expanding as countries attempt to reduce further indebtedness by negotiating with private sector firms to construct dams on a 'build, own, operate and transfer' (BOOT) basis. One example involved AES Corporation's failed attempt to operate alone with the intention of constructing the Bujagali Dam on the White Nile.

Private firms may also act as project authorities in a consortium that includes government parastatals, as in the case of Laos' Nam Theun 2 Dam.

While it is too early to assess the strengths and weaknesses of the private sector's increasing role, it has potential for a number of reasons. Historically private sector firms have played an important role in planning and implementing complex development projects. What several authors consider to be the most successful regional development project in Latin America was planned and executed by a private development company (Nelson, 1973, p121; Katzman, 1977, p53). This was the Parana Land Development Company that the Government of Brazil authorized to pioneer the regional development of a sparsely populated hinterland zone. While that development did not involve the construction of large dams, it did involve tens of thousands of poor rural settlers whose living standards were similar to those of the majority of dam resettlers.

The Parana scheme involved the rural and urban development of over one million hectares that the company bought. After careful planning, settlement began in 1928 on small-scale coffee holdings. It was phased with urban development along a railroad that was extended into the company zone as settlement proceeded. Many of the contemporary problems plaguing dam resettlers were dealt with during the planning process. Location of farms and larger settlement areas, for example, was based on careful soil surveys. Cleared land titles were presented to each rural family so as to avoid the type of land disputes that characterize dam resettlement in India, as elsewhere, and to facilitate access to credit. Construction of the 150km railroad, with market towns spaced at 15km intervals, was synchronized with receipt of funds from land sales.

In terms of my model of the settlement/resettlement process, the large majority of farm households had passed successfully through Stage 3 and had reached Stage 4 (handing over and incorporation) during the 1960s, by which time urban residents outnumbered rural residents. Growing faster than in neighbouring areas, population was estimated at 100,000 by 1940. By 1950 it had reached 400,000, climbing to about one million in the mid-1960s. According to Nelson, by 1968 the population had climbed to approximately 1.7 million 'of which 40–50 percent was urban' (1973, p123). Since the number of small farms was 39,000, agricultural development based on smallholder coffee had had a major multiplier effect with the likelihood that more than one non-farming job 'had been created for every farm job' (Scudder, 1981b, p169).

Of course, the big difference between the Parana Development Company and private sector engineering firms involved in dam planning and construction is that the former's profit depended on a successful process of regional development involving large-scale land settlement. While that also should be the goal of large dam construction, the responsibility of private sector engineering firms focuses too narrowly on dam construction and construction supervision. But there is precedent for taking a wider approach, including examples from my own experience. For the development of the

Senegal River Basin, it was the engineering firm of Gannett Flemming that first pointed out the importance of flood recession agriculture for over half a million people and hence the need to consider a controlled flood release from the proposed Manantali Dam.

Alexander Gibb, when consulting engineers for the first stage of the Kariba Project, drafted in 1960 what remains the most intriguing option for adding downstream irrigation for resettlers and hosts to Kariba's single-purpose role as a hydropower generator. Pumping water from the reservoir's northern corner, that option would deliver water a short distance to a downstream Zambezi tributary that could channel water to three densely settled chieftaincies with a combined population of over 20,000. The Kariba project authority, whose sole interest was generation of hydropower, ignored the Gibb report, although such a scheme for food-deficient hosts and resettlers appeared to be technically and economically feasible.[6] Today, when the existence of the Southern African Power Pool no longer requires Kariba or any other installation to restrict itself to power generation alone, the Gibb scheme seems even more advisable.

In the future some private sector firms may be more concerned with resettler and environmental issues than in the past. The International Commission on Large Dams, founded in 1928 'for the exchange of knowledge and experience in dam engineering,' published in November 1995 its *Position Paper on Dams and Environment*. Although only advisory for its member countries and engineering firms, the guidelines presented are superior to those of the large majority of countries where most future dams will be built and to the guidelines adopted by the World Bank and the regional banks. The key paragraph states 'We must cooperate conscientiously with nature's inherent dynamism without ever overtaxing its powers of regeneration, its ability to adapt to a new but ecologically equivalent equilibrium. And we must ensure that the people directly affected by a dam project are the first to benefit from it' (ICOLD, 1995, p5).

More recently, some important private sector firms including Siemens in Germany, ABB in Sweden–Switzerland, Harza in the US and Hydro-Quebec in Canada have come out in support of the WCD Final Report. While it remains to be seen what such support means, Hydro-Quebec has entered an agreement with the Cree Nation that the Cree leadership, rightly or wrongly, considered a genuine partnership (Chapter 6). And the private sector firms involved have claimed that planning for the Bujagali and Nam Theun 2 Projects meets WCD criteria, although opinions vary as to their success. A gradually increasing number of donors, on which private sector firms are dependent for financing and partial risk guarantees, have either been supportive of the WCD report or have their own guidelines for resettlement and environment issues. That they can have influence is indicated by the withdrawal of the Federal Republic of Germany's support for India's Maheshwar Dam following complaints about resettlement policies and actions that violated the human rights of villagers.

THE PRIVATE SECTOR: ENGINEERING FIRMS

Private sector engineering firms are key institutions in the powerful coalition of politicians, parastatals and line ministries advocating large-scale dams and other river basin infrastructure. They carry out the necessary feasibility studies and infrastructure design. They build and increasingly manage and operate dams. And as agents to governments they supervise, as consulting engineers, the planning, design and implementation work of other engineering firms. While their application of known engineering principles and technology makes them the most efficient institutions involved in water resources development, their focus tends to be restricted to infrastructure development. That narrow focus has weaknesses as well as obvious strengths.

The construction of the Kariba Dam shows the strengths. Working in a remote, incredibly hot and disease-ridden environment, Impresit completed Kariba's construction ahead of schedule and in spite of a record flood that overtopped a coffer dam and swept away the temporary bridge spanning the gorge. Now part of Impregilo, Impresit was one of a relatively small number of firms that had the capacity and experience to bid for constructing World Bank-funded dams where the Bank required international competitive bidding.

Such strengths, however, can bring to the fore weaknesses in other components of the project. Early completion of Kariba Dam, for example, gave the Federal Power Board the opportunity to close the dam ahead of schedule in order to commence reservoir filling during the 1958–1959 rainy season. That required resettlement on the north bank to become a crash programme that indirectly was responsible for the Chisamu War that resulted in the death of at least nine Gwembe Tonga at the hands of the Northern Rhodesian police. Elsewhere, as in India, Guatemala and Mexico, inadequate synchronization between construction and development required resettlers to be housed in temporary quarters.

In addition to the synchronization problem, another problem lies in the way in which international engineering firms work closely with their own governments to push large dams and other infrastructural projects to serve their own interests in developing countries. One example is Bangladesh's Flood Action Plan where pre-feasibility studies were completed by a French engineering consortium in partnership with a host country firm while the French Government pushed for the implementation of a flawed US$10 billion plan for construction of levees that would involve French firms.[7]

To build the Diama and Manantali Dams in the Senegal River Basin, European countries competed with each other by promising funding to the tripartite river basin authority. The French firms that secured the Diama contract and the German ones building Manantali then gave subcontracts to 'firms from their homes of origin. This implies that most of the funds raised for the projects were immediately paid outside the contracting states, particularly to France and the Federal Republic of Germany' (Okidi, 1987a, pp66–67). Since nearly half of the funding for the two dams came from Middle

Eastern petroleum dollars (ibid, p66), approximately US$400 million dollars were recycled from the Arab world and Iran to Europe with minimal impact on improving the capacity of local firms despite the fact that some of the few that received subcontracts did competent jobs and completed their work on time. The response of the Senegal River Authority at the 15th meeting of its Consultative Committee in 1983 was to express concern 'at the fact that the volume of work sub-contracted to the economic operators of the OMVS states did not exceed 2% of the amount of the Diama and Manantali contracts' (as quoted by Okidi, 1987a, p44). Their concern was twofold – loss of income and loss of opportunity 'to gain experience in the major works, thus, promote the strengthening of local institutions for future works' (ibid).

Other weaknesses are more directly related to private sector engineering firms as competing institutions within a highly competitive industry (firms which, in the Lesotho case, are being sued for bribe-giving). Because such firms want to build dams they should not also be contracted to carry out environmental and social impact assessments. That conclusion was brought home to me during my involvement with the IUCN evaluation of Botswana's SOIWDP (Chapter 6). In that case Snowy Mountains Engineering Corporation had completed all planning and design studies including an inadequate environmental impact assessment. Although there are exceptions, such firms rarely have the necessary expertise. If consultants are hired, they remain under close supervision of engineers who want additional contracts. Their numbers also tend to be inadequate, as in the Snowy Mountains case.

The Lahmeyer–McDonald Consortium in Lesotho underestimated the number of resettlers and affected people during feasibility studies for the Highlands Water Project in the 1980s. They also underestimated the negative impact of reduced downstream flows from Katse and Mohale reservoirs. Elsewhere, a director of the consulting firm AFRIDEV complained about the pressure placed upon his firm by one of the engineering firms responsible for environmental and social impact assessments in connection with Namibia's proposed Epupa Dam (communication from Jack Hennessy).

Another weakness relates to a lack of emphasis on the recruitment and training of affected people and other host country nationals as part of a project's labour force. While the preference of contractors to bring with them skilled and experienced staff from completed projects is understandable, more effort should be paid to recruiting local workers for unskilled jobs as well as providing training for some local workers. It is hard to overemphasize this point because it has an important relationship to a host country's capacity to industrialize. The Aswan High Dam is a good example in which Egyptian–Russian cooperation included the training of literally thousands of skilled Egyptian workers who subsequently contributed to development throughout the country. Such training, along with increased subcontracting to local firms, should be required by donors and built into contracts.

OTHER PRIVATE SECTOR FIRMS

Introduction

Other private sector firms can be divided into two categories. One includes firms participating as contractors in the resettlement process. The other includes firms implementing secondary contracts for the project authority or responding to other opportunities provided by dam construction and reservoir formation. The first category involves resettlement planning, implementation and monitoring activities. The second category includes, on the one hand, firms constructing access roads, construction townships and worker camps, and transmission lines, and, on the other hand, those seeking opportunities such as tourism, fisheries and agribusiness associated with the reservoir.

Firms participating in the resettlement process

The extent to which local and international firms participate in resettlement planning depends largely on the capacity of the host country and government policies. Small countries such as Laos and Lesotho are more dependent on private sector expertise than major dam-building countries such as Brazil, China, India and Turkey. In planning for Laos' Nam Theun 2 project, the project authority hired individual expatriate experts and international firms to work with the government's resettlement committee to complete an integrated environment and social management plan.

In Lesotho, the Highlands Development Authority contracted Phase 1A development planning and training to over ten international firms as well as to one international NGO. Learning from the difficulties experienced, planning for Phase 1B went to a single consortium that did a credible job of planning for resettlement in the Mohale Basin but an inadequate one for the majority of resettlers wishing to move to the foothills and the lowlands. In regard to affected people living downstream, the in-stream flow requirement study was contracted to a South African firm that subcontracted assessment of social impacts to a local firm, which received a subsequent contract to work with the project authority and downstream communities in researching mitigation and development options.

To ensure that the resettlement is planned and implemented as a project component and cost, and is synchronized with the construction schedule, governments should play a major role, if not the major role, in the actual implementation of resettlement. Whether implementation responsibilities should fall under the project authority (preferably working with other government agencies to ease future handing over) or under another government agency needs to be carefully assessed in each case since there is no 'best model'. In Egypt the Ministry of Social Affairs did a credible job with Nubian resettlement, whereas in Lesotho, the project authority was the logical agency to handle implementation because of superior resources. However, Lesotho's Highlands Development Authority contracted out specific implementation activities such as water and sanitation, community forestry and fisheries to a wide range of local and international agencies including NGOs, private firms and universities.

As for monitoring, the global experience is that it should be carried out by an organization independent of the project authority, which, however, should have the capacity to evaluate and act upon results. Again there is no best type of institution to carry out monitoring, but local expertise including knowledge of resettler languages, social organization and culture is essential. In some countries, such as India, that expertise is available in a wide variety of local agencies including NGOs, private firms and universities. Unlike the situation with planning, even in small countries sufficient local expertise is increasingly available and should be used provided it is independent of the project authority and the government. In Lesotho, a local firm, Sechaba Consultants, has the necessary expertise, as does the National University of Lesotho. While local NGOs also have the necessary capacity to monitor resettlement conditions in the field, most need further capacity building to be effective contractors.

Other firms

In my experience, other firms tend to ignore resettler and host community interests at those communities' expense. Contractors building roads, construction site facilities and transmission lines often bring their own labour force. They are seldom willing to train local people and they also are hesitant to recruit those who have been trained by project authorities or their consultants in special courses (usually of short duration) that do not qualify trainees for appropriate certificates. The situation is aggravated, sometimes to the point of causing conflict, when politicians and project officials attempt to justify projects to local communities, as they often do, by the promise of jobs that are then not forthcoming. Solutions lie largely with the project authority and local government. The former can stipulate in contracts the extent to which local people should be recruited and trained, while the latter can canvas local expertise and provide firms with registers of the names and expertise of job seekers.

A more difficult problem relates to firms seeking, as immigrant agencies, to profit from new opportunities provided by the dam, the construction township, and especially a major reservoir when in a picturesque setting. While researching material for the '50 dam survey' I found resettler and host communities frequently excluded from opportunities associated with tourism. The situation at Kariba and in connection with Lesotho's Highlands Water Project is not exceptional. With spectacular scenery, the Kariba Lake Basin has become an important destination for tourism operators. Type 'Kariba tourism' into an internet search engine and literally hundreds of websites appear. Of the first 30 found on Netscape, the large majority are on the Zimbabwe side of the reservoir, most of which has been set aside as recreation areas (including national parks and safari camps) at the expense of Gwembe Tonga settlement. Such websites advertise photography, fishing and walking safaris, and in the

Matusadona National Park, camping, safari lodges, houseboats and sailing are available, none of which involve the Gwembe Tonga except as low paid labourers.

On the Zambian side one website advertises a safari camp that provides game walks, bird watching, fishing and canoeing. It too involves Gwembe Tonga only as low paid labourers. There are similar camps on the islands and on the mainland. Conflicts between island safari operators and Tonga and other artisanal fishers for fishing and landing rights are an ongoing problem. As for mainland sites in Gwembe Tonga communal lands, the most spectacular is Kota Kota Hill that juts out into the reservoir and was acquired by a reclusive Italian. He evicted resident fisher-farmers, fenced off the peninsula and stocked it with elephants (that periodically graze in village fields outside the reserve) and with other game.

Legal and illegal efforts by entrepreneurs to gain access to other island and mainland sites at the expense of Gwembe Tonga common property tenure are ongoing. Some are legal, whereby islands, for example, are leased from a district council. Others are illegal and include bribing chiefs and other officials. One particularly brazen episode affected an NGO, Harvest Help/Zambia, which was bringing social services and development opportunities to some of the most isolated and poorest villages in the Valley. The directors woke up one morning to the sound of stakes being driven into the ground. On investigation they found surveyors who claimed that a Harvest Help project area including several villages had been 'given' by the local chief to an entrepreneur. In that case the chief was forced to back down when confronted by the NGO and the irate headmen whose land was involved. But the threat continues to be ongoing given the grandeur of the setting.

Competition for access to sites for tourism in Lesotho's Katse and Mohale reservoir basins is already underway at the expense of LHDA planning and local participation. One example relates to a proposed high altitude training and recreation centre on which construction began in 2002 on the prize Mohale basin site that will become a spectacular island in the centre of the reservoir. The project authority's failure to produce timely zoning regulations allowed the originating entrepreneur, a British firm, to bypass the Authority and national environmental legislation entirely by forming a partnership with several government ministers. The situation is particularly unacceptable for the resettlers who not only have customary tenure over the future island but also will have sufficient capital, received from loss of communal resources, to form a joint venture with a private firm to develop the site themselves.

In the Kariba case, private sector agribusinesses also have disadvantaged Gwembe residents. In the 1980s the Zambian Government initiated a policy to establish joint ventures with multinational agribusiness. Three were proposed for the Middle Zambezi Valley, none of which were intended to involve the village sector except as low paid labourers. One adjacent to the Lusitu River was stopped during the early stages of land clearing by local opposition. That land is now being cultivated by villagers. In the second case, a local chief downstream from the Gwembe Tonga agreed to the allocation of

1000ha of unoccupied but fertile land to an Irish company that grows marigolds and paprika for food colouring. Because Gwembe Tonga lands were not taken in this case and because Middle Zambezi Valley labour receives preferential recruitment, that enterprise at least provides wages to hundreds of villagers during the picking season, though it would have been far better, for villager income generation, to have experimented with the incorporation of small-scale outgrowers, as has proved successful elsewhere in Zambia.

The third agribusiness, the Gwembe Valley Development Company, took over land close to Lake Kariba. It was a joint venture in which a US agricultural services corporation held 70 per cent of the shares. Ten per cent each went to the remaining three shareholders: the Zambian subsidiary of a large German chemical company, a Zambian Government parastatal for marketing cotton and, as an inducement to the local chief and elite, a cooperative with an undefined membership and role. Twenty-one hundred hectares were acquired for the double cropping of cotton and wheat by sprinkler irrigation using 25 central pivots, each of which would cover 83 acres.

The project was a disaster for the nine villages dependent on that land for farming, grazing and a wide variety of natural resources. Although no census of the affected population was ever completed, partial data suggests that over 1750 people were dependent on one or more fields in the area, with over 5000 cattle and goats at least partially dependent on grazing and browse. Three of the nine villages were located within the boundaries of the Gwembe Valley Development Company and were forced to move. Compensation was based on cash as opposed to replacement land and was totally inadequate. Those cultivating cotton fields, for example, received little more than the value of one year's harvest.

Following a visit to the project in its early days of development, I wrote a critical report in which I concluded that 'granted the number of people involved and the degree of land scarcity, the only long term solution would appear to be incorporating the affected population ... as outgrowers clustered around a nucleus estate' (Scudder, 1986, p18). Such an approach made sense not just in terms of human rights but also in terms of economics. Not only were Gwembe Tonga already cultivating cotton but the Gwembe Valley had become the number one peasant cotton growing area in Zambia. Not only would Gwembe Tonga outgrowers produce cotton for the company but village labour would be available for picking cotton on the nucleus estate in which the owners had intended to use mechanized cotton picking machinery.

I had arranged for my report to go to a high government official en route to President Kaunda in hopes of having some influence on policy while there was time. The government reaction, however, was to repudiate the report, with the company proceeding as initially planned. Subsequently it went bankrupt. The estate was then acquired by a South African family business, which leased some of the pivots out to village farmers and purchased village cotton elsewhere within the district; they too went bankrupt due, I suspect, to the scale of the enterprise. The negative effects of the scheme extend far beyond its boundaries. Because of land scarcity, an unknown number of those who lost their land moved onto the adjacent escarpment where their cultivation of steep slopes is causing increasing deforestation and land degradation.

Fishing provides another example of local exclusion, even though local people have shown the capacity throughout the world to produce and market the resource if given the necessary access, training and credit. In India state governments continue to lease fishing and marketing rights on some reservoirs to outside firms, whereas the Government of Laos has given the marketing monopoly for the Nam Ngum reservoir to an entrepreneur from the capital who buys fish from the large population of artisanal fishers at below-market prices.

Elsewhere local fishers are not provided with the training and credit to compete successfully with more experienced fishers and entrepreneurs who are soon attracted to new reservoirs. In such cases local people may need preferential access during the initial years, as happened at Kariba. There, the more committed Gwembe Tonga fishers were able to compete with immigrants after the fishery was opened to all comers five years later. They have not, however, been able to compete successfully in the commercial open-water 'sardine' (*kapenta*) fishery. While participation there would be more difficult given the capital, equipment and management requirements, the Binga District Council on the Zimbabwe side of the reservoir has been harvesting *kapenta* for several years. This shows that the potential is there for properly organized local people.

Tourism, agribusiness and fisheries are three examples of how immigrants with superior resources, including access to political power, are taking over opportunities created by dams and reservoir basins around the world at the expense of local populations that could benefit if appropriate policies were implemented by project authorities with government and other agency support. Although examples are far too few, sufficient examples exist of private sector firms working with resettler populations and other river basin village populations to show the potential that is there. Two of the best examples involve efforts by Hatton's National Bank and the Ceylon Tobacco Corporation in the Mahaweli project (Chapter 5).

LOCAL INSTITUTIONS AND LOCAL LEADERS

Introduction

The potential of local institutions, along with the ability and effectiveness of their leaders, to participate in the resettlement with development process has increased significantly over the years. Several interconnected reasons are involved, which include positions taken by UN and other agencies, the emergence of networks and organizations of indigenous people, and increasing capacity of local institutions and leadership as well as active NGO involvement, which will be dealt with in the next section. Nonetheless, in terms of experience, financial resources and political clout, local institutions remain the weakest of the different categories of stakeholders in water resources development. They need strengthening, for they represent the major risk-takers.

United Nations and other agency positions

Because signed by member countries, though not necessarily observed, UN positions are especially important, starting with the 1947 Universal Declaration of Human Rights (WCD, 2000). Of special relevance to indigenous people, who have been disproportionately displaced by dams, the International Labour Organization's Convention Number 107 of 1957 deals with the 'rights of tribal people to retain their traditional cultures and *lands*' (my emphasis). Also important was the 1986 UN Declaration on the Right to Development.

Important positions taken by other organizations include IUCN's 1980 World Conservation Strategy, which for the first time linked natural resource management not just with the development of local populations but with their active involvement in planning, implementation and management activities. In 1982, following the initial 1981 publication of Robert Goodland's *Tribal Peoples and Economic Development: Human Ecological Considerations*, the World Bank published its Operational Manual Statement on *Tribal People in Bank-Financed Projects*. Apart from the World Bank's guidelines, none of these statements were targeted directly at dam resettlers. All, however, provided important support to the growing capacity of resettlers to influence decision-making processes.

Networks and organizations of indigenous people

Networks and organizations of indigenous people are important because in countries such as Canada, India and the US indigenous people have been involuntarily resettled disproportionately to their numbers in the population. In India, for example, where indigenous people make up less than 8 per cent of the population, they are estimated to be approximately 40 per cent of dam resettlers (McCully, 1996, p70). Among resettlers such people also tend to be the poorest and the least educated and politically connected.

Although regional networks of indigenous people have existed for over 50 years in North America and Scandinavia, the First International Conference on Indigenous Peoples was held in 1975. It led that same year to the formation of the World Council of Indigenous People. Since then indigenous networks, often working closely with individual NGOs and NGO networks, have proliferated, with an increasing number representing the interests of dam-affected people. The Cordillera People's Alliance in the Philippines is an impressive example not just of the nature of such an organization and the difficulties that must be overcome in its formation but also of its effectiveness in suspending and stopping the construction of major dams.[8]

Unifying nine previously separated bands, the Grand Council of the Crees is the second example of a coalition that has been able to stop one major dam while forging a partnership with the governments of Quebec and Canada to profit from future dam construction. The Organizacion Mapuche Ad-Mapu includes Mapuche currently fighting the construction of six dams along Chile's Biobio River, which threaten 'about 4000 people with the loss of their homes and land',[9] while the Lakota Nation includes Sioux reservations that have been disrupted by dams along the Missouri River in the US.

The origins of the Cordillera People's Alliance dates back to 1975 when 150 tribal leaders representing the Igorot people made a peace pact to end previous hostilities in order to fight four dams planned for the Chico River in Luzon. Its formation was the 'turning point in the Chico Struggle' (Carino, 1991), which ended with the cancellation of the Chico Dam and the suspension of the other three. The peace pact also led through several stages to 130 indigenous peoples' organizations in the Philippines federating themselves as the Cordillera People's Alliance in 1984.

The United Nations has been especially supportive of indigenous people and their networks, with 1993 being declared the International Year for the World's Indigenous People. It led in 1995 to the International Decade of the World's Indigenous People. Among indigenous peoples' networks with consultative status with the United Nations Economic and Social Council are several, including the Grand Council of the Crees and the Nordic Saami Council, which have played an important role not just as advocates for dam-affected indigenous people but as key players in the cancellation or modification of major projects (Quebec's Grande Baleine Dam and Norway's Alta Dam, for example).

Local institutions and leaders

Introduction

While the emphasis in this section is on resettler institutions, local institutions also include a range of self-governing institutions such as county, district and municipal councils that include host populations and other adjacent communities. Their involvement is especially important during options assessment, and should a dam be selected, they have an important role to play in representing the interests of resettlers and hosts. And their active involvement is essential if resettlement areas are to be successfully incorporated within the wider society and political economy during the final stage of the resettlement process (Stage 4).

The support of outsiders has also been historically important. The case studies discussed deal first with the US and Canada, followed by cases from Asia, Latin America and Africa. While they emphasize situations where local institutions have played an important role in influencing decision-making in ways beneficial to local people, it is important to emphasize that such cases are a minority because worldwide the majority of affected people continue to be impoverished by large dams. For example, in the 44 cases analysed during the 50 dam survey, living standards of the majority of resettlers worsened following removal in 36 cases (82 per cent).

The US and Canada

For North America, the focus will be primarily upon indigenous peoples since they illustrate in a more dramatic fashion the minority of cases in which local institutions have influenced major policy decisions and which in Canada, where large dams are still being planned, could bode well for the future.

Dam displacement in the US and Canada affected a disproportionate number of Native Americans. They were relatively powerless at first, but over the years their capacity to represent their interests has steadily grown to the extent that two large dam projects – Orme Dam in Arizona and Grande Baleine in Quebec – were stopped.

Just as the Tennessee Valley Authority overrode Black American resettlers during the 1930s (McDonald and Muldowny, 1982), the US Army Corps of Engineers rode roughshod over the interests of Native Americans resettled in connection with the construction in the 1950s and early 1960s of the Garrison, Oahe and Fort Berthold Dams on the Missouri River.[10] At Garrison, members of the affected Sioux Indian reservation had yet to be informed about the project when construction started in 1946. Although dam design was altered to protect the town of Willison, nothing was done to protect the Sioux who lost over 90 per cent of their farmlands, with the reservoir splitting their reservation into five sections. Exploiting the peoples' ignorance, the Corps even tried to use illegal means to acquire their land. Compensation was cash based with no funds for tribal development. In the following years unemployment rates rose as high as 79 per cent and 'many tribal members were driven to a life of despair in nearby urban centers' (Lawson, 1994, p61).

The record of the Bureau of Reclamation, the other major government construction agency, was little better, partly because the Bureau did not receive legislative authority from Congress to involve itself in resettlement activities until the 1960s (Ortolano et al, 2000, p3.6-3). The construction of the Grand Coulee Dam in the late 1930s and early 1940s caused the relocation of approximately 2350 members of two tribes (no proper census was carried out). The two tribal towns that required removal lost services 'because Congress did not provide Reclamation with the authority to finance new water, electrical or telephone services' (ibid, p3.7-8). Because of dependence on salmon, which had provided 40–50 per cent of the people's diet before the dam stopped their migration, both the economy and the culture of the people were devastated: 'important salmon-based cultural and ritual ceremonies were eliminated, parts of language and crafts associated with fishing disappeared, and tribal members' diets changed significantly' (ibid, pxv).

Also involving the Bureau of Reclamation, planning for the Orme Dam in the 1950s and 1960s as part of the Central Arizona Project proceeded 'with a minimum of consultation with the people to be most affected by it, the Ft McDowell Yavapai' (Khera and Mariella, 1982, p170). That was in spite of the fact that the reservoir would inundate approximately two-thirds of the

Yavapai Reservation – 'All the fertile agricultural land, grazing land, and trees would disappear' (ibid). Having been forcibly resettled several times during the 19th century before being allowed to return to their homeland along the Verde River in 1900, a large majority of the Yavapai were not prepared to be displaced again without a fight.[11]

Assisted by a politically savvy Mexican-American woman and two anthropologists, they initiated a campaign against that dam that included sending representatives to Washington in 1975 who were able to meet with government officials and members of Congress. Opposition activities increased after the Bureau prepared an inadequate environmental impact assessment (ibid, p172). Success was realized in 1981 when the Secretary of the US Department of Interior 'announced that Orme Dam would not be built' (Ft McDowell Yavapai Nation website). Since that time the Tribe has celebrated that day with an annual Yavapai Nation holiday which is one of two – the other celebrating their successful fight (against the State of Arizona) to run a casino.

In Canada, where a policy of assimilation was not dropped until the 1970s (Ortolano et al, 2000, p3.8-2), the central and state governments' record with Native American resettlement historically is even worse than in the US. For example, Canadian First Nations adversely affected by the Grand Coulee Dam, and dams in British Columbia further up the Columbia River, 'have not had access to the mitigation and compensation mechanisms and funds that are available to US Native American tribes' (ibid, p3.8-4).[12]

On the other hand, the successful resistance of the James Bay Cree to Hydro-Quebec's Grande Baleine Project had an influence extending to other states. As discussed in Chapter 6, their campaign against the dam and Hydro-Quebec combined an increasingly effective Cree leadership with a coalition of outside individuals and NGOs. With the contacts of Cree leaders, and especially their Grand Chief, extending to the United Nations, the Governor of New York and the Pope, the Cree played the major role in getting Quebec to suspend the Grande Baleine Project in 1994. That suspension became 'permanent' in 2002 as part of the partnership agreement that the Cree signed with the governments of Canada and Quebec.

Again it is important to emphasize that the Orme Dam and Grande Baleine Dam represent the small minority of large projects that have been stopped or at least suspended. More typical are an increasing number of cases in which construction is completed but opposition strengthens the capacity of local institutions and leaders to negotiate, either at the time, or subsequently, for better compensation and development benefits. This process was studied in detail by Bilharz (1998) while assessing the impact of the Kinzua Dam on the Allegany Seneca in New York and Pennsylvania. Although construction did not begin until the 1960s, Seneca resistance to the Kinzua Dam actually dates back to 1927 (Weist, 1994, p11). They fought the dam in the courts and even hired Arthur Morgan, TVA's first commissioner, to advocate an alternate, less disadvantageous, site. When such efforts failed, 'they turned their efforts to obtaining the most compensation monies possible' (ibid). A final settlement in

1964 provided more funds than in past dam resettlement to the tribal authority – in this case the Seneca Nation. The Nation was also given authority over those portions of the reservoir that had inundated tribal land. This 'included the right to license hunting and fishing by non-Senecas and to regulate access to the shoreline, provided that free public access be provided' (Bilharz, 1998, p72).

Throughout her analysis Bilharz makes it clear how fighting the dam strengthened Seneca leadership within both the Seneca community and within the wider region where Seneca became involved in a range of economic and social issues of importance to them (ibid, p83). Especially important was the impact on women, with Bilharz suggesting that the fight against the dam sped up women's becoming a force in the affairs of the Seneca Nation.

Late-industrializing countries

Outside the industrial countries, what success local institutions and leaders have had influencing the dam-building process has depended even more on their participation in increasingly important coalitions of national and international NGOs and other organizations and individuals. There are earlier exceptions, however, which have occurred under all sorts of governing regimes including colonial governments, democracies, and communist and other one-party states. In the 1950s, the Gwembe Tonga Rural Council under the leadership of E. Habanyama pressured the British colonial government to agree to ten conditions for improving resettlement outcomes. Starting in the 1960s, urban associations of Egyptian Nubians first influenced Aswan High Dam resettlement policies and then obtained the permission of the Egyptian Government to recolonize the shores of Lake Nasser. In the 1970s and 1980s the Igorot people played the key role in stopping the construction of the Chico Dam in the Philippines. Although with little influence on decision-making aside from being consulted on resettlement sites and development opportunities, village and other local institutions have also played an important implementation role in China since the end of the 1980s. There the complexity of the country in size and numbers of people has required the central government to delegate governing authority to local government.

Even where coalitions have played a major role, local institutions have still played a dominant role. Such was the case in 1990 when the Batawana's resistance to Botswana's SOIWDP not only was the largest opposition to government policy since independence in 1966 but played a major role in that project's cancellation. Yet that outcome probably would not have happened without IUCN's detailed review, and rejection, of the project and strong support from local and international NGOs and the safari industry.

Affected people also played the key opposition role to Thailand's Pak Mun Dam and, after construction, the key role in changing how the dam was operated so as to allow partial restoration of interrupted fish migrations. Local resistance stiffened with the approval of the project in 1989 by the Thai Council of Ministers. During the 1990s 'not less than 20 mass protests and demonstrations have been organized by the affected villagers to demand

EGAT and the government to solve the problems that they faced' (Amornsakchai et al, 2000, pp13–14). Throughout that period they received promises that were broken and endured violence at the hand of government forces. Efforts paid off in June 2001 when EGAT agreed to an experimental opening of the dam's sluice gates during the fish migration and spawning season. Continued pressure from affected people combined with the results of preliminary research on the experiment's success led to EGAT agreeing to sluice gate opening on an annual basis (IRN Mekong website, 2002; *Bangkok Post*, 2002). Since then, opposition has continued to build that now champions decommissioning of the dam. Throughout it has not been compensation issues that have generated the most opposition but 'the risk to livelihood and the right to the environment upon which affected people depend for their living' (Amornsakchai et al, 2000, p14).

It is doubtful if the Pak Mun outcome would have happened without strong coalition and other support dating back to the early 1990s. In 1993, for example, fishery biologist Tyson Roberts criticized in a published article the project's expected impact on fish populations – fisheries being the key component of the majority's production system, contrary to the opinions of the government and the World Bank. In 1994 IRN's *World Rivers Review* published an article stating that the project's 'impact on the river's fisheries is already extreme'. Coalition forces against the project increased and strengthened thereafter. Important roles are being played, for example, by Thai universities (one of which studied the impact on fisheries of opening Pak Mun's sluices), by TERRA[13] and its journal *Watershed* (People's Forum on Ecology), and by the US-based International Rivers Network (IRN).

In Central and South America local institutions and leaders are also playing an increasingly important role. In the case of Mexico's Zimapan Dam, completed in 1994, Aronsson (2002) details the negotiation process between the resettling peasants of Ejido Vista Hermosa and the project authority. Advised by the country's national peasant organization, resettlers played the dominant role throughout the planning and implementation process. Although local leadership was strengthened, the outcome was still unsatisfactory in that the negotiation process 'failed to re-establish a functioning production base' (ibid, p244).

McCully (1996, pp293–296) describes the participation of locally affected institutions and people in coalitions concerned with dam construction in Brazil's Uruguay and Amazon River basins. Resistance to parastatal plans to build 22 dams along the Uruguay River dated back to the late 1970s. In 1981 affected people, Catholic Church representatives and leaders of rural workers' unions formed the Comissão Regional de Atingidos por Barragens for 'gathering, explaining to and organizing the people directly and indirectly harmed by constructed or projected dams in the Uruguay River Basin, defending their rights against the companies, authorities or any other bodies which are in any way involved in this matter' (quoted by Bermann, 1999, p1). A major advance achieved after two communities had been resettled by the government parastatal responsible for the Itá Dam was community management of the funds provided for a subsequent resettlement. As of 1999, however, major problems remained. Of '1,100 families registered as beneficiaries of resettlement, only 462 have actually received such benefits' (ibid).

In 1989 the First National Conference of Dam-Affected People was held in Brasilia. It led to the formation of the National Movement of Dam-Affected People (MAB). During the World Commission on Dams' Second Regional Consultation, held in Sao Paulo in August 1999, hundreds of MAB members attended. In representing the interests of dam-affected people throughout Brazil, MAB representative Sadi Baron presented a submission in which MAB 'called on the Brazilian Government to not begun [sic] construction of a single dam until the critical situation facing dam-affected populations is resolved by being repaired or through compensation'. Dams mentioned were Itaparica, Castanhão, Tucurui, Itá, Machadinho, Itaipu, and Ilha Grande. The Consultation in Sao Paulo also provided the opportunity for an indigenous leader to highlight the massacres inflicted on Maya resettlers in connection with Guatemala's Chixoy Project (Chen, 1999).

NON-GOVERNMENTAL ORGANIZATIONS (NGOS)

NGOs have been by far the most important advocates for the rights of dam-affected people since the end of the 1970s. They have also played an important research role. Yet to be realized is their potential for helping local organizations to build institutions that can play a stronger role during options assessment and, should a dam be selected, during the planning and implementation of resettlement with development for both resettlers and hosts.

The NGOs involved cover a wide range of interests. Least directly involved in advocacy is IUCN, which is a union of NGO and government members. Initially concentrating on protection of the world's life support systems, IUCN has evolved to the extent that their world conservation strategy of 1980 broke new ground by linking conservation with poverty alleviation. In the mid-1990s IUCN joined with the World Bank in sponsoring the World Commission on Dams and, unlike the Bank, supported the Commission's Final Report. Neither anti-dam nor pro-dam, IUCN and other natural resource-oriented NGOs such as the Wildlife Conservation Society (WCS) are willing to work with governments and project authorities to improve the environmental and social outcomes of development projects, including dams. IUCN and WCS contracts dealing with Laos' Nam Theun 2 Dam are examples. Other NGOs, such as Oxfam, emphasize poverty alleviation. Where they see injustice, as in the case of India's Sardar Sarovar Dam, they speak out on behalf of affected people.

Most active in support of populations affected by dam construction, however, are NGOs that have become increasingly anti-dam because of the lack of concern or inability of project authorities to deal with the adverse effects of dam construction on the environment and on resettlers and downstream populations. The first were based primarily in Europe, Canada and the US. Since the 1980s, they have been joined by an increasing number of

NGOs in the late-industrializing countries where most dams are currently being built.

In the chapter 'We Will Not Move: The International Anti-Dam Movement', McCully (1996) reviews the history of NGO involvement. His title reflects the anti-dam emphasis that continues to this day. The NGOs involved cover a wide range of interests that include 'environmentalists, human rights and democracy activists, peasants' and indigenous peoples' organizations, fishers and recreationalists' (ibid, p281). Because of their critical role in supporting the rights of affected people to be the first among beneficiaries, I am a supporter of such NGOs to the extent of being a member of the IRN, which I consider to be the most important NGO network dealing with dams, and more specifically, resettlement.

IRN's origins date back to 1985 when hydrologist and civil engineer Phillip Williams played a major role in the publication of the first issue of the *International Dams Newsletter*.[14] In 1987 IRN was set up as an NGO with the newsletter subsequently renamed the *World Rivers Review*, which has a worldwide coverage. In 1988 IRN held a major meeting in San Francisco that I attended and which brought together an international group of participants.

IRN's full-time staff of approximately 20 members, which include McCully as Executive Director, work out of a Berkeley office with good library resources. Several staff members concentrate their activities on particular regions and within those regions on specific river basins and projects. Aviva Imhof, for example, covers the Mekong River Basin. The editor of *World Rivers Review*, Lori Pottinger, has a special interest in Africa. Monti Aguirre and Glenn Switkes cover Latin America.

IRN has been especially effective in encouraging and working with individual NGOs and NGO networks in developing countries in Africa, Asia and Latin America, bringing their concerns to the World Bank and other funding agencies and to the public, and publicizing major NGO network declarations. Starting with IRN's 1988 San Francisco Declaration, declarations include the 1994 Manibeli Declaration, the 1997 Curitiba Declaration, the 2002 Posadas Declaration, and the 2003 Rasi Salai Declaration. Named after one of the first villages inundated by India's SSP, the Manibeli Declaration was drafted by IRN, endorsed by 326 signatories from 44 countries and presented to the World Bank president during the Bank's 50th anniversary celebrations (McCully, 1996, p308 and Appendix 2). It called for a moratorium on World Bank funding for large dams until inequities caused by previous ones had been corrected.

Approved at the First International Meeting of People Affected by Dams, the Curitiba Declaration sought an international moratorium on future construction of all large dams until appropriate reparations and other corrective actions had occurred. Drawing NGO representatives from 20 countries in Africa, Asia and Latin America, it was signed in Curitiba, Brazil, at a meeting organized by MAB with IRN assistance and that of a committee including India's Save the Narmada Movement (NBA), Chile's Biobio Action Group and France's European Rivers Network.

The Posadas Declaration followed the Third Meeting of the Latin American Network against Dams and for Rivers that met in Posadas, Argentina, at the edge of the reservoir behind the Yacyretá Dam. Its 19th resolution was 'to repeat and to disseminate the demand "No more dams in the world" '. Signatories included 50 organizations from nine Latin American Countries plus IRN and Spain's Coalición Ríos Vivos. The 2003 Rasi Salai Declaration was produced during the Second International Meeting of Dam-Affected People and their Allies (28 November to 3 December) in Thailand. The meeting included four days of presentations on a wide range of topics and a field trip to the Pak Mun Dam hosted by the dam-affected community of Rasi Salai. IRN and two Thai NGOs were the organizers with NGOs on the International Agenda Committee coming from Latin and North America; Africa; and East, South and Southeast Asia. Major funding came from a number of countries with funders including Action Aid Asia, the Ford Foundation, Oxfam America, and the Swedish Society for Nature Conservation. The more than 300 people in attendance came from 62 countries. The four-page declaration included sections on achievements, challenges and demands – with demands affirming 'the principles and demands of the Curitiba Declaration of 1997'.

Other major international players include the Bern Declaration (Switzerland-based), The Corner House (UK), Wadebridge Ecological Centre (UK),[15] Probe International (Canada) and Environmental Defense (US). Concentrating on indigenous people issues, including dam resettlement, are the International Working Group for Indigenous Affairs (IWGIA), Survival International (UK) and Cultural Survival (US). Major regional players are MAB in Brazil, NBA in India, the Environmental Monitoring Group (GEM) in South Africa, Sobreviviencia in Argentina and Paraguay, and TERRA in the Mekong River Basin.

I have criticized the 'no large dams' emphasis of IRN and other NGOs elsewhere (Scudder, 1995c). Such a stance I consider to be too fundamentalist. Among other criticisms, it runs the risk of overemphasizing, indeed exaggerating, problem areas while intentionally ignoring benefits. I have observed this tendency in regard to criticisms of both Lesotho's Highlands Water Project and Laos' Nam Theun 2 project. In the Nam Theun 2 case, NGO reports exaggerated the biodiversity importance of the future reservoir basin, much of which was already degraded before project-related logging began. Also ignored is the extreme impoverishment of the local population, due partly to intensive US bombing during the Vietnam War, and the need of the Government of Laos for foreign exchange. Without the project, the people's impoverishment will continue. With the project they have the potential of improving their living standards significantly. As for foreign exchange, far better for that to be provided by the export of hydropower than of timber from what are Southeast Asia's best remaining forests.

NGO criticisms also ignore the fact that future large dams are going to be built in Laos as well as elsewhere in Asia, the Middle East, Africa and Latin America in spite of the anti-dam movement. A Korean company built the Houay

Ho Dam during the 1990s in southern Laos and currently the Chinese and the Vietnamese are involved in other dam projects in Laos. Both Houay Ho and the Chinese project have environmental and social problems. The same can be expected if Nam Theun 2 is built without World Bank involvement. It would be far better if the Bank were involved because if current environmental and resettlement plans, which are state of the art, are implemented, they can show the way forward for dealing with environmental and social issues in other late-industrializing countries.

LHWP is another example where dams have been planned to provide a major source of foreign exchange. LHWP's major purpose is to supply water to the urban industrial hub of drought-prone South Africa, the development and stability of which is essential for the development and stability of Southern and Central Africa. National benefits for Lesotho are revenue from water sales, which is intended to be used for national development purposes, and self-sufficiency in electricity from hydropower generated by the 'Muela Dam as water is transferred to South Africa.

I also consider the anti-dams movement's emphasis on 'no further dams until past injustices have been addressed' as unrealistic given the number of existing dams involved and the crisis-based need for new dams in the future. On the other hand, I believe that an anti-dam approach is necessary to alert pro-dam governments, institutions and individuals to the risks that continuing neglect of environmental, economic and affected people issues present to the ongoing and future financing and construction of large dams. It is not that too much emphasis has been placed on stopping bad dams or improving entitlements when dams are built. On the contrary, those activities are crucial. But I do believe that the anti-dam focus has resulted in underemphasizing the importance that some dams could play in national efforts to alleviate poverty. I also see an opportunity being lost for local institution building and working with resettling communities to achieve better outcomes once dam construction is underway. In other contexts, institution-building NGOs such as Oxfam have a proven record around the world in facilitating local development efforts. There is much room, and need, for anti-dam NGOs to undertake similar efforts.

While the anti-dam NGOs are closely attuned to the problems of indigenous people, I believe that they are less aware of the desperate situation of the much larger majority of other poor rural and urban peoples. One example of such lack of awareness involves the Hidrovia Navigation Project being planned for the Paraguay-Parana river system that involves five South American countries. While NGO critics of that project correctly targeted its adverse environmental impacts and impacts on indigenous people, adverse impacts on tens of thousands of poor rural farmers were ignored until pointed out by Clemens and myself (EDF-CEBRAC, 1997).

Another example relates to Lesotho's Highlands Water Project where John Gay and I believed that Environmental Defense and IRN critiques of the Katse Dam ignored its importance for South Africa. In a 1995 e-mail to those NGOs, Gay summed up our concerns as follows: 'Ted and I see water as one of the keys to success of the great South African experiment, and we see the LHDA as a critical element in that success... (I)t does not help to take what I call the "little Lesotho" position, in which all that matters is the situation in the mountains of Lesotho. There is an old tradition in Lesotho which looks inward rather than outward, a tradition which tries to ignore the economic and political realities of the larger southern African region. I fear that some of the advice that you are getting relates to the "little Lesotho" tradition. It certainly does not represent a national consensus.'

Another weakness is criticism of, or efforts to manipulate, other NGOs that may favour specific dams or be willing to work with specific project authorities. One example is IRN's criticism of support by WCS's Director for Asia of World Bank involvement in Laos' Nam Theun 2 Project as a means for protecting the biodiversity of the catchment area (*World Rivers Review*, April 1996, pp6–7). Within India's Narmada Basin, criticism by NBA of ARCH-Vahini's willingness to join a committee seeking land for Gujarat resettlers is another. Still more unfortunate was the vehemence with which ARCH-Vahini responded to NBA, because that may have made irreparable the split between two NGOs with shared interests in resettler welfare. Whether or not ARCH-Vahini's subsequent split with Gujarat project authorities because of their non-compliance with promises made to ARCH-Vahini will lead to a rapprochement remains to be seen.

THE WORLD BANK GROUP AND OTHER DONORS

Introduction

It is appropriate to concentrate on the World Bank in this section for a number of reasons. Four are especially important, the first two of which are only briefly dealt with. These two are the Bank's importance as the world's number one development institution and the Bank's influence on other donors and importance to borrowers. The third and fourth reasons relate more specifically to dams. On the one hand, the Bank has been the largest donor financing large dams; on the other hand, it has pioneered or contributed to important, but still inadequate, approaches to make Bank staff and borrowers more responsive to resettlement and environmental needs.

In recent years, the Bank has begun to falter as the lead donor dealing with large dam issues. The International Finance Corporation (IFC), the private sector member of the World Bank Group, arguably has become a more active force with its appointment of Meg Taylor as Compliance Adviser/Ombudsman for both the IFC and the Bank Group's Multilateral Investment Guarantee Agency (MIGA), and IFC's role in working with international banks and financial services firms in drafting their own social and environmental guidelines and in staff training.

The various regional banks also continue to play an active role as financiers of large dams. Indeed, when the World Bank cut back its large dam funding activities, the Asian Development Bank may have become the most active multilateral agency dealing with large dams. In the process, it has been recruiting new resettlement expertise at a time when the Bank's expertise has been weakened through resignations and retirements. Elsewhere, the Africa Development Bank has been considering providing finance for the construction of Mali's Talo Dam, while the Inter-American Development Bank has played an active role in Latin America, including as a major financier for Costa Rica's Arenal Dam.

Other multilateral agencies are also important players. UNEP is currently hosting the Dams and Development Project as a follow-on activity to the World Commission on Dams, while UNDP and FAO were the key agencies implementing an important series of studies on the major African man-made lakes, including those backed up behind the Akosombo, Aswan High, Kainji, Kariba and Kossou Dams. FAO's David Butcher also produced in 1976 the first manual dealing with resettlement issues. WHO was the key agency implementing the ambitious onchocerciasis control programme in West Africa and has also carried out important research on dam-induced changes in human health.

Among governments' bilateral donors, currently the most active are the Canadian International Development Agency (CIDA) and the Scandinavian aid agencies, in particular Norway's (NORAD) and Sweden's (SIDA). CIDA has been especially active in funding feasibility studies on specific dams. In the mid-1980s, CIDA funded a major feasibility study of China's Three Gorges Project by a consortium of Canadian firms that included Acres International, British Columbia Hydro, Hydro-Quebec and SNC-Lavalin. More recently, CIDA has funded environmental and feasibility studies for Belize's Chalillo Dam as well as a study dealing with the mainstream development of the Mekong River.

Apart from CIDA and the Scandinavian agencies, dam-related funding from other government aid agencies has been relatively minor; one example being funding for a study of development-induced displacement by Britain's Department for International Development (DFID). During the 1980s the US Agency for International Development funded Vimaladharma's and my series of surveys of the settlement component of the Accelerated Mahaweli Project. In addition to more active financing of environmental and feasibility studies, NORAD and SIDA have also funded evaluations, the IUCN SOIWDP Review being a major example.

The World Bank

Introduction
The key player in the funding of large dams, the World Bank, has on the one hand played a pioneering role in developing environmental and social guidelines, while on the other hand, the Bank's involvement has been part of the problem. This conflicting role, especially in regard to the resettlement issues on which I concentrate my analysis, makes such analysis difficult. Without

doubt, the Bank deserves credit. This is presented in the section 'Pioneering aspects of the World Bank's reactions to resettlement issues'. In many cases, however, the Bank's activities have failed to achieve satisfactory outcomes. Reasons for this are discussed in the section 'Weaknesses in the Bank's approach to resettlement issues'.

The Bank deserves credit for its pioneering activities. These require borrowers to recruit panels of experts to provide advice on environmental and resettlement issues relating to the Bank's more controversial large projects. The Bank has also established its own Inspection Panel to provide affected peoples a means for bringing planning and implementation problems to the Bank's attention. Other pioneering activities include the creation of the first resettlement guidelines, which have subsequently been followed by other donors as well as individual nations. More recently, although not as pioneer, the Bank has begun funding resettlement as a separate component of a dam project. It is also revisiting a few projects in an effort to correct past resettlement inequities.

Important as these initiatives are, the Bank admits that they have not produced satisfactory resettlement outcomes. As with studies in the early 1990s by the Bank's Operation Evaluations Department, the Environment Department's 1994 *Resettlement and Development* concluded 'that projects have too often not succeeded in reestablishing resettlers at a better or equal living standards and that unsatisfactory performance still persists on a wide scale' (1994a, p4/7), and more damning, 'existing evidence points to unsatisfactory income restoration more frequently than to satisfactory outcomes' (ibid, p4/2). After examining ten dam projects with a major resettlement component, the Bank's *Involuntary Resettlement: Comparative Perspectives* stated that 'The World Bank acknowledges that the record on restoring – let alone improving – incomes has been unsatisfactory... Other recent Bank reports ... concede that successful interventions are in the minority' (Picciotto et al, 2001, p9).

My analysis of why this unsatisfactory record has occurred differs markedly from the Bank's. It is based on my World Bank consultancies since the mid-1960s and on my non-Bank-financed research and consulting on such Bank-funded projects as Kariba, Akosombo, Kainji, and Mahaweli. For several years in the mid-1960s I participated, as the Bank's first consultant social anthropologist, in a very detailed, five-person study led by Bank economist John C. de Wilde of the experiences of small-scale farmers with agricultural development in tropical Africa (de Wilde, 1967).

In 1977 Michael Cernea asked me to prepare a paper on government-sponsored settlement schemes for an in-house training workshop in a sociology lecture series that he had organized to familiarize Bank staff with the contributions that social scientists other than economists could make to development planning.[16] Having completed insufficient research on such schemes at that time, I suggested that I talk instead on impacts of Bank-funded projects on involuntarily resettled people, a topic on which I had already published. That was agreed, with my talk on 25 May advertised within the

Bank as a presentation 'focusing on the sociological problems involved in resettling displaced people'. Titled 'Some Policy Implications of Compulsory Relocation in Connection with River Basin Development and Other Projects Impacting Upon Low Income Populations', my paper's content included the Bank's Kariba, Akosombo and Kainji projects in Africa and Sobradinho in Brazil.

Based on additional documents provided by the Bank, including some on Nepal's Kulekhani Hydroelectric Project, Brazil's Paulo Afonso IV and Ghana's Kpong, I submitted a further set of comments on 31 May. Together I believe that these two papers were the first to alert Bank staff to the extent that Bank-financed projects involving involuntary relocation were having an adverse impact on a majority of those resettled. In fairness to the Bank, planning for resettlement had been slowly improving during the mid-1970s for a few projects. In regard to Kpong, the Bank actually had in hand a resettlement plan during appraisal of the project. With construction to start within a few months, however, there was insufficient time for any necessary revisions; hence my May 1977 conclusion in full capital letters that 'There is no substitute for appraisal of resettlement needs by experts during the feasibility studies', a requirement that I was pleased to see included when the Bank's first resettlement guidelines were published in 1980. That was one favourable impact of the May 1977 discussions. Recruitment of more social scientists to deal with resettlement issues was another. The most important was Cernea's decision to make involuntary resettlement a priority issue.

Thanks to Cernea's influence, I was the Bank's principal resettlement consultant in connection with India's SSP during the 1980s as well as resettlement adviser to the Canadian-funded CIPM Yangtze Joint Venture feasibility study for the Three Gorges Project (CIPM, 1988). Through the Institute for Development Anthropology I also directed, with the assistance of research assistant Sethu Palaniappan and World Bank Task Manager Gottfried Ablasser, a desk study of 34 Bank-financed government-sponsored land settlement projects (World Bank, 1985a). Additional experience with Bank projects followed from my membership on LHDA's environment and social panel between 1989 and 2002 and my current membership on a similar panel for Laos' Nam Theun 2 project since 1997.

I remain convinced that there is a major need for an international bank for reconstruction and development. Despite structural and policy weaknesses,[17] the World Bank has played an important role in facilitating improved living standards in middle-income countries. While its record is more open to criticism in less developed countries such as Zambia, there, as elsewhere, Bank assistance for education has been important as is more recent health-related assistance throughout tropical Africa.

World Bank funding for large dams

The majority of large dams, as in major dam-building countries such as China, India, Japan, Russia and the US, have been financed with domestic funds. During the early 1990s the Bank estimated that it provided funding for only

2 per cent of large dams constructed during the early 1990s versus approximately 6 per cent in the first half of the 1980s (World Bank, 1994a, p2/10). Bank-funded dams, however, tended to be some of the largest being built in Latin America, Africa and Asia. Funding for Kariba toward the end of the 1950s provided the largest loan that the Bank had given in Africa up to that date. The Bank also provided funding for Ghana's Akosombo Dam and Nigeria's Kainji Dam, and would have supplied funds for the Aswan High Dam if US influence and other political events had not intervened. Such projects involved far more people requiring resettlement than the majority of other large dams, ranging from over 80,000 at Akosombo to over 40,000 in connection with Kainji.

Pioneering aspects of the World Bank's reactions to resettlement issues

Resettlement guidelines

Although critics tend to view the World Bank as a monolithic organization, such a view fails to recognize the important role that individual Bank officials have played in pushing new initiatives. Deserving special mention in connection with large dams are two recent advisers to the Bank's Environment Department. Now retired, they are Michael Cernea and Robert Goodland, with Cernea taking the initiative throughout the 1980s and the 1990s to draft and update, with the help of other social science colleagues in the Bank, the first donor resettlement guidelines.

Gradually strengthened during the 1980s and in 1990, these guidelines emphasized for the first time that resettlement must be a project cost, that it should be minimized to the extent possible, that a plan acceptable to the Bank must be submitted during appraisal, and – especially emphasized in the 1990 update – that resettlement projects must be development projects. During the 1990s those guidelines also served as models for the regional banks and for the OECD countries as well as for China and other countries.

Panels of experts

To complement earlier dam safety panels, in the late 1980s the World Bank began to require borrowers to appoint advisory panels dealing with environmental and social issues. To date the majority of such panels have been formed in connection with large dam projects. Still in existence, the panel for Lesotho's Highlands Development Authority began in 1989, while that for Laos' Nam Theun 2 project dates back to 1997. Other panels were associated with Yacyretá in Brazil–Paraguay and with Ertan and Xiaolangdi in China. As with the Bank's resettlement guidelines, other donors, countries and project authorities have followed the Bank's example with panels of experts. Among the regional banks, the Asian Development Bank required the formation of the Kali Gandaki panel in Nepal, whereas the Komati Basin Authority authorized such a panel to advise the Government of Swaziland's Maguga Project. In Uganda, the panel reported to the private sector firm AES, until its withdrawal from the project, rather than to the government.

As a World Bank requirement, the Bank usually provides funding to a government parastatal or ministry for costs associated with each panel. Hiring and firing of individual panel members must be approved by the Bank. Should the borrower so wish, the Bank will suggest names of experts with relevant natural science, public health and resettlement expertise. Panel members can investigate all issues that they consider important that are additional to terms of reference from the panel's employer. Once comments have been received and dealt with, panel reports are supposed to become public documents.

The inspection panel
The Inspection Panel was created in 1993 on request by the World Bank's board of executive directors to which it reports. It describes itself on its website as 'the first body of its kind to give voice to private citizens in an international context' and as a three-member body 'to provide an independent forum to private citizens who believe that they or their interests have been or could be directly harmed by a project financed by the World Bank' (www.inspection panel.org). Instructions for making submissions are included on the website. Submissions received are forwarded to the Bank's management for comments that the Panel then evaluates. If the Panel concludes that the submission has merit, it recommends to the Board that the claims of the affected people be investigated. On approval by the Board, a similar review process is followed on receipt of the Panel's report after which 'the Board takes the final decision on what should be done' (ibid).[18]

Between 1994, when operations began, and July 2002, 25 submissions were received.[19] Of the eight that involved dam projects, the Board recommended that four be investigated. One involved Nepal's Arun III Hydroelectric Project that the Bank subsequently cancelled. Another case was Uganda's Bujagali where the Inspection Panel's 2001 investigation found violations of Bank policies. The third and fourth involved Yacyretá. In the third case Sobreviviencia and other NGOs made a submission in 1997, with Sobreviviencia claiming that the investigation 'marked the beginning of increased participation and actions of the affected communities to claim their rights' (Peña, 1999, p2). Inadequate response, however, on the part of the project authority led to another submission in May 2002. That was approved by the Bank's Board with the February 2004 report of the Inspection Panel also finding the project authority to be out of compliance with Bank policies. In a World Bank press release on 7 May 2004, the Inspection Panel's chair was quoted as having told the Board that 'it is essential for affected people to have an impartial forum for their concerns'. Providing such a forum would be an important, and necessary, task for the International Adjudication and Compliance Board that I have recommended.

Bank-funded resettlement project components of dam projects
In the 1980s the World Bank began to consider the possibility of financing resettlement implementation, responsibility for which, including funding, had previously been considered a borrower obligation.[20] While a number of candidates were suggested, including India's SSP, the Bank financed only one 'free-standing involuntary resettlement project' during the 1980s. That was

Brazil's Itaparica Resettlement and Irrigation Project, which was appraised in 1987.

Neither SSP nor Itaparica were good candidates for pioneering a long-overdue approach to improving resettlement. In the SSP case, not proceeding was fortunate since none of the project authorities had the political will to deal with resettlement issues. As for Itaparica, the dam was not a World Bank project so that the Bank was 'unable to influence critical project design features, including the choice of rural resettlement areas and the choice of irrigated agricultural development systems' (World Bank, 1989). Longstanding problems have continued as reflected in an affected people's submission to the Inspection Panel in 1997.

Fortunately the problems with Itaparica have not kept the Bank from further experimentation. By far the largest example, indeed the only major one in the 1990s, has been a Bank loan of over US$100 million to finance about 10 per cent of the resettlement component associated with China's multibillion-dollar Xiaolangdi project on the Yellow River. More recently, the Bank has provided a small loan to the Government of Laos that anticipates additional funding for environmental and social purposes.

Revisiting resettlement associated with previous Bank-funded projects

The ability of affected people as individuals or as groups to win court cases against governments to increase cash compensation payments dates back at least to the 1940s in the US. Using the courts to increase payments to individual households has also been successfully pursued since independence in India. Starting in the late 1980s, China may have been the first country to establish 'remaining problems funds' for helping poorly resettled households and communities improve their living standards decades after their removal. I first became aware of such a fund's effectiveness during a visit to the Danjiangkou Dam and Reservoir in the mid-1980s. There, revenue from hydropower generation was placed in a revolving fund that was being effectively used to provide credit for a range of household and community development initiatives.

The 1994 Manibeli Declaration sought a moratorium on World Bank funding for dams until various conditions had been met. One included 'a fund to provide reparations to the people forcibly evicted from their homes and lands by Bank-funded large dams without adequate compensation and rehabilitation'. Probably not a total coincidence, approval in December 1995 of a World Bank loan for Pakistan's Ghazi Barotha Dam 'was made conditional on a process for the resolution of disputes over compensation for people displaced 20 years before by the Tarbela Dam' (WCD, 2000, p128). I do not know if the Bank provided partial funds for that purpose, but such funds were provided for the Gwembe Tonga Rehabilitation and Development Program, which was inaugurated in December 1998 as part of the Bank-funded Zambia Power Rehabilitation Project. Arising from a 1995 report of mine, and also involving South Africa's Development Bank of Southern Africa, that programme includes road construction; water resource development; and rain-fed, reservoir drawdown and irrigation agriculture as well as other components. Although a similar project has been suggested for the Bank-funded Chixoy Dam in Guatemala,[21] the extent to which the Bank will involve itself in such projects remains to be seen.

Weaknesses in the Bank's approach to resettlement issues

Structural and policy issues

There is a range of structural and policy issues that undermine the Bank's ability to deal seriously with resettlement issues. They include pressure on staff to move funds, which favours larger projects over smaller ones and interferes with the time-consuming involvement of local people in options assessment and planning. Local involvement is also hindered by the continued difficulty of getting Bank reports, although in that regard the Bank has become more transparent than most project authorities.

Another generic reason is the Bank's relatively weak project supervision as well as infrequent evaluations of outcomes five to ten years after the end of each project cycle. And because the resettlement process continues after the end of Bank involvement in the large majority of its projects, the shortness (seldom over five years) of the Bank's project cycle is a constraint to ongoing monitoring and evaluation. It may also lead to erroneous conclusions about success, as happened in the Kariba and Pak Mun cases.

In a recent exhortation to the Bank to get its act together, Wade's criticism of what he refers to as matrix management is especially appropriate to staff dealing with social and environmental issues. The World Bank has six regional vice presidents each of whom oversees a number of country departments, 'the director of which has control of virtually all the budget for the Bank's work in that country or cluster of countries' (Wade, 2001, p14). The operational staff, however, on which each such director is dependent are largely in sector departments 'which have little budget of their own'. For that reason sector staff have 'to negotiate with the country director on the terms on which they will take responsibility for preparing a project in the director's country. In this way the country director is able to give the staff who work on projects for his or her country a quiet indication of how much to comply with which operational directives' (ibid), including, of course, those on resettlement, indigenous people and the environment. While environmental staff might seem to have more independence because they have to sign off on each project, they are constrained by the fact that they are expected to 'sell 42 weeks of their time to project officers, to help in the design of projects' (ibid). As Wade notes this arrangement can be expected to affect their work since those perceived as too critical would find it more difficult to sell their services.

Does the Bank care?

I am unable to provide a positive answer to this question. Without doubt there are individuals in the Bank, and especially in the Environment and Social Groups, who care deeply about resettlement with development. There are also project task managers who take seriously implementation of the Bank's guidelines. Two that I have worked closely with on LHWP are John Roome and Andrew Macoun. Another whose concern I respect is Robert Mertz in regard to Laos' Nam Theun 2 Project. I suspect, however, that they are in the minority, with the majority of task managers as well as country directors seeing resettlement as well as environment issues as slowing up the funding for an already too slow project cycle.

Although many of the Bank's operational directives relate to dams, efforts to compress and simplify them in a dam-specific policy directive have never succeeded. The same applies to an overall policy directive relating to social assessment as opposed to individual topics such as resettlement and indigenous people. And in those cases, I believe that the attention paid by the Bank is more a reactive response to NGO and other criticism than a proactive response based on realization of the adverse effect of the large majority of Bank-financed dams on project-affected people.

The Bank's resettlement guidelines[22]

There is no doubt that the Bank's resettlement guidelines have had a major impact on minimizing the number requiring resettlement. They have also improved planning and implementation to the extent that the majority of resettlers are made less poor than would have otherwise been the case. But, as the Bank is the first to admit, in the majority of cases their income-earning capacity and living standards have not been restored.

It is unacceptable for resettlers, who are a dam project's main risk-takers and who are predominately poor people (including a disproportionate percentage of indigenous people), not to become beneficiaries of projects funded by an institution that claims poverty alleviation as its main goal. It becomes even more unacceptable when one realizes that large Bank-financed dams are often the largest single development project in a borrower's portfolio.

While there is no question about resettlement being an incredibly complicated activity, I believe that a major reason why the Bank's record continues to be unsatisfactory is that from their very beginning the guidelines have been part of the problem. As ICOLD recognized in 1997, resettlers must become project beneficiaries (1995, p11). That requires resettlement with development as emphasized in the Final Report of the World Commission on Dams. While the World Bank's guidelines also state on the first page that resettlement projects should be development projects, that statement is immediately undercut by providing borrowers with the fallback option of merely restoring living standards.

Take, for example, the Bank's revised 1990 guidelines, which remain the strongest that the Bank has produced. The content of the initial paragraphs is excellent. Noting 'the severe long-term hardship, impoverishment, and environmental damage' that may occur 'unless appropriate measures are carefully planned and carried out', the guidelines then state that 'Involuntary resettlement should be avoided or minimized where feasible.' They go on to state that 'where displacement is unavoidable … all involuntary resettlement should be conceived and executed as <u>development programs</u>, with resettlers provided sufficient investment resources and opportunities to <u>share in project benefits</u>' (the Bank's underlining). Then, however, that outstanding introduction is undercut by providing borrowers with the fallback option of merely restoring living standards.

Global research on dam displacement has shown that the 'living standards restoration' option is almost guaranteed to leave a majority of the resettlers worse off. Yet, because it is less expensive in the short run, it is the option that project authorities have tended to take. That, in my opinion, is the major reason why the Bank's guidelines have played an impoverishing role in the past and why the Bank's recently weakened guidelines will continue to play such a role in the future. Such a conclusion is not a recent one. In 1979 Cernea asked me to comment on an early draft of the original 1980 guidelines in which stated Bank policy was 'to ensure that the displaced will regain at least their previous income levels after a transition period' (World Bank, 1979, p1). In my reply of 17 May 1979, I wrote '... the planned benefits should be higher than their previous standard of living...; hence I consider this policy statement to be inadequate.' It was inadequate then and the guidelines are still inadequate today.

Dealing with different parts of the resettlement process, in what follows I analyse five reasons as to why the Bank's guidelines cause impoverishment. The first three relate to Stage 1 (Planning). One relates to the nature of the lengthy planning process, a 10–20 year planning horizon not being exceptional. During this period, living standards for the majority can be expected to drop for a number of reasons. Governments, private sector entrepreneurs, NGOs and project-affected people themselves are much less likely to make investments within a future reservoir basin. Hence, by the time a decision is made to proceed with major feasibility studies, including 'base-line studies' to determine pre-project living standards of future resettlers, those people's living standards will already be lower than those of neighbours living outside the project area.

Once people realize that relocation may be forthcoming, housing improvements are less likely to be made and local innovators and entrepreneurs are less likely to invest in new enterprises. In the case of the Swaziland–South African Maguga Dam, local people who wanted to start cattle cooperatives and other business ventures over ten years before the commencement of construction were told by the authorities not to proceed. When removal is imminent, labour migrants often return home to help their families, with those families losing access to remittances. Because of uncertainty over removal dates, people may also be less likely to harvest good crops, having planted a smaller area or being told by the authorities not to plant at all because removal, subsequently delayed, was imminent.

A second reason relates to what the World Bank refers to as pre-project 'base-line studies'. Current guidelines are based on the inaccurate assumption that such studies accurately reflect pre-project income and living standards and hence constitute a basis against which restoration can be measured. Yet even where pre-resettlement surveys are undertaken – and adequate ones are rare – there is a general tendency to underestimate people's incomes at that time so that restoration targets remain too low. Reasons include forgetfulness on the part of those providing data (especially common in regard to assessment by the household head of contributions from other family members), failure to give value to the utilization of soon-to-be-lost common property natural resources for food and other purposes, fear of being taxed and the unflattering or illegal nature of some income-generating activities.

The World Bank's own evaluations refer to the inadequacy of such studies as a base-line against which to measure subsequent restoration. Thailand's Pak Mun Dam is a good example. In this case, 'There is no true baseline study, only preliminary surveys in 1982 and 1983' (World Bank, 1998c, p19). Furthermore, the Pak Mun preliminary surveys considered only income, and that incompletely since income from the most important activity, fishing, was excluded; in addition, they dealt only with households requiring physical removal. Completed seven to eight years before construction began, results were considered so inadequate that a second survey was carried out. Although considered a base-line study by the project authorities, that survey was actually done four months after the dam had been completed and resettlers had moved into their new houses. While it dealt with activities over the previous 12 months, including eight months before reservoir inundation, surveys undertaken during the year of removal cannot be expected to provide a reliable record. Moreover, 'the base-line data on fishing income was inadequate' (ibid, p6).

A third reason why the Bank's guidelines are part of the problem is that project authorities following the 'restorations option' tend to emphasize compensation, as happened in Lesotho's Highlands Water Project and India's Sardar Sarovar, as opposed to providing the sort of development opportunities that are necessary even to restore living standards, let alone improve them. As stated in Chapter 4, the Bank's latest guidelines place disproportionate emphasis on compensation, mentioned 19 times, whereas development is mentioned only four times.

A fourth reason becomes salient immediately following removal, when adjusting to new habitats, hosts and government programmes during Stage 2 reduces time and energy for restoring living standards. During this period, which can be expected to last at least two years, as illustrated by the 50 dam survey in Chapter 3, living standards for the majority can be expected to drop. Policies based on restoration do not take into consideration the extent to which living standards have been adversely affected during those years. Nor do they consider situations where living standards have been rising outside the project area because of non-project-related national development activities. In these situations the living standards of resettlers have worsened in comparison with neighbours unaffected by the project.

Also post removal, a fifth reason relates to the majority of cases where farmland and access to common property resources are lost or reduced. Following removal, household expenses are often greater than before.

Increased costs are especially a problem for resettlers who have to purchase food supplies that previously they were able to produce, or where less fertile soils require the purchase of inputs such as improved seed and fertilizers, or where new production techniques require loans that lead to indebtedness. Another reason why loss of arable land to a project tends to leave households worse off is that such land, unlike cash compensation and jobs, is a resource that usually is inherited from one generation to the next.

The Bank's 2001 guidelines cover only direct economic and social impacts. That is another major weakness. Excluded are a wide range of negative cultural effects reported in study after study that relate to loss of home, burial grounds, religious sites, and ideological and political control over a familiar habitat. Nor do they cover the public health implications of such psychological impacts as 'grieving for a lost home' and 'anxiety for the future', which are especially serious for indigenous people and for many ethnic minorities and peasant communities with strong ties to the land and limited mobility. As Cernea has emphasized, there is no way that the Bank's use of cost–benefit analysis can accurately reflect the hardships involved.[23] Resettlement must be planned and implemented as a development project to offset such costs by helping resettlers become project beneficiaries.

Other prominent resettlement researchers have also concluded that policies that find restoration satisfactory are no longer adequate. Among others they include Martin ter Woort and Theodore Downing. Ter Woort is the leading economist dealing with resettlement issues. His activities include working with host-country and other colleagues to prepare national resettlement policies for Laos, Sri Lanka, Uganda and Vietnam.

Anthropologist Downing's assessment of the revised and weakened World Bank 2001 guidelines is especially damning. After acknowledging impoverishment risks associated with resettlement, the Bank policy fails 'to propose measures to address them. Instead, it falls back on the same flawed economic analysis and methodologies that have been responsible for decades of unacceptable performance.' Emphasizing compensation as opposed to the necessary development, 'the revisions sidestep the need for viable rehabilitation'. Furthermore, the distinction between direct and indirect costs 'leads to an understatement of total project costs' and 'excludes the critical costs of reintegrating and restarting disrupted economies, social institutions and educational systems' (Downing, 2002a, pp13–14).

Downing also believes the 2001 policy 'institutionalizes a negotiating system that potentially violates human rights'. Why, for example, does it not address resettlers' 'lack of information and legal representation' that 'has consistently undermined the capacity of project-affected people to understand and negotiate for their economic reconstruction'? And why does the policy 'permit the Bank to underwrite the borrower's cost of negotiating with the displaced, but not vice versa'? (ibid).

Even within the Bank, individual officials had begun to emphasize the need to move beyond the 'restoration option'. Robert Goodland was perhaps the first to emphasize that position. More recently he stated that 'Making oustees

"no worse off" at some, often long, time after their move is impoverishment...
In my opinion, oustees must be made immediately and clearly better off after
their move' (2000, pp9–10).[24] In the Bank's Operations Evaluation
Department's (OED) 1998 review of dam-induced resettlement, the authors
stated that 'The emphasis should shift from restoring income levels, which
suggest stagnation at pre-dam lifestyles, to improving income levels, which
brings the displacees into the development process along with the project's
primary beneficiaries' (World Bank, 1998a, p7). An updated version published
by the Bank as a book in 2001 was even more emphatic: 'Above all, displacees
must be beneficiaries of the project. Merely aiming to restore standards of living
and lifestyles common to isolated river valleys can be a dead-end development
strategy. The opportunity must be taken to establish new and dynamic sources
of sustainable growth' (Picciotto et al, 2001, p140). In 1999 in the Bank's *The
Economics of Involuntary Resettlement: Questions and Challenges*, published
after his retirement, Cernea emphasized that 'The primary goal of any
involuntary resettlement process is to prevent impoverishment and to improve
the livelihood of resettlers' (Cernea 1999, p6).

Given such opinions of weaknesses, including those of senior staff within
the Bank, why is it that the Bank's resettlement guidelines continue to accept
the 'restoration option'? The question is the more perplexing given the Bank's
emphasis on 'A World Free of Poverty'. Resettlement experts within the World
Bank's Social Development Department explain this paradox in terms of strong
resistance within the World Bank and from Bank members to revising the
guidelines to require improvement. In commenting on the OED belief that
'there is strong case for strengthening' the guidelines (World Bank, 1998a,
p10), the Bank management response to the recommendation 'to change the
policy benchmark from restoration of incomes of affected people to
improvement' was that 'Bank policies already establish high standards for
dealing with involuntary resettlement' and 'Management sees the
implementation of existing policy as the key priority' (ibid, p16).

Two other reasons are also mentioned for not altering the 'restoration'
stance. One is that in shifting from the Bank's Operational Directives to the
new Operational Policies/Bank Procedures format, those involved are
instructed to convert previous documents to a new format but not to revise
them. This argument is not convincing, at least with the resettlement
guidelines, since in fact they have been revised to include a wider range of
resettlement situations and to weaken previous policies.

The second reason relates to the wider range of resettlement situations that
the guidelines now cover, including removal of people from new biosphere and
other reserves and from national parks, or restriction of access to such reserves
and parks. A result of including people involuntarily resettled under the widest
possible range of circumstances, as opposed to emphasizing resettlement in
connection with urban development, mining and dams, which involves the
large majority of people, is to end up with a 'least common denominator' set
of guidelines. If mere restoration is acceptable in some such cases, and I do not
accept that it is, then a single uniform policy for all types of involuntary

resettlement is no longer acceptable. At a time when WCD had the responsibility to develop guidelines and criteria, it was inappropriate for the Bank to pre-empt the WCD process by not only drafting new guidelines for one of the most controversial issues relating to dams, but also to draft guidelines which allow the replication of poverty.

The main argument, however, by opponents within the Bank against shifting from restoration to improvement relates to the failure of the existing guidelines to even achieve their goal of restoration. Why revise goals upward to require improvement, they argue, when 'The Bank has acknowledged that the record on restoring – let alone improving – incomes has been unsatisfactory' (ibid, p2).

I reject that argument for two major reasons. The first is that the emphasis throughout on compensation and restoration as opposed to development is a major reason for the failure of the Bank's guidelines to restore income and living standards. Because of that emphasis, potential development opportunities are not being sought during the planning process. Indeed, as the 1998 OED study notes, 'the weakest part of planning is on economic rehabilitation' (ibid, p6). No wonder the Bank's guidelines fail to achieve results since development planning and implementation is necessary even for income and living standard restoration.

The second reason that I reject the argument that failure to restore in itself is reason enough not to seek the goal of improvement is that, according to the Bank's own studies, the most successful cases of dam-induced resettlement are those where the policy of the implementing agency or the national government is to improve living standards. One such case recently analysed by the Bank is China's Shuikou Project (Picciotto et al, 2001, pp41–53).

The failure of the World Bank's current guidelines to recognize the further impoverishing impacts of mere restoration not only causes those guidelines to be inadequate, but also encourages borrower countries to emulate them. That is the case even in countries with improved national policies for resettlement. China is a case in point. According to Article 3 of 'Land Acquisition and Resettlement Regulation for the Construction of Large and Medium-Sized Water Conservancy Projects' of 25 January 1991, 'the Government advocates and supports resettlement with development.' Yet the next article follows the World Bank's guidelines when it states that 'all resettlers shall be assisted to improve or at least restore their former living standard in steps.' In the case of Lesotho's Highlands Water Project, the binational policy-making commission has continued to reject development initiatives necessary even for living standard restoration by claiming that they go beyond the Bank's restoration requirement.

Panels of Experts and the Inspection Panel

Panels of Environment and Social Experts have two major weaknesses. The first relates to their terms of reference and the second to the way in which the World Bank handles projects involving large dams. According to their terms of reference, such panels have only advisory functions. What clout they have is restricted to their ability to convince project authorities to take recommended courses of action or to influence Bank supervisory missions to insist on the implementation of those recommendations.

The second weakness relates to the reduced clout that the World Bank has once its loans are disbursed. To date those loans have been almost entirely for activities during the project's construction phase – funding for infrastructure in particular. But resettlement activities, and especially those that will determine resettler living standards, continue well beyond the completion of dam construction. By then Bank loans have been disbursed and Bank ability to influence project authority actions is reduced. A case in point relates to the Panel of Experts for LHWP. Having served on that Panel since 1989, I resigned in April 2002 after the completion of the final dam. Although recruitment of a replacement to deal with resettlement issues was a World Bank requirement, it took over 18 months for a replacement to be named in spite of Bank support for several excellent, and available, candidates.

More Bank funding for environment and resettlement that extends beyond the end of the construction phase would be a partial solution. What is really needed, however, is to give the Panel of Experts more authority, coupled with the necessary safeguards against abuse of that authority, to ensure that recommendations are implemented. Such authority has been built into the Concession Agreement that has been drafted for Laos' Nam Theun 2 Project. In that project the Panel is supposed to have the responsibility for deciding when plans intended to improve resettler living standards have been adequately implemented.

The major weakness of the Inspection Panel is easy to identify. It is the disinclination of the Bank's Board of Directors, and perhaps the Bank's senior management, to give it more authority in selecting cases to investigate and more authority to ensure that recommendations for cases undertaken are implemented.

Bank-funded resettlement components and revisited projects
The main weakness of Bank-funded resettlement components and revisited projects is that there are so few. Their lack is perhaps the major reason why I have asked the question, 'Does the Bank care?' On the one hand, the Bank has produced report after report on resettlement issues, all of which deal with institutional, financial, implementation and other explanations as to why outcomes do not meet expectations. Yet, on the other hand, apart from funding Panels of Experts, some technical assistance and a couple of projects, the Bank has avoided providing funding for dam-induced resettlement. I have never heard an adequate explanation as to why that is the case.

As for revisiting previous resettlement in connection with dam-financed projects I am aware of only two examples. One is a conditionality in the loan agreement for Pakistan's Ghazi Barotha Project that disbursement is linked to addressing outstanding resettlement issues associated with the Bank-funded Tarbela project. The other is the Gwembe Tonga component of Zambia's Power Rehabilitation Project. Why so few? And in the case of the Zambian

Project, why did the Bank hand over to the Development Bank of Southern Africa the responsibility for the most important and most expensive activity, the funding and supervision of which has been inadequate?

FINANCIAL INSTITUTIONS

Introduction

The emphasis in this section is on export credit agencies, international banks and financial services firms. As multilateral donors and bilateral donors cut back on their funding of large dams, export credit agencies, private banks and financial services firms have become an increasingly important source of funds and fund raising for a wide range of projects, including dams, in emerging markets. While countries such as Brazil, China and India often can fund large dams with national resources, they are still dependent on the international community for massive projects such as Tucurui, Three Gorges and Sardar Sarovar. In such cases, resettlers and other affected people continue to be disadvantaged as a result of the lack of emphasis on the part of these financiers on transparency, public participation, and environmental and social guidelines.

Export credit and investment insurance agencies

The *ECA Watch*[25] lists 20 national export credit and investment insurance agencies (ECAs). Fourteen are in Europe; three in the Canada and the US, two in Japan and one in Australia. They are public agencies that provide government-supported loans, political risk guarantees and insurance to enable their own business communities to export goods and services to emerging market countries. Competing among themselves to finance their respective private sectors, they have become the most important single source of development assistance and of debt in late-industrializing countries. In 1996, for example, they accounted for 24 per cent of emerging market debt and 56 per cent of debt owed to official agencies. Large-scale infrastructure, including dams, is funded in this way. Such projects include China's Three Gorges Dam and the Philippines' San Roque Dam. ECAs from Germany, Switzerland and Canada, for example, have provided nearly US$1.3 billion in loans and loan guarantees to Siemans and ERG (Germany), ABB and Sulzer Escher-Wyss (Switzerland), and Agra, Inc and General Electric Canada (Canada) for Three Gorges contracts (Udall, 2000).

ECAs are among the last of the major donors to take on responsibility for addressing the impacts of projects on resettlers, other affected communities and river basin habitats. Although the most important in terms of financial outlays, they continue, as a group, to resist formulating their own environmentally and socially responsible guidelines. Pressures for change from NGOs and from other government agencies in the various ECA countries and within OECD, however, are increasing. Especially telling are NGO criticisms that countries that require environmental and social policies for their aid agencies do not apply the same policies to their export credit agencies, and NGO emphasis 'on the issue of the severe financial, social and political damage resulting from corruption, both in the countries that receive corruption-tainted exports and in the exporting countries themselves' (Transparency International, 2000).[26]

NGOs began active monitoring of ECAs in mid-1996. In May 1999, a total of 163 NGOs from 46 countries signed the Mesum Declaration, which lobbied ECAs to agree on 'a common set of environmental and social standards based on existing international standards' and to increase information disclosure and participation (Udall, 2000, p2). Also in 1999, government participants at the G-8 Ministerial Meeting in Cologne stated in their September communiqué that 'We will work within the OECD towards common environmental guidelines for export finance agencies' (as quoted by Udall, 2000).

A year later at a meeting in Indonesia, NGOs from 45 countries issued the Jakarta Declaration for Reform of Official Export Credit and Insurance Agencies. Following up on the Mesum Declaration, the Jakarta Declaration called for 'Transparency, public access to information, and consultation with civil society and affected people; binding common environmental and social guidelines and standards; the adoption of explicit human rights criteria; [and] the adoption of binding criteria and guidelines to end ECAs' abetting of corruption' (www.eca-watch.org/goals/jakartadec.html).

Increasing criticism is having an effect on some ECAs and putting pressure on the others. According to Udall, the US Export-Import Bank, the Export Development Corporation of Canada, the UK's Export Credit and Guarantee Department and the Japanese Bank for International Cooperation 'are far ahead of other OECD Export Credit Agencies in environmental assessment and guidelines' (op cit, p3). The US Export-Import Bank has 'the most developed set of guidelines and procedures' (ibid, p5) among the four and is pushing for common standards for all ECAs so as to improve its own competitive ability.[27] The UK's Export Credit and Guarantee Department (ECGD) has the weakest guidelines of the four with no projects through 1999 turned down on environmental grounds (ibid, p8).

The history of the UK's public financing mechanisms illustrates the extent to which economic and political pressures can conflict a nation's government and institutions by getting involved in hydropolitics at the expense of sound project funding. In the early 1990s pressures from the private sector and the government resulted in large loans being offered to Malaysia for constructing the Pergau Dam. Two large construction firms, both major funders of the party in power, were 'given the two biggest contracts on Pergau – without going through the normal process of competitive bidding' (McCully, 2001, p262). Loans were said to total over UK£230 million for a project that the UK Government's Overseas Development Administration labelled a 'bad buy' for Malaysia. What McCully labels the 'stink of sleaze' worsened when it was learned that the loans were offered 'to encourage the signing of a protocol providing for the sale of UK£1.3 billion worth of British arms' (ibid). Late in 1994 the High Court ruled as illegal the intended funding 'on the grounds that it was not of economic or humanitarian benefit to the Malaysian people' (Hutchinson Encyclopedia).

It is not clear what lessons, if any, have been learned from this case. In early 1999 the UK Government announced its support for Turkey's Ilisu Dam, with the Export Credit and Guarantee Department to provide UK£200 million to support the involvement of Balfour Beatty (one of the two major firms involved in the Pergau case) in the dam's construction. Ilisu, like Pergau, was highly controversial, having been refused funding by the World Bank. Sited on the Tigris River, the dam would not only have adverse effects on downstream flows to Iraq, with whom there was no water use treaty, but it would also flood important historic sites and current settlements of Turkey's Kurdish minority. According to critics, the project 'contravenes the UK Government's rules on ethical foreign policy and its recently announced environmental guidelines' (BBC News, 1999). NGO opposition was especially strong and was channelled through the Ilisu Dam Campaign. In November 2001 Balfour Beatty withdrew its involvement in the project with the result that ECGD and the British Government also were no longer involved.[28] What their involvement would have been if Balfour Beatty had not withdrawn is an interesting question.

Looking to the future, continuing pressure is likely to require ECAs to formulate the recommended guidelines. At the November 2002 session of the OECD Working Party on Export Credits and Credit Guarantees, members 'agreed to public dissemination of information on the policies and procedures adopted to deter and combat bribery, to ensure that transactions supported to the Heavily Indebted Poor Countries are not for unproductive expenditure, to contribute to the protection of the environment and to support small and medium-sized enterprises'.[29] That is an important statement; it remains to be seen how well it is implemented.

Private banks and financial services firms

The increasing involvement of the private sector in dam construction includes banks as well as construction and consultancy firms. Like ECAs, banks in the past have been quite willing to fund projects with inadequate environmental and social protections, especially if they have received risk guarantees from ECAs or multilateral donors. Cases exist where they are also willing to contribute financing to projects after members of the World Bank Group are either unwilling to get involved (as with the Three Gorges Project) or have pulled out (as with World Bank involvement in India's Sardar Sarovar and IFC involvement in Chile's Pangue Dam).

Times are changing, however. Again NGOs have been the driving force. One hundred and two NGOs signed the Collevechio Declaration on Financial Institutions, which was submitted in January 2003 at the Davos World Economic Forum. For advancing social and environmental sustainability, six principles were emphasized: commitment to sustainability, to 'do no harm', responsibility, accountability, transparency, and sustainable markets and governance. Less than five months later, on 4 June 2003, ten international banks adopted the Equator Principles as their guidelines 'for project financing in emerging markets, in the first industry-wide attempt to encourage socially responsible lending' (*Financial Times*, 2003). ABN Amro, Barclays, Citigroup and WestLB drafted the guidelines, to which six other banks committed themselves. According to the Principles, the banks agreed to 'not provide loans directly to projects where the borrower will not or is unable to comply with our environmental and social policies and processes'. They were based on the IFC's social and environmental guidelines for sustainable development and drafted with IFC collaboration and agreement to help with necessary staff training. While welcomed as an important first step, NGOs involved in drafting the Collevechio Declaration were quick to emphasize that implementation of accountability and transparency would be required if the Principles were to be taken seriously.[30]

UNIVERSITIES, NON-PROFIT RESEARCH-ORIENTED INSTITUTES AND NGOS

Introduction

Project authorities have neglected to avail themselves of the range of contributions that universities and non-profit research institutions could make to the project cycle. In addition to the independent monitoring and evaluation that is so important, they could also play an important role in broadening the water resources and energy development options assessment process. Relatively inexpensive as well as objective, dissertation research by degree candidates could be especially helpful for increasing knowledge about the development process.

In my own research, including the writing of this book, I have found PhD dissertations to be especially useful. Examples in North, Central and South America include Bilhartz's dissertation on the US Kinzua Dam, Aronsson's on Mexico's Zimapan, Wali's on Bayano, and Ribeiro's on Argentina–Paraguay's Yacyretá. Yet I am aware of no cases where project authorities have encouraged, let alone financed, such research. Although not specifically related to dam construction, the precedent is there. Following recommendations from the Ford Foundation, the Rahad Corporation in the Sudan supported research of relevance to the large-scale Rahad irrigation project by university masters degree students. Far more use could be made of this kind of research for clarifying impacts of, and needs associated with, the resettlement process and other topics.

I have also found independent research by environmental, human rights and other NGOs to provide an important critique of the adverse environmental and social impact of large dams as well as of dams that are currently on the drawing boards or being implemented. Historically important was the Wadebridge Ecological Centre's two volume study of the *Social and*

Environmental Effects of Large Dams, while McCully's 2001 update of his *Silenced Rivers* remains the best critique of the large-dam-building process from an anti-dam perspective. IRN's various websites are the best means for keeping up with 'current events' relating to specific dams in the major dam-building regions of the world. Provided one keeps in mind their anti-dam agenda, specific IRN, Probe International, and other NGO studies of specific dams such as Laos' Nam Theun 2, Uganda's Bujagali and Lesotho's Highlands Water Project are not only useful sources of information but are also means for putting pressure on project authorities, governments, and donors to do a better job.

Options assessment

Options assessment continues to be dominated by project authorities, with the result that the limitations of such organizations too often result in a flawed assessment that limits the range of options considered and overemphasizes the benefits of the option selected. In addition to involving relevant stakeholders in negotiated agreements, as recommended by WCD, more use should also be made of non-project research organizations. If, for example, the Government of Botswana had invited IUCN's assistance at an earlier date for evaluating development options for the Okavango region, it is likely that an option other than the flawed and subsequently suspended SOIWDP would have been selected. Not only would tens of millions of dollars have been saved, but a major, yet to begin, conservation and development process could have been underway by the early 1990s (Scudder et al, 1993).

Planning

Although their expertise remains seriously under-utilized by project authorities, universities, research councils and institutes, and research-oriented NGOs already have a proven track record in assisting planning efforts during both the design and the operations phases of specific dams, as well as assessing institutional capacities to carry out planning activities. In the US the National Research Council of the National Academy of Sciences has been asked by US Government institutions on various occasions to assess 'overseas' river basin development options as well as the terms of reference for agencies such as the US Corps of Army Engineers with in-country river basin responsibilities. At the request of USAID, a Council expert panel provided advice to a US private sector firm with feasibility study responsibilities for a possible dam on Somalia's Juba River, while the National Science Foundation requested that a similar panel be set up to advise a University of Michigan feasibility study of a dam proposed for the Gambia River. In 2002 the Council was asked by the US Congress to evaluate the planning activities of the US Corps of Army Engineers as a result of which four panels were established to assess such different issues as overall planning and adaptive management.

In the late 1980s and early 1990s, USAID funded a four-year study proposed by the non-profit Institute for Development Anthropology to assess the advantages and disadvantages of environmental flow releases from Mali's Manantali Dam. While that research showed such releases to be both environmentally and economically advantageous, the study's recommendations have yet to be implemented (Chapter 7). The same is true for IUCN and other research that has shown the environmental and economic benefits of environmental flows for Nigeria's Hadejia-Nguru system. More successful in influencing planning has been IUCN research for the restoration of the floodplains in the delta of the Senegal River below the Diama Dam and reservoir in Mauritania (Hamerlynck and Duvail, 2003) and below the Semry rice project on the Logone River in Cameroon (Loth, 2004). Also successful was IUCN and WCS research in the catchment of Laos' Nam Theun 2 Dam for authorizing and influencing the terms of reference for a catchment management authority. In Cameroon and Laos the involvement of project authorities has contributed to successful outcomes.

Monitoring and evaluation

To be effective in identifying problem areas, long-term independent monitoring is essential throughout the development process as is the capacity of project authorities to evaluate and act upon monitoring results. While monitoring has been the main activity of universities and non-profit research institutions, it has characterized only a small minority of large dams. And where it has been carried out, it is due usually to the insistence of international donors, with project authorities either ignoring monitoring entirely or doing it themselves.

Evaluations well after the end of the project cycle are essential if lessons are to be learned about outcomes and applied to future options assessment and decision-making. Whether by project authorities, donors such as the World Bank, or research agencies, 'broad evaluations of completed projects appear to be few in number, narrow in scope, poorly integrated across impact categories and scales, and inadequately linked with dam operations decisions' (Westcoat, 2000, p5). The absence of such studies was 'one of the most disturbing findings' of the WCD (2000, p184), an absence that 'signals a failure to actively engage in learning from experience in both the adaptive management of existing facilities and in the design and appraisal of new dams' (ibid). Although complex, since ex post evaluations need to be 'comprehensive, integrated, long-term, cumulative, and adaptive' (Westcoat, op cit), they are not beyond the capabilities of universities and research institutions, nor of advanced students undertaking PhD research. Another option that can produce results more rapidly, and was used for WCD case studies, could involve a consortium of researchers from different types of institutions, in which university faculty and students play a major role. Examples include the Grand Coulee (US), Pak Mun (Thailand) and Tucurui (Brazil) case studies.

CONCLUSIONS

The record to date suggests that regardless of type, project authorities working alone or with active central government involvement are incapable of dealing adequately with resettling and downstream communities as well as with environmental issues. Although their characteristics can vary with different stages of the project cycle, during all stages other institutions should be involved. Throughout the options assessment process, institutions should be involved that represent 'all those whose rights are involved and who bear the risks of different options' (WCD, 2000, pxxviii). If a dam is the selected option, institutions should be involved that represent the interests of all key stakeholders during all stages of planning, design, implementation, monitoring and evaluation, and decommissioning.

It is especially important that institutions representing the interests of project-affected people be involved throughout, with NGOs actively involved in the building of those institutions where they do not exist. At the same time it is essential for donors such as the World Bank Group to be willing to protect the interests of affected communities in the same way that they provide grants and loans to project authorities and governments and guarantees to private sector firms. Protecting those interests would include providing for whatever legal representation and institution building is necessary.

Environmental and social guidelines of multilateral and bilateral agencies, of nations and of private banks and financial services firms continue to be inadequate, while those of ICOLD and other professional organizations have no clout because they are only advisory to their members. All donors need to do a better job where competitive international bidding is involved to require that some funding for each major contract is available for training in borrower nations and for involvement of national firms. After all, large dams are major development interventions and hence should be planned and implemented in ways that achieve a wider range of national development goals.

Not only should environmental and social impact assessments be required through national legislation, but where donors are involved, they should be completed by institutions other than the project authority and their principal engineering contractors. Independent long-term monitoring is also essential, as is an increasing number of ex post evaluations to better assess outcomes and lessons learned for application elsewhere.

9

The Future of Large Dams and the Way Forward

INTRODUCTION

In this chapter conclusions are presented in two major sections. The first section deals with the future of large dams. It starts with a key message. An introduction then briefly reviews the global context in which water resource planning should occur. It is followed first by consideration of conditions under which dams remain a legitimate development option and then by a consideration of circumstances under which they should not be built. The second section concentrates on the procedures for decision-making, planning, implementation, and operations and management dealing with water resource development where a large dam is a possible option. It utilizes WCD's Seven Strategic Priorities and includes dealing with existing dams.

Recommendations are presented in a box under each strategic priority. Their observance would not eliminate the large dam option, but it would significantly reduce the number built, including some dams that are already 'in the pipeline'.

THE FUTURE OF LARGE DAMS

Introduction

It is important to remind readers that the emphasis in this book is on large dams of 60m and higher. Such dams make up 78 per cent of the 50 dam survey of Chapter 3, but dams of 60m and higher comprise only 11 per cent of those in ICOLD's 1998 register of 22,748 large dams. Emphasis has also been on dams requiring the resettlement of over 1000 people, as was the case with over 90 per cent of the dams in the 50 dam survey.

It is these larger dams that politicians and project authorities extol; for which international contractors and consultants compete for feasibility, design and construction contracts; and which have dominated the large dams dispute. They are also the dams that have had the most adverse impacts on ecosystems, including irreversible impacts because they are usually built on mainstreams

---

BOX 9.1 KEY MESSAGE

Adverse environmental and social impacts of large dams are contributing to serious degradation of global life support systems. Environmental impacts are degrading river basin ecosystems that, in many countries, are national heartlands. Social impacts are further impoverishing tens of millions of river basin residents who, to survive, cause further degradation of surrounding natural resources. Furthermore, the development potential of large dams is seldom realized because of the complexity involved, because of institutional inadequacies, because of implementation uncertainties and because of corruption.

Yet large dams remain a necessary development option for providing water and energy resources to populations in late-developing countries that are in crisis because they have expanded beyond the carrying capacity of their environment. Even then, a decision to build a large dam should only be based on an open and transparent options assessment process in which relevant stakeholders are fully informed of the risks involved. If a decision is made to proceed, state-of-the-art guidelines should be followed in order to reduce known disadvantages, some irreversible, to the extent possible and to increase an equitable distribution of advantages.

---

and major tributaries. That said, I do not mean to imply that smaller dams may not have equally adverse environmental impacts, especially if they are built on the lower reaches of a major tributary. Thailand's 17m Pak Mun is an example of this. Adverse effects can also be expected where a large number of small and medium-sized dams (less than 15m in height) are built in a relatively restricted area, because they can significantly reduce downstream water supplies. Dams built in the escarpment country of Zambia and Zimbabwe that surrounds the Lake Kariba Basin seem to have done just this. In Southern California sediment check dams in national forests fringing the Pacific Ocean are responsible for coastal erosion.

On the other hand, it is important to remember that dams smaller than 30m constitute 58 per cent of those on ICOLD's 1998 list. An unknown proportion of these are built for the benefit of rural villages to control land degradation; add to the supply of arable land; recharge aquifers; and provide water for irrigation, villagers and livestock. Of the 'best practice' examples discussed in this volume, one involves the hundreds of sediment control and water supply dams that China has built during the 1990s in the upper catchment of the Yellow River (World Bank, 2003); the other involves Bunga village's 15 and 16m high check dams in India (Malik and Bhatia, 2003). Analysed in Chapter 3 as one of the dams in the 50 dam survey, Sri Lanka's 18m high Pimburetewa Dam is another example. Such dams, sometimes incorporated within a cascade of dams on the upper reaches of tributaries, can raise village living standards without degrading their environment.

A point inadequately made in the literature is that the larger dams dealt with in this book do not constitute environmentally sustainable development.

Not only do they alter river regimes causing irreversible damage to wetlands and, in some cases, to deltas, but with sedimentation rates averaging between 0.5 per cent and 1 per cent per year, they have a finite life span. Not only are decommissioning costs not factored into a project's rate of return, but the science and engineering of how to accomplish decommissioning does not exist,[1] let alone the science for restoring damaged deltas and floodplains. Looking to the future, a new development paradigm is needed that can wean societies from the need for more and more large dams.

In presenting the conclusions of the German Government to the WCD Final Report, conclusions that were very supportive of WCD's strategic priorities and the 26 guidelines, the German representative asked the following very important questions at the 2001 Symposium on the Benefits and Concerns about Dams that was organized as part of ICOLD's 69th Annual Meeting in Dresden:

- What sort of development should we be aiming at?
- How can we ensure that this development involves the equitable distribution of benefits and burdens, opportunities and risks?
- How can we ensure that human rights are observed?
- How can we ensure that account is taken of the ecosystems' limited ability to cope?

The last point is especially important in regard to the state of the global environment, about which the most knowledgeable biological and social scientists are getting increasingly concerned and which is relevant to large dams because of their impact on river basins. In an article on the concept of environmental sustainability, the now-retired senior environmentalist at the World Bank wrote 'what is not contestable is that the modes of production prevailing in most parts of the global economy are causing the exhaustion and dispersion of a one-time inheritance of natural capital – topsoil, groundwater, tropical forests and biodiversity' (Goodland, 1995, p7). Several years later, I sent out 89 questionnaires to leading development and social anthropologists who had been studying local communities in the major regions of the world. One of three questions asked them to identify three environmental issues that they considered to be the most serious constraints to a sustainable future during the 21st century.

Of the 60 per cent who replied, the number one constraint (noted by 74 per cent) was misuse of natural resources. That actually underestimated the magnitude of the concern because the percentage would have been higher 'if several colleagues had not taken me to task for splitting off environmental from social issues' (Scudder, 1999, p354). Answers were illuminating. A World Bank staff member from Cameroon wrote 'in my work in sub-Saharan Africa the evidence suggests that as natural resources are diminishing, there has been a strong re-emergence of confrontational ethnicity.' Another, with experience in Latin America, Africa and Asia wrote that 'As economic conditions deteriorate, more and more people resort to common resources to survive, destroying those resources and causing conflict among themselves.' The second most important concern, involving over 50 per cent, was water scarcity and pollution, both of which were emphasized by anthropologists from Egypt and Turkey.

It is important to recognize that such concerns are also shared by residents in both industrialized and late-industrializing countries. The Gallup International Institute completed a global poll in 1993. Twenty-four nations were included from different areas of the world and at different levels of development. They included, for example, Brazil, Mexico, Nigeria, Turkey, India and the Philippines, on the one hand, and the US, Canada, various European countries and Japan, on the other hand. Results were unexpected: 'Strikingly, environmental quality is widely seen as a serious problem throughout the countries and as more serious among residents of the developing nations than among those of the industrialized countries... Environmental problems are no longer viewed as just a threat to quality of life ... but are considered a fundamental threat to human welfare' (Dunlap et al, 1993, p11 and p15).

Values change; concerns change. When the most knowledgeable scientists are concerned about the health of the world's life support systems, 'business as usual' must change. Global institutions recognize the need for change in other areas of concern; examples being various UN covenants addressing human rights and the establishment of the International Court of Justice (ICJ). The time is overdue for enforceable covenants relating to the global ecosystem. As for dam-induced human rights violations, a major recommendation of this book is the need to establish an international board for arbitration and compliance to which affected people, NGOs and other in-country institutions can appeal. While 'The State remains the ultimate arbiter' as Kader Asmal noted in his address before the 2001 ICOLD symposium, State decisions can be expected to be more in accord with 'best practice' if policy-makers are aware that 'bad decisions' not only will affect international capital flows but also can be appealed to an international board.

As global population and consumption continue to increase so too does the disconnect between people and their environmental life support systems. In some cases, large dams will be necessary to deal with near-crisis and crisis situations as short- and medium-term solutions. But, in the longer run, most will worsen environmental conditions still further. In other cases, as with Laos' NT2 Dam, the dam option makes sense not because it is a good option, but only because it is the best option available for gaining the necessary foreign exchange for poverty alleviation. These points, along with the 'big project' problem (Scott, 1998) and other large-dam-related risks must be kept in mind while assessing the case for large dams.

Should large dams be built?

The unfortunate answer is yes, but only after a 'best practice' options assessment process that gives sufficient emphasis to environmental and social issues and only where adequate policies exist and are implemented and where project authorities, contractors and consultants have a legal responsibility to follow whatever contractual conditionalities are necessary to implement the project as intended.[2] Those requirements do not exist at present. Let us examine briefly the current situation as it relates to the existence and implementation of adequate guidelines and policies, starting with the World Bank, which should be the pioneer in strengthening guidelines, in reorganizing its structure to facilitate their implementation, and in the funding of pilot and other projects. On all three activities the Bank is deficient. Although an agency committed to a world without poverty, the Bank's resettlement guidelines do not require those relocated in connection with its largest development projects to become project beneficiaries. Nor are indigenous people allowed the possibility of informed consent. As for the Bank's organization for enforcing its guidelines, environmental and social group staff are dependent on task managers – whose job it is to move projects forward – for financing their involvement in specific projects. A very serious constraint to good practice has been the meagre amount of Bank funding available for the resettlement process. Rather, funds are concentrated on infrastructure with the result that once the construction phase is ended or loans disbursed, Bank influence as a major donor is reduced at the very time that the most critical resettlement phase – that of community formation and economic development – is getting underway.

Moving on to bilateral export–import agencies, they have yet to agree to a common set of guidelines, with Canada's Export Development Corporation providing loans to China's Three Gorges Project of CAN$153 million, which is tied to construction of turbines by a Canadian company, while the Export–Import Bank in the US is unwilling to provide financing for the Three Gorges. Although the first group of private banks signed the Equator Principles, involving social and environmental sustainability, in June 2003, almost immediately Barclay's Bank, one of four drafters of the principles, arranged a loan from a group of banks for the environmentally contentious Karahnjukar Hydropower Project in Iceland.[3]

What about project authorities? In the US the Corps of Engineers, though mandated by Congress to pay more attention to environmental responsibilities, initially refused in July 2003 to implement a court order to manage its dams on the Missouri River in a more environmentally friendly way.[4] Why was that? Hard to escape is the conclusion that the Corps does not take seriously its environmental responsibilities when they conflict, as in this case, with such traditional responsibilities as navigation. In China, the way in which Three Gorges resettlement is being implemented is contrary to the government's national policy, while Gujarat, Maharashtra, Madhya Pradesh and the central government ignore the requirements of the Narmada Water Disputes Tribunal for resettlement in connection with India's SSP. In Africa, the Lesotho's Highlands Water Project continues to be in non-compliance with various environmental, social and other World Bank conditionalities and requirements.

As for private contractors and consultants, senior officials of such private sector associations as ICOLD and IHA continue their efforts to marginalize the WCD Final Report, a latest effort, fortunately thwarted, being to remove UNEP's Dams and Development Project as a co-sponsor for the Dams and Sustainable Development Theme at the Third World Water Forum, Kyoto, 2003. In Lesotho two major firms – Canada's Acres International and Germany's Lahmeyer International – have been convicted after lengthy corruption trials of giving bribes to LHDA's first chief executive officer who is now serving a 15-year prison sentence. Trials of other major international firms, that have been similarly accused, are to follow.

As dam advocates, it is very much in the interest of professional societies such as ICOLD, IHA and ICID to evolve with the times by adding a regulatory role to their current advisory one. For if the countries representing their member associations are unable or unwilling to commit themselves to the implementation of state-of-the-art guidelines, further unacceptable results can be expected to increase opposition to dams under any circumstance.

Following a 'best practice' options assessment process will continue to reduce the number of dams built in the future. That is as it should be, given the association of dams with irreversible impacts, the difficulties of implementing them according to 'best practice' guidelines even where the best of intentions are present, and the temptation of governments to build them more for political than economic reasons. But large dams remain legitimate development options under two kinds of conditions. In both cases, there is a need first for a national water resource development planning process involving relevant stakeholders that produces a ranking of projects, as has been done in Nepal with hydropower development.

The first set of conditions is where export of hydropower is seen as the best option for providing small late-industrializing countries such as Laos and Nepal with the foreign exchange that is necessary for raising the incomes of their very poor majority. The second set of conditions is where an increasing disconnect between a nation's growing population and its life supporting natural resource base requires major dam construction to meet immediate and near-future needs for water (and urban water supplies in particular) and for food. One water supply example that involved an extensive options assessment process was South Africa's Skuifraam Dam, which was designed to provide water to Cape Town as well as to the poor, to farmers, and to industry in the Western Cape. Another is the Olivenhain Dam in San Diego, California. Even more important are inter-basin transfers to regions facing present or future water crises. The North China plain is an example in which major cities (including Beijing) and rural areas inhabited by several hundred million people face a critical drop in aquifers and shortfall in surface water. Another example is the inter-basin transfer from Lesotho to South Africa's industrial hub of Gauteng.

India's need for food and water for its exploding population presents an especially difficult situation because such needs are currently being fulfilled at the expense of its life support systems including dropping aquifers. The situation is compounded by a monsoon climate that concentrates rainfall within a relatively short time period. In this situation, it is hard to see an alternative to some large storage reservoirs. As in China, dams should be multipurpose with hydropower to pay the bills and storage for irrigation and meeting urban needs for water. This would require a shift away from current practices where a single ministry or State parastatal does the planning with inadequate involvement of other stakeholders, including government agencies and affected people. And it would require much more attention to be paid to environmental and social issues so as to avoid the ongoing violation of human rights associated with SSP. Before new Indian dams are built, however, the priority should be a major national programme for rehabilitating existing infrastructure, for extending incomplete irrigation projects and increasing the productivity of under-performing ones, and for addressing adverse resettlement outcomes.

Where irrigation is the number one priority, governments are presented with a difficult decision as to irrigation's role in the national economy. As globalization proceeds, a government's efforts to obtain food self-sufficiency where other national resources provide a comparative advantage make little sense. It is far wiser for countries such as Botswana, with its diamond, tourist and rain-fed livestock resources, to import cheaper food staples such as rice from exporting countries such as Thailand and Vietnam. Such a world requires, of course, a more stable global political economy, the achievement of which could play a major role in reducing the need for large dams for irrigation purposes, as would more emphasis on small-scale irrigation options and rain-fed agriculture that would benefit larger numbers of low-income households.

At current prices, cereal staples cannot be expected to move hundreds of millions of rural residents beyond subsistence in countries such as China and India. Where future irrigation is stressed, it would be far better to include higher value crops in the crop mix and to combine agriculture with village industry, as has been done in China or in agro-industrial zones in Brazil's São Francisco River Basin, so as to increase the secondary and induced benefits (multiplier effects) associated with farming and non-farming employment generation and enterprise development.

In addition to hydropower, urban water supply and irrigation, 'flood control' continues to be emphasized as a major benefit associated with large dams. The magnitude of the problem, however, can be reduced by implementing a flood management programme that incorporates such features as learning to live with floods so as to benefit from their existence,[5] improved catchment management, improved dam operations including coordination of flood releases from multiple dams, environmental flows (Acreman et al, 2000; Dyson et al, 2003) and improved floodplain management.

When large dams should not be built

Large dams should not be built in international river basins without either a treaty between the basin states or a willingness on the part of the dam-building nation to abide by the guidelines incorporated within the yet-to-be-approved United Nation's Convention on the Law of the Non-Navigational Uses of International Watercourses. More generally, large dams should not be built where other options exist to meet water resource, energy, agricultural and flood management requirements. This is because of their disproportionately adverse environmental impacts in comparison to other options. It is also because the involuntary resettlement associated with dams is the most adverse type of development-induced removal since it adversely affects a people's total livelihood, unlike urban redevelopment, which seldom eliminates the household economies of the majority. Other reasons for avoiding large dam construction where possible is their complexity, associated uncertainty (including the frequency of unexpected events), and susceptibility to political interference and corruption.

Dams should not be constructed where a participatory planning process involving the full range of affected stakeholders has been neglected and where efforts have not been made to avoid mainstream dams and dams that threaten cultures and require the resettlement of thousands of people. Such conditions would, for example, stop the construction of further dams on the Mekong, including those within China. They would also avoid the construction of dams along the Amazon and the Salween River bordering Myanmar and Thailand.

THE WAY FORWARD: IMPLEMENTING THE SEVEN STRATEGIC PRIORITIES

Introduction

WCD's Seven Strategic Priorities evolved from the Commission's consideration of future directions that was based on the most detailed analysis yet undertaken of the performance of existing dams. Fundamental to future decision-making was a rights and risks approach that 'sought to draw on the broader trends and developments that reflect the changing context and international development discourse' (WCD, 2000, p204). Especially important were a series of UN covenants starting with the 1948 Universal Declaration of Human Rights and including the 1986 UN Declaration on the Right to Development and the 1992 Rio Declaration on Environment and Development. According to the 1986 Declaration, 'every human person and all peoples are entitled to participate in, contribute to, and enjoy economic, social, cultural and political development.'

The Right to Development most certainly would apply to large dams, which are justified by politicians and planners as major development projects, with some being the largest single investment at the time of construction in a government's development portfolio. Specifically, the decision-making process requires cost–benefit analysis to be complemented by distributional analysis since 'Reference to the human rights framework means that those policies that deny the rights of some to fulfil those of others cannot be adopted' (ibid, p200). In his WCD Contributing Paper, Rajogopal (2000, pp10–11) also argues that the right to participation and the right to remedy would also apply to stakeholders such as resettlers.[6]

In the past, risks and risk analysis were applied primarily to project authorities and investors. WCD broke new ground by applying risk not just to resettlers, hosts and downstream communities but also to future generations and to the environment. The Commission also applied the precautionary approach whereby 'Decision-makers faced with scientific uncertainty and public concerns have a duty to provide answers where risks and irreversibility are considered unacceptable by society' (op cit, Box 7.3, p207).

Strategic Priority 1: Gaining public acceptance[7]

Introduction

For the Commission, gaining public acceptance of key decisions is an essential component of the options assessment process (Strategic Priority 2). It requires decision-making processes and mechanisms 'that enable informed participation by all groups of people and result in the demonstrable acceptance of key decisions' (op cit, p215). Four issues warrant further consideration. The first concerns the feasibility of what has been called 'open planning' whereby the planning arena is opened to all concerned. The three others are the role and selection of stakeholders in a decision-making process for gaining public acceptance, the concept of informed consent, and an institutional mechanism for dealing with irresolvable conflicts.

In the 1950s when Colson and I began our Kariba research, scant attention was paid to such issues as public acceptance. Then the decision-making process for large dams was made within ministries and parastatal agencies with the strong support of heads of state. Social values were changing, however, with emphasis on stakeholder involvement growing during the 1960s as the public sought greater participation in making decisions relating to the environment, good governance and other issues of importance to their lives. At first, planners were concerned that incorporating more actors in the decision-making process would cause 'gridlock' and would cause them to lose their influence and/or would result in uninformed people making poor decisions. Early on, the danger of gridlock seemed a legitimate concern; indeed, one I shared in the 1970s when involved in land use planning for a seasonal watercourse near my own residence. More recent experimental and field research and surveys, as

---

BOX 9.2 RECOMMENDATIONS

- Gaining public acceptance should start at the beginning of the options assessment process.
- For public acceptance to occur, all relevant risk-takers as well as categories of citizens should be involved.
- During options assessment, a major effort should be made to obtain the consent of major stakeholders.
- Stakeholders should have access to an International Adjudication and Compliance Board if governments are unable to resolve conflicts among stakeholders.

well as case studies, have shown that a well thought-out and implemented stakeholder process is both feasible and desirable as a means for improving planning outcomes, their legitimacy and the financial cost of project implementation.[8]

The process for gaining public acceptance should start from the very beginning of the options assessment process. Less clear, is when it should end. Should, for example, the same stakeholders be involved in monitoring implementation, dealing with non-compliance, and making decisions relating to decommissioning at the end of a project's lifespan? As for consent, how to obtain it and what to do if it could not be obtained was one of the most difficult issues dealt with by the Commission. Should key stakeholders such as indigenous people have, for example, a veto? That word never occurred in the Commission's Final Report. Rather it was dealt with indirectly by emphasizing the need for good faith negotiations, 'with disagreements referred to a designated judicial body' (WCD, 2000, p219). For me, that judicial body should be an International Adjudication and Compliance Board.

Is it possible to provide more specific guidelines on these four issues than WCD was able to give? I believe that it is, even though variation among cases will require flexibility. Especially important is the existence within nations and within the community of nations of an institutional mechanism for conflict resolution. In exploring the four issues further, it is important to add the word 'responsibilities' to the 'rights and risks' approach, which then becomes a 'rights, risks and responsibilities' approach.[9] Responsibilities should be explained to stakeholder representatives at the commencement of proceedings as being their involvement in a dialogue in which each participant attempts to listen respectfully to viewpoints other than one's own and to arguments for compromise when they are raised.

Public involvement makes good sense

Based on case studies in China, Nepal, South Africa, Venezuela and elsewhere,[10] the World Bank estimates that public involvement in options assessment and subsequent project planning and implementation requires an additional two years. It also increases upfront financial costs. That additional time and finance is an excellent investment since it should result in selection of better and more legitimate options, and less contentious implementation. Moreover, it is far better to increase the early stages of the planning process than to run the risk of a limited public acceptance process either stopping a poorly explained project or, at a later date, resulting in more financially costly implementation delays.

This view is supported by several impressive case studies (World Bank, 2003). In Venezuela opposition in both river basins stopped the government-planned Yacambú – Quíbor inter-basin transfer project in the mid-1980s. In response, the government formed a public company with a representative board with the mandate to solicit public input into the pros and cons of the project through a broad-based Consulting Council. Concerns in the sending basin had been primarily related to extraction of their water resources, whereas citizens in the receiving basin had been concerned about how the water would be divided between rural and urban users, and smaller and larger farms in areas to be irrigated. Once such concerns had been dealt with, consensus was reached; the project was refinanced and implemented with important benefits in both basins.

Other examples include multi-stakeholder involvement in the screening and ranking of medium-sized hydropower projects in Nepal and conservation and development on China's Loess Plateau. In Nepal, an initial inventory of 138 sites was reduced to 24 for fine ranking, with further public consultation to select 7 options from the 24. In China, government agencies, including local government, worked with farm communities in two World Bank-financed projects to select and build over 450 small, medium and large (a few up to 30m) dams to provide sediment control. Actively involved, community farmers benefited in a number of ways including improved water supplies, local flood control and increased arable land with more secure land tenure. Multi-stakeholder involvement also played a major role in decision-making that led to San Diego's Olivenhain Dam, for which the San Diego County Water Authority 'sought and received comment from the general public and special interest groups, and initiated a comprehensive outreach program to gain public support' (Reed et al, 2003).

As for financial savings, the World Bank states that '... the impact of delays in the very early stages on the economic or financial viability of a dam project is rather small. Delays when a major part of the capital expenditures have been made, on the other hand, are much more severe' (2003, p28). The Bank estimates that the cost caused by delays in the construction of India's Sardar Sarovar Project as a result of strong local, national and international opposition exceeds US$200 million a year. Losses exceeding US$200 million a year are also attributed to the inability of the Yacyretá authorities to deal equitably with affected people in Argentina and Paraguay.

Involving stakeholders in the options assessment process

Options assessment requires strategic planning that can result in selection of specific projects. For public acceptance to occur, all categories of risk-takers as well as other concerned citizens should be involved from the very beginning. Prior to that time, there should be an appropriate legislative framework as well as a stakeholder communication strategy, the nature of which can be expected to vary from country to country. Such a communication strategy should include how to prepare a preliminary listing of stakeholders (and including those based on self-identification) as well as information on the role and responsibilities of stakeholders whether they represent government and project authority interests, or those of affected people. From the start, it should be recognized that selection of a representative group of stakeholders is at the same time critical to success and a difficult undertaking.

Active stakeholder involvement in decision-making, and subsequently in the implementation, management and evaluation of whichever option, or options, is/are selected, is what participation is all about. That said, it is important to emphasize that the relatively recent emphasis on the importance of participation has occurred at the same time that civil society has been undergoing dynamic changes in the complexity of its social organization and values. Such changes also apply to what WCD labels as tribal and indigenous societies that are becoming more open-ended systems. Increasingly, affected communities tend to be split between those who might favour a dam because of assumed employment, commercial and other opportunities and those who are more likely to oppose it. Given such increasing complexity, which can also be expected to be accompanied by conflicting views about the meaning of development as represented by dam construction, how stakeholder categories are selected assumes increased importance as does the means whereby each category of stakeholders selects those who will represent their interests.

Once stakeholder representatives have been identified, they should be instructed about the nature and objectives of the decision-making process, their role and responsibilities in that process and which stakeholders, if any, might have the option of 'consent'. In regard to their role, stakeholders need to understand the level of influence they can realistically expect to have on outcomes and to understand whether or not their involvement stops once an option is selected or may continue during the planning, implementation and operational phases of a specific project.[11] They also need access to the necessary information on options under consideration and they should be instructed about whatever institutional mechanisms will be used to deal with unresolved conflicts. So as to create as 'level a playing field' as possible, resources should be available to provide the less experienced and educated stakeholders with whatever financial, legal and technical assistance may be necessary. As for their responsibilities, stakeholders should understand that while they are expected to represent their interests, they are also expected to value the efficiency and fairness of options under consideration.

In addition to whatever agency is driving the options assessment exercise, experience shows the need for an independent facilitator as well as for a team of experts for explaining technical, economic, social and other details. The dynamics of a stakeholder-driven options assessment process can be expected to vary from one situation, and from one country, to another once the stakeholders are on board. Integrating them into a forum worked well in establishing and monitoring WCD, as did the formation of a small stakeholder advisory group from the membership of the forum. While that advisory group played an active decision-making role in the resolution of conflicts over the selection of Commission members, unresolved conflicts dealing with options assessment require, I wish to emphasize, an independent institutional mechanism for conflict resolution at both the national and international level.

Consent

Issues relating to consent can be expected to be difficult and perhaps irresolvable in the absence of an acceptable process of adjudication, involving both national and international institutions, which is dealt with in the next section. To whom consent applies is a question that needs to be addressed prior to the commencement of the decision-making process associated with options assessment. According to WCD, 'where projects affect indigenous and tribal peoples [decision-making] processes are guided by their free, prior and informed consent' (2000, p215). Both categories of people are included based on the tendency of the United Nations to include an undetermined number of tribal people in Africa, Asia and the Pacific as indigenous people and both are granted 'free, prior and informed consent' based on instruments of international law including 'Conventions 107 and 169 of the International Labour Organization and the evolving United Nations *Draft Declaration on the Rights of Indigenous Peoples*' (ibid, p216).

The World Bank's definition of indigenous people is much narrower and does not incorporate prior and informed consent. Rather, the Bank's emphasis is on avoiding projects involving indigenous people to the extent possible and, where indigenous people are present, involving them in a process of informed participation during all stages of the project cycle.

Neither the World Bank nor the WCD approach is satisfactory. Both, for example, are associated with problems of definition. Take the broader WCD category of indigenous and tribal people. When does a tribal or an indigenous society become an ethnic minority, or in the Indian case cease to be a tribe because of conversion to the Hindu religion and absorption within the caste system? Take the Gwembe Tonga, for example. At the time of their resettlement in the late 1950s, they were considered one of Zambia's most isolated and least developed 'tribes'. If another dam is built in the Middle Zambezi Valley, and two have been under consideration that would require some Gwembe Tonga resettlement, should they still be considered a tribal population with the right of consent? Even though some have served as ministers in Zambian national governments, others fly jets in the Zambian air force, thousands have received a secondary school education and hundreds a university education which has enabled them to move into middle class occupations? If the answer is yes, then it would apply to the large majority of the population of Southern, Central and East Africa. Does that mean that no dam could be built in nearly 15 countries in the absence of consent? That would be an untenable position. Should it arise, it would present the type of conflict that requires adjudication by, preferably, an international institution.

But even if the definitional problem can be dealt with, it is hardly fair to restrict consent to a limited number of affected people. What about situations where tens of thousands of peasants, or even hundreds, will lose both their homes and livelihoods, or where dam construction threatens socio-cultural systems? Most, but not all, threats to cultural survival would involve indigenous and tribal people. One example of an indigenous society at risk would be that of the James Bay Cree if Hydro-Quebec's Grande Baleine Project had been constructed (Chapter 6). Future examples would be dams in the Amazon that severely reduce customary tenure over territory at the expense of the socio-cultural systems of affected Native Americans.

But there are also situations that involve societies that are neither indigenous nor tribal. As examples, I suspect that a case could be made for the Nubians and related groups in connection with the planned construction of the Meroe and Kajbar Dams in the Northern Sudan and for the Kurds in connection with Turkey's Ilisu Dam. In both cases important archaeological sites would also be at risk in addition to the contemporary cultures of the two ethnic minorities. There are, of course, other reasons for rejecting the Ilisu Dam, such as there being no international treaty dealing with the Tigris River. The archaeological risks there also are compounded by the decision of the Government of Iraq to build the Makhool Dam, which will flood key sites, including the royal capital of Assyria (*Science*, 2002), to offset reduced flows that will result from the completion of the Ilisu Dam.

Based on the Meroe and Ilisu cases, WCD's restriction of free, prior and informed consent to indigenous and tribal[12] communities is not broad enough. Moreover, it does not explain why indigenous and tribal people should be willing to give their consent regardless of how transparent and participatory negotiations are. In many future cases is it not wishful thinking that a majority of resettlers will 'consent' to be relocated given the fact that all community relocation is stressful, that successful outcomes are uncertain, and that resettlers in the future will be better informed of the risks involved even if the policy of governments and project authorities is to help them become beneficiaries? Moreover, even under the best of circumstances, the majority of resettlers can expect their living standards to drop during the years of uncertainty throughout the lengthy planning process associated with most large dams, during their physical removal, and for a year or more following their resettlement.

Also problematic is what categories of indigenous, tribal or other stakeholders should have informed consent: resettlers alone, or resettlers and hosts? And what about downstream communities who belong to the same ethnic groups, tribes, and/or indigenous people whose livelihoods will be adversely affected? This is an issue that can only be resolved on a case-by-case basis, and then within the context of a participatory decision-making process. Yet another issue deals with cases, such as India's SSP, where affected people, in this case all resettlers, include peasants and town dwellers as well as tribal people in various stages of emulating Hindu culture. Does consent relate only to the latter, and if so, would some tribal people be excluded because of the degree to which they have been incorporated within Hindu society? Yet another contentious issue concerns how consent might be obtained and what it means. Was the process really based on free, prior and informed consent or was it biased and corrupt? Regarding the Sainte-Marguerite 3 hydro project, a Montagnais group calling themselves Innu traditionalists opposed the project and the 1994 agreement that they claimed was voted upon by the two communities after preparatory works on the project had begun. They also claimed that the members of their Band Council had been corrupted by the project with those opposing the project intimidated and some jailed.[13]

To conclude, the consent of all stakeholders should be sought for whatever decision is made during a legitimate water resources development options assessment process, irrespective of whether or not that decision involves dam construction. But what if consent is not possible in cases where a large dam is selected as the best option to deal with an immediate crisis involving the well-being of a much larger number of people? Or, in a worst-case scenario, a decision is made to build a major dam without adequate stakeholder involvement in the decision-making process or to build one that will have adverse environmental effects? That is when the right of appeal, by a project authority or a government in the first case, or affected people in the second, to what I have called an international adjudication and compliance board is necessary.

Adjudication and the need for an international adjudication and compliance board

All protagonists see stakeholder participation as a better means for informing decision-makers about options for water resource development. For the WCD, the World Bank and the International Association for Public Participation,[14] the final decision-maker is assumed to be the government. That makes sense as a general principle. On the other hand, the impact of dams on the public interest, on human and other rights, on mainstreams, on rivers whose basins involve national heartlands, and on international rivers is too important for global life support resources and internationally accepted covenants for project authorities and governments not to be subject to review at the international level. A mechanism for dispute resolution and compliance is needed that can involve adjudication at both the national and international levels and to which any stakeholder, including affected persons, project authorities, governments, NGOs and donors can apply.

Current disagreements in the US about the release of environmental flows from Missouri River dams illustrate the need for an adjudication process for situations where special interests impede the operation of dams according to changing social values and the recommendations of scientists (Chapter 7). The present Congress is unable to adjudicate an issue that its members see as being at the expense of two lower basin states for the benefit of three upper basin states, whereas the current President, prior to his election, supported the status quo because he needed the votes of one of the lower basin states. As for the Corps of Army Engineers, which operates the dams, initially they resisted a July 2003 court order to mimic reduced summer flows for the benefit of biodiversity protected under the 1973 *Endangered Species Act*. Although subsequently they did reduce river flows following another court order, by then it was too late in the season to properly mimic pre-dam flows. Meanwhile the degradation of the Missouri River Basin continues.

The Missouri River situation is not unique in the US. In September 2003 the district judge who had been overseeing implementation of the Comprehensive Everglades Restoration Plan in Florida was replaced after ten years following complaints from the sugar industry that he was biased toward environmental interests because of his attempts to ensure that programme requirements to improve water quality were carried out as scheduled (*Los Angeles Times*, 2003b).

Two arbitration levels are needed in the US and elsewhere. The first would be at the national level and would have the authority to settle all types of complaints dealing with the options assessment process and the design, implementation and operation of whatever option was selected as well as with decommissioning of a dam. Its authority would include irresolvable conflicts between stakeholders and between stakeholders and project authorities in regard to options selected, implemented and operated. Lack of compliance dealing, for example, with environmental and resettlement issues, would also be included. Designed to deal with the failure of national arbitration, the second level would be international.

How the arbitration process was structured at the national level would vary under different systems of governance. The approach suggested by the authors of the National Research Council's report on the Missouri River would be sanctioned by the US Congress. It would be an ad hoc approach whereby arbitration would be the responsibility of a 'formal multiple-stakeholder group' that drew its members from the involved states, government agencies, NGOs and other interested parties and was complemented by an independent panel of scientists with relevant expertise. Similar arrangements could deal with water resource conflicts elsewhere in the US. While the option of rejecting their recommendations would remain with the national government, ignoring their conclusions would have political costs.

A permanent Arbitration and Compliance Board would be needed at the international level that should include members with water resources expertise. It might be institutionalized under the International Court of Justice (ICJ) or the United Nations. An extension of the current UNEP–Dams and Development Project might be considered since it involves an existing organization. But in that event it would need major reorganization in order to have the authority to render decisions under the type of binding dispute resolution that characterizes the World Trade Organization. Compliance could be facilitated in a number of ways. The very existence of such an international mechanism would presumably serve as a stimulus to governments to make every effort to resolve conflicts at the national level. Where brought to an international board, pressure could be provided in a number of ways including constraints on accessing international capital from multilateral and bilateral sources as well as other types of sanctions.

Precedents already exist for extending international authority to such vital life support systems as water resources and river basins. The International Monetary Fund and the World Bank Group influence the economies of member countries that wish to receive grants and loans and set conditions on how funds received are spent. There is also a gradual widening of World Bank Group conditionalities concerning large dams. At first the World Bank only required a Dam Safety Panel of international experts whose job it was to ensure that design, construction and operations met international standards.

Operational Guidelines to be followed by Bank staff and host country counterparts followed, starting with OMS 2.33 on Involuntary Resettlement in 1980. Later in the 1980s panels with environmental, public health and resettlement expertise were added for the Bank's more contentious projects – most of which have been large dams.

In response to criticisms of Bank involvement in India's SSP, the Bank agreed to an Independent Review that issued a highly critical report in 1992 of both the Bank and the various Indian project authorities. Influenced by the Independent Review but wanting more control over the review process, the Bank established its own Inspection Panel to which local NGOs and other stakeholders could, and did, make complaints. In the second half of the 1990s a Quality Assurance and Compliance Unit was established under the Vice President for Environmentally and Socially Sustainable Development to ensure that the Bank's ten key safety-net policies would be systematically and uniformly applied in all Bank operations. Other multilateral organizations, including the regional banks, have moved in the same direction, while two other members of the World Bank Group – the International Finance Corporation (IFC) and Multilateral Investment Guarantee Agency (MIGA) – established the Office of the Compliance Adviser/Ombudsman in fiscal year 2000, which reports directly to the World Bank President.

The World Trade Organization (WTO), with over 130 members, has a binding dispute resolution mechanism for settling conflicts between member nations that include both OECD and late-industrializing countries. A world court (ICJ) has recently been established to deal with human rights and other abuses of the world citizenry, while influential leaders have begun calling for more effective global governance. Renato Ruggiero, while still WTO Director General, gave a 1999 speech in which he emphasized the need for building 'a global system for the third millennium,' and the need for the 'international rule of law' since 'our globalizing world demands global solutions'.

Concerned by 'the prospect of environmental collapse,' Ruggiero became one of a number of prominent supporters of a Global Environmental Organization for global environmental governance. Other supporters include French President Jacques Chirac and former USSR President Mikhail Gorbachev. While such an organization might also provide a 'home' for an International Adjudication and Compliance Board for large dams, it would be preferable to link it to an already existing organization. Moreover, environmental issues would be only one of a number of important issues to be addressed by the Board.

Strategic Priority 2: Comprehensive options assessment

The importance and nature of comprehensive options assessment is presented with clarity and emphasis in the WCD Final Report. To be effective, options assessment should be a process that extends from the beginning of the decision-making process to the end of a programme's or a project's operation, which in the event of a dam would include decommissioning. The composition of

---

BOX 9.3 RECOMMENDATIONS

- Comprehensive options assessment should commence at the beginning of the decision-making process for water resource development and continue throughout the operation of whatever programme or project is selected.
- All relevant stakeholders and categories of concerned people should be involved.
- Economic, financial and technical issues should be complemented by equal consideration of environmental, institutional and social issues.
- Where a dam is selected, interdepartmental and interdisciplinary oversight is needed for increasing potential benefits and decreasing potential costs. Such oversight, with an influential political leader as chair and backed up by sufficient finance to bring in other institutions, should be required for all large dams whether backed by a single ministry or other agency.

---

stakeholders could be expected to change as a programme or project evolved. Done correctly, the options assessment process requires additional 'upfront' funding. On the other hand, it reduces the likelihood of more expensive delays and opposition at a later date such as those that characterize India's SSP.

Based on an assessment of needs for water resource development and involving strategic planning, comprehensive options assessment 'must precede selection of any specific development plan'. It must also acknowledge from the start that 'Alternatives to dams do often exist' (WCD, 2000, pp221–224) and that options must include improving the performance and sustainability of existing dams. And throughout, the options assessment process should be guided by the core WCD values of equity, efficiency, participatory decision-making, sustainability and accountability.

During the assessment process, economic, environmental, financial, social and technical aspects should have the 'same significance' while being assessed (ibid, p221). My experience indicates that institutional capacity should also be included. This is especially the case with environmental and social aspects and with resettlement in particular. Even though the definition of capacity in the 50 dam survey was restricted to staff numbers and expertise (Chapter 3), outcomes were adverse in every one of the cases where a major lack of capacity was coded. Capacity is also highly relevant for flood management once a dam is operational.

If a dam is selected as the most desirable option, oversight is important because of the breadth, importance and uncertainty associated with outcomes and the complexity of the planning and implementation process. Provided by an overseeing government committee, such oversight should be interdepartmental and interdisciplinary. It should be required for all dams advocated by one ministry (such as energy or irrigation) or other agency because of the risk of 'tunnel vision' that ignores potential benefits and potential costs. Oversight committees should be chaired by a politically influential leader, such as a deputy prime minister for mainstream dams on large rivers and tributaries. They should also have the finance necessary to bring other government agencies, NGOs, and research institutions, for example, into the planning and implementation process – functions that lie outside the responsibilities of stakeholders involved in comprehensive options assessment.

Strategic Priority 3: Addressing existing dams

Introduction

The majority of the world's large dams already exist. The development potential of far too many is under-utilized, which is why their modernization should be given priority as a development option over the construction of new dams. Single-purpose dams, in particular, could often be operated or rehabilitated in ways that would reduce adverse impacts and realize a wider range of benefits. Modernizing operations are considered in the sections that follow under a number of headings: Taking a basin-wide perspective, Evaluation and monitoring, Dam safety licensing and relicensing, Dealing with under-utilized potential, Retrofitting and rehabilitation, and Restoration and reparations.

Taking a basin-wide perspective

With all dams, operations should be carried out within a river basin context, which may involve two or more rivers where inter-basin transfers occur. That is especially the case where a cascade of dams exists and where changes in how one or more dams are operated can have a negative or positive impact on those downstream. In the early 1990s when China's Longtan Dam was still a

---

BOX 9.4 RECOMMENDATIONS

- Modernizing existing dams should take priority over building new dams.
- The operation of multiple dams within a river basin should be coordinated.
- Additional attention should be paid to the environmental and socio-economic impacts of inter-basin transfers on the receiving river.
- Uncertain outcomes associated with modernization require an adaptive management approach based on ongoing monitoring and evaluation.
- The safety of all large dams requires licensing and periodic relicensing, with the licensing process used as an opportunity to address issues associated with modernization and decommissioning.
- Modernization should include the extent to which underperformance can be addressed by adding additional functions to single-purpose dams and, as societal values change, extending and upgrading irrigation systems and achieving unrealized multiplier effects.
- Retrofitting and rehabilitation should be an ongoing process.
- The World Bank Group, as the largest donor funding large dams, should take the lead through their Inspection Panel and Compliance Adviser/Ombudsman in piloting procedures for environmental restoration and social reparations.

candidate for World Bank funding and I was on the environment and resettlement panel, I was intrigued by the potential that this high dam at the top of China's third largest river system had for improving the efficiencies of the downstream cascade of dams.

Flood management is an example of the need for taking a basin-wide perspective. It is also a reason why institutional capacity should be an important issue during options assessment. The severity of floods that killed hundreds and dislocated thousands in 2001 and 2002 along the middle and lower Zambezi was due in part to the unwillingness of operators of the Kariba and Cahora Bassa Dams, both of which are single-purpose hydro installations, to lower reservoir levels before the advent of the rainy season and to manage flood releases thereafter (Davies, 2001). Also in the past few years a similar criticism has been made in Nigeria about the operation of the Kainji Dam on the Niger, the Shiroro Dam on the Kaduna, and the Tiga and Challawa Dams at the top of the Hadejia-Nguru system.[15]

Another type of mismanagement has been the unwillingness of the operators of Mali's Manantali Dam to make controlled releases for the benefit of downstream communities in spite of the fact that economic studies had shown that such releases would be a win–win situation.[16] Where inter-basin transfers occur, scant attention has been paid to impacts on the receiving river. Because inter-basin transfers from Laos' Nam Theun 2 Project will double the flow of the Xe Bang Fai, I was concerned, as a POE member, about the impact of an altered flow regime on the productivity and socio-economics of the existing fishery. I learned that there was virtually no research on that topic for rivers in the tropics and subtropics. Even more disturbing is that an increasing number of such transfers are occurring worldwide 'despite a lack of adequate knowledge of the effects of such schemes' (Snaddon et al, 1999, piv).

Evaluation and monitoring

A major constraint to carrying out the WCD process as well as my own 50 dam survey was the lack of information on the extent to which even major dams have met the goals that they were supposed to achieve. That is an amazing conclusion given that such dams often are a nation's largest single development project at the time of their construction. Optimizing how existing dams are to be operated in the future will require more information on their past impacts and far more monitoring in the future of the changes implemented. Of eight lessons learned by the authors of the WCD Grand Coulee Dam case study, two dealt with the need for periodic and planned re-evaluations of project operations. According to the first, re-evaluations 'provide a mechanism for incorporating temporal changes in social values', while the second states that 'they provide a mechanism for incorporating changes in science and technology' (Ortolano et al, 2000, p8-2 and p8-3). Changes in science would include an increasing emphasis on the need for adaptive management to deal with the amount of uncertainty associated with such major human experiments as dam construction.

Dam safety licensing and relicensing

All large dams should be licensed and subject to relicensing, and yet an unknown number are unlicensed or, if they are licensed, have not been periodically relicensed. Relicensing should be not just for safety reasons but also because the relicensing process gives the public the opportunity to participate in deciding whether or not relicensing should proceed, and if it should, under what conditions (including implementation of environmental flows).

Dealing with under-utilized potential

Dealing with under-utilized potential is applicable to all existing large dams, and especially to those older than 50 years, as a result of changing social values. Reassessment and extension of potential is especially relevant for single-purpose dams designed by a specific ministry or parastatal organization and for dams that include irrigation. The two mainstream dams on the Zambezi were built and operated to generate electricity by single-purpose agencies that resist utilization of stored water for other purposes in spite of significant environmental costs to downstream habitats (because of regularization of river flows) and economic and social costs to communities (because of poorly managing flood releases and an underdeveloped irrigation potential). Now that both dams have been integrated within the Southern African Power Pool (SAPP), the opportunity exists for managing both to achieve a wider range of goals. This is especially the case with Cahora Bassa in Mozambique where Beilfuss (2001 and 2003) and Gammelsrød (1992) have demonstrated how environmental flows could provide important ecological (especially within the Zambezi Delta) and economic (through an increase in the off-take of shrimp which is one of Mozambique's more important sources of foreign exchange) benefits without jeopardizing hydropower generation.[17]

Dams built primarily for irrigation or with a major irrigation component are notorious for underperformance. Those within the WCD knowledge base 'fell well short of targets in terms of development of command area (and infrastructure), area actually irrigated, and to a lesser extent the intensity with which areas are actually irrigated' (WCD, 2000, p43). In some cases, especially where projections of area to be irrigated were based on inadequate soil surveys,[18] extension and performance improvement would not be possible. Elsewhere, governments and project authorities have a wide range of options. Conventional ones include improving canal infrastructure and water management via such means as drainage. Especially important is more emphasis on a system's operation and maintenance (O&M), a frequently reported tendency being for project authorities to emphasize construction while underemphasizing, and especially underfunding, O&M. Another less frequently noted inadequacy, especially where the project authority is a construction and engineering-oriented ministry of irrigation, is failure to integrate agricultural research, on-farm extension and marketing into systems operation.

Working with individual farm households to raise their disposable income and with farmers' water user associations is a win–win situation. Higher incomes are important, for example, to enable farmers to purchase pumps to expedite the conjunctive use of ground and surface water, improved use of the former giving farmers greater control over water supplies and further raising farmer disposable income. As discussed in Chapter 3, the increasing incomes of many farming households are the engine that drives development during the early stages of industrialization. Accelerating the global trend of involving farmer-run water user associations in system management will further decrease the financial costs of O&M activities and may increase productivity. Working more closely with farmers will also enable project authorities to gain familiarity with how farming households can use water for a wider range of purposes including livestock management and aquaculture, which will further increase productivity and income.

Potential for extending irrigation systems and increasing output is especially great in India, where WCD's India Case Study reports 'a persistent gap between the created irrigation potential and its utilization,' with there being some evidence that the discrepancy may be increasing (Banerji et al, 2000, pix). Part of the problem, especially on inter-state rivers, is because rivers are under state rather than central government control, with states on inter-state rivers hurrying to increase access to scarce water supplies by building dams for reservoir storage. But the emphasis on dam construction the authors also relate to an engineering bias 'in project preparation at the State level, and examination at the Central level,' there being 'no *inter-disciplinary planning* [the authors' emphasis] in the proper sense of the term' (ibid, pviii). Although some states have begun experimenting with farmer-run water user associations, another constraint is that planning and implementation remains primarily in the hands of government agencies. Moreover, because irrigation benefits have gone mainly to larger-scale farmers, 'dams not only help maintain the current inequities in the Indian society but, in some ways, exacerbate them (ibid, pxiv).

Retrofitting and rehabilitation

Retrofitting should be an ongoing process to improve safety, development potential and a project's lifespan. The possibility that global warming will increase storm, and hence flood, events will require improving capability to release outflow and to improve downstream 'early warning systems'. Productivity can be increased by updating equipment and operational systems. As one example, improved decision support systems used in conjunction with accurate data on river flows 'can increase hydroelectric benefits by 5 to 10% over rule-based operating criteria' even without affecting existing water uses (WCD, 2000, p226). While WCD notes that lifespan can be increased by enlarging reservoir capacity in most late-industrializing countries, enlargement of capacity can be expected not just to require more resettlement but also a second resettlement for those communities that had opted to remain within the reservoir basin when the dam was built. If selected, such an option should only occur on the basis of 'free, prior and informed consent' during the options assessment process. A far better alternative to enlarging reservoir capacity is to consider the feasibility of installing improved techniques for sediment flushing.

Restoration and reparations

In addressing existing dams, WCD's key message emphasized two types of opportunities. One was to 'optimize benefits'. The other was to 'address outstanding social issues and strengthen environmental mitigation and restoration measures' (WCD, 2000, p225). In both industrialized and late-industrializing countries there are useful examples of what could be done, but little sustained action. In fact, in Europe and the US more attention has been paid to decommissioning relatively small dams in an attempt to improve ecological services than to operating existing dams in ways that will improve their services. A few countries, including Australia, Cameroon, South Africa and the US, have experimented with environmental flows on a few rivers, while others, Nigeria included, have considered the possibility but done nothing. Examples also include efforts, as along the Mississippi and the Rhine, to restore some wetlands by removing levees, with the US government even resettling some communities in the process.

Inadequate as the environmental examples are, they have occurred more frequently than efforts by project authorities and donors to address outstanding social issues. In the US, Native American tribes have had to rely on the courts for reparations. Courts in India have also been used to appeal compensation offered to individual households by project authorities. Only in China is there a national policy for project authorities to address outstanding issues associated with previous resettlement. This involves a revolving 'remaining problems fund'. Although I have not seen any reviews of its general effectiveness, several decades after resettlement I found it playing an important role in rehabilitating Danjiangkou resettlers in the mid-1980s.

The only examples that I am aware of where a multilateral donor has addressed a reparation issue at a later date is the Gwembe Tonga component of Zambia and the World Bank's Power Rehabilitation Project, and Bank funding for Pakistan's Ghazi Barotha Hydropower Project. It remains to be seen if either sets a precedent. Not only was the incorporation of the Gwembe Tonga component into the Zambian project suggested by a third party, but – due, especially, to inadequate funding – it remains to be seen if implementation achieves more than being just another project that raised, but did not meet, the legitimate expectations of affected people.

In the Ghazi Barotha case, the Bank tied a US$350 million loan not just to meeting the Bank's environmental and resettlement guidelines during project implementation but also to addressing outstanding resettlement issues arising from the construction of the Tarbela Dam in the 1970s. In a December 2002 release, the Bank threatened to suspend, and possibly cancel, the Ghazi Barotha loan because of non-compliance with various loan agreements including those addressing Tarbela resettlement in regard to which the Bank reported minimal progress. It is too early to know the extent to which the Bank will insist on their implementation. While the Independent Review of the SSP was highly critical of both the World Bank and the project authorities in its 1992 report, the resettlement record of the central government and the three state governments has worsened since that time with no substantive reaction from the Bank. Although the Bank is no longer directly involved in SSP, by its own admission its responsibilities did not end following its withdrawal.

Looking to the future, the best approach for project authorities is to reduce the need for reparations by two approaches. One, currently being pioneered by Canada's Hydro-Quebec, is to bring resettlers, hosts and other affected communities into a project as partners. The other, as is happening in Brazil and China, is to set aside a portion of project revenue for benefiting affected people. In regard to existing dams, I believe that the World Bank Group, and the regional banks, as major funders of large dams should take on the responsibility, at the very least, of establishing guidelines for dealing with reparation issues based on carefully planned and implemented pilot projects. As stated in the previous chapter, it is not clear that the World Bank really cares about addressing poverty issues associated with the implementation of its largest infrastructure projects. Why, for example, has so little funding been given for implementing the Bank's requirement that 'resettlement activities should be conceived and executed as sustainable development programs' (World Bank, 2001, p1)?

The World Bank Group has the means for taking action by giving the Bank's Inspection Panel and the IFC/MIGA Compliance Adviser/Ombudsman (CAO) the authority to deal with restoration and reparations issues. Both are already dealing with stakeholder complaints concerning dams. Surely it makes sense to give them, or at least their parent institutions, more authority to see that substantiated complaints are addressed. Of the 25 submissions to the Inspection Panel by mid-2002, the Board recommended that three of the eight involving large dams be investigated. As for CAO, its most recent complaint assessment is a May 2003 report dealing with Chile's Pangue project. Critical of IFC's involvement prior to its July 2002 exit from the project, the report stated that 'IFC should consider that it has some outstanding obligations to those affected so that they may be in the best position to continue building a sustainable relationship' with the project authority and relevant others (IFC, 2003, p4). Moreover, the report states that 'The CAO may assist the complainant further in resolving the issues of concern if the complainant so wishes' (ibid, p3). This might require a special project that it should be IFC responsibility to fund and supervise.

Strategic Priority 4: Sustaining rivers and livelihoods

Introduction

This priority deals with river basin ecosystems and draws on Chapter 3 of WCD's Final Report. A multilayered approach is recommended that 'prioritizes avoidance, especially in sensitive areas, and has in-built checks and balances that adapt and respond to changes' (WCD, 2000, p235). Avoidance is crucial. Greater emphasis on making affected people project beneficiaries at least has the potential for improving livelihoods. Such is not the case with some environmental impacts of major dams on mainstreams and tributaries where impacts on deltas, for example, are often irreversible.

BOX 9.5 RECOMMENDATIONS

- More attention should be paid during the options assessment process to the irreversibility of the environmental impacts of large dams.
- More comparative research on the provision of life support systems by free-flowing rivers should be undertaken.
- More comparative research on the environmental impacts of large dams should be a global priority, with special emphasis on aquifers, wetlands, deltas and offshore marine conditions and resources.
- Future guidelines should include indicators of environmental impacts, including those that are irreversible, during options assessment.
- The role of environmental flows for the benefit of ecosystems and downstream people should be featured in the planning of future dams.
- Environmental planning for reservoir basins should be based on the assumption that a majority of resettlers would prefer to remain as close as possible to their present location.
- Environmental planning for catchments should include the land and water use systems of existing communities within a conservation and development approach.
- Wherever possible, new dams should be built on already dammed rivers.
- Required environmental set-asides should include designation of free-flowing rivers.

On the other hand, it is hard to prioritize avoidance when so little is known about the downstream environmental impacts of dams. That is why the recommendations for more before-and-after dam construction research, which are the main recommendations for further research in this book, are so important. Research results can then be incorporated within guidelines as the type of criteria for distinguishing between 'good dams and bad dams' (Ledec et al, 1999) that are discussed below.

Deltas

A major reason for the caution expressed in Chapter 4 against using beneficial multiplier effects from large dams and associated irrigation as a reason for dam construction is the difficulty of assessing the cultural, economic and life support system value of whatever irreversible environmental effects may be involved. This is especially the case where mainstream dams have an irreversible impact on important deltas, as was the case of the Colorado and Mississippi Rivers in the US, the Zambezi and Nile in Africa, and the Indus in India and Pakistan (Chapter 7). I am aware of no comprehensive and quantitative studies of the ecological, economic and socio-cultural costs in such cases. The same applies where upstream dams share responsibility for the periodic drying out of the lower reaches of rivers such as China's Yellow River and Australia's Murray–Darling River System.

Because of such irreversible effects, future dams on mainstream rivers should be selected as an option only under the most pressing national needs that cannot be met by other options. A partial exception might be where other dams have already been built on the mainstream. Then a cascade of dams might be an acceptable option, especially where a mainstream dam had been built across the river's lower reaches. In Brazil, for example, a cascade of dams in the Tocantins–Araguaia Basin should be considered as an alternative to future dams within the Amazon Basin because of the location of the Tucurui Dam on the lower Tocantins. On the other hand, the existence of Chinese dams on the Upper Mekong River should not be used to justify mainstream dams in the downstream countries because of the livelihood dependence of millions of people living in riverine communities on flood recession agriculture and grazing, and on flood-dependent fisheries and other natural resources.

Consideration of a cascade of dams would apply even more to already dammed tributaries. In Laos, for example, the NT2 POE has suggested that dam construction be restricted, at least for the foreseeable future, to several rivers. In addition to the costs of mainstream dams to riverine ecosystems, another factor to be considered is the need – also stressed by WCD – to maintain some free-flowing rivers in a world where already 60 per cent have been dammed. Such an option should be emphasized in the environmental guidelines of donors with environmental set-asides including a requirement that another free-flowing river not be dammed. That is an option that could, and should be, followed in countries such as Brazil, Ethiopia, Laos, Nepal, Vietnam and Zambia.

Environmental flows

Planning for all future dams should include consideration of environmental flows to 'help maintain downstream ecosystems and the communities that depend on them' (WCD, 2000, p234). On the other hand, environmental flows should not be considered as a substitute for natural flow regimes. Rather they are an important means for mitigating what would otherwise be more severe environmental and social impacts. Case studies in Australia, Cameroon, South Africa and the US have shown their benefit. The science is there. Jackie King and her South African colleagues have broadened methodologies originally developed for aquatic resources, fish especially, to incorporate people's livelihoods (King et al, 2000), and such methodologies have been applied to Lesotho's Highland Water Project. The March 2002 international working conference in Cape Town on Environmental Flows for River Systems dealt with people as well as with ecosystems.[19] Since then the World Bank has appointed an advisory committee on Environmental Flows, and IUCN has published its 2003 manual on the importance of environmental flows and how to implement them. There is no longer any excuse for planners to ignore the role of environmental flows in the planning of future dams.

Reservoir basins

Especially in late-industrializing countries, many rural resettlers can be expected to prefer resettlement within future reservoir basins so as to remain in as familiar a habitat (host populations included) as possible. Opportunities for helping them to become project beneficiaries should be designed, through participatory planning, to avoid environmental degradation and especially the risk of increasing siltation and decreasing water quality in the reservoir. Especially important is for plans to include ways for local communities to help manage, and benefit financially from, tourism and whatever parks and biodiversity reserves are to be implemented, and to develop the means for competing with immigrants.

Catchments

In industrial countries, as well as in such late-industrializing countries as China, South Africa and Zimbabwe, governments and project authorities are paying increasing attention to improved environmental management of middle and upper basin catchments by involving relevant stakeholders in sub-catchment management committees and development implementation. Especially impressive is China's Loess Plateau Watershed Rehabilitation Project on the middle and upper reaches of the Yellow River where the Yellow River Conservancy Commission, assisted by World Bank funding, is working with local government and local communities to implement hundreds of sub-catchment dams for sediment control linked to increasing arable land and for water supply to villagers and their livestock (World Bank, 2003).

In Zimbabwe the government is experimenting with sub-catchment management committees with one of the first two experiments involving a tributary draining into Lake Kariba. Similar committees are being developed in South Africa, with government agencies and local stakeholders working in the Olifants River Basin with the African office of the International Water Management Institute. Relatively recent, all such efforts suggest the way forward that planners should take elsewhere.

In Laos, the government has been working closely with IUCN, WCS and the World Bank to protect the entire 3500km^2 catchment of the proposed Nam Theun 2 Dam within a National Biological Conservation Area. To be administered by a Watershed Management and Protection Authority established in 2000, planning for the conservation area will include working with 6000 indigenous people in a way that will benefit from their indigenous knowledge, incorporate their communities in management activities including biodiversity research and control of poachers, and include environmentally sustainable development activities designed to improve and stabilize their land and water use systems.

Environmental set-asides, complementary approaches and restrictions

Implementation of environmental set-asides has not proved satisfactory in the past. Supposed to replace inundated forest area, mitigate impacts on biodiversity and offset possible use of forest reserves for resettlement purposes, adequate set-asides have been hard to find and will be still harder to find in late-industrializing countries as populations continue to increase. India's SSP illustrates some of the difficulties involved when the large majority of the 3000 resettlers from Maharashtra preferred to remain in their State and to resettle in nearby forest reserves.

Complementary approaches are needed. Although not likely to duplicate environmental resources lost, one would be to set aside one free-flowing river for every one proposed to be dammed in the future. There should also be environmental restrictions equivalent to those involving affected people. Just as dams, such as China's Three Gorges and India's Sardar Sarovar, should not be built that require the relocation of large numbers of people and where inadequate land, jobs and other resources are available for rehabilitation, so too should environmental restrictions be formulated as suggested by Goodland, Ledec and other World Bank colleagues for selecting sites for hydropower projects.

Goodland considered 'intact habitat lost' to be 'the single most relevant proxy for environmental impact' (1997, p84), and to be measured as hectares lost per megawatt generated (Goodland et al, 1993, p125). Also important, especially in the tropics with their high biodiversity, was 'a thorough biotic inventory', reduced 'reservoir water retention time', and siting above undammed tributaries (hence in the upper reaches of a river where possible) with new dams preferred on already dammed rivers (Goodland, 1995, pp124–126). High sedimentation rates that can be expected to adversely affect live storage (Goodland, 1996, p39) would be another indicator of a 'bad dam' that deserves increasing attention because of the expectation of more extreme climatic events associated with global warming. Goodland's two most important social indicators were number of resettlers per megawatt generated and presence of vulnerable ethnic minorities followed by risk of water-borne diseases.

Following up on Goodland's work, Ledec, Quintero and Mejía use seven key environmental and social indicators to distinguish between 'good dams and bad dams' (1999) that are both quantitative and easily calculated. They are (1) reservoir surface area (especially ratio of inundated hectares per megawatt), (2) numbers of resettlers (again measured by number displaced per megawatt generated), (3) water retention time in reservoir, (4) biomass flooded, (5) length of river impounded, (6) number of downriver tributaries and (7) access roads through forests. They also suggest nine other indicators that they consider useful but less powerful and that require more data collection. Derivative indicators would include production of greenhouse gases and aquatic weed infestation so that shallow reservoirs in the tropics such as Brokopondo (Surinam) and Balbina (Brazil) would be avoided in the future. It is important to emphasize that such indicators tend to be more negative in the late-developing countries, where the majority of future dams will be built, because of their location in the tropics and subtropics and/or because of larger numbers of resettlers.

Strategic Priority 5: Recognizing entitlements and sharing benefits

Introduction

WCD's introduction to this Strategic Priority includes the statements that 'Successful mitigation, resettlement and development are fundamental commitments and responsibilities of the State and the developer... Impact assessment includes all people in the reservoir, upstream, downstream and in catchment areas whose properties, livelihoods and non-material resources are affected' (2000, p240). Moreover, 'Adversely affected people are recognized as first among the beneficiaries of the project.'

The analysis of resettlement in Chapter 3 draws on a statistical analysis of 44 cases. It documents the nature of the four-stage resettlement process, the impoverishment risks that must be avoided, and the conditions and procedures that are necessary for a successful outcome. Chapter 4 documents that sufficient opportunities often exist to enable resettlers to become project beneficiaries. Catchment examples discussed under the fourth Strategic Priority indicates that the same is true for upstream residents. Unfortunately insufficient research has been done on affected people living below dams to know whether or not their livelihoods can be improved. As in the case of deltas, some adverse impacts may be irreversible. This is especially likely to be the case in late-industrializing countries where most future dams will be built and where the economies of tens of thousands, and even millions of people –

BOX 9.6 RECOMMENDATIONS

- Affected people in reservoir basins, downstream of dams and in catchment areas should be project beneficiaries.
- Large dams should not be built where opportunities do not exist for improving the lifestyles of affected people. Increasing attention should be paid to opportunities whereby affected people become partners with project authorities.
- Large dams should not be built where the political will is not present for implementing the opportunities necessary for improving living standards.
- Affected people should always be included in the options assessment process as full participants.
- International adjudication should be available to affected people where prior informed consent has not been obtained.
- Planning and implementing resettlement should be the responsibility of the project authority.
- Budgets for resettlement purposes should be stand-alone because the resettlement process can be expected to extend well beyond the end of the construction phase.
- Budgeting for resettlement should include the host population and should anticipate the need for additional finance as a result of undercounting, population increase, construction delays, the need for additional staff and staff training, the complexities involved and unexpected events.

as along the Mekong – are sustained by natural flood regimes. This risk is one of the major reasons why I believe large dams on mainstreams should be considered only as a last option in the future.

Resettlement

This section should be read in conjunction with Chapter 4, which details how to implement a beneficial resettlement process. In anticipation of criticism of WCD's resettlement guidelines, it is important to emphasize that similar guidelines had been previously published by the International Commission on Large Dams (ICOLD) in their November 1995 *Position Paper on Dams and Environment*. On the first page ICOLD states that 'we must ensure that the people directly affected by a dam project are first to benefit from it,' while the fourth page emphasizes that 'For the population involved, resettlement must result in a clear improvement of their living standard.' Case studies not only show that improvement is possible but they have replicable features such as irrigation and fisheries that can be implemented elsewhere.

Seeking improvement is a win–win situation, for it also contributes to the stream of project benefits and lowers the risks of a reduced project life because of increasing sedimentation. On the other hand, implementing a successful resettlement process needs to be recognized as a complicated development process in which political will on the part of the government and the project authority, adequate institutional capacity including experienced staff and funding over an extended time period, and participation by affected people are all important, while adequate opportunities that are available to resettlers for improving living standards are essential. Where such opportunities are available, the evidence indicates that a majority of resettlers will grasp them, although in the process they may need training and credit so as to be able to compete with immigrants. Involving the host population as beneficiaries is also essential; otherwise competition over limited land, grazing, fuel and building materials, jobs, commercial opportunities and social services can result in conflict and lead to impoverishment risks (Cernea, 1999a; Cernea and McDowell, 2000) for both resettlers and hosts.

It must also be recognized that successful resettlement takes time. Because of associated stress and hardship, resettlement involves a transition stage following physical removal that often lasts several years and during which living standards of the majority can be expected to drop. On the other hand, once resettlers get back on their feet by coming to terms with their new habitat and neighbours and achieving self-sufficiency, resettlement theory (Chapter 2) based on case study analysis documents their readiness to build new communities and adopt new economic opportunities. These need to be environmentally, economically, institutionally and culturally sustainable into the second generation of resettlers.

Downstream communities

I find it appalling that only recently have a few donors and project authorities considered dam impacts on downstream communities during feasibility studies. To repeat previous statements in this monograph, numbers of affected people are likely to far exceed the number affected by reservoir formation. In industrial countries the large majority of downstream residents tend to live in cities along major water courses and can expect to benefit from upstream dams as a result of improved energy and food supplies, flood management and navigation. While the same is likely to apply to rural residents, including farmers, in industrial countries, it does not apply to late-industrializing countries where the livelihoods of many millions of people are still dependent on natural river flows.

A few African examples warrant repeating. In the Senegal River Basin, construction of the Manantali Dam has adversely affected up to a million downstream residents (Horowitz and Salem-Murdock, 1990; Salem-Murdock, 1996; Adams, 1999). In Eastern Nigeria hundreds of thousands of flood-dependent rural residents living below the junction of the Hadejia and Jama'are Rivers have been adversely affected by the upriver Tiga Dam, despite benefits per unit of water being higher for use in associated wetlands than for irrigation provided by the dam (Barbier et al, 1997). Along the lower Zambezi, hundreds of thousands of villagers have been adversely affected by Mozambique's Cahora Bassa Dam (Muhai, 1997; Isaacman, 2001). Elsewhere dams on the Indus have adversely affected millions in Pakistan's Sind Province, while suggested mainstream dams on the Middle and Upper Mekong can also be expected to adversely affect millions.

Looking to the future, options assessment that includes dams needs to consider in a more participatory fashion, and in much more detail, impacts on downstream communities, including those affected by inter-basin transfers. Where a dam option is selected, feasibility studies should include assessing not just the avoidance and mitigation of adverse impacts but how to enable downstream communities to become project beneficiaries. One way, effectively used by Brazil in the middle São Francisco basin (Scatasta, 2003) is to incorporate irrigation within agro-industrial development districts, thereby increasing multiplier effects from both farming and non-farming employment and enterprise development. At the very least, release of environmental flows can be an important means for reducing adverse impacts on flood-dependent communities.

Strategic Priority 6: Ensuring compliance

As emphasized by WCD, a generalized set of compliance guidelines is needed, with a compliance plan incorporated into the documentation and budgeting for each project prior to commencement. Ensuring compliance is costly so that a project's ability to deliver 'must be explicitly addressed in the multi-criteria analysis to assess options' (WCD, 2000, p248). Compliance implementation should be subject to 'independent and transparent review' (ibid, p244). An Independent Review Panel is suggested as the best way to assess whether or not compliance commitments have been met 'in order to restore trust and confidence in the process' – wording which illustrates the unsatisfactory nature

---

BOX 9.7 RECOMMENDATIONS

- Compliance requirements, adequately budgeted, should be incorporated within legally binding contracts.
- Realistically budgeted performance bonds and/or trusts dealing with relevant environmental and social issues should be a legally binding requirement.
- Compliance review should be a function of an international adjudication and compliance board as recommended under Strategic Priority 1.

---

of the compliance process to date.[20] Drawing up WCD's recommended list of accredited experts could be a function of the International Adjudication and Compliance Board for dams that I recommended under Strategic Priority 1. Another function of the Board could be drawing up an international certification system such as WCD also recommends. Examples given included certification of forest products advocated by the Forestry Stewardship Council and a certification standard for dams under the International Organization for Standardization (ISO).

Regulatory frameworks at the national level not only should incorporate 'best practice' guidelines, but ensure that those relating to compliance be included within legally binding contracts. For tasks such as resettlement, as well as programmes for downstream users and integrated catchment management, adequately financed pre-project performance bonds are necessary, or in the case of government parastatals such as Lesotho's Highlands Development Authority, trust funds. As for corruption, though WCD also notes voluntary integrity pacts, strong sanctions are needed that include public exposure and permanent or temporary debarment 'from participation in tenders and contracts' (ibid, p250).

Strategic Priority 7: Sharing rivers for peace, development and security

WCD's Strategic Priority 7 relates to the world's 261 international river basins. Global concern over the risk of water wars has been growing over the past ten

---

BOX 9.8 RECOMMENDATIONS

- Good faith negotiations between countries sharing river basins should be backed up by international law.
- A first step should be ratification of the 1997 UN Convention on the Law of Non-Navigational Uses of International Waters.
- A second step should be the creation of an International Adjudication and Compliance Board under either the International Court of Justice or UN auspices.

years as awareness of the growing water crisis has increased.[21] During the 1990–1993 period, the project on Environmental Change and Acute Conflict of the University of Toronto and the American Academy of Arts and Sciences carried out a number of country case studies, with co-principal investigator Homer-Dixon concluding that 'the renewable resource most likely to stimulate interstate resource war is river water' (Homer-Dixon, 1994, p19). WCD, however, took a different tack by concentrating on how sharing international waters can also propagate peace, a theme which WCD chair Kader Asmal emphasized in his speech as recipient of the Year 2000 Stockholm Water Prize. What are needed are good faith negotiations that involve a 'shift in focus from the narrow approach of allocating a finite resource to the sharing of rivers and their associated benefits' (WCD, 2000, p251).

An example of what the Commission has in mind is the Nile Basin Initiative, which is a partnership of the ten basin countries that began in 1999. It was initiated with the help of the World Bank Group, UNDP and Canada's International Development Agency (CIDA), with funds pledged by more than ten donors during 2001. A Shared Vision was formulated 'to achieve sustainable socio-economic development through the equitable utilization of, and benefit from, the common Nile Basin water resources'. The Initiative is organized around a Council of Ministers, a Technical Advisory Committee and a Secretariat. The initial emphasis has been on electricity. In June 2003 the responsible ministers from all ten countries concluded their meeting by signing a 'Dar Es Salaam Declaration on Regional Electric Power Trade'.[22]

Just setting up the Initiative has been a major accomplishment, given previous tension between Egypt and Ethiopia in the lower basin states, and between the lower basin states of Egypt and the Sudan and the six upper basin states over the 1929 (between Egypt and the UK) and 1959 (between Egypt and the Sudan) Nile Waters Treaties. But as Nabil M. El-Khodari pointed out in late 2002, much more needs to be done. A legally binding agreement has yet to be endorsed by the member states; indeed, El-Khodari states that 'as of August 15th, 2002, none of the Nile Basin countries have ratified the Convention on the Law of the Non-Navigational Uses of International Watercourses' (United Nations, 1997). He is also concerned about the lack of transparency surrounding Initiative activities, the delayed appearance of information on the Initiative's website, and the non-involvement of such UN organizations as FAO, UNEP and UNESCO. Given the Shared Vision's emphasis on poverty alleviation, there also appears to be an overemphasis on macro-economic planning while the environmental component does not include 'the notion of water for the ecosystem' (El-Khodari, 2002). One also wonders how the other member states will cope with the Sudan's proceeding with the Merowe Dam on the Nile mainstream and Ethiopia's commencement of construction during 2002 of the Tekeze Dam on a Blue Nile tributary.

A second example could arise as a result of the Challenge Program on Water and Food under the Consultative Group for International Agricultural Research (CGIAR). Involving 13 river basins in Africa, Asia, Latin America and the Middle East, with more to be added in Africa and over half of which are international, one of five themes is Integrated Basin Water Management Systems. As with the Nile Basin Initiative, however, the current focus is both macro and technical with little apparent attention paid to the many millions of people living along, and dependent upon, those river basins.

The major problem in implementing Strategic Priority 7 is that current principles and covenants relating to international rivers 'have no status in international law' (WCD, 2000, p252). That applies to the 1966 Helsinki Rules as well as to the 1997 UN Convention on the Law of the Non-Navigational Uses of International Waters that has yet to be ratified by the necessary number of countries. While WCD sees ratification as the way to go, once again the problem of compliance looms. This is especially the case in countries such as China and Turkey that have the resources to build dams on international rivers without international finance. As for countries that need such finance, the logical solution is tying the finance to treaties or at least to agreements between basin states that are based on such principles in the UN Convention as 'equitable and reasonable utilization', 'no significant harm' and 'prior information' where a project will have an impact on neighbouring states.

Where disputes and conflicts cannot be resolved, WCD states that 'the international community needs to take a strong and concerted stand' (ibid, p255) and recommends an independent panel such as defined in the 1997 Convention in the hope that good faith negotiations will 'lead to mutually agreeable outcomes' (ibid, p254). And if they do not, then a dispute could go to the International Court of Justice (ICJ) or to the type of adjudication and compliance board that I recommend should be set up under either ICJ or UN auspices.

Notes

CHAPTER 1

1   The seven strategic priorities are: (1) gaining public acceptance; (2) comprehensive options assessment; (3) addressing existing dams; (4) sustaining rivers and livelihoods; (5) recognizing entitlements and sharing benefits; (6) ensuring compliance; and (7) sharing rivers for peace, development and security.

2   See WCDs' *Dams and Development: A New Framework for Decision-Making*, 2000, pp15–17. Robert Goodland, the World Bank's senior environmental adviser until his recent retirement, considered resettlement 'arguably the most serious issue of hydro-projects nowadays' (1994, p149). Asit Biswas and Cecilia Tortajada of the Third World Centre for Water Management state that: 'Probably the most critical issue facing large dams at present is the issue of resettlement of people from the inundation caused by their construction' (2001, p20).

3   To become project beneficiaries, a majority of resettlers must be able to raise their living standards as a result of project opportunities. To contribute to the stream of project benefits, their disposable income must be sufficient to purchase a widening range of goods and services.

4   Robinson (2003) *Rights and Risks: The Causes, Consequences, and Challenges of Development-Induced Displacement*. See also Theodore E. Downing (2002b, p3) '*Avoiding New Poverty: Mining-Induced Displacement and Resettlement*', International Institute for Environment and Development and, in reference to dams, Balakrishnan Rajagopal (2000), *Human Rights and Development*, Contributing Paper to WCD's Thematic Review on Regulation, Compliance and Implementation.

5   Kader Asmal, at the time South Africa's Minister of Water Affairs and Forestry, was the Commission's Chair and Lakshmi Jain, then India's High Commissioner to South Africa, was Vice-Chair.

6   TenLinks.com and Umwelt-Online.

7   'A fast server in North America (www.damsreport.org) met the demand for the downloadable version of the report, as our own server was running at maximum capacity for most of the five days following the report's release' (*DAMS*, 2000).

8   Statement by UNEP's Director General at the Third Meeting of the Forum, 25–27 February 2001.

9   The core values were equity, efficiency, participatory decision-making, sustainability and accountability.

10 WCD had never intended the guidelines to be binding but rather had expected each country to adapt them to national conditions.

11 I have chosen to use the Kariba case to illustrate specific points throughout the text, rather than to present it as a detailed case history. For readers interested in more detail, the World Commission on Dam's Kariba case history (Soils Inc,

2000) provides a recent review. Resettlement is covered in Elizabeth Colson (1971) *The Social Consequences of Resettlement*, which I consider still to be the best single case study of dam resettlement. A more recent update can be downloaded from my website.

12 Perlman (1976) observed the same tendency in low-income urban settlements (*favelas*) involved in urban redevelopment in Brazil.

CHAPTER 2

1 A confusing term because of its many meanings, model is nonetheless used by a number of writers on resettlement, including Cernea. The meaning that I give to the term is that of an abstraction that attempts to simplify the dynamics of complex systems and in the case of my four-stage framework to predict how resettlers will respond to the actions of project authorities.

2 In Northern Rhodesia, the African National Congress was against the Kariba Dam and Gwembe Tonga resettlement as part of their opposition to the Central African Federation. Ill-informed about the resettlement process, the ANC's assistance was restricted to making appeals to the British Crown and the United Nations and, although banned in the Gwembe District, to local agitation against the dam and resettlement (Colson, 1971, p39). Neither activity was effective; indeed the government later blamed ANC resistance for what the Gwembe Tonga refer to as the Chisamu War, when panicking government police killed eight resisters and wounded more than 30.

3 Proceedings of the first conference was published as McDowell (1996) *Understanding Impoverishment – The Consequences of Development-Induced Displacement*. The published proceedings of the second was titled *Risks and Reconstruction: Experiences of Resettlers and Refugees* (Cernea and McDowell, 2000). The 2000 volume was specifically organized around the eight impoverishment risks.

4 Mahapatra, as is the case with other researchers, appears not to have realized that the four-stage framework applies only to cases with *successful* outcomes. While that would explain its inapplicability to the Indian situation, my reading of Mahapatra's case study of resettlement in connection with India's Ramial Dam (1999b, Annexure 1) is that the-four stage framework is applicable to the small minority who were able to improve their living standards because they could benefit from irrigation in the project's command area (see Chapter 3, this volume).

5 Rew et al (2000) were more explicit about this conclusion at a later date where they contrast 'top of the hill' policies with the 'swamp' of ground level implementation where policies can be renegotiated or transformed.

6 These include Colson, 1999; Koenig, 1995; and Mehta and Srinivasan, 2000.

7 Koenig as well as Mehta and Srinivasan rely heavily on Colson's Kariba data.

CHAPTER 3

1 This chapter is an abbreviated version of the original draft that Earthscan's reader and the editor thought was too technical and detailed in regard to analytical

procedures, statistical tables and additional discussion of data biases and significance. In total, 5 of the initial 18 tables are included, however. The first lists the 50 dams on which the statistical analysis was based. The other four illustrate the type of statistical analysis undertaken. Readers interested in more detail can download the original version titled 'Fifty Dam Survey' from my website.

2   Clarke, 2000, p50. Large dams, such as those in the high mountains of Switzerland and the Scandinavian countries, do not always cause resettlement. However, in some of the replies to the WCD survey some resettlement is known to have occurred even though no information on resettlement was received. Venezuela's Guri Dam is one example.

3   In two cases no data were included on the cultural status of the resettling population.

4   Aswan, Pimburetewa and Arenal.

5   Shuikou, Kainji, Victoria, Kossou and Yantan. Although the majority of the Ramial resettlers studied by the Mahapatras may have restored their living standards, they constituted a relatively small proportion of the resettled population. What evidence is available suggests that the living standards of the majority worsened after resettlement.

6   Yantan, Kossou and Ramial.

7   According to the Bank's 1994 *Resettlement and Development: The Bankwide Review of Projects Involving Involuntary Resettlement 1986–1993*, 'The general conclusion of the resettlement review is that the quality of the Bank's resettlement project portfolio has improved, particularly after 1991' (p8/1), while 'The Bank made significant progress during 1986 to 1993 in ... assisting borrowers in improving the circumstances of resettlers and their ability to restore their income' (pix).

8   The *Bankwide Review* came to the same conclusion as previous OED studies 'that although the data are weak, projects appear often not to have succeeded in re-establishing resettlers at a better or equal living standard and that unsatisfactory performance still persists on a wide scale' (1994a, px). The Bank's more recent (Picciotto et al, 2001) *Involuntary Resettlement: Comparative Perspectives*, which analyses resettlement outcomes from seven dam projects states the unsatisfactory nature of outcomes more forcefully: '**The Income Restoration Record is Unsatisfactory**' (p9, with bold lettering being a Bank section heading).

9   The role of resettlers and other stakeholders in the options assessment process and in the planning, implementation, management and evaluation of dam projects is dealt with in detail in Chapter 9 under Strategic Priority 1.

10   The World Bank's 1980 guidelines subsequently influenced the regional banks, the OECD countries and individual countries such as China.

11   Political will was present in all eight of the cases in which living standards appeared to have either improved or been restored.

12   The key component in the project authority's initial RAP was an irrigation project in a different river basin combined with improved housing and social services. That plan was dropped when the resettlers stated their desire to remain as close as possible to their pre-project sites.

13   Aswan, Shuikou and Arenal.

14   See, for example, Ledec et al (1999) '*Good Dams and Bad Dams: Environmental and Social Criteria for Choosing Hydroelectric Project Sites*', The World Bank.

15   While it is conceivable that unexpected events might improve outcomes, outcomes are more likely to be unfavourable simply because such events create additional

uncertainty in an already stressful situation and create conditions that were not anticipated by either planners or resettlers.

16　The five were landlessness, joblessness, food insecurity, marginality and loss of access to common property. The 44 cases included 18 in which all four stages had been completed at the time of last data collection, 5 where a majority of resettlers had at least begun Stage 3, and 21 where the majority remained in Stage 2. Because a majority of resettlers in the 21 cases had been in Stage 2 for seven or more years, that was indicative of a failing resettlement process.

17　The other three impoverishment risks were increased morbidity and mortality, social disarticulation and homelessness. In spite of increasing evidence that involuntary resettlement is associated with ill effects on health, inadequate data were available for analysis of resettlement-associated morbidity and mortality (although necessary for assessing post-project health impacts, no pre-project health surveys were carried out in 33 of the 44 cases where data existed. In only 5 of the 11 cases where such surveys were completed were they adequate). Least problematic of Cernea's impoverishment risks was homelessness, provision of housing being the most successful resettlement component worldwide. Housing was considered adequate in 38 (81 per cent) of 47 cases and inadequate in none (in seven cases inadequate housing posed a problem for a minority of households and in two other cases resettler housing was associated with some host jealousy but no major problems). Social disarticulation arises from a loss of social capital due especially to the inability or unwillingness of project authorities to resettle people in communities and social units of their choice. It proved to be a problem for a majority of resettlers in 15 (34 per cent) of 44 cases.

18　It was a problem for a majority of resettlers in 35 of the 44 cases and a problem for a minority in another three cases.

19　Joblessness was a problem for a majority of resettlers in 21 (51 per cent) of 41 cases and for a minority in 12 other cases (29 per cent).

20　The same would also apply to important cultural concepts relating to time and place (Downing, 1996). Where case studies do include such issues, impacts have been overwhelmingly negative, suggesting that outcomes would be even worse than those dealing largely with variables that can be more easily quantified.

21　Hussein Fahim's publications provide the most detailed analysis of the Egyptian Nubian resettlement process. They and other relevant publications are listed in the bibliography. Readers interested in an up-to-date case study of the High Dam are referred to the Third World Centre for Water Management's forthcoming Oxford University Press publication on the Aswan High, Ataturk and Bhakra Dams.

22　During the final war years Pimburetewa was under government control during the day time and Tamil Tiger control at night.

23　Bank appraisal and supervisory missions included resettlement specialists such as Cernea as well as Zong-cheng Lin who had written his PhD dissertation on Shuikou relocation.

24　Based on results of a 1995 survey of 34,063 resettlers, Bank consultant Youxuan Zhu reports that 49 per cent resettled in 'traditional agriculture,' while jobs of 19 per cent were in enterprises and 14 per cent in services (World Bank, 1998b, Annex A, p30). Enterprises included jobs in old and newly created industries and what the Chinese refer to as 'sidelines', which include raising livestock, mushrooms and fish for the market. Services are defined as including small village shops and other commercial activities as well as less-certain migratory wage labour to coastal and other areas outside the reservoir basin.

25   Two of the five affected districts lost over 20 per cent of their land to the reservoir; land that in two districts supported 40 and 70 per cent of their inhabitants.

26   That was Béoumi. Although losing more of its land to the reservoir (70 per cent) than any of the other districts, only 13,000 of the 75,000 resettlers were involved. Another factor complicating the assessment of outcomes was the presence of two ethnic groups. Although the large majority of resettlers belonged to the ethnic group that Lassailly-Jacob studied, a minority belonged to a second group on which virtually no information is available.

27   In a 1994 lecture at the World Bank, Lassailly-Jacob also faults the AVB for ignoring the irrigation potential of the Kossou project and that of drawdown agriculture.

28   Although unlikely under present climatic conditions, should the reservoir eventually fill, the living standards of those involved would worsen unless they could find occupations other than farming.

29   Even if that was true, Yantan provides a good example of why the World Bank's policy of allowing mere restoration is deficient. Even with restoration, incomes remained below the province's poverty threshold. Moreover, as the Bank reports 'resettler incomes are below the incomes of unaffected people in the same jurisdictions, and that gap has also been widening' (1998b, p22). The further statement that 'Local officials say that this is attributable to the lag time in establishing the new enterprises and bringing them to maturity..., and that eventually the resettlers will catch up' is not very reassuring given the risks and uncertainty associated with those new enterprises.

30   See Chapter 4 for the potential multiplier effects that can accompany well-planned and implemented irrigation projects.

31   Statement by Shri K. P. Singh on July 25, 2001 (http://164.100.24.208/lsdeb/ls13/ses7/250701.html).

32   According to Mahapatra (1999a, p127), a book on *Irrigation in Orissa* published by the state government's Water and Land Management Institute in most cases does not even include the number of affected villages, let alone households.

33   I agree with that assessment. Furthermore, rehabilitation efforts should be based on project-derived opportunities rather than on non-project-related macro-economic trends at the national and international levels.

34   Compounding the loss of arable land and fish production was project-related sale of livestock because the fencing of remaining land that could be farmed reduced the availability of grazing.

CHAPTER 4

1   Egypt's Aswan High Dam and Sri Lanka's Pimburetewa and Victoria Dams.

2   India's Ramial Dam, Mexico's Aleman and Cerro de Oro Dams and the Pantabangan Dam in the Philippines.

3   A point emphasized by Chris Perry during discussions following the World Commission on Dams' London January 2000 workshop on Social Impacts.

4   This section draws heavily from the draft reports of the World Bank Task Force on Multiplier Effects of which Rita Cestti was Task Manager. Because the final report (Bhatia et al, *Indirect Economic Impacts of Dams: Methodological Issues and Summary Results of Case Studies in Brazil, Egypt and India*. Volumes I and II) was forthcoming at the time of writing, I have quoted from the 2003 drafts of

the Brazil, Indian and Aswan studies. See also Bhatia et al's preliminary 2003 report prepared for the Third World Water Forum, Kyoto, Japan; Bhatia and Cestti's Power Point presentation at the Third World Water Forum; and Cestti and Scatasta's paper presented at the World Bank's Water Week, 2003. While the emphasis is on the irrigation component of large dams, a similar section could be written on the hydro component. Kariba is one example (Soils Inc, 2000), while Biswas and Tortajada associate the export of power to India from Bhutan's Chukha I and II projects as being 'responsible for lifting the per capita GDP of that country from being the lowest in South Asia in 1960 to the second highest in the region at present' (2001, p13).

5   The Aswan High Dam study dealt primarily with direct benefits at the national level, concluding that the dam 'was, and is, a good investment, yielding significant annual net returns'. They could have been considerably higher if more emphasis had been placed on high value crops. Instead the dam's existence allowed the government 'to pursue policies that distorted agricultural production, yielding a cropping pattern that favored low-value crops that made inefficient use of both water and land' (Robinson et al, 2003, p45).

6   Within the São Francisco River Basin, the cost of new job creation in irrigation varied from US$2,000 to US$20,000, whereas the next lowest cost, for wood processing, ranged from US$9,000 to US$128,400 (Scatasta, 2003, Table 14).

7   A Social Accounting Matrix-based model was used 'to compute the values of relevant variables in the "with project" situation with their counterparts in the hypothetical case that the project had not been undertaken' (Bhatia and Malik, 2003, p3).

8   Average income gains for marginal farmers were 50 per cent and for large farmers 43 per cent. Landless workers, at 23 per cent, gained least, in part because relatively small holdings meant that farm households relied mainly on family labour (Bhatia and Cestti, 2003). Rather, their gains came from milk production and provision of services. What employment generation occurred appeared to be in such off-farm activities as construction, including construction of additional shops.

9   Results of El-Tayeb's survey were published in Scudder, 1981b, pp180–182.

10 Cage culture is a form of aquaculture whereby nets (approximately 7 x 7m and 2.5m deep) enclose water under bamboo rafts that float on top of empty barrels. They are stocked with carp fed on commercial feed (Soemarwoto, 1988, p118).

11 Volta reservoir was rapidly colonized by professional fishers who lived below the dam but had fished the tidal and other waters in a number of nations. In the Ivory Coast, the armed forces were used to protect the new fishery behind the Kossou Dam from thousands of professional fishers from Mali, while other immigrant fishers rapidly colonized the new reservoir fisheries behind the Selingue and Manantali Dams within Mali. In Laos, professional fishers on the reservoir behind the Nam Ngum Dam already have begun to ask about fishing the reservoir behind the still-to-be constructed Nam Theun 2 Dam.

12 Since the mid-1950s, aquaculture in the two reservoirs has been 'neither environmentally nor socially sustainable. The benefits of floating cage aquaculture, which originally were guaranteed to the displaced people by provincial legislation ... have been usurped by the politically powerful and consolidated into the hands of the urban rich from Bandung and Jakarta' (Costa-Pierce, 1998). An estimated 25,558 cages on Cirata and 8199 on Saguling in 1996 'have been developed haphazardly in very few areas of the reservoir where market

access is good, rather than where the environments are suitable, further degrading the aquatic environment' (ibid) which experts estimate has a carrying capacity of 16,400 cages, or approximately half the 1996 total.

13   Community involvement was less obvious in a third that involved a high altitude wetland habitat.

14   The second, also on the first page, is that 'resettlement activities should be conceived and executed as sustainable development programs, providing sufficient investment resources to enable the persons displaced by the project to share in project benefits'.

15   Chapter 1, this volume, p6. See for example, Lowe-McConnell's (editor) (1966) proceedings of a 1965 symposium on man-made lakes at London's Royal Geographical Society that included six papers dealing with environmental, public health and socio-economic problems.

16   The revised compensation policy approved by the project authority and the commission did not incorporate the recommendation of the Mohale consultants (Contract 1012) and the POE to provide the resettlement option to households that lose over 50 per cent of their arable land to inundation. The large majority, perhaps numbering over 100 households, may not be able to assess the impact of such losses on their living standards until several years after inundation occurs. It took several years of persuasion before LHDA and the commission agreed to extend resettlement benefits to them and to set aside the necessary funds for up to 150 households.

17   Though Cernea has written an excellent critique of the compensation principle in economics (Cernea, 2002), his most recent (1999 and 2002) thinking on an economics for resettlement has not influenced World Bank policy.

18   That was established by the NGO ARCH-Vahini, which had prepared a listing of landlords who were willing to sell land.

CHAPTER 5

1   Another 3000–4000 displaced by the Kotmale and Victoria Dams chose to resettle in upland areas in the two reservoir basins or elsewhere. A small minority of the 75,000 downstream households were spontaneous settling households that had immigrated into the project area before the AMP began.

2   Tamil, a Dravidian language, is the dominant language of South India.

3   This section draws heavily on Disanayaka's 2000 *Water Heritage of Sri Lanka* and Wickremaratne's chapter in Muller and Hettige's 1995 *The Blurring of a Vision – The Mahaweli*.

4   The Mahaweli Project irrigation system layout was to channel main canal water into a number of secondary or distributary canals which in turn served tertiary or turnout channels for providing water to a small number of farmers who were expected to work together in turnout operation and maintenance.

5   Of the various sources used in this section, the most important were the 1997 and 1999 Mahaweli Statistical Handbooks prepared by MASL's Planning and Monitoring Unit.

6   Called 'evacuees' in the Sri Lankan literature.

7   The small number of Tamil-speaking Hindu and Muslim households in the sample is because the greater proportion of those minorities lived as host populations in the northern portion of System B, which was still in the process of being developed when USAID funding for our study stopped.

8　There were 39.70 rupees to the US dollar at 1989 exchange rates.

9　At that time Additional Secretary, Ministry of Mahaweli Development, and former Director General of the MEA.

CHAPTER 6

1　Relevant source material on Kariba as well as on the other seven cases is included in this volume's bibliography.

2　This is a very conservative estimate, especially if dam-related irrigation works are included – as they should be. According to Fernandes and Paranjpye, 16–38 million people may have undergone forced relocation in India as a result of dam construction (1997, p17).

3　As quoted by Jain (2001, p3) from the 2000 Planning Commission report.

4　In January 1995, because of the demonstrated inadequacy of resettlement, India's Supreme Court required construction to stop at 80m. Under pressure from the strong political and economic forces behind the dam, and the development paradigm that it represented, the Supreme Court gave an interim order in February 1999 allowing the dam's height to be increased to 85m. On 18 October 2000, the Court by a two to one majority gave an order mandating construction to go forward in stages to the dam's full height of 138m in spite of further deterioration of resettlement implementation contrary to the requirements of the Tribunal, various state resolutions, the High Court of Gujarat and the Supreme Court itself. So prejudicial, biased in regard to development options, and ill-informed was the order of the majority, that the third justice disassociated himself from it – 'I have read the judgment proposed... I regret my inability to agree therewith.' In support of this statement, see Jain's 2001 *Dam vs. Drinking Water – Exploring the Narmada Judgment* (96pp). A former member of India's Planning Commission and High Commissioner to South Africa, Jain was appointed by the Government of India in 1993 as a member of the independent Five Member Group for assessing controversial SSP issues. While Indian High Commissioner in South Africa, he joined WCD in 1998 as Vice-Chair.

5　Ramsar is the Convention on Wetlands of International Importance that was signed in Ramsar, Iran, in 1971. As of October 2003 there were 138 Contracting Parties and 1316 listed wetlands.

6　My most important single source on the Okavango region and the water development project is *The IUCN Review of the Southern Okavango Integrated Water Development Project* (Scudder et al, 1993, 543pp). The next most important source is my own field notes kept while I was resident in the area between October 1991 and June 1992 and during subsequent revisits, the most recent being in 2002. The Okavango region is defined as including the entire delta, its semi-arid hinterland on all three sides, and the Boteti River and riverine communities.

7　Hydro-Quebec officials played an active role contributing to the Commission's thematic review of the social impacts of large dams that included attending meetings as well as preparing a paper on 'Dams and Benefit Sharing. A Submission from Hydro-Quebec'.

8　As reported on 19 March 1999 by Eric Siblin in the *Montreal Gazette* and distributed on their website by the International Rivers Network 6 May 1999.

CHAPTER 7

1   See, for example, Rogers' chapter 'Assessing the Socioeconomic Consequences of Climate Change on Water Resources' (1994) and his chapter 'Engineering Design and Uncertainties Related to Climate Change' (1997).
2   See, for example, Friedl and Wüest's 2002 article 'Disrupting biogeochemical cycles – Consequences of damming'.
3   FCFA is the franc of the African Financial Community (franc de la Communauté Financière d'Afrique), made up of 14 West and Central African countries.
4   McCully, 2001, p36 based on Bourke's 'Subduing the Seas' Onslaught' in *South*, July 1988.
5   The section on Vietnam's Yali Dam is based on a 23 September 2003 Press Advisory from the Canadian NGO Probe International titled 'Leaked Report Criticizes Vietnam for Unsafe Dam Operations'.
6   Draft 12/09/2000 IUCN Policy for the Sustainable Use of Deltas.
7   Submission to the World Commission on Dams by Aslam Khwaja on 'Some Aspects of Opposing Kalabagh Dam'.
8   *Dawn* was reporting on the gist of speakers at a ceremony for the publication of Karim Khwaja's book, *Indus Valley – Environmental and Delta Crisis*.
9   Erik Eckholm, 'A battle over Indus River water', in *International Herald Tribune* 24 April 2003.
10 The Indus Delta 'experiences the highest wave energy of any river in the world' (Asianics, 2000, p107).
11 This case is based on the following sources: Wesseling et al, 1996; Acreman et al, 2000; and Loth, 2004 .

CHAPTER 8

1   See the chapter by Tumbare (2000) 'The importance of politicians in water related development projects'.
2   Fahim, 1981, p14 after Heikel, 1973, p62.
3   See also Aaron Wolf's 1995 *Hydropolitics along the Jordan River: Scarce Water and Its Impact on the Arab-Israeli Conflict*.
4   Parastatals are specialized government agencies that are established to undertake specific tasks. National and international river basin authorities would be an example of parastatals established to deal with water resource and energy development.
5   As new countries gain their independence the number of international river basins has been steadily increasing. For a recent assessment see Wolf et al, 1999. On the importance of international river basins see relevant volumes in the series of publications resulting from the United Nations University's Programme on Integrated Basin Management. Especially important is Biswas and Uitto's 2001 edited volume on the Ganges–Brahmaputra–Meghna Basins, which includes nearly 550 million people who constitute the world's largest aggregate of poor people. Also relevant is Biswas et al's 1999 volume on Latin America's Amazon and Plata Basins plus the São Francisco within Brazil.
6   In 2002 the most serious drought in the oral and recorded histories of the Middle

Zambezi Valley had left that population literally starving at the time this chapter was written.

7   The Bangladesh Centre for Advanced Studies' 1994 *Rivers of Life* documents how existing levees were poorly maintained and frequently breached. Denying access to floodplains, they also had reduced annual fish production by 45,000 tonnes while not increasing agricultural production. See also Rogers et al (1989) *Eastern Waters Study: Strategies to Manage Flood and Drought in the Ganges-Brahmaputra Basin.*

8   The section on the Cordillera People's Alliance is based on a 1991 background paper delivered by Joji Carino at The Other Economic Summit convened when the G-7 nations met in London. See also Drucker, 1985.

9   Quoted from the Mapuche section of the website (www.unpo.org) for the Unrepresented Nations and Peoples Organization.

10   The information that follows comes primarily from Lawson's 1994 *Dammed Indians.*

11   In a 1976 referendum 144 Yavapai voted against the dam and 57 for it with Khera and Mariella speculating that the yes votes may have involved Yavapai living off the reservation who might have been more interested in cash compensation than protecting tribal land or perhaps were confused by 'misleading wording of the ballots' (Khera and Mariella, 1982, p173).

12   The mechanisms and funds that the authors are referring to are from successful law suits (claims cases) that Native Americans along both the Columbia and Missouri Rivers have won against the US Government since the late 1970s.

13   TERRA (Towards Ecological Recovery and Regional Alliance) was founded in 1991 to focus on local communities and ecosystems within the Mekong River Basin. It draws its expertise from a coalition of supporters in all of the Mekong countries except China, and works closely with Thailand's Project for Ecological Recovery that was started in 1986.

14   The history of IRN in this paragraph is from McCully, 1996, p307.

15   Especially important is the Centre's two volumes (1984 and 1986) *The Social and Environmental Effects of Large Dams* and the journal *The Ecologist.*

16   Cernea had been hired in 1974 as the Bank's first permanent sociologist. The lecture series he organized served as the basis for his 1985 volume *Putting People First: Sociological Variables in Rural Development.*

17   See Robert Wade's 2001 paper, 'The US Role in the Malaise at the World Bank: Get Up, Gulliver' for a recent review of World Bank weaknesses by an academic who also believes in the need for a world bank. Wade is especially critical of the extent of the US influence on Bank's policies. One result, in my opinion, is the Bank's unwillingness to fund or push land reform as a means to free up land for resettlement in host areas.

18   For one analysis of the Inspection Panel see CIEL (1997) *A Citizen's Guide to the World Bank Inspection Panel.*

19   These are outlined in a July 2002 compilation by the Bank Information Center on which most of the information that follows is based. Two of the four submissions that the Panel decided not to investigate involved separate issues dealing with the Lesotho's Highlands Water Project. Those, the Panel decided, were not sufficiently related to Bank involvement. The third submission, dealing with Chile's Pangue Dam, was rejected because the Panel's jurisdiction does not include IFC projects. Instead the Bank's President appointed an independent investigator (Hair et al, 1997). Itaparica was the fourth case. Although the Panel

recommended investigation, Board approval was not forthcoming because of ongoing implementation of a government action plan that was supposed to address the resettlement component's major deficiencies.

20   Though perhaps not the pioneering donor, during the 1980s the US Agency for International Development provided funding to the Government of Mali for physical removal of 11,000 resettlers in connection with the construction of the Manantali Dam.

21   Personal communication from Barbara Rose Johnston.

22   Resettlement guidelines were pioneered by the World Bank in 1980 as the Bank's Operational Manual Statement (OMS) 2.33 'Social Issues Associated with Involuntary Resettlement in Bank-Financed Projects'. They were revised in 1990 as Operational Directive 4.30, 'Involuntary Resettlement'. They were revised again, and weakened, in 2001 as Operational Policy 4.12, Involuntary Resettlement, OP 4.12, Annex A – Involuntary Resettlement Instruments, and Bank Procedures 4.12, Involuntary Resettlement.

23   See also Cernea, 1999, pp19–22 for a detailed discussion of the inability of cost–benefit analysis to deal with involuntary resettlement.

24   Because of the nature of the resettlement process, and especially the tendency for living standards of the majority to drop during Stage 2, I believe 'immediate' improvement will only be possible under quite exceptional circumstances and where small numbers of resettlers are involved.

25   *ECA Watch* is a publication of the International NGO Campaign on Export Credit Agencies whose website is www.eca-watch.org.

26   TI Working Paper 'OECD Working Party on Export Credits and Credit Guarantees', Informal Consultation in Paris on 16 November 2000.

27   See Nancy Dunne, 'The Americas & Middle East: Export credit agencies hunt for common ground'. *Financial Times*, 11 July 2001.

28   See ECGD website (www.ecgd.gov.uk) 2 July 2003 on the Ilisu project.

29   www.oecd.org/pdf/M00037000/M00.

30   See 'NGO Collective Analysis of the Equator Principles', *Focus on Finance*, June 2003 on the Global Policy Forum website (www.globalpolicy.org/socecon/ffd/2003/06ngos.htm).

Chapter 9

1   During the National Research Council's 2003 review of the activities of the US Army Corps of Engineers, one recommendation – given that the dam-building era in the US is over – was that the Corps would be the logical lead organization to study the decommissioning problem and to pioneer the necessary science and engineering of removal.

2   The phrase 'as intended' as opposed to 'as planned' is important since unexpected events and other happenings require an adaptive planning process.

3   The *Independent*, London, 7 July 2003, as reported on IRN's WCD website.

4   'Judges Order Contempt Hearing for Army Corps of Engineers', *Los Angeles Times* (2003a). At issue was the Corps failure to operate Missouri River Dams for the benefit of endangered species as required by the *Endangered Species Act*.

5   As has been recommended for Bangladesh (Rogers et al, 1989).

6   The 'Rights and Risks' approach is more recently emphasized in the Brookings Institution's 2003 *Rights and Risks: The Causes, Consequences, and Challenges*

of Development-Induced Displacement (Robinson, 2003), while Cernea, in a series of papers starting in the mid-1990s, was the first systematically to apply a risks approach to resettlers.

7   In addition to the WCD process, my thinking in this section has been influenced by two more recent activities. The most important was as a member of the 2002–2003 Advisory Panel to the World Bank's task force on Stakeholders' Involvement in Options Assessment. As one of a number of Bank responses to the WCD report, the purpose of the task force was to produce a sourcebook on stakeholder involvement for Bank task managers and host country counterparts. Two consultants, Kees Blok and Larry Haas, were the principal researchers; J. Richard Davis was the World Bank Task Manager. The second activity, also during 2002–2003, was serving as a member of a US National Academy of Sciences – National Research Council multipanel effort to advise the Corps of Army Engineers and the US Congress on the Corps' future direction and activities.

8   See World Bank, July 2003, for a well-referenced yet brief assessment of the relevance of research and case studies to a participatory decision-making process. Developed by social and behavioural scientists, supportive are 'normative theories relating to social justice in decision-making. These include the theories of equity, procedural and distributive justice, and, more recently, fairness theory' (p13). As for the fear of planners losing influence, recent research in Australia shows that while the public wants involvement, a partnership with planners is the desired mechanism (see McCreddin et al, 1994).

9   Referred to as the 3-Rs, Blok, Haas and Davis emphasized the importance of adding 'responsibilities' to the WCD 'rights and risks' approach.

10 Though fewer dams will be built there, additional cases from industrialized countries would include Australia (Murray–Darling Basin Commission and Moore River catchment), US (Deschutes Resources Conservancy in the Columbia River Basin) and Canada (stakeholder involvement undertaken by British Columbia Hydro).

11 Blok, Haas and Davis postulated a community liaison group for a project's construction phase and a consultation group or committee for the operational phase. I am a strong believer in continuity, so I believe a single stakeholders' group makes sense provided there is a mechanism for adding and resigning members according to the needs of different stages in the water resources development process.

12 Among social scientists, both these terms are contentious because they reify the socio-cultural systems of the people to whom they apply. I use them only because they continue to be used by donors such as the World Bank as well as by NGOs concerned about development's adverse impacts on the ethnic minorities for which the terms are used.

13 14 May 1994, Press Release from the Coalition for Nitassinan.

14 A product of the 1990s, the International Association for Public Participation (IAP2) advocates that the public, defined as all relevant stakeholders, 'should have a say in decisions about actions that affect their lives' (the first of seven IAP2 Core Values for the Practice of Public Participation).

15 See, for example, the article by Hope E. Ogbeide on NGO/Civil Society Dialogue on the Report of the World Commission on Dams in Nigeria posted 11 July 2003 on the IRN-Africa website.

16 See Chapters by Hollis and Salem-Murdock in Acreman and Hollis, 1996, and A. Adams, 1999.

17　Studies undertaken by the Institute for Development Anthropology have also shown that environmental flows released from Mali's Manantali Dam would benefit over half a million downstream residents without loss of hydropower generating capacity.

18　Examples would include Kenya's World Bank-financed Bura Irrigation Project in which initial proposals and planning for a 14,000ha scheme were reduced to a 6700ha scheme prior to appraisal based on soils surveys that should have been carried out at an earlier date. The Bank's approval of the 6700ha scheme in 1977 was itself based on an overoptimistic assessment of still inadequate soil surveys. In the mid-1980s the scheme was again reduced – this time to less than 3000ha. According the Bank's mid-term review, 'In hindsight the donors' decision at appraisal neither to cancel nor postpone the project until new feasibility studies were completed was unwise. Further research or a pilot project was desirable to test soil/water relationships and crop yields' (World Bank Mid-Term Evaluation, Bura Irrigation Settlement Project, Annex II on Farm Budgets, January 1985, pp43–44).

19　A CD-ROM containing the Conference Proceedings is available through Southern Waters Ecological Research and Consulting (Pty) Ltd (admin@southern waters.co.za).

20　On page 245 of the Final Report, WCD states that 'Trust and confidence in the capacity and commitment to meet obligations must be restored if new projects are to create more positive development outcomes and avoid the level of conflict that has occurred in the past. This requires the formation of new relationships and new and more effective means of ensuring compliance.'

21　Especially influential in alerting people to the magnitude of the water quantity and quality problem has been Gleick's 1993 volume on *Water in Crisis: A Guide to the World's Fresh Water Resources* and articles by Falkenmark.

22　See www.nilebasin.org/Energy_Ministers_Meeting.htm.

References

Abeygunawardena, W. (1980) 'Agricultural Development in the Mahaweli Project – An Analysis', Manuscript, Colombo, Sri Lanka

Acreman, M. C. and Hollis, G. E. (eds) (1996) *Water Management and Wetlands in Sub-Saharan Africa*, Gland, Switzerland, International Union for the Conservation of Nature and Natural Resources (IUCN/World Conservation Union)

Acreman, M. C., Farquharson, F. A. K., McCartney, M. P. et al (2000) 'Managed Flood Releases from Reservoirs: Issues and Guidance', Report to DFID and the World Commission on Dams, Centre for Ecology and Hydrology, Wallingford

Adams, A. (1999) 'Social Impacts of an African Dam: Equity and Distributional Issues in the Senegal River Valley', Contributing Paper to WCD Thematic Review 1.1, Capetown, WCD

Adams, W. M. (1985) 'The downstream impacts of dam construction: A case study from Nigeria', *Transactions of the Institute of British Geographers N.S.*, vol 10, pp292–302

Adams, W. M. (1992) *Wasting the Rain: Rivers, People and Planning in Africa*, London, Earthscan

Adams, W. M. (1993) 'Development's deaf ear: Downstream users and water releases from the Bakolori Dam, Nigeria', *World Development*, vol 21, no 9, pp1405–1416

Adams, W. M. (1996) 'Economics and hydrological management of African floodplains', in Acreman, M. C. and Hollis, G. E. (eds) *Water Management and Wetlands in Sub-Saharan Africa*, Gland, Switzerland, International Union for the Conservation of Nature and Natural Resources (IUCN/World Conservation Union)

Adams, W. M. (2000) 'The Social Impact of Large Dams: Equity and Distribution Issues', Thematic Review I.1 prepared as an input to the World Commission on Dams, Cape Town, available at www.dams.org

Adekolu-John, E. O. (1980) 'The probable impact of the proposed Jebba Dam on health aspects of the River Niger Basin of Nigeria', *Public Health, London*, vol 94, pp235–242

Adeniyi, E. O. (1973) 'Downstream impact of the Kainji Dam', in Mabogunje, A. L. (ed) *Kainji: A Nigerian Man-Made Lake, Socio-Economic Conditions*, Kainji Lake Studies, vol 2, Ibadan, Nigeria, University of Nigeria Press for Nigerian Institute of Social and Economic Research

Agouba, M. I. (1979) 'Social Change in Rural Sudanese Communities: A Case Study of an Agricultural Development Scheme in the Sudan', PhD Dissertation, Khartoum, University of Khartoum

Ahmed, M., Navy, H., Vuthy, L. and Tiongco, M. (1998) *Socio-Economic Assessment of Freshwater Capture Fisheries of Cambodia: Report of a Household Survey*, Phnom Penh, Mekong River Commission

Amnesty International (1990) 'Mauritania – Human Rights Violations in the Senegal River Valley (Summary)', London, Amnesty International

Amornsakchai, S., Annez, P., Vongvisessomjai, S. et al (2000) 'Pak Mun Dam, Mekong River Basin, Thailand', A WCD case study prepared as an input to the World Commission on Dams, Cape Town, available at www.dams.org

Aronsson, I.-L. (2002) 'Negotiating Involuntary Resettlement: A Study of Local Bargaining during the Construction of the Zimapan Dam', Occasional Papers 17, Uppsala, Uppsala University

Asian Development Bank (ADB) (1998) *Aide Memoir: Special Review Mission Loan No 1329–LAO (SF): Theun Hinboun Hydropower Project*, 18–28 November, Manila, ADB

Asianics Agro-Dev, International (Pvt) Ltd (2000) 'Tarbela Dam and Related Aspects of the Indus River Basin, Pakistan', A WCD case study prepared as an input to the World Commission on Dams, Cape Town, available at www.dams.org

Asmal, K. (2003) 10 April, letter to the Chair (Margaret Catley-Carlson) of the Global Water Partnership, Pasadena, Scudder archives

Associates in Rural Development (ARD) (1989) *Jubba Environmental and Socioeconomic Studies*, Vol III, Burlington, Vt., Associates in Rural Development for the Ministry of National Planning and Jubba Valley Development and the United States Agency for International Development

Audy, J. R. (1971) 'Measurement and diagnosis of health', in Shepard, P. and McKinley, D. *Environ-Mental*, Boston, Houghton Mifflin

Awachi, B. J. E. (1979) 'On fishing and fisheries management in large tropical African rivers with particular reference to Nigeria', in Welcomme, R. (ed) *Fisheries Management in Large Rivers*, FAO Technical Report no 194, Rome, United Nations Food and Agriculture Organization

Ayeni, J. S. O., Roder, W. and Ayanda, J. O. P. (1994) 'The Kainji Lake experience in Nigeria', in Cook, C. C. (ed) *Involuntary Resettlement in Africa*, World Bank Technical Paper Number 227, Africa Technical Department Series, Washington, DC, World Bank

Bakhsh, H., Ghaffar, A. and Sario, P. (1999) 'Stop Damning the Indus', Submission to the first World Commission on Dams' Regional Consultation, Colombo

Balon, E. K. (1974) *Fishes of Lake Kariba, Africa*, Neptune City, New Jersey, T.F.H. Publications

Bandara, C. M. M. (1985) 'Heartland and its Development', in Hullugalle, L. (ed) *Gamini Dissanayake, 50: A Beginning*, Colombo, Hullugalle L.

Bandaragoda, D. J. (1987) 'Social development in the Kalawewa Settlement Project of the Accelerated Mahaweli Development Programme', *Regional Development Dialogue*, vol 8, no 2, pp159–195

Banerji, P., Iyer, R.R., Rangachari, R., Sengupta, N. and Singh, S. (2000) 'India Country Study', Prepared as an input to the World Commission on Dams, Cape Town, available at www.dams.org

Bangkok Post (1999) 7 February, 'More dam controversy'

Bangkok Post (2002) 12 June, article dealing with EGAT agreement to annual opening of Pak Mun Dam sluice gates

Bangladesh Centre for Advanced Studies (1994) 'Rivers of Life', Reports by journalists, edited by Haggart, K., Dhaka, BCAS

Bank Information Center (2002) 'Table 1: Official Responses to World Bank Inspection Panel Claims', Before the 2nd Review of the Panel, Bank Information Center, available at www.bicusa.org/mdbs/wbg/inspect

Barbier, E. B. and Thompson, J. R. (1996) 'The value of water: Floodplain versus large-scale irrigation benefits in northern Nigeria', *Ambio*, vol 27, no 6, pp434–440

Barbier, E. B., Acreman, M. and Knowler, D. (1997) *Economic Valuation of Wetlands: A Guide for Policy Makers and Planners*, Gland, Switzerland, Ramsar Convention Bureau

Baron, S. (1999) 'Reparations and Indemnification for Losses Suffered by Dam-Affected Populations', Submission to the second WCD Regional Consultation, Sao Paulo, Brazil

Bartolomé, L. (1991) 'The Yacyretá experience with urban resettlement: Some lessons and insights', in Cernea, M. and Guggenheim, S. (eds) *Anthropological Approaches to Involuntary Resettlement: Policy, Practice and Theory*, Boulder, Colorado, Westview Press

Bartolomé, L. J., de Wet, C., Mander, H. and Nagaraj, V. K. (2000) 'Displacement, Resettlement, Rehabilitation, Reparation and Development', WCD Thematic Review 1.3 prepared as an input to the World Commission on Dams, Cape Town, available at www.dams.org

Barutciski, M. (2000) *Addressing Legal Constraints and Improving Outcomes in Development-Induced Displacement and Resettlement Projects*, Refugee Studies Centre, Oxford, University of Oxford

Bavadam, L. (2003) 'Sardar Sarovar Dam – Woes of the displaced', *Frontline*, vol 20, issue 18 (30 August–12 September)

Baviskar, A. (1999) 'Commentary: A Grain of Sand on the Banks of Narmada', *EPW*, 7–13 August, available at www.narmada.org/articles/epw/amita.baviskar.html

Baxi, U. (1989) 'Notes on constitutional and legal aspects of rehabilitation and development', in Fernandes, W. and Thukral, E. G. (eds) *Development Displacement and Rehabilitation*, New Delhi, Indian Social Institute

Bayley, P. B. and Petrere, M. Jr (1989) 'Assessment methods, current status and management options', in Dodge, D. P. (ed) Proceedings of the International Large River Symposium, *Canadian Special Publication of Fisheries and Aquatic Sciences*, vol 106, pp385–398

BBC News (1999) 1 March, World: Middle East Turkish dam gets UK support, available at http://news.bbc.co.uk/1/hi/world/middle_east/288183.stm

BBC News (2000) 6 March, Flooding destroys Zambian crops, available at http://news.bbc.co.uk/1/hi/world/africa/667450.stm

Beilfuss, R. D. (2001) 'Prescribed Flooding and Restoration Potential in the Zambezi Delta, Mozambique', Working Paper No 3 of the Program for the Sustainable Management of Cahora Bassa Dam and the Lower Zambezi Valley, Baraboo, Wisconsin, International Crane Foundation

Beilfuss, R. D. (2003) 'Modeling Water Availability for the Rehabilitation of the Lower Zambezi River and Delta, Mozambique', Under Review

Beilfuss, R. D. and Bento, C. M. (1997) 'Impacts of Hydrological Changes on the Marromeu Complex of the Zambezi Delta, with Special Attention to the Avifauna', Paper presented at the Workshop on the Sustainable Use of Cahora Bassa Dam and the Zambezi Valley, 29 September–2 October, Songo, Mozambique

Beilfuss, R. D., Dutton, P. and Moore, D. (2000) 'Land cover and land use changes in the Zambezi Delta', in Timberlake, J. (ed) *Biodiversity of the Zambezi Basin Wetlands*, Vol III, *Land Use Change and Human Impacts*, Consultancy report for IUCN ROSA, Bulawayo, Biodiversity Foundation for Africa and Harare/The Zambezi Society

Beilfuss, R. D., Moore, D., Dutton, P. and Bento, C. (2001) 'Patterns of Vegetation Change in the Zambezi Delta, Mozambique', Working Paper No 2 of the Program for the Sustainable Management of Cahora Bassa Dam and the Lower Zambezi Valley, Baraboo, Wisconsin, International Crane Foundation

Bell, C., Hazell, P. and Slade, R. (1982) *Project Evaluation in Regional Perspective: A Study of an Irrigation Project in Northwest Malaysia*, Baltimore, Johns Hopkins University Press

Bento, C. M. (2002) 'The Status and Prospects of Wattled Cranes *Bugeranus carunculatus* in the Marromeu Complex of the Zambezi Delta', MSc Thesis, Cape Town, University of Cape Town

Bergkamp, G., McCartney, M., Dugan, P., McNeely, J. and Acreman, M. (2000) 'Dams, Ecosystems Functions and Environmental Restoration', Thematic Review II.1 prepared as an input to the World Commission on Dams, Cape Town, available at www.dams.org

Bermann, C. (1999) 'Community-Managed Resettlement: The Case of Itá Dam', Submission abstract for the second World Commission on Dams Regional Consultation, Sao Paulo, Brazil

Besteman, C. and Cassanelli, L. V. (eds) (1996) *Struggle for Land in Southern Somalia: The War Behind the War*, Boulder, Colorado, Westview Press

Besteman, C. and Roth, M. (1988) 'JESS Report on Land Tenure in the Middle Jubba Valley: Issues and Policy Recommendations', JESS Report no 34, Burlington, Vermont, Associates in Rural Development

Bhalla, G. S., Chadha, G. K., Kashyap, S. P. and Sharma, R. K. (1990) *Agricultural Growth and Structural Changes in the Punjab Economy: An Input-Output Analysis*, Washington, DC, IFPRI

Bhatia, B. (1997) 'Forced Evictions in the Narmada Valley', in Drèze, J., Samson, M. and Singh, S. (eds) *The Dam and the Nation: Displacement and Resettlement in the Narmada Valley*, Delhi, Oxford University Press

Bhatia, R. and Cestti, R. (2003) 'PowerPoint Presentation on Study of the Multiplier Effects of Dams', Third World Water Forum, Kyoto, Japan, 16–23 March

Bhatia, R. and Malik, R. P. S. (2003) 'Multiplier Effects of Dams: A Case Study of the Bhakra Multipurpose Dam, India', Draft Report for World Bank Task Force on Multiplier Effects, Washington, DC

Bhatia, R. and Scatasta, M. (2003) 'Multiplier Effects of Dam Study: A Review of Past Studies and Methodological Issues', Report prepared for the World Bank Task Force on Multiplier Effects, Washington, DC

Bhatia, R., Scatasta, M. and Cestii, R. (2003) 'Study of the Multiplier Effects of Dams: Methodology Issues and Preliminary Results', Preliminary report prepared for the Third World Water Forum, Kyoto, Japan, 16–23 March

Bhatia, R., Scatasta, M. and Cestii, R. (forthcoming) *Indirect Economic Impacts of Dams: Methodological Issues and Summary Results of Case Studies in Brazil, Egypt and India*, Vols I and II, Washington, DC, World Bank

Bilharz, J. A. (1998) *The Allegany Senecas and Kinzua Dam: Forced Relocation Through Two Generations*, Lincoln, University of Nebraska Press

Bingham, M. (1982) 'The livestock potential of the Kafue Flats', in Howard, G. and Williams, G. (eds) *Proceedings of the National Seminar on Environment and Change: The Consequences of Hydroelectric Power Development on the Utilization of the Kafue Flats*, April 1978, Lusaka, Kafue Basin Research Committee of the University of Zambia

BioScience (1995) Special Section on 'The ecology of large rivers', vol 45, no 3 (March)

BioScience (1998) Special Section on 'Flooding: Natural and managed disturbances', a special issue of *BioScience* devoted to flooding as a disturbance, vol 48, no 9 (September)

BioScience (2000) Special Issue, 'Hydrological alterations cause global environmental change', vol 50, no 9 (September)

Bissell, R. E., Singh, S. and Warth, H. (2000) 'Maheshwar Hydroelectric Project: Resettlement and Rehabilitation', An independent review conducted for the Ministry of Economic Cooperation and Development (BMZ), Government of Germany, 15 June

Biswas, A. K. (2002) 'Aswan Dam revisited: The benefits of a much-maligned dam', *Development and Cooperation*, no 6 (November/December), pp25–27

Biswas, A. K. and Tortajada, C. (2001) 'Development and large dams: A global perspective', *Water Resources Development*, vol 17, no 1, pp9–21

Biswas, A. K. and Uitto, J. I. (eds) (2001) *Sustainable Development of the Ganges-Brahmaputra-Meghna Basins*, Tokyo, United Nations University Press

Biswas, A. K., Cordeiro, N. V., Braga, B. P. F. and Tortajada, C. (eds) (1999) *Management of Latin American River Basins: Amazon, Plata, and São Francisco*, Tokyo, United Nations University Press

Black, M. (2001) 'The day of judgment', *New Internationalist*, Issue 336 (July): pp9–28

Bond, V. and Ndubani, P. (2001) 'Situation in Chiawa Following Floods', Chiawa field report for UNICEF, 14 March, Lusaka

Botswana, Government of (1985) Sixth National Development Plan (NDP 6) 1985–1991, Gaborone, Ministry of Finance and Development Planning

Botswana, Government of (1989) Central Statistical Office, Data on regional poverty, Gaborone

Botswana, Government of (1991) Seventh National Development Plan (NDP 7) 1991–1997, Gaborone, Ministry of Finance and Development Planning

Boughey, A. S. (1962) 'The explosive development of a floating weed vegetation in Lake Kariba', *Adansonia*, vol III, no 1, pp49–61

Bourdillon, M. F. C., Cheater, A. and Murphree, M. (1985) *Studies of Fishing on Lake Kariba*, Gweru, Mambo Press

Bourke, G. (1988) 'Subduing the seas' onslaught', *South*, July

Bourne, S. P. (1957) 30 May, letter replying to request from the Gwembe District Commissioner for background information on the Lusitu resettlement area, Pasadena, California, Scudder archives

Brind, W. G. (1954) *The Okavango Delta: Report on the 1951–1953 Field Surveys*, Gaborone, Department of Water Affairs

Brokensha, D. (1963) 'Volta resettlement and anthropological research', *Human Organization*, vol 22, pp286–290

Brokensha, D. and Scudder, T. (1968) 'Resettlement', in Warren, W. M. and Rubin, N. (eds) *Dams in Africa: An Interdisciplinary Study of Man Made Lakes in Africa*, London, Frank Cass and Co.

Bruwer, C., Poultney, C. and Nyathi, Z. (1996) 'Community based hydrological management of the Phongolo Floodplain', in Acreman, M. C. and Hollis, G. E. (eds) *Water Management and Wetlands in Sub-Saharan Africa*, Gland, Switzerland, International Union for the Conservation of Nature and Natural Resources (IUCN/World Conservation Union)

Buchan, A. (1988) 'Grazing Resources of the Makatini Flats and Pongolo Floodplain: Production, Use and Significance in the Local Socio-Economy', Investigative Report no 32, Institute of Natural Resources, University of Natal, Pietermaritzburg

Butcher, D. A. P. (1971) *An Operational Manual for Resettlement: A Systematic Approach to the Resettlement Problem created by Man-Made Lakes, with Special Relevance for West Africa*, Rome, FAO

Campbell, A. C. (1976) 'Traditional Utilization of the Okavango Delta', Symposium on the Okavango Delta and its Future Utilization, Gaborone, The Botswana Society

Cano, G. (1989) Unpublished Outline on the Legal and Institutional Aspects concerning the Environment relating to LHDA, Maseru

Capistrano, D. and Stackhouse, J. (1997) 'Bangladesh's troubled waters: Finding a better way to manage a precious resource', Ford Foundation Report, Winter, 2833, available at www.fordfound.org/publications/ff_report/

CARE International (1996) 'Socio-economic and Cultural Survey – Nam Theun 2 Project Area, Lao PDR' (Chamberlain, J. R., Alton, C., Silavong, L. and Philavong, B.), Vientiane, CARE International

Carino, J. (1991) 'Background Paper on the Cordillera People's Alliance' (delivered at The Other Economic Summit convened when the G-7 Nations met in London), London

Caufield, C. (1996) *Masters of Illusion: The World Bank and the Poverty of Nations*, New York, Henry Holt and Company

Center for International Environmental Law (CIEL) (1997) *A Citizen's Guide to the Work Bank Inspection Panel*, Washington DC, CIEL

Center for International Environmental Law (2000) 'Issue Brief for the World Summit on Sustainable Development 26 August – 4 September', Washington, DC, CIEL

Central African Council (1951) 'Annual Report on the Kariba/Kafue Hydro-Electric Power Committee', Salisbury

Central Bank of Ceylon (1981) *Economic and Social Statistics of Sri Lanka*, vol 4, no 1, Colombo, Central Bank

Centre for Science and Environment (CSE) (1982) *The State of India's Environment: The Citizens' Fifth Report*, New Delhi, CSE

Centre for Social Studies, Surat (1997) 'Resettlement and Rehabilitation in Gujarat', in Drèze, J., Samson, M. and Singh, S. (eds) *The Dam and the Nation: Displacement and Resettlement in the Narmada Valley*, Delhi, Oxford University Press

Cernea, M. M. (ed) (1985) *Putting People First: Sociological Variables in Rural Development*, New York, Oxford University Press for the World Bank

Cernea, M. M. (1986) 'Involuntary Resettlement in Bank-Assisted Projects: A Review of the Application of Bank Policies and Procedures in FY 1979–1985 Projects', Processed, Agriculture and Rural Development Department, Washington, DC, World Bank

Cernea, M. M. (1988) 'Involuntary Resettlement in Development Projects: Policy Guidelines in World Bank Assisted Projects', World Bank Technical Paper no 80, Washington, DC

Cernea, M. M. (1990) 'Poverty Risks from Population Displacement in Water Resources Development', Development Discussion Paper no 355, Cambridge, Massachusetts, Harvard University Institute for International Development

Cernea, M. M. (ed) (1991) *Putting People First: Sociological Variables in Rural Development*, Second Edition: Revised and Expanded, New York, Oxford University Press for the World Bank

Cernea, M. M. (1993) 'Anthropological and sociological research for policy development on population resettlement', in Cernea, M. M. and Guggenheim, S. E. (eds) *Anthropological Approaches to Resettlement: Policy, Practice, and Theory*, Boulder, Colorado, Westview Press

Cernea, M. M. (1994) 'Population resettlement and development', *Finance and Development*, September, pp46–49

Cernea, M. M. (1995) 'Understanding and preventing impoverishment from displacement', Keynote Opening Address, International Conference on Development-Induced Displacement and Impoverishment, Oxford, 3–7 January, *Journal of Refugee Studies* vol 8, no 3, pp245–264

Cernea, M. M. (1996) 'Understanding and preventing impoverishment from displacement', in McDowell, C. (ed) *Understanding Impoverishment: The Consequences of Development-Induced Displacement*, Oxford, Berghahn Books

Cernea, M. M. (1997a) 'Hydropower Dams and Social Impacts: A Sociological Perspective', Paper, Social Assessment Series no 44, Washington, DC, World Bank Environment Department

Cernea, M. M. (1997b) 'African Involuntary Population Resettlement in a Global Context', Paper, Social Assessment Series no 45, Washington, DC, World Bank Environment Department

Cernea, M. M. (1999a) 'Why economic analysis is essential to resettlement: A sociologist's view', in Cernea, M. M. (ed) *The Economics of Involuntary Resettlement: Questions and Challenges*, Washington, DC, World Bank

Cernea, M. M. (ed) (1999b) *The Economics of Involuntary Resettlement: Questions and Challenges*, Washington, DC, World Bank

Cernea, M. M. (2002) 'For a new economics of resettlement: A sociological critique of the compensation principle', in Cernea, M. M. and Kanbur, R. (eds) (2002) *An Exchange on the Compensation Principle in Resettlement*, Ithaca, Cornell University

Cernea, M. M. and Guggenheim, S. E. (eds) (1993) *Anthropological Approaches to Resettlement: Policy, Practice and Theory*, Boulder, Colorado, Westview Press

Cernea, M. M. and McDowell, C. (eds) (2000) *Risks and Reconstruction: Experiences of Resettlers and Refugees*, Washington, DC, World Bank

Cestti, R. and Scatasta, M. (2003) 'Towards a Full Assessment of the Impacts of Dams: Improving Our Understanding of Indirect and Induced Impacts', Paper presented at Water Week 2003, 4–6 March, Washington, DC, World Bank

Chamberlain, J. R. (1997) *Nature and Culture in the Nakai – Nam Theun Conservation Area*, Vientiane, Chamberlain, J. R.

Chambers, R. (1969) *Settlement Schemes in Tropical Africa: A Study of Organizations and Development*, New York, Prager

Chen, C. (1999) 'The Chixoy Dam Case', Submission at the World Commission on Dams' Second Regional Consultation, Sao Paulo, Brazil

Chibnik, M. (1994) *Risky Rivers: The Economics and Politics of Floodplain Farming in Amazonia*, Tucson, University of Arizona Press

Chicago Tribune (2002) 14 December, article on reparations for Native American Ft. Randall Dam resettlers

Chuta, E. and Liedholm, C. (1979) 'Rural Non-Farm Employment: A Review of the State of the Art', Michigan State University Rural Development Papers no 4, East Lansing, Michigan State University, Department of Agricultural Economics

CIPM Yangtze Joint Venture (CYJV) (1988) *Three Gorges Water Control Project Feasibility Report*, Vol 9 – *Resettlement*, Appendix 9B: *World and China Resettlement Experience*, CIPM Yangtze Joint Venture

Clark, S. J. (2001) 'An Investigation into the Impact of HIV on Population Dynamics in Africa', PhD Dissertation in Demography, Philadelphia, University of Pennsylvania

Clark, S. J., Colson, E., Lee, J. and Scudder, T. (1995) 'Ten thousand Tonga: A longitudinal anthropological study from Southern Zambia, 1956–1991', *Population Studies*, vol 49, pp91–109

Clarke, C. (2000) 'Cross-Check Survey: Final Report', A WCD Survey prepared as an input to the World Commission on Dams, Cape Town, available at www.dams.org

Clements, F. (1959) *Kariba: The Struggle with the River God*, London, Methuen and Co

Cliggett, L. and Colson, E. F. (2001) 'All This Theft: Property and Loss', draft manuscript, El Cerrito, CA

Coalition for Nitassinan (1994) 14 May, Press Release, available at http://nativenet.uthscsa.edu/archives/nl/9405/0268.html

Cockcroft, I. G. (1949) 'Removal of Natives Consequent upon the Kariba Gorge Hydro-Electric Power Scheme', Report to the Chief Native Commissioner, Southern Rhodesia, Gokwe

Coke, M. and Pott, R. (1970) *The Pongolo Floodplain Pans: A Plan for Conservation*, Mimeographed manuscript, Natal Parks Board, South Africa, Pietermaritzburg

Colson, E. F. (1971) *The Social Consequences of Resettlement*, Manchester, Manchester University Press

Colson, E. (1994) Lecture, Refugee Studies Programme, Oxford, University of Oxford

Colson, E. F. (1999) 'Gendering those uprooted by development', in Indra, D. (ed) *Engendering Forced Migration: Theory and Practice*, Oxford, Berghahn Press

Colson, E. F. (2000) 'The father as witch', *Africa*, vol 70, no 3, pp333–358

Confluence: Newsletter of the Dams and Development Project (2002a) Number 1 (May), available at http://www.unep-dams.org/

Confluence: Newsletter of the Dams and Development Project (2002b) Number 2 (December), available at http://www.unep-dams.org/

Cook, C. C. (ed) (1994) 'Involuntary Resettlement in Africa', World Bank Technical Paper Number 227, Africa Technical Department Series, Washington, DC, World Bank

Cooke, V. J. R. S. (1992) 'The Mahaweli Development Programme', in Hullugalle, L. (ed) *Gamini Dissanayake, 50: A Beginning*, Colombo, Hullugalle, L.

Coomaraswamy, R. (1992) 'Raising funds for the Mahaweli', in Hullugalle, L. (ed) *Gamini Dissanayake, 50: A Beginning*, Colombo, Hullugalle, L.

Coppola, S. R. and Agadzi, K. (1977) 'Evolution of the Fishing Industry over Time at Volta Lake', Development Project Statistical Studies, September, Rome, FAO

Costa-Pierce, B. A. (1998) 'Constraints to the sustainability of cage aquaculture for resettlement from hydropower dams in Asia: An Indonesian case study', *Journal of Environment and Development*, vol 7, no 4, pp333–368

Cumanzula, F. (2000) 'Zimbabwe: The resettlement of the Tonga community will never be justified', in Environmental Monitoring Group (EMG) *Once There Was A Community...*, Southern African Hearings for Communities Affected by Large Dams, Cape Town 11–12 November 1999, Final Report, Cape Town, EMG

Curitiba Declaration (1997) *Affirming the Right to Life and Livelihood of People Affected by Dams*, 14 March, available at http://www.irn.org/programs/curitiba.html

Curry, B. (1993a) 'Human Responses to Riverine Hazards in Bangladesh: A Consideration for Sustainable Development', Unpublished manuscript

Curry, B. (1993b) 'Living with Water in Bangladesh', Unpublished manuscript

DAMS, 'The Eternal Website', Official Newsletter of the World Commission on Dams (2000) no 8, p4

DAMS, Official Newsletter of the World Commission on Dams (2001) no 9

Davies, B. (1976) 'Cahora Bassa hazards', *Nature*, vol 254, pp477–478

Davies, B. (2000) Communication to WCD

Davies, B. (2001) 7 November, e-mail to IRN's Ryan Hoover on dam-induced Zambezi River flooding

Davies, B. R., Hall, A. and Jackson, P. B. N. (1975) 'Some ecological effects of the Cahora Bassa Dam', *Biological Conservation*, vol 8, pp189–201

Davis, G. J. (1976) 'Parigi: A Social History of Balinese Movement to Central Sulawesi, 1907–1964', PhD Dissertation, Palo Alto, Stanford University

Dawn (2003) February internet edition with reference to the Indus Delta, available at http://www.dawn.com/2003/02/18/nat22.htm

De Silva, J. (1986) 'River runoff and shrimp abundance in a tropical coastal ecosystem – the example of the Sofala Bank (Central Mozambique)', in Skreslet, S. (ed) *NATO ASI Series,* vol 67, pp329–344, Berlin/Heidelberg, Springer-Verlag

De Silva, K. M. (1981) *A History of Sri Lanka*, Delhi, Oxford University Press

De Wet, C. (1993) 'A spatial analysis of involuntary community relocation: A South African case study', in Cernea, M. M. and Guggenheim, S. E. (eds) *Anthropological Approaches to Resettlement: Policy, Practice and Theory*, Boulder, Colorado, Westview Press

De Wet, C. (2003) 'Why Do Things So Often Go Wrong in Resettlement Projects? How Should We Try to Improve Matters?' Paper delivered at a January conference in Addis Ababa, Ethiopia

De Wilde, J. C. (1967) *Experiences with Agricultural Development in Tropical Africa*, Vols 1 and 2, Baltimore, Johns Hopkins University Press

Diarra, L. (1988) 'Changes in *Vetiveria nigritiana* and *Eragrostis barteri* grasslands in the Niger Floodplain, Central Mali', *ILCA Bulletin*, no 31, pp14–18

Dickson, I. J., Goodland, R., Leblond, P. H., Leistriz, F.L., Limoges, C. and Scudder, T. (1994) 'Hydro-Quebec's Grande-Baleine Environmental Impact Study: An Assessment Report', Report prepared for Hydro-Quebec, Quebec City

Dincer, T. (1985) *Okavango Swamp Model – Phase II*, Gaborone, Department of Water Affairs

Dincer, T., Child, S. and Khupe, B. B. J. (1987) 'A simple mathematical model of a complex hydrologic system', *Journal of Hydrology*, vol 93, pp41–65

Disanayaka, J. B. (2000) *Water Heritage of Sri Lanka*, Colombo, Disanayaka, J. B.

Downing, T. E. (1996) 'Mitigating social impoverishment when people are involuntarily displaced', in McDowell, C. (ed) *Resisting Impoverishment – Tackling the Consequences of Development-Induced Impoverishment*, Oxford, Berghahn Books

Downing, T. E. (2002a) 'Creating poverty: the flawed economic logic of the World Bank's revised involuntary resettlement policy', *Forced Migration Review*, vol 12 (February), pp13–14

Downing, T. E. (2002b) 'Avoiding New Poverty: Mining-Induced Displacement and Resettlement', Report commissioned by the Mining, Minerals and Sustainable Development Project of the International Institute for Environment and Development, Tucson

Drèze, J., Samson, M. and Singh, S. (eds) (1997) *The Dam and the Nation: Displacement and Resettlement in the Narmada Valley*, Delhi, Oxford University Press

Drucker, C. (1985) 'Dam the Chico: Hydropower development and tribal resistance', *The Ecologist*, vol 15, no 4, pp149–157

Dubash, N. K., Dupar, M., Kothari, S. and Lissu, T. (2001) *A Watershed in Global Governance? An Independent Assessment of the World Commission on Dams*, Washington, DC, World Resources Institute and Lokayan

Dubowski, Y. (1997) 'The Environmental Effects of the High Dam at Aswan', June talk at the California Institute of Technology

Dunlap, R. E., Gallup, G. H. Jr and Gallup, A. M. (1993) 'Of global concern: Results of the health of the planet survey', *Environment*, vol 35, no 9, pp7–15, 33–39

Dunne, N. (2001) 'The Americas and Middle East: Export credit agencies hunt for common ground', *Financial Times*, 11 July

Dyson, M., Bergkamp, G. and Scanlon, J. (eds) (2003) *Flow: The Essentials of Environmental Flows*, Gland, Switzerland, IUCN

Eastend Investments (1997) 'Maun Groundwater Development Project, Phase 1: Exploration and Resource Assessment', Executive Summary, Final Report to the Department of Water Affairs, Ministry of Minerals, Energy and Water Affairs (Botswana), May, Gaborone

ECA Watch (a publication of the International NGO Campaign on Export Credit Agencies available at www.eca-watch.org)

Eder, J. (1982) *Who Shall Succeed? Agricultural Development and Social Inequality on the Philippine Frontier*, Cambridge, Cambridge University Press

Egré, D., Roquet, V. and Durocher, C. (2002) 'Benefit Sharing From Dam Projects – Phase 1: Desk Study', Montreal, Vincent Roquet and Associates for the World Bank

El-Abd, S. (1979) 'Land reclamation and resettlement in Egypt', in El-Hamamsy, L. and Garrison, J. (eds) *Human Settlements on New Lands: Their Design and Development*, Cairo, American University in Cairo Press

El-Khodari, N. M. (2002) 'The Nile Basin Initiative: Business as Usual?' Paper prepared for the International Conference on Basin Organizations, Madrid, Spain, 4–6 November

El-Tayeb, E. H. (1981) May-June data on non-farm employment on the New Halfa Scheme, Sudan, published in Scudder, 1981b

Engineering News (2001) 'Are dams damning Southern African development?' 27 April–3 May issue

Environmental Defense Fund (EDF) and Fundação Centro Brasileiro de Referência e Apoio Cultural (CEBRAC) (1997) *The Hidrovía Paraguay-Paraná Navigation Project: Report of an Independent Review*, Washington, DC and Brasília, EDF/CEBRAC

Eriksen, J. H. (1999) 'Comparing the economic planning for voluntary and involuntary resettlement', in Cernea, M. M. (ed) *The Economics of Involuntary Resettlement: Questions and Challenges*, Washington, DC, World Bank

Fahim, H. M. (no date) 'Negative Implications of International Food Aid to Development: The Nubian Case', Unpublished Manuscript

Fahim, H. M. (1968) 'The Resettlement of Egyptian Nubians: A Case Study in Development Change', PhD Dissertation, Berkeley, University of California

Fahim, H. M. (1971) 'The Evaluative Research on the Egyptian Scheme of Nubian Resettlement', Paper delivered at the April Meeting of the Society for Applied Anthropology

Fahim, H. M. (1972) 'Nubian Settlers and Government Administrators: A Preliminary Analysis of a Cross Cultural Setting', January, Paper for Seminar on Development Administration in Egypt, Social Research Center, Cairo, American University in Cairo

Fahim, H. M. (1973) 'Nubian resettlement in the Sudan', *Ekistics*, vol 36, no 212, pp42–49

Fahim, H. M. (1974) 'Basic Information on the Newly Settled Nubian Community in Kom Ombo, Upper Egypt', Report prepared for the Egyptian Authority for the Cultivation and Development of Reclaimed Lands, May, Social Research Center, Cairo, American University in Cairo

Fahim, H. M. (1975) 'The Nubian Settlement in Kom Ombo Region, Upper Egypt', Survey study prepared for the Department of Health, Education and Welfare, Social Research Center, Cairo, American University in Cairo

Fahim, H. M. (1979) 'Community-Health aspects of the Nubian resettlement in Egypt', in Clark, M., Kemper, R. and Nelson, C. (eds) *From Tzintzuntzan to the 'Image of*

Limited Good': Essays in the Honor of George M, Foster, Berkeley, California, The Kroeber Anthropological Society Papers

Fahim, H. M. (1981) *Dams, People and Development: The Aswan High Dam Case*, New York, Pergamon Press

Fahim, H. M. (1983) *Egyptian Nubians: Resettlement and Years of Coping*, Salt Lake City, University of Utah Press

Farid, M. A. (1975) 'The Aswan High Dam Development Project', in Stanley, N. F. and Alpers, M. P. (eds) *Man-Made Lakes and Human Health*, London, Academic Press

Farvar, M. T. and Milton, J. P. (eds) (1972) *The Careless Technology: Ecology and International Development*, Garden City, New York, Natural History Press

Feit, H. A. (1982) 'The Future of hunters within nation-states: Anthropology and the James Bay Cree', in Leacock, E. and Lee, R. (eds) *Politics and History in Band Societies*, Cambridge, Cambridge University Press

Feit, H. A. (1995) 'Hunting and the quest for power: The James Bay Cree and whitemen in the 20th century', in Morrison, R. B. and Wilson, C. R. (eds) *Native Peoples: The Canadian Experience*, Toronto, McCelland and Steward

Fernandes, W. and Paranjpye, V. (eds) (1997) *Rehabilitation Policy and Law in India: A Right to Livelihood*, ISI, Pune, Delhi and Iconet

Fernandes, W. and Raj, A. (1992) *Development, Displacement and Rehabilitation in the Tribal Areas of Orissa, Report*, New Delhi, Indian Social Institute

Fernando, C. H. and Holcik, J. (1991) 'Fish in reservoirs', *International Review of Hydrobiology*, vol 79, pp149–167

Fernea, E. W., Fernea, R. A. and Rouchdy, A. (1991) *Nubian Ethnographies*, Prospect Heights, Illinois, Waveland Press

Fernea, R. A. (1962) 'The Use of Pilot Communities as an Approach to Nubian Resettlement', Report submitted the Egyptian Ministry of Social Affairs, Cairo

Fernea, R. A. (ed) (1966) *Contemporary Egyptian Nubia*, in two volumes, New Haven, Human Relations Area Files

Fernea, R. A. and Kennedy, J. G. (1966) 'Initial Adaptations to Resettlement: A New Life for Egyptians' *Current Anthropology*, vol 7, pp349–354

Fernea, R. A. and Rouchdy, A. (1987) 'Contemporary Egyptian Nubians', in Hagg, T. (ed) *Nubian Culture: Past and Present*, Main papers presented at the Sixth International Conference for Nubian Studies in Uppsala, Stockholm, Akmqvist and Wiksell International

Fernea, R. A. and Rouchdy, A. (1991) 'Part III, Epilogue, Contemporary Egyptian Nubians', in Fernea, E. W., Fernea, R. A. and Rouchdy, A. (eds) *Nubian Ethnographies*, Prospect Heights, Illinois, Waveland Press

Financial Times (2003) 4 June, 'Environment groups hold banks to their green promises', Demetri Sevastopulo

Food and Agriculture Organization of the United Nations (FAO) (1973) *Settlement of Lake Nasser Fishermen*, Based on the work of Van Heck, B., Rome, FAO

Foster, G., Scudder, T., Colson, E. F. and Van Kemper, R. (eds) (1979) *Long-Term Field Research in Social Anthropology*, London, Academic Press

Frederiksen, H. D. (1992) 'Water Resources Institutions: Some Principles and Practices', World Bank Technical Paper no 191, Washington, DC, World Bank

Fried, M. (1963) 'Grieving for a lost home', in Duhl, L. (ed) *The Urban Condition*, New York, Basic Books,

Friedl, G. and Wüest, A. (2002) 'Disrupting biogeochemical cycles – Consequences of damming', *Aquatic Science*, vol 64, pp55–65

Ft. McDowell Yavapai Nation website, www.ftmcdowell.org

Gadd, K. G., Nixon, L. C., Taube, E. and Webster, M. H. (1962) 'The Lusitu Tragedy', *Central African Journal of Medicine*, supplement to vol 8, pp491–508

Gallais, J. (1967) *La Delta Interieur du Niger: Etude de Geographie Regionale*, in two vols, Dakar, Institut Fondamental d'Afrique Noire

Gammelsrød, T. (1992) 'Variation in shrimp abundance on the Sofala Bank, Mozambique, and its relation to the Zambezi River runoff', *Estuarine, Coastal and Shelf Science*, vol 35, pp91–103

Gannett, Fleming, Corddry and Carpenter Inc (1978) 'Assessment of Environmental Effects of the Proposed Developments in the Senegal River Basin', Dakar, OMVS

Gay, J. (1995) October e-mail to International Rivers Network/Environmental Defense

Gazette, The (1994) Authier, P. and Hamilton, G., 'Quebec Shelves Great Whale', 19 November

Geiser, P. (1973) 'The myth of the dam', *American Anthropologist*, vol 75, pp184–194

Geiser, P. (1986) *The Egyptian Nubian: A Study in Social Symbiosis*, Cairo, American University in Cairo Press

Germany, Government of (2001) Statement at ICOLD'S 69th Annual Meeting during the Symposium on the Benefits and Concerns about Dams, ICOLD, Dresden, 9–15 September

Gibb, Alexander, Electricité de France and EUROCONSULT (1986) 'Etude de la Gestion des Ouvrages Communs de l'OMVS: Rapports Phase 2, Volume 2C, Réflexions sur les systèmes de tarification', Electricité de France and Euroconsult, Dakar, OMVS

Gibb, Alexander, Electricité de France and EUROCONSULT (1987) 'Etude de la Gestion des Ouvrages Communs de l'OMVS', 4 vols, Electricité de France and Euroconsult, Dakar, OMVS

Gibb, Alexander & Partners (1961) 'Proposed Kariba Irrigation Project', unpublished report

Gill, S. J. (1993) *A Short History of Lesotho From the Late Stone Age Until the 1993 Elections*, Morija, Lesotho, Morija Museum and Archives

Gleason, J. E., Tittagalla, N. P. and Dinatissa, W. H. A. S. (1990) 'Report on Optimal Crop Combinations Maha 1989/90; Mahaweli System B', MARD/MDS Projects, Agricultural Economics Report no 8

Gleick, P. H. (ed) (1993) *Water in Crisis: A Guide to the World's Fresh Water Resources*, New York and Oxford, Oxford University Press

Global Policy Forum (2003) 'NGO collective analysis of the Equator Principles', *Focus on Finance*, June, available at www.globalpolicy.org/socecon/ffd/(2003)/06ngos.htm

Goldsmith, E. and Hildyard, N. (eds) (1984) *The Social and Environmental Effects of Large Dams: Volume 1 Overview*, Camelford, Cornwall, Wadebridge Ecological Centre

Goldsmith, E. and Hildyard, N. (eds) (1986) *The Social and Environmental Effects of Large Dams: Volume 2 Case Studies*, Camelford, Cornwall, Wadebridge Ecological Centre

Goodland, R. (1981) *Tribal Peoples and Economic Development: Human Ecological Considerations*, Washington, DC, World Bank

Goodland, R. (1994) 'Ethical Priorities in Environmentally Sustainable Energy Systems: The Case of Tropical Hydropower', in Shea, W. R. (ed) *Energy Needs in the Year 2000: Ethical and Environmental Perspectives*, Canton, Mass., Watson Publishing International

Goodland, R. (1995) 'The concept of environmental sustainability', *Annual Review of Ecology and Systematics*, no 26, pp1–25

Goodland, R. (1996) 'The environmental sustainability challenge for the hydro industry', *Hydropower and Dams*, Issue One, pp37–42

Goodland, R. (1997) 'Environmental sustainability in the hydro industry: Disaggregating the debate', in Dorsey, T. (ed) *Large Dams: Learning from the Past – Looking at the Future*, Washington, DC and Gland, Switzerland, IUCN in partnership with the World Bank

Goodland, R. (1999) 'The Evolution of Environmental Assessment in the World Bank: From "Approval" to Results', Environmental Paper 67, Washington, DC, World Bank

Goodland, R. (2000) 'Social and Environmental Assessment to Promote Sustainability', Environmental Paper 74, Washington, DC, World Bank

Goodland, R. (2003) 'Extractive Industries Review, Recommendations on Resettlement', Discussion Draft

Goodland, R., Juras, A. and Pachauri, R. (1993) 'Can hydro-reservoirs in tropical moist forests be environmentally sustainable?' *Environmental Conservation*, vol 20, no 2, Summer, pp122–130

Grand Council of the Crees (1999) 18 March, Speech by the Grand Council's Director of Relations to the Quebec electricity industry association (AIEQ), available at www.gcc.ca

Grand Council of the Crees (2001) 18 December, Speech by Ted Moses, Grand Chief of the Crees, to AIEQ, available at www.gcc.ca

Grand Council of the Crees website, www.gcc.ca

Grant, N. L. (1990) *TVA and Black Americans: Planning for the Status Quo*, Philadelphia, Temple University Press

Great Whale Public Review Support Office (1994) Joint Report on the Conformity and Quality of the Environmental Impact Statement for the Proposed Great Whale River Hydroelectric Project, 18 November

Guardian, The (2003) 24 July, Vidal J., 'Troubled waters for Bangladesh as India presses on with plan to divert major rivers', available at www.guardian.co.uk/international/story/0,,1004769,00.html

Guggenheim, S. (1993) 'Peasants, planners, and participation: Resettlement in Mexico', in Cernea, M. M. and Guggenheim, S. (eds) *Anthropological Approaches to Resettlement: Policy, Practice and Theory*, Boulder, Colorado, Westview Press

Guggenheim, S. (1994) 'Involuntary Resettlement: An Annotated Reference Bibliography for Development Research', Environment Working Paper no 64, Washington, DC, World Bank

Gunaratna, M. H. (1988) *For a Sovereign State*, Ratmalana, Sri Lanka, Sarvodaya Book Publishing Services

Gwembe Commission (1958) 'Report of the Commission Appointed to Inquire into the Circumstances Leading up to and Surrounding the Recent Deaths and Injuries Caused by the Use of Firearms in the Gwembe District and Matters Relating Thereto', Lusaka, Government Printer

Gwembe District (1956) November District Officer Tour Report, Gwembe Boma

Gwembe District (1957a) September District Officer Tour Report, Gwembe Boma

Gwembe District (1957b) Annual Report of the District Commissioner, Gwembe Boma

Gwembe District Council (1956) Annual Report, Muyumbwe

Gwembe District Council (1957) Annual Report, Muyumbwe

Gwembe District Council (1960) 10 March, Letter rejecting setting up a Kariba Lake Development Company as suggested by Central African Federation and Southern Rhodesian officials, Muyumbwe

Hair, J. D., Dysart, B. C., Danielson, L. J. and Rubalcava, A. O. (1997) 'Pangue Hydroelectric Project (Chile): An Independent Review of the International Finance Corporation's Compliance with Applicable World Bank Group Environmental and Social Requirements', Pangue Audit Team, Santiago

Hakim, R. (1995) 'The Implications of Resettlement on Vasava Identity: A Study of a Community Displaced by the Sardar Sarovar (Narmada) Dam Project, India', PhD Dissertation, Cambridge, Cambridge University

Hakim, R. (1996) 'Resettlement and rehabilitation in the context of Vasava culture: some reflections', in Dréze, J., Samson, M. and Singh, S. (eds) *The Dam and the Nation: Displacement and Resettlement in the Narmada Valley*, New Delhi, Oxford University Press

Hakim, R. (2000) 'From corn to cotton: Changing indicators of food security among resettled Vasavas', in Cernea, M. M. and McDowell, C. (eds) *Risks and Reconstruction: Experiences of Resettlers and Refugees*, Washington, DC, World Bank

Hamerlynck, O. and Duvail, S. (2003) *The Rehabilitation of the Delta of the Senegal River in Mauritania: Fielding the Ecosystem Approach*, Gland, IUCN

Hansen, A. and Oliver-Smith, A. (eds) (1982) *Involuntary Migration and Resettlement: The Problems and Responses of Dislocated People*, Boulder, Colorado, Westview Press

Hartman, C. W. (1974) *Yerba Buena: Land Grab and Community Resistance in San Francisco*, San Francisco, Glide Publications for Earl Warren Legal Institute, University of California, Berkeley

Heaver, R. (1983) 'Bureaucratic Politics and Incentives in the Management of Rural Development', World Bank Staff Working Paper no 537, Washington, DC, World Bank

Heikel, H. (1973) *The Cairo Documents*, Garden City, New York, Doubleday

Hilton, T. E. and Kowu-Tsri, J. Y. (1973) 'The impact of the Volta Scheme on the lower Volta floodplains', *Journal of Tropical Geography*, pp29–37

Hollis, G. E. (1996) 'Hydrological inputs to management policy for the Senegal River and its floodplain', in Acreman, M. C. and Hollis, G. E. (eds) *Water Management and Wetlands in Sub-Saharan Africa*, Gland, Switzerland, International Union for the Conservation of Nature and Natural Resources (IUCN/World Conservation Union)

Hollis, G. E., Adams, W. M. and Aminu-Kano, M. (1993) *The Hadejia-Nguru Wetlands: Environment, Economy and Sustainable Development of a Sahelian Floodplain Wetland*, Gland, Switzerland, IUCN

Homer-Dixon, T. F. (1994) 'Environmental scarcities and violent conflict: Evidence from cases', *International Security*, vol 19, no 1, pp5–40

Hoover, R. (2001) *Pipe Dreams: The World Bank's Failed Efforts to Restore Lives and Livelihoods of Dam-Affected People in Lesotho*, Berkeley, International Rivers Network

Horowitz, M. M. (1989) 'Victims of development', *Development Anthropology Network*, vol 7, no 2, pp1–8

Horowitz, M. M. (1991) 'Victims upstream and down', *Journal of Refugee Studies*, vol 2, pp164–181

Horowitz, M. M. and Salem-Murdock, M. (1990) *The Senegal River Basin Monitoring Activity: Synthesis Report*, Binghamton, New York, Institute for Development Anthropology

Horowitz, M. M., Salem-Murdock, M., Grimm, C. et al (1991) *The Senegal River Basin Monitoring Activity, Phase 1: Final Report*, May (revised), Binghamton, New York, Institute for Development Anthropology

Hughes, F. M. R. (1988) 'The ecology of African floodplain forests in semi-arid and arid zones: A review', *Journal of Biogeography*, vol 15, pp127–140

Hughes, F. M. R. (1992) 'Environmental Change, Disturbance and Regeneration in Semi-Arid Floodplain Forests', Unpublished manuscript, Cambridge, UK (see also 1990, 'The influence of flooding regimes on forest distribution and composition in the Tana River Floodplain, Kenya', *Journal of Applied Ecology*, vol 27, pp475–491)

Hullugalle, L. (1992) *Gamini Dissanayake, 50: A Beginning*, Colombo, Hullugalle, L.

Hunting Technical Services – Consult 4 Joint Venture (1997) *Adjudication*, volume 4, *Resettlement and Development Study*, Maseru, Lesotho

Hurst, H. E. et al (1931–1966) *The Nile Basin*, 10 volumes and 21 supplements, Cairo

Hutchinson Encyclopedia on Malaysia's Pergau Dam Project, Oxford, Helicon Publishing

Hydro-Quebec (1986) *La Grande Agreement*, Montreal, Hydro-Quebec

Hydro-Quebec (1992) Map of Hydroelectric Development and Native Communities of Northern Quebec, Montreal, Hydro-Quebec

Hydro-Quebec (1993) *Grande Baleine Feasibility Study*, Part 2, Book 8, Montreal, Hydro-Quebec

Hydro-Quebec (1999) 'Dams and Benefit Sharing, A Submission from Hydro-Quebec' prepared for the World Commission on Dams

Hydro-Quebec website, www.hydro.qc.ca/en/

Independent, The (2003) 7 July, Article on Iceland's Karahnjukar Hydropower Project as reported on IRN's WCD site (owner-irn-wcd@netvista.net)

International Advisory Group (IAG) of the World Bank (1997) 'Terms of Reference', Appendix 2, 'World Bank's handling of social and environmental issues in the proposed Nam Theun 2 hydropower project in Lao PDR', Report of the International Advisory Group, 19 August

International Commission on Large Dams (ICOLD) (1995) Position Paper On Dams and the Environment, Paris, ICOLD

International Commission on Large Dams (ICOLD) (1998) *Register of Large Dams*, Paris, ICOLD

International Council of Scientific Unions (1972) 'Man-Made Lakes as Modified Ecosystems', SCOPE Report 2, Paris, ICSU

International Finance Corporation (2003) Assessment by the Office of the Compliance Adviser/Ombudsman in relation to a complaint filed against IFC's investment in ENDESA Pangue S.A., May, Compliance Adviser/Ombudsman, Washington, DC, IFC

International Fund for Agricultural Development (IFAD) (1993) *World Rural Poverty Report*, Rome, IFAD

International Herald Tribune (2002) 24 April, 'A battle over Indus River water', Eckholm, E.

International Labour Organization (ILO) (1957) Convention 107 on Indigenous and Tribal Populations, Addis Ababa, ILO

International Labour Organization (ILO) (1981) *Basic Need in an Economy Under Pressure*, Addis Ababa, ILO

International Labour Organization (ILO) (1989) Convention 169 concerning Indigenous and Tribal Peoples in Independent Countries, Addis Ababa, ILO

International Rivers Network (IRN) (1999a) 'Resettlement gone wrong: The case for reparations', *World Rivers Review*, vol 14, no 9 (December) pp8–9

International Rivers Network (IRN) (1999b) Report on the Cree, 6 May, Berkeley

International Rivers Network (IRN) (2001a) Report from Lao Atakpu of Nigeria's
   African Network for Environmental and Economic Justice on Dam-induced
   Flooding, available on request to irn-safrica@netvista.net
International Rivers Network (IRN) (2001b), 12 July, item on rising aquifer salinity
   threatening Luxor temple, available on request to irn-safrica@netvista.net
International Rivers Network (IRN) (2002), 21 June, item on Pak Mun Dam, available
   on request to irn-mekong@netvista.net
International Rivers Network (IRN) (2003), 11 July, article by Hope E. Ogbeide on
   NGO/Civil Society Dialogue on the Report of the World Commission on Dams in
   Nigeria, available on request to irn-safrica@netvista.net
International Rivers Network (IRN)/Environmental Defense (ED) (1995) 28 September,
   letter to the World Bank's Vice President for Africa, Berkeley and Washington, DC,
   IRN and ED
Isaacman, A. (2001) 'Domesticating a white elephant: Sustainability and struggles over
   water, the case of Cahora Bassa Dam', *Zambezia*, vol XXVIII, no ii, pp199–228
IUCN/Government of Botswana (1991) Memorandum of Understanding for the IUCN
   Review of the Southern Okavango Integrated Water Development Project, 11
   October, Gland and Gaborone, IUCN and Government of Botswana
IUCN/World Bank (1997) *Large Dams: Learning from the Past, Looking at the Future*,
   Gland, Switzerland, IUCN-World Bank
IUCN/World Conservation Union (1991) Inception Report of the IUCN SOIWDP
   Review Team, October, Gaborone, IUCN
IUCN/World Conservation Union (1992a) 'The IUCN Review of the Southern
   Okavango Integrated Water Development Project', Draft Final Report, May,
   Gaborone, IUCN SOIWDP Review Team
IUCN/World Conservation Union (1992b) 'The IUCN Review of the Southern
   Okavango Integrated Water Development Project', Final Report, October, Gland
   Switzerland, IUCN
IUCN/World Conservation Union (1997) 'Environment and Social Management Plan
   for Nakai-Nam Theun Catchment and Corridor Areas', July, Vientiane, IUCN
IUCN/World Conservation Union (2000a) 17 June, News Release, 'At Expo (2000) –
   Hanover, Germany – IUCN project awarded', IUCN Waza-Logone Project
IUCN/World Conservation Union (2000b) 9 December, Draft Policy for the Sustainable
   Use of Deltas, Gland, Switzerland
Jackson, P. B. N. (1961) *The Fish of the Middle Zambezi*, Kariba Studies, Ichthyology,
   Manchester, Manchester University Press
Jain, L. C. (2001) *Dam vs Drinking Water – Exploring the Narmada Judgment*, Pune,
   India, Parisar
Jenness, J. (1970) 'Fishermen of the Kainji Basin', Rome, FAO
Jing, J. (1999) 'Displacement, Resettlement, Rehabilitation, Reparation and
   Development – China Report', Contributing Paper to Thematic Review I.3 prepared
   as an input to the World Commission on Dams, Cape Town, available at
   www.dams.org
Jobin, W. (1999) *Dams and Disease: Ecological Design and Health Impacts of Large
   Dams, Canals and Irrigation Systems*, London, E and FN Spon
Jogaratnam, T. (1995) 'Accelerated Mahaweli Development Programme: Its
   implications for the economy of Sri Lanka', in Muller, H. P. and Hettige, S. T. (eds)
   The Blurring of a Vision – The Mahaweli, Ratmalana, Sri Lanka, Sarvodaya Book
   Publishing Services

Johnston, B. F. and Kilby, P. (1975) *Agriculture and Structural Transformation: Economic Strategies in Late Developing Countries*, New York, Oxford University Press

Johnston, B. R. (2000) 'Reparations and the Right to Remedy', Contributing Paper to Thematic Review V.4 prepared as an input to the World Commission on Dams, Cape Town, available at www.dams.org

Joint Permanent Technical Commission/Lesotho Highlands Water Commission (1991) 3 October, letter to the LHDA Chief Executive requesting withdrawal of the September (1991) LHDA POE Report, Maseru, JPTC

Joint Permanent Technical Commission/Lesotho Highlands Water Commission (1992) 30 January, letter to LHDA POE members disassociating the JPTC from the POE September Report, Maseru, JPTC

Joshi, V. (1983) 'Studies on Rehabilitation of Submerging Villages: A Summary of the General Report', Centre for Social Studies, Surat

Kamwanga, J. and Chosani N. (1997) *Development Strategies and Rehabilitation Programs for the Peoples Affected by the Construction of the Kariba Dam: Proposed Implementation Plan* (vol 1) and *Final Composite Report* (vol 2), Institute for Economic and Social Research, Lusaka, University of Zambia for the World Bank

Kassas, M. (1972) 'Impact of river control schemes on the shoreline of the Nile Delta', in Farvar, M. T. and Milton, J. P. (eds) *The Careless Technology: Ecology and International Development*, Garden City, New York, Natural History Press

Katzman, M. T. (1977) *Cities and Frontiers in Brazil: Regional Dimensions of Economic Development*, Cambridge, Harvard University Press

Kemper, R. V. and Royce, A. P. (eds) (2002) *Chronicling Cultures: Long-Term Field Research in Anthropology*, Walnut Creek, California, Altamira Press

Kennedy, J. (1977) *Struggle for Change in a Nubian Community*, Palo Alto, Mayfield

Khera, S. and Mariella, P. S. (1982) 'The Fort McDowell Yavapai: A case of long-term resistance to relocation', in Hansen, A. and Oliver-Smith, A. (eds), *Involuntary Migration and Resettlement: The Problems and Responses of Dislocated People*, Boulder, Colorado, Westview Press

Khwaja, A. (1998) 'Some Aspects of Opposing Kalabagh Dam', Submission for the first World Commission on Dams' Regional Consultation, Colombo, Sri Lanka

King, J. M., Tharme, R. E. and de Villiers, M. S. (2000) 'Environmental Flow Assessments for Rivers: Manual for the Building Block Methodology', WRC Report no TT131/00, Pretoria, Water Research Commission

Koenig, D. (1995) 'Women and resettlement', in Gallin, R. and Ferguson, A. (eds) *The Women and International Development Annual*, Boulder, Colorado, Westview Press

Koenig, D. (2002) 'Toward Local Development and Mitigating Impoverishment in Development-Induced Displacement and Impoverishment', RSC Working Paper 8, Refugee Studies Centre, Oxford, University of Oxford

Koenig, D. and Diarra, T. (2000) 'The effects of resettlement on access to common property resources', in Cernea, M. M. and McDowell, C. (eds) *Risks and Reconstruction: Experiences of Resettlers and Refugees*, Washington, DC, World Bank

Lagus, C. (1959) *Operation Noah*, London, William Kimber

Lahmeyer-MacDonald C. (1986) *Lesotho Highlands Water Project, Feasibility Study Report*, Maseru, Lahmeyer-MacDonald

Lassailly-Jacob, V. (1990) 'Village Resettlement in New Nubia, Egypt: The Modification of a Development Project through a Case Study', Paris, Lassailly-Jacob

Lassailly-Jacob, V. (1994) 'Resettlers after 25 Years: The Kossou Hydro-Electric Project, Ivory Coast', Paper presented on 6 June at a Seminar at the World Bank

Lawson, M. L. (1994) *The Dammed Indians: The Pick-Sloan Plan and the Missouri River Sioux, 1944–1980*, Norman, University of Oklahoma Press

Leach, E. R. (1961) *Pul Eliya – A Village in Ceylon: A Study of Land Tenure and Kinship*, Cambridge, Cambridge University Press

Ledec, G., Quintero, J. D. and Mejía, M. C. (1999) 'Good Dams and Bad Dams: Environmental and Social Criteria for Choosing Hydroelectric Project Sites', Washington, DC, World Bank

LeMarquand, D. G. (1982) 'International Development of the Senegal River', PhD Dissertation, Oxford, Oxford University College

Lerer, L. B. and Scudder, T. (1999) 'Health impacts of large dams', *Environmental Impact Assessment Review*, vol 19, pp113–123

Lesotho, Government of (2003) 'Report of the Ombudsman on the Lesotho Highlands Water Project', Maseru, GOL

Lesotho Highlands Development Authority (LHDA) (1986) Government of Lesotho Order 23 (14 November) Establishing the Lesotho Highlands Development Authority, Maseru, GOL

Lesotho Highlands Development Authority (LHDA) (1990) Phase 1A Compensation Plan, LHDA, Maseru

Lesotho Highlands Development Authority (LHDA) (1997) *Environmental Action Plan* and especially Volume 3 *Resettlement and Development Action Plan*, LHDA, Maseru

Lesotho Highlands Water Project (LHWP) (1986) Treaty on the Lesotho Highlands Water Project between the Government of the Republic of South Africa and the Government of the Kingdom of Lesotho, Signed 24 October

LHDA POE (1989) First Report of the Panel of Experts on Environmental Issues, February, Maseru, LHDA

LHDA POE (1990) Report of the Panel of Environmental Experts, March, Maseru, LHDA

LHDA POE (1991) Report of the Panel of Environmental Experts, August, Maseru, LHDA

LHDA POE (1992) Report of the Panel of Environmental Experts, August, Maseru, LHDA

LHDA POE (1995a) Report of the Panel of Environmental Experts, April, Maseru, LHDA

LHDA POE (1995b) Report of the Panel of Environmental Experts, December, Maseru, LHDA

LHDA POE (1996) Report of the Panel of Environmental Experts, June, Maseru, LHDA

LHDA POE (1997) Report of the Panel of Environmental Experts, July, Maseru, LHDA

LHDA POE (1999) Report of the Panel of Environmental Experts, March, Maseru, LHDA

LHDA POE (2000a) Report of the Panel of Environmental Experts, April, Maseru, LHDA

LHDA POE (2000b) Report of the Panel of Environmental Experts, November, Maseru, LHDA

LHDA POE (2001) Report of the Panel of Environmental Experts, August, Maseru, LHDA

LHDA POE (2002) Report of the Panel of Environmental Experts, April, Maseru, LHDA

LHDA POE (2003) Draft Report of the Panel of Environmental Experts, September, Maseru, LHDA

Linares, O. (1981) 'From tidal swamp to inland valley: On the social organization of wet rice cultivation among the Diola of Senegal', *Africa*, vol 51, p557

Los Angeles Times (1985) 22 June, excerpts from a speech by Sri Lanka's President Jayewardene on the Mahaweli Project

Los Angeles Times (2003a) 13 July, 'Judges order contempt hearing for army corps of engineers'

Los Angeles Times (2003b) 24 September, 'Judge taken off Everglades case following complaints'

Loth, P. (ed) (2004) *The Return of the Water: Restoring the Waza Logone Floodplain in Cameroon*, Gland, IUCN

Lowe-McConnell, R. H. (ed) (1966) *Man-Made Lakes*, New York, Academic Press

Lund, R. (1978) *A Survey of Women's Working and Living Conditions in a Mahaweli Settlement Area with Special Emphasis on Household Budgets and Household Surplus*, Research Department, Colombo, People's Bank Study Papers

MacGregor, R. (1990) *Chief: The Fearless Vision of Billy Diamond*, Ontario, Penguin Books

Maema, M. and Reynolds, N. (1995) 'Lesotho Highlands Water Project-induced displacement: Context, impacts, rehabilitation strategies, implementation experience, and future options', in McDowell, C. (ed) *Resisting Impoverishment: Tackling the Consequences of Development-Induced Displacement*, Oxford, Berghahn Books

Mahapatra, L. L. (1999a) *Resettlement, Impoverishment, and Reconstruction in India: Development for the Deprived*, New Delhi, Vikas Publishing House Pvt Ltd

Mahapatra, L. L. (1999b) 'Testing the risks and reconstruction model on India's resettlement experiences', in Cernea, M. M. (ed) *The Economics of Involuntary Resettlement: Questions and Challenges*, Washington, DC, World Bank

Mahaweli Authority of Sri Lanka (1997) Mahaweli Statistical Handbook prepared by the MASL's Planning and Monitoring Unit (PMU), Colombo

Mahaweli Authority of Sri Lanka (1999) Mahaweli Statistical Handbook prepared by the MASL's Planning and Monitoring Unit (PMU), Colombo

Mahaweli Development Board (1977) Summary Reports on Projects, November, Mahaweli Development Board, Colombo

Mahaweli Economic Agency (1985) Unpublished paper presented at a seminar on land settlement in Sri Lanka, Colombo

Malasha, I. (1999) 'The Justification for and Implementation of a New Management Regime in the Lake Kariba Fishery', Draft manuscript, Harare, University of Zimbabwe

Malik, R. P. S. and Bhatia, R. (2003) 'A Case Study of the Sukhomajri-Bunga Check Dams, India', March Draft Report for the World Bank Task Force on the Multiplier Effects of Dams, Washington DC, World Bank

Malila, I. (1999) 'Maun Socio-economic and Housing Survey: Mabudutsa and Mabudutsane Wards', Gaborone, Republic of Botswana, Ministry of Local Government and Lands, Applied Research Unit

Manibeli Declaration (1994) Calling for a Moratorium on World Bank Funding of Large Dams, June, reproduced in McCully, P. (2001)

Mankodi, K. and Gangopadhyay, T. (1983) *Rehabilitation: Ecological and Economic Costs*, Surat, Centre for Social Studies

Manley, R. E. and Wright, E. P. (1996) 'The review of the Southern Okavango Integrated Water Development Project', in Acreman, M. C. and Hollis, G. E. (eds) *Water Management and Wetlands in Sub-Saharan Africa*, Gland, Switzerland,

International Union for the Conservation of Nature and Natural Resources (IUCN/World Conservation Union)

Marcus, C. (1994) 'Environmental memories', in Low, S. and Altman, I. (eds) *Place Attachment*, New York, Plenum Press

Margolis, M. (1980) 'Natural disaster and socioeconomic change: Post-Frost adjustments in Parana, Brazil', *Disasters*, vol 4, pp231–235

Marshall, B. E., Junor, F. J. R. and Langerman, J. D. (1982) 'Fisheries and Fish Production on the Zimbabwe Side of Lake Kariba', Kariba Studies Paper number 10, pp175–231, Bulawayo, National Museums and Monuments of Zimbabwe

Martin, R. B. (1986) *Communal Areas Management Programme for Indigenous Resources*, Branch of Terrestrial Ecology, Department of National Parks and Wildlife Management, Harare

Mathur, H.M. (1995) 'Struggling to Regain Livelihood: The Case of People Displaced by the Pong Dam in India', Paper presented at the International Conference on Development-Induced Displacement and Impoverishment, Oxford, Oxford University, 3–7 January

Mathur, H. M. (1997) 'Managing Projects that Involve Resettlement: Case Studies from Rajasthan, India', Economic Development Institute (EDI Working Papers), Washington, DC, World Bank

McCreddin, J. A., Syme, G. J., Nancarrow, B. E. and George, D. R. (1994) 'Developing Fair and Equitable Land and Water Allocation in Near Urban Locations: Principles, Processes and Decision-Making', Consultancy Report 96/60, Perth, CSIRO, Division of Water Resources

McCully, P. (1996) *Silenced Rivers: The Ecology and Politics of Large Dams*, London, Zed Books

McCully, P. (2001) *Silenced Rivers: The Ecology and Politics of Large Dams*, enlarged and updated edition, London, Zed Books

McDonald, M. J. and Muldowny, J. (1982) *TVA and the Dispossessed: The Resettlement of Population in the Norris Dam Area*, Knoxville, University of Tennessee Press

McDowell, C. (ed) (1996) *Understanding Impoverishment: The Consequences of Development-Induced Displacement*, Oxford, Berghahn Books

McElwee, P. and Horowitz, M. M. (1999) 'Environment and Society in the Lower Mekong Basin: A Landscaping Review', IDA Working Paper, no 99, Binghamton, Institute for Development Anthropology for the Mekong River Basin Research and Capacity Building Initiative, Oxfam America SEA

McMillan, D. F. (1995) *Sahel Visions: Planned Settlement and River Blindness Control in Burkina Faso*, Tucson, University of Arizona Press

Mehta, L. and Srinivasan, B. (2000) 'Balancing Pains and Gains: A Perspective Paper on Gender and Large Dams', Contributing Paper for WCD Thematic Review 1.1, Cape Town, World Commission on Dams

Mejía, M. C. (1996) 'Involuntary Resettlement of Urban Population: Experiences in World Bank-Financed Development Projects in Latin America', Paper presented at the World Bank's Urban Resettlement Workshop in Ouro Preto, Brazil, 25–29 September, Washington, DC, World Bank

Mejía, M. C. (1999) 'Economic dimensions of urban resettlement: Experiences from Latin America', in Cernea, M. M. (ed) *The Economics of Involuntary Resettlement: Questions and Challenges*, Washington, DC, World Bank

METSI Consultants (2000) 'Consulting Services for the Establishment and Monitoring of the Instream Flow Requirements for River Courses Downstream of Lesotho

Highlands Water Project Dams', Final Report, Lesotho Highlands Water Project, Maseru

Midweek Sun (1994) 3 March, Headline that the President of Botswana 'Longs for Okavango Delta utilization'

Mitchell, D. S. (1973) 'Aquatic weeds in man-made lakes', in Ackermann, W. C., White, G. F. and Worthington, E. B. (eds) *Man-Made Lakes: Their Problems and Environmental Effects*, Washington, DC, American Geophysical Union

Montreal Gazette (1999) 19 March, 'Crees grapple with future: Truce with Hydro-Quebec leads to new challenges', Siblin, E., as distributed on IRN's website

Montreal Gazette (2001) 27 September, article on Hydro-Quebec (no title listed), Doughherty, K.

Montreal Gazette (2001) 10 December, '$3.6 billion Cree-Quebec deal unraveling', Roslin, A.

Montreal Hour (2000) 22 June, 'Lucien's power play' Stewart, L.

Moran, E. (1989) 'Adaptation and maladaptation', in Schumann, D. A. and Partridge, W. L. (eds) *The Human Ecology of Tropical Land Settlement in Latin America*, Boulder, Colorado, Westview Press

Morse, B., Berger, T., Gamble, D. and Brody, H. (1992) *Sardar Sarovar: The Report of the Independent Review*, Ottawa, Resources Futures International

Morton, A. J. and Obot, E. A. (1984) 'The Control of *Echinochloa stagnina* (Retz) P. Beauv. by harvesting for dry season livestock fodder in Lake Kainji, Nigeria – A modeling approach', *Journal of Applied Ecology*, vol 21, pp687–694

Muhai, A. (1997) 'Cahora Bassa and the Lower Zambezi Workshop', Conference Proceedings of Workshop Sobre O Uso Sustentavel da Barrágem de Cahora Bassa e do Vale do Rio Zambese, 29 September–2 October, Songo, Mozambique

Muller, H. P. and Hettige, S. T. (eds) (1995) *The Blurring of a Vision – The Mahaweli*, Ratmalana, Sri Lanka, Sarvodaya Book Publishing Services

Murray-Hudson, M. and Crisman, T. L. (2003) 'Ecotourism as a sustainable land-use option in African wetlands', in Crisman, T. L., Chapman, L. J., Chapman, C. A. and Kaufman, L. S. (eds) *Conservation, Ecology, and Management of African Fresh Waters*, Gainesville, University Press of Florida

Nam Theun 2 Electricity Consortium (NTEC) (1997) *Nam Theun 2 Hydroelectric Project Resettlement Action Plan*, Vientiane, Lao PDR, NTEC

Nam Theun 2 Electricity Consortium (NTEC) (2002) *Nam Theun 2 Hydroelectric Project Resettlement Action Plan*, Vientiane, Lao PDR, NTEC

Nam Theun 2 Panel of Experts (1997) Report of the International Environmental and Social Panel of Experts, Vientiane, Hydropower Office, Government of Laos

Nam Theun 2 Panel of Experts (2001) Fifth Report of the International Environmental and Social Panel of Experts, Vientiane, Hydropower Office, Government of Laos

Nam Theun 2 Panel of Experts (2003) Sixth Report of the International Environmental and Social Panel of Experts, Vientiane, Hydropower Office, Government of Laos

Narmada Water Disputes Tribunal (1979) Decision of the Tribunal under the Interstate Water Disputes Act, 1956, Delhi, Government of India

Nation, The (2001) 29 October, 'Cree leaders cut a deal and surrender the Rupert' (Commentary on Cree Public Reactions to 'The Agreement in Principle')

National Academy of Sciences – National Research Council (1966) *Alternatives in Water Management*, Publication 1408, Washington, DC, NAS-NRC

National Research Council (2002) *The Missouri River Ecosystem: Exploring the Prospects for Recovery*, Washington, DC, National Academy Press

Nelson, M. (1973) *The Development of Tropical Lands: Policy Issues in Latin America*, Baltimore, Johns Hopkins University Press for Resources for the Future

Netherlands Engineering Consultants (NEDECO) (1979) Mahaweli Ganga Development Program Implementation Strategy Study, The Hague, The Netherlands

New Africa (1985) 'Report on coastal erosion due to the Akosombo Dam', vol 27

New York Times (2001) 7 August, 'A foolish dam and a writer's freedom', Rushdie, S.

New York Times (2002) 19 August, 'Taming the untouchable corps', editorial

Niezen, R. (1998) *Defending the Land: Sovereignty and Forest Life in James Bay Cree Society*, Boston, Allyn and Bacon for Cultural Survival Studies in Ethnicity and Change

Nigam (see Sardar Sarovar Narmada Nigam Ltd)

Nile Basin Initiative (2003) 'Dar es Salaam Declaration on Regional Electric Power Trade', Council of Ministers, June, Entebbe, Nile Basin Initiative Secretariat

Niyangoda, S. M. S. B. (2001) 'Mahaweli Then and Now', Manuscript, Colombo, Ministry of Mahaweli Development

OECD (2000) Report on the November session of the Working Party on Export Credits and Credit Guarantees, Paris, OECD

Ohly, J. J. and Junk, W. J. (1999) 'Multiple use of Central Amazon Floodplains: Combining ecological conditions, requirements for environmental protection, and socioeconomic needs', in Padoch, C., Ayres, J. M., Pinedo-Vasquez, M. and Henderson, A. (eds) *Várzea: Diversity, Development, and Conservation of Amazonia's Whitewater Floodplains*, Bronx, New York, New York Botanical Garden Press

Okavango Observer (1993) October, Article in which the Principle Water Engineer for Operations and Maintenance is quoted as saying future Maun water demand will be met by combined use of surface and ground water

Okavango Observer (1993) 3 December, 'President Speaks at Maun Kgotla'

Okavango Observer (1994a) 18 March, 'Comment'

Okavango Observer (1994b) 14 October, 'Is government punishing Maun?', Scudder, T.

Okavango Observer (1994c) 4 November, 'Ngami land water problem', Scudder, T.

Okavango Observer (1994d) 15 April, 'Vice president excited'

Okavango Observer (1994e) 12–18 July, 'Interview with His Excellency: President on campaign trail'

Okavango Observer (1995) 30 June, 'Dream of a dam', Mogae, F.

Okidi, C. O. (1987a) 'Development and the Environment in the Senegal Basin under the OMVS Treaty', Discussion Paper no 283, Nairobi, Institute for Development Studies, University of Nairobi

Okidi, C. O. (1987b) 'The Role of the State in the Management of International River and Lake Basins in Africa', Discussion Paper no 285, Nairobi, Institute for Development Studies, University of Nairobi

Oliver-Smith, A. (1991) 'Successes and failures in post-disaster resettlement', *Disasters: The Journal of Disaster Studies and Management*, vol 15, no 1, pp12–23

Oliver-Smith, A. (2002) 'Displacement, Resistance and the Critique of Development: From the Grass-Roots to the Global', RSC Working Paper no 9, Refugee Studies Centre, Oxford, University of Oxford

Ortolano, L., Cushing, K. (2000) 'Grand Coulee Dam and Columbia Basin Project, USA', Case study report prepared as an input to the World Commission on Dams, Cape Town, available at www.dams.org

Osman, H. (1999) 'Hydro Development in Egypt – Lessons from Aswan High Dam', Submission at the World Commission on Dams' Third Regional Consultation, Cairo, Egypt

Oyedipe, F. A. P. (1983) *Adjustment to Resettlement: A Study of the Resettled People in the Kainji Lake Basin*, Ibadan, University Press Ltd

Padoch, C., Ayres, J. M., Pinedo-Vasquez, M. and Henderson, A. (eds) (1999) *Várzea: Diversity, Development, and Conservation of Amazonia's Whitewater Floodplains*, Bronx, New York, New York Botanical Garden Press

Paranjpye, V. (1990) *High Dams on the Narmada: A Holistic Analysis of the River Valley Projects*, Studies in Ecology and Sustainable Development – 3, New Delhi, Indian National Trust for Art and Cultural Heritage

Parasuraman, S. (1999) *The Development Dilemma: Displacement in India*, The Hague, Institute of Social Studies

Parker, H. (1984) *Ancient Ceylon*, New Delhi, Asian Educational Services (reprint)

Partridge, W. L. (1983) 'Comparative Analysis of Bid Experience with Resettlement, Based on Evaluations of the Arenal and Chixoy Projects', Report to the Inter-American Development Bank (IDB), Washington, DC, IDB

Partridge, W. L. (1989) 'Involuntary resettlement in development projects', *Journal of Refugee Studies*, vol 2, no 3, pp373–384

Partridge, W. L. (1993) 'Successful involuntary resettlement: Lessons from the Costa Rican Arenal Hydroelectric Project', in Cernea, M. M. and Guggenheim, S. E. (eds) *Anthropological Approaches to Resettlement: Policy, Practice and Theory*, Boulder, Colorado, Westview Press

Partridge, W. L., Brown, A. B. and Nugent, J. B. (1982) 'The Papaloapan Dam and resettlement project: Human ecology and health impacts', in Hansen, A. and Oliver-Smith, A. (eds) *Involuntary Migration and Resettlement: The Problems and Responses of Dislocated People*, Boulder, Colorado, Westview Press

Patel, A. (1997) 'Resettlement politics and tribal interests', in Drèze, J., Samson, M. and Singh, S. (eds) *The Dam and the Nation: Displacement and Resettlement in the Narmada Valley*, Delhi, Oxford University Press

Pearce, F. (1992) *The Dammed: Rivers, Dams, and the Coming World Water Crisis*, London, Bodley Head

Peña, E. D. (1999) 'Yacyretá Hydro Electric Project: The Struggle for Participation', Submission abstract for the Second Regional Consultation of the World Commission on Dams, Sao Paulo, Brazil

Perlman, J. E. (1976) *The Myth of Marginality: Urban Poverty and Politics in Rio de Janeiro*, Berkeley, University of California Press

Perritt, R. (1988) *An Analysis of the Volta River Basin and Development in Ghana as Administered by the Volta River Authority*, USAID Cooperative Agreement on Settlement and Resource Systems Analysis, Worcester, Massachusetts, Clark University, Binghamton, New York, Institute for Development Anthropology

Petit, C., Scudder, T. and Lambin, E. (2001) 'Quantifying processes of land-cover change by remote sensing: Resettlement and rapid land-cover changes in South-Eastern Zambia', *International Journal of Remote Sensing*, vol 22, no 17, pp3435–3456

Philadelphia Inquirer (1991) 14 January, 'Plan to dredge Botswana river threatens vast, fragile swamps', Lyman, R.

Picciotto, R., Van Wicklin, W. and Rice, E. (eds) (2001) *Involuntary Resettlement: Comparative Perspectives*, World Bank Series on Evaluation and Development, vol 2, New Brunswick, Transaction Publishers

Pinedo-Vasquez, M. (1999) 'Changes in social formation and vegetation on silt bars and backslopes of levees following intensive production of rice and jute', in Padoch, C., Ayres, J. M., Pinedo-Vasquez, M. and Henderson, A. (eds) *Várzea: Diversity,*

Development, and Conservation of Amazonia's Whitewater Floodplains, Advances in Economic Botany, vol 13, Bronx, New York, New York Botanical Garden Press

Poeschke, R. (1996) *Nubians in Egypt and Sudan: Constraints and Coping Strategies*, Saarbrucken, Verlag fur Entwicklungspolitic

Portères, R. (1976) 'African cereals: Eleusine, fonio, black fonio, teff, *brachiaria, paspalum, pennisetum*, and African rice', in Harlan, J. R., De Wet, J. M. J. and Stemler, A. B. L. (eds) *Origins of African Plant Domestication*, The Hague, Mouton Publishers

Posadas Declaration (2002) 'Mega dams, a history of destruction which repeats itself', available through IRN (http://www.irn.org/programs/)

Postel, S. (1996) *Dividing the Waters, Food Security, Ecosystem Health, and the New Politics of Scarcity*, Worldwatch Paper 132, Washington, DC, Worldwatch Institute

Postel, S. and Richter, B. (2003) *Rivers for Life: Managing Water for People and Nature*, Washington, DC, Island Press

Poultney, C. (2001) 'People and Environment Again at Risk – The Pongolapoort Dam', Lubombo Waterways Programme, Mboza, KwaZulu-Natal, Mboza Village Project

Probe International (2003) 23 September, Press Advisory 'Leaked Report Criticizes Vietnam for Unsafe Dam Operations', Toronto, Probe International

Quartey, E. L. (1988) *Volta River Project*, USAID Cooperative Agreement on Settlement and Resource Systems Analysis, Worcester, Massachusetts, Clark University, Binghamton, New York, Institute for Development Anthropology

Quebec Provincial Government (1991) *The James Bay and Northern Quebec Agreement and Complementary Agreements*, Quebec, Les Publications of Quebec

Quebec Provincial Government (1999) Agreement in Principle (between the Grand Council of the Crees and the Province of Quebec), Quebec

Rajogopal, B. (2000) 'Human Rights and Development', Contributing Paper to Thematic Review V.4 prepared as an input to the World Commission on Dams, Cape Town, available at www.dams.org

Rasi Salai Declaration (2003) 'Rivers for Life: Second International Meeting of Dam-Affected People and their Allies', available through IRN (http://www.irn.org/riversforlife/)

Reed, G. E., Steele, K. A., Verigin, S. W. and Ehasz, J. L. (2003) 'Olivenhain Dam "Partnering" approach creates commitment, success', *Hydro Review*, vol XXII, no 5 (October), pp10–17

Rew, A. W. (1996) 'Policy implications of the involuntary ownership of resettlement negotiations: Examples from Asia of resettlement practice', in McDowell, C. (ed) *Resisting Impoverishment – Tackling the Consequences of Development-Induced Impoverishment*, Oxford, Berghahn Books

Rew, A. W. and Driver, P. A. (1986) *Evaluation of the Victoria Dam Project in Sri Lanka*, Vol III, *Initial Evaluation of the Social and Environmental Impact of the Victoria Dam Project*, Evaluation Report EV 392, Evaluation Department, Overseas Development Administration, London

Rew, A. W., Fisher, E. and Pandey, B. (2000) 'Addressing Policy Constraints and Improving Outcomes in Development-Induced Displacement and Resettlement Projects', Refugee Studies Centre, Oxford, University of Oxford

Reynolds, N. (1981) 'The Design of Rural Development: Proposals for the Evolution of a Social Contract Suited to Conditions in Southern Africa', Parts I and II, Working Papers 40 and 41, Cape Town, Southern Africa Labour and Development Research Unit

Reynolds, N. (1992) 'Community Development and Resource Management', Paper written for the IUCN SOIWDP Review Team, Pasadena, Scudder archives

Ribeiro, G. L. (1994) *Transnational Capitalism and Hydropolitics in Argentina: The Yacyretá High Dam*, Gainesville, University Press of Florida

Roberts, T. (1993) 'Just another dammed river? Negative impacts of Pak Mun Dam on fishes of the Mekong Basin', *Natural History Bulletin of the Siam Society*, vol 41, pp105–133

Roberts, T. (2001) Draft Manuscript on the Pak Mun Fish Ladder, Bangkok

Robinson, W. C. (2003) 'Rights and Risks: The Causes, Consequences and Challenges of Development-Induced Displacement', An Occasional Paper, Brookings Institution–SAIS Project on Internal Displacement, May, Washington, DC, Brookings Institution

Robinson, S., Strzepek, K., El-Said, M. and Lofgren, H. (2003) 'The High Dam at Aswan: An Analysis of Its Benefits and Costs for the Egyptian Economy', 15 March, Draft Report for the World Bank Task Force on Multiplier Effects, Washington, DC, World Bank

Robichaud, W. (1997) *Saola Conservation Action Plan for Lao PDR: Environmental and Social Action Plan for Nakai-Nam Theun Catchment and Corridor Areas*, Vientiane, Lao PDR, Wildlife Conservation Society

Roder, W. (1970) *The Irrigation Farmers of the Kainji Lake Region, Nigeria*, Rome, FAO

Roder, W. (1994) *Human Adjustment to Kainji Reservoir in Nigeria: An Assessment of the Economic and Environmental Consequences of a Major Man-made Lake in Africa*, Lanham, New York, University Press of America

Rodrigo, M. L. (1991) 'Resources and Peasant Livelihood: Differential Response to Agrarian Change and Planned Development: A Case Study from the Mahaweli Irrigation Project in Sri Lanka', PhD Dissertation, Ithaca, Cornell University

Rogers, P. (1994) 'Assessing the socioeconomic consequences of climate change on water resources', in Frederick, K. D. and Rosenberg, N. J. (eds) *Assessing the Impacts of Climate Change on Natural Resource Systems*, Boston, Kluwer Academic Publishers

Rogers, P. (1997) 'Engineering design and uncertainties related to climate change', in Frederick, K. D., Major, D. C. and Stakhiv, E. Z. (eds) *Climate Change and Water Resources Planning Criteria*, Boston, Kluwer Academic Publishers

Rogers, P., Lydon, P. and Seckler, D. (1989) *Eastern Waters Study: Strategies to Manage Flood and Drought in the Ganges-Brahmaputra Basin*, Irrigation Support Project for Asia and the Near East (SPAN) for United States Agency for International Development, Arlington, Virginia

Roosevelt, A. C. (1991) *Moundbuilders of the Amazon: Geophysical Archaeology in Majaro Island, Brazil*, San Diego, Academic Press

Roosevelt, A. C. (1999) 'Twelve thousand years of human–environment interaction in the Amazon floodplain', in Padoch, C. (ed) *Várzea: Diversity, Development, and Conservation of Amazonia's Whitewater Floodplains*, Advances in Economic Botany, vol 13, New York, New York Botanical Garden

Rosa, E. A. (1998) 'Metatheoretical foundations for post-normal risk', *Journal of Risk Research*, vol 1, no1, pp15–44

Ruggiero, R. (1999) 12 April, Geneva Speech, 'Beyond the Multilateral Trading System', WTO News: 1995–1999 Speeches

Rutland Herald (2000) 18 June, 'Hydro-Quebec gets freer rein on rates, dams', Dillon, J.

Sakthivadivel, R., Thiruvengadachari, S., Amerasinghe, U., Bastiaanssen, W. G. M. and Molden, D. (1999) 'Performance Evaluation of the Bhakra Irrigation System, India, Using Remote Sensing and GIS Techniques', Research Report 28, Colombo, International Water Management Institute

Salem-Murdock, M. (1989) *Arabs and Nubians in New Halfa: A Study of Settlement and Irrigation*, Salt Lake City, Utah, University of Utah Press

Salem-Murdock, M. (1996) 'Social science inputs to water management and wetland conservation in the Senegal River Valley', in Acreman, M. C. and Hollis, G. E. (eds) *Water Management and Wetlands in Sub-Saharan Africa*, Gland, Switzerland, International Union for the Conservation of Nature and Natural Resources (IUCN/World Conservation Union)

Salem-Murdock, M. and Niasse, M. (1993) *Senegal River Basin Monitoring Activity II: Executive Summary*, Binghamton, New York, Institute for Development Anthropology

Salisbury, R. F. (1986) *A Homeland for the Cree: Regional Development in James Bay 1971–1981*, Quebec, McGill-Queen's University Press

Sam, I. (1992) 29 April, Letter from the World Bank's Sam, I. (Chief, Infrastructure Operations, Southern Africa Department) to the LHDA POE noting that LHDA, to which the POE reports, has accepted the Panel's Report and, like the Bank, shares the Panel's Concerns, Washington, DC, World Bank

Sardar Sarovar Narmada Nigam Ltd (Nigam) (1989) *Ist Year – A Look At Major Achievement*, 11 July, Nigam, Gandhinagar

Saturday Star (1990) 9 December, 'On local resistance to the Southern Okavango Integrated Water Development Project'

Scatasta, M. (2003) 'Sobradinho Dam and the Cascade of Reservoirs on the Sub-Médio São Francisco River, Brazil', 4 April, Draft Report for the World Bank Task Force on Multiplier Effects of Dams, Washington, DC, World Bank

Science (2002) 'Dam Threatens Iraqi Ancient Sites', vol 295 (22 March)

Scientific Committee on Problems of the Environment (SCOPE) (1972) 'Man-Made Lakes as Modified Ecosystems', Scope Report 2, International Council of Scientific Unions (ICSU), Paris, ICSU

Scott, J. C. (1998) *Seeing Like A State: How Certain Schemes to Improve the Human Condition Have Failed*, New Haven, Yale University Press

Scudder, T. (1960) 'Fishermen of the Zambezi', *Rhodes-Livingstone Journal*, no 27, pp41–49

Scudder, T. (1962) *The Ecology of the Gwembe Tonga*, Manchester, Manchester University Press for Rhodes-Livingstone Institute

Scudder, T. (1965) 'The Kariba case: Man-made lakes and resource development in Africa', *Bulletin of the Atomic Scientists*, December pp6–11

Scudder, T. (1968) 'Social anthropology, man-made lakes and population relocation in Africa', *Anthropological Quarterly*, vol 41, no 3, pp168–176

Scudder, T. (1971a) 'Gathering among African Woodland Savannah Cultivators – A Case Study: The Gwembe Tonga', Zambian Papers, no 5, Manchester, Manchester University Press for the Institute for African Studies, University of Zambia

Scudder, T. (1971b) 'The Gwembe Tonga and the Kariba Lake Basin', Unpublished manuscript, Pasadena, Scudder archives

Scudder, T. (1972) 'Ecological bottlenecks and the development of the Kariba Lake Basin', in Farvar, M. T. and Milton, J. P. (eds) *The Careless Technology: Ecology and International Development*, New York, Natural History Press

Scudder, T. (1973) 'The human ecology of big projects: River basin development and resettlement', in Siegel, B. (ed) *Annual Review of Anthropology*, Palo Alto, California, Annual Reviews

Scudder, T. (1975) 'Resettlement', in Stanley, N. F. and Alpers, M. P. (eds) *Man-Made Lakes and Human Health*, London, Academic Press for Institute of Biology

Scudder, T. (1979) 'Evaluatory Report on Mission to Sri Lankan Settlement Projects: A Discussion of Some Basic Issues', Report no 1 prepared for USAID, Colombo

Scudder, T. (1980) 'The Accelerated Mahaweli Programme (AMP) and Dry Zone Development: Some Aspects of Settlement', Report no 2, Colombo, Institute for Development Anthropology for USAID

Scudder, T. (1981a) 'What it means to be dammed: The anthropology of large-scale development projects in the tropics and subtropics', *Engineering and Science*, vol 54, no 4, pp9–15

Scudder, T. (1981b) *The Development Potential of New Lands Settlement in the Tropics and Subtropics: A Global State-of-the-Art Evaluation with Specific Emphasis on Policy Implications*, Binghamton, New York, Institute for Development Anthropology

Scudder, T. (1981c) 'The Accelerated Mahaweli Programme (AMP) and Dry Zone Development: Some Aspects of Settlement', Report no 3, Clark University and Institute for Development Anthropology Cooperative Agreement sponsored by USAID, Colombo

Scudder, T. (1983) *The Relocation Component in Connection with the Sardar Sarovar (Narmada) Project*, Binghamton, Institute for Development Anthropology for the World Bank

Scudder, T. (1985) 'A sociological framework for the analysis of new lands settlements', in Cernea, M. M. (ed) *Putting People First: Sociological Variables in Rural Development*, New York, Oxford University Press for the World Bank

Scudder, T. (1986) 'The Gwembe Valley Development Company in Relationship to the Development of the Southern Portion of Gwembe District', Unpublished Report, Pasadena, Scudder archives

Scudder, T. (1988) *Overview of the African Experience with River Basin Development: Achievements to Date, the Role of Institutions, and Strategies for the Future*, Worcester, Massachusetts, Clark University, Binghamton, New York, Institute for Development Anthropology Cooperative Agreement sponsored by USAID

Scudder, T. (1989) 'Supervisory Report on the Resettlement and Rehabilitation (R and R) Component of the Sardar Sarovar Project (SSP)', Binghamton, New York, Institute for Development Anthropology for World Bank

Scudder, T. (1991) 'The need and justification for maintaining transboundary flood regimes: The Africa case', Special issue, The International Law of the Hydrologic Cycle, *Natural Resources Journal*, vol 31, no 1, pp75–107

Scudder, T. (1993a) 'Development-induced relocation and refugee studies: 37 years of change and continuity among Zambia's Gwembe Tonga', *Journal of Refugee Studies*, vol 6, no 2, pp123–152

Scudder, T. (1993b) 'Monitoring a large-scale resettlement program with repeated household interviews', in Kumar, K. (ed), *Rapid Appraisal Methods*, Regional and Sectoral Studies, Washington, DC, World Bank

Scudder, T. (1993c) 'Development Strategies for Botswana's Okavango Delta', in Shen, H. W., Su, S. T. and Wen, F. (eds) *Hydraulic Engineering 93*. Proceedings of the 1993 Conference on Hydraulic Engineering and International Symposium on Engineering Hydrology, New York, American Society of Civil Engineers

Scudder, T. (1995a) 'Constraints to the development of settler incomes and production oriented participatory organizations in large-scale government sponsored projects: The Mahaweli case', in Muller, H. P. and Hettige, S. T. (eds) *The Blurring of a Vision – The Mahaweli: Its Social, Economic and Political Implications*, Ratmalana, Sri Lanka, Sarvodaya Book Publishing Services

Scudder, T. (1995b) 'Reflexions sur le deplacement des populations en relation avec la construction des barrages', in Conac, F. (ed) *Barrages Internationaux et Cooperation*, Paris, Karthala

Scudder, T. (1995c) 'The big dam controversy and environmental fundamentalism: Musings of an anthropologist', *Development Anthropologist*, vol 13, nos 1 and 2, pp8–18

Scudder, T. (1996) 'Development-induced impoverishment, resistance, and river basin development', in McDowell, C. (ed) *Resisting Impoverishment – Tackling the Consequences of Development-Induced Displacement*, Oxford, Berghahn Books

Scudder, T (1997a) 'Social Impacts of Large Dams', in Dorcey, T., *Large Dams: Learning from the past, looking at the future*, Workshop Proceedings, Gland, 11–12 April, IUCN/World Bank

Scudder, T. (1997b) Chapters on 'Resettlement' and 'Social Impacts', in Biswas, A. K. (ed) *Water Resources: Environmental Planning, Management and Development*, New York, McGraw Hill

Scudder, T. (1999) 'The emerging global crisis and development anthropology: Can we have an impact?' Malinowski Award Lecture, *Human Organization*, vol 58, no 4, pp351–364

Scudder, T. (2001) 'The World Commission on Dams and the need for a new development paradigm', *International Journal of Water Resources Development*, vol 17, no 3, pp329–341

Scudder, T. and Colson, E. (1980) *Secondary Education and the Formation of an Elite: The Impact of Education on Gwembe District, Zambia*, London, Academic Press

Scudder, T. and Colson, E. (1982) 'From welfare to development: A conceptual framework for the analysis of dislocated people', in Hansen, A. and Oliver-Smith, A. (eds) *Involuntary Migration and Resettlement: The Problems and Responses of Dislocated People*, Boulder, Colorado, Westview Press

Scudder, T. and Mahapatra, L. K. (1985) 'Narmada River Development – Gujarat Sardar Sarovar Dam and Power Project Resettlement and Rehabilitation: Review and Findings', Binghamton, Institute for Development Anthropology for the World Bank

Scudder, T. and Scudder, M. E. D. (1981) 'The Social Impacts of the John Wayne Airport of Orange County', Consultancy report commissioned by Mariners Community Association, Pasadena, Scudder archives

Scudder, T. and Wimaladharma, K. P. (1983) 'The Accelerated Mahaweli Programme (AMP) and Dry Zone Development' Report no 4, USAID Cooperative Agreement on Settlement and Resource Systems Analysis, Worcester, Massachusetts, Clark University, Binghamton, New York, Institute for Development Anthropology

Scudder, T. and Wimaladharma, K. P. (1985) 'The Accelerated Mahaweli Programme (AMP) and Dry Zone Development' Report no 5, IDA Working Paper 23, USAID Cooperative Agreement on Settlement and Resource Systems Analysis, Worcester, Massachusetts, Clark University, Binghamton, New York, Institute for Development Anthropology

Scudder, T. and Wimaladharma, K. P. (1989) 'The Accelerated Mahaweli Programme (AMP) and Dry Zone Development' Report no 7, IDA Working Paper 47, USAID Cooperative Agreement on Settlement and Resource Systems Analysis, Worcester, Massachusetts, Clark University, Binghamton, New York, Institute for Development Anthropology

Scudder, T., Manley, R. E., Coley, R. W., Davis, R. K., Green, J., Howard, G.W., Lawry, S.W., Martz, D., Rogers, P.P., Taylor, A.R.D. et al (1993) *IUCN Review of the*

Southern Okavango Integrated Water Development Project, The IUCN Wetlands Programme, Gland, Switzerland, Samara Publishing Company for IUCN (World Conservation Union)

SEATEC International (2000) Draft Nam Theun 2 Hydroelectric Project Environmental Assessment and Management Plan, Bangkok, SEATEC International

Sechaba Consultants (2000) *Poverty and Livelihood in Lesotho: More than a Mapping Exercise,* Maseru, Sechaba Consultants

Seckler, D. (1996) 'The New Era of Water Resources Management: From "Dry" to "Wet" Water Savings', Washington, DC, Consultative Group on International Agricultural Research

Seidman, A. (1979) 'The economics of eliminating poverty and the distorted growth of import substitution industry', in Turuk, B. (ed) *Development in Zambia: A Reader,* London, Zed Press

Senete, S. A. (2000) From a draft manuscript on his life history, Sikagoma Adam Senete, Mazulu Village, Zambia

Shenouda, W. (1999) 'Benefits of and concerns about Aswan High Dam – case study (Egypt)', in Turfan, M. (ed) *Benefits of and Concerns about Dams: Case Studies,* Ankara, Turkish National Committee on Large Dams

Shoemaker, B. (1998) 'Trouble on the Theun-Hinboun: A Field Report on the Socio-Economic and Environmental Effects of the Nam Theun-Hinboun Hydropower Project in Laos', Berkeley, California, International Rivers Network

Shoemaker, B. (2000) 'Theun-Hinboun Update: A Review of the Theun-Hinboun Power Company's Mitigation and Compensation Program', December Report, Berkeley, California, International Rivers Network

Silva, K. T. and Kumara, W. D. N. R. P. 'Suicide and Sexual Anomie in a New Settlement in Sri Lanka', in de Silva, P. (ed) *Suicide in Sri Lanka*', Proceedings of a Workshop at the Institute of Fundamental Studies, Kandy, Pasadena, Scudder archives

Simon, J. (1979) 'Zambia's urban situation', in Turok, B. (ed) *Development in Zambia: A Reader*, London, Zed Press

Snaddon, C. D., Davies, B. R. and Wishart, M. J. (1999) 'A Global Overview on Inter-Basin Water Transfer Schemes, with an Appraisal of their Ecological, Socio-Economic and Socio-Political Implications, and Recommendations for their Management', Pretoria, South Africa, Water Research Commission

Snowy Mountains Engineering Corporation (SMEC) (1987a) 'Southern Okavango Integrated Water Development, Phase I, Final Report Technical Study', 5 volumes, Report to the Department of Water Affairs, June, Gaborone

Snowy Mountains Engineering Corporation (SMEC) (1987b) 'Volume III: Sukwane Reservoir Impact Assessment', Report to the Department of Water Affairs, Gaborone

Snowy Mountains Engineering Corporation (SMEC) (1991) 'Southern Okavango Integrated Water Development, Environmental Impact Study, Sukwane Reservoir and Pipeline to Mopipi', Report to the Department of Water Affairs, Gaborone

Soemarwoto, O. (1988) 'Dams as agents of rural development', in Charoenwatana, T. and Rambo, A. T. (eds) *Sustainable Rural Development in Asia*, Proceedings of the SUAN IV Regional Symposium on Agroecosystem Research, Farming Systems Research Project and Southeast Asia Universities Agrosystem Network, Khon Kaen, Thailand

Softestad, L. T. (1990) 'On evacuation of people in the Kotmale Hydro Power Project: Experience from a socio-economic impact study', *Bistandsantropologen*, no 15, pp22–32

Soils Incorporated (Pty) Ltd and Chalo Environmental and Sustainable Development Consultants (2000) 'Kariba Dam Case Study' prepared as an input to the World Commission on Dams, Cape Town, available at www.dams.org

Sole, M. E. (1984) 'The Tennessee Valley Authority Experience, Are There Some Lessons to be Learned?', Unpublished paper, Maseru, Lesotho Highlands Development Authority

Sørbø, G. M. (1977) 'Lake Nasser Fishermen', Oslo, NORAD

Sorensen, B. R. (1996) *Relocated Lives: Displacement and Resettlement within the Mahaweli Project*, Sri Lanka, Amsterdam, VU University Press

Southerland, A. J. (1992) 'Impressions of Change and Prospects for Future Development in Ngamiland – with Specific Reference to Molapo Farming Areas in Gomare and Shorobe', Paper written for the IUCN SOIWDP Review Team, Pasadena, Scudder archives

Sparkes, S. (1997) 'Observations Relating to the Resettlement of People on the Nakai Plateau', Report prepared for the Nam Theun 2 Electricity Consortium, May

Sparkes, S. (2000) 'Case Study 3: Theun Hinboun Hydropower Project', Manuscript

Sri Lanka, Government of (1978) *The Programme*, Foreword, Ministry of Lands and Land Development, Government Printer, Colombo

Sri Lanka, Government of (2001) Portion of the 14 February presentation of the National Budget dealing with the restructuring of the MASL into a River Basin Management Agency, Colombo

Stanley, D. J. and Warne, A. G. (1993) 'Nile Delta: Recent geological evolution and human impact', *Science*, vol 260, pp628–634

Sugg, A. St J (1957) 21 May, letter to S. P. Bourne requesting information on Lusitu resettlement area, Pasadena, California, content noted in Scudder archives

Sunday Times (1990) 9 December, 'Local resistance to the Southern Okavango Integrated Water Development Project'

Suwanmontri, M. (1996) 'An analysis on involuntary resettlers', *R and R Research Series*, no 3

Suwanmontri, M. (1999a) 'Agriculture-based Resettlement Design and Management for Hydrodams: The Thai Experience', Paper presented at the 2nd International Conference, World Council of Power Utility, China, October

Suwanmontri, M. (1999b) 'Establishment of a Resettlement Concept', Paper presented at the 2nd International Conference, World Council of Power Utility, China, October

Tata Institute for Social Science (1997) 'Experiences with resettlement and rehabilitation in Maharashtra', in Drèze, J., Samson, M. and Singh, S. (eds) *The Dam and the Nation: Displacement and Resettlement in the Narmada Valley*, Delhi, Oxford University Press

Tinley, K. (1994) 'Description of Gorongosa-Marrameu Natural Resource Management Area, Section 2: Ecological Profile of the Region (Form, Content, Process)', Harare, IUCN Regional Office for Southern Africa

Tjitradjaja, I. (1997) 'Drawdown Farming at Jatiluhur Dam, West Java: A Case Study of Local Resources to New Conditions', PhD dissertation, New Brunswick, New Jersey, Rutgers University

Toronto Globe and Mail (1994) 22 November, article on a possible Grande Baleine future

Transparency International (2000) 'OECD Working Party on Export Credits and Credit Guarantees', Working Paper, Informal Consultation in Paris, 16 November

Tremmel, M. (1994) *The People of the Great River: The Tonga Hoped the Water Would Follow Them*, Silveira House Social Series no 9, Gweru, Zimbabwe, Mambo Press

Tribune, The (2001) 6 December, 'Dam oustees await rehabilitation'

Trigger, B. G. (1985) *History and Settlement in Lower Nubia*, New Haven, Yale University Press

Tumbare, M. J. (1999) 'Some Lessons Learned from the Management of the Binational Kariba Dam for Future Large Dam Projects', Submission to the Third Regional Consultation (8–9 December, Cairo, Egypt) of the World Commission on Dams

Tumbare, M. J. (2000) 'The importance of politicians in water related development projects', in Tumbare, M. J. (ed) *Management of River Basins and Dams: The Zambezi River Basin*, Rotterdam, AA Balkema

Udall, L. (2000) 'Export Credit Agencies', Contributing Paper to Thematic Review V.4 prepared as an input to the World Commission on Dams, Cape Town, available at www.dams.org

United Kingdom Export Credit and Guarantee Department ECGD (2003) 2 July, information on the Ilisu project, available at www.ecdg.gov.uk

United Nations (1948) Universal Declaration of Human Rights

United Nations (1986) UN Declaration on the Right to Development

United Nations (1992) Rio Declaration on Environment and Development

United Nations (1997) Convention on the Law of the non-Navigational Uses of International Watercourses

United Nations Development Programme (UNDP) (1978) Recommendations of the Programming Mission for Socio Economic Studies and Planning Related to Mahaweli Development, Colombo, UNDP

United Nations Development Programme (UNDP)/Food and Agriculture Organization of the United Nations (FAO) (1975) 'Lake Nasser Development Centre, Aswan, Egypt: Project Findings and Recommendations', Terminal Report *(FI:DP/EGY/66/558)*, Rome, FAO

United Nations Development Programme (UNDP)/Food and Agriculture Organization of the United Nations (FAO) (1977) *Investigation of the Okavango Delta as a Primary Water Resource: Botswana, Project Findings and Recommendations*, Rome, FAO

United Nations Educational, Scientific and Cultural Organization (UNESCO)/UNDP (1997) 'Technical Support for and Review of the Environmental Impact Assessment of Phase 1B of the Lesotho Highlands Water Project', Fifth Mission Report: Comments on the Interim Environmental Action Plan for Phase 1B of the Lesotho Highlands Water Project, Compiled and Edited by David Bourn, Oxford, Environmental Research Group Oxford Ltd for UNESCO/UNDP

United Nations High Commissioner for Human Rights (1994) Draft Declaration on the Rights of Indigenous People

UXO Lao PDR Trust Fund (1995) Report on Unexploded Ordinance, Vientiane, Lao National UXO Programme, Ministry of Labour and Social Welfare

Van de Schalie, H. (1972) 'World Health Organization Project Egypt 10: A case history of a Schistosomiasis Control Project', in Farvar, M. T. and Milton, J. P. (eds) *The Careless Technology: Ecology and International Development*, Garden City, New York, Natural History Press

Van der Hoek, F., Konradsen, F., Athukorala, K. and Wanigadewa, T. (1998) 'Pesticide poisoning: A major health problem in Sri Lanka', *Social Science Medicine*, vol 46, nos 4–5, pp495–504

Vermillion, D. L. and Merrey, D. J. (1998) 'What the 21st century will demand of water management institutions', *Zeitschrift fur Bewasserungswirtscraft*, vol 33, no 2, pp165–187

Vidanapathirana, U. (1984) *A Study of People's Bank Crop Cultivation Financing in the Mahaweli 'H' Area*, Colombo, A People's Bank Research Department Publication

Vientiane Times (2001) 12–15 January, issue notes cultivation area of Gnommalath Community Irrigation Project

Vincent Uhl Associates, available at www.vuawater.com

Wade, R. H. (2001) 'The US Role in the Malaise at the World Bank: Get Up, Gulliver', Paper presented at the 28–30 August Annual Meeting of the American Political Science Association, San Francisco

Wali, A. (1989) *Kilowatts and Crisis: Hydroelectric Power and Social Dislocation in Eastern Panama*, Boulder, Colorado, Westview Press

Wanigaratne, R. (1984) 'Subsistence Maintenance and Agricultural Transformation on the Frontier in Sri Lanka: The Kaltota Irrigated Settlement Project', PhD, Dissertation, Madison, University of Wisconsin

Wanigaratne, R. (1998) 'Mahaweli Settler Household Incomes: Trends, determinants, constraints and choices', unpublished paper, Planning and Monitoring Unit, Colombo, Mahaweli Authority of Sri Lanka

Wanigaratne, R. and Vimaladharma, K. (2001) 'The Ninth Field Report on the Mahaweli Programme of Sri Lanka – Development Trends and Possibilities', 23 June, Manuscript, Pasadena, Scudder archives

Warren, T. J. (1999) 'A Monitoring Study to Assess the Localized Impacts Created by the Nam Theun-Hinboun Hydro-Scheme on Fisheries and Fish Populations', Report Prepared for the Theun-Hinboun Power Company (THPC), June, Vientiane, Lao PDR

Washington Post (2000) 10 September, 'The corps' controversial projects'

Waterbury, J. (1979) *Hydropolitics of the Nile Valley*, Syracuse, New York, Syracuse University Press

Webster, M. H. (1975) 'Medical aspects of the Kariba Hydro-Electric Scheme', in Stanley, N. F. and Alpers, M. P. (eds) *Man-Made Lakes and Human Health*, London, Academic Press

Weissman, M. M., and Paykel, E. S. (1972) 'Moving', New Haven, *Yale Alumni Magazine*, October, pp16–19

Weist, K. (1994) 'Development Refugees: Indians, Africans and Big Dams', 1994 Annual Elizabeth Colson Lecture, Oxford University, Refugees Study Programme

Wellington, J. H. (1949a) 'Zambezi-Okavango Development Projects', *The Geographical Review*, vol XXXIX, no 4, pp566–567

Wellington, J. H. (1949b) 'A new development scheme for the Okovango Delta, Northern Kalahari', *The Geographical Journal*, vol CXII (January–June)

Wesseling, J. W., Naah, E., Drijver, C. A. and Ngantou, D. (1996) 'Rehabilitation of Logone Floodplain, Cameroon, through hydrological management', in Acreman, M. C. and Hollis, G. E. (eds) *Water Management and Wetlands in Sub-Saharan Africa*, Gland, Switzerland, International Union for the Conservation of Nature and Natural Resources (IUCN/World Conservation Union)

Westcoat, J. (2000) 'Ex-Post Evaluation of Dams and Related Water Projects', Contributing Paper to Thematic Review IV.5 prepared as an input to the World Commission on Dams, Cape Town, available at www.dams.org

White, G. F. (1988) 'The environmental effects of the High Dam at Aswan', *Environment*, vol 30, no 7, pp5–11, 34–40

Wickremaratne, M. L. H. (1995) 'The rationale of the Accelerated Mahaweli Programme', in Muller, H. P. and Hettige, S. T. (eds) *The Blurring of a Vision – The*

Mahaweli, Ratmalana, Sri Lanka, Sarvodaya Book Publishing Services

Williams, G. J. (1985) 'Resource sharing: The development of hydropower on the Middle Zambezi River', in Handlos, W. L. and Williams, G. W. (eds) *Development Prospects for the Zambezi Valley in Zambia*, Kafue Basin Research Committee, Lusaka, University of Zambia

Williams, P. B. (1993) 'Assessing the True Value of Flood Control Reservoirs: The Experience of Folsom Dam in the February 1986 Flood', Paper presented at the 1993 American Society of Civil Engineers National Conference on Hydraulic Engineering and International Symposium on Engineering Hydrology, San Francisco, 25–30 July

Williams, G. J. and Howard G. W. (eds) (1977) 'Development and Ecology in the Lower Kafue Basin in the Nineteen Seventies', Papers from the Kafue Basin Research Committee of the University of Zambia, Lusaka

Wilson, K. (1997) presented at the Workshop on the Sustainable Use of Cahora Bassa Dam and the Zambezi Valley, 29 September to 2 October, Songo, Mozambique

Wimaladharma, K. (1981) Unpublished manuscript and field notes on Sri Lanka's Minneriya project, Kandy

Wimaladharma, K. (1982) 'Non-farm employment in the major settlements in Sri Lanka', in Wimaladharma, K. (ed) *Land Settlement Experiences in Sri Lanka*, Colombo, Wimaladharma, K.

Wimaladharma, K. (1984) 'An Anecdotal Early History of the Mahaweli Development Board and It's Thinking on Settlements', Manuscript, Colombo and Pasadena, Scudder archives

Winarto, Y. T. (1992) 'The management of secondary consequences in dam projects: The case of drawdown agriculture in Indonesia', *World Development*, vol 20, no 3, pp457–465

Wolf, A. T. (1995) *Hydropolitics along the Jordan River: Scarce Water and Its Impact on the Arab-Israeli Conflict*, Tokyo, United Nations University Press

Wolf, A. T., Natharius, J. A., Danielson, J. J., Ward, B. S. and Pender, J. K. (1999) 'International river basins of the world', *International Journal of Water Resources Development*, vol 15, no 4, pp387–427

World Bank (1978a) 'Rural Enterprise and Non Farm Employment', A World Bank Paper, Washington, DC, World Bank

World Bank (1978b) 'Agricultural Land Settlement', A World Bank Issues Paper, Washington, DC, World Bank

World Bank (1979) Draft 'Social Issues Associated with Involuntary Resettlement in Bank-Financed Projects', Washington, DC, World Bank

World Bank (1980) 'Social Issues Associated with Involuntary Resettlement in Bank-Financed Projects', Operational Manual Statement 2.33, Washington, DC, World Bank

World Bank (1981) *Accelerated Development in Sub-Saharan Africa: An Agenda for Action*, Washington, DC, World Bank

World Bank (1982) 'Tribal People in Bank-Financed Projects', Operational Manual Statement 2.34, Washington, DC, World Bank

World Bank (1983a) 'Zambia: Kariba North Hydroelectric Project', Project Performance Audit Report, August, Washington, DC, World Bank

World Bank (1983b) 'Sri Lanka: Mahaweli Ganga Development Project II', Full Supervision Report, 13 April, Annex 1, Washington, DC, World Bank

World Bank (1984) *Staff Appraisal Report. India Narmada River Development – Gujarat Sardar Sarovar Dam and Power Project*, 16 October, Washington, DC, World Bank

World Bank (1985a) 'The Experience of the World Bank with Government-Sponsored Land Settlement', Report no 5625, Operations Evaluation Department, Washington, DC, World Bank

World Bank (1985b) 'Republic of Kenya: Bura Irrigation Settlement Project Mid-Term Evaluation Report 1984', Annex II: Farm Budgets, January, Washington, DC, World Bank

World Bank (1986) 'Operations Policy Issues in the Treatment of Involuntary Resettlement', Operational Manual Statement no 10.08, Washington, DC, World Bank

World Bank (1989) 'Brazil – Itaparica Resettlement and Irrigation Project', 10 July Office Memorandum, Washington, DC, World Bank

World Bank (1990) 'Involuntary Resettlement', Operational Directive no 4.30, Washington, DC, World Bank

World Bank (1993) *Early Experience with Involuntary Resettlement*, Operations Evaluation Department, Washington, DC, World Bank

World Bank (1994a) *Resettlement and Development: The Bankwide Review of Projects Involving Involuntary Resettlement* 1986–1993, Environment Department, Washington, DC, World Bank

World Bank (1994b) 'Zambia Poverty Assessment', Report no 12985-ZA, vol 1, Main Report, Washington, DC, World Bank

World Bank (1995) 'Terms of Reference: Assessment and Implementation Study for Rehabilitation and Development Strategies for Kariba Dam Construction Affected Gwembe Tonga and Affected Downstream Riverine Areas', Zambia, Power Rehabilitation Project, Annex 5, Washington, DC, World Bank

World Bank (1996) *The World Bank's Experience with Large Dams: A Preliminary Review of Impacts*, Operations Evaluation Department, Washington, DC, World Bank

World Bank (1997) 'Project Appraisal Document to the Republic of Zambia for a Power Rehabilitation Project', Report no 17019-ZA, Washington, DC, World Bank,

World Bank (1998a) 'Recent Experiences with Involuntary Resettlement', Operations Evaluation Department, Washington, DC, World Bank

World Bank (1998b) 'Recent Experiences with Involuntary Resettlement: China – Shuikou (and Yantan)', Report no 17539, Operations Evaluation Department, Washington, DC, World Bank

World Bank (1998c) 'Recent Experiences with Involuntary Resettlement: Thailand – Pak Mun', Report no 17541, Operations Evaluation Department, Washington, DC, World Bank

World Bank (2001) 'Involuntary Resettlement: Comparative Perspectives', OP 4.12, Washington, DC, World Bank

World Bank (2003) Stakeholder Involvement in Options Assessment: Promoting Dialogue in Meeting Water and Energy Needs – A Sourcebook, Washington, DC, World Bank

World Bank (2004) 'Argentina: World Bank Board Discusses Yacyretá Hydroelectric Project', News Release no (2004)/266/7

World Bank Annex 1, 'Planning the Sardar Sarovar Project', Washington, DC, World Bank

World Commission on Dams (2000) 'Dams and Development: A New Framework for Decision-Making', The Report of the World Commission on Dams, London, Earthscan

World Health Organization (2000a) 'HIV/AIDS Statistics for Africa', Geneva, WHO

World Health Organization (2000b) 30 November, Response to the WCD Final Report, Geneva, WHO

World Rivers Review (formerly *International Dams Newsletter)* (1994) *Mun River Fisheries Lost to Pak Mun Dam*, vol 9, no 1, p11

World Rivers Review (formerly *International Dams Newsletter*) (1996), Berkeley, California, International Rivers Network, April, pp6–7

World Rivers Review (2001) *Dam-Related Flooding Ravages Northern Nigeria*, vol 16, no 5, Berkeley, California, International Rivers Network

Worley International (see under Probe International)

Worthington, E. B. (1972) 'The Nile catchment – Technological change and aquatic biology', in Farvar, M. T. and Milton, J. P. (eds) *The Careless Technology: Ecology and International Development*, Garden City, New York, Natural History Press

Yambayamba, E. S. K., Mweene, A. S., Banda, D. J. and Kang'omba, S. (2001) 'An Investigation into Groundwater Pollution in the Gwembe Valley: The Case of Lusitu', September Report, Lusaka, Ministry of Environment and Natural Resources

Zambezi River Authority (1996) *Kariba Dam's Operation Noah Re-Launched*, June Draft, Pasadena, Scudder archives

Zambezi Society, The (2001) 6 April, Press Release on the four volume *Wetlands Biodiversity Report*. Harare, available at www.zamsoc.org/

Zein, A. H. E. (1966) 'Socio-economic implications of the water-wheel in Adindan, Nubia', in Fernea, R. A. (ed) *Contemporary Egyptian Nubia*, vol 2, HRAFlex Book MR8 001, HRAF, New Haven, Yale University

Zhu, Y. (1998) 'Economic Rehabilitation in Shuikou Reservoir Area', Annex A, *Recent Experiences with Involuntary Resettlement: China – Shuikou (and Yantan)*, Report no 17539, Operations Evaluation Department, Washington, DC, World Bank

Index